Fodor's

ESSENTIAL
NEW ZEALAND

P9-CRZ-403

Welcome to New Zealand

From the Bay of Islands' pristine beaches in the north to the soaring pinnacles of Milford Sound in the south, New Zealand is a stunner. Glaciated mountains, steaming volcanoes, and lush forests give adventurers a vast array of ecological playgrounds to explore. While hikers retreat to 14 national parks, bird-watchers find their bliss on peaceful Stewart Island. But it's not all parks and rec. Māori enclaves display deep native heritage, idyllic vineyards produce world-class wines, and vibrant dining and arts scenes thrive in cities like Auckland and Wellington.

TOP REASONS TO GO

★ **Landscapes:** Deep blue lakes, alpine peaks, green valleys—the scenery is breathtaking.

★ **Superb Wine:** Hawkes Bay's Bordeaux blends, Marlborough's Sauvignon Blancs, and more.

★ **Hobbits:** Lord of the Rings tours in Glenorchy and Matamata take fans to Middle Earth.

★ **Water Sports:** Incredible sailing, surfing, rafting, kayaking, and diving.

★ **Māori Culture:** Native traditions are shared in craft workshops and ceremonial feasts.

★ **The Great Walks:** Ten famous trails, including the Milford Track, entice hikers.

Contents

Fodor's Features

6

Contents

MAPS

EXPERIENCE NEW ZEALAND

25 ULTIMATE EXPERIENCES

New Zealand offers terrific experiences that should be on every traveler's list. Here are Fodor's top picks for a memorable trip.

1 Abel Tasman National Park

As New Zealand's smallest and most visited park, Abel Tasman offers visitors golden beaches, limestone caves, and awesome rock formations, all easily accessible via hiking or kayaking. *(Ch. 9)*

2 Wineries

From Marlborough to Hawke's Bay to Wairapa, New Zealand is world-famous for fine white wines and rich reds, thanks to its cool winters and mild summers. *(Ch. 6–10)*

3 The Lord of the Rings Filming Locations

Thanks to its role as the filming location for the *Lord of the Rings* movies, New Zealand has become synonymous with Middle-earth. Multiple tours will take you from Hobbiton to Mt. Doom. *(Ch. 6, 8)*

4 Wellington

New Zealand's capital city is filled with fascinating museums, a blossoming art scene, and some of the country's best culinary offerings. *(Ch. 8)*

5 Christchurch

After a series of earthquakes, this quirky city has reinvented itself as an artsy mecca, thanks to projects like its cardboard cathedral and the stunning Center of Contemporary Art. *(Ch. 10)*

6 Stewart Island

On this small remote island, explore Rakiura, the country's newest national park, glimpse kiwi birds in their natural habitats, and spot the stunning southern lights. *(Ch. 12)*

7 The Coromandel Peninsula

A remote getaway of white-sand beaches, native forest, and quirky cafés, this low-key part of the country is filled with fishing, cycling, and relaxing with locals. *(Ch. 5)*

8 Glacier-Trekking

The country's Southern Alps serve as a wonderland of glacier-filled landscapes, with plenty of opportunities to trek and explore these icy behemoths up-close. *(Ch. 9, 11)*

9 Rugby

As New Zealand's national sport, rugby union is serious business here, with fans rooting feverishly for the All Blacks Rugby team. Catch a match at a stadium or just watch a game at a bar for an authentic Kiwi experience. *(Ch. 3, 8)*

10 Whanganui National Park

New Zealand's longest navigable river serves as the centerpiece of this park, and you can explore the Whanganui via canoe, kayak, or raft. *(Ch. 7)*

11 Waitomo Glowworm Caves

This massive system of underground limestone caves is filled with electric blue inhabitants that give off an otherworldly glow. *(Ch. 7)*

12 Aoraki/Mount Cook National Park

Rising 12,316 feet, Aroraki is New Zealand's largest mountain. Its national park also offers turquoise glacial lakes and high alpine tundra hikes. *(Ch. 11)*

13 Rotorua Hot Springs

Sitting on top of the most active segment of the Taupo Volcanic Zone, Rotorua offers a multitude of volcanic springs and thermal pools that serve as nature's hot tubs. *(Ch. 6)*

14 Milford Sound

Within glacier-carved Fiordland National Park, you'll find sublime Milford Sound and its dramatic waterfalls, glacial lakes, and awe-inspiring mountain peaks. *(Ch. 11)*

15 The Bay of Islands

A collection of 144 islands, the Bay of Islands is a stronghold of both New Zealand and Māori history, along with chances for scenic kayaking and fishing. *(Ch. 4)*

16 The Great Walks

Scattered over New Zealand's national parks are 10 Great Walks, ranging from day hikes to multiday tracks that explore the country's diverse and spectacular scenery. *(Ch. 3–12)*

17 Bird-Watching

From kiwis on Stewart Island to royal albatrosses in Otago to penguins in Fiordland, you don't have to be a bird nerd to appreciate New Zealand's diverse feathered population. *(Ch. 12)*

18 Beaches

New Zealand has over 9,300 miles of coastline, which ripples and zigzags to create bays, coves, fjords, and countless beaches perfect for surfing, sunbathing, and swimming. *(Ch. 3–7)*

19 Tongariro National Park

If you've ever wanted to hike a volcano, New Zealand's oldest national park is home to three (including the one that stood in for Mt. Doom in the *Lord of the Ring* movies). *(Ch. 6)*

20 Auckland

New Zealand's biggest city is the entryway for most visitors to the country, welcoming travelers with its vibrant restaurants, gorgeous beaches, and active harbor filled with chances to set sail. *(Ch. 3)*

21 Whale-Watching in Kaikoura

The Pacific coastline of Kaikoura is the country's best spot for whale-watching and one of the only places in the world where you have the chance to spot a sperm whale. *(Ch. 9)*

22 Queenstown

Long known as the Adventure Capital of the World, this small and lively city is a jumble of ski slopes, rivers, and alpine areas that make it a haven for everything adrenaline-pumping. *(Ch. 11)*

23 Māori Culture

There are many ways to learn about the vibrant culture of the Māori, the indigenous people of New Zealand, from visiting the Te Papa Museum to participating in a traditional *hāngi*. *(Ch. 6, 8)*

24 Skiing

With all its mountains, New Zealand is a skier's paradise, from volcanic cones like Mt. Ruapehu in the North Island to the massive Southern Alps on the South Island. *(Ch. 6, 11)*

25 Extreme Sports

If you've ever wanted to sky-dive, cliff-dive, or bungee-jump, New Zealand has the best variety of adventure activities, in unbelievably gorgeous settings. *(Ch. 11)*

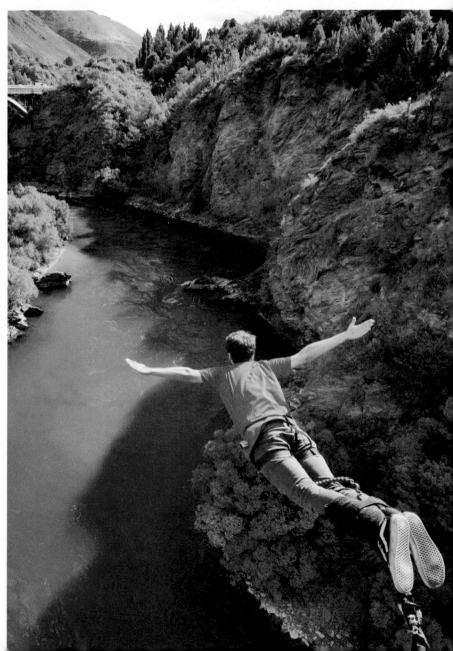

WHAT'S WHERE

1 Auckland. Auckland, the City of Sails, is New Zealand's biggest city, its economic capital, and its most multicultural city, home to Polynesians, Asians, and other immigrants. Dynamic, driven, and gorgeous, Auckland is the perfect introduction to New Zealand.

2 Northland and the Bay of Islands. Northland has a large population of Māori, ancient kauri forests, salty harbors, and ocean inlets. The Bay of Islands is known for diving, sailing, and sunning on and around the isolated beaches on its 100-plus islands.

3 The Coromandel and the Bay of Plenty. Close to Auckland, the Coromandel and the Bay of Plenty have white-sand beaches, blue seas, native birds, and steep hills carpeted with forest. The Coromandel has a café-and-board-shorts culture, while the Bay of Plenty is a Māori cultural hub.

4 East Coast and the Volcanic Zone. Taupo, a vibrant city next to New Zealand's largest lake, is bordered by volcanoes in Tongariro National Park; nearby Turangi claims to be the trout-fishing capital of the world. Te Urewera's wilderness contrasts with the mix of arty café towns like Napier, wineries, and beach towns like Ruatoria and Tolaga Bay, where Māori community life is still present.

5 North Island's West Coast. Mt. Taranaki broods over Egmont National Park and the rural industrial area affectionately known as the 'Naki. A thin highway loops through surf towns, tropical coastline, black-sand beaches, and the lower West Coast farmland. Outside of Wellington, SH1 is bordered by Kapiti Coast beach towns, farmland, and the Tararua Ranges. Kapiti Island is a protected reserve where endangered birdlife thrives.

6 Wellington and the Wairarapa. Cafés, art galleries, and cinemas overflow in the capital city, giving it a vibrant quality. It's bordered by steep hillsides studded with Victorian homes and an expansive harbor and crowned by Te Papa, New Zealand's largest museum. Lyall and Houghton bays attract surfers, while the Miramar Peninsula is home to Peter Jackson's film empire. The Wairarapa, northeast of Wellington, features some of New Zealand's best wine country and windswept coasts.

Paihia○ ○Russell
Bay of Islands
NORTHLAND
2 ○Whangarei

Pacific Ocean

Tasman Sea

Hauraki Gulf

Coromandel
1 ○Whitianga
Auckland **3** ○Tairua
○Thames ○Whangamata

Whakaari
White Island

Cape Runaway

Hamilton ○Tauranga *Bay of Plenty* *East Cape*
Cambridge○ ○Whakatone
Raglan○ WAIKATO ○Opotiki ○Ruatoria
○Tokoroa *Lake Rotorua* EASTLAND
○Rotorua **4** ○Tolaga Bay

Awakino○ *Lake Taupo* ○Taupo
Te Urewera ○Gisborne
New Plymouth○ ○Turangi HAWKE'S *Nat'l Park*
TARANAKI BAY
Egmont ○Ohakune *Tongariro* ○Wairoa *Mahia Peninsula*
National Park Stratford○ *National Park*
Whanganui ○Waiouru ○Napier
Nat'l Park
5 *Hawke Bay*

Whanganui○
Bulls○ *South Pacific Ocean*
Palmerston North○
MANAWATU

Kapiti
Island *TARARUA RANGES*
○Masterton
○Martinborough
Picton○ **6** WAIRARAPA
Tasman Bay ★ 0 ────── 50 mi
Nelson○ *Cook Strait* WELLINGTON 0 ────── 50 km
○Blenheim

WHAT'S WHERE

7 Upper South Island and the West Coast. Across the Cook Strait is the Marlborough Sounds, known for seafood, sunshine, Sauvignon Blanc, sailing, and the Queen Charlotte Track. To the southeast, the wineries of Blenheim rise up into snowcapped mountains plunging to the Kaikoura coastline. To the west, the artistic town of Nelson gives way to Abel Tasman National Park. The West Coast is rugged with sights like the Punakaiki Pancake Rocks and the twin glaciers, Franz Josef and Fox.

8 Christchurch and Canterbury. Easygoing Christchurch, with its British-style gardens and meandering Avon River, is bordered in the north by the thermal resort town, Hanmer Springs. To the east is the Banks Peninsula, another volcanic remnant of green hills and hidden ocean inlets, as well as the French-flavored town of Akaroa. To the west, the flat, vast Canterbury Plains extends to remote Arthur's Pass and the Southern Alps and Aoraki (Mt. Cook), New Zealand's tallest peak.

9 The Southern Alps and Fiordland. The Southern Alps is populated by alpine towns. Queenstown is known as the Adventure Capital of the World and offers up any extreme sport you can think of. Wanaka is quieter, though no less scenic, while artsy Arrowtown displays the area's gold-rush history. Remote Glenorchy is the gateway to spectacular hiking tracks. Best known for the Milford Sound and track, Fiordland is a raw, brooding forest.

10 Otago, Invercargill, and Stewart Island. The southern part of the South Island has two main towns: Invercargill and Dunedin. Dunedin is the livelier of the two, due in part to its university. The towns are bordered by the Otago Peninsula, rich in albatrosses, seals, and penguin colonies, and the Catlins, known for its bird-rich forests. To the very south lies Stewart Island, with its colonies of kiwi birds and Rakiura National Park.

What to Eat and Drink

PAVLOVA
The country's most beloved dessert is this meringue-based concoction with a soft inside and crispy crust outside, served with whipped cream and fruit. It's typically made at home during the holidays, but many bakeries sell it year-round too.

WINE
Wine is huge here, with a variety of popular regions all over the country producing high-quality whites and reds. Popular regions include Marlborough, Hawke's Bay, Gisborne, and Central Otago. Sauvignon Blancs and Pinot Noirs are particularly well-regarded here.

LAMB
No matter where you go in New Zealand, lamb is bound to be on the menu. Sheep farms are everywhere, and lambs raised on Kiwi farms are grass-fed and have a more pronounced flavor with a tenderer cut. You'll find lamb in the form of chops, steaks, and racks, and it tends to be much cheaper than in the United States.

L&P
Lemon & Paeroa, otherwise known as L&P, is New Zealand's most famous soft drink. It's a carbonated lemon-flavored drink (even sweeter than Sprite), and it's what you'll get if you ever order a lemonade here.

FISH-AND-CHIPS
Originally an export from the British colony days, fish-and-chips has continued to remain popular thanks to the country's reliance on the fishing industry. Just like in England, expect lightly battered fish (typically snapper, hoki, or terakihi) served alongside crispy fries.

KUMARA FRIES
One of the most well-known New Zealand vegetables, a kumara is like a sweet potato or yam. Seasoned in various ways, kumara fries are a common choice for a side to a fast food or pub meal.

HOKEY POKEY ICE CREAM
Fresh dairy is delicious here, and one of the most popular ice cream flavors is called Hokey Pokey. It consists of vanilla ice cream mixed with golden honeycomb toffee, and it is a mainstay at most ice cream shops in the country.

GREENSHELL MUSSELLS
Native to New Zealand, Greenshell mussels are found in the area of the Marlborough Sounds; the town of Havelock is known as the Greenshell mussel capital of the world. They have a green hue to their edges, and are usually larger than other mussels. Also called green-lipped mussels, enjoy them doused in a butter-garlic sauce.

CRAYFISH
Not to be confused with the smaller shrimp-like species common in the American south, New Zealand crayfish are hard-shelled lobsters ranging in colors from speckled orange to purple, with eight small legs instead of two large front claws. Their flavor is a bit different than lobster, but the meat's consistency is the same.

A New Zealand winery

SPEIGHT'S BEER

One of New Zealand's most beloved brands of beer, Speight's is available at just about every store and bar in the whole country. The most common is a draught-style lager, and variations include Speight's Summit, with all-natural ingredients, and Speight's Traverse, a low-carb option.

HĀNGI

A Māori hāngi is a culinary experience and a classic Māori cultural tradition. The preparation involves steaming meat, seafood, and vegetables for several hours in a large underground pit. It's often paired with a concert (similar to a Hawaiian luau).

BLUFF OYSTERS

If you're used to garnishing your oysters with lemon juice and cocktail sauce to mask the flavor, think again. The Bluff oyster is one of the largest and tastiest you'll ever try, and it's considered by many to be the most delicious oyster species in the world. Found in the Foveaux Strait, between the South Island and Stewart Island, they are served all over the country, but are most common in the south. Other names include dredge oysters, mud oysters, and flat oysters.

MUTTONBIRD

For those who appreciate delicacies, muttonbird (also known as sooty shearwater) is a species of seabird that is served saturated in bull kelp, giving it a briny taste. The more south you travel, the fresher it gets, because muttonbirds are mostly found on Australia's Muttonbird Island, located off the coast of Stewart Island. It's very rarely even talked about outside of Australia and New Zealand, so this is certainly one flavor you can't get elsewhere.

VEGEMITE

A condiment as common as peanut butter and jelly is in the States, New Zealanders put vegemite on their toast in the morning or snack on it any time of the day. (You might also hear about its close cousin, Marmite, which is the same flavor, but with a different name). This thick black spread is made from leftover brewers' yeast extract with various spices added in, and often has a bitter saltiness. This means it's an acquired taste (don't just go for a straight spoonful out of the jar), but add it to your toast with some eggs and bacon, and it just might inspire your taste buds.

What to Buy

ABALONE

You'll find the iridescent blue-gray abalone (or paua) shell inlaid on wooden homewares or silver jewelry. The shells come from a species of sea snail found throughout New Zealand's coasts, and you can even beachcomb to find slivers in the sand that wash ashore all over the country.

KETE BAGS

Woven out of New Zealand flax leaves and traditionally made by the Māori, kete products usually come in the form of backpacks, handbags, or wallets. The weaving process, called raranga, is the same process used to weave floor mats and belts.

WILD FERN'S BEE VENOM

The skincare industry is thriving in New Zealand, with companies like Wild Fern using ethical and sustainable local sources for their products. One of the most popular is their bee venom, which you'll find used in eye creams, face masks, moisturizers, and lip plumpers.

CARVED WOOD

The art of wood-carving, also called *whakairo rakau*, is considered an ancient and respected Māori skill. You'll see beautifully Māori-carved wood products for sale throughout the country, everywhere from boutique shops to airports.

POUNAMU

Also known as greenstone or jade, this is the national gem of New Zealand. Local lore says buying it for yourself is bad luck, so have a travel companion officially purchase it for you. The stone is mostly made into ornamental pieces or jewelry, but it's often carved into different symbols, which all have specific meanings and stories.

MERINO WOOL

New Zealand is the world's second largest wool producer (after Australia), and high-country merino wool is the most sought after. Merino wool clothing and products are sold nearly everywhere (just make sure the label confirms it was actually made here). Wool sweaters, leggings, hats, scarves, and gloves all make for great (and warm) souvenirs.

WHITTAKER'S CHOCOLATE

A native New Zealand brand, Whittaker's is the second leading chocolate company in the country after Cadbury. The family has been making chocolate for more than 120 years, and a visit to their headquarters in Porirua is sure to result in some sweet souvenirs.

Pounamu, or jade carving

OLIVE OIL
More than 20 varieties of olive trees are available in New Zealand and olives are grown from Northland to Central Otago, but New Zealand's nascent olive oil industry varies widely in quality. The best olive oils have smooth, non-cloying texture and nutty, peppery flavors. Simunovich Olive Estate (south of Auckland) and Frog's End Estate (outside Nelson) have earned accolades for their extra virgin presses.

MANUKA HONEY
Produced by bees that pollinate the manuka bush, manuka honey is used in all sorts of medicines, beauty products, and herbal remedies. It's also a delicious natural sweetener that makes a great souvenir you can purchase from a health food store or local farm.

PUKEKO
The pukeko, or swamp hen, is a ubiquitous native bird, but it took artist Kevin Kilsby to turn the bright blue and red creature into an icon. His whimsical, decorative clay creations—with big red beaks, impossibly long, skinny legs, and gumboot-clad feet—come in several sizes and designs. Find the statuettes in souvenir shops all over the country, or go to the source: Kilsby's shop in Auckland.

RUGBY GEAR
As the world's leading rugby union team, the New Zealand All Blacks have quite the fan following here. So do your best to fit in by purchasing a jersey, scarf, or hat and show your support for the All Blacks, whether or not you make it to a game or just cheer them on from a bar.

Best National Park Adventures

KAYAKING IN NELSON LAKES NATIONAL PARK
This national park is focused around two gorgeous glacier-formed lakes: Rotoiti and Rotoroa, both of which are excellent places to kayak. Pull up to a quiet stretch of pebble beach to observe the park's rocky peaks and intense greenery, where all you will hear are the birds and the breeze.

SWIMMING IN ABEL TASMAN NATIONAL PARK
Abel Tasman offers gorgeous scenery in the form of beaches, golden sand, and limestone caves, and one of the most unique ways to see it all is by taking it in via a sky-dive.

CAVING IN KAHURANGI NATIONAL PARK
Within New Zealand's second largest park, you'll find some of the country's most interesting rock formations as well as a spectacular network of underground caves. Local guides can take you on cave tours and cave-diving in the Pearce and Riwaka rivers.

HIKING IN MOUNT ASPIRING NATIONAL PARK
No roads go through Mount Aspiring, which means you'll need to hike, fly, or boat to explore it. But luckily this breathtaking, unspoiled landscape is made for hiking, and invites you to explore its river valleys, deep wilderness, and unusual Red Hills.

BOAT CRUISING IN FIORDLAND NATIONAL PARK
The country's biggest park offers scores of boat trips that take you through its two main sounds: Milford and Doubtful, and get you close to waterfalls, penguins, and dolphins.

VOLCANO HIKING IN TONGARIRO NATIONAL PARK
Home to three spectacular volcanoes (Tongariro, Ruepehu, and Ngauruhue, which doubles as Mt. Doom), the famed Tongariro Alpine Crossing has been described as the best one-day hike in the world, taking you over red craters, green and blue lakes, and wild open countryside.

FLIGHT-SEEING IN AORAKI /MOUNT COOK NATIONAL PARK
In the heart of the Southern Alps lies New Zealand's largest mountain, Aoraki. The best way to get close is via a flight-seeing tour; certain tours can also take you to land and trek on the famed Tasman Glacier.

SCENIC DRIVING IN EGMONT NATIONAL PARK
Within New Zealand's second oldest park, Mt. Taranaki rises 8,261 feet, dominating the landscape. Actually climbing the volcano is for serious mountaineers only, but you can drive up three access roads that lead you to the forest-lined lower slopes, offering stunning views.

BIRD-WATCHING IN RAKIURA NATIONAL PARK
Taking up 85% of Stewart Island, this park and its impenetrable wilderness are home to a striking variety of birds. Water taxi companies can drop you off at bird sanctuary Ulva Island, or take off on a hike on your own and spot a few of the island's 20,000 kiwi birds.

CANOEING IN WHANGANUI NATIONAL PARK
New Zealand's most canoed river is the heart of this national park, thanks to its gentle gradient and calm rapids. Paddle through the lush wilderness to Pipiriki, or head out to the lower reaches to explore historic Māori riverside settlements.

Best Wineries

MT. DIFFICULTY, OTAGO

The Central Otago wine region is filled with vineyards hemmed in by staggering white-capped mountain ranges, producing earthy rich reds. Mt. Difficulty Wines is known for its sustainable and organic wines, which you can taste in its gorgeous setting.

ALLEN SCOTT FAMILY WINEMAKERS, MARLBOROUGH

New Zealand's largest, most well-known wine region is Marlborough, which produces 70% of the national crop and some world-class Sauvignon Blancs. One highlight of the area is Allen Scott Family Winemakers, a family operation that produces excellent Chardonnay, Pinot Noir, and Riesling.

FROMM WINERY, MARLBOROUGH

Also in the Marlborough region, Fromm is a Swiss-based company with both Kiwi and European roots. Having planted their first vines over 25 years ago, they have the oldest Malbec vineyard in the country and continue to produce an especially delicious Pinot Noir.

HUNTER'S WINES, MARLBOROUGH

One of the most well-known women in the New Zealand wine business, Jane Hunter is a pioneer of wine-making in Marlborough. Within the rustic farm house that doubles as a wine cellar, you can taste Sauvignon Blancs, Pinot Noirs, and Māori-inspired bubbly. The garden showcases a collection of rare native plants, and the rotating artists-in-residence regularly contribute to the decor.

WAIRAU RIVER WINES, MARLBOROUGH

Established in 1978, this family-owned winery in Blenheim was one of the first official grape growers in the region. Today, they have multiple vineyards producing excellent Sauvignon Blanc, along with an on-site restaurant specializing in wine parings.

KAHURANGI ESTATE, NELSON

Located close to Kahurangi National Park, this winery specializes in aromatic grapes that produce sweeter than usual wines. It also has one of the oldest Riesling vines on the South Island and it's one of the most scenic places to enjoy a glass or two, thanks to Mt. Arthur in the background.

NEUDORF VINEYARD, NELSON

For an example of how impressive a small winery can be, head to Neudorf Vineyard, which has been producing wine in the Moutere Valley since 1978. Thanks to a worldwide reputation for excellent Pinot Noirs and Chardonnays, the owners are able to pack a one-two punch of delicious wine amid an intimate, friendly setting.

BLACK ESTATE, WAIPARA VALLEY

A local landmark, Black Estate is home to two vineyards and an award-winning restaurant. Some of their most popular wines include Cabernet Franc, Chenin Blanc, Pinot Noir, and Chardonnay.

Allan Scott Family Winemakers

PEGASUS BAY, WAIPARA VALLEY
Entirely family-owned and run, Pegasus Bay is open for tastings, education, and, of course, for purchasing delicious wine. Pinot Gris, Chardonnay, and Pinot Noir are highlights, as is the winery's natural amphitheater that regularly hosts classical concerts and operas.

MARTINBOROUGH VINEYARD, THE WAIRARAPA
This region is known for small wineries like Martinborough Vineyard, which produces some of New Zealand's best Pinot Noirs. Their Chardonnay is also excellent.

MISSION ESTATE WINERY, HAWKE'S BAY
The country's second-largest wine region, Hawke's Bay is famous for Chardonnays, Cabernet Sauvignons, Syrahs, and

Merlots. You'll find them all here, at the oldest winery in New Zealand (it dates back to 1851).

CRAGGY RANGE WINERY, HAWKE'S BAY
For Hawke's Bay's most picturesque winery, visit Craggy Range, which offers breathtaking views of Te Mata Peak. Sample the excellent Chardonnays, Merlots, and Syrahs and be sure to spend some time at the excellent French-inspired restaurant on-site.

GIBBSTON VALLEY WINES, OTAGO
As the best known winery in Central Otago, Gibbston Valley also has the honor of being home to the first vines planted in the region. Today, it offers premium wines in a beautiful setting along with an impressive cheese plate and sandwich menu. For an intimate wine tasting, be sure to visit the wine cellar/cave for a tour.

GOLDIE VINEYARD, AUCKLAND
This winery was the first to plant grapes on Waiheke Island, part of the Hauraki Gulf Islands in Auckland. There's a wine resarch institute on-site for those who are truly interested in the wine-making process; casual fans can just enjoy a personalized tour or, if you're lucky, the specactular nine-course degustation menu that is served just four times a year.

Best Beaches

WHARARIKI BEACH

South Island beaches are captivating, particularly in Abel Tasman National Park and neighboring Golden Bay. The sands are indeed golden, and the water is jade green; Wharariki Beach has one of the most breathtaking coastlines in the whole country.

90 MILE BEACH

Actually stretching just 89 miles, this beach spans the length of the Aupouri Peninsula from Kaiaia to Cape Regina. Part of the Te Araroa Trail (one of the world's longest walking trails), it's perfect for surfing, swimming, and fishing.

RAGLAN

A world-renowned surfing paradise, Raglan is a town in the Waikato region ripe with opportunities for water adventures, including kayaking and paddleboarding. The best beaches for surfing are Manu Bay and Ngarunui Beach, with plenty of classes for newbies too.

COROMANDEL-WAIHI BEACH

Located at the bottom of Coromandel Peninsula, Waihi is a town on the western coast of the Bay of Plenty, which has one of the most beautiful coastlines in New Zealand. With a 9 km (5½ mile) shore, it's perfect for safe surfing, swimming, and long walks.

OHOPE BEACH

On the eastern side of the Bay of Plenty, Ohope stretches for 11 km (7 miles), surrounded by forest trails that can take you into the foot of Te Urewera National Park. The gentle waves and warm water means this is a great place to learn how to surf.

FITZROY BEACH

Located in New Plymouth, Fitzroy runs alongside the Coastal Walkway, and is a popular destination for swimming and surfing. It's especially suitable for families.

ST. CLAIR BEACH

In Otago, St. Clair lies on the outskirts of Dunedin, an excellent break from the bustling city center. It has consistent surf breaks, easy swimming, and the only heated salt water pool in the country.

Fitzroy Beach

WAIHEKE ISLAND
Part of the Hauraki Gulf Islands right outside Auckland, Waiheke is a former hippie hideaway turned upscale vacation retreat filled with vineyards and local cafés. Luckily, it's still filled with charming beaches like Oneroa Beach, Palm Beach, and Onetangi.

KAITERITERI BEACH
With access to Abel Tasman, Kaiteriteri is one of the region's prettiest beaches, thanks to its golden sand, rocky islets, and deep clear water. You can even cycle here from Nelson via the Great Taste Trail.

CATHEDRAL COVE
One of Coromandel's most distinctive features is this slice of beach by the town of Hahei. The stunning rock arch makes for a gorgeous setting to swim and snorkel in the cove's calm waters. It can be reached via hiking, kayaking, or a water taxi.

TAYLOR'S MISTAKE
This beach just outside of Christchurch has the best surfing waves in the area, but is still calm enough for swimmers to enjoy. Hikers and bikers also enjoy coming here for the excellent clifftop views; be on the look-out for dolphins playing in the waters.

KAREKARE BEACH
Known for its black volcanic sand, Karakare is a 50-minute drive from downtown Auckland and offers surfing, walking, and picnicking in setting filled with waterfalls and rain forest landscapes.

New Zealand Today

Kia ora, or welcome, to the "Youngest Country on Earth." New Zealand's moniker may specifically reference its place as the last landmass to be discovered, but it also speaks to the constant geological, social, and political shifts the country has undergone as it has tried to find its national identity. Tectonic hotbeds include three active volcanoes—Tongariro, Ngauruhoe, and Ruapehu—on the Central Plateau of the North Island and the still-growing Southern Alps on the South Island. In a nation of farmers with frontier ancestors, Georgina Beyer, a transgender former sex worker, won a rural seat against a conservative opponent in 1999, and today, Prime Minister Jacinda Ardern is the world's youngest female head of government, and only the second elected head of government to give birth while in office. New Zealand's Ernest Rutherford was the first person to split the atom, but the country remains passionately anti–nuclear technology. The national rugby team, the All Blacks, continues to dominate the field as one of the best rugby teams in the world, though many Kiwis still consider themselves to be underdogs in sport.

A TALE OF TWO ISLANDS

Together, the North and South Islands make up the majority of *Aotearoa*—Land of the Long White Cloud. New Zealand is roughly the size of Colorado (with a slightly smaller population), but you are never more than 150 miles from the sea. New Zealand's two main islands are more than 1,000 miles long and together encompass nearly every environment on the planet: glaciers, white-sand beaches, fjords, rain forests, alpine forest and lakes, agricultural plains, and volcanic craters and cones.

The South Island is the stunner: the colorful beaches, inlets, and sunny vineyards of the north give way to the Southern Alps, a mountain range that can only be crossed in three places (Arthur's Pass, Lewis Pass, and Haast Pass). Aoraki/Mount Cook National Park contains New Zealand's tallest mountain (Aoraki/Mt. Cook, 12,316 feet) and another 19 peaks that are more than 10,000 feet. Forty percent of the park is covered by glaciers. On the West Coast, dense native forest, wild weather, and a sparse population provide a frontier feel. At the southern end of the West Coast is primeval Fiordland National Park, more than 3 million acres of raw wilderness. Together, Fiordland, Aoraki/Mount Cook, Westland Tai Poutini, and Mount Aspiring national parks form Te Wāhiponamu, a UNESCO World Heritage site encompassing 6.4 million acres, nearly 10% of New Zealand's total landmass.

On the East Coast of the South Island, sea life ranges from the giant 65-foot male sperm whale to the 5-foot Hector's Dolphin. On land, ideas of preserving the wildlife are different from what you'd expect. Saving birds and trees entails ridding the area of possums and cats— mammals that are not native to New Zealand.

Fourteen miles separate the North and South Islands over the rough Cook Strait, but the two islands are worlds apart. Due to its volcanic origins, the North Island has fertile farmlands and rejuvenated native forest. More than three-quarters of New Zealand's 4.2 million people live on the North Island, which tends to have milder weather and a more forgiving landscape. Long beaches sweep up both coasts past small communities (many still predominantly Māori). Te Urewera National Park and two out of three of New Zealand's longest rivers (Waikato and Wanganui) are found near the Central Plateau. Here you'll also discover New Zealand's largest lake (Taupo).

A TALE OF TWO CULTURES

New Zealand is 900 miles from the nearest landmass. Its relative isolation and geographical diversity have affected its population. On a whole, New Zealanders are genial, reserved, and friendly, but they don't suffer fools or braggarts lightly. An isolated past, when things were either unavailable or expensive, led to a nation of inventors: Kiwis invented the jet-boat, bungy jumping, and the electric fence, to name a few. They were the first to climb Mt. Everest, and the first to give women the vote.

New Zealand is a bicultural nation. New Zealanders of European descent (*Pākehā*) make up 80% of the population, while Māori make up 15% (the rest is largely Pacific Islanders and Asian), and the future is still unclear. There are two camps: most New Zealanders want to move forward as "one New Zealand," but a significant portion still sees Māoridom as a culture set apart. Although some New Zealanders consider the reconciliation process to be labored and an impediment to forward progress, Māori is an oral culture, and others feel that continuing to discuss the past is a way of making certain it isn't lost in the present.

KIWI QUALITY OF LIFE

New Zealand is consistently rated as one of the best places to live and is one of the most active nations: Kiwis seem to be born with a love of the outdoors, and families tramp, caravan, sail, and play rugby, cricket, and netball together. Most New Zealanders are well educated. They value travel highly, with one-quarter of the population traveling overseas every year, often for their post-school O.E. (overseas experience). Kiwis don't tend to be religious, with two-thirds lightly following one of the four main Christian religions (Catholic, Methodist, Presbyterian, and Anglican). New Zealand isn't a

wealthy nation, either: most Kiwis prefer a good work–life balance to an overflowing bank account.

100% PURE

Despite their quality of life, many New Zealanders express concern for the country's future. The Department of Conservation now focuses on environmental issues, reflecting the national love of the outdoors and the importance of the landscape to the country's burgeoning tourism industry. Although New Zealand is making great strides in sustainability, the country aims for a "100% Pure" lifestyle and is still introducing initatives (including heavy fines for littering) as part of a Keep New Zealand Beautiful campaign. New Zealand is also facing a challenge in rising obesity in 25% of adults, a binge-drinking problem, youth gang culture and violent crime, and an increase in poverty. Basically, New Zealand is facing many of the same problems as the Western world—just on a smaller scale.

New Zealand History

AOTEAROA

According to Māori legend, the demigod Maui sailed from Hawaiki (believed to be one of the French Polynesian islands) in his canoe, and he caught a huge fish, which he dragged to the surface. The fish is the North Island; Maui's canoe is the South Island.

This legend describes New Zealand's history, which is one of hardship, fortitude, and discovery. This brave, isolated, and young country is still creating its history, day by day.

Māori oral traditions say it began with the moa hunters, believed to have arrived in the 9th century, possibly from east Polynesia, which could make them related to present-day Māori. In AD 925, Kupe sailed from Hawaiki and discovered New Zealand. He returned to Hawaiki, named it Aotearoa (Land of the Long White Cloud), and passed on the sailing coordinates. In AD 1350, eight war canoes landed in New Zealand, marking the beginning of Māori culture on the landmass. Their existence was a battle of brutality and beauty. Warriors were trained at a young age, and tribal warfare and sheer survival led to a low life expectancy. At the same time, Māori became accomplished tattoo, carving, and weaving artists.

EUROPEANS ARRIVE

In 1642, the Dutch captain Abel Tasman sighted the South Island, near Punakaiki, and officially put New Zealand on the map. Captain Tasman never actually set foot in New Zealand, though—he left after his boat was attacked by Māori in Golden Bay.

In 1767, Captain James Cook visited "Nieuw Zeeland" (as it had been named) in the *Endeavour,* and he is responsible for accurately charting the coastline. The whalers and sealers arrived in the 1790s, nearly obliterating sea-life populations in a matter of decades. Māori also suffered from the introduction of European diseases and firearms, which they used on each other in their brutal land wars.

THE TREATY OF WAITANGI

The date February 6, 1840, is one of the most important dates in New Zealand history. Māori signed the Treaty of Waitangi with the British. The Treaty guaranteed Māori rights to their land, but it gave the British sovereignty. The hope of this treaty was that it would end land wars, tame lawlessness, and put New Zealand beyond the reach of French settlement. The New Zealand capital was moved from Russell in the Bay of Islands to Auckland, where it remained for 25 years.

But Māori continued to lose their land to both the government and local settlers. When *Pākehā* (Europeans) outnumbered Māori for the first time in 1858, Māori tribes banded together, declaring Waikato's Te Wherowhero the first Māori king. This only galvanized the British further, and violent land wars continued well into the 1860s.

BOOM YEARS AND SOCIAL CHANGES

Meanwhile, on the South Island, gold was discovered, leading to a booming period of growth in the areas around Queenstown, Arrowtown, and Otago, including the establishment of New Zealand's first university in 1869 in Dunedin. The nation's capital was also moved to Wellington (1865), and Māori were given representation in parliament two years later. By 1880, the government had established free public schooling, and railroads and roads were beginning to crisscross the country. New Zealand also became the first country to legalize unions in 1878, and it was the first country to give women the vote in 1893.

Although well versed in land wars, New Zealand got its first taste of international war in 1899, when it backed the British in the Boer War. New Zealand's allegiance to the Crown made for a bloody 50 years. In World War I, New Zealanders were part of the epic battle at Gallipoli in Turkey; 10% of the population joined the Australian and New Zealand Army Corps (ANZAC), which helped to form the strange and unique bond with Australia, but nearly 17,000 New Zealanders died in the conflict. New Zealand also entered the fray in World War II, once again sustaining heavy casualties that rocked the tiny country's population.

THE POST-WWII YEARS

The 1950s through the 1980s were a time of huge economic growth, then bust, populated with local tragedies. In 1952 the country's population soared to more than 2 million, and in 1953 local boy Edmund Hillary with Sherpa Tenzing Norgay became the first to summit Mt. Everest. Postwar, the economy was at an all-time high. Within the next few decades, however, disaster struck again and again, including the 1953 Mt. Ruapehu eruption that killed 151 people when a lahar derailed a train, the sinking of the ferry *Wahine* off Wellington's coast in 1968, and the plane crash in Antarctica in 1979 that killed all 257 passengers. The economy went into a slump, and mad-dash government efforts only seemed to make things worse.

The 1980s were defined by stands that started to give New Zealand her own identity. In 1981 much of the population was in an uproar about the South African rugby team touring New Zealand. Apartheid protesters flocked to the streets and clashed with Kiwis who felt that politics had no place in rugby. In 1984, the Labour government put a ban on nuclear-powered or-armed ships, despite pressure from the United States because of its anti-nuke stand. In 1985, the Greenpeace ship *Rainbow Warrior* was blown up in Auckland by the French. In 1987, New Zealand won the inaugural Rugby World Cup—a feat it repeated in 2011 and 2015.

IN THE NEW MILLENNIUM

Māori culture has experienced a resurgence and greater integration, but in 2003 a new debate flared as Māori requested a legal inquiry into their precolonial customary ownership of the seabed and shore. Thousands of protesters marched on Parliament in support of Māori claims. New Zealand ratified the Kyoto Treaty in late 2002; it bound itself to new environmental regulations. On February 22, 2011, a magnitude 6.3 earthquake caused massive destruction in Christchurch and killed 181 people. In the past decade, New Zealand has seen its tourism numbers grow, thanks largely to its fame as the setting of Peter Jackson's *Lord of the Rings* trilogy.

What to Read and Watch Before You Go

THE LUMINARIES BY ELEANOR CATTON

Young author Eleanor Catton penned this ambitious, 800-page novel that went on to win the UK's prestigious Man Booker Prize. Organized into astrologically inspired sections, the book's intriguing characters meet each other during an 1860s gold rush on the South Island's West Coast, when many Europeans flocked to the area after word spread that two Māori men had struck gold.

TOP OF THE LAKE

This eerie television show about sordid crimes in a gorgeous region of New Zealand (shot mostly in Queenstown and Glenorchy on the South Island) was a BBC Original that's also currently available on Netflix. Its binge-worthy, cliffhanger episodes and creepy plot are responsible for many lost nights of sleep. In a stunning performance (but with a questionable New Zealand accent), Elizabeth Moss plays a troubled detective with mysterious issues around returning home for the first time. The show takes place in a remote mountain town and centers on the mysterious pregnancy of a 12-year-old girl.

HUNT FOR THE WILDERPEOPLE

The story of a Māori preteen and his unlikely foster father's adventure in the Bush is a feel-good, laugh-out-loud choice for anyone looking to venture to New Zealand. The heartwarming film takes you on a single-camera trek through the Central Plateau and Waitakere Ranges of the Auckland region. Director Taika Waititi's other film Boy, a coming-of-age story in Waihau Bay, is worth seeing as well.

THE LORD OF THE RINGS SERIES

You'd have to be living under a rock not to know that Peter Jackson's film adaptations of JRR Tolkien's fantasy book series were filmed exclusively throughout New Zealand. Today Lord of the Rings super-fans visit New Zealand just to experience the real-life Middle Earth that surrounds them, even inspiring guided tours and other LOTR-specific tourism to pop up in recent years. Even if you aren't obsessed, the six movies (the three in the original trilogy and the three in The Hobbit trilogy that came after) are a fun way to get psyched about a trip to the only land that could re-create such a fantasy world.

TO THE IS-LAND BY JANET FRAME

Perhaps New Zealand's most celebrated and prolific female writer, Janet Frame wrote dozens of novels, short story collections, poems, and autobiographies. Her autobiographies (To The Is-Land, followed by An Angel at My Table) tell the story of Frame's life, starting with her childhood in 1920s New Zealand. Her fascinating, somewhat volatile life is marked by poverty, psychiatric (mis)treatment and hospitalizations, and eventual outstanding literary achievement.

POUNAMU POUNAMU BY WITI IHIMAERA

Witi Ihimaera's short stories are about the Māori people living on the East Coast of New Zealand, both in traditional rural communities living traditional ways of life, and in their transitions to urban environments. Ihimaera and others started a wider trend for Māori art and literature, helping the Māori as a whole to become better recognized and celebrated by mainstream (European) New Zealand and international cultures.

THE BONE PEOPLE BY KERI HULME

In her novel that won the Man Booker prize in 1984, Keri Hulme creates a moving mystery full of complex characters and themes of love, loss, isolation, and grief. With her mixed cast of characters, outsiders, and recluses of both European and Māori identities, Hulme tells a larger story of New Zealand's historical relations.

THE WHALE RIDER BY WITI IHIMAERA

First a novel by Māori writer Witi Ihimaera and then a 2003 film, *The Whale Rider* is a glimpse into the Māori community and its heritage, and how it has evolved in the modern era. It tells the story of a 12-year-old Māori girl who wants to follow in the tradition of her ancestor (the "Whale Rider") and become a warrior and leader, but is prohibited by her elders because of her gender. True to the book's specific setting, the movie version was filmed in the community of Whangara, on the Northeast coast of the North Island.

ISLAND OF THE LOST BY JOAN DRUETT

A book of nonfiction pieced together from memoirs and historical accounts, *Island of the Lost* tells the stories of two shipwrecks on New Zealand's Auckland Island, occurring months apart from each other in 1864. Through these survival tales (both the successes and failures), the reader discovers the harsh environment, rare flora and fauna, and all elements of life on this unique island.

NOBODY IS EVER MISSING BY CATHERINE LACEY

In Catherine Lacey's raw and emotional novel, a young American woman—haunted by her past and confused about her present—escapes life by hopping on a plane to New Zealand, planning to traverse a country she knows little about. The beauty of the prose is enough to get lost in itself, but it's also fun to discover New Zealand alongside the narrator as she hitchhikes across the country, treks the cities and wilderness, and meets local personalities along the way.

THE CHRONICLES OF NARNIA SERIES

Director and New Zealand native Andrew Adamson took filming back to his home country when creating the movie versions of author C.S. Lewis's *Chronicles of Narnia*, the beloved children's fantasy series. The story begins with *The Lion, The Witch, and The Wardrobe* (2005), when a family of children in post–World War II London escape to a faraway, enchanted land and adventure ensues. A grand scope of New Zealand serves as a backdrop (with a lot of special effects in the foreground), including scenes in Flock Hill, Woodhill Forest, Waitaki District, and Purakaunui Bay.

THE PIANO

A bleak and unruly 19th-century New Zealand sets the background for this eerie love story that went on to win multiple Oscars, including Best Actress and Best Supporting Actress for Holly Hunter and a young Anna Paquin. Director Jane Campion explores ideas of class barriers, British imperialism, and challenges to antiquated British ideals on the "wild" island, and received critical acclaim for the movie's artsy strangeness and talented dramatic performances.

Best Tours in New Zealand

You can always travel without a guide, but in unfamiliar territory you'll learn more with a knowledgeable local by your side. If you're interested in a multiday excursion book it at least several weeks in advance. The companies listed here cover large regions of one or both islands.

With most adventure-tour companies, the guides' knowledge of the environment is matched by a level of competence that ensures your safety even in dangerous situations. The safety record of adventure operators is extremely good. Be aware, however, that most adventure-tour operators require you to sign waivers absolving the company of responsibility in the event of an accident. Courts normally uphold such waivers except in cases of significant negligence.

Bicycling

Season: October–March.

Best Locations: Countrywide.

Cost: Multiday tours start around NZ$1,700 per person, including food, lodging, and guide services. Supplemental fees are commonly charged for single riders.

New Zealand Pedaltours. New Zealand Pedaltours operates on both islands, with tours of 2 to 37 days. Tour options include the Coromandel Peninsula, the Southern Alps, and the Central Otago Rail Trail. Both islands. ⊠ *45 Tarawera Terr., Kohimarama, Auckland* ☎ *09/585–1338, 09/585–1339* ⊕ *www.pedaltours.co.nz.*

SOUTH ISLAND CONTACTS Adventure South. ⊠ *29 Iversen Terr., Christchurch* ☎ *0800/00–1166* ⊕ *www.advsouth.co.nz.* **Pacific Cycle Tours.** ⊠ *Unit 3, 14 Kennaway Rd., Christchurch* ☎ *03/982–9933* ⊕ *www.bike-nz.com.*

Canoeing

Season: Year-round, best October–April.

Best Locations: Whanganui River, North Island.

Cost: From NZ$80 per person for single-day tours to NZ$225 per person for five-day trips. Tents, sleeping bags, and bedrolls can be rented for an additional fee.

Blazing Paddles Canoe Adventures. Blazing Paddles Canoe Adventures runs one- to five-day trips on the Whanganui River, during which you can ride mild rapids, and see waterfalls, pristine forests, and birdlife. Overnight stays are spent camping or in huts, depending on the trip. Blazing Paddles has a provisional OutdoorsMark safety rating and now holds a DOC concession for self-catered guiding trips on the Whanganui River. ⊠ *1033 State Hwy. 4, Taumarunui* ☎ *07/895–5261, 0800/252–9464* ⊕ *www. blazingpaddles.co.nz.*

Cross-Country Skiing

Season: July–September.

Best Location: Aoraki (Mount Cook) and Wanaka, South Island.

Cost: Around NZ$850 for two to five days, NZ$1,170–NZ$1,700 for five days high on Mt. Cook alpine skiing, which includes equipment, meals, hut accommodation, a guide, and transport.

Alpine Recreation Canterbury. In winter (July–September), Alpine Recreation Canterbury runs multiday backcountry skiing trips on the glaciers of Aoraki/Mount Cook and Westland national parks and in the Two Thumb Range above Lake Tekapo, with terrains to suit all reasonably fit skiers. In the National Parks, Alpine and

Telemark Tours typically start with a flight to the alpine hut that becomes your base; from there the group sets out each day. In the Lake Tekapo High Country you hike three hours to a private hut, from which you do day tours. Snowshoeing tours are also possible from here.

In summer (November–April), Alpine Recreation Canterbury runs guided treks, mountaineering courses, and guided ascents in Aoraki/Mount Cook and Westland national parks. They have their own private hut straight opposite the mighty Caroline Face of Mt. Cook, which is used for the Aoraki Mt. Cook Trek, the Ball Pass Crossing, and climbing courses. ✉ *30 Murray Pl., Lake Tekapo, Christchurch* ☎ *03/680–6736, 0800/006–096* ⊕ *www.alpinerecreation.com.*

Diving

Season: Year-round.

Best Locations: Bay of Islands, Poor Knights Islands, Great Barrier Island, Goat Island Marine Reserve, and the Coromandel Peninsula, North Island. Also, Milford Sound, South Island.

Cost: A two-dive day trip without rental gear runs about NZ$150, with gear around NZ$240.

Yukon Dive. Pacific Hideaway Charters runs dives at the Poor Knights Islands, Mokohinau Islands, and the coastal regions around Tutukaka—all of which are home to manta rays, large kingfish, and lots of other sea life. Day trips include tea, coffee, and snacks, as well as kayaks to borrow if you want to stay on the surface. ✉ *Marina A8, Tutukaka* ☎ *09/434–4506, 0800/693–483* ⊕ *yukon. co.nz/pacifichideaway.*

NORTH ISLAND CONTACTS Paihia Dive Hire and Charter. ☎ *0800/107–551, 09/402–7551* ⊕ *www.divenz.com.*

Fishing

Licenses and Limits: Different regions require different licenses when fishing for trout, so check at the local tackle store or visit ⊕ *www.fishandgame.org. nz.* Fees are approximately NZ$124 per year, but at most tackle shops, you can purchase a daily or weekly license. No license is needed for saltwater fishing.

Season: Varies by region.

Best Locations: Countrywide.

Cost: Big-game fishing: NZ$300 per person, per day. Heli-fishing: from NZ$560 per person, per day. Trolling and fly-fishing for lake trout: from NZ$90 per hour (one to four people). Charter costs vary widely.

NORTH ISLAND CONTACTS Blue Ocean Charters. ☎ *0800/224–278* ⊕ *www.blue-ocean.co.nz.* **Brett Cameron Central Plateau Fishing.** ☎ *07/378–8192* ⊕ *www.cpf.net. nz.* **Te Ra Charters.** ☎ *07/865–8681* ⊕ *tera. whangamata.co.nz.*

SOUTH ISLAND CONTACTS New Zealand Fly Fishing Guide. ☎ *03/442–7061* ⊕ *www.flyfishing.net.nz* **Toa Tai Charters.** ☎ *021/169–2257* ⊕ *www.toatai.co.nz.*

Hiking

Season: October–March for high-altitude walks, year-round for others.

Best Locations: Any of the national parks or New Zealand's ten Great Walks.

Cost: One- to three-day guided hikes are NZ$170 to NZ$1,070. Prices for longer hikes vary widely.

Hiking New Zealand. Hiking New Zealand has hiking tours to suit everyone on both islands, from 5 to 20 days. ☎ *0800/697–232, 03/310–8188* ⊕ *www. HikingNewZealand.com.*

NORTH ISLAND CONTACTS Bush and Beach. ☎ *09/837–4130, 0800/423–224* ⊕ *www.bushandbeach.co.nz.* **Kiwi Dundee Adventures, Ltd.** ☎ *07/865–8809* ⊕ *www.kiwidundee.co.nz.*

SOUTH ISLAND CONTACTS Alpine Guides Ltd. ☎ *03/435–1834* ⊕ *www.alpineguides. co.nz .* **Alpine Recreation.** ☎ *03/680–6736* ⊕ *www.alpinerecreation.com .* **Guided Walks New Zealand Ltd.** ☎ *03/442–3000, 0800/832–226* ⊕ *www.nzwalks.com .* **Marlborough Sounds Adventure Company.** ✉ *London Quay, Picton* ☎ *03/573–6078* ⊕ *www.marlboroughsounds.co.nz.* **Ultimate Hikes.** ✉ *The Station Bldg., Duke St. Entrance, Queenstown* ☎ *03/450–1940* ⊕ *www.ultimatehikes.co.nz.* **Wild West Adventure Co.** ✉ *8 Whall St., Greymouth* ☎ *03/768–6649, 0800/946–543* ⊕ *www. fun-nz.com.*

Horse Trekking

Season: All year-round on the North Island; may be weather dependent on the South Island.

Best Locations: Northland and the Coromandel Peninsula in the North Island, Nelson and Canterbury high country in the South Island.

Cost: Prices range from about NZ$125 for two hours to NZ$240 for a day trip, or NZ$500 for overnight; contact outfitters for specifics on shorter or multiday trips.

SOUTH ISLAND CONTACTS
Cape Farewell Horse Treks. ✉ *23 McGowan St., Puponga* ☎ *03/524–8031* ⊕ *www.horsetreksnz.com* ☎ *From NZ$80.*

Dart Stables Glenorchy. ✉ *58 Coll St., Glenorchy* ☎ *03/442–5688, 0800/474–3464* ⊕ *www.dartstables.com.*

NORTH ISLAND CONTACTS
Pakiri Beach Horse Rides. ✉ *317 Rahuikiri Rd., Pakiri Beach, R.D. 2, Wellsford* ☎ *09/422–6275* ⊕ *www.horseride-nz. co.nz* ☎ *NZ$175 half day, NZ$299 full day, including packed lunch.*

Sailing

Season: Year-round.

Best Locations: Bay of Islands, Auckland and Wellington in the North Island, upper and lower South Island, including the Marlborough Sounds.

Cost: Bay of Islands from NZ$90 for a day trip to NZ$700 to NZ$850; Doubtful Sound from NZ$1,750 for five days; Fiordland National Park from NZ$3,700 for eight days.

SOUTH ISLAND CONTACTS Abel Tasman Sailing Adventures. ✉ *46 Martin St., Nelson* ☎ *03/547–6666, 0800/467–245* ⊕ *www.sailingadventures.co.nz* **Heritage Expeditions.** ☎ *03/365–3500* ⊕ *www. heritage-expeditions.com.*

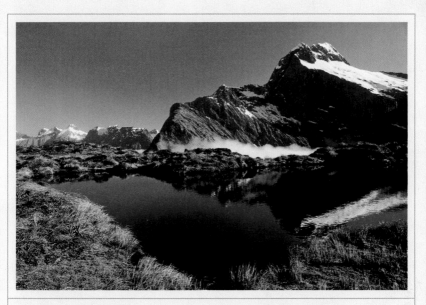

TRAMPING NEW ZEALAND

Tramping (hiking) in the backcountry is a sacred Kiwi pastime. Pristine coastal beaches, meandering rivers, glaciated peaks, steaming volcanoes, isolated lakes, cascading waterfalls, and lush native forest are often just an hour's drive from the major cities. You can "get amongst it" all with short walks, one-day tramps, or multiday hikes.

Many of New Zealand's best tramps are within the 14 national parks. The Department of Conservation (DOC) manages these parks and additional lands totaling over 5 million hectares, almost 30 percent of New Zealand. DOC maintains a range of tracks, walkways, huts, and campgrounds throughout these areas.

The Great Walks are the ten most renowned hiking (though one is technically a canoeing route) tracks, which traverse the country's volcanic plateau beaches, temperate rainforest, fjords, and mountain ranges. The most famous, Milford Track, is commonly called "the finest walk in the world." Collectively the Great Walks see over 86,000 trampers annually.

However, hundreds of other tracks and routes crisscross the country, ranging from gruelling week-long, self-guided adventures to mellow, half-hour strolls through native bush. Often on these tracks you'll have the scenery to yourself. The range of difficulty and variety of terrain means almost anyone can experience tramping in New Zealand.

Milford Track.

PLANNING TIPS

■ During summer book accommodations well in advance, especially for the Milford Track.

■ DOC lowers fees from May to September. However alpine tracks may be impassable or closed.

■ Skip popular day walks such as the Tongariro Alpine Crossing over long weekends to avoid crowds.

■ Many tracks require transport. Book in advance through local tour operators.

BEST ONE-DAY HIKES

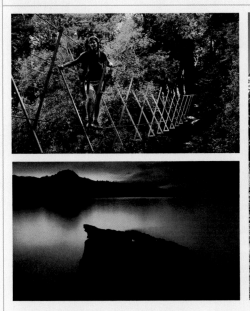

You don't need to commit to a three-day trek in order to see New Zealand by foot. These one-day hikes will give you a sense of New Zealand's landscapes sans huts and tents.

Tongariro Alpine Crossing: Explore the central North Island's alpine scenery, steaming fumaroles, volcanic craters, and brilliant emerald lakes on the country's most popular day walk. In summer the hike is somewhat strenuous, though not technically difficult. In winter it requires high-alpine experience. Hikers generally walk from Mangatepopo to Ketetahi, with side trips to the summits of Ngauruhoe and Tongariro.

Abel Tasman National Park: The park's easily-accessible, golden-sand coastlines require limited fitness. Perhaps the best of the many day walks on the Abel Tasman Coast Track is from Totaranui to Separation Point, where seals are visible in winter and autumn. Water taxi from Marahau transport visitors to a number of different points along the track.

Fiordland National Park: There are a number of short walks from the roadside on the drive to Milford Sound. These range from easy to difficult and from 30 minutes to a day. Key Summit (medium) and Gertrude Saddle (difficult) take in some of New Zealand's most amazing mountain scenery. Don't miss Bowen Falls, an easy 30 minute walk along Milford Sound's foreshore.

Queenstown: A number of day walks start at Glenorchy at Lake Wakatipu's north end. You can access short sections of the Routeburn, Caples, and Gr eenstone tracks, where alpine scenery is the star. The walk to Routeburn Falls is particularly spectacular, well graded, and of medium difficulty.

(top left) Hollyford Track, Fiordland National Park. (right) Routeburn Falls, Mt. Aspiring National Park. (bottom left) Anchorage Hut, Abel Tasman National Park. (opposite page) Routeburn Track.

GREAT WALKS

ISLAND TRACK	DIFFICULTY	ACTIVITIES / ATTRACTIONS
LAKE WAIKAREMOANA TRACK, Te Urewera National Park (Ch. 6) 46 km (28.5mi), 3–4 days	Moderate. The tougest part is the climb from lake edge to Panekiri Bluffs. Heavy rain, mosquitoes and sandflies are common.	Much of the track runs through podocarp forest. Track condition is generally good. The best views are from Panekiri Bluffs. See a variety of birds: kaka, parakeets, paradise ducks, whiteheads, fantails, silvereyes, morepork (native owl) kiwi. Don't miss the short uphill side trip to Korokoro waterfall. Advance booking advised.
TONGARIRO NORTHERN CIRCUIT, Tongariro National Park (Ch. 6) 41 km (25 mi), 3–4 days	Moderate. Take good gear especially for the toughest section, the "Staircase." Do not attempt the track in rain or snow. Volcano erruptions are possible; stay back from steam vents.	This is one of New Zealand's best walks, with wonderful alpine and volcanic vistas, warm blue-green lakes, and steam vents, but mountains are often in heavy clouds. You'll see Mt. Ngauruhoe—a.k.a Mt. Doom in The Lord of the Rings.
WHANGANUI JOURNEY, Whanganui National Park, near Taumarunui (Ch. 9) Full Trip: 145 km (90 mi,) 5 days Short Trip: 88 km (54.5 mi,) 3 days	Moderate. Those with experience can swim, canoe, and kayak. Be prepared for rain and floods.	Although a river journey, Whanganui is a Great Walk, and there is a 3-day version from Whakahoro to Pipiriki. The Whanganui river takes a twisting path to sea; en route, expect narrow gorges, high cliffs, waterfalls, glowworm grottos. Tieke Marae has good huts and facilities, but you'll follow Maori protocol; koha (a gift of money) will be expected. Book trip and hire kayaks in advance from operators in Turangi, Taumaruni, or Ohakune.
ABEL TASMAN COAST TRACK, Abel Tasman National Park, near Nelson (Ch. 9) 54 km (34 mi), 3–5 days	Moderate. In autumn and winter, walking and weather conditions are good and the track is less crowded.	Follow the coast across beautiful golden sand beaches, rocks, and regenerating rain forests (with nikau palms, ferns, and forest gians). The two estuaries are only passable around low tide. You may spot seals and penguins.
HEAPHY TRACK, Kahurangie National Park, near Nelson (Ch. 9) 78 km (48 mi), 4–6 days	Moderate. The most difficult section is between Brown and Perry Saddle huts. While normally a drier area, it does rain on the western slopes.	The track begins in dense beech and podocarp forest in north; continues up to snow tussock plateaus; and descends into palm-studded forests, rugged West Coast beaches. See bird, including kiwis and pipits, along one of the country's finest routes. This is primarily a summer route; snow can block the track in winter.

ISLAND TRACK	DIFFICULTY	ACTIVITIES/ATTRACTIONS
PAPAROA TRACK, Paparoa National Park (Ch. 9) 55 km (34 mi), 2–3 days	Moderate. Paparoa National Park averages over 200 inches of rain a year, so prepare for some wet weather and the occasional high winds.	New Zealand's newest Great Walk takes you through the Paparoa Range, past lush rain forests, limestone cliffs, and subtropical palms. Explore the area's unique mining history while enjoying gorgeous sunsets from the Moonlight Tops Hut and expansive views of the Tasman Sea. It was also designed to be equally accessible to cyclists.
ROUTEBURN TRACK, Mount Aspiring and Fiordland national parks (Ch. 11) 32 km (20 mi), 2–3 days	Moderate. Heavy rain, clouds, snow, and ice can be factors. On mountaintops, winter avalanches are possible.	Travel in either direction through beech forest and onto exposed mountaintops for spectacular scenery. In summer flowers, many unique to New Zealand, cover the alpine slopes. You'll need good equipment to travel this route.
MILFORD TRACK, Fiordland National Park, near Te Anau (Ch. 11) 54 km (33.5 mi), 4–5 days.	Moderate. There are two strenuous climbs, one with a very steep descent. It frequently rains. Beware of avalanche conditions at Mackinnon Pass in winter.	You can only hike in one direction (south to north) along New Zealand's most popular track. Clinton River (often muddy) crosses Mackinnon Pass, goes through alpine meadows, and passes waterfalls, including NZ's highest, Sutherland Falls. Thick forests bookend the track, and lots of kea (mountain parrots) greet trampers. Book at least four months ahead; sandfly repellent is a must.
KEPLER TRACK, Fiordland National Park, near Te Anau (Ch. 11) 60 km (37 mi), 3–4 days	Moderate. Day one includes a steep climb from lake to tops.	The hike goes through beech forests to sometimes snow-covered tussock tops with wonderful views in clear weather. Geology buffs will appreciate this trek, especially Mt. Luxmore. Detour to Iris Burn waterfall, 20-minute walk from Iris Burn hut.
RAKIURA TRACK, Rakiura National Park, Steward Island (Ch. 12) 36 km (22 mi, including road walk), 3 days.	Moderate. There are two short uphill climbs. Be prepared to get muddy in the wet changeable weather. Expect mosquitoes and sandflies.	Follows the coastline through beech forest, subalpine scrub, and remote beaches. Mt. Anglem, a 3–4 hour side trip (one-way), provides wonderful views. Birdlife includes kiwi, bellbirds, tui, fantails, and parakeets. You may see seals and penguins. Hut tickets are required; there's some camping. Pack extra food and insect repellent.

WHAT TO BRING

Weather in New Zealand is unpredictable to say the least, so it is extremely important to be prepared and to carry the right equipment. In the mountains you should prepare for cold, wet weather year-round; in the north you can generally travel a little lighter, but there is nothing worse than walking for five hours shivering and wet because you forgot a decent jacket.

Tramping gear is widely available throughout New Zealand for rental or purchase, but is usually more expensive than in the United States. You must declare all used camping and hiking equipment on arrival. The Ministry of Agriculture and Fisheries (MAF) will inspect and sterilize your equipment, which is usually available for immediate collection. By not declaring your gear you risk not only a hefty fine but also the fragile New Zealand ecosystem, which is extremely susceptible to invasive foreign species.

The equipment you carry and the fitness required depends hugely on where you are heading and how long and at what time of year you're going. In general you should carry:

A good-quality three-season hiking tent (for overnighters).

Tramping clothes, i.e., polypropylene underwear, fleece, etc.

Warm sleeping bag in the winter (year-round in the South Island).

Personal first-aid kit and insect repellent.

Topographic maps (widely available throughout the country). Though not required for the majority of marked tracks, they should be carried when venturing into the back country.

Three-season Tent

Sleeping bag

Fleece jacket

Polypropylene underwear tights and top

WHAT TO WEAR

BASE LAYER: Wear lightweight thermal underwear, preferably polypropylene or other moisture wicking synthetic fabric.

MID LAYER: Fleece, wool, or synthetic jer (preferable for their lighter weight and rapid drying time) go over the base layer. This layer should keep you warm when wet (no cotton sweatshirts).

BACKPACK: Take a sturdy, comfortable pack that fits you well. Take a larger pack for longer tracks. Strong canvas fabric is best.

GAITERS: If walking through thick mud, water, or snow, tramping gaiters (covers for your shoes and pants) are a must.

The key thing to remember is layering. Wearing multiple layers of clothing allows you to rapidly adjust to changing temperatures and different exertion levels. Modern synthetic fabrics are preferable for their lightweight, quick drying times, and ability to keep you warm when wet.

HAT AND GLOVES: Bring a warm hat and gloves made from wool or synthetic.

SUN PROTECTION: Bring a sunhat and sunglasses.

OUTER LAYER: A water- and windproof outer layer, is necessary. In addition to a jacket bring overtrousers for many tracks, especially in the winter.

TROUSERS/SHORTS: Strong synthetic fabrics are best because they dry quickly when wet. No jeans!

SOCKS: Wool or synthetic hiking socks to keep your feet warm.

FOOTWEAR: The most important part, boots should be strong, sturdy, and waterproof. For longer, more rugged tramps full leather boots are best, but on shorter tramps and day walks lightweight fabric boots are often sufficient.

CHOOSING YOUR TRACK

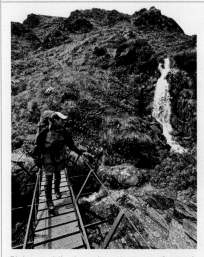

Pick your hike based on the type of experience you're looking for and the time of year you plan on visiting. The DOC has five classifications for walks to help you decide which tracks are best suited for your experience and fitness level.

Short Walks: These easy walks last up to an hour along an even, graded surface and are suitable for all fitness levels.

Walking Tracks: These easy to moderate walks take from a few minutes to a day on reasonably well-formed but occassionally steep tracks. They are clearly signposted and suitable for people with low to moderate fitness. You may need light hiking boots in winter.

Easy Tramping Tracks: These single or multiday, signposted tracks for people of moderate fitness are well formed but may be steep and muddy. Wear light hiking boots. This category includes all the Great Walks.

Tramping Tracks: Trampers need good fitness and moderate back country experience, including navigation and survival skills, to walk these challenging single or multiday unformed trails. Generally marked with poles or rock cairns, trails may include unbridged river crossings; appropriate equipment, sturdy hiking boots, and preparation are required.

Route: You need a lot of backcountry survival and navigational experience, a high level of fitness, sturdy hiking boots and equipment, and preparation for these treks through natural terrain. Tracks may have basic markings, but trampers should be self-sufficient.

Visit DOC's information offices, in all major towns and the national parks, for information and lists of experienced guides, and to register your intentions. Inexperienced trampers should consider guided trips, which remove some of the organizational hassle and provide additional safety. Guides are generally friendly and extremely knowledgeable, and group trips are a great way to meet other travelers.

HUTS

DOC maintains a network of over 950 backcountry huts throughout New Zealand's conservation areas that are available for a small fee. Accommodations range from basic 4-person shelters offering a roof and a mattress to 20-person buildings complete with cooking facilities, toilets, lights, and heating. It's best to book huts well in advance. Book huts on the DOC Web site or by contacting the local DOC office. During the busy months custodians check for payment; however in the off season, respect the honesty system. Fees keep these places pristine and accessible to the public.

Chapter 2

TRAVEL SMART
NEW ZEALAND

Updated by
Kathy Ombler

★ **CAPITAL:**
Wellington

⚑ **POPULATION:**
4,885,300

💬 **LANGUAGE:**
English, Māori

$ **CURRENCY:**
New Zealand dollar

☎ **COUNTRY CODE:**
64

⚠ **EMERGENCIES:**
111

🚗 **DRIVING:**
On the left

⚡ **ELECTRICITY:**
230-40V/50Hz; electrical
plugs have two flat prongs
in a V

🕗 **TIME:**
16 hours ahead of New York

🌐 **WEB RESOURCES:**
NZ Tourism:
🌐 www.newzealand.
com, NZ Tourism Guide:
🌐 www.tourism.net.nz,
The New Zealand Herald:
🌐 www.nzherald.co.nz

Auckland

NEW
ZEALAND

NORTH
ISLAND

Wellington

TASMAN
SEA

SOUTH
ISLAND

SOUTH
PACIFIC
OCEAN

What You Need to Know Before You Visit New Zealand

KNOW WHAT TO DO IF AN EARTHQUAKE HAPPENS

It's nothing to be super concerned about, safety-wise, but earthquakes do happen in this small country constantly. There's a chance you might experience a small earthquake while here at least once, so it's important to know what safety precautions to take in the event one does occur. The biggest safety tips are to have an earthquake plan with your fellow travelers, stay indoors until the shaking stops and it's safe to exit, take cover under a desk or table, and stay away from windows and bookcases or anything that can fall on you. If you're outdoors, move to a clear spot away from buildings and trees, and drop to the ground; if you're in a car, drive to a clear place and stay inside the car. New Zealand's most recent major earthquake was in Christchurch in 2011, which was quite devastating, but the country has not seen one as severe since.

GET TO KNOW SOME VOCABULARY/ PRONUNCIATION

Kiwi English can be mystifying. The colloquialisms alone, not to mention rural slang, can make things puzzling. Known as "cow cockie" talk, this is what you'll hear when "girls" refers to someone's cows, and "gummies" (galoshes) are the favored footwear. The last thing you want to do is offend someone, so it can be helpful to look up a list of slang locals use, so you don't get your verbs and nouns mixed up. People often refer to getting drunk as getting "pissed," so it doesn't always mean someone is angry. New Zealanders refer to dinner as "tea," and afternoon as "arvo." Things are also often pronounced differently here. When traveling around, you'll often see signs for cities and small towns that have a "wh" in the word; it's actually pronounced with an "F" sound: for example, Kaiwharawhara is pronounced kai-futuh-futuh when you add a Kiwi twang to it. Many place-names are Māori as well and can be so long as to seem unpronounceable. (In fact, one of these can claim itself as the longest place-name in the world.) The biggest communication glitch between New Zealanders and visitors often involves the Kiwis' eloquent use of the understatement. This facet of Kiwi speech is both blessing and curse. Everything sounds relaxed and easygoing, but if you're trying to judge something like distance or difficulty, you may run into trouble. No matter how far away something is, people often say it's "just down the road" or "just over the hill." Ask specific questions to avoid a misunderstanding.

PASSES CAN HELP YOU SAVE MONEY

Look into the New Zealand Travelpass to save money by combining bus, ferry, and train costs. The Travelpass has no fixed itineraries and gives you 3,000 different stops to choose from. You choose from a certain number of days of travel and kinds of transportation; there's also an option to tack on air travel. Most Travelpasses are valid for one year; the bus-only version is valid for unlimited travel on InterCity and Newmans coaches over a one-, two-, or three-month period, with an incremental-rate structure. Ask at a local tourist i-SITE visitor information center about hotel and local transportation packages that include tickets to major museum exhibits or other special events.

DON'T MIX UP NEW ZEALAND AND AUSTRALIA

You'll find in your travels that many people don't quite know the difference between Kiwis and Ozzies. Since New Zealand is close to Australia and the two do have several cultural aspects in common, they can easily get mixed up. However, there are differences in the accents, and the indigenous cultures are drastically different. Be careful not to assume the two cultures are that much alike, as New Zealanders are a proud folk and appreciate when people realize that although they are small, they are still a distinct country ripe with great wine, mountain ranges, and an amazing rugby team.

NEW ZEALAND SUN IS STRONGER THAN MOST PLACES SO BRING SUNSCREEN

You won't notice it at first, but once you stay out in the sun on a summer day in New Zealand, you'll begin to feel just how much sharper the sun's rays hit you. It's important to wear sunglasses especially if your eyes are sensitive to sunlight. There isn't a direct hole in the ozone layer over New Zealand, but the thinning layer does send pockets of ozone-depleted air over certain parts of the country starting in the spring. Certain days can hit you harder than others, so make sure you keep yourself protected at all times.

BE RESPECTFUL OF MĀORI CULTURE

As New Zealand's indigenous people, the culture of the Māori is embedded throughout the fabric of the country. The history between the native Māori and the European colonizers who settled New Zealand is long, and often fraught with violence. Recent years have seen a wonderful resurgence in Māori culture and pride, but there are still debates regarding the legal ownership of the land. Tourists especially should be respectful toward Māori history, culture, and tradition. If you don't know anything about the Māori prior to your trip, it's helpful to do some quick reading on the airplane before you land. For instance, the marae, the area in front of a Māori meetinghouse, should not be entered unless you are invited or unless it's in use as a cultural center. Only use the traditional *hongi* (touching foreheads and nose in greeting) if someone else initiates it. You're likely to see a lot of Māori culture on your trip; the Māori Haka is a ceremonial dance or challenge used to intimidate rivals or opponents with chants, the stomping of feet, and extreme facial expressions. The national rugby teams perform it before a game to demonstrate their strength and power to the opposite team. It is also performed at funerals as a memorial to someone's spirit.

IT HELPS TO KNOW WHEN THINGS ARE CLOSED

On Christmas Day, Good Friday, Easter Sunday, and the morning of ANZAC Day (April 25), everything closes down in New Zealand except for a few gas stations, some shops selling essential food items, and emergency facilities. On other public holidays many museums and attractions stay open, as do transportation systems, though on a reduced schedule. Local anniversary days, which vary regionally, pop up as once-a-year three-day weekends in each particular area; some businesses close but hotels and restaurants stay open.

THERE ARE STRICT RULES ABOUT WHAT YOU CAN BRING INTO THE COUNTRY

New Zealand has stringent regulations governing the import of weapons, foodstuffs, and certain plant and animal material. Most stringent is the agricultural quarantine. New Zealand is highly dependent on its agriculture and horticulture industries and cannot risk unwanted introduction of pest plants or animals or disease. The authorities don't want any nonnative seeds (or popcorn kernels or honey) haplessly transported into the country. You must declare even a single piece of fruit, and all camping and hiking gear must be declared and inspected at customs. You'll be hit with an instant NZ$400 fine if you're caught bringing in fruit. And be truthful about your camping gear because they *will* want to take a look at it, unravel your tent and sleeping bag, and check for grass and muck. Do yourself a favor and make sure any camping gear and hiking boots are reasonably clean when entering the country. If you are unsure, simply declare it on the immigration card. An official will ask what you're declaring and if it's okay (like chocolate, for example), he'll send you straight through.

Getting Here and Around

✈ Air Travel

The most common method of arriving in New Zealand is via airplane, typically into Auckland International Airport. Although air travel within New Zealand can be expensive compared with bus travel, the one-way fare system does make it easy to get around, especially if you don't want to spend all your time on the road. These days, booking your domestic flights in conjunction with your international flight won't necessarily save you any money, but it can help if connecting flights are running late—they will hold your next flight for you if possible. Some airlines give great deals if you add stopovers to your flight itinerary. You'll need to stop in at a Pacific destination like Tahiti or Fiji for a limited time before heading to New Zealand. Check with the airline and see what they're offering; make sure that New Zealand is included in Pacific deals because sometimes it's the one exception. Qantas has a low-budget airline called Jetstar, which serves trans-Tasman and between major New Zealand hubs Auckland, Christchurch, Wellington, and Queenstown. When booking domestic flights with either Jetstar or Air New Zealand make sure you read the fine print regarding baggage allowance, as the cheaper fares have zero checked baggage allowance. If you hold an international student identification card, you'll save even more. But make sure you check in well before time! Jetstar is notorious for turning away passengers if they arrive even one second after cutoff time.

From New York to Auckland (via Los Angeles) flights take about 19 hours; from Chicago, about 17 hours; from Los Angeles to Auckland (nonstop), about 12 hours. From the United States and Canada, you will have to connect to a New Zealand–bound flight in Los Angeles, San Francisco, or Houston.

AIRPORTS

The major airport is Auckland International Airport (AKL). It is usually a bit cheaper to fly into and out of this airport, but the supplemental fees for flights to Wellington (WLG) or Christchurch (CHC) are reasonable. New Zealand's airports are relatively compact and easy to negotiate.

Auckland's international and domestic terminals are in separate buildings, a 10-minute walk apart. Free bus shuttles run constantly (however, after an incoming long-haul flight you may find that the walk and fresh air is great for the soul!). Christchurch International Airport is the main gateway to southern tourism destinations.

New Zealand has a dense network of domestic air routes, so hopping from one area to another is fairly easy, if not inexpensive. Air New Zealand partners with other international airlines and serves some smaller regional airports, so you can make these flight arrangements when booking your international flight. If you are sure of your dates well ahead of time, it's worth checking Air New Zealand's Grab A Seat program for one-off domestic specials. Fares between the main cities (Auckland, Wellington, Christchurch, and Queenstown) can be reasonable, but others are often more expensive. For other cities, it's worth checking the websites of smaller regional airlines (Sounds Air and Chathams Air, for example), who have picked up routes the bigger airlines have deemed not worthwhile.

FLIGHTS

Air New Zealand flies two to three times a day from Los Angeles to Auckland and is the only carrier that extends a daily nonstop flight from San Francisco to

Auckland. Qantas flies from Los Angeles to New Zealand daily, mostly through Sydney. United and Air Canada, affiliates of Air New Zealand, connect from points in North America to Los Angeles. Fiji Airways connects from Los Angeles through Nadi, Fiji, with Auckland, Wellington, and Christchurch.

Within New Zealand, Air New Zealand and Jetstar compete on intercity trunk routes, along with smaller airlines Sounds Air, and Air Chathams who fly several intercity routes. Several airlines provide services to Australia: trans-Tasman flights are available from Auckland, Wellington, Christchurch, Dunedin, and Queenstown.

🚢 Boat Travel

To travel between the North Island and the South Island, take either the Interislander or Bluebridge ferry between Wellington and Picton. Both ferries carry cars. They also connect with KiwiRail trains. A free shuttle is available between the railway station and InterIslander ferry terminal in Wellington. The Bluebridge terminal is right across the road from the station. The Picton railway station is a few minutes' walk from the ferry terminals. Both ferries travel four to five times a day. Standard one-way passenger fare can be as much as NZ$70, but there are off-peak deals to be had for as low as NZ$39. The fare for a medium-size sedan starts at NZ$175 (including driver). Be sure to ask about specials, including ferry-train package deals through KiwiRail, when you book.

Schedules are available at i-SITE visitor information centers around the country. Most will arrange Interislander and Bluebridge ferry bookings. You can also check schedules and fares and book online via the Interislander and Bluebridge websites. Some fares allow you to make schedule changes up to the last minute and guarantee a full refund if you cancel prior to check-in. Discount fares can be booked once in New Zealand; these have some restrictions. No matter how you go about it, it's a good idea to reserve in advance, especially during holiday periods.

🚌 Bus Travel

New Zealand is served by an extensive bus network. The InterCity Group operates the main bus lines, InterCity and Newmans. Some Newmans and InterCity bus routes overlap, but Newmans tends to have fewer stops and sticks to the key tourism routes, for example Christchurch to Queenstown and the West Coast. InterCity buses, on the other hand, cover more remote areas.

There are also many regional bus services. For instance, Bottom Bus, operated by Travel Head First, runs from Dunedin through the Catlins to Southland, Queenstown, and Fiordland; while Atomic Travel links Christchurch with Dunedin.

Take a hop-on, hop-off bus if you prefer a more flexible itinerary, typically valid for 12 months. InterCity offers this, along with "backpacker-target" companies like Kiwi Experience and Stray Bus. Some passes cover all of New Zealand, whereas others are limited to specific regions. Most of the backpacker buses have affiliations with accommodation and activities and can offer priority bookings and special deals.

FARES AND PASSES
Fares vary greatly. A standard full fare between Auckland and Wellington is NZ$95 but can be obtained for as low as NZ$34. A certain number of seats are

Getting Here and Around

sold at a discounted rate, so book your tickets as early as possible, especially during the holidays. Individual company's websites are the best way to find out about special fares.

Look into the various flexible passes that allow coach travel over a set route in a given time frame, usually three or six months. You can travel whenever you like, without paying extra, as long as you stick to the stops covered by your pass. The Flexipass is sold in blocks of time during which you're eligible to travel on regular InterCity bus routes. This is such a good deal that locals even use this pass for their daily commute. Typically valid for a year, you can hop on and off, changing your plans without a penalty at least two hours prior to your departure. You must schedule in advance, as independent bus ticketing windows don't track your Flexipass hours.

There is also the New Zealand TravelPass, which allows unlimited travel on buses and trains and on the Interislander ferries that link the North and South Islands. Kiwi Experience and Stray Bus also visit some pretty cool destinations with special accommodations not found on the mainstream traveler networks—remote farming settlements, small town pubs, and Māori *marae* (villages), for example.

🚗 Car Travel

Nothing beats the freedom and mobility of a car for exploring. Even if you're nervous about driving on the "wrong" side of the road, driving here is relatively easy. Many rental cars will have a sticker right next to the steering wheel reading "stay to the left." Having said this, as tourism numbers increase so, too, have the number of driving accidents involving tourists. Tourism organizations have prepared a

voluntary Code of Practice to help rental vehicle companies advise their clients, and the Drive Safe website (⊕ *www. drivesafe.org.nz*) gives some handy tips.

Remember this simple axiom: drive left, look right. That means keep to the left lane, and when turning right or left from a stop sign, the closest lane of traffic will be coming from the right, so look in that direction first. By the same token, pedestrians should look right before crossing the street. Americans and Canadians can blindly step into the path of an oncoming car by looking left as they do when crossing streets at home. You'll find yourself in a constant comedy of errors when you go to use directional signals and windshield wipers—on Kiwi roads it's the reverse of what you're used to.

RENTAL CARS

Japanese brands dominate rental agencies in New Zealand. Most major agencies also offer higher end options, for example convertibles and esteemed European models such as BMWs. Domestic agency Smart Car Rentals specializes in luxury rentals such as Mercedes and Audi convertibles. Most Kiwi cars these days are automatic, though some stick shifts (manual) are included in hire fleets, so specify if you prefer an automatic.

Many Kiwi companies (the largest is Maui-Rentals) hire out a wide selection of small campers and larger motor homes. Most major international car rental companies operate here; there are also reputable domestic agencies. Rates in New Zealand begin at about NZ$35 a day and NZ$320 a week—although you can sometimes get even cheaper deals on economy cars with unlimited mileage. This does not include tax on car rentals, which is 12.5%. Reserve a vehicle well in advance if renting during holiday seasons, especially Christmas.

Most major international companies (and some local companies) have a convenient service if you are taking the ferry between the North and South Islands and want to continue your rental contract. You simply drop off the car in Wellington and on the same contract pick up a car in Picton, or vice versa. It saves you from paying the fare for taking a car across on the ferry (though you will have to organize your luggage into carry-on). Your rental contract is terminated only at the far end of your trip, wherever you end up. In this system, there is no drop-off charge for one-way rentals, making an Auckland–Queenstown rental as easy as it could be. Check for rates based on a south-to-north itinerary; it may be less expensive as it's against the normal flow. Special rates should be available whether you book from abroad or within New Zealand.

In New Zealand your own driver's license is acceptable. Still, an International Driver's Permit is a good idea; it's available from the American Automobile Association. These international permits are universally recognized, and having one in your wallet may save you problems with the local authorities. For most major rental companies in New Zealand, 21 is the minimum age for renting a car. With some local rental companies, however, drivers under 21 years old can rent a car but may be liable for a higher deductible. Children's car seats are mandatory for kids under seven years old. Car-rental companies may ask drivers not to take their cars onto certain (rough) roads, so ask about such restrictions.

ROAD CONDITIONS
Roads are well maintained and generally not crowded (except for leaving major cities at peak holiday weekends). In rural areas, you may find some unpaved roads. On most highways, it's easier to use the signposted names of upcoming towns to navigate rather than route numbers.

Due to the less-than-flat terrain, many New Zealand roads are "wonky," or crooked. So when mapping out your itinerary, don't plan on averaging the speed limit of 100 kph (62 mph) too often. Expect two or three lanes; there are no special multi-occupant lanes on the major highways. In areas where there is only one lane for each direction, cars can pass, with care, while facing oncoming traffic, except where there is a double-yellow center line. Rural areas still have some one-lane roads. One-lane bridges are common. *See Rules of the Road.*

Dangerous overtaking, speeders, lack of turn signal, tailgating, and slow drivers in passing lanes are all afflictions suffered on New Zealand highways.

RULES OF THE ROAD
The speed limit is 100 kph (62 mph) on the open road, 50 kph (31 mph) in towns and cities, and 70 kph (44 mph) or 80 kph (50 mph) in some "in between" areas. Watch for the signs that show where these change. A circular sign with the letters LSZ (Limited Speed Zone) means speed should be governed by prevailing road conditions but still not exceed 100 kph. Speed cameras, particularly in city suburbs and on approaches to and exits from small towns, will snap your number plate if you're driving too fast. Fines start at about NZ$60 for speeds 10 kph (6 mph) over the speed limit. (If you're driving a rental, the company will track you down for payment.) It's easier and safer for everyone to obey the speed limit.

New Zealand law states that you must always wear a seat belt, whether you are driving or are a passenger. As the driver, you can be fined for any passenger not wearing a seat belt or approved child

Getting Here and Around

restraint if under the age of seven. If you are caught without a seat belt and you are clearly not a New Zealander, the result is likely to be a friendly but firm warning. Drunk drivers are not tolerated in New Zealand. The blood alcohol limit is 250 micrograms (mcg) of alcohol per liter of breath. This equates to about 1½ standard drinks, but everyone reacts differently. It's safest to avoid driving altogether if you've had a drink. If you are caught driving over the limit you will possibly be taken to the nearest police station to dry out and be required to pay a high fine. Repeat offenses or instances of causing injury or death while under the influence of alcohol are likely to result in jail terms.

When driving in rural New Zealand, cross one-lane bridges with caution—there are plenty of them. A yellow sign with parallel black lines will usually warn you that you are approaching a one-lane bridge, and another sign will tell you whether you have the right-of-way. A rectangular blue sign with a bigger white arrow on the left side of a smaller red arrow means you have the right-of-way, and a circular sign with a red border and red arrow on the left side of a white arrow means you must pull over to the left and wait to cross until oncoming traffic has passed. Even when you have the right-of-way, slow down and take care. Roundabouts can be particularly confusing for newcomers. When entering a roundabout, yield to all vehicles coming from the right. A blue sign with a white arrow indicates that you should keep to the left of the traffic island as you come up to the roundabout. In a multilane roundabout, stay in the lane closest to the island until ready to exit the circle. You must indicate left just before you exit.

You can only pass on the left if there are two or more lanes on your side of

the center line or if the vehicle ahead is signaling a right turn. At all other times, you must pass on the right, and only when you have enough clear road to do so. When you encounter fog, try putting your headlights on low beam; this sometimes helps as high beams refract light and decrease visibility. It is illegal to drive with only your parking lights on.

In cities and towns, the usual fine for parking over the time limit on meters is NZ$10–NZ$15. In the last few years "pay-and-display" meters have been put up in cities. You'll need to drop a couple of dollars' worth of coins in the meter, take the dispensed ticket, and put it in view on the dashboard of your car. Alternatively look for the parking lot number on the street beside your car and enter that into the nearest machine, along with your money. The fine for running over the time for these meters runs about NZ$12, but if you don't make any attempt at all to pay, the fine will be at least NZ$40 and you may risk being towed. So carry a few coins at all times—any denomination will usually do (gold coins only in Auckland and Wellington). Credit cards also work in some machines. Make sure to observe all "no parking" signs, especially at peak commuter times in cities, when parking on some busy streets is not permitted (signs will show this). If you don't, your car is highly likely to be towed away. It will cost about NZ$100 to NZ$200 to have the car released, and most tow companies won't accept anything but cash. For more road rules and safety tips, check the New Zealand Transport Agency website ⊕ *www.nzta.govt.nz.*

🛳 Cruise Travel

Cruise companies are increasingly drawn to Auckland and Wellington's superb harbors, as well as to the gorgeous scenery, nature tourism, culture, food, and wine found in places such as the Bay of Islands, Tauranga, Napier, Marlborough Sounds, Akaroa, Dunedin, Fiordland, and Stewart Island. World-cruise itineraries with Crystal Cruises and Regent Seven Seas Cruises now include New Zealand. But some of the best cruising programs are those that concentrate entirely on the South Pacific and combine New Zealand with destinations such as Fiji, New Caledonia, Tonga, Samoa, and Australia. Generally, such cruises start and finish in Auckland and visit South Pacific islands in between, or travel around New Zealand then cross the Tasman Sea to visit Australian east coast ports.

P&O Cruises runs a couple of cruises out of Auckland to the South Pacific. Another choice is Holland America Line with its cruises around New Zealand, Australia, and the South Pacific.

🚆 Train Travel

Don't rely on trains to get you around; train travel in New Zealand is limited to three routes operated by Kiwi Rail Scenic Journeys and commuter services in Wellington and Auckland. That said, the three long journeys are indeed scenic. They include the daily TranzAlpine Express, a spectacular ride over Arthur's Pass and the mountainous spine of the South Island between Greymouth, on the West Coast, and Christchurch on the east. The Coastal Pacific runs from Christchurch along the stunning Kaikoura coast (between mountains and sea), to Marlborough wine country and Picton. This service recommenced in the summer of 2018, after two years of rebuilding following a devastating 2016 earthquake, and the journey now showcases the incredible sea floor uplift that occurred in the quake. The Coastal Pacific runs daily between October and April and a few days a week through winter months (timetable varies). The Northern Explorer travels from Wellington to Auckland, departing Auckland on Monday, Thursday, and Saturday and Wellington Tuesday, Friday, and Sunday.

The trains do leave and arrive on time as a rule. They have one class, with standard comfortable seats and a basic food service selling light meals, snacks, beer, wine, and spirits. Special meals (diabetic, wheat free, or vegetarian) can be arranged, but you have to order at least 48 hours before you board the train. Most carriages have large windows from which to view the spectacular passing scenery, and you'll hear a commentary on passing points of interest. Most trains also have a viewing carriage at the rear.

Travelers can purchase a New Zealand Travelpass for unlimited travel by train, bus, and Interislander ferry for a variety of periods. Senior citizens (over 60) get a 20% discount with proof of age. You can obtain both schedules and tickets at i-SITE visitor information centers and at train stations. Reservations are advised, particularly in the summer months. Book at least 48 hours in advance.

Before You Go

🌐 Passport

For American travelers, a valid passport is required for traveling to New Zealand. Your passport must be valid for at least three months after your planned departure date.

💳 Visa

For American travelers, a tourist visa is not required for stays of less than three months. For other countries, visas might be required; check before you go.

✏️ Immunizations

No specific immunizations or vaccinations are required for visits to New Zealand.

📅 When to Go

High Season: It's best to visit from October to April, especially in alpine areas. The summer holidays (mid-December to February) can be crowded, with scarce car rentals and accommodations and expensive flights.

Low Season: June through September (winter) is the least expensive time to visit New Zealand, although flights from the United States may not be at their lowest. Prices in ski areas do remain high June through August but accommodations on weekdays will not be hard to come by.

Value Season: March to May and September to November, fall and spring respectively, offer the best combination of temperature, weather, and moderate prices. One exception is Easter weekend, when many families take vacations.

SAFETY

New Zealand is generally safe for travelers, but international visitors have been known to get into trouble when they take their safety for granted. Use common sense, particularly if walking around cities at night. Stay in populated areas, and avoid deserted alleys. Although New Zealand is an affluent society by world standards, it has its share of poor and homeless, and violent gangs and drug problems do exist. Avoid bus and train stations or city squares and parks late at night.

Women will not attract more unwanted attention than in most other Western societies, nor will they be immune from the usual hassles. In cities at night, stick to well-lighted areas and avoid being totally alone. Hotel staff will be happy to give tips on any areas to avoid, and the times to avoid them. New Zealand is relatively safe for women, but don't be complacent. Female travelers have been victims of sexual assault in New Zealand; hitchhiking is not recommended, especially for solo females.

New Zealand is generally very safe and accepting for LGBTQ travelers, with the major cities in particular being very friendly and having their own vibrant communities (same sex marriage has been legal in New Zealand since 2013). As with most countries in the world, it is smart to practice caution when in more rural areas.

Essentials

🛏 Lodging

You'll find a wide variety of accommodatoins in New Zealand, from youth-oriented hostels to quaint B&Bs to breathtaking luxury lodges. Tourism New Zealand publishes an online accommodation directory listing all properties that are accredited by Qualmark, the national tourism–quality assurance organization. While most reputable properties are Qualmark registered, some outstanding places to stay are not. Another online directory, ⊕ *www.nztourism.net.nz*, also publishes a comprehensive accommodation directory.

BED-AND-BREAKFASTS

There are some helpful resources on the Web for researching and booking B&B choices. On websites such as those maintained by the Bed and Breakfast Association, you'll find hundreds of listings and advertisements for reputable B&Bs throughout the country. Heritage & Character Inns of New Zealand specializes in higher-end B&Bs.

Once in New Zealand you will find the *New Zealand Bed & Breakfast Book* in most major bookstores, or you can look at their listings online for free. It lists about 1,000 B&Bs, but be aware that property owners, not independent writers, provide the editorial copy.

HOME AND FARM STAYS

If you think green acres is the place to be, New Zealand has plenty of them. Home and farm stays provide not only comfortable accommodations, but a chance to experience the countryside and the renowned Kiwi hospitality. Most operate on a B&B basis, though some also serve evening meals. Farm accommodations vary from modest shearers' cabins to elegant homesteads. Some hosts offer day trips, as well as horseback riding, hiking, and fishing. For two

people, the average cost ranges from NZ$90 to NZ$400 per night, including meals. Check farmstay accommodation on Tourism New Zealand's ⊕ *www. newzealand.com* for options.

Farm Helpers in New Zealand (FHINZ) advertises dozens of positions throughout the country where you can stay for free in exchange for working on a farm. Tasks include fruit picking, gardening, and light carpentry.

Homestays, the urban equivalent of farm stays, are less expensive. Many New Zealanders seem to have vacation homes, called *baches* in the North Island, *cribs* in the South Island; these are frequently available for rent. New Zealand Vacation Homes lists houses and apartments for rent on both the North and South Islands. Baches and Holiday Homes to Rent Ltd. publishes an annual directory of rental homes throughout the country, with color photos for each listing.

LUXURY LODGES

New Zealand does luxury lodges very, very well. At the high end of the price scale, luxury lodges put forth the best of country life, elegant dining, and superb accommodations. Some specialize in fishing, others in golf, but there is always a range of outdoor activities for nonanglers and nongolfers. Tariffs run about NZ$400–NZ$2,000 per day for two people; meals are generally included. For information, visit the New Zealand Lodge Association's website, where you can download an electronic catalog of New Zealand lodges. These properties are also listed in their very own Luxury Lodge category on the Qualmark website.

MOTELS

Motels are popular accommodations, and most provide comfortable rooms with excellent self-service kitchen facilities for

Essentials

NZ$70–NZ$195 per night. Unlike in the United States, motels in New Zealand are not always below the standard of hotels. Many are set up like stylish apartments, with living and kitchen areas as well as bedrooms. Some motels are called "motor lodges." Accommodations with more basic facilities are called "serviced motels." The Motel Association of New Zealand (MANZ) is an independent organization with nearly 1,000 members. Its website allows you to find properties by region or by motel name.

MOTOR CAMPS

The least expensive accommodations are the tourist cabins and flats in most of the country's 400 motor camps, or holiday parks as they are now described. Many of these also offer excellent motel and apartment units, as well as camping and powered sites. Tourist cabins provide basic accommodation and shared cooking, laundry, and bathroom facilities. Bedding and towels are usually provided. A notch higher up the comfort scale tourist flats provide fully equipped kitchens and private bathrooms. Tent sites and powered caravan or motor home sites usually cost less than NZ$50 and overnight rates for cabins range anywhere from NZ$50 to NZ$100. More fully equipped tourist flats will cost NZ$80 to NZ$150.

🍴 Dining

The New Zealand dining scene comes from a long tradition of Māori staples, like fish, birds, and root vegetables, typically cooked slowly in an underground oven known as a *hāngi*. With the Europeans came livestock (sheep, cattle, and pigs) and a meat-and-potato diet. But the past few decades have seen a move towards farm-to-table and local fare, with farmers and consumers quickly developing a taste and reputation for sustainable, seasonable dishes. The food here is sometimes described as "Pacific Rim" or "Pacific Rim fusion," which is an expansive term that incorporates Asian and Pacific Island influences, with traditional European-style mainstays.

Burgers are a staple for a quick bite. However, you'll find there's a whole lot more than two all-beef patties and a bun—two of the most popular fillings are beetroot and a fried egg. Cheese on burgers (and sandwiches) is often grated bits sprinkled on top. Another Kiwi snack staple, meat pies, is sold just about everywhere. The classic steak-and-mince fillings are getting gussied up these days with cheese or mushrooms. And who could forget good ol' fish-and-chips in this former British colony? Appropriately called "greasies," this mainstay is often made of shark but called lemon fish or flake. You might notice bowls by the cash registers of take-out shops containing packets of tartar sauce or tomato sauce (ketchup). These are usually not free for the taking; they cost about 50¢ each. Be aware that "bacon" might consist of a thick blubbery slice of ham or a processed fatty, pink, spongy substance. If you love your bacon streaky and crisp, politely inquire what kind of bacon they serve before ordering a BLT.

When in New Zealand, taste the lamb. No matter where you go in the country, it's sure to be on the menu along with locally farmed beef. Cervena, or farm-raised venison, is another local delicacy available all over New Zealand. Don't miss a Māori hāngi. This culinary experience is most likely to be available in conjunction with a cultural show, or marae visit. The traditional preparation involves steaming meat, seafood, and vegetables, for several hours, in a large underground pit. Also be sure to try the locally grown *kūmara,* or sweet potato.

Some Kiwi folk view muttonbird (the cute name for young sooty shearwaters, harvested from their burrows on little islands around Stewart Island) as a special treat, but others balk at its peculiar smell and strong flavor. It is an acquired taste, but if you're an adventurous eater it's definitely one to try.

Of course, seafood is a specialty, and much of the fish is not exported so this is your chance to try it. The tastiest fish around is snapper in the North, and blue cod (not a true cod relative) in the South. Grouper (often listed by its Māori name of *hāpuku*), terakihi, and marine-farmed salmon are also menu toppers, as is whitebait, the juvenile of several fish species, in the whitebait-fishing season of spring. As for shellfish: try the Bluff oysters (in season March–August), Green-shell mussels (also known as green-lipped or New Zealand green mussels), scallops, crayfish (spiny lobster), and local clamlike shellfish, *pipi* and *tuatua*.

Hotel restaurants serve breakfast roughly between 7 and 10; cafés and restaurants often serve breakfast/brunch to 11 am, or even an "all-day breakfast." Lunch usually starts about noon and is over by 3. Dinners are usually served from 6 pm, but the most popular dining time is around 7 to 8. Restaurants in cities and resort areas will serve dinner well into the night, but some places in small towns or rural areas still shut their doors at around 8.

Some restaurants serve a fixed-price dinner, but the majority are à la carte. Remember that "entrée" in Kiwi English is the equivalent of an appetizer. Increasingly, restaurants are offering smaller, tapas-style plates for sharing. It's wise to make a reservation and inquire if the restaurant has a liquor license or is "BYOB" or "BYO" (Bring Your Own Bottle)—a few places have both. This only pertains to wine, not bottles of beer or liquor. Be

prepared to pay a corkage fee, which can be up to NZ$10. Many restaurants add a 15% surcharge on public holidays. Employers are required by law to pay staff a higher wage during holidays. This amount will be itemized separately on your bill.

🍸 Nightlife

New Zealand is well known for its wines, particularly whites such as Sauvignon Blanc, Riesling, Pinot Gris, and Chardonnay. The country has also gained a reputation for red wines such as Cabernet Sauvignon, Pinot Noir, and Merlot. The main wine-producing areas are Hawke's Bay, Wairarapa, Marlborough, Nelson, Waipara (north Canterbury), and Central Otago. Restaurants almost without exception serve New Zealand products on their wine list.

When ordering a beer, you'll get either a handle (mug), a one-liter jug (pitcher) with glasses, or a "stubby" (small bottle). If you've asked for one of these (a bottle), you might need to request a glass if you don't want to glug straight from the bottle (depending how casual the bar is). Two large mainstream breweries, DB and Lion, produce their own products along with smaller, well-known brands that initially started as independent breweries, such as Macs, Monteiths, and Speights. They also dispense international brands Steinlager, Stella Artois, Heinekin, and more. The big trend in recent years, however, has been to boutique micro-breweries and craft beers. Innovation, international awards, and ever-changing brews are the features of brands where even the brewery names are interesting, for example Garage Project, Parrotdog, and 8 Wired Brewing. Each brand has its own fan base and the good pubs will have at least a couple of ever-changing

Essentials

taps serving up these tasty brews. Most restaurants and liquor stores also sell beers from Australia, Europe, and other parts of the world. Some of the beer in New Zealand, especially the craft beers, is stronger than the 4% alcohol per volume brew that is the norm in the United States. Many go up to 7% or 8% alcohol per volume, so check that number before downing your usual number of drinks.

Beer and wine can be purchased in supermarkets, specialized shops, and even little corner suburban shops—seven days a week. People under 18 are not permitted by law to purchase alcohol, and shops, bars, and restaurants strictly enforce this. If you look younger than you are, carry photo identification to prove your age.

➕ Health

The most common types of illnesses are caused by contaminated food and water. In New Zealand that really shouldn't be an issue. New Zealand has high hygiene standards and strict health regulations when it comes to serving food and beverage from shops, restaurants, cafés, and bars. The tap water is fine to drink. Locals do it all the time.

General health standards in New Zealand are high, and it would be hard to find a more pristine natural environment. The major health hazard in New Zealand is sunburn or sunstroke. Even people who are not normally bothered by strong sun should cover up with a long-sleeve shirt, a hat, and pants or a beach wrap. At higher altitudes you will burn more easily, so apply sunscreen liberally before you go out—even for a half hour—and wear a visor or sunglasses.

Dehydration is another serious danger that can be easily avoided, so be sure to carry water and drink often. Limit the amount of time you spend in the sun for the first few days until you are acclimatized, and avoid sunbathing in the middle of the day.

There are no venomous snakes, and the only native poisonous spider, the *katipo,* is a rarity. The whitetail spider, an unwelcome and accidental import from Australia, packs a nasty bite and can cause discomfort but is also rarely encountered (and easily identified by it's white tail). One New Zealander you will come to loathe is the tiny black sand fly, common mainly in the western half of the South Island, which inflicts a painful bite that can itch for several days. In other parts of the country, especially around rivers and lakes in the evenings, you may be pestered by mosquitoes. Be sure to use insect repellent.

One of New Zealand's rare health hazards involves its pristine-looking bodies of water; as a precaution don't drink water from natural outdoor sources. Although the country's alpine lakes might look like backdrops for mineral-water ads, some in the South Island harbor a tiny organism that can cause "duck itch," a temporary but intense skin irritation. The organism is found only on the shallow lake margins, so the chances of infection are greatly reduced if you stick to deeper water. Streams can be infected by giardia, a waterborne protozoal parasite that can cause gastrointestinal disorders, including acute diarrhea. Giardia is most likely contracted when drinking from streams that pass through an area inhabited by mammals (such as cattle or possums). There is no risk of infection if you drink from streams above the tree line.

Less common, but a risk nevertheless, is the possibility of contracting amoebic meningitis from the water in geothermal pools. The illness is caused by an organism that can enter the body when the water is forced up the nose. The organism is quite rare, but you should avoid putting your head underwater in thermal pools or jumping in them. Also remember not to drink geothermic water.

OVER-THE-COUNTER REMEDIES
Popular headache, pain, and flu medicines are Nurofen (contains ibuprofen), Panadol (contains acetaminophen), and Dispirin (contains aspirin). Dispirin often comes as large tabs, which you must dissolve in water. Many Kiwi households and wheelhouses have a green tube of Berocca, the soluble vitamin supplement often taken the morning after a big night out.

Tipping

Tipping is not as widely practiced in New Zealand as in the United States or Europe, but in city restaurants and hotels it's appreciated if you acknowledge good service with at least a 15% tip. Tour guides and drivers are also used to receiving some gesture, even though it isn't mandatory.

Taxi drivers will appreciate rounding up the fare to the nearest NZ$5 amount, but don't feel you have to do this. Porters will be happy with a NZ$1 or NZ$2 coin. Most other people, like bartenders, theater attendants, gas-station attendants, or barbers, will probably wonder what you are doing if you try to give them a tip. The nice thing about this is good service in New Zealand is given because the person means it, not because they're aiming for a good tip.

Visitor Information

Tourism New Zealand is a government agency that markets New Zealand internationally. Their North American office is in Santa Monica. They have a website (⊕ newzealand.com) that lists all you'll want or need to know about your New Zealand holiday. There are also 30 locally funded Regional Tourism Organizations (RTOs) based throughout the country, some of these also market internationally, and they run most of the i-SITE visitor centers. Many of these have computerized booking systems in place, so rather than driving from lodge to B&B to hotel, making inquiries, the i-SITE can be a good place to let you know instantly which places are vacant. They also offer knowledgeable, independent advice about local attractions, activities, and transport. These centers are marked with blue signs and a white lowercase letter i.

Speak Like a Local

From the moment you begin your New Zealand (or *Aotearoa,* as you'll learn in the airport) adventure, you'll confront the mélange of Māori words, Briticisms, and uniquely Kiwi phrases that make the language vibrant, but perhaps a bit hard for American ears to navigate.

New Zealand is a bilingual nation, as reflected in its national anthem. Although Māori isn't conversational language, a basic knowledge of Māori is essential for understanding phrases and the meaning of place-names, as well as the pronunciation of certain words or place-names. ■TIP➔ **For a crash course in the best way to pronounce New Zealand place-names, the best thing to do is watch the weather report on the news.**

Talking Kiwi is not as daunting as Māori pronunciations for those with the English language under their belt. New Zealanders tend to use the Queen's English, colored up with their unique brand of abbreviated slang. Most Kiwi turns-of-phrase are easy to unravel—a *car park* is a parking lot, for example. Others, like *dairy* (a convenience or corner store), can be confused with American terminology. Only occasionally will you find yourself at a complete loss (with words like *jandal,* for example—Kiwi for flip-flop), and even then New Zealanders will be happy to set you right. Below are common Māori and Kiwi phrases that you'll likely hear throughout the country.

MĀORI PRONUNCIATION

Knowing how to pronounce Māori words can be important while traveling around New Zealand. Even if you have a natural facility for picking up languages, you'll find many Māori words to be quite baffling. The West Coast town of Punakaiki (pronounced poon-ah- *kye*-kee) is relatively straightforward, but when you get to places such as Whakatane, the going gets tricky—the opening *wh* is pronounced like an *f,* and the accent is placed on the last syllable: "fa-ca-tawn-e." Sometimes it is the mere length of words that makes them difficult, as in the case of Waitakaruru (why- *ta*-ka-ru-ru) or Whakarewarewa (fa-ca- *re*-wa- *re*-wa). You'll notice that the ends of both of these have repeats—of "ru" and "rewa," which is something to look out for to make longer words more manageable. In other instances, a relatively straightforward name like Taupo can sound completely different than you expected (Toe-paw). Town names like Waikanea (*why*-can-eye) you'll just have to repeat to yourself a few times before saying them without pause.

The Māori *r* is rolled so that it sounds a little like a *d.* Thus the Northland town of Whangarei is pronounced "fang-ah-day," and the word *Māori* is pronounced "mah- *aw*-dee," or sometimes "mo-dee," with the *o* sounding like it does in the word *mold,* and a rolled *r.* A macron indicates a lengthened vowel. In general, *a* is pronounced *ah* as in "car"; *e* is said as the *ea* in "weather." *O* is pronounced like "awe," rather than *oh,* and *u* sounds like the *u* of "June." *Ng,* meanwhile, has a soft, blunted sound, as the *ng* in "singing." All of this is a little too complicated for those who still choose not to bother with Māori pronunciations. So in some places, if you say you've just driven over from "fahng-ah-ma- *ta,*" the reply might be: "You mean 'wang-ah- *ma*-tuh'." You can pronounce these words either way, but more and more people these days are pronouncing Māori words correctly.

MĀORI GLOSSARY
COMMON MĀORI WORDS

Aotearoa: Land of the long white cloud (New Zealand's Māori name)

Haere mai: Welcome, come here

Haere rā: Farewell, good-bye

Haka: "Dance," implies history, life-force, rhythm, words and meaning of the haka, made internationally famous by the All Blacks, who perform it before each match

Hāngi: Earth oven, food from an earth oven, also used to describe a feast

Hongi: Press noses in greeting

Hui: Gathering

Iwi: People, tribe

Ka pai: Good, excellent

Kai: Food, eat, dine

Karakia: Ritual chant, prayer, religious service

Kaumātua: Elder

Kia ora: Hello, thank you

Koha: Customary gift, donation

Kūmara: Sweet potato

Mana: Influence, prestige, power

Marae: Traditional gathering place, sacred ground

Moko: Tattoo

Pā: Fortified village

Pākehā: Non-Māori, European, Caucasian

Pounamu: Greenstone

Rangatira: Chief, person of rank

Reo: Language

Tāne: Man

Tangata whenua: People of the land, local people

Taonga: Treasure

Tapu: Sacred, under religious restriction, taboo

Wahine: Woman

Waiata: Sing, song

Waka: Canoe

Whakapapa: Genealogy, cultural identity

Whānau: Family

KIWI GLOSSARY
COMMON KIWI WORDS

Across the ditch: Over the Tasman Sea in Australia (Australians are called Aussies)

Bach: Vacation house (pronounced *batch*)

Cabbage: Stupid

Crook: Sick

Fanny: Woman's privates (considered obscene)

Footie: Rugby football

Gutted: Very upset

Kiwi: A native, brown flightless bird; the people of New Zealand; or the furry fruit

Knackered: Tired

Nappie: Diaper

Pissed: Drunk

Sealed road: Paved road

Shout: Buy a round of drinks

Sticking plaster or plaster: Adhesive bandage

Stuffed up: Made a mistake

Sweet as: All good

Ta: Thanks

Torch: Flashlight

Tramping: Hiking

Whinge: To whine

Great Itineraries

Best of the North Island, 8 to 10 Days

It can be difficult to decide which island to focus on, but this much is true: each of the islands is uniquely memorable, so no matter where you go, you will bring home a story. You will find volcanic springs, worm caves, and subterranean excitement in the North Island. Most of your time can be spent exploring the busy cities and close-to-ground activities. It's generally quicker and easier to get from place to place by car. If you travel by bus, consider adding a few hours to the itinerary, since buses make frequent stops and weave in and out of towns.

Fly in: Auckland Airport (AKL)

Fly out: Auckland Airport (AKL)

DAYS 1 AND 2: AUCKLAND

After a long international flight, stretch your legs and invigorate your circulation with a walk around the city center, with perhaps stops at **Auckland Museum** and **Auckland Domain** or **Albert Park.** Head to the harbor (or "harbour") and take a ferry ride round-trip between Auckland and Devonport for a great view of the city from the water. Have an early dinner and turn in to get over the worst of the jet lag.

On your second day, you'll have more wind in your sails to explore the City of Sails. Depending on your interests, head to **Kelly Tarlton's Antarctic Encounter and Underwater World,** the **New Zealand National Maritime Museum,** the **Auckland Art Gallery,** or the **Parnell** neighborhood for window-shopping. If you're feeling energetic, you can even do a bit of kayaking (or just sunbathing) at **Mission Bay** or **Karekare Beach.**

DAYS 3 AND 4: WAITOMO AND ROTORUA

Waitomo is known for what's beneath the surface—intricate limestone caves filled with stalactites, stalagmites, and galaxies of glowworms. If this is up your alley, get an early start from **Auckland** to arrive here before 11 am and sign up for a cave tour. Afterward, continue on to **Rotorua,** which seethes with geothermal activity. In the late afternoon you should have time for a walk around the town center, strolling through the **Government Gardens,** and perhaps also **Kuirau Park.** If you decide to skip the **Waitomo** worms, you can zip straight down from Auckland to Rotorua. In addition to the town proper, visit some of the eye-popping thermal areas nearby, such as **Waikite Valley Thermal Pools.** At night, be a guest at a *hāngi,* a Māori feast accompanied by a cultural performance. On the next day, you can either see some of the outlying thermal areas or continue south to **Taupo.** Another option is to take a detour to **Hobbiton,** the movie set that stood in for the Shire in the *Lord of the Ring* movies, located an hour northwest of Rotorua (1½ hours north of Taupo) in the town of Matamata. Even if you're not a fan of the books or movies, it's still a magical experience to explore the Hobbit holes and have a second breakfast. **Logistics:** 3–3½ hours by car.

DAY 5: TAUPO

Midway between Auckland and Wellington, the resort town of **Taupo,** on its giant namesake lake, is the perfect base for a day full of aquatic activities. If you're at all interested in trout fishing, this is the place to do it. You can also bathe in the volcanic springs in the park that is open to the public night and day. **Logistics:** 1–1½ hours by car.

DAY 6: NAPIER

The small town of **Napier** is an art deco period piece; after a devastating Richter 7.9 earthquake in 1931, the center of town was rebuilt in the distinctive style, and it's been carefully preserved ever since. Take a guided or self-guided walk around the heritage (historically significant) neighborhood. If you have a car, drive out of town and visit one of the 30-odd wineries around **Hawke's Bay.** In the afternoon, take a drive to the top of **Te Mata Peak,** or visit nearby towns **Hastings** or **Havelock North.** Otherwise, hang out at the waterfront or visit the aquarium. **Logistics:** 1½–2 hours by car.

DAYS 7 AND 8: WELLINGTON

New Zealand's capital, **Wellington,** is a terrific walking city, and there's even a cable car to help you with the hills. The big cultural draw is **Te Papa Tongarewa**—the Museum of New Zealand, which, with five floors and great interactive activities for kids, can take a full day to explore. You may wish to spend the rest of your first day here along the waterfront, winding up with dinner in the area. Be sure to check out the entertainment listings, too; you could be in town during one of the many festivals or catch a cool local band. On your second day, explore more of the urban highlights, like the **City Gallery** and the **Museum of Wellington City & Sea,** followed by a bit of browsing on the main shopping drags or a trip up into the hills to the **Botanic Garden.** If you'd prefer more time out in the country and have a car, drive up the **Kapiti Coast** and book to visit **Kapiti Island Nature Reserve,** or sip acclaimed Pinot Noir in the wine center of **Martinborough. Logistics:** 4–5 hours by car.

OTHER TOP OPTIONS

With at least one more day at your disposal, you could squeeze in one of the following destinations. **The Tongariro**

Crossing, a challenging but spectacular daylong hike, could be added to your Taupo stay. You'll "tramp" up close to three volcanoes: **Tongariro, Ngauruhoe,** and **Ruapehu.** If you have two days and are keen on swimming with dolphins or doing some diving, loop up to **Paihia,** a small seaside town and gateway to the **Bay of Islands,** after your initial two days in Auckland. You can dip into the mellow, rural **Coromandel Peninsula,** perhaps the gateway town of **Thames,** before going south to Rotorua. Most places on the Coromandel are within 1 to 1½ hours' drive from the Thames township.

Great Itineraries

Best of the South Island, 10 to 13 Days

The South Island is where you'll find yourself recharging that camera battery. For breathtaking scenery and daredevil activities like skydiving, skiing, exotic wildlife viewing, and trekking, this island has the most to offer. Spend a few days on a biking or hiking trip, and a few days on a wine tour, and you've got yourself quite a suitable itinerary. Driving on this island can take longer between towns since the roads weave in and out of mountains.

Fly in: Wellington International Airport (WLG)

Fly out: Wellington International Airport (WLG)

DAYS 1 AND 2: PICTON AND BLENHEIM

Hop or drive onto the ferry from Wellington to Picton. This small seaside township is the Marlborough region's main commercial port, and the gateway to the gorgeously scalloped coastline of **Marlborough Sounds.** Hop on a mail boat, which makes stops at coves and islands along the Sounds; take a day walk along the famous **Queen Charlotte Track** for spectacular water views; or join a kayak tour (you might just see some seals and dolphins as you paddle around). Have dinner along the foreshore and turn in early.

The next morning, head out of town to the **Blenheim** region, where the rolling hills are covered with grapevines and filled with scores of wineries. Stop in for tastings at esteemed spots like the **Seresin Estate, Cloudy Bay,** and **Allan Scott Wines**; if you've made reservations, you might also be able to dine at **Herzog** or **Hunter's Garden Cafe.** Be sure to pick up a few bottles of wine and olive oil to take with you.

DAY 3: KAIKOURA

Get an early start and continue down the South Island's eastern coast to the seaside settlement of **Kaikoura,** where you can go whale-watching, reef diving, swimming with dolphins or seals, or stay on land and indulge in a big crayfish lunch ("Kaikoura" actually means "meal of crayfish" in the Māori language). **Logistics:** 1–3 hours by car.

DAYS 4 AND 5: CHRISTCHURCH

2010 and 2011 brought three significant earthquakes that rocked **Christchurch,** the South Island's largest city. The city center and some outlying suburbs were significantly damaged and are in the process of being rebuilt. Although this will take some time, "The Garden City" still lives up to its name: after you arrive from Kaikoura, spend the afternoon strolling around 395-acre **Hagley Park** and the neighboring **Christchurch Botanic Gardens,** a sprawling wonderland with more than 10,000 exotic and indigenous plants. Or take a punt on the meandering **Avon River,** followed by a coffee at a local café. For a two-day stay, fit in a couple of hours at the **International Antarctic Centre,** or spend the day in **Akaroa,** swimming with the endangered Hector's dolphins or enjoying the French-influenced atmosphere. The next morning, get an early start to make the push to Queenstown. **Logistics:** 2 hours from Kaikoura.

DAYS 6 THROUGH 8: QUEENSTOWN

Depending on your appetite for adventure, **Queenstown** may be the focus of your South Island trip. Take the plunge with **AJ Hackett Bungy,** free-fall on the **Shotover Canyon Swing,** try a jet-boat ride, or go rafting. As the town is set on **Lake Wakatipu** with the jagged peaks of the **Remarkables** mountains around it, you won't lack for scenic distractions. If you're interested in the area's gold-mining history, detour to nearby **Arrowtown** and see the **Lake District Museum & Gallery.** If the area looks familiar, you're not dreaming: many scenes from the *Lord of the Rings* film trilogy were shot here. **Logistics:** 5–6 hours by car.

DAYS 9 AND 10: FIORDLAND NATIONAL PARK

Follow your extreme sports adventure with some extremely splendid landscapes. At **Milford and Doubtful sounds** in **Fiordland National Park,** deep green slopes fall steeply down to crystalline waters. Rare species live in the unique underwater environment here, so try to visit the **Milford Deep Underwater Observatory.** Drink in the views by catamaran, by kayak, or by flightseeing. Whatever you do, don't forget your rain gear and bug repellent! If pressed, you could make a trip to Milford Sound a long day's trip from Queenstown.

■ TIP→ **The road to Milford Sound can be a bit precarious. You can get more out of taking a bus through Fiordland National Park as the bus driver also serves as a tour guide, and stops at various attractions. The bus trip is 4–5 hours, and you can ogle the mountains from the windows.**

OTHER TOP OPTIONS

With more time in your schedule, build in a couple of low-key days to offset the thrills-and-chills outdoor activities. After you arrive at Picton, you can drive or take a bus to Nelson, a relaxed waterfront town that's a good base for arts-and-crafts shopping and wine tasting. One fun stop is the **World of Wearable Art & Classic Cars Museum.** If ice is on your mind and you're willing to brave rainy conditions, push on down the rugged West Coast, stopping at the **Pancake Rocks**—columns of limestone resembling stacks of pancakes—on your way to the **Fox** or **Franz Josef Glacier** in **Westland Tai**

Poutini National Park. Their flow rates are up to 10 times the speed of most valley glaciers. (To do this, plan on three days, as it's a long drive and you'll want at least one full day at the glaciers.)

Contacts

✈ Air Travel

Auckland International Airport. ☎ 09/275–0789 ⊕ www.aucklandairport.co.nz. **Christchurch International Airport.** ☎ 03/358–5029 ⊕ www.christchurchairport.co.nz. **Wellington International Airport.** ☎ 04/385–5100 ⊕ www.wellingtonairport.co.nz.

⛴ Boat Travel

Bluebridge. ☎ 0800/844–844 toll-free in New Zealand ⊕ www.bluebridge.co.nz. **Interislander.** ☎ 644/498–3302 in U.S., 0800/802–802 toll-free in New Zealand ⊕ www.greatjourneysofnz.co.nz.

🚌 Bus Travel

Atomic Travel. ☎ 03/349–0697 in NZ ⊕ www.atomictravel.co.nz. **Bottom Bus.** ☎ 03/477–9083 ⊕ www.travelheadfirst.com. **InterCity.** ☎ 09/583–5780 ⊕ www.intercity.co.nz. **Flexipass.** ⊕ www.intercity.co.nz/bus-pass/flexipass. **Kiwi Experience.** ☎ 09/336–4286 ⊕ www.kiwiexperience.com. **Newmans.** ☎ 09/583–5780 ⊕ www.intercity.co.nz. **Stray Bus.** ☎ 09/526–2140 ⊕ www.straytravel.com. **Stray Travel.** ☎ 09/526–2140 ⊕ www.straytravel.co.nz.

🚗 Car Travel

Apex Rental Car. ☎ 800/7001–8001 toll-free in U.S., 0800/500–660 toll-free in New Zealand ⊕ www.apexrentals.co.nz. **Maui-Rentals.** ☎ 800/2008–0801 toll-free in U.S., 0800/688–558 toll-free in New Zealand ⊕ www.maui-rentals.com. **Smart Car Rentals.** ☎ 09/307–3553, 0800/458–987 toll-free in New Zealand ⊕ www.smartcarrental.co.nz. **New Zealand Transport Agency.** ☎ 0800/822–422 toll-free in New Zealand, 06/953–6200 ⊕ www.nzta.govt.nz.

🚢 Cruise Travel

Crystal Cruises. ☎ 888/722–0021 ⊕ www.crystalcruises.com. **Holland America Line.** ☎ 877/932–4259 ⊕ www.hollandamerica.com. **P&O Cruises.** ☎ 0800/780–716 toll-free in New Zealand ⊕ www.pocruises.co.nz. **Princess Cruises.** ☎ 0800/780–717 toll-free in New Zealand ⊕ www.princess.com. **Regent Seven Seas Cruises.** ☎ 954/776–6123 ⊕ www.rssc.com.

💲 Discounts

New Zealand Travelpass. ☎ 0800/339–966 toll-free in New Zealand ⊕ www.travelpass.co.nz.

🚆 Train Travel

InterCity Travel Centres. ☎ 09/583–5780 in Auckland, 03/365–1113 in Christchurch, 04/385–0520 in Wellington ⊕ www.intercity.co.nz/travel-info. **Great Journeys of New Zealand.** ☎ 04/495–0775, 0800/802–802 toll-free in New Zealand for bookings ⊕ www.greatjourneysofnz.co.nz.

Chapter 3

AUCKLAND

Updated by
Richard Pamatatau

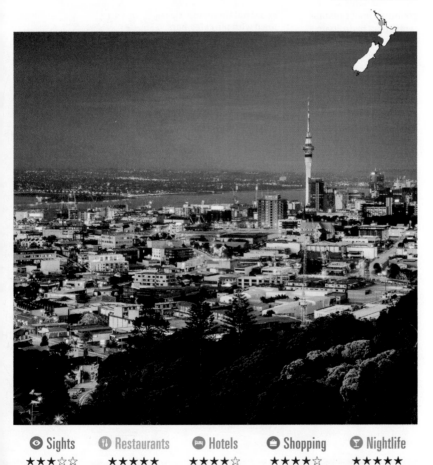

◉ Sights	🍴 Restaurants	🛏 Hotels	🛍 Shopping	🍸 Nightlife
★★★☆☆	★★★★★	★★★★☆	★★★★☆	★★★★★

WELCOME TO AUCKLAND

TOP REASONS TO GO

★ **Boating and Sailing:** Aucklanders love boating. You can join them on a commuter ferry, a sailboat, or a racing yacht.

★ **Cuisine and Café Culture:** You'll find some of the country's finest restaurants, plus bistro bars, noodle houses, and vibrant neighborhood eateries.

★ **Year-Round Golf:** Auckland has more than 20 golf courses, from informal to challenging championship level. The Muriwai Golf Club fronts a great surf beach.

★ **Art and Culture:** The award-winning Auckland Art Gallery, Auckland Museum, theater companies, and live music scene draw crowds.

★ **Gorgeous Beaches:** The West Coast's black-sand beaches attract surfers from around the world; the safest swimming is on the East Coast. Takapuna Beach and Mission Bay are good places to swim but are very crowded on a sunny day. Remember to swim between the flags and slather on the sunscreen.

1 City Center and Parnell. The main pulse of the city is the waterfront and Queen Street. To the east of the city center, Parnell has historic buildings, good restaurants, and water views.

2 Ponsonby. Explore narrow streets lined with wooden Victorian villas and stroll the main strip lined with hip cafés, bars, restaurants, and local designer clothing stores.

3 Western Springs. A park and suburb west of Auckland, and named after the springs that bubble into the lake, this makes a nice retreat from the city.

4 Devonport. Across Waitemata Harbour, this suburb favored by the well-to-do has great views of the harbor, cafés, and a grand dame hotel.

5 Hauraki Gulf Islands. Rangitoto, Waiheke, Rakino, and Motutapu islands have great walking and nature sites while Waiheke draws visitors to its wineries, restaurants, and Easter Jazz Festival.

6 Greater Auckland. The area surrounding Auckland runs for 57 miles from north to south, with everything from parks and dormant volcanic cones to beaches and forests.

HAURAKI
GULF ISLANDS 5

DEVONPORT 4

Waitemata
Harbour

Princes Wharf
Queens Wharf
Captain Cook Wharf
Marsden Wharf

Kings
Wharf

Bledisloe
Wharf

Jellicoe Wharf

Freyberg
Wharf

Fergusson
Wharf

Western Viaduct
Viaduct
Basin

Jellicoe St.
Madden St.

St. W

Customs

Sturdee St.
Fanshawe St.

Halsey St.

Fanshawe St.

Victoria
Park

Wyndham St.

Halsey St.

Nelson St.

Victoria St. W.

Wellesley St. W.

Hobson St.

Cook St.

Union St.

Tyler St.
Customs St. E

Queen St.

Shortland St.

CITY
CENTER

Beach Rd.

6

Tooley St.

Quay St.

6

The Strand

The Strand

Balfour Rd.

1

Fraser Park

Parnell Rise

PARNELL

Albert
Park

Kitchener St.

Princes St.

Auckland
University

Auckland
Art Gallery

Wellesley St. E.

Symonds St.

Alten Rd.

Stanley St.

Carlaw
Park

Garfield St.

Scarborough
Reserve

Cheshire St.

Parnell Rd.

Aotea
Sq.

Wakefield St.

Grafton Rd.

16

Vincent St.

Mayoral Dr.

Pitt St.

Greys Ave.

Myers
Park

Liverpool St.

NEWTON

Queen St.

1

Karangahape Rd.

16

GRAFTON

Park Rd.

Auckland
Domain

Auckland
War Memorial
Museum

Newmarket
Park

Ian McKinnon Dr.

Newton
Rd.

Upper Queen St.

Symonds St.

Grafton Rd.

Seafield View Rd.

Claremont St.

Park Ave.

Carlton Gore Rd.

George St.

Titoki St.

Morgan St.

NEWMARKET

EDEN TERRACE

4

Basque
Road Res.

Dominion Rd.

New North Rd.

23

Burleigh St.

Nugent St.

15

Boston Rd.

1

Khyber Pass Rd.

Broadway

12

REMUERA

GREATER
AUCKLAND

6

Auckland is called the City of Sails, and visitors flying in will see why. On the East Coast is the Waitemata Harbour—a Māori word meaning sparkling waters—which is bordered by the Hauraki Gulf, an aquatic playground peppered with small islands where many Aucklanders can be found "mucking around in boats."

Not surprisingly, Auckland has some 70,000-plus boats. About one in four households in Auckland has a seacraft of some kind, and there are 102 beaches within an hour's drive depending on the traffic; during the week many are quite empty except for the two weeks that include Christmas and New Year. Even the airport is by the water; it borders the Manukau Harbour, which also takes its name from the Māori language and means "solitary bird."

According to Māori tradition, the Auckland isthmus was originally peopled by a race of giants and fairy folk. When Europeans arrived in the early 19th century, however, the Ngāti-Whātua tribe was firmly in control of the region. The British began "negotiations" with the Ngāti-Whātua in 1840 to purchase the isthmus and establish the colony's first capital. (The Government is still dealing with the fallout from the British negotiations and redress for land theft continues between Ngāti-Whātua and the Crown.) In September of that year the British flag was hoisted to mark the township's foundation, and Auckland remained the capital until 1865, when the seat of government was moved to Wellington. Aucklanders expected to suffer from the shift; it hurt their pride

but not their pockets. As the terminal for the South Sea shipping routes, Auckland was already an established commercial center. Since then urban sprawl and massive immigration has made this city of approximately 1.6 million people one of the world's largest geographically.

A couple of days in the city will reveal just how developed and sophisticated Auckland is—the Mercer City Survey 2018 saw it ranked as the third-highest city for quality of life—though those seeking a New York in the South Pacific will be disappointed. Auckland is more get-up and go-outside than get-dressed-up and go-out. That said, most shops are open daily, central bars and a few nightclubs buzz well into the wee hours, especially Thursday through Saturday, and a mix of Māori, Pacific people, Asians, and Europeans contributes to the cultural milieu. Auckland has the world's largest single population of Pacific Islanders living outside their home countries, though many of them live outside the central parts of the city and in Manukau to the south. The Samoan language is the second most spoken in New Zealand. Most Pacific people came to New Zealand seeking a better life. When the plentiful, low-skilled work that attracted them dried up, the dream soured, and the population has suffered with poor health and education. Luckily, policies are now addressing that, and change is slowly coming. The Pacifica Festival in March is the region's biggest cultural event, attracting thousands to Western Springs with fantastic food, stunning performances, and art and craft from the region. The annual Pacific Island Secondary Schools' Competition, also in March, sees young Pacific Islander and Asian students compete in traditional dance, drumming, and singing. This event is open to the public.

At the geographical center of Auckland city is the 1,082-foot Sky Tower, a convenient landmark for those exploring on foot and some say a visible sign of the city's naked aspiration. The Waitemata Harbour has become better known since New Zealand staged its first defense of the America's Cup in 2000 and the successful Louis Vuitton Pacific Series in early 2009. The first regatta saw major redevelopment of the waterfront and more work is currently underway with the Cup challenge being held in 2021. The area, where many of the city's most popular bars, cafés, and restaurants are located, is now known as Viaduct Basin or, more commonly, the Viaduct. A recent expansion has created another area, Wynyard Quarter, which is packed with eateries.

GETTING ORIENTED

The drive from the airport is often slow as the city's road network is being revamped to accommodate rapid population growth. As you leave the airport, you'll pass some dramatic landscapes along with sculpture and industrial parks before you hit New Zealand proper. The suburban landscape is dominated by the city's 50 or so volcanic hills. Many of these hills have been set aside as parks, some with livestock and all with great views from their summits that can be reached on foot. The Auckland region is geographically diverse, and Auckland city sits on an isthmus between Waitemata

Harbour (to the east) and Manukau Harbour (to the southwest). At its narrowest point the isthmus is only 1 km (½ mile) wide. The Orakei and Panmure basins, which are east of the city, are actually large craters that have been invaded by the sea. There's plenty of outdoor activity on the easy rolling terrain outside the central suburban areas and in some of the city's big parks. The many islands of the Hauraki Gulf, off Auckland's East Coast, are a must; ferries go to most at least once a day.

Planning

When to Go

Auckland's weather can be unpredictable, but don't let that put you off. There is always something to do whatever the weather. The warmest months are December through April and a sun hat is a good idea. Winter is between July and October. It can be humid in summer and quite chilly in winter. It often rains, so be prepared.

Planning Your Time

You can get around city center and the suburbs close to the harbor like Ponsonby, Devonport, and Parnell, on foot, by bus, and by ferry. Elsewhere, Auckland is not as easy to explore. The neighborhoods and suburbs sprawl from the Waitemata and Manukau harbors to rural areas, and complicated roads, frequent construction, and heavy traffic can make road travel a challenge. Still it's best to have a car for getting between neighborhoods and some city center sights. What might look like an easy walking distance on a map can turn out to be a 20- to 30-minute hilly trek, and stringing a few of those together can get frustrating.

If you're nervous about driving on the left, especially when you first arrive, purchase a one-day Link Bus Pass that covers the inner-city neighborhoods and central business district (CBD) or, for a circuit of the main sights, a Discovery Pass. Take a bus to get acquainted with the city layout. Getting around Auckland by bus is easy and inexpensive. The region's bus services are coordinated through the Auckland Transport. You can buy electronic Hop cards which can be used on buses, trains and ferries and its website can provide door-to-door information, including bus route numbers, to most places in the greater Auckland area. Timetables are available at most information centers.

Getting Here and Around

AIR TRAVEL
Auckland International Airport (AKL) lies 21 km (13 miles) southwest of the city center, about a 30-minute drive away depending on traffic. It has adopted a "quiet airport" policy, so it doesn't use loudspeakers to announce boarding times. Look for flight info on screens, which abound.

A free inter-terminal bus links the international and domestic terminals from 6 am to 10 pm. Otherwise, the walk between the two terminals takes about 10 minutes. Luggage for flights aboard the two major domestic airlines, Air New Zealand and Qantas Airways, can be checked at the international terminal.

Air New Zealand and Jetstar, Qantas's budget airline, are the main domestic carriers serving Auckland. Air New Zealand connects with 20 domestic cities a day, and makes about 10 flights a day to Australia. Jetstar also connects Auckland with many cities and complements Qantas's cross-Tasman service; Jetstar is now competing with Air New Zealand on some regional flights. It can have unpredictable service and requires check-in one hour before departure.

CONTACTS Auckland International Airport. ✉ *Ray Emery Dr.* ☎ *09/275–0789* ⊕ *www.aucklandairport.co.nz.*

AIRPORT TRANSFERS
The SkyBus (NZ$18 one-way; NZ$32 round-trip) leaves the international terminal on a regular basis, 24 hours a day. You can request a stop at any bus stop or hotel along the 60-minute route between the airport and the Ferry Building in downtown Auckland. The bus leaves the Ferry Building at 20-minute intervals between 5 am and 6 pm, and then every 30 minutes until the morning.

Limo Hire Auckland runs between the airport and the city (NZ$350 one-way or NZ$650 return). Taxi fare to the city is NZ$90 to NZ$100. Super Shuttle has service between the airport and any address in the city center (NZ$20 per person). Allow an hour's traveling time.

CONTACTS Limo Hire Auckland. ☎ *09/948-2554* ⊕ *www.limohireauckland.co.nz.* **SkyBus.** ✉ *Auckland International and Domestic Airport, Ray Emery Dr.* ☎ *0800/759-287* ⊕ *www.skybus.co.nz.* **SuperShuttle.** ✉ *Newmarket* ☎ *09/522-5100* ⊕ *www.supershuttle.co.nz.*

BUS TRAVEL WITHIN AUCKLAND
The easily recognizable red, green, and orange Link Buses circle the inner city and close suburbs every 10 minutes between 6 am and 7 pm weekdays, and then every 15 minutes until about 11:30 pm. Weekend service runs from 7 am to 6 pm. The route includes the Britomart Centre between Customs and Quay streets, Queen Street, Parnell, Newmarket (near the Auckland War Memorial Museum), Ponsonby, and Karangahape Road. The fares range from NZ$1 for the inner city to NZ$4.50 for the close suburbs. You can pay in cash using change or else buy a Hop prepay card available widely.

Auckland's bus and train network offers a joint electronic ticket. If you're not feeling intrepid, hire a car or take a taxi. For travel farther afield, Auckland Transport offers bus services as far north as Orewa on the Hibiscus Coast and south to Puke-kohe. You can buy a range of day passes from the ferry office. The information office at Britomart provides maps and timetables.

CONTACTS Information Office. ✉ *137 Quay St., City Center* ☎ *09/365–9914 public service number* ⊕ *www.auckland-nz.com/visit/discover/i-SITE-Visitor-Infor-mation-Centres.*

BUS TRAVEL FROM AUCKLAND
The Sky City Coach Terminal is the hub for InterCity Coaches and Newmans Coaches. InterCity links Auckland to most other major cities at least once a day. Newmans has daily routes to Wellington daily via Hamilton and Taupo, and to Rotorua and Napier. Kiwi Experi-ence goes to many more out-of-the-way destinations such as the East Cape; the "Funky Chicken" round-trip pass allows you to hop on and off where you please along the route. The buses depart from the Parnell office.

BUS CONTACTS InterCity Coaches. ☎ *09/583–5780* ⊕ *www.intercity.co.nz.* **Kiwi Experience.** ✉ *Parnell* ☎ *09/336–4286* ⊕ *www.kiwiexperience.com.* **Sky City Coach Terminal.** ✉ *102 Hobson St., City Center* ☎ *09/583–5780* ⊕ *www.intercity.co.nz.*

CAR AND TAXI TRAVEL
Auckland traffic is unpredictable due to a road network groaning under the pres-sure of a rapidly growing population. An incident on any part of the road network leads to gridlock across the whole city. Local rush hours last from 5:30 to 10 am and then 3 to 7 pm, but if it's raining add an hour at least. Massive road upgrades are under way across the motorway system, so traffic can be disrupted at any time. The main motorways all have convenient city turnoffs, but watch the signs carefully. The main road into and out of Auckland is State Highway 1. Off-ramps are clearly marked. Most areas have meter parking where you can pay by credit card. Fines are hefty if you overstay your time.

Auckland taxi rates vary with the com-pany. Most are around NZ$2 per km (½ mile), but some charge as much as NZ$4. Flag-fall, when the meters start, is usually NZ$2. The rates are listed on the driver's door. Most taxis accept major credit cards.

TAXI CONTACTS Alert Taxis. ☎ *09/309–2000* ⊕ *www.alerttaxis.co.nz.* **Auckland Cooperative Taxi Service.** ☎ *09/300–3000* ⊕ *www.cooptaxi.co.nz.* **Corporate Cabs.** ☎ *09/377–0773* ⊕ *www.corporatecabs.co.nz.*

TRAIN TRAVEL
KiwiRail, New Zealand's train operator, has a terminal and booking office at the **Britomart Transportation Centre,** on the harbor end of Queen Street. Service leaves Auckland for Wellington Monday, Thursday, and Saturday at 7:45 am and returns Tuesday, Friday, and Sunday.

Britomart Transport Centre
The hub of Auckland's growing rail net-work system is built in the city's historic central post office with a modern annex that houses the train hub. There is a currency exchange in the renovated old building that is adjacent to the fast-grow-ing Britomart Precinct, with its trendy eateries and fashion stores. ✉ *Queen Elizabeth Sq., Queen and Quay Sts.* ☎ *0800/467–536* ⊕ *www.britomart.co.nz.*

Restaurants

Princes Wharf and adjoining Viaduct Quay, an easy stroll from the city's major thoroughfare, Queen Street, offer dozens of eateries in every style from cheap-and-cheerful to superposh. High Street, running parallel to Queen Street on the Albert Park side of town, is a busy café and restaurant strip. Vulcan Lane, between Queen and High streets, has some pleasant bars. Asian immigrants have created a market for a slew of cheap noodle and sushi bars throughout the inner city; the more crowded, the better.

Outside the city center, the top restaurant areas are a 10-minute bus or cab ride away on Ponsonby and Parnell roads. Dominion and Mt. Eden roads in the city, as well as Hurstmere Road in the seaside suburb of Takapuna (just over the Harbour Bridge) are also worth exploring with the creation of a dining precinct called The Commons. The mix is eclectic—Indian, Chinese, Japanese, Italian, and Thai eateries sit alongside casual taverns, pizzerias, and high-end restaurants.

Restaurant and hotel reviews have been shortened. For full information, visit Fodors.com. Restaurant prices are the average cost of a main course at dinner, or if dinner is not served, at lunch. Hotel prices are the lowest cost of a standard double room in high season, including 12.5% tax.

What It Costs			
$	$$	$$$	$$$$
RESTAURANTS			
under NZ$15	NZ$15–NZ$20	NZ$21–NZ$30	over NZ$30
HOTELS			
under NZ$125	NZ$125–NZ$200	NZ$201–NZ$300	over NZ$300

Hotels

As New Zealand's gateway city, Auckland has most of the large international chain hotels, as well as a range of comfortable bed-and-breakfasts. Many of the large brand-name hotels cluster around the central business district (CBD), whereas B&Bs are found in trendier neighborhoods. Many of the best are in suburbs close to the city center like Devonport and Ponsonby.

November to March are the busiest months for Auckland hotels, so it pays to book by August to ensure you get your first choice. All the major hotels have parking at a price while a number of the B&Bs offer parking as part of your lodging package. Wi-Fi access is standard. B&B owners offer insider knowledge on what's best close by, and many will make reservations or other arrangements for you. Only the hotels tend to have air-conditioning, but this isn't a problem when you can fling open the windows and let in the fresh air.

Tours

Several companies run city orientation tours or special-interest excursions outside town.

BUS TOURS

InterCity's TravelPass (☎ 0800/222–146 ⊕ flexipass.intercity.co.nz) provides set itineraries on comfortable buses and commentary on the passing scenery. For the independent traveler, the **InterCity Flexipass** lets you travel where and when it suits you. Based on hours of travel, it lets you hop on and off and stay as long as you like. Passes are valid for 12 months from activation.

Explorer Bus

BUS TOURS | FAMILY | This yellow double-decker stops at 18 city attractions; you can hop on and off anywhere along the way. Buses begin at the Ferry Building between 9 and 4 daily. Buy tickets with a range of options from the driver or at the Fullers office in the Ferry Building. ✉ Ferry Bldg., Queen's Wharf, 30 Custom St. ☎ 0800/439–756 ⊕ www.explorerbus. co.nz ⌖ From NZ$45 a day.

Grayline Tours

BUS TOURS | A variety of guided bus tours leave from Hobson Street, behind the Sky City Hotel. Itineraries can take in city highlights or West Coast beaches. ⊠ *Sky City Coach Terminal, 102 Hobson St.* ☎ *09/583–5764* ⊕ *www.graylinetours. co.nz* ⚲ *From NZ$64.*

HORSE TREKKING

Pakiri Beach Horse Rides

GUIDED TOURS | **FAMILY** | North of Auckland, Pakiri Beach Horse Rides runs trips from several hours to several days, all incorporating a ride on the namesake white-sand beach. You might ride through groves of *pohutukawa,* which are ablaze with red flowers in the summer, or across the sand dunes with inspiring views of islands on the horizon or even go from the East to the West Coast. The proprietors are very conscious of horse welfare and don't take riders who weigh more than 210 pounds without prior arrangement. ⊠ *317 Rahuikiri Rd., Pakiri Beach, R.D. 2, Wellsford* ☎ *09/422–6275* ⊕ *www.horseride-nz.co.nz* ⚲ *From NZ$275.*

MĀORI TOURS

★ Potiki Adventures

SPECIAL-INTEREST | **FAMILY** | This company cultivates an air of intimacy with its small groups and friendly, open tour guides. You'll travel to Waiheke Island by ferry for an experience that includes a trip around the island, a visit to an ancient fortified village, a weaving demonstration, an olive oil tasting, and the chance to hear and play Māori musical instruments. Lunch is at one of the many cafés on the island. Potiki also offers customized private tours that include meeting Māori artists and gallery visits. ⊠ *68 Ocean Rd., Waiheke Island, Hauraki Gulf Islands* ☎ *09/372– 3477* ⊕ *www.potikiadventures.co.nz* ⚲ *From NZ$150 excluding ferry fares.*

★ TIME Unlimited

SPECIAL-INTEREST | **FAMILY** | You'll have the time of your life on any of the tours offered by TIME Unlimited. The company integrates Māori culture with activities like kayak-fishing and trail walking and can arrange an overnight stay at a *marae* (meetinghouse). TIME, through its concessions with the Department of Conservation and Māori tribes, can take visitors to places often out of reach of other tours, and they will customize a tour to meet your specific needs and time frame. Transport is in late-model Mercedes vehicles. ⊠ *Auckland* ☎ *09/846–3469* ⊕ *www.newzealand-tours.travel* ⚲ *From NZ$275.*

WILDERNESS TOURS

Bush and Beach Ltd.

GUIDED TOURS | Whether you are a *Lord of the Rings* fan, an outdoor adventurer, or a wine buff you'll find something from Bush and Beach to meet your needs and time frame. Tours range from a quick-ish tour of *Lord of the Rings* set Hobbiton to a full-day excursion that includes rain forest plus black-sand West Coast beaches, wineries, and a visit to where Jane Campion's *The Piano* was filmed. There are also tours of Great Barrier Island in the Hauraki Gulf. Custom tours are also available. ⊠ *Auckland* ☎ *09/837–4130* ⊕ *www.bushandbeach.co.nz* ⚲ *From NZ$80.*

WINE TOURS

Fine Wine Tours

SPECIAL-INTEREST | The four-hour West Auckland tour takes in several wineries and includes a picnic lunch and, weather permitting, a visit to a black-sand beach. The full-day Waiheke Island tour covers a number of wineries and lunch. Tour host Phil Parker is an authority on New Zealand wines and he has published a guide to the country's wine regions. Custom tours can be arranged. ☎ *09/845–6971* ⊕ *www.insidertouring.co.nz* ⚲ *From NZ$302.*

NZWinePro Auckland Wine Tours

SPECIAL-INTEREST | If you are pushed for time, but still want to fit in a vineyard, these four-hour tours may be the ticket. They are based around wine-growing areas to Auckland's north and west, plus Waiheke Island. The company also tailors tours to your grape or wine choice. ⊠ *417a Tamaki Dr.* ☎ *09/575–1958* ⊕ *www.nzwinepro.co.nz* ✉ *From NZ$195.*

Visitor Information

Need some travel advice? Drop in at one of Auckland's many i-SITEs and other visitor centers. Employees will help plan trips, provide sightseeing information, and point you toward a well-priced lunch.

CONTACTS Auckland International Airport Visitor Centre. ⊠ *Ray Emery Dr., next to arrivals exit, ground fl., International terminal* ☎ *09/275–0789.* **Auckland i-SITE Visitor Centre.** ⊠ *Atrium, Sky City, Victoria and Federal Sts.* ☎ *09/367–6009* ⊕ *www. aucklandnz.com.*

City Center and Parnell

Auckland's city center includes the working port area, much of it reclaimed from the sea in the latter half of the 19th century. While it's easy to walk around this area, some of the best views can be marred by the container and car import terminal which is behind a large red iron fence. Successive city administrators neglected Auckland's older buildings, too, so Queen Street and its surroundings are a mix of glass-tower office buildings and a dwindling number of older, some say more gracious, properties. Tucked away in Lorne and High streets, running parallel with Queen Street, are good examples of the city's early architecture, now home to the shops of some of New Zealand's leading fashion designers. The central business district (CBD) has been energized by a residential surge since the late 1990s and a move to create pedestrian-friendly strips, which is boosted by apartment development and an influx of Asian students. The Auckland

Domain and Parnell areas have the city's preeminent museums and art gallery as well as historic homes and shops. Parnell was Auckland's first suburb, established in 1841, and is a good place to look for arts and crafts or to sample some of Auckland's most popular cafés, bars, and restaurants.

A dozen "city ambassadors" patrol the city center on weekdays between 8:30 and 5, providing directions and answering questions. They're identified by their yellow-and-gray uniforms with "ambassador" written on their tops in red.

◉ Sights

Albert Park

BUILDING | FAMILY | These 15 acres of formal gardens contain a mix of established and seasonal plantings, a fountain, and statue- and sculpture-studded lawns. They are a favorite of Aucklanders, who pour out of nearby office buildings, and two adjacent universities to eat lunch and lounge under trees on sunny days. Good cafés at the universities serve well-priced take-out food and coffee. The park is built on the site of an 1840s–50s garrison, which kept settlers apart from neighboring Māori tribes. On the park's east side, behind Auckland University's general library, are remnants of stone walls with rifle slits. The park is home to festivals throughout the summer and the Auckland Art Gallery is on its edge. ⊠ *Bounded by Wellesley St. W, Kitchener St., Waterloo Quad, City Center.*

★ Auckland Art Gallery Toi o Tāmaki

ARTS VENUE | The modernist addition to the Auckland Art Gallery has breathed life and light into a structure built in the 1880s. The soaring glass, wood, and stone addition, which some say looks like stylized trees, both complements and contrasts with the formal château-like main gallery. A courtyard and fountain space at the front is home to ever-changing works. The gallery, adjacent to Albert Park has some 15,000 items dating from the 12th century but also shows innovative and challenging contemporary art that draws big crowds. Historic portraits of Māori chiefs by well-known New Zealand painters C.F. Goldie and Gottfried Lindauer offer an ethnocentric view of people once seen as fiercely martial. Goldie often used the same subject repeatedly—odd, considering his desire to document what he considered a dying race. New Zealand artists Frances Hodgkins, Doris Lusk, and Colin McCahon are also here, as are shows and performances. The gallery has made a tilt to offering more international exhibitions so check with the website for the latest show. Free collection tours are given at 11:30 and 1:30. The café is hip and busy and the gift shop offers a range of books, original artworks, and keepsakes. ⊠ *5 Kitchener St., at Wellesley St. E, City Center* ☎ *09/379–1349* ⊕ *www. aucklandartgallery.com* ☞ *Free, except for special exhibits.*

Auckland Domain
BUILDING | FAMILY | Saturday cricketers, Sunday picnickers, and all-day runners are some of the Aucklanders who enjoy this rolling, 340-acre park—not to mention loads of walkers, often with dogs. Running trails range from easy to challenging, and organized 10-km (6-mile) runs occur throughout the year. The Domain contains some magnificent sculpture as well as the domed **Wintergardens** (open daily 10–4), which houses tropical and seasonally displayed hothouse plants. In summer watch the local paper for free weekend-evening concerts, which usually include opera and fireworks. Take a bottle of wine and a basket of goodies and join the locals—up to 300,000 per show. ⚠ **While the Domain is safe during the day it is not a place to be at night unless you're there for a concert with a big crowd.** ⊠ *Entrances at Stanley St., Park Rd., Carlton Gore Rd., and Maunsell Rd., Parnell.*

★ Auckland War Memorial Museum
ARTS VENUE | FAMILY | The Māori artifact collection here is one of the largest in the world, housed in a Greek Revival building in one of the city's finest parks, with views to match. Must-sees include a fine example of a *pātaka* (storehouse), a fixture in Māori villages, and Te Toki a Tapiri, the last great Māori *waka* (canoe). Made of a single log and measuring 85 feet long, it could carry 100 warriors, and its figurehead shows tremendous carving. To learn more about Māori culture, attend one of the performances, held at least three times daily, that demonstrate Māori song, dance, weaponry, and the *haka* (a ceremonial dance the All Blacks rugby team has adopted as an intimidating pregame warm-up). The museum also holds an exceptional collection of Pacific artifacts and hosts high-quality visiting or issue-specific exhibitions. If you want a bit of talk and music in the evening check out the once-a-month panel discussion followed by live music known as Late at the Museum. On Anzac Day (April 25), thousands gather in front of the museum in a dawn service to recognize the gallantry of the country's servicemen and women. ⊠ *Auckland Domain, Park Rd., Parnell* ☎ *09/309–0443* ⊕ *www.auckland-museum.com* ☞ *From NZ$25.*

Civic Theatre
ARTS VENUE | FAMILY | This extravagant art nouveau movie theater was the talk of the town when it opened in 1929, but nine months later the owner, Thomas O'Brien, went bust and fled, taking the week's revenues and an usherette with him. During World War II a cabaret show in the basement was popular with Allied servicemen. One of the entertainers, Freda Stark, is said to have appeared regularly wearing nothing more than a coat of gold paint. Now the café at the front of the Civic bears her name. When you sit down to a show or movie you'll see a simulated night sky on the ceiling and giant lions with lights for eyes on stage. The theater is host to an ever-changing

City Center, Parnell & Ponsonby

One of the best walks to take in Auckland is to the summit of One Tree Hill, an extinct volcano and the site of three Māori *pā* (fortifications).

raft of movie premieres, intimate rock concerts, live theater, and dance parties. ⊠ *Queen and Wellesley Sts., City Center* ☎ *09/309–2677.*

Ferry Building

MARINA | This magnificent 1912 Edwardian building continues to stand out on Auckland's waterfront. It's still used for its original purpose, launching ferries to Devonport as well as to Waiheke and other Hauraki Gulf islands. The building also houses bars and restaurants. ⊠ *Quay St., City Center.*

★ Kelly Tarlton's Sealife Aquarium

ZOO | **FAMILY** | This harborside marine park—the creation of New Zealand's most celebrated undersea explorer and treasure hunter—offers a fish's-eye view of the sea. A transparent tunnel, 120 yards long, makes a bewitching circuit past moray eels, lobsters, sharks, and stingrays. You can also have an encounter with King and Gentoo penguins and their keepers in their icy home, and take home photos to prove it. This attraction is popular and limited to four people a

day so it pays to book ahead. ⊠ *Orakei Wharf, 23 Tamaki Dr., 5 km (3 miles) east of downtown Auckland* ☎ *09/531–5065* ⊕ *www.kellytarltons.co.nz* ✉ *NZ$39.*

New Zealand Maritime Museum

MUSEUM | **FAMILY** | New Zealand's rich seafaring history is on display at this marina complex on Auckland Harbour. The collection includes Pacific and Māori seagoing canoes as well as a range of European sailing boats. There are detailed exhibits on early whaling and a superb collection of yachts and ship models, including *KZ1*, the 133-foot racing sloop built for the America's Cup challenge in 1988. A scow conducts short harbor trips twice a day on Tuesday, Thursday, and weekends, and there's a wharf-side eatery. ⊠ *Eastern Viaduct, Quay St., City Center* ☎ *09/373–0800* ⊕ *www.maritimemuseum.co.nz* ✉ *From NZ$25.*

One Tree Hill

ARCHAEOLOGICAL SITE | **FAMILY** | The largest of Auckland's extinct volcanoes and one of the best lookout points, One Tree Hill, or Maungakiekie, was the site of three

Māori *pā* (fortifications). It used to have a single pine tree on its summit, but that was attacked several times by activists who saw it as a symbol of colonialism, and in 2000 it was taken down. Sir John Logan Campbell, the European founding father of the city, is buried on the summit. There is fantastic walking and running in the surrounding acreage known as Cornwall Park, with avenues of oaks, a kauri plantation, and an old olive grove. Or just take a mat and read under an old tree. Free electric barbecue sites are also available. Because the park is a working farm of sheep and cattle, you'll need to be wary of cows with their calves along the paths. There's also a cricket club with old-style seating, where you can watch a game in summer, and a pavilion where you can buy refreshments. ⊠ *Greenlane Rd. W, Parnell* ⊕ *www.cornwallpark. co.nz.*

Parnell Rose Gardens

GARDEN | FAMILY | When you tire of boutiques and cafés, take 10 minutes (or more) to gaze upon and sniff this collection of some 5,000 rosebushes. The main beds contain mostly modern hybrids, with new introductions planted regularly. The adjacent **Nancy Steen Garden** has antique varieties. And don't miss the incredible trees. There is a 200-year-old *pohutukawa* (puh-hoo-too- ka-wa), whose weighty branches touch the ground and rise up again, and a *kanuka* that is one of Auckland's oldest trees. In summer it's a popular site for wedding photographs. ⊠ *85 Gladstone Rd., Parnell* ⌕ *Free.*

Parnell Village

TOWN | The lovely Victorian timber villas along the upper slope of Parnell Road have been transformed into antique shops, designer boutiques, cafés, and restaurants. Parnell Village is the creation of Les Harvey, who saw the potential of the old, run-down shops and houses and almost single-handedly snatched them from the jaws of the developers' bulldozers in the early 1960s by buying

them, renovating them, and leasing them out. Today this village of trim pink-and-white timber facades is one of the most delightful parts of the city. At night, the area's restaurants and bars attract Auckland's well-heeled set. ⊠ *Parnell Rd. between St. Stephen's Ave. and Augustus Rd., Parnell* ⊕ *www.parnell.net.nz.*

St. Mary's Church in Holy Trinity

RELIGIOUS SITE | This Gothic Revival wooden church was built in 1886, by the early Anglican missionary Bishop Selwyn. The craftsmanship inside the kauri church is remarkable, down to the hand-finished columns. One of the carpenters left his trademark, an owl, sitting in the beams to the right of the pulpit. If you stand in the pulpit and clasp the lectern, you'll feel something lumpy under your left hand—a mouse, the trademark of another of the craftsmen who made the lectern, the so-called Mouse Man of Kilburn. The story of the church's relocation is also remarkable. St. Mary's originally stood on the other side of Parnell Road, and in 1982 the entire structure was moved across the street to be next to the new church, the Cathedral of the Holy Trinity. ⊠ *Parnell Rd. and St. Stephen's Ave., Parnell* ⊕ *www.holy-trinity.org.nz.*

Sky Tower

OBSERVATORY | FAMILY | This 1,082-foot beacon is the first place many Aucklanders take visiting friends to give them a view of the city. Up at the main observation level, glass floor panels let you look past your feet to the street hundreds of yards below. Adults step gingerly onto the glass, while kids delight in jumping up and down on it. Through glass panels in the floor of the elevator you can see the counterweight of the **Sky Jump,** a controlled leap off the 630-foot observation deck that provides an adrenaline rush. ⊠ *Victoria and Federal Sts., City Center* ☎ *09/912–6000* ⊕ *www.skycity.co.nz* ⌕ *From NZ$29.*

🍴 Restaurants

★ Cibo

$$$$ | MODERN NEW ZEALAND | When you are in the mood for superb food without any drama head to Cibo. The name means "good food" in Italian, and it is apt for this restaurant, which has been around for more than 20 years. **Known for:** excellent innovative Italian food; exceptional wine list; the best place for a long lunch. $ *Average main: NZ$45* ✉ *91 St. Georges Bay Rd., Parnell* ☎ *09/303–9660* ⊕ *www.cibo.co.nz* ⊘ *Closed Sun. No lunch Sat.*

★ Fish

$$$$ | NEW ZEALAND | This light-filled restaurant with floor-to-ceiling glass looks across the harbor to trendy Devonport and the Bayswater boat marina. The menu is based on high-quality fresh local produce, particularly fish and meat cooked to perfection. **Known for:** superb seasonal and local dishes; bright and buzzy ambience; excellent views. $ *Average main: NZ$38* ✉ *Hilton Auckland, Princes Wharf, 147 Quay St., City Center* ☎ *09/978–2000* ⊕ *www.fishrestaurant. co.nz.*

★ Giraffe Restaurant

$$$$ | NEW ZEALAND | FAMILY | Located in the buzzy heart of the viaduct, Giraffe unites the best local foods with flair and fun. It's open from breakfast until late and whether you are a meat eater or a vegan, the menu will leave you satisfied. **Known for:** regularly changing menu of high-quality food; locally focused wine list; relaxed atmosphere with great service. $ *Average main: NZ$34* ✉ *Viaduct Harbour, City Center* ☎ *09/358–1093* ⊕ *www.girafferestaurant.co.nz.*

Harbourside Ocean Bar Grill

$$$$ | SEAFOOD | Overlooking the water from the upper level of the restored Ferry Building, this seafood restaurant is an Auckland institution that draws foodies and families alike. It serves seasonal New Zealand seafood on a menu that references a number of cuisine styles. **Known for:** high-quality seafood; unique and tasty meat options, including venison; stunning harbor views. $ *Average main: NZ$50* ✉ *Ferry Bldg., Quay St., City Center* ☎ *09/307–0486* ⊕ *www. harbourside.co.*

Mexican Café

$$$ | MEXICAN | FAMILY | This very busy café has been serving up great Mexican-style food since 1983. People go as much for the noisy, friendly vibe as they do for the food such as the chicken fajitas or vegetarian burritos. **Known for:** tasty Mexican food; great value; big crowds during prime mealtimes. $ *Average main: NZ$25* ✉ *67 Victoria St. W, City Center* ☎ *09/373–2311* ⊕ *www.mexicancafe. co.nz.*

Non Solo Pizza

$$$$ | ITALIAN | FAMILY | If you've had a busy day and want to roll on and be surrounded by animated diners this place is for you. The food can be ordered individually or with bowls to be shared by the table. **Known for:** delicious pizza; great range of pastas; fabulous desserts. $ *Average main: NZ$35* ✉ *259 Parnell Rd., Parnell* ☎ *09/379–5358* ⊕ *www. nonsolopizza.co.nz.*

★ O'Connell Street Bistro

$$$$ | NEW ZEALAND | This former bank vault, on one of the city's fashionable backstreets, has a cozy bar from which you can watch passersby through thin venetian blinds. It has garnered a loyal clientele who keep returning for the food and service. **Known for:** large and varied wine list; intimate and sophisticated atmosphere; superb, ever-changing menu. $ *Average main: NZ$42* ✉ *3 O'Connell St., City Center* ☎ *09/377– 1884* ⊕ *www.oconnellstbistro.com* ⊘ *Closed Sun. No lunch Sat.*

Ostro Brasserie and Bar

$$$$ | MODERN NEW ZEALAND | Housed in the artfully renovated Seafarers Building overlooking the harbor, Ostro has a

Did You Know?

Although the Ferry Building was built in the Edwardian style, a new section of piers evokes a ship anchored behind the original structure. Look for the curved sail-shape roof and smokestack-like turrets.

New Zealand Snacks

Hokey-Pokey Ice Cream. Go for the full-fat version of this vanilla ice cream dotted with toffee bits.

Kūmara Fries. Packed with potassium and fiber, *kūmara* fries are guilt-free delicious snacks. The kūmara, or sweet potato, has a rich heritage as a Māori food staple. Red, gold, and orange varieties are plentiful in New Zealand today. Orange is the sweetest, especially good fried and served with sweet chili sauce and sour cream. These fries are soft rather than crunchy.

Pavlova. Like the ballerina for whom it was named, this national dessert is feather light—a meringue topped with fruit, sauce, and fresh cream. The confection is essentially hollow, but it forms the tough core of one of the many Kiwi and Aussie rivalries: who invented it and named it after Anna Pavlova? So far, Kiwis have the edge: their recipe predates the Australian one by six years.

Whitebait Fritters. The Kiwi passion for this seafood, a smeltlike fish caught as juveniles as they head upriver to spawn, is so intense that the media reports the start of whitebait season. Find the pancake-size fritters at markets or as a daily special in cafés. Strict controls and high demand make it a delicious and pricey delicacy.

buzzy bar, superb food, and some of the best people-watching in Auckland. Enjoy lunch, dinner, or something in-between in a relaxed brasserie style. **Known for:** seasonal menu of New Zealand classics; excellent wine list; waterfront views. ⑤ *Average main: NZ$40* ✉ *Seafarers Bldg., Tyler St.* ☎ *09/302–9888* ⊕ *www. seafarers.co.nz.*

Soul Bar and Bistro
$$$$ | **NEW ZEALAND** | There's always something to see at the Soul Bar and Bistro, which fronts the Viaduct Basin on the harbor. The menu is modern with a traditional twist (pork belly with pork-and-apple strudel, parsnip puree, and parsley slaw, for example) and always good whether your want fresh fish, meat, or something from the plant family. **Known for:** sensational wine list; hip atmosphere; outside seating on terrace. ⑤ *Average main: NZ$39* ✉ *Viaduct Harbour, City Center* ☎ *09/356–7249* ⊕ *www.soulbar. co.nz.*

The Sugar Club
$$$$ | **MODERN NEW ZEALAND** | For a high-end dining experience, this is the place to go—53 floors up in the Sky Tower. The decor is reminiscent of 1930s Italy, while the food and views attract a range of diners. **Known for:** interesting food combinations served small plate-style; gorgeous citywide views; high prices. ⑤ *Average main: NZ$90* ✉ *Level 53, Sky Tower, Federal and Victoria Sts., City Center* ☎ *09/363–6365* ⊕ *www.skycityauckland. co.nz/restaurants/the-sugar-club.*

Tanuki's Cave
$$$ | **JAPANESE** | A flight of dimly lighted stairs leads down to this buzzing Japanese yakitori and sake bar. The oblong bar is usually jammed with film-festival types, the young art and fashion crowd, or classical music lovers eating before a concert in the nearby Town Hall. **Known for:** Japanese small plates; wide range of sake; hip crowds. ⑤ *Average main: NZ$28* ✉ *319B Queen St., City Center* ☎ *09/379–5151* ⊕ *www.sakebars.co.nz/ cave* ☉ *No lunch.*

Hotels

★ Braemar Bed & Breakfast

$$$$ | B&B/INN | This gorgeous Edwardian town house in the heart of the city is close to all of Auckland's enchantments, including the art gallery, restaurants, parks, museums, and designer shops. **Pros:** lovely historic building; endearing hosts; proximity to the city. **Cons:** no outdoor space; parking is difficult; no views. $ *Rooms from: NZ$350* ⊠ *7 Parliament St., City Center* ☎ *09/377–5463* ⊕ *www. parliamentstreet.co.nz* ↩ *4 rooms* ⊙ *Breakfast.*

Crowne Plaza

$$$$ | HOTEL | FAMILY | Close to everything in the city, all of the rooms at the Crowne Plaza have city views. **Pros:** close to town; well priced; good café. **Cons:** often frequented by conference-goers; nearby shopping center is drab; breakfast not included. $ *Rooms from: NZ$550* ⊠ *128 Albert St., City Center* ☎ *09/302–1111* ⊕ *www.crowneplazaauckland.co.nz* ↩ *352 rooms* ⊙ *No meals.*

Grand Millenium Auckland

$$ | HOTEL | This hotel is close to the Aotea Centre performance venue and its central locale close to many well-priced restaurants appeals to business travelers. **Pros:** central to the city; very comfortable pillows; good Japanese restaurant. **Cons:** decor needs a refresh; streets outside can be noisy; often busy with conferences. $ *Rooms from: NZ$200* ⊠ *Mayoral Dr. at Vincent St., City Center* ☎ *09/366–3000* ⊕ *www.rendezvoushotels.com* ↩ *455 rooms* ⊙ *No meals.*

Heritage Auckland

$$$$ | HOTEL | FAMILY | This hotel in a former department store unites the historic with the contemporary. **Pros:** close to city center; delicious restaurant; rooftop pool. **Cons:** limited Wi-Fi; often busy with conference-goers; not all rooms have great views. $ *Rooms from: NZ$450* ⊠ *35 Hobson St., City Center* ☎ *09/379–8553*

⊕ *www.heritagehotels.co.nz* ↩ *467 rooms.*

★ Hilton Auckland

$$$$ | HOTEL | Standing on the end of Princes Wharf, the Hilton resembles the cruise ships that dock alongside it, with white walls and neutral furnishings in chic rooms that allow your eyes to drift to the great views. **Pros:** lovely views; decent on-site eating and drinking; close to central city and ferry terminal. **Cons:** ships mooring nearby can be noisy; wharf can be busy with revelers; some may find the short walk from town a hassle. $ *Rooms from: NZ$369* ⊠ *Princes Wharf, 147 Quay St., City Center* ☎ *09/978–2000* ⊕ *www.hilton.com* ↩ *201 rooms* ⊙ *No meals.*

Pullman Hotel Auckland

$$$ | HOTEL | FAMILY | With its great location across from Auckland University, Pullman offers a mix of hotel rooms and apartments; the Residences wing has beautiful balconied rooms, some with partial harbor views, while the Tower offers more conventional rooms and suites. **Pros:** close to city center; reliable service; nice spa. **Cons:** can be busy with conferences; steep walk from city central; street outside can be noisy at night. $ *Rooms from: NZ$280* ⊠ *Princes St. and Waterloo Quadrant, City Center* ☎ *09/353–1000* ⊕ *www.pullmanhotels. com* ↩ *394 rooms.*

Sky City Grand Hotel

$$$ | HOTEL | FAMILY | A bonus of staying at this central city hotel is the specially commissioned artwork by top New Zealand artists hanging in the soaring lobby. **Pros:** close to the city center; excellent restaurants; gorgeous design throughout. **Cons:** can be busy with conferences; noisy at night; expensive valet parking. $ *Rooms from: NZ$250* ⊠ *90 Federal St., City Center* ☎ *09/363–7000* ⊕ *www. skycitygrand.co.nz* ↩ *316 rooms.*

Sofitel Auckland Viaduct

$$$ | HOTEL | This waterfront hotel presents the customer with both luxury and a friendly environment, as well as views of the ever-changing Viaduct Basin from some rooms. **Pros:** well situated, with waterside dining; excellent rooms; close to Victoria Park. **Cons:** Viaduct area can be noisy; breakfast not included; no free parking. ⑤ *Rooms from: NZ$300* ✉ *21 Viaduct Harbour Ave., City Center* ☏ *09/909–9000* ⊕ *www.sofitel-auckland. com* ⇦ *172 suites.*

Stamford Plaza

$$$ | HOTEL | Constant upgrades, noteworthy service, and attention to detail keep this mid-city hotel at the top of its game. **Pros:** close to town; good service and lovely staff; excellent rooms. **Cons:** tends to get busy with group tours; fronts a very busy street; not many good views. ⑤ *Rooms from: NZ$225* ✉ *Albert St. and Swanson St., City Center* ☏ *09/309–8888* ⊕ *www.stamford.com.au/spak* ⇦ *329 rooms.*

Nightlife

For the latest information on nightclubs get your hands on *What's On Auckland,* a pocket-size booklet available at all visitor information bureaus. The monthly *Metro* magazine, available at newsstands, has a guide to theater, arts, and music, and can also give you a helpful nightlife scoop. The Friday and Saturday editions of the *New Zealand Herald* run a gig guide and full cinema and theater listings.

After sunset the bar action is split across four distinct areas, with the waterfront and central city a common ground between the largely loyal Parnell and Ponsonby crowds. Auckland can be quite unpleasant in the small hours of the morning when young people from the far suburbs spill out of bars drunk and rowdy. To avoid this, head to Parnell where the restaurants and bars are frequented by a polished, free-spending crowd,

or for a more relaxed scene, head to Ponsonby Road, west of the city center, where you'll find street-side dining and packed bars. If you prefer to stay in the city center, the place to be for bars is the Viaduct, particularly in summer, or High Street and nearby O'Connell Street, with a sprinkling of bars in between. At the Queen Street end of Karangahape Road (just north of Highway 1) you'll find shops, lively bars, cafés, and nightspots. Note that not many venues are aimed at the gay and lesbian market in Auckland, but the best place to scout for bars is the gay news site *GayNZ.com.* Nightclubs, meanwhile, are transient animals with names and addresses changing monthly if not weekly.

There is also a growing nightlife scene on the North Shore—particularly in the upmarket seaside suburb of Takapuna. If you make the trip over the bridge, you'll be rewarded by bars and restaurants with a particularly relaxed vibe and great beach views.

COMEDY

Classic Comedy & Bar

COMEDY CLUBS | Auckland's main venue for live comedy has established itself on the international circuit with many well-known acts coming here to perform along with the best of New Zealand's rising talent. In April the venue hosts the International Laugh Festival. ✉ *321 Queen St., City Center* ☏ *09/373–4321* ⊕ *www.comedy.co.nz.*

LIVE MUSIC AND NIGHTCLUBS

The live music scene in Auckland is growing—bands often perform in unexpected and sometimes out-of-the-way locations (a bowling alley isn't unheard of), so keep an eye on the entertainment guides. Live bands tend to start late so make sure you eat first because at most venues food is not a priority and the scene is more grunge than lounge. If you like up-and-coming bands, then head to Karangahape Road at the top of Queen Street. There you'll find smaller venues, which are often the launch pad for local bands. For live indie music, Whammy, also on Karangahape Road, is a good bet.

🎭 Performing Arts

The Auckland arts scene is busy, particularly in the area of visual arts, with some 60 dealer galleries operating. Theater is on the rise and more touring exhibitions and performing companies are coming through the city than ever before. The Auckland Philharmonia Orchestra performs regularly, including at the summer series of free concerts in the park at the Domain, when thousands of music lovers sit with picnics under the stars. The Spark Arena by the harbor attracts plenty of rock acts, too.

ART GALLERIES

Artspace

ART GALLERIES—ARTS | This independent contemporary gallery shows both international and local artists plus occasionally hosts talks and seminars. ✉ *300 Karangahape Rd., City Center* ☎ *09/303–4965* ⊕ *www.artspace.org.nz.*

Masterworks

ART GALLERIES—ARTS | This gallery exhibits and sells contemporary New Zealand art, glass, ceramics, and jewelry and is the place to go if you are looking for something different. Its location on Upper Queen Street is an easy walk from the center of town. Masterworks holds some 15 group and individual exhibitions a year including student work and will pack and ship any item purchased. ✉ *71 Upper Queen St., City Center* ☎ *09/373–5446* ⊕ *www.masterworksgallery.co.nz* ⏱ *Closed Sun. and Mon.*

MUSIC AND OPERA

Aotea Centre

CONCERTS | Auckland's main venue for the performing arts and medium-size conferences is in the center of the city and often mounts free art exhibitions in its public spaces. There is a good café on the steps leading into the main foyer. The

New Zealand Opera performs three annual main-stage seasons here, accompanied by either the **Auckland Philharmonia Orchestra** or the **New Zealand Symphony Orchestra**. ✉ *Aotea Sq., 50 Mayoral Dr., City Center* ☎ *09/309–2677* ⊕ *www.aucklandlive.co.nz/venue/aotea-centre.*

Auckland Town Hall

ARTS CENTERS | The New Zealand Symphony and Auckland Philharmonia Orchestras perform here in the Great Hall, which holds up to 1,529 people on three levels. Some say it has some of the finest acoustics in the world. It also features the largest musical instrument in the country, the Town Hall Organ. More intimate concerts take place in the Concert Chamber. ✉ *303 Queen St., City Center* ☎ *09/309–2677* ⊕ *www.aucklandlive.co.nz/venue/auckland-town-hall.*

Civic Theatre

ARTS CENTERS | This theater hosts many performances by international touring companies and artists. ✉ *Queen and Wellesley Sts., City Center* ☎ *09/309–2677* ⊕ *www.aucklandlive.co.nz/venue/the-civic.*

🛍 Shopping

Auckland's main shopping precincts for clothes and shoes are Queen Street, High Street, and the Britomart precinct behind the train station. Queen Street is particularly good for outdoor gear, duty-free goods, greenstone jewelry, and souvenirs and big-name international brands. O'Connell and High streets also have a good smattering of designer boutiques, bookstores, and other specialty shops.

BOOKS

Unity Books

BOOKS/STATIONERY | If you are after New Zealand–related books, travel, and fiction, this is the place for you. Smart staff will help you find that special text. ✉ *19 High St., City Center* ☎ *09/307–0731* ⊕ *www.unitybooks.co.nz.*

CLOTHING AND ACCESSORIES
★ Fingers

JEWELRY/ACCESSORIES | This store show-cases unique contemporary work by about 45 New Zealand artists, working with fine metals and stones to create beautiful jewelry. Many of the artists have works in the New Zealand National Collection, and customers who pur-chased items at an early stage of a maker's career are being rewarded with significant increases in value. Look out for works that combine precious metal with more mundane materials like rocks, seashells, or even plastic. ⊠ *2 Kitchener St., City Center* ☎ *09/373–3974* ⊕ *www. fingers.co.nz.*

★ Zambesi

CLOTHING | Always among the top New Zealand designers, this fashion label run by an informed family team has always charted its own course. You'll find its garments for men and women are never dated and are worn by very influential people who want a look that is both strong and understated. ⊠ *56 Tyler St., near Britomart, City Center* ☎ *09/303– 1701* ⊕ *www.zambesistore.com.*

DEPARTMENT STORES
Smith and Caughey's Ltd.

DEPARTMENT STORES | This is a good place to see plenty of local and international brands under one roof, coupled with extremely good service and the largest cosmetics hall in the city. ⊠ *253–261 Queen St., City Center* ☎ *09/377–4770* ⊕ *www.smithandcaugheys.co.nz.*

SOUVENIRS AND GIFTS
Pauanesia

GIFTS/SOUVENIRS | The sign hanging above this gift shop sets the tone—the letters are shaped from *paua* shell, which resembles abalone. You'll find one-off bags, place mats, picture frames, cushions, jewelry, and many other hand-made items. ⊠ *35 High St., City Center* ☎ *09/366–7282* ⊕ *www.pauanesia.co.nz.*

🏃 Activities

Aucklanders love sports, whether as spectators or participants. The nation's psyche is embedded in rugby—where men (most of the time) chase an elliptical ball around hoping to land it under goal-posts to score what is known as a "try." The city is home to two rugby teams— the Auckland Blues and the North Harbour team known as Harbour.

For those not in love with rugby there is soccer and, in summer, cricket. Increas-ingly, more people are taking up cycling and mountain biking, and it's easy to rent a bike. For many women the big sport is netball, which is akin to basketball. There are a number of venues around the city.

For those who prefer water sports, Auckland has plenty of sailing, surfing, and kite-surfing. Beaches—commonly categorized as east, west, or north—gen-erally have great views and are good for walking. The eastern beaches, such as those along Tamaki Drive on the south side of the harbor, are closer to the city and don't have heavy surf. West coast black-sand beaches are popular (and hot) in summer, and can have rough seas with sudden rips and holes. (Surfboards can be rented at Muriwai and Piha.) And across Waitemata Harbour from the city, a chain of magnificent beaches stretches north as far as the Whangaparoa Peninsula.

BOATING AND SAILING

In Auckland, you're never far from the water; on the East Coast it's the Wait-emata Harbour and Hauraki Gulf, and on the West Coast, dramatic surf beaches. Residents make the most of it all and the number of watercraft make it clear why they call Auckland the City of Sails. There are lots of opportunities for you to take part in the fun. If you're in Auckland in February, be sure to check out the Auckland Anniversary Regatta (⊕ *www. regatta.org.nz*). The Yachting New Zealand website has a calendar of events through-out the year (⊕ *www.yachtingnz.org.nz*).

INDEPENDENT MULTIDAY TRIPS

If you'd like an independent trip, but you'd rather someone else take the actual helm, New Zealand ports offer scores of options for skippered personalized itineraries. Choices include high-speed catamarans, luxury yachts, and restored tall ships, and these vessels run the gamut from basic to swank (which, unsurprisingly, directly corresponds to cost). Skippered boats during peak season cost anywhere from NZ$1,000 to NZ$3,000 a day. While most have habitual cruising grounds near their home ports, many skippers are happy to discuss an itinerary that includes destinations far and wide.

TOURS
Fullers

BOAT TOURS | To get a sense of Auckland, the Auckland skyline, and the size of Sky Tower, take a 1½-hour Auckland Harbour cruise that leaves from the Ferry Building. Commentary runs while the boat passes the Harbour Bridge, Devonport's naval base, and Bean Rock Lighthouse. There's a brief stopover on Rangitoto Island in the Harauki Gulf. Various day tours of Waiheke Island are also available. ✉ *Ferry Bldg., 99 Quay St.* ☎ *09/367–9111* ⊕ *www.fullers.co.nz* ✉ *From NZ$45.*

★ Sail NZ

BOAT TOURS | No experience is necessary to sail on America's Cup yachts with Sail NZ. Help sail with a racing crew or relax while they do the work. For more thrills, participate in the America's Cup Match Racing trip, a three-hour experience that includes practice drills followed by a race against other yachts with a race crew. If you want a more relaxed activity, the company has a range of options that allow you to see the harbor without the pressure of racing. There are lunch and dinner options. ✉ *Viaduct Harbour* ☎ *09/359–5987* ⊕ *www.exploregroup. co.nz/en/unique-experiences/ameri- cas-cup-sail-auckland* ✉ *From NZ$99.*

BUNGEE-JUMPING
AJ Hackett Bungy—Auckland Harbour Bridge

LOCAL SPORTS | The only bungy (New Zealand spelling for bungee) jumping in Auckland, this company operates off the Harbour Bridge year-round. The Harbour Bridge Experience is a 1½-hour bridge climb with commentary on the history of the bridge and the region. Needless to say, views from the bridge walk are outstanding. There are three trips a day, and reservations are essential. ✉ *Westhaven Reserve, Curran St., Herne Bay* ☎ *09/360–7748* ⊕ *www.bungy.co.nz* ✉ *From NZ$150 for the walk and NZ$225 for the bungy.*

SPORTS VENUES
Eden Park

SPECTATOR SPORTS | The city's major stadium is the best place (in winter) to see New Zealand's sporting icon: the All Blacks, one of the best rugby teams in the world. More frequently, it sees the Auckland Blues, a Super 15 rugby team that plays professional franchise opponents from Australia, South Africa, and other parts of New Zealand. Cricket teams arrive in summer. For information on sporting events, check out *What's On Auckland,* a monthly guide available from the Auckland i-SITE Visitor Centre. ✉ *Reimers Ave.* ⊕ *www.edenpark.co.nz.*

Ponsonby

Some of the city's best cafés are on Ponsonby Road. Breakfast is a specialty because of the high demand from locals looking to grab a coffee and something to eat before heading to a glass tower, media company, or studio downtown. It's difficult to single out any café as all are pretty good because the competition and expectations are high. If you are an architecture buff wander the streets and look at how smart renovation brings modern living and life to former working-class homes.

Rugby Madness

Rugby evolved out of soccer in 19th-century Britain. It was born at the elitist English school of Rugby, where in 1823 a schoolboy by the name of William Webb Ellis became bored with kicking a soccer ball and picked it up and ran with it. Rugby is similar to American football, except players are not allowed to pass the ball forward and they wear no protective gear. There's a World Cup for the sport, every four years since 1987.

Rugby developed among the upper classes of Britain, whereas soccer remained a predominantly working-class game. However, in colonial New Zealand, a country largely free from the rigid class structure of Britain, the game developed as the nation's number-one winter sport. One reason was the success of New Zealand teams in the late 19th and early 20th centuries. This remote outpost of the then British empire, with a population of only 750,000 in 1900, was an impressive rugby force, and it became a source of great national pride. Today, in a country of 4-plus million, the national sport is played by 250,000 New Zealanders at the club level.

The top-class rugby season in the southern hemisphere kicks off in February with the Super 15, which pits professional teams from provincial franchises in New Zealand, South Africa, and Australia against one another. New Zealand's matches are generally held in main cities, and you should be able to get tickets without too much trouble. The international season runs from June to late August. This is your best chance to see the national team, the All Blacks, and the major cities are again the place to be. National provincial championship games hit towns all over the country from late August to mid-October. A winner-takes-all game decides who attains the domestic rugby Holy Grail, the Ranfurly Shield. If you can't catch a live game, you can always join a crowd watching a televised match at a local pub or sports bar. There is also a growing number of women playing rugby here, including at the professional level.

Restaurants

Bambina Ponsonby

$$ | INTERNATIONAL | FAMILY | This café is part of the Ponsonby Road old guard and has been serving its loyal customers for over 20 years. The menu offers breakfast staples like eggs and bacon, but you can also mix it up with coconut yogurt, muesli, and superb salads at lunchtime. **Known for:** great coffee; fresh seasonal food; classic Auckland café experience. $ *Average main: NZ$20* ✉ *268 Ponsonby Rd., Ponsonby* ☎ *09/360–4000* ⊕ *www. bambinaponsonby.co.nz.*

Dida's Wine Lounge & Tapas

$$$ | SPANISH | In 1941 a grocer's shop stood on this site, run by a Croatian, Joseph Jakicevich, who also made his own wine and three generations later, his descendants run this lively wine-and-tapas bar in the same building. More than 100 wines are offered by the glass to accompany a menu of around 18 tapas— all Spanish with a Kiwi twist—which vary depending on the season. **Known for:** superb by-the-glass wine list; tempting small plates to share; local crowds so it can get busy. $ *Average main: NZ$22* ✉ *54 Jervois Rd., Ponsonby* ☎ *09/376– 2813* ⊕ *www.didas.co.nz.*

★ Dizengoff

$$ | ISRAELI | One of the area's most popular breakfast and lunch places, Dizengoff serves hearty Jewish (but not kosher) food to an eclectic clientele. The coffee is among the best around and there is an ever-changing selection of New Zealand art. **Known for:** superb scrambled eggs and veal sausages; long waits especially on weekends; perfect chicken salad. ⑤ *Average main: NZ$20* ✉ *256 Ponsonby Rd., Ponsonby* ☎ *09/360–0108* ☾ *No dinner.*

★ Prego Restaurant

$$$$ | ITALIAN | It's no mean feat being the longest-running restaurant in Ponsonby, where the locals and their guests are fussy. The broad Italian menu includes wood-fired pizzas and good pasta. **Known for:** superb modern Italian food; great wine list; noisy and bustling atmosphere. ⑤ *Average main: NZ$39* ✉ *226 Ponsonby Rd., Ponsonby* ☎ *09/376–3095* ⊕ *www.prego.co.nz.*

★ Sidart

$$$$ | MODERN NEW ZEALAND | This spot and its tasting menus bring modern cooking to a whole new level. The chefs take a slew of the finest ingredients and combine them in ways that will delight and astound the most jaded palate. **Known for:** innovative use of produce; new recipes offered at Tuesday night test kitchen; beautiful city views. ⑤ *Average main: NZ$150* ✉ *Three Lamps Plaza, 283 Ponsonby Rd.* ☎ *09/360–2122* ⊕ *www.sidart.co.nz* ☾ *Closed Sun. and Mon.*

SPQR Cafe & Bar

$$$$ | ITALIAN | This former motorcycle shop is one of the best places on Ponsonby Road for people-watching. The excellent food is largely Italian, and it's known for its thin-crust pizzas. **Known for:** excellent food and wine; hip (sometimes too hip) ambience; fun outdoor seating. ⑤ *Average main: NZ$35* ✉ *150 Ponsonby Rd., Ponsonby* ☎ *09/360–1710* ⊕ *www.spqrnz.co.nz.*

🛏 Hotels

Great Ponsonby Art Hotel

$$$$ | B&B/INN | Local original art gives this villa hotel on a quiet street off Ponsonby Road a special touch. **Pros:** friendly and relaxed atmosphere; tasty breakfasts; central Ponsonby location. **Cons:** sophisticates may find it a bit too homey; half an hour walk to the city; rooms on the smaller side. ⑤ *Rooms from: NZ$355* ✉ *30 Ponsonby Terr., Ponsonby* ☎ *09/376–5989* ⊕ *www.greatpons.co.nz* ⟳ *13 rooms* ⍟ *Breakfast.*

🌙 Nightlife

BARS

Lime

BARS/PUBS | You might as well leave your inhibitions at the door when you enter, because everybody else does. People pack this friendly and often noisy, narrow bar on the weekend. ✉ *167 Ponsonby Rd., Ponsonby* ☎ *09/360–7167.*

Western Springs

Western Springs Park is both a suburb and a park in the inner west part of Auckland. It takes its name from the lake there, fed by a natural spring. Today the park, which houses the zoo and the Museum of Transport and Technology, is home to Pacifica, the giant culture, food, and art festival that takes place in summer, generally in March. The speedway sometimes hosts rock concerts.

The lake, which is full of eels, swans, and ducks, has many surrounding paths popular with dog walkers and joggers alike. See native plants and wild fowl, including native pūkeko, teal, Australian coot, and shovelers, around the shores and wetlands.

Across the road from Western Springs is the Chamberlain Park Golf Course, which is open to the public. Western Springs is a good place to read a book or have a picnic.

◉ Sights

Auckland Zoo

ZOO | **FAMILY** | Since the 1990s, this zoo, 6 km (4 miles) west of Auckland, has focused on providing its animals with the most natural habitats possible, as well as on breeding and conservation. To catch a glimpse of New Zealand flora and fauna, spend time in the New Zealand Native Aviary, where you walk among the birds, and the Kiwi and Tuatara Nocturnal House. A number of music events are held in summer in the zoo grounds. ⊠ *Motions Rd., Western Springs ⊹ By car, take Karangahape Rd. (which turns into Great North Rd.) west out of city, past Western Springs. Take right onto Motions Rd. Buses from city stop opposite Motions Rd.* ☎ *09/360–3805* ⊕ *www. aucklandzoo.co.nz* ⊠ *NZ$24.*

Museum of Transport & Technology

MUSEUM | **FAMILY** | Six km (4 miles) west of Auckland, this is a fantastic place for anyone with a technical bent. A fascinating collection of vehicles, telephones, cameras, locomotives, steam engines, and farm equipment is a tribute to Kiwi ingenuity. The aviation collection includes the only surviving Solent flying boat. One of the most intriguing exhibits is the remains of an aircraft built by New Zealand aviation pioneer Robert Pearse. There is a reproduction of another he built in which he made a successful powered flight around the time the Wright brothers first took to the skies. The flight ended inauspiciously when his plane crashed into a hedge. But Pearse, considered a wild eccentric by his farming neighbors, is recognized today as a mechanical genius. MOTAT, as the museum is called, also has the scooter that former Prime Minister Helen Clark once rode. ⊠ *825 Great North Rd., off Northwestern Motorway (Rte. 16), Western Springs* ☎ *09/846–0199* ⊕ *www. motat.org.nz* ⊠ *NZ$19.*

🏃 Activities

BIKING

Auckland can be good for cycling if you stick to certain areas, such as around the waterfront where there are cycle lanes. With a road bike, you can join a "bunch ride." Cyclists leave designated points most mornings and welcome guests; cycle shops can point you in the right direction. On weekends bunch rides can cover up to 150 km (93 miles) and will show you parts of the countryside that most won't get to see, plus stop off for a mandatory coffee.

★ Adventure Cycles

BICYCLING | This outfit can provide maps of biking routes that avoid pitfalls such as traffic and roadwork (and there's always roadwork in Auckland). Bikes run from NZ$30 for a full day to NZ$260 for a month. A full range of related gear, like panniers, helmets, and lights can also be rented. Though the company does not organize bike tours, it provides as much information as needed. ⊠ *9 Premier Ave., Western Springs* ☎ *09/940–2453* ⊕ *www.adventure-auckland.co.nz/ adventurecycles.*

GOLF

Chamberlain Park Golf Course

GOLF | This 18-hole public course in a parkland is a five-minute drive off Northwestern Motorway (Route 16) from the city. It's a popular course with open fairways, controlled rough, and big old specimen trees. The course is popular with the first tee at 6 am. Because it is publicly owned you don't need membership anywhere else to play, but call ahead to book because Chamberlain Park is busy. The club shop rents clubs, shoes, and carts. It's one of the cheapest golf courses in Auckland, and because it's on volcanic rock, the course holds up in wet weather. ⊠ *46 Linwood Ave., Western Springs* ☎ *09/815–4999* ⊕ *www.chamberlainpark. co.nz* ⊠ *NZ$30* 🏌 *18 holes, 5553 yards, par 69.*

Devonport

The 20-minute ferry to Devonport across Waitemata Harbour provides a fine view of Auckland's busy harbor. Originally known as Flagstaff, after the signal station on the summit of Mt. Victoria, Devonport was the first settlement on the north side of the harbor. Later the area drew some of the city's wealthiest traders, who built their homes where they could watch their sailing ships arriving with cargo from Europe. Aucklanders have fixed up and repopulated its great old houses, laying claim to the suburb's relaxed and moneyed seaside aura.

The Esplanade Hotel is one of the first things you'll see as you leave the ferry terminal. It stands at the harbor end of Victoria Road, a pleasant street for stopping at a shop, a bookstore, or a café; pick-up some fish-and-chips to eat under the giant Moreton Bay fig tree on the green across the street.

GETTING HERE AND AROUND

Various companies serve Waitemata Harbour; one of the best and least expensive is Fullers. The ferry terminal is on the harbor side of the Ferry Building on Quay Street, near the corner of Albert Street. Boats leave here for Devonport Monday through Thursday 6:15 am–11 pm, Friday and Saturday 6:15 am–1 am, and Sunday 7:15 am–10 pm at half-hour intervals, except for one 45-minute interval between the 9:15 am and 10 am sailings. From 8 pm Monday through Thursday and from 7 pm on Sunday they sail on the hour. The cost is NZ$12 round-trip.

FERRY INFORMATION Fullers Booking Office. ⊠ *Ferry Bldg., Quay St.* ☎ *09/367–9111* ⊕ *www.fullers.co.nz.*

◉ Sights

Mt. Victoria

ARCHAEOLOGICAL SITE | FAMILY | Long before European settlement, this ancient volcano was the site of a Māori pā (fortified village) of the local Kawerau tribe. On the northern and eastern flanks of the hill you can still see traces of the terraces once protected by palisades of sharpened stakes. Don't be put off by its name—this is more molehill than mountain. The climb is easy and the views are outstanding. Mt. Victoria is signposted on Victoria Road, a few minutes' walk from the Esplanade Hotel. ⊠ *Kerr St., off Victoria Rd., Devonport.*

National Museum of the Royal New Zealand Navy

MUSEUM | The role of New Zealand's navy is recognized in this small museum. Also known as Te Waka Huia O Te Taua Moana O Aoteoroa, or Torpedo Bay Navy Museum, it holds a trove of material that reflects the country from a naval perspective. You'll see not only predictable naval material like firearms, swords, and militaria but also memorabilia from those connected to the Navy. ⊠ *64 King Edward Parade, Torpedo Bay, Devonport* ☎ *09/446–1824* ⊕ *www.navymuseum. co.nz* ⊠ *Free; donations welcome.*

North Head

MILITARY SITE | Jutting out from Devonport into Auckland's harbor, the position of an ancient Māori defense site was enough to convince European settlers that they, too, should use North Head for strategic purposes. Rumor has it that veteran aircraft are still stored in the dark, twisting tunnels under the Head, but plenty of curious explorers have not found any. You can still get into most tunnels (they're safe), climb all over the abandoned antiaircraft guns, and get great views of Auckland and the islands to the east. It's one of the best places to watch yacht racing on the harbor. North Head is a 20-minute walk east of the ferry terminal on King Edward Parade, left onto Cheltenham Street, and then out Takarunga Road. The visitor information center can say when the local folk-music club will have events in one of the old bunkers. ⊠ *Takarunga Rd., Devonport.*

🍴 Restaurants

Manuka

$$$ | NEW ZEALAND | FAMILY | A corner on Devonport's main street is a good place to people-watch and rest after exploring, and Manuka is a relaxed spot with wooden tables and stacks of newspapers and magazines. Wood-fired pizzas are available all day, with toppings ranging from classic pepperoni to smoked chicken, Brie, and roasted cashews. **Known for:** delicious pizza; great coffee; home-style baked goods. $ *Average main: NZ$28* ⊠ *49 Victoria Rd., Devonport* ☎ *09/445–7732* ⊕ *www.manukarestaurant.co.nz.*

🛏 Hotels

Esplanade Hotel

$$$ | HOTEL | FAMILY | Commanding the corner opposite the pier, this turn-of-the-20th-century Edwardian baroque-revival hotel is the first thing you see when approaching Devonport by ferry. **Pros:** stunning views; charming decor; good restaurant. **Cons:** poor parking lot; road access into Devonport can be slow; outside environment can be busy and noisy. $ *Rooms from: NZ$300* ⊠ *1 Victoria Rd., Devonport* ☎ *09/445–1291* ⊕ *www.esplanadehotel.co.nz* ⌇ *17 rooms* ❏❍❏ *Breakfast.*

Peace and Plenty Inn

$$$ | B&B/INN | FAMILY | Antiques give this lovely B&B a mix of luxury and simplicity. **Pros:** lovely environment; great breakfast; good location in Devonport. **Cons:** some may find the antiques too fussy; accessing Devonport by car can be problematic; at least 30 minutes from the central city. $ *Rooms from: NZ$265* ⊠ *6 Flagstaff Terr., Devonport* ☎ *09/445–2925* ⊕ *www.*

peaceandplenty.co.nz ⌇ *7 rooms* ❏❍❏ *Breakfast.*

👜 Shopping

Takapuna Market

OUTDOOR/FLEA/GREEN MARKETS | FAMILY | The Takapuna parking lot comes alive on Sunday mornings, with organic cheese, meat, vegetables, homemade jams, small goods, and a slew of sweet and savory items from boutique bakers on sale. There's also clothing from young designers. ⊠ *Corner Lake Rd. and Anzac St.* ☎ *021/127–2529.*

Hauraki Gulf Islands

More than 50 islands lie in the Hauraki Gulf, forming the Hauraki Gulf Marine Park, managed by the Department of Conservation (DOC). Many of the islands are nature reserves, like Hauturu, Little Barrier, home to endangered plants and birds, and public access to these is restricted. Others like TiriTiri Matangi are public reserves that can be reached by ferry, and a few are privately owned. Rakino is also popular, but you will need to pack a lunch.

GETTING HERE AND AROUND

Fullers operates ferries year-round to Rangitoto daily at 9:15 and 12:15, departing the island at 12:45 and 3:30. The fare is NZ$29 round-trip; boats leave from the Ferry Building. Fullers also arranges Volcanic Explorer tours, which include a guided ride to the summit in a covered carriage. It's NZ$60 for the tour and ferry ride, and you must book in advance.

Fullers ferries make the 35-minute run from the Ferry Building to Waiheke Island from 5:30 am to 11:45 pm at a cost of NZ$36 round-trip. Return ferries leave every hour on the hour, and every half hour at peak commuter times. Buses meet ferries at the Waiheke terminal and loop the island. If you're planning on

Rangitoto Island emerged from the sea in a dramatic volcanic eruption 600 years ago.

going farther afield on the island, you can purchase an all-day bus pass from Fullers Booking Office (NZ$9 to Oneroa, Palm Beach, Onetangi, and Rocky Bay), but you need to take the 10 am ferry (return time optional). Fullers also provides tours, after which passengers may use their ticket to travel free on regular island buses that day. Note that crossings can be canceled if seas are rough and that ferries are very crowded on busy holiday weekends.

SeaLink runs car and passenger ferries to Waiheke, leaving from Halfmoon Bay in the east of the city. The round-trip fare is NZ$152 per car, plus NZ$36.50 for each adult. On Waiheke you can also take a shuttle to beaches or vineyards; Waiheke Shuttles has reliable service, but it pays to book well ahead in summer.

FERRY AND BUS INFORMATION SeaLink. ⊠ *Ara-Tai Dr., Halfmoon Bay* ☎ *09/300–5900* ⊕ *www.sealink.co.nz* **Waiheke Shuttles.** ☎ *09/372–2966* ⊕ *www.wai-hekeshuttles.co.nz.*

◉ Sights

★ Goldie Vineyard
WINERY/DISTILLERY | First to plant grapes on Waiheke were Kim and Jeanette Goldwater, whose eponymous wines have since earned a reputation for excellence. It's also home to Auckland University's Wine Research Institute for postgraduate research into wine as well the Goldie Room, a fantastic eatery that offers superb food and, of course, wine. Personalized tours can be arranged. The estate is known for the Long Lunch, which is a nine-course degustation menu that is held about four times a year and sells out very quickly. ⊠ *18 Causeway Rd., Waiheke Island, Surfdale* ☎ *09/372–7493* ⊕ *www.goldieestate.co.nz.*

Great Barrier Island
ISLAND | FAMILY | Also known as Aotea, Great Barrier Island is the largest in the gulf with a population of around 1,100, and is mostly agricultural. It's popular with surfers—particularly Awana

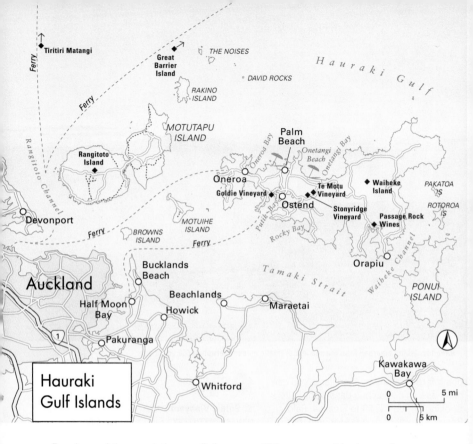

Hauraki Gulf Islands

Beach—and the population swells in summer as the boating crowd moves in, mooring in its many sheltered bays. Access is by ferry, air, or yacht.

Passage Rock Wines

WINERY/DISTILLERY | On the eastern end of the island, this vineyard in its own little valley with a view to Passage Rock has pricey and highly regarded wines. It's especially known for Chardonnays, Viogniers, and Syrahs. The vineyard has a good bistro that is very popular with locals but be sure to check the opening hours. Tastings are Friday through Sunday, noon through 4 pm. ⊠ *Waiheke Island, 438 Orapiu Rd., Ostend* ☎ *09/372–7257* ⊕ *www.passagerockwines.co.nz.*

★ Rangitoto Island

ISLAND | When Rangitoto Island emerged from the sea in a series of fiery eruptions 600 years ago, it had an audience: footprints in the solidified ash on its close neighbor Motutapu Island prove that Māori people watched Rangitoto's birth. It is the largest and youngest of about 50 volcanic cones and craters in the Auckland volcanic field, and scientists are confident it will not blow again. During the 1920s and '30s hundreds of prisoners built roads and trails on the island, some of which are still used as walkways. Small beach houses were erected by families in the early 20th century. Many were pulled down in the 1970s before their historical significance was recognized. Thirty-two remain, and a few are still used by leaseholders, who are allowed to use them during their lifetimes. (Afterward, they'll be relinquished to the DOC.) The island's most popular activity is the one-hour summit walk, beginning at Rangitoto Wharf and climbing through lava fields and forest to the peak. At the top, walkers are rewarded with panoramic views of Auckland and the Hauraki Gulf. Short detours lead to lava caves and to the remnants of a botanical park planned in 1915. Wear sturdy shoes and carry water because parts of the walk are on exposed lava flows, which are hot in the sun. You can swim at Islington Bay and at the Rangitoto Wharf in a specially made pool. ⊕ *www.rangitoto.org.*

★ Stonyridge Vineyard

WINERY/DISTILLERY | This vineyard has followers all over the world. The Stonyridge Larose, made from the classic Bordeaux varieties, is excellent and the vintage often sells out. Reservations for lunch at the Veranda Café, which uses local produce including olive oil and wine, are essential. This place is popular with the helicopter-in crowd. ⊠ *80 Onetangi Rd., Waiheke Island, Ostend* ☎ *09/372–8822* ⊕ *www.stonyridge.co.nz.*

★ Te Motu Vineyard

WINERY/DISTILLERY | The friendly Dunleavy family started planting vines in 1989. Now its Te Motu Bordeaux blend, which is made only when conditions are right, is on the wine list at many Michelin-starred restaurants in France. The winery gives tastings, but it's best to call first to check for times. Don't be fooled by the restaurant's name, the Shed; it caters to a fussy clientele for its grown-on-site garden-to-plate cooking. The wine list, which always features Te Motu wines from the heritage cellar, changes monthly. Reservations are essential. ⊠ *76 Onetangi Rd., Waiheke Island, Onetangi* ☎ *09/372–6884* ⊕ *www.temotu.co.nz.*

★ Tiritiri Matangi

ISLAND | You can see rare native birds up close at Tiritiri Matangi, a bird sanctuary open to the public and accessible by ferry from Auckland or Gulf Harbour on the Whangaparoa Peninsula. Gentle, well-maintained, signposted trails lead to the top of the island and the oldest

lighthouse in the gulf, still in operation. The island is free from predators, and the birds are unafraid. Tiritiri is home to at least 18 *takahe,* large blue-and-green flightless birds with red beaks that are part of a nationwide breeding program for the rare species; you can usually spot them eating grass near the lighthouse. ⊕ *www.tiritirimatangi.org.nz.*

★ Waiheke Island

ISLAND | **FAMILY** | Once a sleepy summer vacation retreat and hippie haven with beach houses dotting its edges, Waiheke is now home to 35 vineyards (many the passion projects of their owners), architectural holiday homes owned by the well heeled, and old-school tiny weekend escapes. The island has earned an international reputation for its vineyards, and many local cafés stock Waiheke wines unavailable elsewhere. The annual Waiheke Jazz Festival at Easter attracts renowned overseas performers. From the ferry landing at Matiatia Wharf you can walk five minutes to the small town of **Oneroa,** the island's hub, with its shops, cafés, bars, and real estate agents. Another minute's walk gets you to **Oneroa Beach,** one of the most accessible beaches. The north-facing beaches—sheltered bays with little surf—are the best for swimming. The most popular is **Palm Beach,** 10 minutes by bus from Oneroa. Around the rocks to the left is **Little Palm Beach,** one of Auckland's three nudist beaches. Another great beach, **Onetangi,** is on the north side of the island, 20 minutes from Matiatia by bus. **Whakanewha Regional Park,** on the south side, is a lovely bush reserve leading down to a half-moon bay. You can hike and picnic here, and the wetlands is home to rare birds such as the New Zealand dotterel. You can get to the park from Oneroa by shuttle bus. If you go in summer or on weekends, it pays to get ferry tickets early as the island draws big crowds on fine days.

🍴 Restaurants

Mudbrick Vineyard and Restaurant

$$$$ | **EUROPEAN** | This vineyard produces a small portfolio of whites and reds, many of which never make it off the island. The food emphasis is on red meat; particular favorites are the rack of lamb and Black Angus eye fillet. **Known for:** exceptional local wine; stunning views; excellent lamb. ⑤ *Average main: NZ$50* ✉ *Church Bay Rd., Hauraki Gulf Islands* ☎ *09/372–9050* ⊕ *www.mudbrick.co.nz.*

Vino Vino

$$$ | **MEDITERRANEAN** | **FAMILY** | Waiheke's longest-running restaurant perches on Oneroa's main street, with a large all-weather deck overlooking the bay. The platters—Mediterranean, grilled (with Italian sausages and calamari), or seafood—are perennial favorites. **Known for:** eclectic menu; good wine list; gorgeous views. ⑤ *Average main: NZ$30* ✉ *3/153 Ocean View Rd., Oneroa, Hauraki Gulf Islands* ☎ *09/372–9888* ⊕ *www.vinovino. co.nz.*

🛏 Hotels

The Boatshed

$$$$ | **HOTEL** | If you feel like staying in a "lighthouse" without being responsible for the ships, this two-story turret suite at The Boatshed may be the place for you. **Pros:** gorgeous location with bay views; lovely rooms and decks; excellent food. **Cons:** pricey; some find the rooms small; rooms close together. ⑤ *Rooms from: NZ$800* ✉ *Tawa and Huia Sts., Little Oneroa, Waiheke Island, Hauraki Gulf Islands* ☎ *09/372–3242* ⊕ *www. boatshed.co.nz* ⇗ *7 rooms* ⑩ *Breakfast.*

The Moorings

$$$$ | **RENTAL** | From the bright guest rooms of this L-shape Mediterranean farmhouse-style home, you can look outward or inward: out onto Matiatia Bay or into a sheltered courtyard with lavender hedges and lemon trees. **Pros:**

great views; informal atmosphere; lovely location. **Cons:** no room service; some may find decor basic; small kitchen. ⑤ *Rooms from: NZ$350* ✉ *9 Oceanview Rd., Oneroa, Waiheke Island, Hauraki Gulf Islands* ☎ *027/550–3888* ⊕ *www. themoorings.gen.nz* ⇗ *2 rooms* ⑩ *No meals.*

🏃 Activities

KAYAKING

Ferg's Kayaks

KAYAKING | **FAMILY** | Instead of taking the ferry to Rangitoto, why not paddle? Ferg's Kayaks leads guided trips to the island twice daily, leaving at 9:30 am and 5:30 pm. The round-trip takes about six hours, including two to paddle each way and one to climb the volcano. On the later trip you paddle back in the dark toward the city lights. Booking is essential, and trips are dependent on weather and numbers. ✉ *12 Tamaki Dr.* ☎ *09/529–2230* ⊕ *www.fergskayaks.co.nz* ⊠ *From NZ$160.*

Ross Adventures

KAYAKING | **FAMILY** | There's more to Waiheke Island than relaxed beaches and wineries. Half, full-day, and overnight kayaking trips take paddlers past coastal cliffs and inlets. Explore caves, beaches, and Māori pā sites, and have coffee and snacks or lunch at a private beach depending on the day's route. Half and full-day trips include swimming and snorkeling, and you may spot blue penguins or dolphins as you kayak. ✉ *Matiatia Wharf, Ocean View Rd.* ☎ *09/372–5550* ⊕ *www.kayakwaiheke.co.nz* ⊠ *From NZ$125.*

Greater Auckland

West Auckland has black-sand KareKare and Muriwai beaches, the former with a famous gannett bird colony, as well as vineyards. North Auckland includes Takapuna Beach, a ritzy seaside suburb.

Volcano Views

Auckland is built on and around 48 volcanoes, and the tops provide sweeping views of the city.

Mt. Eden. This is the highest volcano on the Auckland isthmus. Several bus tours include this central site, but you have to walk to the summit. It's a popular spot at night when the city's lights below make a spectacular show, and many go there to canoodle or even propose. At the base of the mountain is Mount Eden village, known for its good places to eat and shop at boutique stores. ⊕ *www.mounteden. co.nz*

One Tree Hill. One Tree Hill, the largest of Auckland's extinct volcanoes, was the site of an early Māori settlement. The surrounding park is great for picnics and running or walking. ⊕ *www.cornwallpark.co.nz*

Rangitoto Island. Rangitoto Island has an even better vista than One Tree Hill. This volcano emerged from the sea 600 years ago, no doubt much to the wonder of the Māori people living next door on Motutapu Island. Take a ferry to the island; then take a short ride on a covered carriage towed by a jeep or walk to the top to get a 360-degree view of the city and the Hauraki Gulf islands. There are paths around the island along which you can take a peek at some holiday homes. ⊕ *www.rangitoto.org*

It's thought that Māori settled on the volcanoes beginning in the 14th century, taking advantage of the fertile soils. There's evidence that in the 16th century the Māori used the cones as defensive pā (fortified villages). Remains of complex earthworks can be seen on Mt. Eden and One Tree Hill, where Māori cleared volcanic stone to develop garden plots and formed the terraces that are features of pā.

Sights

Babich Wines
WINERY/DISTILLERY | The Babich family has been making wine in New Zealand since 1916, beginning first in the far north, where Josip Babich joined his brothers from Croatia and planted grapes near the gum fields. The 72-acre Henderson cellar site has a range of tastings and snacks; years ago it was amid farmland but now is almost surrounded by houses as the population in west Auckland has grown. ✉ *15 Babich Rd., Henderson, Waitakere City* ☎ *09/833–7859* ⊕ *www.babich-wines.co.nz.*

Villa Maria Winery
WINERY/DISTILLERY | This winery has grown from a small company founded by the Fistonich family to one of the country's biggest producers, with a wide range of wines using different grapes. It is recognized for its consistency, and Sir George Fistonich, the founder, has done much for the grape industry in New Zealand. The tasting room offers selections from most of the company's vineyards (shipping can be arranged if you decide to buy). Villa Maria also hosts outdoor summer concerts from jazz to classical. ✉ *118 Montgomerie Rd., Mangere, Manukau City* ☎ *09/255–0660* ⊕ *www.villamaria.co.nz.*

Beaches

KareKare
BEACH—SIGHT | **FAMILY** | Film buffs will recognize KareKare and its black sand from the dramatic opening scenes of *The Piano*. Its size means you will never feel

Auckland see detail map

Haoraki Islands see detail map

Greater Auckland

Hauraki Gulf

Whangaparaoa

Helensville

Coatesville

Albany

Waimauku

Motutapu Island

Waiheke Island

Takapuna Beach

Rangitoto Island

Oneroa

Onetangi

Ostend

Muriwai Beach

Waitakere

Waitematā Harbour

Devonport

Western Springs

Mission Bay

Babich Wines

Newmarket

Bethells

Titirangi

Remuera

Panmure

Howick

Piha

WAITAKERE RANGES

Mt. Eden

Villa Maria Winery

Mt. Wellington

Karekare

Auckland see detail map

Kawakawa Bay

Whatipu

Papatoetoe

Manukau Harbour

Manukau

NORTH ISLAND

Tasman Sea

Papakura

0 ——— 10 miles

0 ——— 10 kilometers

hemmed in, even in the peak summer months when it attracts big visitor numbers despite the steep road access. You'll need to pack a lunch as there are no shops. The pounding waves make for great swimming and surfing, but again, go in only when the surf patrol is operating as there are strong rips and undertows. Fit walkers should explore the southern end of the beach. You can venture past the point but only go at low tide because getting back is difficult when the tide comes in. The sunsets are spectacular anytime of year. **Amenities:** lifeguards in summer; free parking and toilets; picnic areas. **Best for:** surfing; swimming; sunset; walking. ⊠ *KareKare Rd.*

Mission Bay

BEACH—SIGHT | FAMILY | About 10 minutes' drive from the central city, Mission

Bay off Tamaki Drive draws the crowds year-round and summertime can see families and community groups from all of Auckland picnicking side by side. Dining options run the gamut from fast food to formal-ish restaurants. Three extremely good ice-cream parlors and an abundance of good coffee round out the culinary options, and it's not uncommon to see long lines at each joint and then people eating sitting on the seawall. Be aware though it can get very busy in summer and finding a place to park can be a nightmare. **Amenities:** food and drink; showers; toilets; parking. **Best for:** sunrise; swimming. ⊠ *Tamaki Dr.*

Muriwai Beach

BEACH—SIGHT | FAMILY | The black sand of Muriwai Beach is a must for those exploring the West Coast. Combine a trip here with a visit to any of the many wineries in the area. The beach is great for surfing, kitesurfing, walking, and swimming, but don't venture into the water if the surf patrol is not operating, and always swim between the red and yellow flags. It is a great spot for a long walk and in summer it draws huge crowds. In winter you may be accompanied by wild winds, but it's still enjoyable if you're warmly dressed. Alternatively, get up-close-and-personal with the local gannet colony from the DOC viewing platforms; you can see the chicks in December and January. **Amenities:** food and drink; lifeguards in summer; parking; showers; toilets. **Best for:** sunset; walking; swimming. ⊠ *Motutara Rd.*

Takapuna Beach

BEACH—SIGHT | FAMILY | You'll see some of New Zealand's most expensive houses along Takapuna Beach on Auckland's North Shore. If architecture (or being nosey) isn't your thing, it's a safe swimming beach in summer and there are many picnic areas, but be sure to check the water quality signs at its entrances first; after heavy rains, the water can be polluted with rain run-off. It's good for walking and in the mornings and evenings it's where the well-sneakered walk their pooches. Sailors, kayakers, and triathletes all use this beach for training. Stand-up paddle boarding is also very popular here. The many cafés in Takapuna township are two minutes away from the sand. **Amenities:** food and drink; parking; showers; toilets; water sports. **Best for:** sunrise; swimming; walking. ⊠ *The Promenade.*

 Restaurants

★ **The Food Vault**

$$ | MODERN NEW ZEALAND | The fresh-baked goods, plumber's breakfast (a hearty plate of eggs, hash brown, sausage, bacon, mushrooms, and anything else the chef adds) and coffee make this a great place to spend a morning. The atmosphere is friendly, with customers ranging from cyclists stopping for a fix

to locals looking for a hearty breakfast or lunch. ⑤ *Average main: NZ$20* ⊠ *10 Matua Rd., Huapai* ☎ *09/412–5085* ⊕ *www.thefoodvault.co.nz.*

🎭 Performing Arts

ART GALLERIES

★ **Fresh Gallery Otara**

ART GALLERIES—ARTS | This Auckland Council-funded gallery is off-the-beaten art track in the Otara Town Centre, but it's well worth visiting for the extraordinary work it shows. Emerging artists, many from the Pacific, test boundaries not only in materials used, but also with content and techniques. The space is also used by the South Auckland Poets' Collective for performance poetry that plays to packed houses. ⊠ *5/46 Fairmall, Otara Town Centre, Otara* ☎ *09/271–6019* ⊙ *Closed Sun.*

West Coast Gallery Piha

ART GALLERIES—ARTS | It's well worth driving the winding road to this West Coast beach to see work by some 200 artists living in the region; there's everything from paintings, ceramics, sculpture, and jewelry to photography, glasswork, books, and CDs. Prices range from NZ$20 or NZ$30 to thousands of dollars. The gallery hosts regular events and occasional themed art projects that get locals involved. ⊠ *Seaview Rd., Piha* ⊕ *www.westcoastgallery.co.nz* ⊙ *Closed Mon. and Tues.*

🛍 Shopping

Otara Market

OUTDOOR/FLEA/GREEN MARKETS | For many years people from all over Auckland have headed south on a Saturday morning looking for bargains to the sounds of hip-hop beats and island music. Vegetable stalls groan with produce such as taro, yams, and coconuts. More Asian food stalls are joining the traditional Polynesian tapa cloths, paua-shell jewelry, greenstone, and bone carvings, reflecting the city's increasingly multicultural profile, but sadly some junky stuff is creeping in. The market opens around 6, and stalls come down around midday. Exit the Southern Motorway at the East Tamaki off-ramp, turn left, and take the second left. ⊠ *Newbury St., Otara.*

Activities

GOLF

Gulf Harbour Country Club

GOLF | Designed by Robert Trent Jones Jr. (some say the world's finest designer of classic golf courses), this course is about 40 minutes north of Auckland (if the traffic is flowing) on the East Coast's Whangaparaoa Peninisula. Some have called it the Pebble Beach of New Zealand and there's a dress code here: collared shirts, golf slacks or shorts, and no metal spike shoes with socks. The first nine holes are hilly while the last nine offer amazing views of the Hauraki Gulf. Winter specials are posted on the website. After a round, take a stroll around the Gulf Harbour Marina to look at the range of yachts and launches. ⊠ *Gulf Harbour Dr., Rodney District* ☎ *09/424–0971* ⊕ *www.gulfharbourcountryclub.co.nz* ✉ *NZ$115* ⚲ *18 holes, 7000 yards, par 72.*

Muriwai Golf Club

GOLF | A 40-minute drive (depending on traffic) northwest of the city brings you to this links course near a bird sanctuary, with outstanding views of the coast, even from the "19th hole." Because the links are on sandy soil, they can be played even if the rest of Auckland is sodden and the course is often home to tournaments and training. If your partner is not a golfer there are some great beach and forest walks close by. ⊠ *Coast Rd., Muriwai Beach* ☎ *09/411–8454* ⊕ *www.muriwaigolfclub.co.nz* ✉ *NZ$90* ⚲ *18 holes, 6800 yards, par 72.*

Titirangi Golf Club

GOLF | Designed by renowned golf architect Alister MacKenzie, this is one of the country's finest (and oldest) 18-hole courses. The club was established in 1909 and takes pride in its rolling fairways, and challenging bunkers and greens. Golfers might be distracted by the magnificent setting and specimen trees. Nonmembers are welcome to play provided they contact the course in advance (and get through the painful automated phone system). Once booked, you must show evidence of membership at an overseas club and the dress code must be adhered to. Tailored shirts and pants are a must and no beachwear of any kind is allowed. ⊠ *Links Rd., Waitakere City* ☎ *09/827–5749* ⊕ *www.titirangigolf.co.nz* ✉ *NZ$150* ⚲ *18 holes, 6600 yards, par 70.*

HIKING

Waitakere Ranges

HIKING/WALKING | These scenic hills west of Auckland are a favorite walking and picnic spot for locals. The bush-clad ranges, rising sharply from West Coast beaches, are threaded by streams and waterfalls, but currently many trails are closed because of a virus that is affecting the great Kauri trees found in the forest. The Arataki Visitor Centre, which also displays modern Māori carvings, will update you on which paths are open. To get to the Waitakeres, head along the Northwestern Motorway (Route 16) from central Auckland, take the Waterview turnoff, and keep heading west to the gateway village of Titirangi. A sculpture, ironically depicting fungal growth, tells you you're heading in the right direction. From here the best route to follow is Scenic Drive, with spectacular views of Auckland and its two harbors. The visitor center is 5 km (3 miles) along the drive. ⊠ *300 Scenic Dr.* ☎ *09/817–0077* ⊕ *regionalparks.aucklandcouncil.govt.nz/aratakivisitorcentre.*

Chapter 4

NORTHLAND AND
THE BAY OF ISLANDS

Updated by
Richard Pamatatau

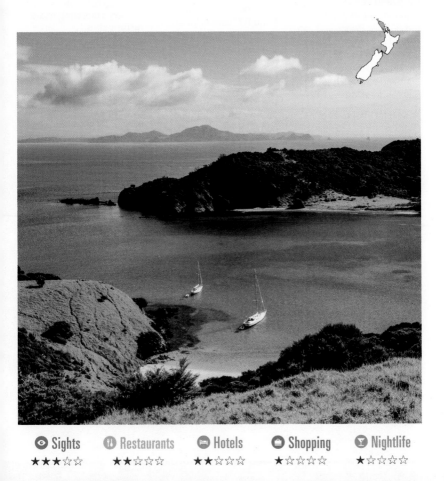

👁 **Sights** 🍴 **Restaurants** 🛏 **Hotels** 🛍 **Shopping** 🍸 **Nightlife**
★★★☆☆   ★★☆☆☆   ★★☆☆☆   ★☆☆☆☆   ★☆☆☆☆

WELCOME TO NORTHLAND AND THE BAY OF ISLANDS

TOP REASONS TO GO

★ **Boating and Fishing:** Take a cruise to an island, whale-watch, swim with dolphins, or fish with the Bay of Islands as the hub.

★ **Bountiful Beaches:** Most Northland beaches are safe for swimming. On the 90 Mile Beach you can swim in both the Tasman Sea and the Pacific Ocean. Experienced surfers head to Shipwreck Bay for great waves.

★ **Coastal Views:** Take the Old Coast Road to Russell for superb views of islands and (almost) hidden bays and places to picnic.

★ **Superb Diving:** Dive at the Poor Knights Islands, known for their huge variety of subtropical fish, or the wreck of the Greenpeace vessel Rainbow Warrior, sunk by French agents in 1985.

★ **Walking and Hiking:** Superb bushwalking (hiking) provides a close look at ancient kauri trees (a local species of pine) and interesting birds, such as tūī (too-ee), fantails, and wood pigeons.

The northernmost part of New Zealand features a stunning collection of islands known, fittingly, as the Bay of Islands. The West Coast, from Dargaville to Cape Reinga seems empty, and the unassuming little towns along the way and the lumbering Kohu Ra Tuama Hokianga Harbour ferry contrast the luxurious lodges and fancy yachts around the Bay of Islands. No matter where you are in the North, you're never far from the water and a combination of coastline, rolling pastures, and ancient native forest.

1 Warkworth. This small town with a working class history is a good stopping point for visitors to the nearby Goat Island marine reserve.

2 Whangarei. The only city in Northland has an interesting Māori past and an up-and-coming artistic present.

3 Hokianga and the Kauri Coast. This quiet area has small towns and access to gorgeous giant kauri trees in Waipoua State Forest.

4 Paihia and Waitangi. The small town of Paihia is the main vacation base for the region, while Waitangi holds one of the country's most important historic sites.

5 Russell. This relaxed and charming beach town has a fascinating Wild West–esque history.

6 Kerikeri. Considered the cradle of the nation, most of New Zealand's earliest history can be traced back to this small town.

Northland is the place to go when you seek more than great restaurants and shopping. You'll be best served on a trip here by taking in inspiring views from winding coastal roads or reading on a quiet beach with some fruit from owner-operated shops. While there are pockets of relative sophistication that offer good coffee and fancy food, much of this part of the country is about the views.

Yet there's also a rawness to the North. Social tensions are exacerbated by political neglect and high unemployment, particularly among the area's Māori population, but the scenery is truly majestic, going from rugged to pastoral in a matter of kilometers. You will notice the change about an hour after leaving the sometimes-confusing jumble that makes up Auckland. With the city behind you the air starts to clear and you can see what some call the Northland light. The lack of industry in Northland alongside a declining population means less pollution, and may account for the fact that it seems brighter the farther north you go, even on overcast days.

The Tasman Sea to the west and the Pacific Ocean to the east meet at the top of North Island at Cape Reinga. No matter what route you take, you'll pass farms and forests, marvelous beaches, and great open spaces. Even though the East Coast, up to the Bay of Islands, is Northland's most densely populated, often with cashed-up migrants from bigger cities, it still feels uncrowded.

The first decision on the drive north comes at the foot of the Brynderwyn Hills. Turning left will take you up the West Coast through areas once covered with forests and now used for either agricultural or horticulture. Driving over "the Brynderwyns," as they are known, takes you to Whangarei, the only city in Northland. If you're in the mood for a diversion, you can slip to the beautiful coastline and take in Waipu Cove, an area settled by Scots, and Laings Beach, where million-dollar homes sit next to small Kiwi beach houses.

An hour's drive farther north is the Bay of Islands, known all over the world for its beauty. Here you will find lush forests, splendid beaches, and shimmering harbors. The Treaty of Waitangi was signed here in 1840 between Māori and the British Crown, establishing the basis for the modern New Zealand state. Every year on February 6, the extremely beautiful Waitangi Treaty Ground (the name means weeping waters) is the site of a commemoration of the treaty, and of protests by Māori unhappy with it.

Continuing north on the East Coast, the agricultural backbone of the region is even more evident and a series of winding loop roads off the main highway leads to beaches that are both beautiful and isolated where you can swim, dive, picnic, or just laze. The West Coast is even less populated, and the coastline is rugged and windswept. In the Waipoua Forest, you will find some of New Zealand's oldest and largest kauri trees (although a disease has recently spread, affecting the trees and closing some trails to them); the winding road will also take you past mangrove swamps.

Crowning the region is the spiritually significant Cape Reinga, the headland at the top of the vast stretch of 90 Mile Beach, from where it's believed Māori souls depart after death. Today Māori make up roughly a quarter of the area's population (compared with the national average of about 15%). The legendary Māori navigator Kupe was said to have landed on the shores of Hokianga Harbour, where the first arrivals made their home. Many different *iwi* (tribes) lived throughout Northland, including Ngapuhi (the largest), Te Roroa, Ngāti Wai, Ngāti Kuri, Te Aupouri, Ngaitakoto, Ngāti Kahu, and Te Rarawa. Many Māori here can trace their ancestry to the earliest inhabitants.

MAJOR REGIONS

Northland. *Te Tai Tokerau,* or Northland, with its no-frills, tiny, friendly towns and high rates of unemployment, is extremely different from the affluent Bay of Islands. However, the scenery is just as stunning. But without the infrastructure that goes along with organized tourism you will feel a little off the beaten path (in addition, many New Zealanders joke that cannabis cultivation fuels a giant hidden economy). Heading north from Auckland, you'll reach **Warkworth** first, a low-key base for stops like Goat Island and nearby wineries. Heading farther north, the largest town is **Whangarei,** which serves as the main center for the region.

On the west coast, you'll find the area known as **Hokianga Harbour** and its harbor along with the **Kauri Coast,** which features the unique kauri trees of Waipoua State Forest.

The Bay of Islands. This sweep of coastline is home to 144 islands amid a mild, subtropical climate and excellent game-fishing waters. That combination makes the Bay of Islands ideal—with a slew of things to do while visiting. You can base yourself in popular **Paihia,** take in history at **Waitangi** and **Kerikeri,** or relax at the nearby beaches of low-key **Russell.**

Planning

Planning Your Time

Plan to spend three days in Northland. On Day 1 take in the main town of Paihia, and then catch the ferry to Russell for lunch and sightseeing. Drive north on the second day, stopping at beaches and Cape Reinga. Meander home via the Hokianga on Day 3 by winding south through the forests along the West Coast to Kohukohu. Ferry south across serene Hokianga Harbour to Rawene. From Opononi, closer to the harbor's mouth, continue down the Kauri Coast to the Waipoua Forest. From there, Highway 12 runs to Brynderwyn, where you rejoin State Highway 1 about an hour north of Auckland.

When to Go

Snow doesn't fall in the "winterless north," but it can get cool. The best time to go is between mid-November and mid-April; peak season is December through March. During the quiet months of July and August it can be quite rainy. For game fishing, arrive from February to June.

Getting Here and Around

BOAT AND FERRY TRAVEL

Three passenger boats cross between Paihia and Russell, with departures at least once every 20 minutes in each direction from 7:20 am to 10:30 pm from Paihia, and 7 am to 10 pm from Russell. The one-way fare is NZ$6. Or, join the car ferry at nearby Opua, about 5 km (3 miles) south of Paihia. It operates from 6:50 am to 9:50 pm, with departures at approximately 10-minute intervals from either shore. The last boat leaves from Okiato on the Russell side at 9:50 pm. The one-way fare is NZ$13 for car and driver plus NZ$1 for each adult passenger. Buy your tickets on board (cash only). Save time by crossing the Hokianga Harbour between Rawene and Kohukohu (with or without a car) by ferry.

BUS TRAVEL

Taking a bus is a cheap and also easy alternative to driving. Several companies serve all but the most out-of-the-way spots. InterCity (contact the Paihia branch) runs several times daily between Auckland and the Bay of Islands and connects to the other Northland centers at least once a day. Auckland to Paihia takes about 4½ hours depending on traffic and to Kerikeri about 5½ hours.

CONTACTS InterCity. ☎ *09/583–5780* ⊕ *www.intercity.co.nz.*

CAR TRAVEL

It's best to see Northland's many lovely bays, sandy beaches, and worthwhile sights by car. Northland roads are generally just two lanes wide with many one-lane bridges in remote areas. Take care on the narrow—and often unsealed—roads that thread through the region. Don't risk a drive along 90 Mile Beach; the quicksand and tides can leave you stuck, and your rental car insurance won't cover any accidents here. You can easily find a tour company to take you along 90 Mile Beach.

From Auckland, drive up the East Coast on State Highway 1 and return down the West Coast on Highway 12 (or vice versa), but make sure to check out smaller, winding coastal roads with their stunning coastlines and dramatic island views.

Restaurants

Seafood abounds in the north with scallops and oysters farmed throughout the region, though occasional sewerage scares and algae blooms put them off-limits. Snapper and kingfish are available year-round, and marlin and broad-bill swordfish are abundant between January and June. The region also prides itself on its local produce.

People eat earlier in Northland than in the cities, with restaurants filling around 7. Dress is casual—jeans are acceptable in all but the most upscale lodges. From May through September, many restaurants close or reduce their opening hours, some to four nights a week. October sees regular hours resume.

Hotels

Northland accommodations vary from basic motels to luxury lodges. Hosts, particularly in the bed-and-breakfasts, are eager to share their local knowledge and are a great resource on less-obvious attractions. Paihia is considered a hub for Northland and has plenty of vacation apartments and standard motels. You'll also find a range of B&Bs and lodges in places like Russell.

Paihia is a hub for Northland and has plenty of vacation apartments and standard motels. You'll also find, in places like Russell, a range of B&Bs and lodges. High season runs from December through March. Some lodges have shoulder seasons in April and May, and September and October. Overall, room rates drop between May and October though many places also close for a break.

Restaurant and hotel reviews have been shortened. For full information, visit Fodors.com. Restaurant prices are the average cost of a main course at dinner or, if dinner is not served, at lunch. Hotel prices are the lowest cost of a standard double room in high season.

What It Costs			
$	$$	$$$	$$$$
RESTAURANTS			
under NZ$15	NZ$15–NZ$20	NZ$21–NZ$30	over NZ$30
HOTELS			
under NZ$125	NZ$125–NZ$200	NZ$201–NZ$300	over NZ$300

Visitor Information

Local visitor bureaus, many known as i-SITEs, have information on the whole region, with more extensive information on their particular environs. Destination Northland, a regional tourism organization, is a good resource for the entire region (⊕ *www.northlandnz.com*). In addition, some helpful community Web resources include ⊕ *www.kerikeri.co.nz* and ⊕ *www.paihia.co.nz*.

Warkworth

59 km (36 miles) north of Auckland.

A sleepy town on the banks of the Mahurangi River, Warkworth was established in 1853. With lime mined from the local river, it became the first cement-manufacturing site in the southern hemisphere. Today, race boatbuilding and refitting are the main industries, though slowly boutique food producers are opening shop. Warkworth also serves as a service town for the surrounding farms and market gardens.

It's a convenient stopping point en route to nearby marine reserve Goat Island or the superb vineyards at Matakana.

GETTING HERE AND AROUND

There are two ways to get to Warkworth: bus or car. It's on the major bus routes north, and all you need to do is let the driver know where you want to get off. InterCity has ticketing options that let you explore, and regular service. However, bus travel can be limiting because attractions are spread out. For more flexibility rent a car and rove the countryside more freely, especially if you are heading to Matakana to explore the wineries. There are about 100 white-sand beaches in the area, which are easy to get to and often deserted.

VISITOR INFORMATION

CONTACTS Warkworth Visitor Information Centre. ✉ *1 Baxter St.* ☎ *09/425–9081* ⊕ *www.matakanacoast.co.nz.*

 Sights

Goat Island

BEACH—SIGHT | FAMILY | Take a trip to the Goat Island (also known as Te Hawere-a-Maki Marine Reserve), where fishing is prohibited and marine life has returned in abundance. Prominent species include blue *maomao* fish, snapper, and cod. It does get crowded here, and midweek is best. You can put on a snorkel and get up-close-and-personal with a school of maomao. The beach area is good for a picnic as well. Another fun activity is to take a glass-bottom boat tour. Just as the name promises, Glass Bottom Boat takes a glass-bottom boat around the island and gives you an aquarium eye view of waters teeming with fish. If the weather isn't ideal, there is an inner reef trip. Call ahead, because trips don't run if there is too much of a swell. You can also rent flippers, masks, and snorkels if you want to get in the water. To get to Goat Island head toward Leigh, 21 km (13 miles) northeast of Warkworth.

From Leigh, take a left turn and follow the signs for a couple of miles. If you arrive by 10 am, you should avoid the masses especially midweek and in winter. If you want to stay the night, there are camping grounds nearby; the Warkworth Visitor Centre will direct you. ⊠ *Goat Island Rd.* ⊕ *www.discovergoatisland.co.nz/reserve.html.*

SheepWorld

AMUSEMENT PARK/WATER PARK | FAMILY | Head for SheepWorld about an hour north of Auckland for a taste of life on a typical New Zealand sheep farm. Twice a day demonstrations show working farm dogs rounding up sheep before the shearers take over. An ecotrail meanders through the bush, providing information on native trees, birds (and their calls), and *weta* (large, ugly—yet impressive—native insects). On the weekends, the farm dogs even herd ducks. Children can take pony rides, and, in August, bottle-feed lambs. Depending on the weather there is also eel feeding. ⊠ *324 State Hwy. 1* ☎ *09/425–7444* ⊕ *www.sheepworld. co.nz* ⊠ *NZ$35.*

Warkworth Museum

MUSEUM | FAMILY | For a glimpse of Northland's pioneering past pay a visit to the Warkworth District Museum. It's a must if you are interested in learning about how smaller settlements in New Zealand developed. This eclectic collection includes Māori artifacts plus farming and domestic implements from the early days of the European settlement including tools used to dig for kauri gum. Rotating textile displays cover clothing and lace dating to the late 1700s. There is also a display of a school dental clinic—what Kiwi children called the "murder house." Outside is a collection of old buildings, including a bushman's hut and an army hut used by Americans stationed at Warkworth during World War II. ⊠ *Tudor Collins Dr.* ☎ *09/425–7093* ⊕ *warkworth-museum.co.nz* ⊠ *NZ$7.*

Whangarei

127 km (79 miles) north of Warkworth, 196 km (123 miles) north of Auckland.

The main center in Northland is the Whangarei (*fahng*-ar-ay) District; Whangarei Harbour was traditionally a meeting place for Māori tribes traveling south by *waka* (canoe). The full Māori name of the harbor, Whangarei Terenga Paraoa, means "swimming place of whales" but is also interpreted as "the meeting place of chiefs." Europeans started to settle in the area from the mid-1800s; now it's a town of roughly 45,000 people, rooted in the agriculture, forestry, and fishing industries. Boatbuilding is a traditional business, manufacturing everything from superyachts to charter boats. There is also a growing community of artists who have retreated to the North where housing is cheaper. The mouth of the harbor is dominated by the volcanic peaks of Whangarei Heads, atop Bream Bay. The drive from town to the Whangarei Heads takes about 20 minutes heading out on Riverside Drive, past mangrove-lined bays. At the Heads are stunning white-sand beaches and coves with safe swimming as well as several hikes, including up the peaks of Mt. Manaia.

GETTING HERE AND AROUND

Whangarei is about two hours by car from Auckland on State Highway 1. Bus services also travel this route but take longer as they stop at many small towns along the way.

You can fly from Auckland to Whangarei, but factoring arriving at the airport and checking in, it's often quicker to drive to Whangarei. There is no train service.

VISITOR INFORMATION

CONTACTS Northland Coach and Travel Centre. ⊠ *The Hub Information Centre, 91 Dent St.* ☎ *09/430–1188.* **Whangarei Visitor Information Centre.** ⊠ *92 Otaika Rd.* ☎ *09/438–1079* ⊕ *whangareinz.com.*

The Treaty of Waitangi

The controversial cornerstone of New Zealand's Māori and Pākehā relations is the 1840 Treaty of Waitangi, the first formal document that bound the Māori to the British crown. This contract became the basis for Britain's claim to the entire country as its colony.

In the mid-1830s, Britain became increasingly concerned about advances by French settlers and the inroads made by the New Zealand Company, a private emigration organization. The British government had an official Resident at Waitangi, James Busby, but no actual means to protect its interests. In 1835, Busby helped orchestrate an alliance among more than 30 North Island Māori chiefs.

In 1840, Captain William Hobson arrived in Waitangi to negotiate a transfer of sovereignty. Hobson and Busby hurriedly drew up a treaty in both English and Māori, and presented it to the Māori confederation on February 5, 1840. On the following day, about 40 chiefs signed the treaty.

But there were significant differences between the Māori and English versions. In the first article, the English version said the Māori would cede sovereignty to the Queen of England. But the Māori translation used the word *kāwanatanga* (governorship), which did not mean that the Māori were ceding the right to *mana* (self-determination).

The second article guaranteed the chiefs the "full, exclusive and undisturbed possession of their lands, estates, forests, fisheries, and other properties," but granted the right of preemption to the crown. The Māori translation did not convey the crown's exclusive right to buy Māori land, which caused friction over the decades. The third article granted the Māori protection as British citizens—and thus held them accountable to British law.

After the initial wave of signatures at Waitangi, signatures were gathered elsewhere in the North Island and on the South Island. In spring 1840 Hobson claimed all of New Zealand as a British colony. He had not, however, gotten signatures from some of the most powerful Māori chiefs, and this came back to haunt the crown during the Land Wars of 1860.

What wasn't confiscated after the Land Wars was taken by legislation. In 1877 Chief Justice Prendergast ruled that the treaty was "a simple nullity" that lacked legal validity because one could not make a treaty with "barbarians." At first European contact, 66.5 million acres of land was under Māori control, but by 1979 only 3 million remained—of mostly marginal lands.

The battle to have the treaty honored and reinterpreted is ongoing. In 1973, February 6 was proclaimed the official Waitangi Day holiday. From the get-go, the holiday sparked debate, as Māori activists protest the celebration of such a divisive document. The Waitangi Tribunal was established in 1975 to allow Māori to rule on alleged breaches of the treaty, and in 1985 the tribunal's powers were made retrospective to 1840. It has its hands full, as the claims continue to be one of New Zealand's largest sociopolitical issues. The treaty is now in the National Archives in Wellington.

4

Northland and the Bay of Islands WHANGAREI

Did You Know?

According to Māori legend, the dead leap off the Pōhutukawa tree at Cape Reinga's point to begin their trip to the underworld. Turbulent waters churn below, where the Pacific Ocean and the Tasman Sea meet.

Scuba divers examine the notoriously friendly subtropical fish in the Poor Knights Islands Marine Reserve.

◉ Sights

Claphams Clocks—The National Clock Museum

MUSEUM | FAMILY | If you want to while away some time this clock museum is the place for you. About every conceivable method of telling time is represented. The collection of more than 1,500 clocks includes primitive water clocks, ships' chronometers, and ornate masterworks from Paris and Vienna. Ironically, the one thing you won't find here is the correct time. If all the bells, chimes, gongs, and cuckoos went off together, the noise would be deafening, so the clocks are set to different times. ⊠ *Town Basin, Dent St.* ☎ *09/438–3993* ⊕ *www. claphamsclocks.com* ✉ *NZ$10.*

Kiwi North

MUSEUM | FAMILY | Minutes out of town, this 61-acre park is home to a nocturnal kiwi house, several Heritage buildings, and the Whangarei Museum. The museum has some 40,000 items in its collection including fine examples of pre-European Māori cloaks, *waka* (canoes), and tools. Photographers will love the early pictures of the area. You can also check out Glorat, an original 1886 kauri homestead, and the world's smallest consecrated chapel, built in 1859 from a single kauri tree. On the third Sunday of every month and on selected "Live Days" (call for dates), you can cruise around the park on model reproductions of steam and electric trains, as well as on a full-size diesel train. ⊠ *500 State Hwy. 14, Maunu* ☎ *09/438–9630* ⊕ *www.kiwinorth.co.nz* ✉ *Park free; Kiwi House and Whangarei Museum NZ$20.*

Reyburn House Art Gallery

HOUSE | This is the oldest kauri villa in Whangarei. It is home to the Northland Society of Arts and regularly hosts exhibitions from New Zealand artists. Original works from well-known artists are available for purchase. The permanent collection focuses on the 1880s to the present and several well-known New Zealand artists are represented. ⊠ *Town*

The Poor Knights Islands

Jacques Cousteau once placed the Poor Knights Islands among the world's top 10 dive locations. Underwater archways, tunnels, caves, and rocky cliffs provide endless opportunities for viewing many species of subtropical fish. On a good day you'll see soft coral, sponge gardens, gorgonian fields, and forests of kelp.

Two large islands and many islets make up the Poor Knights, remnants of an ancient volcanic eruption 12 nautical miles off the stunning Tutukaka coast, a half-hour drive east of Whangarei. The ocean around them is a marine reserve, extending 800 meters (½ mile) from the islands. Indeed the islands themselves are a nature reserve; landing on them is prohibited.

At 7.9 million cubic feet, Rikoriko Cave, on the southern island's northwest side, is one of the world's largest sea caves. It's known for its acoustics. Ferns hang from its roof, and underwater cup coral grows toward the rear of it. (Normally found at depths of 200 meters, the cave light has tricked the coral into thinking it is deeper.) Visibility at the Poor Knights is between 20 and 30 meters, but in Rikoriko Cave it goes up to 35 to 45 meters.

A dense canopy of regenerated *pohutukawa* covers the islands, flowering brilliant scarlet around Christmas time. Native Poor Knights lilies cling to cliff faces, producing bright red flowers in October. Rare bellbirds (*koromikos*) and red-crowned parakeets (*kakarikis*) thrive in the predator-free environment. Between October and May, millions of seabirds come to breed, including the Buller's shearwaters that arrive from the Arctic Circle. But possibly the most distinguished resident is the New Zealand native *tuatara*, a reptile species from the dinosaur age that survives only on offshore islands.

New Zealand fur seals bask on the rocks and feed on the abundant fish life, mostly from July to October, and year-round dolphins, whales, and bronze whaler sharks can be seen in the surrounding waters. In summer you can see minke and rare Bryde's whales, too. In March stingrays stack in the hundreds in the archways for their mating season.

Conditions rarely prevent diving, which is good year-round. That said, don't expect the same experience you'll get diving off Australia's Great Barrier Reef. There aren't as many colorful fish, and the water is cooler. In October, the visibility drops to about 18 to 20 meters because of a spring plankton bloom, though this attracts hungry marine life. The best places for novices are Nursery Cove and shallower parts of the South Harbour.

Basin, Reyburn House La. ☎ 09/438–3074 ⊕ www.reyburnhouse.co.nz ✉ By donation.

Whangarei Falls

LOCAL INTEREST | FAMILY | The falls are a lovely picnic spot, located on Ngunguru Road, 5 km (3 miles) northeast of town.

Viewing platforms are atop the falls, and a short trail runs through the local bush. ✉ 12 Ngunguru Rd., Glenbervie ⊕ www.whangareifalls.co.nz.

Whangarei Town Basin

MARINA | People often bypass Whangarei on their way to the Bay of Islands. It's easy to see why, as the town has a confusing traffic system, but if you can brave it the area known as the Whangarei Town Basin is worth a look. The marina is now a haven for visiting yachts and has cafés, restaurants, galleries, and crafts shops. There's parking behind the basin off Dent Street. ⊠ *Dent St.* ⊕ *www.wdc.govt.nz.*

Restaurants

★ Tonic

$$$$ | FRENCH | This eatery draws diners with its cuisine that fuses fresh local produce with an international flair. The local love for Tonic is intense, so be prepared to wait for a table. **Known for:** innovative cuisine; great NZ-heavy wine list; big local crowds. $ *Average main: NZ$32* ⊠ *239a Kamo Rd.* ☎ *09/437–5558* ⊕ *www.tonicrestaurant.co.nz* ☻ *No lunch.*

Hotels

Chelsea House

$$ | B&B/INN | This beautiful renovated villa offers three lovely rooms that will remind you of a relative's comfortable country house. **Pros:** lovely environment; cozy decor; tasty breakfasts. **Cons:** some may find it a bit basic; 20-minute walk to town; no guest cooking facilities. $ *Rooms from: NZ$145* ⊠ *83 Hatea Dr.* ☎ *09/437–7115* ⊕ *www.chelsea-house. co.nz* ⇨ *3 rooms.*

Lodge Bordeaux

$$$ | B&B/INN | FAMILY | With obvious references to France (but in a very Kiwi way), Lodge Bordeaux offers comfortable and stylish accommodations. **Pros:** big rooms; nice outdoor spaces; smart decor. **Cons:** slightly clinical; on a busy state highway; no dining on-site. $ *Rooms from: NZ$270* ⊠ *361 Western Hills Dr.* ☎ *09/438–0404* ⊕ *www.lodgebordeaux. co.nz* ⇨ *15 rooms.*

Lupton Lodge

$$$$ | B&B/INN | The country setting of Lupton Lodge makes it a perfect place to retreat to after a day's traveling in the North, with five rooms, two apartments, a lovely big swimming pool, and gorgeous gardens. **Pros:** great value; beautiful setting; delicious food. **Cons:** distance from town might be problematic for some guests; not right on the beach; no room service. $ *Rooms from: NZ$310* ⊠ *555 Ngunguru Rd.* ☎ *09/437–2989* ⊕ *www.luptonlodge.co.nz* ⇨ *7 rooms.*

Nightlife

Killer Prawn Restaurant and Bar

BARS/PUBS | This eatery doubles as Whangarei's nightlife hub and is part of the town's scenery. The food is good (but not terribly chic). That said, they do know how to cook prawns. It's a great place if you want a noisy, buzzy evening. ⊠ *28 Bank St.* ☎ *09/430–3333.*

Shopping

★ Burning Issues Gallery

CRAFTS | Burning Issues Gallery is one of the best places in Northland to buy locally made arts and crafts and work from some of the country's best artisans. Look for beautifully carved *pounamu* (New Zealand greenstone) and bone pendants. The silver and gold jewelry and small ceramic items are perfect for tiny take-home gifts. ⊠ *8 Quayside, Town Basin* ☎ *09/438–3108* ⊕ *www.burningissuesgallery.co.nz.*

Quarry Craft Co-op Shop

CRAFTS | A cooperative of local craftspeople, including jewelers, potters, wood turners, and weavers, runs the Quarry Craft Co-op Shop. You will find unique crafts, including jewelry made from kauri gum. The cooperative also runs courses—some only a day long—so check the website; you might end up making your own souvenir. The co-op is also home to residential craftspeople dedicated to preserving the art of wood turning and hand-printing. ✉ *21 Selwyn Ave.* ☎ *09/438–1215* ⊕ *www.quarryarts.org.*

⚡ Activities

DIVING

Dive Tutukaka

TOUR—SPORTS | Dive trips with Dive Tutukaka to the spectacular Poor Knights Islands include rented gear. Lunch is extra but inexpensive. You can also sail on *The Perfect Day,* a 70-foot luxury multilevel boat between November and April. This trip includes a half day of sightseeing, with the option to go kayaking, snorkeling, and diving. Free transfers to and from Whangarei are provided. ✉ *Poor Knights Dive Centre, Marina Rd., Tutukaka* ☎ *09/434–3867* ⊕ *www.diving.co.nz* ✉ *From NZ$299.*

Hokianga and the Kauri Coast

85 km (53 miles) west of Paihia.

A peaceful harbor moves inland into the Hokianga region. It's a quiet area with small towns, unspoiled scenery, and proximity to the giant kauri trees on the Kauri Coast, a 20-minute drive south on Highway 12. Here the highway winds through Waipoua State Forest, then stretches south to Kaipara Harbour. Giant golden sand dunes tower over the mouth of Hokianga Harbour, across the water from the twin settlements of Omapere and Opononi. Opononi is the place where Opo, a tame dolphin, came to play with swimmers in the mid-1950s, putting the town on the national map for the first and only time in its history. A statue in front of the pub commemorates the much-loved creature.

GETTING HERE AND AROUND

The best way to get to the Hokianga is to drive; from Auckland turn left at the bottom of the Bryderwyn Hills and follow the road. There is generally one bus service a day from Auckland, but there is no airport or train service.

VISITOR INFORMATION

CONTACTS Hokianga Visitor Information Centre. ✉ *29 State Hwy. 12, Omapere* ☎ *09/405–8869* ⊕ *www.northlandnz. com.* **Kauri Coast i-SITE Visitor Centre.** ✉ *4 Murdoch St., Dargaville* ☎ *09/439–4975* ⊕ *www.kauriinfocentre.co.nz.*

👁 Sights

Dargaville

TOWN | Sixty-four kilometers (40 miles) south of the Waipoua Forest along the Kaihu River, you'll come to sleepy Dargaville, once a thriving river port and now a good place to stock up if you're planning to camp in any of the nearby forests. It has some good craft stores, too. The surrounding region is best known for its main cash crop, the purple-skinned sweet potato known as *kūmara.* You'll see field after field dedicated to this root vegetable. ✉ *Dargaville* ☎ *09/439–4975* ⊕ *www.dargaville.co.nz.*

Māngungu Mission House

BUILDING | The 1838 Māngungu Mission House is an overlooked stop on the tourist trail. Although Waitangi is the most famous site of New Zealand's founding document, this unassuming spot, which looks out over Hokianga Harbour, was the scene of the second signing of the Treaty. Here, on February 12, 1840, the largest gathering of Māori chiefs signed the Treaty of Waitangi (73 chiefs, compared with about 40 in Waitangi's signing). The house is now a museum, furnished with pre-Treaty missionary items, including portraits, photographs, and furniture. ✉ *Motukiore Rd., Hokianga Harbour, Horeke* ☎ *09/407–0470* ⊕ *www. heritage.org.nz/places/places-to-visit/*

northland-region/mangungu-mission
✉ NZ$10.

Matakohe Kauri Museum

MUSEUM | South of Dargaville is Matakohe, a pocket-size town with an outstanding attraction: the Matakohe Kauri Museum. The museum's intriguing collection of artifacts, tools, photographs, documents, and memorabilia traces the story of the pioneers who settled this area in the second half of the 19th century—a story interwoven with the kauri forests. The furniture and a complete kauri house are among the superb examples of craftsmanship. One of the most fascinating displays is of kauri gum, the transparent lumps of resin that form when the sticky sap of the kauri tree hardens. This gum, which was used to make varnish, can be polished to a warm, lustrous finish that looks remarkably like amber—right down to the occasional insects trapped and preserved inside—and this collection is the biggest in the world. **Volunteers Hall** contains a huge kauri slab running from one end of the hall to the other, and there is also a reproduction of a cabinetmaker's shop, and a chain-saw exhibit. The Steam Saw Mill illustrates how the huge kauri logs were cut into timber. Perhaps the best display is the two-story replica of a late 1800s to early 1900s boardinghouse. Rooms are set up as they were more than 100 years ago; you can walk down the hallways and peer in at the goings-on of the era. If you like the whirring of engines, the best day to visit is Wednesday, when much of the museum's machinery is started up. ✉ 5 Church Rd., Matakohe ☎ 09/431–7417 ⊕ www.kaurimuseum.com ✉ NZ$25.

★ Waipoua State Forest

FOREST | Kauri forests once covered this region, and Waipoua State Forest contains the largest collection of the remaining trees although many are currently under threat from a disease known as Kauri Dieback. Because of this, always check with the center to see if the forest is open the day you visit. If it is open, a short path leads from the parking area on the main road through the forest to **Tane Mahuta,** "Lord of the Forest," and the largest tree in New Zealand. It stands nearly 173 feet high, measures 45 feet around its base, and is 1,200 to 2,500 years old. The second-largest tree, older by some 800 years, is **Te Matua Ngahere,** about a 20-minute walk from the road. If you have a few hours to spare you can visit Te Matua Ngahere and other trees of note. Head to the Kauri Walks parking lot about a mile south of the main Tane Mahuta parking lot. From there you trek past the **Four Sisters,** four kauri trees that have grown together in a circular formation, then the **Yakas Tree** (named after an old kauri-gum digger), and Te Matua Ngahere. The forest has a campground—check at the visitor center before you pitch a tent. Facilities include toilets, hot showers, and a communal cookhouse. When it's wet, you may spot large kauri snails in the forest. Also, the successful eradication of predators such as weasels and stoats has led to a rise in the number of kiwis in the forest. You'll need a flashlight to spot one because the birds only come out at night. The Waipoua campground and Waipoua Visitor Centre is managed by Te Iwi O Te Roroa, the local Māori tribe. ✉ Waipoua Visitor Centre, 1 Waipoua River Rd., Waipoua ☎ 09/439–6445 ⊕ www.kauricoast.com/waipoua-forest-visitors-centre.

🍽 Restaurants

Boatshed Café and Crafts

$ | **NEW ZEALAND** | This café is on the waterfront adjacent to the Rawene supermarket, craft shop, and ferry ramp. It's got a lovely outdoor deck and is a good place to take a coffee and slice of pizza while waiting for the ferry. **Known for:** good coffee; tasty baked goods; nice views. $ Average main: NZ$13 ✉ 8 Clendon Esplanade, Rawene ☎ 09/405–7728 ⊗ No dinner.

Did You Know?

New Zealand's oldest, biggest trees grow in Waipoua Forest. No one knows exactly how old Tane Mahuta ("Lord of the Forest," in Māori), the most famous one, is, but it's been around for 1,200–2,500 years.

Bay of Islands

🛏 Hotels

Copthorne Hotel and Resort Hokianga

$$ | HOTEL | FAMILY | From the deck of this charming seaside hotel you look straight out to the mouth of Hokianga Harbour, where the view hasn't changed since, according to legend, the Polynesian navigator Kupe first arrived in New Zealand 1,000 years ago. **Pros:** on the beach; great views; good-size pool. **Cons:** not all rooms have views; service can be patchy; Wi-Fi and breakfast not included. ⑤ *Rooms from: NZ$199* ⊠ *State Hwy. 12, Omapere* ☎ 09/405–8737 ⊕ *www. millenniumhotels.com/en/hokianga/ copthorne-hotel-and-resort-hokianga* ⤳ *46 rooms.*

★ Waipoua Lodge

$$$$ | B&B/INN | Renovations of this 100-year-old kauri farmhouse and its buildings have created a sophisticated and relaxing place to stay in the northern end of the North Island. **Pros:** excellent food; peaceful, gorgeous location; beautiful gardens. **Cons:** might be too isolated for some; on the pricey side; not located on the beach. ⑤ *Rooms from: NZ$650* ⊠ *State Hwy. 12, Waipoua* ☎ 09/439–0422 ⊕ *www.waipoualodge.co.nz* ⤳ *4 suites* ⑩ *Breakfast.*

Paihia and Waitangi

69 km (43 miles) north of Whangarei.

As the main vacation base for the Bay of Islands, Paihia is an unremarkable stretch of motels at odds with the quiet beauty of the island-studded seascape. With its handful of hostels, plus the long and safe swimming beach, it's popular with a young backpacker crowd. Most of the boat and fishing tours leave from the central wharf, as do the passenger ferries to the historic village of Russell. The nearby suburb of Waitangi, however, is one of the country's most important historic sites. The Treaty Grounds, a lovely nearby park, was where the Treaty of Waitangi, the founding document for modern New Zealand, was signed.

The main Bay of Islands visitor bureau, in Paihia, is open daily. There is a really good toilet facility at the southern end of the strip.

GETTING HERE AND AROUND
BUS DEPOT Paihia. ⊠ *InterCity Travel Centre, Maritime Bldg., Marsden Rd., Paihia* ☎ *09/402–7857.*

VISITOR INFORMATION
CONTACTS Bay of Islands Visitor Information Centre Paihia. ⊠ *Marsden Rd., Paihia* ☎ *09/402–7345* ⊕ *www.bayofislands. co.nz.*

Sights

The Hundertwasser Public Toilets
BUILDING | On the main street of Kawakawa, a nondescript town just off State Highway 1 south of Paihia, stand surely the most outlandish public toilets in the country—a must-go even if you don't need to. Built by Austrian artist and architect Friedensreich Hundertwasser in 1997, the toilets are fronted by brightly colored ceramic columns supporting an arched portico, which in turn supports a garden of grasses. There are no straight lines in the building, which is furnished inside with mostly white tiles, punctuated with primary colors, and set in black grout (something like a Mondrian after a few drinks). Plants sprout from the roof. If you sit in one of the cafés across the road you can watch the tourist buses stop so the visitors can take pictures of the facilities. ⊠ *Gillies St.* ⊕ *www.bay-of-islands-nz.com/hundertwasser.shtml.*

Mt. Bledisloe
VIEWPOINT | FAMILY | On the National Trust Estate beyond the Treaty Grounds, Mt. Bledisloe showcases the splendid view across Paihia and the Bay of Islands. The handsome ceramic marker at the top showing the distances to major world cities was made by Doulton in London and presented by Lord Bledisloe in 1934 during his term as governor-general of New Zealand. The mount is 3 km (2 miles) from the Treaty House, on the other side of the Waitangi Golf Course. From a small parking area on the right of Waitangi Road, a short track rises above a pine forest to the summit. ⊠ *Mt. Bledisloe, Waitangi.*

★ Waitangi National Trust Estate
MEMORIAL | Take in a major site in New Zealand's history at the northern end of Paihia to gain a better understanding of the turbulent relationship between Māori and the British colonizers. The **Treaty House** in Waitangi Treaty Grounds is a simple white-timber cottage, and was prefabricated in New South Wales for British resident James Busby, who arrived in New Zealand in 1832. Busby had been appointed to protect British commerce and put an end to the brutalities of the whaling captains against the Māori, but he lacked the judicial authority and the force of arms necessary to impose peace. The real significance of the Treaty House lies in the events that took place here on February 6, 1840, the day the Treaty of Waitangi was signed by Māori chiefs and Captain William Hobson, representing the British crown. The treaty was the first formal document that bound the Māori to the British crown, and became the basis for Britain's claim to the entire country as its colony. The visitor center presents the events that led to the Treaty of Waitangi. You'll also be able to experience *kapa haka*, a live Māori cultural performance. The center also displays Māori artifacts and weapons, including a musket that belonged to Hone Heke Pokai, the first Māori chief

The Māori National Festival in Waitangi commemorates the signing of the Waitangi treaty.

to sign the treaty, who would later go on to attack the British in their stronghold at Russell. From the visitor center, follow a short track (trail) through the forest to **Ngatoki Matawhaorua** (ng-ga-to-ki ma-ta-*fa*-oh-*roo*-ah), a Māori war canoe. ⊠ *Waitangi Rd., Waitangi* ☎ *09/402–7437* ⊕ *www.waitangi.org.nz* ⊠ *NZ$50.*

🍴 Restaurants

Charlotte's Kitchen

$$$ | **INTERNATIONAL** | This busy restaurant is named after Charlotte Badger, one of the first European women to live in New Zealand; legend says she was actually a pirate. It's pricey, but worth it for the delicious Japan-inspired seafood and gorgeous views from its location at the end of the wharf. **Known for:** excellent oysters; good pizza selection; tasty cocktails. ⑤ *Average main: NZ$28* ⊠ *69 Marsden Rd., Paihia* ☎ *09/402–8296* ⊕ *www. charlotteskitchen.co.nz.*

🛏 Hotels

Abri

$$ | **HOTEL** | These freestanding studio apartments resemble tree houses and provide lovely sea views from the bush behind the Paihia beachfront. **Pros:** close to town; friendly hosts; beautiful decor. **Cons:** no beach or pool; you're on your own for food; some room views are better than others. ⑤ *Rooms from: NZ$190* ⊠ *10–12 Bayview Rd., Paihia* ☎ *09/402–8003* ⊕ *www.abriapartments. co.nz* ⇄ *3 rooms* ⏣ *No meals.*

Copthorne Hotel and Resort Bay of Islands

$$ | **HOTEL** | The biggest hotel north of Auckland and a favorite with tour groups, this complex sprawls along a peninsula within walking distance of the Treaty House. **Pros:** most rooms have a terrace or patio; French-provincial style; lovely location. **Cons:** some rooms need refreshing; often full of conference-goers; limited Wi-Fi (that you have to pay for). ⑤ *Rooms from: NZ$200* ⊠ *Tau Henare Dr., Waitangi* ☎ *09/402–7411* ⊕ *www.*

millenniumhotels.com/en/bay-of-islands/
copthorne-hotel-and-resort-bay-of-islands
🛏 145 rooms ⫶○⫶ Breakfast.

Paihia Beach Resort and Spa

$$$$ | **RESORT** | **FAMILY** | A large *pohutuka-wa* tree stands next to the heated salt-water pool in front, and all of the rooms have bay views, a deck or patio, and a large whirlpool tub in the bathroom. **Pros:** close to town; stunning views; excellent spa. **Cons:** some road noise; decor a bit dated; breakfast not included. ⑤ *Rooms from: NZ$610* ⊠ *116 Marsden Rd., Paihia* ☎ *09/402–0111* ⊕ *www.paihiabeach.co.nz* 🛏 *21 rooms* ⫶○⫶ *Breakfast.*

🏃 Activities

Getting out on the water is a highlight of the Bay of Islands whether on the ferry crossing from Paihia to Russell or on a guided trip. The coastal areas are also lovely places to stroll, especially in summer.

BOATING

Carino NZ Sailing and Dolphin Adventures

BOATING | Get close to dolphins (primarily bottlenose) and penguins. Passengers on the 50-foot red catamaran can just relax or pitch in with sailing. This full-day trip (NZ$134) includes a barbecue lunch at one of the islands, weather permitting, and a full bar is on board. This company has a permit that allows guests to swim with dolphins. The tours do not run in the winter months. ⊠ *Paihia Wharf Marsden Rd.* ☎ *09/402–8040* ⊕ *www.sailingdolphins.co.nz.*

★ Fullers

TOUR—SPORTS | Cruises and sea-based adventure trips depart daily from both Paihia and Russell. The most comprehensive sightseeing trip is the six-hour, summer-only Best of the Bay Supercruise (NZ$127) aboard a high-speed catamaran. You'll follow about half of what was once called the "Cream Trip" route, but nowadays, instead of picking up cream from farms, the boat delivers mail and

supplies to vacation homes. Fullers also visits Urupukapuka Island, once home to a *hapu* (subtribe) of the Ngare Raumati Māori. Little is known about their life, but there are numerous archaeological sites. It's also the only one to go to Otehei Bay, one of the island's most spectacular bays. On this particular trip, the boat stops for 1½ hours on the island, where you can go kayaking, take a short hike, or have lunch at the Zane Grey Café. The trip also takes in the Hole in the Rock, a natural hole at sea level in Piercy Island that boats pass through if the tide is right. During winter there is a shorter NZ$119 trip that is mostly focused on finding dolphins. ⊠ *Maritime Bldg., Marsden Rd., Paihia* ☎ *09/402–7421* ⊕ *www.dolphincruises.co.nz.*

DIVING

The Bay of Islands has some of the finest scuba diving in the country, particularly around Cape Brett, where the marine life includes moray eels, stingrays, and grouper. The wreck of the Greenpeace vessel *Rainbow Warrior*, bombed and sunk by French agents in 1985, is another underwater highlight. The wreck was transported to the Cavalli Islands in 1987 and is now covered in soft corals and jewel anemones; it's full of fish life. Water temperature at the surface varies from 16°C (62°F) in July to 22°C (71°F) in January. From September through November, underwater visibility can be affected by a plankton bloom.

Yukon Dive

SCUBA DIVING | This company will take you around two significant sunken ships: the Greenpeace vessel *Rainbow Warrior* plus the former Royal New Zealand Navy vessel *Canterbury*. Accredited divers can rent equipment and the unaccredited can sign up for dive courses. Prices including equipment begin at NZ$290. ⊠ *7 Williams Rd., Paihia* ☎ *21/261–1779* ⊕ *www.yukon.co.nz.*

Continued on page 136

CARVING

Although pre-European Māori did not have a written language, their traditional carvings served as a historical record. Every piece has a kaupapa (story), which can be read by those who know how. The shape of the heads, position of the body, and surface patterns work together to commemorate important events.

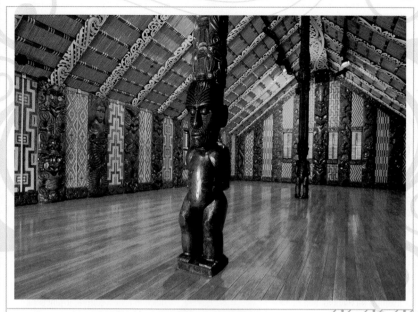

MĀORI ART

Kiwi culture weaves together Māori and *Pakeha* (European) traditions. Māori symbols crop up in everything from the popular whale's tail pendants to a major airline's modernized koru logo. Today Māori art, likewise, melds traditional storytelling with modern concerns.

It wasn't always this way, but since the 1970s there has been a resurgence of, and interest in, Māori culture throughout New Zealand. Days begin with the Māori greeting, "kia ora," literally "be well," offered by Māoris and pakeha alike. Kiwis cheer the world-famous All Blacks rugby squad when they perform the haka—that fierce warrior dance that intimidates opposing teams.

There has even been a renaissance in Māori arts, crafts, and body art. Weavers gather by the hundreds to participate in the hui workshop. Reviving an ancient tradition they work their harakeke (flax) materials into baskets and skirts.

Tens of thousands of spectators attend the biannual Māori performance competition at the Te Matatini arts festival. In Rotorua, center of modern Māori life in New Zealand, there are nightly traditional chants and hangi feasts. Galleries all over New Zealand celebrate works of contemporary artists who express strong or glancing Māori influences in their pieces, and visitors and locals alike mimic traditional Māori moku, or tattoos.

Many Māori artisans see this integration as essential to preserving their culture.

Above: Whare runanga (meeting house), Waitangi

TRADITIONAL ART

Traditional Māori art is symbolic, not literal, and recurring motifs appear on meeting houses, in jewelry, and on objects. Some shapes and symbols come from nature, others represent ancestors or the geographical region of an iwi, or tribe.

Hei Matau—The fish hook is a popular talisman for safe journeys over water. It also represents prosperity.

Hiku—New Zealanders frequently wear the whale's tail, which is a sign of strength and speed.

Koru—The curled fern frond symbolizes beginnings or life, as well as peace and strength.

Hei Tiki—The small human figure with a tilted head depicts a fetus in the womb and symbolizes fertility.

MASKS

North Island styles of face mask include Tai Tokerau, Tai Rawhiti, and Rongowhakaata, and are distinguished by the parallel, angular lines framing the eyes. Koruru, found in the mid-North Island area, are masks characterized by rounded, bulging eyes. The point at the top of the Taranaki mask symbolizes Mount Taranaki. In the Coromandel area, look for tell-tale paua shell eyes in the Pare Hauraki and hollow eye sockets in the Te Whanau a Apanui. The Te Arawa Māori, who live between Rotorua and Lake Taupo, make Ruru masks with pointed ears representing a small owl.

WOOD CARVING

Whakairo (carving) holds an important place in Māori culture; it functions as both an art form and a historical record. Each line and shape has meaning, and each design connects the physical object with mana, or spiritual power. Intricately carved Māori meeting houses and raised storehouses, seen on both islands, demonstrate the Māori practice of designing and patterning objects to imbue them with the spirits of ancestors. For an excellent example, visit the meeting house and war canoe on the Treaty of Waitangi grounds on the North Island.

Apprentice carvers spend upwards of ten years learning their craft.

TEKOTEKO AND OTHER OBJECTS

This ancestral face on an archway greets visitors to a marae.

Tekoteko, carved human figures, adorn Māori meeting houses, homes, and, traditionally, canoe prows. These symbolic ancestors' defiant stances, protruding tongues, and weapons ward off intruders. Other carved items include ceremonial war paddles (*wahaika*), spears (*taiaha*), treasure boxes, and sticks. Look for these carvings at a marae or in museums and galleries.

PAINTINGS (KOWHAIWHAI)

Decorative patterns, called *kowhaiwhai*, are considered less sacred than wood carvings or tattoo-making and can be done by anyone. Find these temporary designs on meeting-house ridgepoles and rafters, canoe bottoms, and paddles. The standard black, white, and red paints mimic the colors produced by red ochre, white clay, and charcoal, the materials used by Māori ancestors. Designs can represent speed and swiftness or hospitality and strength.

Above: The koru symbol is common in Māori style painting.

MĀORI TA MOKO

Unlike contemporary ink tattoos, traditional Māori moku (tattoos) were literally carved into the body with a tool called an uhi, filled with soot from burnt plants or caterpillars, and covered with leaves to heal.

Only those of high rank wore facial tattoos, and they were recognized by these patterns rather than by the natural features we use to describe people today. Segments of the face were reserved for identifying features related to the social rank of the wearer's family; for example, sections on each side of the face depicted the ancestry from the mother's and father's sides.

Markings also commemorated important events in a person's life and, except for some tribes that had tattoos on their legs and buttocks, were confined to the face. Women's tattoos were, and still are, limited to an outline around the lips and thin lines from the lips down the chin. This pattern is still worn in ink tattoos today.

Today, talented Ta Moko artists continue the deeply spiritual traditions of ancient Māori tattooing.

MODERN MĀORI ART

Contemporary Māori artists work in every medium, including music, weaving, crafts, film, and visual entertainment and often contain subtle cultural references or overt interpretations of historic symbols.

Museums, such as the comprehensive **Te Papa** (in Wellington), the **Auckland Art Gallery**, and tiny **Suter Art Gallery** (in Nelson), exhibit a range of art that may include portraits of Māori and their Ta Moku from the last century or modern, mixed-media art by pan-Pacific artists commenting on current events.

Contemporary artwork with traditional Māori influences

MĀORI JEWELRY AND SOUVENIRS

Māori symbols are common in contemporary pendants that are crafted of plastic and wood and hung on a braided cord. More expensive versions are made of greenstone (jade), once used for chisels and weaponry, or bone. These necklaces are popular souvenirs.

Traditional Māori pendant carved from greenstone (jade)

Many contemporary artists take the idea of these traditional pendants and reinterpret motifs in fresh ways. A modern necklace may reference a pattern from a chief's cloak or hint at the fish hook without mimicking the the pattern. While such jewelry may come in greenstone, some artists work with metals like silver or gold instead.

Modern angular and traditional rounded wooden treasure boxes, called wakahuia, incorporate Māori symbols.

Contemporary textile artists blend traditional materials such as flax, tree bark pigments, and feathers with nontraditional colors to craft modern purses and wall hangings.

Popular souvenirs include greenstone, ceramics, synthetic feathers, decorative flax designs, replicas of paddles and war clubs, clothing, and jewelry. The Toi Iho certifies that items were produced by Māori artists (⊕ www.toiiho.co.nz). Not all Māori artists participate in the program; check carefully for authenticity.

This girl wears a greenstone pendant

BUYING MĀORI ART

Woven Kete pikau (back pack)

Māori ceramics with traditional motifs

WHERE TO BUY

Those seriously interested in Māori art and culture should visit Rotorua. Creative Rotorua (⊕ www.creativerotorua.org.nz) is an umbrella organization that links to arts organizations, performances, various area artists, and the local Māori Arts Trail, which maps out studios you can visit. If your trip coincides with Te Matatini, a dance showcase as well as the largest Māori arts festival in the world, scour the booths for authentic crafts (⊕ www.tematatini.org.nz).

If Rotorua isn't on your itinerary, seek out Māori galleries in Christchurch, Queenstown, Auckland, Wellington, and Whangarei. The Te Papa Museum in Wellington has a range of Māori-influenced New Zealand artworks, jewelry and prints. Most museum shops have reproductions of pieces in the collection and rare art books.

HOW TO CHOOSE

Buy what you like or choose a depiction of a place you visited. The connection you feel should motivate you more than the piece's resale value. If quality is important, seek authentication from a dealer.

CUSTOM MADE FOR YOU

New Zealand's small population and informal atmosphere allow for direct contact with artists. Visit their studios, attend a workshop, or chat with them about their pieces. Most artisans and craftspeople will happily custom-make a piece to forward to you at home. There are also dozens of online shops offering various Māori-themed wares if you regret not making a purchase after you return. By purchasing directly from the artist you'll get a one-of-a-kind piece, but don't expect a discount.

USEFUL WEB SITES

⊕ www.maoriart.org.nz

⊕ www.maori.com

The Moko, or facial tattoo, on this carved figure displays ancestral and tribal messages that apply to the wearer. These messages represent the wearer's family, sub-tribal and tribal affiliations, and his place within these social structures. This carving commemorates an ancestor.

Russell

*4 km (2½ miles) east of Paihia by ferry,
13 km (8 miles) by road and car ferry.*

Russell is regarded as the "second"
town in the Bay of Islands, but it's far
more interesting, and pleasant, than
Paihia. Hard as it is to believe, sleepy
little Russell was once dubbed the "Hell-
hole of the Pacific." In the mid- to late
19th century (when it was still known
by its Māori name, Kororareka) it was a
swashbuckling frontier town, a haven for
sealers and whalers who found the East
Coast of New Zealand to be one of the
richest whaling grounds on Earth.

Tales of debauchery abound. British
administrators in New South Wales were
sufficiently concerned to dispatch a British resident agent in 1832 to impose law
and order. After the Treaty of Waitangi,
Russell was the capital until 1844, when
the Māori chief Hone Heke, disgruntled
with newly imposed harbor dues and his
loss of authority, cut down the flagstaff
flying the Union Jack above the town
three times before attacking the British
garrison. Most of the town burned to the
ground in what is known as the Sacking
of Kororareka. Hone Heke was finally
defeated in 1846, but Russell never
recovered its former prominence, and
the seat of government was shifted first
to Auckland, then to Wellington.

Today Russell is a delightful town of
timber houses and big trees that hang
low over the seafront, framing the yachts
and game-fishing boats in the harbor. The
relaxed vibe can best be absorbed in a
stroll along the Strand, the path along the
waterfront. There are several safe swimming beaches, some in secluded bays,
as well as the aptly named Long Beach,
over the hill from the township.

GETTING HERE AND AROUND

The road between Russell and Paihia is
long and tortuous. The best way to travel
between the two is by passenger ferry,
which leaves from the Russell Wharf, or
by car ferry, which departs from Okiato,
about 9 km (5½ miles) southwest of
town.

VISITOR INFORMATION

CONTACTS Russell Information Centre.
⊠ *Russell Wharf* ☎ *09/403–8020* ⊕ *www.
russellinfo.co.nz.*

◉ Sights

Christ Church

BUILDING | One of the donors to the con-
struction of New Zealand's oldest church
was Charles Darwin, who at that time
in 1835 was making his way around the
globe on board the HMS *Beagle*. Behind
the white picket fence that borders the
churchyard, gravestones tell a fascinating
and brutal story of life in the colony's early days. Several graves belong to sailors
from the HMS *Hazard* who were killed in
this churchyard by Hone Heke's warriors
in 1845. Another headstone marks the
grave of a Nantucket sailor from the
whaler *Mohawk*. As you walk around the
church, look for the musket holes made
when Hone Heke besieged the church.
The interior is simple and charming—
embroidered cushions on the pews are
examples of a still-vibrant folk-art tradition ⊠ *Church and Robertson Sts.*

Pompallier Mission

HISTORIC SITE | **FAMILY** | New Zealand's
oldest industrial building, the Pompal-
lier Mission, at the southern end of
the Strand, was named after the first
Catholic bishop of the South Pacific.
Marist missionaries built the original
structure out of rammed earth, because
they lacked the funds to buy timber. For
several years the priests and brothers
operated a press here, printing Bibles
in the Māori language. From December
through April you can visit independently,
but from May to November the mission
organizes tours at set times. ⊠ *The
Strand* ☎ *09/403–9025* ⊕ *www.pompalli-
er.co.nz* ⊠ *NZ$10.*

Restaurants

★ The Gables Restaurant

$$$$ | **MODERN NEW ZEALAND** | One of Russell's oldest buildings (built in 1847) is home to an up-to-the-minute kitchen, serving the finest cuts of meat, fresh fish, and imaginative vegetarian options. The atmosphere is calm, the wine list decent, and the service is on point. **Known for:** smart seasonal cooking; lively atmosphere; great seafood. ⑤ *Average main: NZ$32* ✉ *19 The Strand* ☎ *09/403–7670* ⊕ *www.thegablesrestaurant.co.nz.*

🛏 Hotels

★ Arcadia Lodge

$$$ | **B&B/INN** | This B&B, perched over Matauwhi Bay a few minutes' walk from town, had been supported for more than 100 years by whale vertebrae, which served as the backbones of this turn-of-the-20th-century home. **Pros:** lovely rooms; spectacular views; decadent breakfast. **Cons:** finding the parking lot is tricky so follow the directions on the website; no beach access or pool; no other meals besides breakfast are served. ⑤ *Rooms from: NZ$255* ✉ *10 Florance Ave.* ☎ *09/403–7756* ⊕ *www.arcadialodge.co.nz* ↪ *5 rooms* ❍ *Breakfast.*

Duke of Marlborough Hotel

$$$ | **HOTEL** | This waterfront hotel is a favorite with the yachting fraternity, for whom ready access to the harbor and the bar downstairs are the most important considerations. **Pros:** prime waterfront position; fun crowds; good restaurant. **Cons:** can be too close to the action; quite noisy; little privacy. ⑤ *Rooms from: NZ$290* ✉ *The Strand* ☎ *09/403–7829* ⊕ *www.theduke.co.nz* ↪ *26 rooms* ❍ *Breakfast.*

★ The Homestead at Orongo Bay

$$$$ | **B&B/INN** | Tucked away in gardens off the road between the car-ferry landing and Russell, this historic lodge, built in 1865, soothes with peace and quiet—which is why it has hosted several famous guests who want to relax in peace. **Pros:** gorgeous property; amazing food; lovely garden. **Cons:** slightly out of town; decor might be old-fashioned to some; on the pricier side. ⑤ *Rooms from: NZ$350* ✉ *45 Aucks Rd.* ☎ *09/403–7527* ⊕ *www.thehomestead.co.nz* ↪ *3 rooms* ❍ *Breakfast.*

🏃 Activities

FISHING

Major Tom Charters

FISHING | Chase game fish such as marlin, kingfish, *hapuka* (grouper), snapper, broadbill, and tuna. A full day, with a maximum of four anglers, is NZ$1,750 including lunch (hopefully you catch dinner). ☎ *09/403–8553* ⊕ *www.majortom.co.nz.*

HIKING

There are several pleasant walks around the Russell area; the most challenging—and spectacular—is the **Cape Brett Tramping Track** out to the lighthouse. It takes about eight hours round-trip. It costs NZ$30 to walk the track and you can stay in a hut for NZ$15 a night. You must book and pay in advance, as this is a popular walk. It is not for the unfit, and good shoes are a must. Check with the Russell Information Center on the wharf. For a shorter jaunt on your own (an hour each way), follow the **Whangamumu Walking Track** to the remnants of a whaling station. Many relics such as an old boiler and vats are still left at the station.

Kerikeri

20 km (12 miles) north of Paihia.

Kerikeri is often referred to as the cradle of the nation because so much of New Zealand's earliest history, especially interactions between Māori and Europeans, took place here. A major citrus and kiwifruit growing area, it was once principally a service town for the whole mid-north region. Though newcomers have flocked to Kerikeri for its low-key lifestyle, it still feels like a small town. The Sunday farmers' market is a treat.

The **Kerikeri Proctor Library,** open weekdays 8 to 5, and Saturday from 9:30 to 2, is the only place in Kerikeri that provides visitor information, and it's far less extensive than other bureaus.

GETTING HERE AND AROUND

Kerikeri is about four hours' drive from Auckland following State Highway 1. Buses connect from Auckland directly and from the other centers. There is also a good airport with regular flights, but it is expensive to fly, particularly from Auckland. There is no train service.

VISITOR INFORMATION

CONTACTS Kaitaia Visitor Information Centre. ⊠ *At South and Matthews Rd., Kaitaia* ☎ *09/408–0879.* **Kerikeri Proctor Library.** ⊠ *6 Cobham Rd.* ☎ *09/407–9297* ⊕ *www.kerikeri.co.nz.*

◉ Sights

Kerikeri Farmers' Market

MARKET | FAMILY | If you're in Kerikeri on a Sunday, head to the market to sample and buy the best the region has to offer, from music to fresh produce, local wines, cheeses, preserves, oils, and handmade soaps. Grab a locally roasted coffee and wander among the stalls. ⊠ *Parking lot, off Hobson Ave.* ⊕ *www. bayofislandsfarmersmarket.co.nz.*

Kerikeri Mission Station

BUILDING | FAMILY | The station, which includes the 1821 **Mission House** and the **Stone Store,** provides a fascinating and rare look at pretreaty New Zealand. **Kemp House,** otherwise known as Mission House, has gone through many changes since 1821, but ironically, a major flood in 1981 inspired its "authentic" restoration. The flood washed away the garden and damaged the lower floor, and during

repair much information about the original structure of the house was revealed. Its ground floor and garden have been restored to the style of missionary days, and the upper floor retains its Victorian decoration. **Stone Store,** New Zealand's oldest stone building, is a striking example of early colonial architecture. Designed by Wesleyan missionary John Hobbs and built by an Australian convict stonemason between 1832 and 1836, the Store was meant to house New Zealand mission supplies and large quantities of wheat from the mission farm at Te Waimate. When the wheat failed, the building was mainly leased as a kauri gum-trading store. The ground floor is still a shop. The upper stories display the goods of a culture trying to establish itself in a new country, such as red Hudson Bay blankets, which were sought after by Māori from the *pā* (hilltop fortification), forged goods, steel tools, an old steel flour mill, and tools and flintlock muskets—also prized by local Māori. Guided tours are available; bookings are essential. ⊠ *Kerikeri Historic Basin, Kerikeri Rd.* ☎ *09/407–9236* ⊠ *NZ$12.*

Kororipo Pā

MILITARY SITE | Across the road from the Kerikeri Basin's Stone Store is a path leading to the historic site of Kororipo Pā, the fortified headquarters of legendary chief Hongi Hika. The chief visited England in 1820, where he was showered with gifts. On his way back to New Zealand, during a stop in Sydney, he traded many of these presents for muskets. Having the advantage of these prized weapons, he set in motion plans to conquer other Māori tribes, enemies of his own Ngapuhi people. The return of his raiding parties over five years, with many slaves and gruesome trophies of conquest, put considerable strain between Hongi Hika and the missionaries. Eventually his warring ways were Hongi's undoing. He was shot in 1827 and died from complications from the wound a year later. Untrained eyes may

Northern Northland

Above the Bay of Islands Northland are many small communities. For many the big attraction is **90 Mile Beach,** a 100-km (60-mile) or so long clear stretch of golden sand running up North Island's tip. You access it from **Kaitaia,** a vibrant town with an extremely good café—Birdies—where the omelets are not only delicious, they will set you up for the day. If you want to travel the beach, take a tour; the beach is virtually off-limits to independent travelers, as, thanks to quicksand and incoming tides, rental-car insurance won't cover you here.

Just out of Kaitaia are the beaches at Ahipara and Shipwrecks. Surfers love the long lines and almost perfect waves here. Many surfers head south around the point for even better waves and fewer people.

Cape Reinga, at the peninsula's end, is a sacred Māori area. They believe that spirits depart for the underworld by sliding down the roots of the headland's gnarled *pohutukawa* tree (reputed to be 800 years old) and into the sea. A much-photographed solitary lighthouse stands here.

You can easily drive into the Far North, barring 90 Mile Beach. From the Bay of Islands on State Highway 10 you'll reach Mangonui, a former whaling port on the southeast side of **Doubtless Bay.** Beach lovers should head for the Karikari Peninsula, on Doubtless Bay's northwestern side. From Doubtless Bay it's less than a half-hour drive west to Awanui, near the service town of Kaitaia. Fill your gas tank in one of these two towns, then head north on Highway 1. The last few miles to Cape Reinga aren't paved.

have difficulty figuring out exactly where the *pā* (Māori fortification) was, as no structures are left. The pā was built on a steep-sided promontory between the Kerikeri River and the Wairoa Stream. ⊠ *Kororipo Pā.*

Rewa's Village
MUSEUM | FAMILY | This museum re-creates a *kāinga* (unfortified fishing village) where local Māori lived in peaceful times. In times of war they took refuge in nearby Kororipo Pā. In the village are good reproductions of the chief Hongi Hika's house, the weapons store, and the family enclosure, as well as two original canoes dug up from local swamps and original *hāngi* stones, which were heated by fire and used to cook traditional Māori feasts, found on-site. A "discoverers garden" takes you on a winding path past indigenous herbs and other plants;

information is posted describing the uses of each plant. ⊠ *Kerikeri Historic Basin, Kerikeri Rd.* ☎ *09/407–6454* ⊕ *www. kerikeri.co.nz/Rewas_Village.cfm.*

🍴 Restaurants

Fishbone Café
$$ | CAFÉ | The coffee is good as is the big range of egg dishes, salads, and sandwiches. The menu for meals changes frequently and is built around seasonal produce, much of it from local suppliers. **Known for:** excellent coffee; great wine list; local charm. ⓢ *Average main: NZ$20* ⊠ *88 Kerikeri Rd.* ☎ *09/407–6065* ⊗ *No dinner.*

Marsden Estate Winery and Restaurant
$$$ | ECLECTIC | Named after the missionary Samuel Marsden, who planted New Zealand's first grapevines in Kerikeri in

1819, this winery is a popular lunch spot and for good reason. The seasonal menu is eclectic and is built around fresh local produce. **Known for:** excellent seasonal cuisine; high quality wine; terrace seating. ⑤ *Average main: NZ$32* ✉ *Wiroa Rd.* ☎ *09/407–9398* ⊕ *www.marsdenestate. co.nz* ◷ *No dinner Sun.–Thurs.*

🛏 Hotels

★ Kauri Cliffs Lodge

$$$$ | RESORT | FAMILY | Several holes of a par-72 championship golf course sweep past this cliff-top lodge, which is truly outstanding. **Pros:** absolute luxury; superb scenery; all the amenities you can imagine including pool, spa, and beach access. **Cons:** possibly overwhelming for first-timers; expensive; dress code on the strict side. ⑤ *Rooms from: NZ$935* ✉ *139 Tepene Tablelands Rd., Matauri Bay* ☎ *09/407–0010* ⊕ *www.kauricliffs. com* ⇆ *22 suites* ¶◎¶ *Some meals.*

Kauri Park

$$ | HOTEL | This small cluster of chalets is a notch above the usual, with contemporary style and a magnificent setting among fruit trees adjacent to farmland. **Pros:** relaxed and friendly atmosphere; beautiful rooms; lovely location. **Cons:** not within walking distance of town; no on-site restaurant; some rooms on the small side. ⑤ *Rooms from: NZ$190* ✉ *512 Kerikeri Rd.* ☎ *09/407–7629* ⊕ *www.kauripark.co.nz* ⇆ *9 units* ¶◎¶ *No meals.*

Mangonui Hotel

$ | HOTEL | This classic wooden two-story pub sits just a few feet from Mangonui's harbor and has a New Zealand Historic Places Trust classification. **Pros:** old-fashioned charm; centrally located; great place to meet locals. **Cons:** really basic; can be noisy; no dining on-site. ⑤ *Rooms from: NZ$120* ✉ *Beach Rd., Mangonui* ☎ *09/406–0003* ⊕ *www.mangonuihotel. co.nz* ⇆ *13 rooms* ¶◎¶ *No meals.*

Paheke

$$ | B&B/INN | An enormous cedar of Lebanon stands in front of this gracious 1864 kauri homestead; both the tree and the house are listed with the Historic Places Trust. **Pros:** good value; relaxing atmosphere; stunning grounds. **Cons:** not close to town; some rooms share a bathroom; might be too old-fashioned for some. ⑤ *Rooms from: NZ$195* ✉ *State Hwy. 1, Ohaeawai* ☎ *09/405–9623* ⊕ *www. paheke.co.nz* ⇆ *4 rooms* ¶◎¶ *Breakfast.*

🛍 Shopping

Makana Confections

FOOD/CANDY | FAMILY | The products at this boutique place are fabulous. Favorites include the macadamia butter toffee crunch; chocolate-coated, locally grown macadamias; and liqueur truffles. ✉ *504 Kerikeri Rd.* ☎ *09/407–6800* ⊕ *www. makana.co.nz.*

🤸 Activities

GOLF

Carrington

GOLF | There's an 18-hole, par-72, tournament-quality course, which meanders along 100 acres of coastline. The course shares the land with the Karikari Estate winery, and Carrington Resort, a luxury lodge. Green fees are NZ$135 per person, and clubs cost NZ$20 to rent. ✉ *Matai Bay Rd., Karikari Peninsula* ☎ *09/408–1049* ⊕ *www.carrington.co.nz/ golf.*

★ Kauri Cliffs

GOLF | The spectacular par-72 championship course at Kauri Cliffs has four sets of tees to challenge every skill level. Fifteen holes have views of the Pacific, and six are played alongside the cliffs. Kauri Cliffs is approximately 45 minutes' drive from Kerikeri. ✉ *139 Tepene Tablelands Rd., Matauri Bay* ☎ *09/407–0010* ⊕ *www.rob-ertsonlodges.com/the-lodges/kauri-cliffs* 🖼 *NZ$518 per person, Oct.–Apr.*

Chapter 5

COROMANDEL AND THE BAY OF PLENTY

Updated by
Kathy Ombler

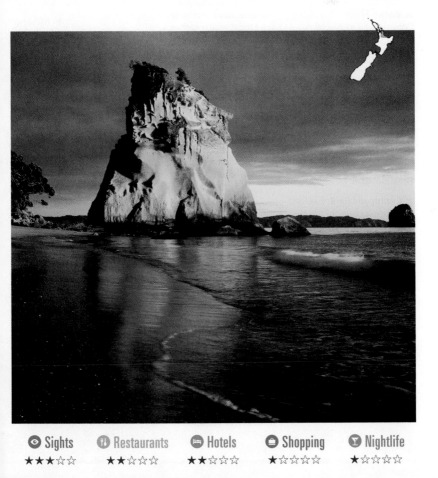

⊙ Sights	🍴 Restaurants	🛏 Hotels	🛍 Shopping	🍸 Nightlife
★★★☆☆	★★☆☆☆	★★☆☆☆	★☆☆☆☆	★☆☆☆☆

WELCOME TO COROMANDEL AND THE BAY OF PLENTY

TOP REASONS TO GO

★ **Beach Bounty:** The seemingly endless coastline here is replete with forest-fringed inlets, sprawling sand dunes, and many of the country's most popular beaches.

★ **Vistas:** From Coromandel's coastal cliffs to the Bay of Plenty's volcanic peak, Mauao, great views abound.

★ **Walking and Hiking:** Climb Mauao (The Mount) for stunning coastal views, or take a forest walk to swim in a lagoon formed by Kaiate Falls. Coromandel Forest Park has a network of trails.

★ **Cycling and Gold:** Explore gold-mining history as you ride the gentle Hauraki Cycle Trail, through forested Karangahake and Waikino gorges.

★ **Watery Wonders:** Dive or snorkel in the region's marine reserves, or swim with dolphins. Charter a deep-sea fishing trip, or kayak beneath glowworms by moonlight.

1 Thames. Coromandel's oldest town and current agricultural center.

2 Tapu-Coroglen Road. Gateway to the gorgeous Rapaura Watergardens.

3 Coromandel Town. The birthplace of the New Zealand gold rush.

4 Colville and Beyond. Coromandel's northmost (and most wild) reaches.

5 Whitianga. A great base for water activities.

6 Around Hahei. Home to the best beaches in the region.

7 Tairua. Another great base for area beaches.

8 Whangamata. A harborside town and summer hotspot.

9 Waihi to Paeroa. The southernmost part of Coromandel.

10 Katikati. Home to a collection of murals depicting the area's fraught history.

11 Tauranga. The Bay of Plenty's biggest city and one of the country's sunniest spots.

12 Whakatane. An important small town for Māori history.

13 Whakarri (White) Island. An eerie island containing New Zealand's most active volcano.

Cuvier
Island

MERCURY
ISLANDS
Great Mercury Island

Mercury Bay

Hahei
6

THE
ALDEMEN
ISLANDS

25

7 Shoe Is.
Tairua
Hikuai Slipper
Island
Opoutere

8
Whangamata

Tuhua
(Mayor Island)

Waihi
Waihi Beach
2
Tahawai
Matakana
Island
10
Katikati

Pacific Ocean

Mauao
(Mount
Maunganui)
Motiti
Island

11 Omanu Beach
Papamoa Beach
Tauranga
29 Te Puke Maketu
Kaiate Bay of Plenty
Kaimai Falls
36 2

33

Whakarri
13 (White)
Island

Matata
2 Thornton Motuhora
Island

Whakatane

Lake
Rotoehu Edgecumbe Wainui Ohope
2 12 2
Lake Opotiki
1 Mourea Rotoma Pekatahi
Lake 30
Rotorua
Ngongotaha Te Ngae

0   10 mi

0   10 km

Beautiful sandy beaches, lush native forests, and some steamy geothermal activity make Coromandel Peninsula and the Bay of Plenty quite a departure from urban Auckland. Many residents live in coastal villages or small rural towns, with the occasional artsy or alternative-lifestyle community thrown in, particularly in parts of Coromandel.

Both areas bask in more than their fair share of sun for much of the year, so avocado, citrus, kiwifruit, nuts, and even subtropical fruits flourish here, and many growers adopt organic practices. Keep an eye out for the ubiquitous unmanned fruit stands accompanied by "honesty boxes."

Both regions are hugely popular holiday spots for New Zealanders: the beaches and bays, the fishing, surfing, and kayaking on the water, and the land-based bush and coastal walks and cycle trails draw people, especially in the summer holidays in January. Join them or, perhaps more wisely, time your trip to avoid the crowds—rest assured, the weather will still be warm.

Follow State Highway 25—the Pacific Coast Highway—as it meanders up the west coast and down the east coast of the peninsula. Traffic can build up on this road, particularly in the busy summer months or weekends. As you drive south down the peninsula's east coast, the Pacific Highway stretches out to the coastal plains and forests of the Bay of Plenty.

From the Bay of Plenty's northern gateway of Katikati as far as Whakatane and Ohope Beach, the coastline consists of huge stretches of sand, interrupted by rivers, estuaries, and sandbars. Inland, the soil is rich and fertile; this is horticulture territory with sprawling canopies of kiwifruit vines, fields of corn and other produce, and pockets of dense native forest. You'll see people fishing in some of the bays, but others have strict conservation rules; signs in the shape of a fish outline whether you can fish.

GETTING ORIENTED

Coromandel and the Bay of Plenty regions are about two to three hours southeast of Auckland and west of the Waikato farming district and are a mix of rugged and forested hill country and rich plains used for horticulture. They are about a seven- to nine-hour drive from Wellington and one to two hours from Hamilton and Rotorua. Many of Coromandel's small settlements are based on former ports, established to transport logs in earlier days, when the forests were milled. Bay of Plenty, with its strong horticultural focus (in particular kiwifruit), is dotted with small rural towns fanning out from Tauranga's large port. You can fly over or take a boat to see an active marine volcano on White Island off the coast of Whakatane. The steaming fissures are dramatic whether viewed by sea, air, or standing on the marine volcano itself.

MAJOR REGIONS

Coromandel. Coromandel Peninsula beckons from the Hauraki Plains like a big lizard lying in the sun—the dark forest on the central mountainous spine promising more than just pretty pictures. When you arrive at the peninsula you'll be surprised how lush the forest growth is, wonder at how the road hugs the coast literally feet above the water, and understand why people like living here. As with so many other lands "discovered" by Europeans, Coromandel was looted for its valuable resources: kauri trees, then kauri gum from the peninsula's forests, and finally gold from the southern hills and around Waihi and Coromandel towns in the 1870s. Relative quiet since the 1930s has allowed the region to recover its natural beauty and attract many life-styler types. In the 1960s and 1970s, dairy farms and orchards sprang up, as did communes, spiritual retreats, and artists' communities. The population is now a mix of artists, those who appreciate the country lifestyle (and the easy access to organic food), and a growing number of Aucklanders looking for a weekend or retirement home.

A craggy range of forest-covered peaks rises sharply to almost 3,000 feet and dominates the center of the peninsula. The west coast cradles the tidal Firth of Thames, and along the east coast the Pacific has carved out a succession of beaches and inlets separated by rearing headlands. Because of its rich soil, the peninsula has many spectacular gardens; some are open to the public. From the town of Thames, the gateway to the region, State Highway 25 will take you up the western coast of the peninsula to the Tapu-Coroglen Road, Coromandel Town, and Colville. Heading south on the eastern peninsula, you'll pass the towns of Whitianga, Hahei, Tairua, Whangamata, and the many beaches surrounding them. The southernmost part of the peninsula stretches between the towns of Waihi and Paeroa.

The Bay of Plenty. People refer to the Bay of Plenty as New Zealand's food bowl—as in plenty of food. Some of the most fertile land for fruit and vegetables is found in the region, and seafood is abundant. Coming from Coromandel, the first main area you'll hit is Katikati, and from there, you'll find the central city base of the Bay, Tauranga and its associated port, Mount Maunganui. Both have retained a relaxed vacation-town vibe despite ongoing expansion. From here and from the next major town along this coast, Whakatane, you can take day trips to beaches, the bush, and offshore attractions such as volcanic White Island. "Laid-back sophistication" is an apt description of what this region can offer its visitors.

The Bay of Plenty also has a significant Māori history; this is the first landing place of *Takitimu, Tainui, Arawa,* and *Mataatua,* four of the seven Māori migration *waka* (canoes) that arrived in New Zealand from the Polynesian Pacific Islands, and from what they call their traditional homeland, Hawaiki. These first arrivals formed the ancestral base for the Māori tribes of the Tauranga region: Ngāti Ranginui, Ngāti Te Rangi, and Ngāti Pūkenga.

Planning

When to Go

These regions are well loved for their beaches, and they are crowded between December and February when the hot summer weather draws thousands of holiday makers; sleepy seaside towns become filled with city folk with a tourist surge during the weeks around Christmas and the New Year. Don't overlook the off-season (March through September). The weather's usually sunny, climate is temperate, prices are lower, and locals have more time to chat. Some of the more hardy locals swim whatever the weather.

Making the Most of Your Time

Set aside four to five days and get a rental car as Bay of Plenty and Coromandel need to be approached with flexibility. These regions have much to provide in a relatively small area. Allow for five-minute stops at the beach to become long coastal walks. Likewise, the many forest walks can be as challenging as you choose—from an hour to a whole day or overnight. You can approach the journey many ways, perhaps as a coastal exploration from Auckland along the "Seabird Coast," home to Miranda, an internationally recognized wetland on the Firth of Thames—then cross the fertile farmland of the Hauraki Plains to the base of Coromandel Peninsula. From here, try a loop of the peninsula that begins in Thames and ends in Whangamata, then continue along the coast to Bay of Plenty, Tauranga, and Whakatane. And be patient—the curvy roads challenge many drivers, especially tourists in campervans.

Getting Here and Around

AIR TRAVEL

There are some tiny airstrips along Coromandel Peninsula and a commercial airport at Tauranga and Whakatane. A number of scenic-flight operators, like Aerius Helicopters, offer trips over the region.

CONTACTS Aerius Helicopters.
☎ 0800/864–354 ⊕ www.aerius.co.nz.
Air Chathams. ☎ 0800/580–127 ⊕ www.

airchathams.co.nz. **Air New Zealand.**
☎ 0800/737–737 ⊕ www.airnewzealand.co.nz.

BUS TRAVEL

Go Kiwi Shuttles links Auckland, Auckland Airport, and towns of Coromandel, and also offers personal charters. InterCity Coachlines also serves the area.

CONTACTS Go Kiwi Shuttles. ☎ 0800/446–549 ⊕ www.go-kiwi.co.nz. **InterCity Coachlines.** ☎ 0800/222–146 ⊕ www.intercity.co.nz.

CAR TRAVEL

The best way to explore the region is by car. Most roads are well maintained and clearly signposted (albeit some can be narrow and winding), and a car gives you the freedom to explore attractions such as short walks and waterfalls along side roads.

There are two main ways to drive to Coromandel from Auckland. First take the Southern Motorway, following signs to Hamilton. Just as you get over the "Bombay Hills," turn left onto State Highway 2 (it's clearly signposted to Coromandel); then take the turnoff to State Highway 25, signposted between the small towns of Maramarua and Mangatarata. Follow the signs to Thames. Allow 1½ to 2½ hours for the 118-km (73-mile) journey. An arguably more scenic—though longer—way is to detour off the Southern Motorway at Manurewa, travel through Clevedon, and follow the Seabird Coast, past tiny Kaiaua village, Miranda thermal springs, and alongside the Firth of Thames, home to thousands of seabirds attracted here to the internationally recognized Ramsar wetland of Miranda. From Thames, State Highway 25 is the main loop that travels around the peninsula, and, though winding, the road is in good condition.

To reach the Bay of Plenty from Auckland, take the Southern Motorway, following signs to Hamilton. Just past the "Bombay Hills," turn left onto State

Highway 2, and stay on Highway 2 all the way to Tauranga, driving through Paeroa, the scenic Karangahake Gorge (stop for walks and photos), Waihi, and Katikati on the way. The driving time between Auckland and Katikati is around 2 hours, 40 minutes. Between Auckland and Tauranga, it's at least 3 hours, 15 minutes.

FERRY TRAVEL

360 Discovery

Auckland ferry company Fullers operates the 360 Discovery ferry service from downtown Auckland to Coromandel, daily during peak summer holiday season, five days per week during the rest of the summer, and three days a week during winter. The sailing takes just under two hours and travels via Waiheke and Rotoroa islands to Hannafords Wharf, 7 km (4 miles) from Coromandel Town. A free shuttle service operates into the town. One-way fare is NZ$64. ☎ 0800/360–3472 ⊕ www.fullers.co.nz.

Restaurants

There are many dining options across Coromandel and the Bay of Plenty. You can buy fruit from roadside orchard stalls and take-out from fish-and-chips joints as well as visit cafés serving sandwiches, burgers, and espresso coffee, right through to fine-dining affairs. Even when restaurants are formal in appearance, diners and hosts tend toward a relaxed country-casualness. Restaurant owners make a point of using the region's abundant resources, like fruit from local orchards and shellfish from nearby mussel and scallop farms.

Dinner service begins about 6 pm in the winter and around 7 pm during the summer months, though many places have "all-day menus." In peak season most places keep serving until at least 9 pm. For many restaurants reservations are a good idea, especially in the summer around Coromandel. In winter, phone

ahead to check if the restaurant will stay open.

Hotels

Like mellow places around the world, you'll find plenty of comfortable bed-and-breakfasts and stylish motels, but both Coromandel and Bay of Plenty also have a sprinkling of luxe boutique lodges tucked away in the forest or along coastal coves. In peak season, from October through March, advance booking is essential across the board and many of the better places have long-term customers who book as much as a year in advance.

Restaurant and hotel reviews have been shortened. For full information, visit Fodors.com. Restaurant prices are the average cost of a main course at dinner or, if dinner is not served, at lunch. Hotel prices are the lowest cost of a standard double room in high season.

What It Costs			
$	**$$**	**$$$**	**$$$$**
RESTAURANTS			
under NZ$15	NZ$15–NZ$20	NZ$21–NZ$30	over NZ$30
HOTELS			
under NZ$125	NZ$125–NZ$200	NZ$201–NZ$300	over NZ$300

Tours

Coromandel Adventures

DRIVING TOURS | If you don't have your own transport, that's not a problem. Coromandel Adventures will happily drive you to any or all of the area's major sights, or simply from town to town. The small tour company has a range of tailor-made tours that will show you the best and some secret spots of Coromandel, including the northern peninsula tip and beautiful

Hot Water Beach and Cathedral Cove on the eastern side. Check the website for online specials. ☎ *0800/462–676* ⊕ *www.coromandeladventures.co.nz* ⊠ *From NZ$25.*

Visitor Information

The Coromandel, Katikati, Tauranga, Thames, Pauanui, Tairua, Waihi, Whakatane, Whangamata, and Whitianga visitor centers are open daily between at least 10 and 4. For tidal information, check the back page of the *New Zealand Herald* newspaper. *Tait's Fun Maps* of Coromandel, Thames, and Whitianga are not drawn to scale, but they clearly mark roads and main attractions. Pick up a copy at almost any hotel, tour-operator office, or visitor center, or check ⊕ *www.coromandelfun.co.nz.*

Thames

120 km (75 miles) southeast of Auckland.

The peninsula's oldest town, Thames has evolved from a gold-mining hotbed in the late 1800s to an agricultural center. Locals have a saying that when the gold ran out, "Thames went to sleep awaiting the kiss of a golden prince—and instead it awoke to the warm breath of a cow." The main street was once lined with nearly 100 hotels (read: bars—gold mining and logging was thirsty work). Only a handful of these hotels still operate, but the town and environs provide glimpses of the mining era. In 1872 two towns, Grahamstown in the north and Shortland in the south, merged to form Thames, and many locals still refer to upper Thames as Grahamstown. Thames today is also the gateway to Kauaeranga Valley, part of Coromandel Forest Park, home to waterfalls, kauri groves, and the dramatic Pinnacles formations. Pinnacles Hut is a popular overnight hiking destination (advance booking required). Thames is

also the northern entry point for the two- to four-day Hauraki Rail Trail. This is part of Nga Haerenga, the New Zealand Cycle Trail. The 173-km (107-mile) trail travels in part on former railway lines, including tunnels (the grade is easy), and explores farmland, the coast around Thames, gold-mining history, and the scenic Karangahake Gorge.

GETTING HERE AND AROUND

If you're not driving, you can take a public bus to Thames from Auckland, Hamilton, Tauranga, or any of the smaller towns on the main road en route from these cities. If you're coming from the nearest big city, a bus ticket shouldn't cost you more than about NZ$30–NZ$42.

You can pick up a rental car at the Auckland airport and drive on down to Coromandel, or you can take a bus and rent a car when you arrive in Thames. At the Thames i-SITE Information Centre, located right where the bus deposits you, ask for rental car advice.

BUS CONTACTS Bus Depot. ⊠ *Thames i-SITE Visitor Infomation Centre, 200 Mary St.* ☎ *07/868–7284.*

CAR RENTALS Saunders Rentals. ⊠ *201 Pollen St.* ☎ *0800/111–110* ⊕ *www.saundersmotorgroup.co.nz.*

VISITOR INFORMATION

CONTACTS Thames i-SITE Visitor Centre. ⊠ *200 Mary St.* ☎ *07/868–7284* ⊕ *www.thamesinfo.co.nz.*

◉ Sights

Bounty Store

MUSEUM | This design store–cum–gallery is Thames's best option for buying local arts and crafts, including jewelry, pottery, weaving, and paintings. ⊠ *644 Pollen St.* ☎ *07/868–8988.*

Goldmine Experience

BUILDING | Take a guided experience to learn about one of the richest gold strikes in the world. The tour includes a

The Coromandel

Did You Know?

The Pinnacles Track was once used to bring supplies to loggers in the valleys. Restored in the 1990s, the trail's stone steps cross three rivers and lead to what was the logging camp.

40-minute underground tour of an 1868 stamper battery. Wear sturdy footwear, as it can be muddy. Advanced booking is recommended. ⊠ *Corner of State Hwy. 25 and Moanawataiari Creek Rd.* ☎ *07/868–8154* ⊕ *www.goldmine-experience.co.nz* ⊠ *NZ$15.*

Grahamstown Saturday Market

MARKET | On Saturday morning, the northern end of Thames's main street is transformed into a bustling market. Stalls line the street, with vendors selling local organic produce, cheeses, and beverages as well as antiques, jewelry, and arts and crafts. Every second Saturday of the month, there's a dedicated craft market, too. ⊠ *Upper Pollen St.*

Thames Historical Museum

MUSEUM | This tiny, volunteer-run museum contains photographic displays of the 1860s gold-rush and logging industries, re-creations of period rooms from the 1800s, and information on the area's first Māori inhabitants and early European settlers. A nice feature on the grounds is the memorial garden, with period roses and other flora that settlers commonly planted; it's a lovely place to rest and reflect. ⊠ *Pollen and Cochrane Sts.* ☎ *07/868–8509* ⊕ *www.thameshistoricalmuseum.weebly.com* ⊠ *NZ$5.*

Thames School of Mines Mineralogical Museum

MUSEUM | From the mid-1800s, the School of Mines was an internationally recognized institution, teaching all aspects of mining. A diploma from here guaranteed a job anywhere in the world. The museum was established in 1900 to exhibit geological samples. The school closed decades ago, but the museum's still kicking, displaying those turn-of-the-20th-century rock specimens along with scales, models of stamper batteries, and other gold-mining paraphernalia. ⊠ *Brown and Cochrane Sts.* ☎ *07/868–6227* ⊕ *www.nzmuseums.co.nz/collections/3309* ⊠ *NZ$10.*

🍴 Restaurants

The Junction Hotel

$$$ | NEW ZEALAND | FAMILY | Within one of the few hotels remaining from the gold rush days, you'll find classy pub grub in a convivial atmosphere. The Grahamstown Bar Diner (GBD) is the main restaurant bar, serving everything from breakfast and lunch to bar snacks and pizzas to evening main courses. **Known for:** decent burgers and fish-and-chips; great tapas menu; late night music on weekends. ⑤ *Average main: NZ$25* ⊠ *700 Pollen St.* ☎ *07/868–6008* ⊕ *www.thejunction.net.nz.*

Sola Café

$ | VEGETARIAN | A consistently good community café, Sola offers an all-vegetarian menu but it's no health food bar. Counter food includes tasty risotto cakes, Florentines, and fresh fruit shortbreads. **Known for:** excellent vegetarian menu; tasty berry friend (a small, sweet cake made from ground almonds and egg whites, often topped or filled with fruit); lots of teas. ⑤ *Average main: NZ$12* ⊠ *720b Pollen St.* ☎ *07/868–8781* ⊗ *Closed Sun.*

🛏 Hotels

Coastal Motor Lodge

$$ | HOTEL | Set amid 3 acres of gardens, with native bushwalks to the rear of the property and the Thames coast just across the road, this is a spacious, scenic spot to stay as you enter Coromandel. **Pros:** close to Thames; lovely views; obliging hosts. **Cons:** basic furnishings; need to book well ahead in summer; on a main road. ⑤ *Rooms from: NZ$172* ⊠ *608 Tararu Rd.* ☎ *07/868–6843* ⊕ *www.stayatcoastal.co.nz* ⇌ *16 units* ❍| *No meals.*

Grafton Cottage & Chalets

$$ | B&B/INN | FAMILY | These six independent units set among a hillside garden overlooking the sea offer a relaxing ambience and great sunsets. **Pros:** great

The farmland outside of Coromandel Town stretches in every direction.

fishing shops, the knowledge is definitely local. ✉ *2 Kapanga Rd., Coromandel* ☎ *07/866-7397* ⊕ *www.topcatch.co.nz.*

HIKING
Kauri Block Track

HIKING/WALKING | On a clear day, head up to the Kauri Block Track (1½ hours return), which provides panoramic views over the town, harbor, and coast. Follow the main road to Coromandel town's western outskirts, where a signpost points out the start of the trail at 356 Wharf Road. The trail goes through native and regenerating bush then a side track leads to a Māori *pā* (fortified village) site on the summit, with spectacular views. The trail continues down through the bush and emerges onto Harbour View Road, which you follow back to town. ✉ *356 Wharf Rd., Coromandel* ⊕ *www. doc.govt.nz* 🎟 *Free.*

Long Bay Scenic Reserve and Kauri Grove

HIKING/WALKING | A gentle 40-minute walk (one-way) leads to Tucks Bay and a beautiful beach. Pack a picnic and enjoy a relaxing afternoon. The track starts at the end of Long Bay Road, at the Long Bay Motor Camp (about 3 km [2 miles] from Coromandel Town). En route it passes through a grove of young kauri trees (and one much bigger, older kauri that happily evaded the early loggers). Either return the way you came, or head across Tucks Bay and follow the coastal track back to the motor camp. ✉ *3200 Long Bay Rd., Coromandel.*

Colville and Beyond

30 km (19 miles) north of Coromandel.

Get closer to the very north of the Coromandel Peninsula—with its rugged coastline, delightful coves, and pastures—and take the 30-minute drive from Coromandel up to **Colville.** The town has a grocery store–gas station, post office, community hall, and café. For something different, there is an interesting Buddha shrine, or stupa, by the Mahamudra Buddhist Centre on the drive in and public toilets with a mosaic worthy of a picture. Colville is the gateway to some of the peninsula's most untamed landscape. Maps of the area are available in Coromandel at the Town Information Centre and in Colville at the General Store.

GETTING HERE AND AROUND

Other than driving to Colville, you can get here by bus or with a small touring company like Coromandel Adventures, which offers excursions and shuttle transport around the area.

Sights

Fletcher Bay

SCENIC DRIVE | Beyond Colville, a twisty, gravel road will take you to Fletcher Bay, the northernmost end of the peninsula. (It's impossible to fully circumnavigate the peninsula by road.) To reach Fletcher Bay, turn left at a T-junction about 5 km (3 miles) north of Colville. This road follows the west coast to a stunning sandy beach at Port Jackson, then continues along the cliff top and down to Fletcher Bay, a smaller, sandy cove banked by green pasture rolling down to the beach. It's 60 km (38 miles) from Coromandel—a 1¼-hour drive. There's a small camping ground here, tracks and beaches to explore, and a great kayaking spot. From Fletcher Bay, hikers can follow the signposted Coromandel Coastal Walkway, an old bridle trail along the very northeastern tip of Coromandel Peninsula, down to Stony Bay. It's a charming three- to four-hour walk, partly along cliff tops with grand views across to the Mercury Islands, and at times dipping down to secluded, forest-fringed beaches.

★ General Store

STORE/MALL | Colville's classic counter-culture General Store is run by a local co-operative. It sells foodstuffs (there's a well-stocked organic section), wine, beer, and gasoline. It's kind of like the general store that used to be in all country areas. It's also the northernmost supplier on the

peninsula, so don't forget to fill your tank. ✉ *2314 Colville Rd.* ☎ *07/866–6805.*

🍽 Restaurants

Hereford 'n' a Pickle

$ | **MODERN NEW ZEALAND** | The meat and produce in this café and store all come from the owner's very own farm, Kairaumati Hereford Stud. The meat is processed on-site, the sausages are made from an old family recipe, and the free-range eggs, honey, vegetables, jams, and pickles are all homegrown. **Known for:** pure homegrown Hereford beef burgers; homemade baked goods; pickles and chutneys. ⑤ *Average main: NZ$10* ✉ *2318 Colville Rd.* ☎ *07/866–6937* ⊕ *www.kairaumatipolledherefords. com.*

🛏 Hotels

Anglers Lodge Motel and Holiday Park

$$ | **HOTEL** | A friendly, family-run business offers appealing cabins, motel units, and campervan and tent sites nestled off the main road at Amodeo Bay. The beach is just over the road, and it's a fisherman's paradise. **Pros:** friendly operators; stunning location with great views; spotless facilities. **Cons:** far from town; gets very busy during Easter and Lodge's annual fishing competition; must book well ahead for summer. ⑤ *Rooms from: NZ$140* ✉ *Amodeo Bay, 1446 Colville Rd., Colville* ☎ *07/866–8584* ⊕ *www. anglers.co.nz* ⤴ *13 units* ⧆ *No meals.*

★ Tangiaro Kiwi Retreat

$$$ | **HOTEL** | It's quite a drive to get there but there are not many places where you can stay in simple, understated luxury and hear kiwi call at night. **Pros:** prolific birdlife—some 50 kiwi live in the local reserve; close to great beaches and forest walks; massage therapist's hut and hot tub in the bush. **Cons:** birdsong might wake you early; long winding drive (or expensive helicopter) to get there; far from shops. ⑤ *Rooms from: NZ$220*

✉ *1299 Port Charles Rd., Coromandel* ☎ *07/866–6614, 0800/826–4276* ⊕ *www. kiwiretreat.co.nz* ⤳ *14 rooms* ❍❘ *No meals.*

Whitianga

46 km (29 miles) southeast of Coromandel.

Nestled between forest-clad hills and the sea on Coromandel's eastern coast is Whitianga, the main township on this side of the peninsula. Here the beachfront is lined with motels and hostels, all within walking distance of shops and the ferry across Whitianga Harbour to Flaxmill Bay and Cooks Beach. Many people use the town as a base for fishing or boating trips, and others stock up for camping at nearby beaches. Over summer it hosts some great rock music and jazz shows, and people use it as a base for enjoying the region's gorgeous beaches.

If you're driving between Whitianga and Coromandel and the sun is shining, make some time to head north toward Whangapoua. Park your car, grab your bathing suit, and make the 30-minute trek over to New Chums Beach, a native forest-fringed bay of golden sand. It's accessible only by foot and you have to wade through an estuary to get there, but the beautiful and secluded beach (rated by locals as among the top 101 things to do in New Zealand) is one of the country's worst-kept secrets.

The Whitianga i-SITE Visitor Centre can help you choose an excursion and has a full list of the many B&Bs in the area.

GETTING HERE AND AROUND

Unless you're driving or on a charter flight from Auckland, the bus is the only way to get to Whitianga (with the exception of those stalwart few who are conquering the Coromandel by bicycle). Bus companies stop at the Whitianga i-SITE Visitor Centre.

A nice way to explore Flaxmill Bay or Whitianga (if you're based at either of these points) is to leave your car near the dock and take the NZ$5 (NZ$7 return) ferry across and explore the beaches or cafés, depending which side you end up, on foot. Or for NZ$1.50 extra, take your bike along.

BUS DEPOT Whitianga. ✉ *Whitianga i-SITE Visitor Information Centre, 66 Albert St.* ☎ *07/866–5555* ⊕ *www.thecoromandel.com.*

TOURS

★ Ocean Leopard Tours

BOAT TOURS | Explore the area's dramatic volcanic coastline from the comfort of a sleek, purpose-built craft that gets right up against sea cliffs, blowholes, and even into sea caves. Skipper Jason has years of experience in showing off his favorite local haunts. His covered boat keeps the rain and sun at bay without spoiling the views. Trips, which leave from both Whitianga Wharf and Ferry Landing (across the estuary), include one-hour and two-hour options (snorkeling can also be added). Booking ahead is essential in summer. ☎ *07/866–4990* ⊕ *www.oceanleopardtours.co.nz* ⤳ *From NZ$70.*

Sea Cave Adventures

BOAT TOURS | This company uses a smaller boat that can get you into the sea caves and blowholes (weather and tide dependent) as well as showcase all the sheer volcanic coastal cliffs and white-sand beaches. The skipper knows the best spots and you can shelter from the sun under the boat's awning. Two-hour trips leave from Whitianga Wharf at 8, 11, 2, and 4:30 (one hour each). Reservations are recommended. ✉ *Whitianga Wharf* ☎ *0800/806–060* ⊕ *www.seacaveadventures.co.nz* ⤳ *From NZ$90.*

FESTIVALS

Whitianga Scallop Festival

FESTIVAL | Held every September, this annual celebration of Whitianga seafood is one of the region's main events. Stalls serve scallops prepared every which way, and there are music performances, kids' activities, and cook-offs. Even though that's only early spring here, the vibes are warm enough. Keep an eye on the website, as tickets sell quickly. ⊕ *www.scallopfestival.co.nz.*

VISITOR INFORMATION

CONTACTS Whitianga i-SITE Visitor Centre. ✉ *66 Albert St.* ☎ *07/866–5555* ⊕ *www.thecoromandel.com.*

 Sights

The Lost Spring

SPA—SIGHT | There are spas, and then there is The Lost Spring: thermal pools set in the middle of town yet landscaped as if they're lost in the forest. The Lost Spring taps into 16,000-year-old mineral water drawn from more than 2,000 feet below ground, and now filling a man-made haven of steaming lagoons, waterfalls, and quartz-studded caves. Lie back in the water and watch native birds eating berries from the trees and ferns while waiters deliver snacks, juices, beer, wine, or cocktails to the water's edge. There's also a restaurant and day spa (be sure to book ahead). ✉ *121 A Cook Dr.* ☎ *07/866–0456* ⊕ *www.thelostspring.co.nz* 🍴 *From NZ$40* ☞ *Restricted to 14 yrs and over.*

 Restaurants

Cafe Nina

$ | **CAFÉ** | Jasmine vines cloak the front porch of this adorable 1890 miner's cottage. Folks come here for breakfast and lunch every day of the week and you might have to wait a bit during holiday time, but locals think it's worth it. **Known for:** classic breakfasts, including a great eggs Benedict; seafood chowder; lots of locals. ⑤ *Average main: NZ$14* ✉ *20 Victoria St.* ☎ *07/866–5440* ⊙ *No dinner.*

Poivre & Sel

$$$$ | **FRENCH FUSION** | The existence in a small seaside town of such a high-quality French fusion eatery pleasantly surprises many visitors. French chef Samuel Goslin remains true to classical French cuisine, at the same time allowing for the Kiwi taste for less salt and less fat. **Known for:** French classics like garlic snails; dish presentation that is more like art; two- or three-course degustation menus. ⑤ *Average main: NZ$60* ✉ *2 Mill Rd.* ☎ *07/866–0053* ⊕ *www.poivresel.co.nz* ⊙ *Closed Sun. and Mon.*

Salt Restaurant and Bar

$$$ | **NEW ZEALAND** | Put a slightly upmarket yet still casual restaurant in a popular local hotel, with a waterside location in a holiday town, and you've got this can't-miss dining spot. There is casual pub dining in the bars, but Salt, with its alfresco dining by the palm-edged marina, is the star. **Known for:** great raw bar with oysters and ceviche; steamed mussels; slow-roasted lamb sharing plate. ⑤ *Average main: NZ$30* ✉ *1 Blacksmith La.* ☎ *07/866–5818* ⊕ *www.salt-whitianga.co.nz* ⊙ *Closed Mon. and Tues.*

 Hotels

Admiralty Lodge

$$$ | **HOTEL** | A mile from the town center, but only across the road from Buffalo Beach, this is a good spot if you're planning on a few days beachside. **Pros:** great views; big swimming pool; beach location. **Cons:** right beside the road; breakfast included, but at café a few minutes' drive away; nearest shops also a few minutes' drive. ⑤ *Rooms from: NZ$290* ✉ *69–71 Buffalo Beach Rd.* ☎ *07/866–0181, 0508/236–472* ⊕ *www.admiraltylodge.co.nz* 🛏 *18 rooms* ⦿ *Breakfast.*

Beachfront Resort

$$$ | **B&B/INN** | You can step out of this tiny, family-run property's garden onto a breathtaking beach. **Pros:** stunning

location; direct beach access; powerful showers. **Cons:** few minutes' walk out of town; no air-conditioning; need to book well in advance for summer. $ *Rooms from: NZ$300* ⊠ *111–113 Buffalo Beach Rd.* ☎ *07/866–5637* ⊕ *www.beachfrontresort.co.nz* ⊅ *8 rooms* ❄️ *Breakfast.*

Oceanside Motel

$$$ | **B&B/INN** | Stylish studio suites or one-bedroom units overlook the beach here. **Pros:** stunning sea views from upstairs rooms; friendly hosts; kayaks and guest barbecue available. **Cons:** small bathrooms in some units; upstairs rooms with a view are more expensive; no air-conditioning. $ *Rooms from: NZ$250* ⊠ *32 Buffalo Beach Rd.* ☎ *07/866–5766* ⊕ *www.oceansidemotel.co.nz* ⊅ *9 rooms* ❄️ *Breakfast.*

🏃 Activities

Fishing, swimming, and diving are popular activities around this seaside town. There's kayaking along the dramatic coastline, with its rock arches and caves, or cruising the clear waters in a glass-bottom boat. Inland, old miner's trails now make interesting forest walks.

BOATING, FISHING, AND DIVING

Cathedral Cove Scenic Cruises

BOATING | Skipper Ken has a wealth of knowledge about the local history, geology, and marine life and he'll share it all with you as he shows you the special spots of this spectacular coastline. He even has an underwater camera installed on his boat, so you can check out the fish without getting wet or you can jump right in and snorkel. Tours leave daily from Whitianga Wharf (with Ferry Landing pick-ups possible). Reservations are recommended. ⊠ *Whitianga Wharf* ☎ *0800/888–688* ⊕ *www.cathedralcovecruises.co.nz* 🚤 *From NZ$70.*

Cave Cruzerze

BOATING | The Cave Cruzer gives you an unusual spin on an ex-Navy rescue boat, exploring Cathedral Cove, blowholes,

and sea caves, with time for snorkeling if you wish. At one point, you'll head into a cave and your guides will provide a surprising acoustical demonstration. Two trip options are the standard 2- to 2½-hour Scenic and Sound, and 1-hour Express. There's no shade on this boat, but lots of personality. ☎ *07/866–0611, 027/663–3449* ⊕ *www.cavecruzer.co.nz* 🚤 *From NZ$60.*

Glass Bottom Boats

BOATING | On these cruises to Te Whanganui-A-Hei Marine Reserve, get in the water with a snorkel or simply sit on board and watch the marine life through the vessel's glass bottom. Informed guides discuss the formation and history of the land, Captain Cook's explorations here during the 1700s, the earliest Māori settlers Ngāti Hei, and the more recent history of Narnia film locations. Several trips daily, year-round (weather permitting) leave from Whitianga Wharf. The trips take two hours, and advanced booking is essential. ☎ *07/867–1962* ⊕ *www.glassbottomboatwhitianga.co.nz* 🚤 *From NZ$105.*

GUIDED HORSE TREKS

Rangihau Ranch

TOUR—SPORTS | **FAMILY** | This ranch offers guided horse rides into the rugged Coromandel ranges. Treks from 30 minutes to two hours will take you through native bush and across open pasture into the hills and valleys surrounded by spectacular views across the peninsula. All abilities are well catered to and even pre-schoolers are welcome. ⊠ *111 Rangihau Rd., Coroglen* ☎ *07/866–3875* ⊕ *www.rangihauranch.co.nz* 🚤 *From NZ$30.*

Around Hahei

57 km (35 miles) southeast of Coromandel, 64 km (40 miles) northeast of Thames.

The beaches, coves, and seaside villages around Hahei make for a great day of exploring—or lounging. If you're craving a true beach vacation, consider basing yourself in Hahei rather than in Whitianga. From Hahei, you can easily reach Cathedral Cove, the Purangi Estuary, Cooks Beach, and Flaxmill Bay (where the little passenger ferry crosses to Whitianga township); the famous Hot Water Beach is only minutes away.

GETTING HERE AND AROUND

If you're day-tripping from Whitianga, take the five-minute ferry ride (which leaves every hour, NZ$6 round-trip) across to Flaxmill Bay and explore by foot. Alternatively, follow State Highway 25 south from Whitianga. The road takes you past the Wilderland Community's roadside stand (selling organic produce and delicious honey from a community-run organic farm) and on a loop around to Hahei, Cooks Beach, and Flaxmill Bay. If you want to explore Cathedral Cove you can walk the steepish track, or simply catch a water taxi off the beach at Hahei.

CONTACTS Cathedral Cove Water Taxi.
☎ 027/919–0563 ⊕ www.cathedralcove-watertaxi.co.nz.

 Sights

Cathedral Cove

VIEWPOINT | The Cathedral Cove rock arch is possibly the most visited feature in Coromandel. The two-hour return walk is steep and the water at the cove is usually calm and clear, so good for swimming and snorkeling. To get there, travel along Hahei Beach Road, turn right toward town and the sea, and then, just past the shops, turn left onto Grange Road and follow the signs. In the height of summer the parking lot at the trailhead is closed and a shuttle bus (NZ$5 return) takes you from Hahei Village. Or you can walk from the northern end of Hahei Beach, adding a 20-minute climb. Another option is to jump on the Cathedral Cove Water Taxi that buzzes from Hahei Beach to Cathedral Cove in a few minutes. Or you

could paddle there with Cathedral Cove Kayaks. A good plan is to visit outside peak summer holiday season, January in particular. ✉ *Trail head car park, End of Grange Rd., Hahei.*

★ **Colenso Country Café and Shop**

RESTAURANT—SIGHT | FAMILY | A cottage café and craft shop are set in a garden full of citrus and olive trees and kitchen herbs. The café serves soups, more-ish country-style pies, salads, and an ever-changing variety of cakes, scones, muffins, slices, and Devonshire teas. In the shop you can procure tasty chutneys, jams, organic honey, and giftware. The open grassy space, play area, and tame donkeys make this an especially good place to stop with kids. It's located on State Highway 25 just south of the Hahei turnoff on the way to Tairua. ✉ *State Hwy. 25, Whenuakite* ☎ *07/866–3725.*

Te Pare Historic Reserve

NATURE PRESERVE | The headland at the south end of Hahei Beach is the site of two former Māori pā (fortified village). Although no trace remains of the defensive terraces and wooden spikes that once ringed the cliffsides, the stunning outlook, which made it an ideal defensive sight in years past, remains. At high tide, the blowhole at the foot of the cliffs adds a booming bass note to the sound of waves. To reach the actual pā site, follow the red arrow down the hill from the parking area at the end of Pa Road. After some 50 meters (164 feet), take the right fork through a grove of giant *pohutukawa* trees, then go through a gate and across an open, grassy hillside. You can also pick up the trail onto the headland from the southern end of Hahei Beach, at mid- to low tide. ✉ *End of Pa Rd., Hahei.*

 Beaches

Cooks Beach

BEACH—SIGHT | This beach lies in Mercury Bay, so named for Captain James Cook's observation of the transit of the planet

Swimmers enjoy the blue waters in Te Whanganui-a-Hei (Cathedral Cove) Marine Reserve, Coromandel Peninsula.

Mercury in 1769. The beach is notable for the captain's landfall, the first here by a European. It's a beautiful expanse of white sandy beach, backed by a growing sprawl of holiday homes. Forest-covered headlands overlook each end (take the walking track to Shakespeare Cliff Scenic and Historic Reserve, on the northern headland for the view). The beach is a safe family swimming spot, likely to be crowded in peak summer months (January) and delightfully quiet at other times of the year. Along with private holiday homes, B&Bs and a holiday park with campsites and cabins are located near the beach. **Amenities**: food and drink; parking; toilets. **Best for**: swimming; sunrise; walking. ⊠ *Marine Parade, Cooks Beach, Coromandel.*

Hot Water Beach

BEACH—SIGHT | This wild and potentially dangerous surf beach is incredibly popular for its under-the-sand thermal spring. By scooping a shallow hole in the sand, you can create a pool of warm water; the deeper you dig, the hotter it becomes.

The phenomenon occurs only at low- to mid-tide, so time your trip accordingly. In summer you'll be joined by hundreds of other spade-toting, wannabe bathers—plan your visit outside of busy January if you can. Hot Water Beach is well signposted off Hahei Beach Road from Whenuakite (fen-oo-ah-kye-tee). ⚠ **Do not swim in the surf at Hot Water Beach; the spot is notorious for drownings.** However, nearby Hahei Beach is one of the finest and safest on this coast. If you need to while away some time before the tide goes out, there are a couple of beachside cafés, plus the Moko Artspace gallery to browse. **Amenities**: food and drink; changing rooms and showers; toilets; parking (small fee). **Best for**: sunbathing; surfing (experienced surfers only); walking. ⊠ *Hot Water Beach Rd.*

🍴 Restaurants

★ Eggsentric Café

$$$$ | **ECLECTIC** | More than just great food, there's a community hub-feel about this restaurant: there are live music sessions, poetry readings, film nights, and a summer sculpture symposium. The dinner menu reaches beyond standard café fare, and there's also a great range of classic breakfasts and fresh baking. **Known for:** scallops, chowders, and other seafood; tasty desserts; community art and music. $ *Average main: NZ$31 ⌧ 1049 Purangi Rd., Flaxmill Bay* 🕾 *07/866–0307* ⊕ *www.eggsentriccafe. co.nz* ⊗ *Closed Mon. and May–Sept.*

Go Vino

$$ | **MODERN NEW ZEALAND** | This café's small shared plates feature an eclectic fusion of Asian and classic European flavors with a strong Kiwi touch. Try the tea leaf salad, Burmese-style, with roasted soy beans, peanuts, *kawakawa* (a pepper-flavored native plant), cabbage, and tomato; ostrich and beef cheek; or the braised octopus with nectarines. **Known for:** great pizzas; selection of fusion dishes; dessert platters. $ *Average main: NZ$18 ⌧ 19 Captain Cook Rd., Cook's Beach* 🕾 *07/867–1215* ⊕ *www.govino. co.nz* ⊗ *Closed Tues. and Wed.*

🛏 Hotels

The Church Accommodation

$$ | **HOTEL** | Set among gardens and native bush and connected by winding paths are these character-filled studios and cottages. **Pros:** range of accommodations; lovely garden; free Wi-Fi throughout. **Cons:** at least 10-minute walk to the beach; must book well ahead in summer; can be shady and cool in winter. $ *Rooms from: NZ$195 ⌧ 87 Hahei Beach Rd., Hahei* 🕾 *07/866–3533* ⊕ *www.thechurchhahei.co.nz* ⊗ *Closed a few wks mid-winter* ⇆ *12 rooms* ⊘ *No meals.*

★ Mussel Bed

$$$$ | **B&B/INN** | Every detail of guest comfort and privacy is considered at this delightful, friendly B&B. **Pros:** down-to-earth, friendly Kiwi hosts; excellent breakfasts and fresh baking; great

location close to the beach. **Cons:** away from town and shops; can't see the beach; can be traffic noise. $ *Rooms from: NZ$325 ⌧ 892 Purangi Rd., Cooks Beach* 🕾 *07/866–5786* ⊕ *www.mus-selbed.co.nz* ⇆ *3 suites, 1 2-bedroom cottage* ⊘ *Breakfast.*

Tatahi Lodge

$$$ | **HOTEL** | This lodge offers a range of accommodations (and prices) and is a four-minute walk from the beach. **Pros:** self-catering options; good for budget travelers; close to cafés, brewery, and beach. **Cons:** can feel a bit crammed; gets busy with young backpackers; some units lack privacy (and private bathrooms). $ *Rooms from: NZ$215 ⌧ 9 Grange Rd., Hahei* 🕾 *07/866–3992* ⊕ *www.tatahilodge.co.nz* ⇆ *10 units* ⊘ *No meals.*

Wairua Lodge

$$$ | **B&B/INN** | Rain-forest retreat describes this place well: four stylish double rooms and one two-bedroom apartment are nestled on a 15-acre property with native forest, bushwalks, streams, and hidden swimming holes for your enjoyment. **Pros:** divine location; fantastic river swimming; treetop bathhouse. **Cons:** some unsealed road access; no shops close by for catering; have to book the balcony bath in one-hour timeslots. $ *Rooms from: NZ$205 ⌧ 251 Old Coach Rd., Hahei* 🕾 *07/866–0304* ⊕ *www.wairualodge.co.nz* ⇆ *5 rooms* ⊘ *Breakfast.*

🏃 Activities

Cathedral Cove Dive and Snorkel Hahei

DIVING/SNORKELING | Cathedral Cove Dive and Snorkel Hahei gives beginner, advanced, and dive-master courses, as well as daily dive trips in the Te Whanga-nui-A-Hei Marine Reserve, Cathedral Cove, and around the outer islands and pinnacles. Most dive sites are a 10-minute boat ride away. They also hire snorkels, and will give tips on the best spots to go snorkeling. ✉ *48 Hahei Rd., Hahei* ☎ *07/866–3955* ⊕ *www.hahei. co.nz/diving.*

⭐ **Cathedral Cove Kayak Tours**
KAYAKING | **FAMILY** | A stunning way to explore this spectacular volcanic coastline is by sea-kayak. This company is happy to work with beginners and families and they pride themselves on showing off places you're unlikely to find on foot. Paddle straight off Hahei Beach and along to famous Cathedral Cove (they're the only kayak company licensed to land here) and be served a cappuccino—and that's just the standard trip. They take groups of eight in double kayaks. Other options, weather permitting, include a full-day paddle (think caves and blowholes) and a remote coastal tour. ✉ *88 Hahei Beach Rd., Hahei* ☎ *07/866–3877, 0800/529–258* ⊕ *www.kayaktours.co.nz* 🖃 *From NZ$115.*

Hahei Explorer
BOATING | *Hahei Explorer,* a sturdy, eight-seater rigid inflatable boat, explores this volcanic coastline's sea caves, blowhole, beaches, headlands, and spectacular Cathedral Cove. One-hour trips depart directly off Hahei Beach (the southeastern end) six times daily (four in winter). Booking ahead is essential; be sure to arrive 15 minutes before departure. ✉ *Hahei* ✥ *South end of beach* ☎ *07/866–3910* ⊕ *www.haheiexplorer.co.nz* 🖃 *NZ$95.*

Tairua

28 km (18 miles) south of Hahei, 37 km (23 miles) north of Whangamata.

Tairua is one of the larger communities along the coast, and one of the prettiest, nestled beside an estuary, harbor, and hills. The twin volcanic peaks of Paku rise up beside the harbor, and there's an ocean beach close by. Because State Highway 25 is the town's main road, it's also a convenient stop en route to other seaside spots around Whitianga

and Hahei. The five-minute ferry ride from Tairua across the harbor to the holiday homes of Pauanui takes you to the immediate area's best beach. The ferry runs hourly throughout most of the summer (NZ$5 round-trip). If you're here at the end of February you can get fully immersed, literally, in the Tairua Wet & Wild weekend, involving lots of watersports fun. For year-round activities and maps check out the Pauanui and Tairua information centers.

GETTING HERE AND AROUND
If you're based in Thames, Tairua is an easy drive across the base of the Coromandel Peninsula along State Highway 25A. Otherwise, whether you're heading up or down the eastern side of Coromandel, you can't miss it. The information center, just down the first road to the right after you cross the bridge coming into town, is a good place to stop in and get your bearings.

VISITOR INFORMATION
CONTACTS Pauanui Information Centre.
✉ *23 Centreway, Pauanui* ☎ *07/864–7101.* **Tairua Information Centre.** ✉ *2 Manaia Rd.* ☎ *07/864–7575* ⊕ *www.tairua.co.nz.*

👁 Sights

Wharekawa Harbour Wildlife Refuge
NATURE PRESERVE | Take a detour to the dazzling, white-sand Opoutere Beach and Wharekawa Harbour Wildlife Refuge, reached by a five-minute drive off SH25, turning left 8½ km (5 miles) south of Tairua. The road follows the Wharekawa Estuary to a parking lot. From here cross a wooden footbridge and follow the trail for 10 minutes through the forest to the long white beach. Much of the estuary and headland area here is a wildlife refuge, a breeding ground for shorebirds, including the endangered New Zealand dotterel. Take care not to enter fenced areas as these protect the barely visible eggs that lie in shallow nests in the sand.

For more information, ask at the Tairua or Whangamata information center.

🍴 Restaurants

Manaia Café and Bar

$$$$ | ECLECTIC | This spacious, centrally located café/restaurant can get busy with both visitors and locals. Breakfast kicks off at 9 am with all the standard Kiwi options and salads, burgers, and fish-and-chips come on the menu for lunch; dinner is still casual but slightly more upmarket fare with a good range of lamb, steak, salmon, pork, and vegetable dishes on offer. **Known for:** woodfire pizzas; breakfast waffles; art and craft store next-door. $ *Average main: NZ$31* ✉ *228 Main Rd.* ☎ *07/864–9050* ⊕ *www.manaia.co.nz* ⊘ *Closed Tues. and Wed.*

Surf and Sand

$ | SEAFOOD | A classic New Zealand takeout experience, this is the spot to get a quintessential Kiwi-style beachside lunch or dinner of fish, shellfish, chips (fries), and burgers. When the fish (battered or crumbed) and chips are done well, they're not too greasy or fatty. **Known for:** classic New Zealand fish-and-chips; Kumara (sweet potato) fries; battered Coromandel oysters. $ *Average main: NZ$12* ✉ *Shop 7, Main Rd.* ☎ *07/864–8617.*

🛏 Hotels

Blue Water Motel

$$$ | HOTEL | These bright and cheery self-contained units are at the southern end of Tairua, across the street from a small sandy beach. **Pros:** simple and charming decor; close to the beach; outstandingly helpful hosts. **Cons:** a bit cramped; beside the main road; there are steps to some rooms. $ *Rooms from: NZ$220* ✉ *213 Main Rd.* ☎ *07/864–8537* ⊕ *www.bluewatermotel.co.nz* ⇨ *10 units* ❍ *No meals.*

Grand Mercure Puka Park Resort

$$$$ | HOTEL | This hillside hideaway, managed by the international Accor hotel chain, is nestled in native bushland near Pauanui Beach. **Pros:** upmarket and well appointed; close to the beach; pool, tennis court, and bikes are among amenities. **Cons:** somewhat formal for the region; access to rooms not easy on steep paths (call for a golf cart); steep climb uphill from the beach. $ *Rooms from: NZ$347* ✉ *Mount Ave., Pauanui* ☎ *07/864–8088* ⊕ *www.pukapark.co.nz* ⇨ *48 rooms* ❍ *No meals.*

Pacific Harbour Lodge

$$$ | HOTEL | With a grand Pacific-style portico, this resort property on the main street in Tairua looks like a tropical island getaway. **Pros:** tropical island ambience; good location; well priced. **Cons:** not all villas have a harbor view; Wi-Fi not free; cable television in lobby only. $ *Rooms from: NZ$298* ✉ *223 Main Rd.* ☎ *07/864–8581* ⊕ *www.pacificharbour.co.nz* ⇨ *31 rooms* ❍ *No meals.*

Whangamata

37 km (23 miles) south of Tairua, 60 km (38 miles) east of Thames.

The Coromandel Ranges back Whangamata (fahng-a-ma- ta), another harborside town, with a population of around 3,500. Once a town of modest houses, it's been discovered by city people wanting to work remotely from the beach, and some mighty big homes have now been constructed here. The harbor, surf beaches, mangroves, and coastal islands are glorious. In summer, the population more than triples. It's a great spot for deep-sea fishing, and for surfers its bar break creates some of the best waves in New Zealand. For classic- and muscle-car enthusiasts, the Whangamata Beach Hop held each year around March is a must-go. You'll see amazing classic cars and listen to some of the best rock-and-roll bands around. In February, British cars and bikes are a feature during the "Brits at the Beach" festival.

GETTING HERE AND AROUND

Whangamata is Coromandel's last coastal port of call, as you travel southward into the Bay of Plenty. If you're only passing through but you've got a couple of hours to spare, check out some of the short bush walks in the area, or, of course, head down to the beach.

VISITOR INFORMATION

CONTACTS Whangamata Information Centre. ✉ *616 Port Rd.* ☎ *07/868–0200* ⊕ *www.whangamatanz.com.*

🍴 Restaurants

Neros Bar & Eatery

$$$ | **ITALIAN** | **FAMILY** | Come to this indoor/outdoor bistro for casual evening dining loosely billed as Italian with pizza, pastas, and risotto on the menu. There's also a great range of Kiwi-modern mains that feature salmon, steak, pork, and the local fish catch. **Known for:** pizzas; Thai curries; wine menu with a focus on NZ wines. $ *Average main: NZ$22* ✉ *711 Port Rd.* ☎ *07/865–6300* ⊕ *www.nerorestaurant. co.nz* ⊘ *No lunch.*

SixfortySix

$$ | **CAFÉ** | This café boasts of being the friendliest place in town, and the day-long crowds support the claim. Inside, you'll find good coffee, fresh pastries, and a paper roll menu (as they call it) listing fresh, wholesome breakfasts and lunches like house-smoked salmon, salads, and classic burgers. **Known for:** spiced breakfast bircher; quality Kokako roast coffee; alfresco dining. $ *Average main: NZ$18* ✉ *646 Port Rd.* ☎ *07/865–6117* ⊕ *www.sixfortysix.co.nz* ⊘ *No dinner Wed.–Fri.*

🛏 Hotels

Brenton Lodge

$$$$ | **B&B/INN** | Looking out over Whangamata and the islands in its harbor from your hillside suite, you'll feel rested and pampered, especially after being greeted with fresh flowers, fruit, and handmade chocolates. **Pros:** peaceful setting; pool and hot tub; breathtaking views. **Cons:** a little too far from town to walk home in the evening; no air-conditioning; some stairs to negotiate. $ *Rooms from: NZ$470* ✉ *2 Brenton Pl.* ☎ *07/865–8400* ⊕ *www.brentonlodge.co.nz* ⊘ *Closed June and July* ⇋ *4 suites* ⦿ *Breakfast.*

Pipinui Motel

$$$ | **HOTEL** | Tucked away down a quiet street, yet just a two-minute walk to Whangamata marina and a 10-minute walk to the beach, this motel has two studios and two one-bedroom units, all self-contained with modern kitchens, big bathrooms, peaceful pastel colors, and small private decks. **Pros:** modern and spacious; well serviced; good location. **Cons:** if you want to stay around Christmas you'll need to book months ahead; breakfast not included; a bit expensive for what you get. $ *Rooms from: NZ$235* ✉ *805 Martyn Rd.* ☎ *07/865–6796* ⊕ *www.pipinuimotel.co.nz* ⇋ *5 rooms* ⦿ *No meals.*

🏃 Activities

The beach is where it's at here. Surfers and swimmers share the waves; farther offshore big-game fishing is popular.

SURFING

Whangamata Surf Shop

SURFING | If you're looking for a quick introduction to the sport, check out the Whangamata Surf Shop, owned by legendary surfing family the Williams (daughter Ella is a former World Junior Champ and now follows the WLS QS Tour). Located in the center of town, the shop has surfboards and boogie boards for rent. If you want to learn what to do with them, they'll send you off for a surfing lesson with their friends down on the beach (at Access 8) who run the Whangamata Surf School. ⊠ *634 Port Rd.* ☎ *07/865–8252* ⊕ *www.whangamata-surfshop.co.nz* ⊠ *NZ$80 (1 hr, including instructor and surfboard).*

TOUR OUTFITTERS

Kiwi Dundee Adventures

TOUR—SPORTS | Doug Johansen (Kiwi Dundee), Jan Poole, and their small family of expert, friendly Kiwi guides offer personalized tours throughout New Zealand but they have a special focus on their home region, Coromandel. Their total enthusiasm for the region rubs off on anyone who takes a Kiwi Dundee tour. There are one-day or three-day walks and tours, plus 14- to 20-day tours all over New Zealand if you'd like more. ☎ *07/865–8809* ⊕ *www.kiwidundee. co.nz.*

WALKING

Wentworth Valley

CAMPING—SPORTS-OUTDOORS | Regenerating forest, gold mine history, and the 150-foot-high Wentworth Falls are all features on these short walks in the hills of southern Coromandel Forest Park, behind Whangamata. There's also a Department of Conservation campsite in the valley, and lots of swimming holes for cooling off on hot summer days. From Whangamata township drive south on SH25 for 2½ km (1½ miles). Turn right off the highway into Wentworth Valley Road. The track starts at the road's end. ⊠ *Wentworth Valley Rd.* ☎ *07/865–7032* ⊕ *www.wentworthvalleycamp.co.nz.*

Waihi to Paeroa

Waihi is 30 km (18.6 miles) south of Whangamata, 20 km (12.4 miles) from Paeroa.

Southern Coromandel is bounded by the historic and scenic Karangahake Gorge

and smaller, adjoining Waikino Gorge. State Highway 2 wends its way through the forest-covered, gorged terrain from small farming town Paeroa, to the gold-mining center of Waihi. While the towns are just 20 km (12.4 miles) apart, there is much to see and do along the way. Try to give yourself some time to explore the forest walks to old mining sites, batteries, and tunnels. Better still, take a bike ride on the Hauraki Rail Trail (including through the tunnels). Check out the gold-mining history in Waihi. If you're not beached-out after Coromandel, head to beautiful Waihi Beach, 11½ km (7 miles) from Waihi.

Gold mining has helped shape the history of this region. From the late 1800s to early 1900s, hundreds of miners toiled in both underground and open pit mines. You can reflect on their efforts at heritage sites and in museums, and even visit a working mine, as mining still continues in Waihi.

Today a new rush of people comes here to explore the walking trails and heritage mining sites and tunnels, to cycle the Hauraki Rail Trail and the Goldfields Heritage Railway, and to visit the cafés and wineries.

GETTING HERE AND AROUND

If you've headed south down the east coast of the Coromandel, Waihi is your last port of call before you arrive into the Bay of Plenty. Consider a break here, or at least a detour to the west on State Highway 2. This will lead you into the Waikino, then Karangahake Gorge in Coromandel Forest Park, then you'll emerge into open farmland country and Paeroa township. InterCity runs daily bus services to the region.

BUS TRAVEL InterCity. ☎ *09/583–5780* ⊕ *www.intercity.co.nz.*

VISITOR INFORMATION

CONTACTS Paeroa Information Hub. ⊠ *101 Normanby Rd., Paeroa* ☎ *07/862–8636* ⊕ *www.thecoromandel.com.* **Waihi i-SITE**

Visitor Centre. ⊠ *126 Seddon St., Waihi* ☎ *07/863–6715* ⊕ *www.thecoromandel. com.*

👁 Sights

Gold Discovery Centre and Gold Mine Tour
FACTORY | FAMILY | Head underground to this interactive museum explaining the region's gold-mining history. The roof is lined with timbers as if you are in a real mine shaft. You can operate a compressor drill, fire the explosives, learn of the local geology and the role of stamper batteries in extracting gold from rock, and understand the social upheavals of striking miners, unions, and bosses. If you want to see the real thing, take a tour (1½ hours) to Waihi's still-working mine. ⊠ *126 Seddon St., Waihi* ☎ *07/863–9015* ⊕ *www.golddiscoverycentre.co.nz* 🖼 *From NZ$25.*

Goldfields Railway
BRIDGE/TUNNEL | FAMILY | This half-hour, 7-km (4½-mile) heritage-train journey into the Karangahake Gorge follows part of the former Waihi to Paeroa line, built in 1905 after five years of challenging construction in the steep gorge country. The train travels from historic Waihi Railway Station to the Waikino Station Café (with great homemade baking). Travel one-way or return, or bring your bike—from Waikino to Paeroa, the former railway line now forms part of the Hauraki Rail Trail for bikers and walkers. Train reservations are recommended. ⊠ *30 Wrigley St.* ☎ *07/863–9020* ⊕ *www.waihirail.co.nz* 🖼 *From NZ$15.*

Martha Mine
ARCHAEOLOGICAL SITE | In the center of Waihi, gaze in awe into the huge open pit of the Martha Mine, one of the world's most significant gold and silver mines of its time. Since the late 1800s, thousands of miners worked here, extracting 174,000 kilograms of gold and more than a million kilos of silver. Cross the road from the Waihi i-SITE Visitor Information Centre to the Cornish Pumphouse (relocated here) for a glimpse into the pit, and perhaps walk around the Pit Rim Walkway (5 km/3 miles). ⊠ *Seddon St., Waihi.*

🏖 Beaches

Waihi Beach
BEACH—SIGHT | Nineteen km (12 miles) north of Katikati, Waihi Beach is ideal for swimming and surfing, and has access to numerous walkways. With 9 km (5½ miles) of sweeping white sand, the beach is one of the region's safest for swimming, surfing, and kayaking, and is particularly popular in peak summer (January). A surf club offers beach patrols at the beach's northern end and in summer at the far Bowentown end in the south, although you'll find people splashing about all along the long white stretch. At low tide, people dig in the sand looking for *tuatua* and *pipi*—delicious shellfish that you boil until they open. Don't miss the drive to the top of the Bowentown heads at the southern end of Waihi Beach. This is an old Māori *pā* (fortified village) with stunning views. A short but steep walk from here leads to Cave Bay directly below the viewing point. ⚠ **Don't swim at Cave Bay; there are dangerous currents here.** The Waihi Beach township encompasses restaurants and shops, and there is a full range of accommodations, from holiday parks to boutique lodges. **Amenities:** food and drink; lifeguard; toilets; parking; surf school. **Best for:** kayaking; swimming; sunrise; surfing; walking; windsurfing. ⊠ *The Esplanade, Waihi Beach* ⊕ *www. waihibeachinfo.co.nz.*

🍴 Restaurants

Bistro at the Falls Retreat
$$$$ | MODERN NEW ZEALAND | It might be way out in the bush but this restaurant could stand proud in any big city. Dine inside or out, beneath the trees, and

watch the chefs in the open kitchen firing up the wood-fired oven for pizzas or creating contemporary cuisine with organic-farmed beef and lamb and vegetables straight from the garden. **Known for:** spicy chicken pizza (and other pizzas); sharing platters; vegetarian salads. $ Average main: NZ$33 ⊠ 25 Waitawheta Rd., Karangahake Gorge ☎ 07/863–8770 ⊕ www.fallsretreat.co.nz ⊗ Closed Mon. and Tues. Apr.–Oct. (approximately).

Down Thyme Restaurant and Cafe
$$$ | **MEDITERRANEAN** | Mediterranean food and ambience are the focus at this quiet restaurant tucked away on the edge of town. The finest local produce, organic where possible, is sourced, and matched with quality international and local craft beers and wines. **Known for:** homemade ice cream; Angus beef cheeks; Mediterranean-style risottos. $ Average main: NZ$29 ⊠ 31 Orchard Rd. ☎ 07/863–8980 ⊕ www.downthyme.nz ⊗ Closed Mon. No lunch Tues.

The Refinery
$ | **CAFÉ** | Hidden down a side street (look for the sign on the main street), you'll find this gourmet home-cooking surprise. This café gem serves breakfasts, muffins, scones, cakes, and shortcakes alongside build-your-own bagels and counter "sammies" crammed with choices of grilled meats, haloumi (salty cheese of goat and sheep's milk), and vegetables. **Known for:** best bagels in the region; cornbread Reuben grilled sandwiches; historic building. $ Average main: NZ$13 ⊠ 5 Willoughby St., Paeroa ☎ 07/862–7678 ⊕ www.the-refinery.co.nz ⊗ Closed Mon. and Tues.

Hotels

Manawa Ridge
$$$$ | **B&B/INN** | A luxury retreat built with artistic architectural flair to exacting eco-standards (recycled beams, mud brick, and straw bale walls), this lodge stands on a farm ridge top with 360-degree views over the Pacific Ocean and Coromandel. **Pros:** 360-degree farm, forest, and coastal views; hospitable hosts; gourmet breakfasts. **Cons:** 9 km (5½ miles) out of town; no facilities or shops so you're committed to in-house dining; rustic quirkiness may not suit all tastes. $ Rooms from: NZ$950 ⊠ 267 Ngatitangata Rd. ☎ 07/863–9400 ⊕ manawaridge.co.nz ⥲ 3 suites ❤️ Breakfast.

Activities

BICYCLING
★ Hauraki Rail Trail
BICYCLING | FAMILY | Join the Kiwi families discovering this gently graded 160-km (100-mile) bike trail. There are six stages: from Waihi, a 24-km (15-mile) stage follows the old railway line through scenic Karangahake Gorge to Paeroa. Heritage gold-mine sites, bridges, and tunnels are part of the drama, so bring a torch, and call at a country café en-route. You can even ride the Goldfields Railway train along with your bike for the first stretch. From Paeroa the trail crosses Hauraki Plains farmland for 34 km (21 miles) to Thames. The southern 60-km (37-mile) stage includes more farmland riding, south from Paeroa to Te Aroha then the Waikato town of Matamata. Or, from Thames, you can follow the Shorebird Coast around internationally important wetland site the Firth of Thames for 55 km (34 miles) to Miranda. The Hauraki Rail Trail is one of the Nga Haerenga-New Zealand Cycle Trails' "Great Rides." ⊠ Karangahake Gorge ⊕ www.haurakirailtrail. co.nz.

HIKING
Karangahake Gorge Walks
HIKING/WALKING | FAMILY | Rivers, waterfalls, and steep, forest-sided ravines, plus old railway tunnels and gold-mining sites, can all be explored on the walkways in Karangahake Gorge. The trails are well maintained by the Department of Conservation (DOC) and designed to showcase

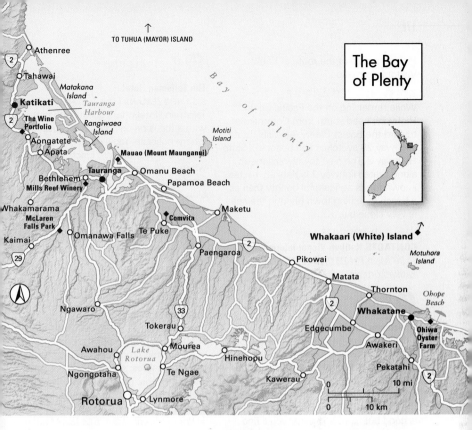

↑
TO TUHUA (MAYOR) ISLAND

The Bay of Plenty

Bay of Plenty

Athenree
Tahawai
Matakana Island
Katikati
The Wine Portfolio
Aongatete
Apata
Tauranga Harbour
Rangiwaea Island
Motiti Island
Mauao (Mount Maunganui)
Tauranga
Omanu Beach
Bethlehem
Mills Reef Winery
Papamoa Beach
Whakamarama
McLaren Falls Park
Omanawa Falls
Te Puke
Comvita
Maketu
Kaimai
29
Paengaroa
Whakaari (White) Island
Motuhora Island
Pikowai
Matata
Thornton
Ohope Beach
Ngawaro
33
Tokerau
Edgecumbe
Whakatane
Ohiwa Oyster Farm
Awahou
Lake Rotorua
Mourea
Hinehopu
Awakeri
Ngongotaha
Te Ngae
Kawerau
Pekatahi
Rotorua
Lynmore

0   10 mi
0   10 km

the best natural and heritage features. Recommended are Rail Tunnel Loop (one hour) and Waikino Historic Walkway (three to four hours, return). Some tracks are shared with bikers on the Hauraki Rail Trail, but there's plenty of room. Look for the large riverside parking lot and DOC signs partway through the gorge, opposite Moresby Road (to tiny Karanga-hake Village). Most tracks begin across a footbridge from here. DOC camping spots and good cafés are also in the area. Pick up a DOC brochure at local i-SITE Visitor Information Centres. ✉ *Karanga-hake* ⊕ *www.doc.govt.nz*.

Katikati

62 km (39 miles) southeast of Thames, 35 km (22 miles) northwest of Tauranga.

The small town of Katikati was founded by Irish Protestant settlers in the 1870s. Long before the Irish arrived, Māori had recognized the area's potential for growing food crops. These days, fruit-growing—particularly kiwifruit and avocado—keeps the Katikati economy afloat, perhaps providing one (of many) explanations for Katikati's name, "to nib-ble" in Māori. Katikati's most noticeable features are more than 50 murals around town, depicting its history. Another inter-esting attraction is the **Haiku Pathway,** a walking trail studded with haiku-etched boulders. The path starts on Katikati's Main Street and leads down to the river.

Pick up a map of the route at Katikati Visitor Information.

GETTING HERE AND AROUND

While remaining on the Pacific Coast Highway, head south from Coromandel toward the Bay of Plenty. At Waihi, State Highway 25 switches and becomes State Highway 2. The next town you'll meet along State Highway 2 is Katikati, better known for its agricultural bounty than as a beach or fishing town (though the sea is very close by).

VISITOR INFORMATION

CONTACTS Katikati Visitor Information.
✉ *36 Main Rd.* ☎ *07/549–1658* ⊕ *www. katikati.org.nz.*

◉ Sights

Lindemann Road Lookout

VIEWPOINT | For great views over the Bay of Plenty, drive a couple of minutes north of Katikati on State Highway 2 to Lindemann Road. The lookout is signposted at the turn off. Drive 3½ km (2 miles) to the road's end and the lookout. The road is good but narrow in parts; you'll find a map embedded in rock to help orient you. If the weather is clear you might see volcanic White Island, to the south. Self-contained campervans can stop here overnight.

The Wine Portfolio

WINERY/DISTILLERY | A handsome, Cape Dutch-style building will probably attract your attention, just south of Katikati on Highway 2. Originally built for Morton Estate Wines, it now houses the cellar door of wine-making business Wine Portfolio. The boutique, specialist winery produces vintages from grapes grown in leading New Zealand wine regions Hawke's Bay and Marlborough. Here's your chance to sample the country's best wines, all in one place. ✉ *2389 Main Rd.* ☎ *07/552–0795* ⊕ *www.wineportfolio. co.nz.*

🍴 Restaurants

The Talisman Hotel

$$$ | NEW ZEALAND | The 1876-built Talisman Hotel offers quality pub fare, with a focus on using local produce where possible. You'll meet the locals here, be it over brunch, lunch, or dinner, where your meal could be anything from crammed-full burgers to chicken cordon bleu. **Known for:** wood-fired pizzas; twice cooked ribs in sticky sauce; impressive wine pairings. ⑤ *Average main: NZ$29* ✉ *7–9 Main Rd., State Hwy. 2* ☎ *07/549–3218* ⊕ *www.talismanhotel.co.nz.*

🛏 Hotels

★ Matahui Lodge

$$$$ | HOTEL | This lodge on 6 acres of manicured gardens and vineyards is an outstanding example of the boutique home-hosted properties popping up in this region. **Pros:** substantial breakfasts; lovely gardens; good wine list. **Cons:** a little far from town for some; some rooms have stair access; books up quickly. ⑤ *Rooms from: NZ$475* ✉ *187 Matahui Rd., 9 km (5½ miles) south of Katikati* ☎ *07/571–8121* ⊕ *www.matahui-lodge. co.nz* ⇄ *3 suites* ❙◎❙ *Breakfast.*

Tauranga

216 km (134 miles) southeast of Auckland.

The population center of the Bay of Plenty, Tauranga is one of New Zealand's fastest-growing cities. Along with neighboring town Whakatane, this seaside city also rates as one of the country's sunniest spots. Unlike most local towns, Tauranga doesn't grind to a halt in the off-season, because it has one of the busiest ports in the country, and the excellent waves at the neighboring beach resort of Mount Maunganui—just across Tauranga's harbor bridge—always draw surfers and holiday folk.

GETTING HERE AND AROUND

Whether you self-drive, catch a bus, or fly, getting to Tauranga is simple. Air New Zealand flies daily from major cities throughout New Zealand to Tauranga Airport. By road, Tauranga is about a 50-minute drive northeast of Rotorua. From Auckland, allow 2½ hours for the drive south. You can travel either on State Highway 2 through the southern Coromandel and northern Bay of Plenty regions (slightly longer but arguably more scenic) or on State Highway 1 to Waikato then State Highway 29, which crosses over the Kaimai Ranges—a steep-ish but scenic drive through farmland and native forest. InterCity buses travel daily to Tauranga from Auckland, Hamilton, and Rotorua. The Tauranga bus depot is in the city center, handy to shops and accommodations.

Once you are here, major and clearly signposted roads lead from Tauranga to coastal resorts, Mount Maunganui and Papamoa, and south through kiwifruit orchard country to Whakatane. A toll expressway bypasses some of these places, for example, Te Puke, should you be in such a hurry on your vacation. Local bus company the Bay Bus (sometimes called the Bay Hopper) travels regularly between Tauranga and regional towns including Mount Maunganui, Te Puke, Katikati, and Whakatane. Activity operators, for example, swim with dolphins, kayaking, fishing, and walking tours, are mostly based in or close to the city and will collect you from your accommodations.

BUS CONTACTS Bay Bus. ☎ 0800/422–928 ⊕ www.baybus.co.nz. **InterCity Tauranga Depot.** ✉ Wharf St. ☎ 07/578–8103 ⊕ www.intercity.co.nz.

VISITOR INFORMATION

CONTACTS Tauranga i-SITE Visitor Information Centre. ✉ 95 Willow St. ☎ 07/578–8103 ⊕ www.bayofplentynz.com.

◉ Sights

To explore the town center, start at **The Strand,** where palm trees separate the shops from the sea. Bars, restaurants, and cafés line The Strand and nearby side streets. If you're interested in the beachier side of Tauranga, head 8 km (5 miles) east out of the city center and over the Harbor Bridge to Mount Maunganui. Here, you'll find one of the best surf spots in the country along the 20-km (12½-mile) shoreline, a sheltered, harborside swimming spot, as well as shopping, restaurants, and walking tracks up and around the prominent, small, and dormant volcano Mauao (Mt. Maunganui or, as locals say, The Mount).

Comvita

STORE/MALL | This company has developed a worldwide following for its honey-based health products and Experience Comvita shows you why. Take a guided tour and interactive 3D experience to learn about the honeybees and the healing properties of native New Zealand plants, in particular the manuka tree. Tours (40 minutes) start at 10, 11, 1, and 2; advanced booking is recommended. You can also relax in their café and explore the retail store, where trained staff will explain the range of health, wellness, and beauty products available. ✉ 23 Wilson Rd., Paengaroa, Te Puke ☎ 07/533–1987, 0800/493–782 ⊕ www.comvita.co.nz ☜ NZ$10 for guided tour.

★ Mauao (Mt. Maunganui)

BEACH—SIGHT | FAMILY | This dormant volcano is the region's visual icon; its rocky cone stands sentinel, 761 feet high at the end of the peninsula that boasts one of New Zealand's best swimming and surfing areas. White-sand beaches with rolling surf stretch for miles away from Mauao. Trails on Mauao include an easy walk around its base and the more strenuous summit climb. To get to Mauao, head toward it along any road running parallel to the beach. The Mount

Maunganui area gets crowded around Christmas and New Year's Eve, so consider early or late summer for your visit or even winter. Beach walks or exploring Mauao is a delight at any time, and the sidewalk cafés are always open.

McLaren Falls Park

BODY OF WATER | FAMILY | Four hundred and ninety-four acres of parkland, alongside a gentle flowing river that tumbles over the small McLaren Falls, make a great spot for a picnic or driving break. Picnic tables, coin-operated barbecues, and toilets are located throughout. Walks include a 10-minute easy bushwalk to the falls and more strenuous walks to look-outs on Pine Tree Knoll or The Ridge. It's located a 15-minute drive south of Tauranga off State Highway 29, one of the main roads into Tauranga. ⊠ *State Hwy. 29* ☎ *07/578–8103.*

Mills Reef Winery

WINERY/DISTILLERY | Mills Reef has built a fine reputation for its award-winning wines and the winery itself is a treat to visit. The spacious, landscaped, 20-acre complex encompasses an art deco–style tasting room and popular restaurant with indoor/outdoor dining. Cellar door staff will guide you through tastings of the winery's favored Bordeaux-style reds, Syrahs, and the highly regarded Elsbeth Range. The 150-seater à la carte restaurant is popular for brunch and lunch, and open occasionally for dinners (check their website). ⊠ *143 Moffat Rd., Bethlehem* ⊹ *About 5 km (3 miles) north of Tauranga* ☎ *07/576–8800* ⊕ *www.millsreef.co.nz* ⊗ *Closed evenings Sun.–Wed.*

Papamoa Hills Regional Park

ARCHAEOLOGICAL SITE | FAMILY | A 45-minute climb through this 108-acre regional park will take you to the summit of a former Māori pā that dates back to 1460. It's one of the earliest archaeological sites in the region. From the parking lot the trail is clearly marked: you climb through pine forest, then open farmland. Stop for the views, if not to catch your breath. The park is a 20-km (12½-mile) drive east of Tauranga (en route to Whakatane). You'll need to get off the tolled Expressway for access. If traveling from Tauranga, take the Papamoa exit then follow the signs indicating free road to Te Puke. Go past Welcome Bay Road then look for Poplar Lane, on the right. The parking lot is at the end of Poplar Lane. ⊠ *Poplar La., Papamoa Hills.*

🍽 Restaurants

Harbourside

$$$$ | MODERN NEW ZEALAND | The food and the view will vie for your attention here, as you dine on contemporary New Zealand cuisine. The menu is created largely from local artisan products, and you can admire Tauranga Harbour from the stunning waterfront location. **Known for:** excellent harbor views; grill menu of local, organic cuts; several duck dishes. ⑤ *Average main: NZ$35* ⊠ *Old Yacht Club Bldg., 150 The Strand* ☎ ⊕ *www.harboursidetauranga.co.nz.*

Love Rosie Bakery

$ | BAKERY | FAMILY | There's a vintage retro feel at this unassuming café that belies the amazing fresh baked goods produced within. Cabinets are crammed with pastries, breads, cakes, panini, and sandwiches and some truly fantastic cakes like the passionfruit curd cake. **Known for:** great coffee; classic Kiwi sausage rolls; local vibe. ⑤ *Average main: NZ$12* ⊠ *50 9th Ave.* ☎ *07/928–1112.*

Macau Restaurant and Lounge

$$$ | ASIAN FUSION | Fresh flavors right from Asia are blended with the best of local New Zealand meats, seafood, and vegetables at this popular-with-the-locals waterfront eatery. As with current restaurant trends, small plates are made for sharing, so you can enjoy a blast of flavors and just keep ordering until you're full. **Known for:** crying tiger grilled beef sirloin; steamed buns, spring rolls, and dumplings; banquet-style menu options.

$ *Average main: NZ$27* ⊠ *59 The Strand* ☎ *07/578–8717* ⊕ *www.dinemacau. co.nz.*

Mount Bistro

$$$$ | **NEW ZEALAND** | The high prices set this restaurant apart from other local options, but then again so does the chef. In the open-plan kitchen nationally renowned chef Stephen Barry fuses quality indigenous meats, seafood, and produce with Pacific Rim flavors. À la carte menu choices range from small tapas to share and appetizers (which can be requested as slightly larger mains) to main courses. **Known for:** signature flambé seafood dish; multicourse degustation menu; dessert tasting platter. $ *Average main: NZ$325* ⊠ *6 Adams Ave., Mount Maunganui* ☎ *07/575–3872* ⊕ *www.mountbistro.nz* ⊗ *Closed Mon. No lunch.*

Postbank Restaurant and Bar

$$$$ | **MODERN NEW ZEALAND** | The modern fusion menu here is described like they are chapters: a nod to the quiet, library theme of this stylish eatery in the historic Postbank building. Undoubtedly one of the resort town's premier dining experiences, the "chapters" blend Mediterranean and Asian influences with top New Zealand produce. **Known for:** good wine list; marinated Ora king salmon; reservations required. $ *Average main: NZ$36* ⊠ *82 Maunganui Rd.* ☎ *07/575–4782* ⊕ *www.postbank.co.nz* ⊗ *Closed Sun. No lunch Sat.–Thurs.*

Sidetrack Cafe

$ | **CAFÉ** | At the base of Mauao and across the street from the beach, this bustling café is a great place for breakfast or lunch after a climb or swim. Grab a table (there are more outside than in) for a blueberry muffin, blue cheese scone, a falafel, a salad, or a dense chocolate brownie. **Known for:** tasty muffins and pies; smoothies to go; excellent coffee. $ *Average main: NZ$12* ⊠ *Shop 3, Marine Parade, Mount Maunganui* ☎ *07/575–2145* ⊗ *No dinner.*

🛏 Hotels

Harbour City Motor Inn

$$ | **HOTEL** | This bright modern inn features spacious self-contained studio and one-bedroom units. **Pros:** central location; units have cooking facilities; bathrooms have spa baths. **Cons:** built around a parking lot; no outdoor spaces; basic design. $ *Rooms from: NZ$190* ⊠ *50 Wharf St.* ☎ *07/571–1435* ⊕ *www.taurangaharbourcity.co.nz* ⇥ *20 rooms.*

Hotel on Devonport

$$$$ | **HOTEL** | This luxurious hotel in central Tauranga has earth-toned guest rooms that look out either over the city or the harbor. **Pros:** smart design; modern architecture; access to the adjacent private members' club. **Cons:** slightly impersonal vibe; not all rooms have sea views; secure parking lot costs extra and must be booked in advance. $ *Rooms from: NZ$460* ⊠ *72 Devonport Rd.* ☎ *07/578–2668* ⊕ *www.hotelondevonport.net.nz* ⇥ *38 rooms* ⦿ *Breakfast.*

Papamoa Beach Resort

$$ | **RESORT** | **FAMILY** | This resort complex has the widest range of accommodations in the area, and they're all on the beach, about a 10-minute drive from the Mount Maunganui crowds. **Pros:** spacious rooms; affordable options; on the beach. **Cons:** gets busy over summer; can be noisy; range of accommodation can be confusing (just choose beachside). $ *Rooms from: NZ$155* ⊠ *535 Papamoa Beach Rd.* ☎ *07/572–0816, 0800/461–222* ⊕ *www.papamoabeach.co.nz* ⇥ *38 units* ⦿ *No meals.*

Trinity Wharf

$$$ | **HOTEL** | Perched over the edge of Tauranga Harbour, this is one of the city's higher-end hotels. **Pros:** fantastic views; comfortable, spacious rooms; handy location not far from airport. **Cons:** 10-minute walk into the city center; some rooms have parking-lot views; traffic noise. $ *Rooms from: NZ$250* ⊠ *51 Dive*

For a relaxing swim, take a dip in the saltwater pools at Mount Hot Pools.

Crescent ☎ 07/577–8700 ⊕ www.trinity-wharf.co.nz ➪ 120 rooms ⧫Ol No meals.

🏃 Activities

Surfing, swimming, kayaking, dolphin watching, fishing, big-game fishing—yes, it's mostly on the water that visitors (and locals) enjoy the outdoors around here. There are great short walks around estuaries and to great viewpoints.

HELICOPTER TOURS
Aerius Helicopters
TOUR—SPORTS | If you think this is a scenic place on the ground, take in the view from a helicopter. Aerius are the local scenic flight specialists; they'll buzz you up and around Mauo (Mt. Maunganui), over the Papamoa Hills (historic Māori fortification sites and kiwifruit country), above the beaches, out to the dramatic active volcanic White Island (landings are optional), or across to Rotorua and its stunning forest-fringed lakes and Mt. Tarawera volcano. Flights leave from Tauranga Airport, Hangar 5. ⊠ Jean Batten Dr., Tauranga Airport ☎ 0800/864–354 ⊕ www.aerius.co.nz ✈ From NZ$115; prices quoted from Tauranga.

KAYAKING
★ **Waimarino Glowworm Kayaking**
KAYAKING | For an excellent regional experience, paddle into the night to a magical canyon filled with the lights of thousands of tiny glowworms. You don't need kayaking expertise; after a taste of local wines and cheeses at dusk, you'll be guided on a gentle, two-hour paddle across Lake McLaren to the glowworms. Floating in the dark and the silence (everyone has to be quiet or the glowworms "turn off") is quite something. Tours last about 3½ hours and include 15-minute shuttles to the lake from Waimarino Adventure Park. Times change as the evenings draw out; check the website. ⊠ 36 Taniwha Pl., Wairoa River, Bethlehem ☎ 07/576–4233 ⊕ www.waimarino.com ✈ From NZ$130.

SURFING
Hibiscus Surf School
SURFING | **FAMILY** | Where better to learn to surf than on one of New Zealand's

premier surfing beaches? These dudes reckon that by the end of your first two-hour lesson, you'll actually be riding the waves. They take care of everyone, from beginner to advanced, from daily lessons to multiday packages; they also rent surfboards, paddleboards, and any other gear you need. They're on Mount Maunganui's Main Beach—look for the red Hibiscus surf trailer parked across from Leisure (Moturiki) Island. ⊠ *Main Beach, Mt. Maunganui* ☎ *027/279–9687* ⊕ *surfschool.co.nz* ✉ *From NZ$75.*

SWIMMING

Mount Hot Pools

LOCAL SPORTS | FAMILY | Heated saltwater bathing is reputed to be a great healer, and these pools offer just that, nestled beneath Mauao, Mt. Maunganui. The complex includes a cooler pool with marked lanes for anyone who wants some serious exercise, but most visitors prefer to soak in the hotter saltwater pools. The four pressure water spouts are fun, too; if that's not enough, book a session with one of the in-house massage therapists. There's also a slightly not-so-hot pool for the kids ⊠ *9 Adams Ave.* ☎ *07/577–8551* ⊕ *www.mounthotpools.co.nz* ✉ *NZ$15.*

SWIMMING WITH DOLPHINS

Swimming with dolphins is a big summer activity in the Bay of Plenty. Most cruises leave from the Tauranga Bridge Marina. Advanced booking is essential and should be arranged at least one day prior. The Department of Conservation licenses and regularly inspects operators and sets limits on the number of boats allowed around any pod of dolphins.

Dolphin Blue

WILDLIFE-WATCHING | Aside from the dolphins, a highlight here is the classic, 54-foot wooden launch you sail in. It makes a comfortable trip into the open waters where the dolphins play. Trips run from 8:30 am to about 4 pm, for small groups of up to 15. There's a "swim rope" for you to hold in the water while the dolphins dart around you. They also have kayaks on board, and might pull into a sheltered spot for a paddle while waiting for dolphins to show. Skipper Paul knows a few things about marine mammals, but if none are spotted you can return for free. The season runs from December to March. ⊠ *Pier 3, Sulphur Point Marina, Keith Allen Dr.* ☎ *027/666–8047* ⊕ *www.dolphinblue.co.nz* ✉ *NZ$150.*

Dolphin Seafaris

LOCAL SPORTS | A completely wild and natural encounter on a purpose-built dolphin-viewing vessel is what you'll get with this company. All guides are qualified marine biologists so you'll be educated, too, and there's a chance of seeing other marine mammals (orcas perhaps) as well as dolphins. Strict rules mean all encounters are on the dolphins' terms, but guests do get to swim with them 85% of the time. Wet suits and snorkels are provided. Trips leave 8 am and return around 1 pm. Be sure to book ahead of time. The season runs from November to April. ⊠ *Berth D1, Tauranga Bridge Marina* ☎ *07/577–0105, 0800/326–8747* ⊕ *www.nzdolphin.com* ✉ *NZ$150.*

Whakatane

100 km (62 miles) southeast of Tauranga.

For yet another chance to laze in the summer haze, Whakatane (fah-kah- *tah*-ne) is regularly rated as the North Island's sunniest town. The harbor here was a landfall site of *Mataatua,* one of the first migratory Māori canoes, and the fertile hinterland was among the first areas of the country to be farmed.

GETTING HERE AND AROUND

Whakatane is an easy one-hour drive down the Tauranga Eastern Link Expressway from Tauranga (NZ$2 toll) or, if you want to see more attractions, about 1½ hours on the old SH2. Whichever you choose you'll travel along a spectacular stretch of coast. Keep your eyes on the road—it's easy to lapse when you've got such spectacular ocean scenery.

BUS DEPOT InterCity Whakatane Depot.
⊠ *Quay and Kakahoroa Sts.* ☎ *0800/942–528* ⊕ *www.intercity.co.nz.*

VISITOR INFORMATION

CONTACTS Whakatane i-SITE Visitor Information Centre. ⊠ *Quay and Kakahoroa Sts., on the Strand* ☎ *07/306–2030, 0800/942–528* ⊕ *www.whakatane.com.*

◉ Sights

★ Mataatua Māori Marae

BUILDING | Mataatua, one of the most beautiful carved *wharenui* (meetinghouses) in Māoridom, endured a 130-year-long indignity; it was dismantled, carted to museums around New Zealand, Australia, and England, and rebuilt in various forms. In 2011 the house was returned home to the local Ngāti Awa people and restored. For a truly enriching cultural experience, let these people host you, explain their protocols, and share their history (including song, chants, and an outstanding light show). They'll also take you for a short coastal walk, tell the story of their ancestors, and show you where they first landed in Aotearoa, New Zealand. ⊠ *105 Muriwai Dr.* ☎ *07/308–4271* ⊕ *www.mataatua.com* 🖂 *From NZ$49.*

Ohiwa Oyster Farm

LOCAL INTEREST | Just beyond Ohope, following Wainui Road around the huge Ohiwa Harbour, it's not uncommon to see locals (plus the prolific number of resident wading birds) out on the mudflats harvesting oysters for dinner. The Ohiwa Oyster Farm grows its own oysters and smokes a variety of fish. They serve it all up takeaway style from a humble little kitchen/hut. The harborside picnic tables are a lovely setting for enjoying these tasty morsels. ⊠ *Wainui Rd., Ohope.*

Whakatane Observatory

OBSERVATORY | If you've a hankering to see the stars from an antipodean perspective, check out the Whakatane Observatory, up on a hill above the town. With no city lights to obscure the view, the skies here rate among the clearest in the country. Showings are obviously weather dependent, however on a good night you will see in stark clarity sights such as the "jewel box," a cluster of multicolor stars near the Southern Cross. Nighttime presentations are informal and informative, led by local astrologer Norm Izett. ⊠ *Hurinui Ave.* ☎ *07/308–6495* 🖂 *NZ$15.*

◉ Beaches

★ Ohope Beach

BEACH—SIGHT | FAMILY | The region's most popular and safest swimming beach is the 11-km (7-mile) laid-back Ohope, just a 10-minute drive east of Whakatane. Pohutukawa Avenue, Ohope's main road, runs parallel to the beach, flanked by native pohutukawa trees, private homes, and grazing cows. You can stay in the Top 10 Holiday Park or choose from a range of holiday homes and B&Bs. There's lots to do here: fishing off the beach, surfing, and walking the Kohi Point coastal walk are just a few options. **Amenities**: food and drink; toilets; lifeguards; parking (free). **Best for:** surfing; swimming; walking. ⊠ *Pohutukawa Ave.* ⊕ *www.ohopebeach.info.*

◉ Restaurants

Babinka Restaurant and Bar

$$ | SRI LANKAN | A delightful blend of cuisines can be found here, from authentic curries from Sri Lanka and India to modern New Zealand classics, including seafood specialties and quality steaks. There's also a breakfast menu, and local and imported beers and wines from the bar. **Known for:** refreshing mango lassi; relaxed ambience; house-baked desserts.

$ Average main: NZ$20 ⊠ 62 The Strand ☎ 07/307–0009 ⊕ www.babinka.co.nz ⊘ Closed 2–5 ▭ No credit cards.

The Bean Cafe and Roastery

$ | CAFÉ | Mellow jazz might be playing in the background, local art graces the walls, and the retro couches and armchairs are a great spot to chill out and enjoy a coffee, which is freshly roasted every day in the café. Snack options include bagels with any filling you desire, egg and bacon rolls, sandwiches, cakes, and slices. **Known for:** in-house coffee roasting; quirky and arty decor; excellent bagels. $ Average main: NZ$14 ⊠ 72 The Strand ☎ 07/307–0494 ⊕ www.thebean-cafe.co.nz ⊘ No dinner.

White Island Café

$ | NEW ZEALAND | Based at White Island Tours, this place specializes in breakfast and lunch. The café opens up early (6:30 am) so if you're preparing for a trip out to White Island, nab a table on the deck to get a glimpse of your destination (weather-permitting), and then fuel up with a hearty Kiwi breakfast or some fresh-baked pastries. **Known for:** great coffee; selection of egg dishes; tasty scones. $ Average main: NZ$15 ⊠ 15 The Strand E ☎ 07/308–9588, 0800/733–529 ⊕ www.whiteisland.co.nz ⊘ No dinner.

🛏 Hotels

Moanarua Beach Cottage

$$ | B&B/INN | Hosts Miria and Taroi Black provide true Māori *manaakitanga* (hospitality) and a cultural homestay experience. **Pros:** welcoming, relaxed environment; close to beach; kayaks available to rent. **Cons:** not luxurious; may be too far off-the-beaten-track for some; minimum two-night stay December–April. $ Rooms from: NZ$180 ⊠ 2 Hoterini St., Ohope Beach ☎ 07/312–5924 ⊕ www.moanarua.co.nz ↪ 2 rooms ❍ Breakfast.

White Island Rendezvous

$$ | HOTEL | Convenient if you're heading out to White Island, this motel, run by the

owners of White Island Tours, is across the road from the marina and within walking distance of town. **Pros:** friendly hosts; clean and relaxed; café on-site. **Cons:** seagulls can be noisy; thin walls in units and loud plumbing; one room upstairs with no elevator. $ Rooms from: NZ$150 ⊠ 15 The Strand E ☎ 07/308–9588, 0800/242–299 ⊕ www.whiteislan-drendezvous.co.nz ↪ 27 rooms.

🏃 Activities

Fishing, diving, and swimming with dolphins and seals are popular activities in the Whakatane area. The water surrounding White Island and Whale Island has some great dive sites, with volcanic formations and abundant marine life. Moutohora (Whale Island) sanctuary is home to many endangered native species.

DOLPHIN- AND SEAL-WATCHING

Dolphin and Seal Encounters

WILDLIFE-WATCHING | FAMILY | For closer encounters of the mammalian kind, these local experts take you on a three- to four-hour cruise from Whakatane Wharf. First you'll check out the dolphins (they give a 97% success rate of finding them), then you'll head to Whale Island where the seals might jump off the rocks and swim out to meet you. Wet suits and snorkels for swimming with the dolphins and seals are provided, or you can just watch. From November through March, cruises run twice daily, usually from 8:30 am or 1:30 pm, weather and passenger numbers permitting. ⊠ 96 The Strand ☎ 0800/354–7737, 07/308–2001 ⊕ www.diveworks-charters.com ➿ From NZ$130.

FISHING AND DIVING

Diveworks

FISHING | FAMILY | Offering specialist diving and fishing trips, Diveworks has an afternoon fishing venture that is especially suited to families. Rods, bait, and filleting the fish you might catch are all included. There's also a full-day option for chasing game fish that includes a White Island experience. Dive trips include a full day exploring the unique volcanic features and teeming marine life around White Island, and a half day closer to shore, around Whale Island. ⊠ *The Strand* ☎ *07/308–2001, 0800/354–7737* ⊕ *www. diveworks-charters.com* ⊠ *From NZ$90.*

HIKING

Hiking Trails

HIKING/WALKING | The native forest reserves around Whakatane provide a range of bushwalks and hiking trails. The 6-km (4-mile) walkway called *Nga Tapuwae o Toi* ("the footprints of Toi") is named for a descendant of Tiwakawaka, one of the first Māori to settle in New Zealand. In total it takes about four hours, and it's also divided into eight shorter walks that take you past historic pā (fortified village) sites, along the coastline and the Whakatane River, around Kohi Point (which separates Whakatane from Ohope), and through the Ohope and Makaroa Bush Scenic Reserves. These shorter sections range from one to three hours. No guide is necessary, and the i-SITE visitor information center in Whakatane stocks free trail maps. The main trailhead starts from Canning Place, behind the Whakatane Hotel on the corner of George Street and the Strand. Follow the steps up the cliff and you'll be at the beginning of the trail. For an easier wander (30 minutes round-trip), start at the west end of Ohope Beach and head over to Otarawairere, a delightful secluded cove. ■TIP→ **Some trail crossings depend on the tidal schedule, so be sure to check low-tide times or you might end up swimming across.** ⊠ *Canning Pl., Whakatane* ⊕ *www.doc.govt.nz.*

Whale Island (Moutohorā) Sanctuary Tours

WILDLIFE-WATCHING | FAMILY | Cruise to this island wildlife reserve, home of endangered species such as kiwi, saddleback, parakeet, and *tuatara.* Your skipper, Phil van Dusschoten, has been a stalwart of the restoration program on Moutohora

(Whale Island), just off shore of Whakatane, for 25 years. Let him share his knowledge as he guides you over the gentle island trails. You'll need to check your bags first, to ensure you're not carrying any sneaky, egg-eating pests, such as rats or mice. Tours (4–5 hours) run on Sunday or other days by demand; call to schedule a cruise. ⊠ *96 The Strand* ☎ *0800/354–7737, 07/308–2001* ⊕ *www. whaleislandtours.com* ⊠ *NZ$120.*

Whakaari (White) Island

49 km (29 miles) off the coast of Whakatane.

With its billowing plumes of steam, the active volcano of Whakaari (White) Island makes for an awesome geothermal experience. The island is New Zealand's only active marine volcano—and New Zealand's most active volcano overall. The last major eruption was in 2012, and steam issues continuously from the many fumaroles (vents) and from the central crater, and the area reeks of sulfur. The island itself is eerie but exquisite, with fluorescent sulfuric crystal formations and boiling mud pools.

TOURS

From Whakatane or Tauranga, you can fly over the island on a fixed-wing plane or land there by helicopter; however, the least expensive way to get there is by boat. As a bonus, you might see dolphins, seals, and even a whale en route.

Kāhu Helicopters

GUIDED TOURS | Kāhu Helicopters fly direct from Whakatane to White Island (20 minutes), circle the island for an amazing aerial perspective, then land. You'll get a one-hour walking tour to see the scarily steamy crater and check the remains of an old sulfur factory, then fly back, away from the sulfuric atmosphere. Advanced booking is essential. ⊠ *216 Aerodrome Rd., Whakatane Airport, Whakatane* ☎ *0800/804–354, 07/308–4188* ⊕ *www.*

whiteislandvolcano.co.nz ✉ *NZ$695 per person (minimum of 2).*

White Island Flights

AIR EXCURSIONS | Take a close look at the steaming island volcano from a safe distance. This company flies fixed-wing aircraft to and over the island and its crater (they can't land). It's an option to consider if the weather is too rough for the boat trip. Flights last one hour, or you could, while you're up in the air, book a double whammy and buzz across to see the chasm of Mt. Tarawera. This volcano, near Rotorua, famously erupted in 1886, burying nearby Māori settlements. ☎ *0800/944–834* ⊕ *www.whiteisland-flights.co.nz* ✉ *From NZ$249.*

White Island Tours

GUIDED TOURS | Jump aboard with the local *iwi* (tribe), the only operators licensed to take people by boat to Whakaari/White Island. The boat trip is about 80 minutes each way (look for dolphins) and island time is up to an hour-and-a-half. You'll be guided to the rim of the sulfurous steaming crater, then through the remains of a sulfur mine. Trips run daily, weather permitting, and leave at 8 am (depending on the tides). Be sure to book in advance. ✉ *15 The Strand E, Whakatane* ☎ *07/308–9588, 0800/733–529 Freephone in New Zealand* ⊕ *www.whiteisland.co.nz* ✉ *NZ$229 per person.*

Chapter 6

EAST COAST AND THE VOLCANIC ZONE

6

Updated by
Richard Pamatatu

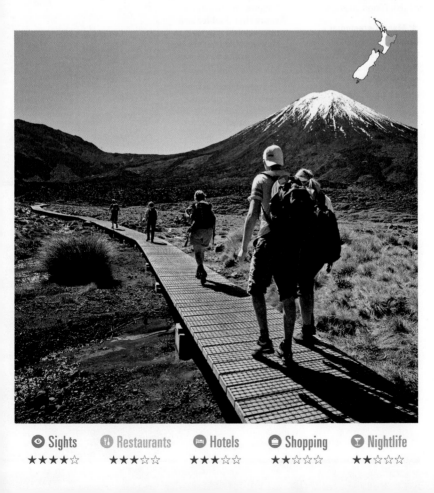

👁 **Sights**
★★★★☆

🍴 **Restaurants**
★★★☆☆

🛏 **Hotels**
★★★☆☆

🛍 **Shopping**
★★☆☆☆

🍸 **Nightlife**
★★☆☆☆

WELCOME TO EAST COAST AND THE VOLCANIC ZONE

TOP REASONS TO GO

★ **Hiking and Walking:** Central North Island has great trails, including the famed Tongariro Alpine Crossing in Tongariro National Park (which stood in for Mordor in the Lord of the Rings movies).

★ **Māori Ceremonial Feasts:** Rotorua may be the best place in New Zealand to indulge in the traditional Māori feast known as a hāngi.

★ **Soaking:** In Rotorua and Taupo, thermal springs are on tap. Soak in your own thermal bath in some Rotorua lodgings or take advantage of public facilities like the Polynesian Spa.

★ **The Shire:** Fans of the Lord of the Rings and The Hobbit movies should make their way to one of New Zealand's most popular tourist attractions: Hobbiton, the movie set that brought the famed hobbits' home to life.

★ **Fishing:** Central North Island is trout country. Local guides know the best spots to nab a catch.

1 Rotorua. A geothermic wonderland and one of the world's first spa towns.

2 Nearby Rotorua. Gorgeous countryside filled with Māori history and a little place called Hobbiton.

3 Taupo. A town on Lake Taupo's northeastern shore that doubles as a major outdoor activities center and one of the best places in the world for rainbow-trout fishing.

4 Tongariro National Park. Three volcanic peaks dominate the oldest and most popular national park in New Zealand.

5 Napier. A coastal city that was devastated by an earthquake in 1931 and rebuilt in colorful art-deco style.

6 Hawke's Bay. A popular vacation area and producer of some of the country's best wines.

7 Gisborne. A mostly quiet, rural place with undiscovered wineries and some important New Zealand history.

8 Te Urewere National Park. A rugged and remote park, with the biggest area of native forest on the North Island.

White Island

Motiti
Island

Cape Runaway   Midway Point

Hicks Bay

Bay of Plenty

35

Te Araroa

Maketu

Te Kaha

Te Puke

Motuhora
Island

Omaio

Tikitiki

Thornton

Whakatane

Ruatoria

Torere

Aorangi   Whareponga

30

Opotiki

Kutarere

Kawerau

Pekatahi

Waioeka

RAUKUMARA RANGE

Waipiro

Toatoa

Te Puia

Lake
Tarawera

Matahi

Oponae

Motu

Tokomaru
Bay

EASTLAND

Waiotapu

Galatea

Matawai

35

Mangatuna

38

Murupara

Rakauroa

Tolaga Bay

Te Whaiti

Te Karaka

8

Hexton   Whangara

Te Urewera
National Park

Manutuke

7

HUIARAU RANGE

Gisborne

Tiniroto

Rangitaiki

Tuai

38

Omahanui

Te Reinga

South Pacific Ocean

5

Pohokura

Marumaru

Tarawera

Rangiahua

Frasertown

2

Ohinepaka

Te Haroto

Wairoa

Nuhaka

2

Waihua

Oraka Beach

Te Pohue

Tutira

Table Cape

Long Point   MAHIA
PENINSULA

Tangoio

Hawke
Bay

Portland Island

Hawke's Bay

6

Rissington

Bay View

Otamauri

5

Napier

Matapiro

Omahu

2

Kereru

50

Hastings

Tikokino

0   20 mi

0   20 km

When you get to Rotorua, after a trip through the rolling, sheep-speckled fields of the Waikato and the wild Mamaku Ranges, the aptly named "Sulfur City"— with its mud pots, geysers, and stinky air—comes as a complete surprise. Rotorua, the mid-island's major city and Māori hub, has been a tourist magnet since the 19th century, when Europeans first heard of the healing powers of local hot springs.

South of Rotorua is the small town of Taupo; it stands alongside the lake of the same name (Australasia's largest) and is the geographical bull's-eye of the North Island. From the lake, you'll have a clear shot at Ruapehu, the island's tallest peak and a top ski area, and its symmetrically cone-shape neighbor, Ngauruhoe. Ruapehu dominates Tongariro National Park, a haunting landscape of craters, volcanoes, and lava flows that ran with molten rock as recently as 1988. As part of the Pacific Ring of Fire (a zone that's earthquake- and volcanic-eruption prone), the area's thermal features remain an ever-present hazard—and a thrilling attraction.

Southeast of Lake Taupo lies Hawke's Bay and the laid-back art deco town of Napier. Laze the days away drinking at the local vineyards or, to truly get off the beaten path, head north to Gisborne; it's the easygoing center of isolated Eastland, the thick thumb of land that's east of Rotorua.

Covering some of the most splendid natural areas in the country, this region lies to the northeast of the North Island. The main towns are busy despite being connected by isolated roads that wind across mountain ranges through vast areas of bush. Expect steaming thermal regions, rolling farmland, or peaceful sun-drenched vineyards.

MAJOR REGIONS
The Rotorua Area. Home of geothermal unrest and oddities, Rotorua today is almost entirely a product of the late 19th-century fad for spa towns; its elaborate bathhouses and formal gardens date to this era. You'll find surreal wonders that include limestone caverns, volcanic wastelands, steaming geysers, and bubbling ponds. Nearby Māori communities offer a fascinating look into the region's most ancient living history as well as beautiful natural landscapes. The area is also where you can most easily access one of the world's most unique landscapes of all: the hobbits' Shire; you can

find it within Hobbiton, the former movie set where many scenes from the *Lord of the Rings* movies were filmed.

Lake Taupo and Tongariro National Park. Fishing and water sports are popular activities in Lake Taupo, New Zealand's largest lake, and on the rivers running into it. The area also has its share of geothermal features. The town of Taupo is the best base for exploring the lake area while Tongariro National Park, dominated by three volcanic peaks, has some great otherworldly hiking trails.

Napier and Hawke's Bay. On the shores of Hawke Bay (Hawke Bay is the body of water, Hawke's Bay is the region), you'll find a fabulous architectural anomaly: the town of Napier, a time capsule of colorful art deco architecture. The countryside here is thick with vineyards, as this is one of the country's major wine-producing areas.

Gisborne and Eastland. Traveling to Eastland takes you well away from the tourist track in the North Island. Once here, you will find rugged coastline, beaches, dense forests, gentle nature trails, and small, predominantly Māori communities. Gisborne is the area's largest town. Above it juts the largely agricultural East Cape, a sparsely populated area ringed with stunning beaches; inland lies the haunting beauty of Te Urewera National Park.

Planning

When to Go

November through mid-April is the best time to visit Central and Eastern North Island. The weather is generally balmy and everything is open. This is also the season for vineyard festivals, so keep an eye on local calendars. Try to avoid the school holidays (from mid-December to late January), when the roads and hotels get clogged with Kiwi vacationers. To see the gannet colony at Cape Kidnappers, you need to go between October and April, when the birds are nesting and raising their young.

Hawke's Bay and Gisborne can be remarkably mild in winter; Rotorua and Taupo, however, can get quite cold and wet. If you want to do some skiing, you can hit the slopes of Tongariro National Park from June through October, but you will be competing with families if you are there during the school break.

Getting Here and Around

AIR TRAVEL

Air New Zealand offers daily direct flights from Wellington, Auckland, and Christchurch to Napier and Rotorua; direct flights from Wellington and Auckland also land in Gisborne. Budget carrier **Jetstar** serves Napier with direct flights from Auckland.

CONTACTS Air New Zealand.
☎ *0800/737–000* ⊕ *www.airnewzealand. co.nz* **Jetstar.** ☎ *0800/800–995* ⊕ *www. jetstar.com.*

BUS TRAVEL

InterCity provides regular bus service for the entire region. Comfortable, reasonably priced, and efficient, it's particularly useful to backpackers and people who are in no particular hurry. The Napier-to-Auckland trip takes 8 hours, Napier–Rotorua is 3½ hours, Napier–Taupo is 2¼ hours, and Napier–Wellington is 6 hours. Frequent local services go between Napier and Hastings. There's also a daily bus to Gisborne from either Auckland, via Rotorua, or from Wellington, via Napier.

CONTACTS InterCity. ☎ *07/348–0366* ⊕ *www.intercity.co.nz.*

CAR TRAVEL

The best way to travel in this region is by car. Rotorua is about three hours from Auckland (could be more than four if you leave Auckland during the rush hour or if there is a motorway holdup). Take Highway 1 south past Hamilton and Cambridge to Tirau, where Highway 5 breaks off to Rotorua. Roads in this region are generally in good condition.

The main route between Napier and the north is Highway 5. Driving time from Taupo is two hours, five if you're coming straight from Auckland. Highway 2 is the main route heading south; it connects Hastings and Napier; from Wellington, driving time is 4½ hours to the former, 5 hours to the latter.

The most direct route from the north to Gisborne is to follow State Highway 2 around the Bay of Plenty to Opotiki, Eastland's northern gateway, then continue to Gisborne through the Waioeka Gorge Scenic Reserve. The drive from Auckland to Gisborne takes seven hours. South from Gisborne, continuing on Highway 2, you pass through Wairoa, about 90 minutes away, before passing Napier, Hawke's Bay, and Wairarapa on the way to Wellington.

TRAIN TRAVEL
Northern Explorer, a scenic 10-hour train connecting Auckland and Wellington, stops at National Park Village and Ohakune. The journey from Wellington passes over five high viaducts. The train from Auckland goes around the remarkable Raurimu Spiral, where the track rises 660 feet in a stretch only 6 km (3½ miles) long.

CONTACTS Northern Explorer.
☎ *0800/872–467* ⊕ *www.kiwirailscenic. co.nz.*

Planning Your Time

Start in Rotorua and then head down to Taupo and the National Park region. If fishing is your game, stop at Turangi. Napier and Hastings, with Hawke's Bay, is an area not to be missed. Prepare for a lengthy drive to Gisborne and the East Cape, and if you have the time (allow for 2½ hours each way and don't forget to fill the tank in Wairoa), take the rugged side road to Lake Waikaremoana. Make sure to save one day for a quick trip to visit Hobbiton, outside of Rotorua.

North Island's East Coast and volcanic zone include some of the country's most popular attractions. Plenty of excellent tours and bus routes hit most highlights, but having your own vehicle gives you the flexibility to seek out an untrammeled scenic spot or that lesser-known-but-outstanding winery.

Information centers known as i-SITEs are found throughout the region. They supply free information and brochures on where to go and how to get there, available accommodations, car rentals, bus services, restaurants, and tourist venues. The centers often serve as bus and tour stops, too.

Restaurants

Rotorua has the area's most diverse dining scene. You can order anything from Indian to Japanese fare, or, for true local flavor, try a Māori *hāngi* (a traditional meal cooked in an earth oven or over a steam vent). Hawke's Bay is another hot spot; its winery restaurants emphasize sophisticated preparations and food-and-wine pairings. Around Eastland, which is so laid-back it's nearly horizontal, the choices are simpler, and you'll be treated with the area's characteristic friendliness. One thing you won't find on any menu is fresh trout. Laws prohibit selling this fish, but if you catch a trout, chefs at most lodging establishments will cook it for you.

Dressing up for dinner, or any other meal, is a rarity, expected at only the most high-end lodges and restaurants.

Hotels

Accommodations range from superexpensive lodges to multistory hotels and budget motels. Bed-and-breakfast establishments—whether in town centers or in the depths of the countryside where you can succumb to the silence, curl up and read a book, or cast a fly in a quiet stream—are another excellent option.

Rotorua has lodgings in all price ranges. If you're willing to stay out of the town center, you can find bargain rates virtually year-round. In both Rotorua and Taupo, many hotels and motels give significant discounts on their standard rates off-season, from June through September. For stays during the school holidays in December and January, book well in advance. Also note that peak season in Tongariro National Park and other ski areas is winter (June–September); summer visitors can usually find empty beds and good deals. Many places, even the fanciest lodges, don't have air-conditioning, as the weather doesn't call for it.

Restaurant and hotel reviews have been shortened. For full information, visit Fodors.com. Restaurant prices are the average cost of a main course at dinner or, if dinner is not served, at lunch. Hotel prices are the lowest cost of a standard double room in high season.

What It Costs

$	$$	$$$	$$$$
RESTAURANTS			
under NZ$15	NZ$15–NZ$20	NZ$21–NZ$30	over NZ$30
HOTELS			
under NZ$125	NZ$125–NZ$200	NZ$201–NZ$300	over NZ$300

Rotorua

Visitors tend to have a love-hate relationship with Rotorua (ro-to-roo-ah). Millions of them—both from New Zealand and abroad—flock in each year, sometimes embracing and sometimes ignoring the unashamedly touristy vibe that has earned it the nickname Rotovegas. In either case, there's no denying that Rotorua has long capitalized on nature's gifts. After all, the influx is nothing new. The "Great South Seas Spa," as the city was once known, ranks among the country's oldest tourism ventures and has been luring vacationers since the late 19th century.

Rotorua's Māori community traces its ancestry to the great Polynesian migration of the 14th century through the Arawa tribe, whose ancestral home is Mokoia Island in Lake Rotorua. The whole area is steeped in Māori history and legend—for hundreds of years, they have settled by the lake and harnessed the geological phenomena, cooking and bathing in the hotpools. Today there are still many places where you can soak in the naturally heated water—and soak up the traditional Māori atmosphere.

Whakarewarewa, at the southern end of Tryon Street, is the most accessible of these and also the most varied. Whaka, as the locals call it, has two parts (the Living Thermal Village and Te Puia), both of which give firsthand exposure to the hotpools and Māori culture. The community was founded by people who moved here from Te Wairoa after the eruption in 1886.

GETTING HERE AND AROUND

Air New Zealand runs daily direct flights from Wellington, Auckland, and Christchurch to the Rotorua Regional Airport (ROT). It's located 10 km (6 miles) from the city center on Highway 33. Taxi fare into the city is NZ$25 to NZ$30. You could also arrange for a ride (NZ$26)

The Rotorua Area

with Super Shuttle; call ahead for a reservation.

In regular traffic, you can drive here from Auckland in about 3 hours; it will take about 5½ to come from Wellington. If you don't have your own vehicle, InterCity provides long-distance bus service.

The city itself is easy to navigate as streets follow a neat grid pattern. Entering Rotorua from Taupo, Fenton Street (the wide main drag) starts around Whakarewarewa. For about 3 km (2 miles), it's lined with lodgings until just before it reaches the lakefront, where shops and restaurants dominate. The Rotorua i-SITE Visitor Information Centre at 1167 Fenton is a good first stop; facilities include a tour-reservation desk and a map shop operated by the Department of Conservation.

AIRPORTS Rotorua Regional Airport . ✉ *Te Ngae Rd.* ☏ *07/345–8800* ⊕ *www.rotorua-airport.co.nz.*

AIRPORT TRANSFERS Rotorua Taxis. ☏ *07/349–6647.* **Super Shuttle.** ☏ *07/345–7790* ⊕ *www.supershuttle.co.nz.*

BUS DEPOT Rotorua Bus Depot. ✉ *Rotorua i-SITE Visitor Information Centre, 1167 Fenton St.*

TOURS
HELICOPTER TOURS
Volcanic Air

AIR EXCURSIONS | Helicopters and float-planes fly from the Volcanic Air office on the Rotorua Lakefront. Trips include over-city flights, crater-lake flights, and excursions to Orakei Korako and White Island. The floatplane trip over the Mount Tarawera volcano is extremely popular.

✉ *Memorial Dr.* ☎ *07/348–9984* ⊕ *www.volcanicair.co.nz* ✉ *From NZ$165.*

VISITOR INFORMATION

Rotorua i-SITE Visitor Information Centre
✉ *1167 Fenton St.* ☎ *07/351–7100* ⊕ *www.rotoruanz.com.*

Sights

Blue Baths
HOT SPRINGS | At the southern end of the Government Gardens you can soak in this thermally heated swimming pool, which was built in the 1930s. ✉ *Queens Dr.* ☎ *07/350–2119* ⊕ *www.bluebaths.co.nz* ✉ *NZ$11.*

Government Gardens
GARDEN | Heading south from Lake Rotorua takes you to the Government Gardens, which occupy a small peninsula. The Māori call this area Whangapiro (fang-ah- *pee*-ro, "evil-smelling place"), an appropriate name for these gardens, where sulfur pits bubble and fume behind manicured rose beds and bowling lawns. The high point is the extraordinary neo-Tudor Bath House. Built as a spa at the turn of the 20th century, it is now the **Rotorua Museum.** One wing on the ground floor is devoted to the eruption of Mt. Tarawera in 1886 and includes artifacts unearthed from the debris plus remarkable photographs of the silica terraces of Rotomahana before the eruption. Be sure to check out the old bathrooms, where some equipment would be right at home in a torture chamber—one soaking tub even administered electric currents to the body. ✉ *Government Gardens, Oruawhata Dr.* ☎ *07/350–1814* ⊕ *www.rotoruamuseum.co.nz* ✉ *NZ$20.*

Kuirau Park
LOCAL INTEREST | FAMILY | This public park is a local hot spot—literally. Mud pools and hot springs sit alongside the flower beds, which at times are almost hidden by floating clouds of steam. You can wander around or join the locals soaking their weary feet in shallow warm pools. Because this thermally active place can change overnight, keep to the paths. ✉ *Kuirau St., south from Lake Rd.* ✉ *Free.*

The Living Thermal Village
HOT SPRINGS | FAMILY | For an introduction to Māori life, visit this authentic village. On a guided tour you'll see thermal pools where villagers bathe, boiling mineral pools, and natural steam vents where residents cook. You can add on a cultural performance and *hāngi* meal to complete the experience. Arts and crafts are available at local shops in case you want to take home a memento. ✉ *17 Tryon St.* ☎ *07/349–3463* ⊕ *www.whakarewarewa.com* ✉ *From NZ$41.*

★ Polynesian Spa
HOT SPRINGS | Considered one of the best spas of its kind, the Polynesian Spa has a wide choice of mineral baths available, from large communal pools and family pools to small, private baths for two. You can also treat yourself to a massage or spa treatments; for a scenic soak, the Lake Spa has exclusive bathing in shallow rock pools overlooking Lake Rotorua. ✉ *Hinemoa St.* ☎ *07/348–1328* ⊕ *www.polynesianspa.co.nz* ✉ *Private pool NZ$20 per ½ hr; lake spa NZ$55; family shared pool from $10.*

St. Faith's
RELIGIOUS SITE | A short walk north from the Rotorua lakefront brings you to the Māori *pā* (fortress) of Ohinemutu, the region's original Māori settlement. It's a still-thriving community, centered on its *marae* (meetinghouse) and St. Faith's, the lakefront Anglican church. The interior of the church is richly decorated with carvings inset with mother-of-pearl. Sunday services feature the sonorous, melodic voices of the Māori choir. The service at 9 am is in Māori and English. ✉ *Tunohopu St.*

Te Puia
LOCAL INTEREST | FAMILY | The grounds here are home to silica terraces, mud

Hāngi: A Traditional Māori Feast

Rotorua is the best place to experience a *hāngi*, a traditional Māori feast featuring food cooked over steaming vents or hot stones. Several local venues offer the opportunity for you to try this slow-cooked treat, paired with a concert—an evening that may remind you of a Hawaiian luau.

As a *manuhiri* (guest), you'll typically get the full treatment, beginning with a *powhiri*, the awe-inspiring Māori welcome that generally includes the *wero* (challenge), the *karanga* (cries of welcome), and the *hongi*, or the pressing together of noses and sharing of breathe/life-force, an age-old Māori gesture that shows friendship and trust.

While the meal cooks, a show begins with haunting harmonious singing, foot stamping, and *poi* twirling (rhythmic swinging of balls on strings). The performance is always followed by food, glorious food. The lifting of the *hāngi* will produce pork, sometimes lamb and chicken, *kūmara* (sweet potato), vegetables, and maybe fish and other seafood, followed by dessert.

Cultural enclaves like the **Living Thermal Village** (✉ *17 Tryon St.* ☎ *07/349–3463* ⊕ *www.whakarewarewa.com NZ$63*) and **Te Puia** (✉ *Hemo Rd.* ☎ *07/348–9047* ⊕ *www.tepuia.com NZ$128*) are only two of the places where you can get a true taste of local flavor.

The **Holiday Inn Rotorua** also has an excellent cultural performance and *hāngi* (✉ *10 Tryon St.* ☎ *07/348–1189* ⊕ *www.holidayinnrotorua.co.nz NZ$69*); and the **Matariki Hāngi and Concert** combines an informative, enthusiastic show with ample, delicious food (✉ *Tutanekai St.* ☎ *07/346–3888* ⊕ *www.accorhotels.com from NZ$39*).

pools, and the Pohutu Geyser (the largest active one in the southern hemisphere). Te Puia also contains the New Zealand Māori Arts & Crafts Institute,where you can watch skilled carvers and weavers at work. Don't miss the Nocturnal Kiwi House, where you might spot one of New Zealand's beloved national birds. Day passes include a guided tour; packages with extras like a cultural performance or *hāngi* feast are also available. ✉ *Hemo Rd.* ☎ *07/348–9047* ⊕ *www.tepuia.com* ✉ *From NZ$56.*

🍴 Restaurants

★ Capers Epicurean

$$$ | **NEW ZEALAND** | **FAMILY** | The pleasing scent of spices may entice you into this large, open restaurant, which serves sustaining meals like chicken shiitake linguine (a grilled chicken breast set on pasta tossed in a creamy mushroom sauce, then topped with crispy prosciutto). Half of the space is a delicatessen that sells preserves and specialty foods, such as chutney made from kūmara (a local sweet potato) and a rub made from kawa kawa (a spicy native herb). **Known for:** interesting cuisine with a local kick; tasty breakfasts; varied dessert cabinet. ⑤ *Average main: NZ$25* ✉ *1181 Eruera St.* ☎ *07/348–8818* ⊕ *www.capers.co.nz.*

Eat Streat

$$$ | **ECLECTIC** | **FAMILY** | If you are not good at making decisions, Eat Streat could drive you crazy. This area at the northern end of Tutanekai Street is covered with a retractable roof and has 15-odd restaurants and bars that tempt tourists and locals with a variety of cuisines. **Known for:** eclectic variety of dishes; good value; buzzy ambience. $ *Average main: NZ$25* ⊠ *Tutanekai St.*

The Fat Dog Café and Bar
$$$ | **ECLECTIC** | **FAMILY** | The eclectic style and fine food here attracts young, old, and everyone in between. The comprehensive menu features a mix of old favorites and seasonal additions. **Known for:** hearty breakfasts; selection of gourmet burgers; relaxing atmosphere. $ *Average main: NZ$28* ⊠ *69 Arawa St.* ☎ *07/347–7586* ⊕ *www.fatdogcafe.co.nz.*

Pig & Whistle
$$$ | **NEW ZEALAND** | The name of this 1940s landmark winks at its previous incarnation—a police station. Expect pub fare at its absolute best, with seafood chowder, Kentucky bourbon pork belly, New Zealand lamb salad, and their famous pigtail fries. **Known for:** great range of beer; live music on weekend and Thursday nights; elevated pub atmosphere. $ *Average main: NZ$27* ⊠ *1182 Tutanekai St.* ☎ *07/347–3025* ⊕ *www. pigandwhistle.co.nz.*

 Hotels

Arista of Rotorua
$$ | **HOTEL** | **FAMILY** | These spacious two-story units, about 1 km (½ mile) from the city center, are a good value—especially for families. **Pros:** within walking distance of town; a parking space for each unit; fenced playground for children. **Cons:** located on busy, sometimes noisy road; check-in time may be restrictive; late check-in fee. $ *Rooms from: NZ$189* ⊠ *296 Fenton St.* ☎ *07/349–0300* ⊕ *www.aristaofrotorua.co.nz* ⟳ *16 rooms* ⊚| *No meals.*

Ashleigh Court Motel
$ | **HOTEL** | **FAMILY** | Each bright, well-maintained unit here has an individual whirlpool tub, which helps distinguish Ashleigh Court from the many motels on Fenton Street. **Pros:** clean and tidy;

reasonably priced; close to Whakarewarewa and the golf course. **Cons:** Fenton Street is busy and can be noisy; no swimming pool; breakfast not included. $ *Rooms from: NZ$124* ⊠ *337 Fenton St.* ☎ *07/348–7456* ⊕ *www.ashleighcourtrotorua.co.nz* ⟳ *13 rooms* ⊚| *No meals.*

★ Holiday Inn Rotorua
$$ | **HOTEL** | From the massive but welcoming entrance foyer with its huge stone fireplace to the lake views from the tower wing, this hotel spells class. **Pros:** good accommodations at all levels; a Māori concert and hāngi on the premise; complimentary shuttle service to town. **Cons:** it's close enough to Whakarewarewa to get more than a whiff of the local vapor; can be crowded with conference attendees; breakfast not included. $ *Rooms from: NZ$149* ⊠ *10 Tryon St.* ☎ *07/348–1189* ⊕ *www.rotorua. holidayinn.com* ⟳ *206 rooms* ⊚| *No meals.*

Princes Gate Hotel
$$$ | **HOTEL** | This ornate timber hotel was built in 1897 on the Coromandel Peninsula; its large, wonderfully appointed guest rooms were transported here in 1920. **Pros:** elegant and sophisticated; has an air of old-fashioned charm; excellent afternoon tea. **Cons:** you'll feel you have to whisper in the lounge; if you want clinical and modern it's not for you; some may find it twee. $ *Rooms from: NZ$220* ⊠ *1057 Arawa St.* ☎ *07/348–1179* ⊕ *www.princesgate.co.nz* ⟳ *50 rooms* ⊚| *No meals.*

Regal Palms 5 Star City Resort
$$$ | **RESORT** | **FAMILY** | The well-appointed studio, one-bedroom, and two-bedroom suites at this resort, located 2 km (1 mile) from downtown Rotorua sit amid spacious grounds. **Pros:** good recreational facilities; roomy accommodations; lovely day spa. **Cons:** you'll need to take the car to town; there may be some traffic noise; breakfast not included. $ *Rooms from: NZ$280* ⊠ *350 Fenton*

St. ☎ 07/350–3232 ⊕ www.regalpalms.
co.nz ⇨ 44 suites ❙❀❙ No meals.

Shopping

Te Puia

CRAFTS | Te Puia was established in 1963 to preserve Māori heritage and crafts. At the institute you can watch wood-carvers and flax weavers at work and see New Zealand greenstone (jade) sculpted into jewelry. The gift shop sells fine examples of this work. ⊠ Hemo Rd. ☎ 07/348–9047 ⊕ www.tepuia.com.

🏃 Activities

BOATING

Kawarau Jet

BOAT TOURS | FAMILY | This company, which is best known for jet-boat trips on Lake Rotorua, has extended its offerings to include parasailing adventures and hot springs excursions. Packages begin at NZ$153 and the team goes out of its way to make sure you have a safe, memorable experience. ⊠ Memorial Dr. ☎ 07/343–7600 ⊕ www.nzjetboat.co.nz.

Lakeland Queen

BOAT TOURS | Licensed for 300 passengers, the Lakeland Queen, a genuine stern-wheel paddle ship, has breakfast, lunch, and dinner cruises. One popular trip includes an onboard barbecue (NZ$59). ⊠ Memorial Dr. ☎ 07/348–0265 ⊕ www.lakelandqueen.com.

Nearby Rotorua

The countryside near Rotorua includes magnificent untamed territory with lakes and rivers full of some of the largest rainbow and brown trout on Earth. From here down through Taupo and on into Tongariro National Park, fishing is a booming business. So if you're dreaming of landing the "big one," this is the place to do it. It's also where you'll find one of New Zealand's most popular man-made

attractions: Hobbiton, the film set that recreated the Shire for the Lord of the Rings movies.

GETTING HERE AND AROUND

Most of the sights outside the Rotorua city area can be reached from State Highway 30, which branches right off Fenton Street at the southern corner of town. The Buried Village is accessed from Highway 30; farther east, you reach the airport, lakes Rotoiti and Rotoma, and Hells Gate. Keeping on Fenton Street will lead to Lake Road and back onto Highway 5, which goes to Paradise Valley, Fairy Springs Road, and farther out of town to Ngongotaha and the Agrodome. If you don't have a car, sightseeing buses operated by Geyser Link Shuttles will transport you to a number of thermal sites in the area, Waimangu and Waiotapu among them; buses leave from Rotorua's i-SITE center on Fenton Street.

BUS CONTACTS Geyser Link Shuttles . ☎ 0800/304–333 ⊕ booking.headfirsttravel.com/geyserlink.

👁 Sights

Agrodome

FARM/RANCH | FAMILY | At this working sheep-and-cattle farm, 6 km (4 miles) north of Rotorua, you can get up close and personal with the animals on a guided tour and pay a visit to the kiwifruit orchard, but the main attraction is the farm show. Well-trained dogs run across the backs of sheep, and there's also a sheep-shearing demonstration. Heads-up to the uninitiated: what the shearer is wearing is not an undershirt but a shearing vest, a classic Kiwi item. Shows are at 9:30, 11, and 2:30 daily. ⊠ 141 Western Rd., Ngongotaha, Rotorua ☎ 07/357–1050 ⊕ www.agrodome.co.nz ⇨ From NZ$37.

Buried Village Te Wairoa

ARCHAEOLOGICAL SITE | At the end of the 19th century, Te Wairoa (tay why- ro-ah, "the buried village") was the starting point for expeditions to the pink-and-white terraces of Rotomahana, on the slopes of Mt. Tarawera. As mineral-rich geyser water cascaded down the mountainside, it formed a series of baths, which became progressively cooler as they neared the lake. In the latter half of the 19th century these fabulous terraces were the country's major attraction, but were destroyed when Mt. Tarawera erupted in 1886, burying the village of Te Wairoa under a sea of mud and hot ash. The village has since been excavated, and of special interest is the *whare* (fahray, "hut") of the *tohunga* (priest) Tuhoto Ariki, who predicted the destruction. An interesting museum contains artifacts, photographs, and models re-creating the day of the disaster, and a number of small dwellings remain basically undisturbed beneath mud and ash. A path circles the excavated village, then continues on as a delightful trail to the waterfall, the lower section of which is steep and slippery in places. Te Wairoa is 14 km (9 miles) southeast of Rotorua. ⊠ *1180 Tarawera Rd., Rotorua* ☎ *07/362–8287* ⊕ *www.buriedvillage.co.nz* ✉ *NZ$35.*

Hells Gate

HOT SPRINGS | Located 15 km (9 miles) east of Rotorua, Hells Gate is arguably the most active thermal reserve in the area. Its 50 acres hiss and bubble with steaming fumaroles and boiling mud pools. Among the attractions here is the Kakahi Falls, reputedly the largest hot waterfall in the southern hemisphere, where, according to legend, Māori warriors bathed their wounds after battle. Warm mud pools are available for public bathing; at the Hellsgate Mud Spa, you can soak in a mud bath or try a *mirimiri* (a traditional Māori massage). ⊠ *State Hwy. 30, Tikitere, Rotorua* ☎ *07/345–3151* ⊕ *www.hellsgate.co.nz* ✉ *NZ$35, spa and mud treatments from NZ$75.*

⭐ Hobbiton

FILM STUDIO | Even if you're not an aficionado of *Lord of the Rings* and *The Hobbit*

movies, a delve into this magic, pretend world of the Shire of Middle Earth (aka the Hobbiton movie set) is rather fascinating. Guides will escort you along the paths of the 12-acre set, stopping at little Hobbit houses set into the hillsides. Along the way, they share secrets about how the movies were made and explain incredible, intricate details of the set design. Like the thirsty Hobbits, you'll enjoy finishing up at the Green Dragon Inn for an exclusively brewed beverage. The standard, two-hour tour costs NZ$84. Meal packages can be added, and transport can be arranged from nearby Matamata and Rotorua. Hobbiton is one of New Zealand's most visited attractions, and reservations are essential for all tours. To think this was once just another New Zealand sheep farm. ⊠ *501 Buckland Rd., Matamata* ☎ *07/888–1505* ⊕ *www.hobbitontours.com* ✉ *From NZ$84.*

⭐ Mitai Māori Village

LOCAL INTEREST | Rewind time by spending an evening at Mitai Māori Village, where you can listen to the harmonious chant of traditionally clad warriors as they paddle a *waka* (war canoe) along the Wai-o-whiro stream, then watch a top-notch cultural show, and enjoy a delicious *hāngi* feast. Getting the chance to see glowworms on a short, guided bush walk is an added bonus. ⊠ *196 Fairy Springs Rd., Rotorua* ☎ *07/343–9132* ⊕ *www.mitai.co.nz* ✉ *NZ$118.*

Skyline Skyrides

AMUSEMENT PARK/WATER PARK | **FAMILY** | A 2,900-foot cable-car system carries you up Mt. Ngongotaha for spectacular views over Lake Rotorua. At the summit, 1,600-feet above sea level, there's a café, a restaurant, and a souvenir shop. As an alternative, try the luge track, where you can take hair-raisingly fast rides on wheeled bobsled-like contraptions (you can also go slowly; a braking system gives you full control of your speed). The track runs partway down the mountain,

The geothermal activity at Waimangu keeps the water of Inferno Crater Lake at a boil.

winding through the redwood trees; from the bottom, you can return to the summit on a separate chairlift. For further thrills, consider zip-lining or mountain biking. ✉ *Fairy Springs Rd., Rotorua* ☎ *07/347–0027* ⊕ *www.skyline.co.nz* 🎞 *Gondola NZ$31, gondola and luge NZ$45.*

★ Waimangu

NATURE SITE | When Mt. Tarawera erupted in 1886, destroying Rotomahana's terraces, not all was lost. A volcanic valley emerged from the ashes, extending southwest from Lake Rotomahana. It's consequently one of the world's newest thermal-activity areas, encompassing the boiling water of the massive Inferno Crater, plus steaming cliffs, bubbling springs, and bush-fringed terraces. A path (one–two hours) runs through the valley down to the lake, where a shuttle bus can get you back to the entrance. You can also cap your trip by taking a cruise on the lake itself. Waimangu is 26 km (16 miles) southeast of Rotorua; to reach it, take Highway 5 south (Taupo direction) and look for the turn after 19 km (12 miles). ✉ *587 Waimangu Rd., Rotorua* ☎ *07/366–6137* ⊕ *www.waimangu.co.nz* 🎞 *From NZ$40.*

Waiotapu

NATURE SITE | This is a freakish landscape of deep, sulfur-crusted pits, jade-color ponds, silica terraces, and a steaming lake edged with red algae and bubbling with tiny beads of carbon dioxide. The **Lady Knox Geyser** erupts precisely at 10:15 daily; other points of interest include the Devil's Ink Pots, a series of evil-looking, bubbling, plopping mud pools, and the spectacular, gold-edged Champagne Pool, which is 195 feet wide and equally deep. Birds nest in holes around the aptly named Birds' Nest Crater—the heat presumably allows the adult birds more time away from the eggs. Waiotapu is 30 km (19 miles) southeast of Rotorua; follow Highway 5 south (Taupo direction) and look for the signs. ✉ *State Hwy. 5, Rotorua* ☎ *07/366–6333* ⊕ *www.waiotapu.co.nz* 🎞 *NZ$33.*

Hotels

★ Solitaire Lodge

$$$$ | HOTEL | Nestled in native bush on a private peninsula, the luxurious Solitaire Lodge commands extensive views over Lake Tarawera and the legendary mountain. **Pros:** quiet, secluded class in superb surroundings; diverse collection of activities offered; high-end wine and food. **Cons:** remote location comes at a high price; no golf course; no swimming pool. ⓢ *Rooms from: NZ$2500* ✉ *16 Ronald Rd., Rotorua* ☎ *07/362–8208* ⊕ *www.solitairelodge.co.nz* ⤳ *11 suites* ⎛⊙⎞ *All-inclusive.*

🛍 Shopping

Amokura Glass

CERAMICS/GLASSWARE | This artist-run hot glass studio and gallery offers live demonstrations four days a week at 12:30 pm. Its collection includes a mix of high-end sculpture, glass tapestries, and souvenirs. ✉ *2 Amokura St., Rotorua* ☎ *07/349–0096* ⊕ *www.amokuraglass. com.*

Mountain Jade

CRAFTS | Look for beautifully made, high-quality jade items in this bright, spacious shop. ✉ *1288 Fenton St., Rotorua* ☎ *07/349–1828* ⊕ *www.mountainjade. co.nz.*

Simply New Zealand

GIFTS/SOUVENIRS | This spot stocks an excellent range of New Zealand gifts and souvenirs. ✉ *1105 Pukuatua St., Rotorua* ☎ *07/348–8273* ⊕ *www.simplynewzea- land.co.nz.*

🏃 Activities

The trout fishing on area lakes, streams, and rivers is some of the finest in the world. For outdoor enthusiasts there is also no shortage of activities such as trail biking, white-water rafting, and bungy jumping.

BIKING

Planet Bike

BICYCLING | FAMILY | First-timers and experts alike will find the perfect mountain-bike adventures with Planet Bike. You can ride for a couple of hours or several days, and some tours combine biking with rafting, kayaking, indoor climbing, or horseback riding. A full day rental (helmet included) starts at NZ$60, depending on the bike. ✉ *8 Waipa Bypass Rd., off Wai- pa State Mill Rd., Rotorua* ☎ *027/280– 2817* ⊕ *www.planetbike.co.nz.*

FISHING

If you want to keep the trout of a lifetime from becoming just another fish story, go with a registered guide. Prices vary, but expect to pay about NZ$120–NZ$150 per hour for a fishing guide and a 20-foot cruiser that takes up to six passengers. The minimum charter period is two hours; gear and tackle are included in the price. A one-day fishing license costs NZ$34 per person and is available on the boat. (You'll need a special license to fish in the Rotorua area and in Taupo.) For general information about local lake and river conditions, check with the Rotorua i-SITE Visitor Information Centre.

Bryan Colman

FISHING | Troll Lake Rotorua or try fly-fishing on the region's many streams, including a private-land source. Bryan takes up to four anglers at a time, and a daylong trip is NZ$860. ✉ *32 Kiwi St., Rotorua* ☎ *07/348–7766* ⊕ *www.TroutFishingRo- torua.com.*

Gordon Randle

FISHING | A trip with Gordon Randle will set you back about NZ$120 per hour; you can also charter the boat (and Gordon) for the day at a cost of NZ$940 plus licenses. ✉ *11 Te Ana Pl., Rotorua* ☎ *07/349–2555, 0274/938–733 boat* ⊕ *www.rotoruatrout.co.nz.*

Scenery in Middle Earth

Some of the most striking elements of the *Lord of the Rings* films weren't created by special effects—they were the astonishing views of New Zealand's countryside. The film crew traveled all over the country, so there are dozens of locales to tempt you to stop and dream awhile.

On the North Island, you can visit a handful of hobbit homes in rural Matamata (⊕ *www.hobbitontours. com*). The volcanic peaks and blasted terrain of Tongariro National Park provided the setting for Mordor. Tackle one of the park's walking trails to see the otherworldly hot springs, lava rocks, and craggy peaks like Ruapehu, the films' Emyn Muil. Take the spectacular Tongariro Crossing trek to pass Ngauruhoe, the volcano the hobbits Frodo and Sam braved as Mount Doom.

Wellington, the film production's home base, is also the hometown of the director, Peter Jackson. Here the orcs, trolls, and the horrible Balrog all came to life, created by Weta Workshop and the production company Three Foot Six (named for the height of a hobbit). Weta's has had its hands full with other major films, including Jackson's *King Kong*. Local wags dub the capital "Wellywood."

The Hutt Valley, east of Wellington, saw plenty of hobbit action. During filming a huge polystyrene castle towered over a quarry by the Western Hutt road. Unsuspecting drivers would pass by Minas Tirith and the fortress of Isengard, where the wizard Gandalf was betrayed and imprisoned. Stay on Highway 2 to reach the beautiful Kaitoke Regional Park, used for the Elven city of Rivendell and a perfect place to picnic on the riverbank.

On the South Island, Highway 6 unrolls south to glacier country. Stop at Franz Josef and look for Mount Gunn, where the beacon burned. Carving through the magnificent landscape, the road leads on to Wanaka, where the ghastly ringwraiths gave chase to Arwen and Frodo.

The breathtaking White Mountains, or Remarkables, at Queenstown were the background for the Ithilien Camp, the giant statues of the Pillars of Argonath, and other scenes. From nearby Glenorchy, you can hire a horse and ride to Paradise, seen as the Elven Lothlórien forest. Farther south, near Te Anau, the brooding silence of the lake district was shot as the Midgewater Marshes, and is prime trout-fishing territory.

RAFTING AND KAYAKING

The Rotorua region has rivers with Grade III to Grade V rapids that make excellent white-water rafting. For scenic beauty—and best for first-timers—the Rangitaiki River (Grades III–IV) is recommended. For experienced rafters, the Wairoa River has exhilarating Grade V rapids. The climax of a rafting trip on the Kaituna River is the drop over the 21-foot Okere Falls, among the highest to be rafted by a commercial operator anywhere. The various operators run similar trips on a daily schedule, though different rivers are open at different times of year, depending on water levels. All equipment and instruction are provided, plus transportation to and from the departure points—which can be up to 80 km (50 miles) from Rotorua. Prices vary depending on the run and the river; many operators sell combination trips.

Kaitiaki Adventures

WHITE-WATER RAFTING | FAMILY | The well-qualified team at Kaitiaki Adventures leads daily rafting trips on the Kaituna River (NZ$109). For a variation on the theme, try white-water sledging—you'll shoot the rapids on a specially designed plastic raft the size of a boogie board, and then soak in a natural hotpool; the cost is NZ$109 to NZ$209, gear included. ✉ *1135 Te Ngae Rd., Rotorua* ☎ *0800/338–736* ⊕ *www.kaitiaki.co.nz.*

River Rats

KAYAKING | FAMILY | Day trips to the main rivers are organized by River Rats; adventure packages are available, too. ✉ *391 State Hwy. 33, Mourea* ☎ *07/345–6543, 0800/333–900* ⊕ *www.riverrats.co.nz.*

Wet 'n' Wild Rafting

KAYAKING | FAMILY | One-day itineraries cover the Rangitaiki, Wairoa, and Kaituna rivers. Wet 'n' Wild Rafting also has multi-adventure and double-trip options. ✉ *2 White St., Rotorua* ☎ *07/348–3191, 0800/462–7238* ⊕ *www.wetnwildrafting. co.nz.*

Taupo

82 km (51 miles) south of Rotorua, 150 km (94 miles) northwest of Napier.

The tidy town of Taupo is the base for exploring Lake Taupo, the country's largest lake. Its shores are backed by volcanic mountains, and in the vicinity you'll see more of the geothermal activity that characterizes this zone. Water sports are popular here—notably sailing, cruising, and waterskiing—but Taupo is best known for fishing. The town is the rainbow-trout capital of the universe: the average Taupo trout weighs in around 4 pounds, and the lake is open year-round. Meanwhile, the backpacker crowd converges on Taupo for its adventure activities. The town has skydiving and bungy-jumping opportunities, and white-water rafting and jet-boating are available on the local rivers.

GETTING HERE AND AROUND

Taupo is four hours from Auckland, depending on traffic, taking Highway 1 the whole way. It's 70 minutes from Rotorua, also via Highway 1. If you are coming by bus, InterCity Buses has daily service to Taupo from Auckland (approximately 5 hours) and from Rotorua (1 hour and 20 minutes).

Within the town, streets are laid out in a grid pattern. Busy Lake Terrace runs along the waterfront; it turns into Tongariro Street as it heads north, crossing the Waikato River and the gates that control the flow of water from the lake. Heu Heu, the main shopping street, runs from the traffic lights on Tongariro Street.

BUS DEPOT Taupo Bus Depot. ✉ *Taupo i-SITE Visitor Information Centre, 30 Tongariro St.*

TOURS

BOAT TOURS

Barbary

BOAT TOURS | This 1920s yacht, believed to have once been the property of golden-age film star Errol Flynn, has short cruises departing at 10:30, 2, and 5. They take in giant carvings on a lakefront cliff face and, depending on the weather, let you swim off the boat when it's moored. On board, you can help hoist the sails or just sit back and dream in one of the big beanbags. ✉ *10 Ferry Rd.* ☎ *07/378–5879* ⊕ *www.sailbarbary.com* ⚓ *From NZ$49.*

Maid of the Falls

BOAT TOURS | FAMILY | Board the *Maid of the Falls* for a Huka Falls cruise. The boat leaves from Aratiatia Dam, 10 km (6 miles) north of Taupo, at 10:30, 12:30, and 2:30; a 4:30 trip is added in summer. The vessel has a viewing platform on the front and takes you up close to the falls, which push a huge amount of water through a narrow gap in the rocks. ✉ *630 Aratiatia Rd.* ☎ *0800/278–336* ⊕ *www. hukafallscruise.co.nz* ⚓ *NZ$39.*

BUS TOURS
Paradise Tours
BUS TOURS | Bus tours operated by this outfit visit attractions in and around Taupo, including Huka Falls and Craters of the Moon. ✉ *Taupo* ☎ *07/378–9955* ⊕ *www.paradisetours.co.nz* ✈ *From NZ$99.*

VISITOR INFORMATION
CONTACTS Taupo i-SITE Visitor Information Centre. ✉ *30 Tongiriro St.* ☎ *07/376–0027* ⊕ *www.greatlaketaupo.com.*

Sights

Aratiatia Dam
DAM | The Waikato River is dammed along its length; the first construction is the Aratiatia Dam, 10 km (6 miles) northeast of Taupo. The river below it is virtually dry most of the time, but three times a day (at 10, noon, and 2), and four times a day in summer (October–March, also at 4), the dam gates are opened and the gorge is dramatically transformed into a raging torrent. Watch the spectacle from the road bridge over the river or from one of two lookout points a 15-minute walk downriver through the bush. To access the dam from Taupo, turn right off Highway 5. ✉ *Aratiatia Rd.*

Craters of the Moon
NATURE SITE | The construction of the local geothermal project had an impressive—and unforeseen—effect. Boiling mud pools, steaming vents, and large craters appeared in an area now known as Craters of the Moon. A marked walkway snakes for 3 km (2 miles) through the belching, sulfurous landscape, past boiling pits and hissing crevices. The craters are up Karapiti Road, across from the Huka Falls turnoffs on Highway 1, 3 km (2 miles) north of Taupo. ✉ *171 Karapiti Rd.* ☎ *0276/564–684* ⊕ *www.cratersofthemoon.co.nz* ✈ *NZ$8.*

Huka Falls
BODY OF WATER | The Waikato River thunders through a narrow chasm and over a 35-foot rock ledge at Huka Falls. The fast-flowing river produces almost 50% of the North Island's required power, and its force is extraordinary, with the falls dropping into a seething, milky-white pool 200 feet across. The view from the footbridge is superb; for an even more impressive look, both the *Maid of the Falls* and vessels operated by Hukafalls Jet get close to the maelstrom. The falls are 3 km (2 miles) north of town; to reach them, turn right off Highway 1 onto Huka Falls Road. ✉ *Huka Falls Rd.*

Huka Prawn Park
AMUSEMENT PARK/WATER PARK | FAMILY | This prawn farm is a curious mix of cheesy and fascinating. Check out the holding tanks where prawns are bred in specially heated river water (in some, baby prawns eat out of your hand). You can also catch your own prawns using a small rod and fishing line, or just buy some on-site; either way you can have them cooked and served as you like in the adjoining café. ✉ *Huka Falls Rd., Wairakei Park* ☎ *07/374–8474* ⊕ *www.hukaprawnpark.co.nz* ✈ *NZ$30.*

Orakei Korako
NATURE SITE | Even if you've seen enough bubbling pools and fuming craters to last a lifetime, the thermal valley of Orakei Korako is still likely to captivate you. Geyser-fed streams hiss and steam as they flow into the waters of the lake, and a cream-and-pink silica terrace is believed to be the largest in the world since the volcanic destruction of the terraces of Rotomahana. At the bottom of Aladdin's Cave, the vent of an ancient volcano, a jade-green pool was once used by Māori women as a beauty parlor, which is where the name *Orakei Korako* (a place of adorning) originated. The valley is 37 km (23 miles) north of Taupo, via Highway 1, and takes about 25 minutes to reach by car; you could always see it en route to or from Rotorua, which lies another 68 km (43 miles) northeast of the valley. ✉ *494 Orakeikorako Rd., Reporoa*

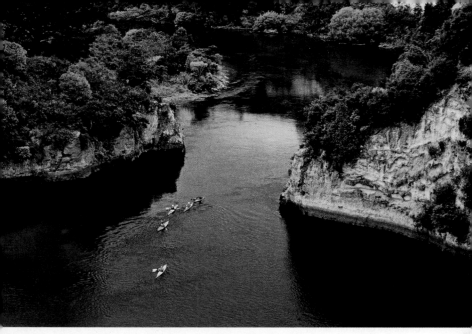

Kayakers paddle the Waikato River, New Zealand's longest waterway.

07/378–3131 ⊕ www.orakeikorako.
co.nz ✉ NZ$36.

Taupo Museum

MUSEUM | FAMILY | You'll find Māori treasures and contemporary art on display at this museum; the volcanic eruptions that have shaped the area are also chronicled. The star attraction, however, is the glorious Ora Garden, which was granted Garden of National Significance status in 2011. ✉ Story Pl. Taupo ☎ 07/376–0414 ⊕ www.taupodc.govt.nz/our-services/libraries-and-museum/museum/Pages/default.aspx ✉ NZ$5.

Restaurants

★ The Bistro

$$$$ | EUROPEAN | This joint aims for simple but nice and has fittingly become an impressive but unpretentious eatery. Large cylindrical lamp shades brighten the modern interior, creating a contemporary bistro vibe; the food follows suit, focusing on what's fresh and seasonal. **Known for:** standard European fare with a local twist; good wine list; excellent pork belly. ⓢ Average main: NZ$32 ✉ 17 Tamamutu St. ☎ 07/377–3111 ⊕ www.thebistro.co.nz ☉ No lunch.

★ Brantry Restaurant

$$$$ | CONTEMPORARY | The menu is updated seasonally at this converted 1950s town house on a suburban street not far from the shores of Lake Taupo. Owners Prue and Felicity Campbell know what they're doing and use the best local ingredients to make delicious things to satisfy all palates. **Known for:** ever-changing innovative menu; high quality ingredients; unique wines. ⓢ Average main: NZ$35 ✉ 45 Rifle Range Rd. ☎ 07/378–0484 ⊕ www.thebrantry.co.nz ☉ Closed Sun. and Mon.

★ The Replete Food Company

$$ | CAFÉ | FAMILY | This café draws the crowds for breakfast and lunch thanks to its outside tables and excellent food. In the morning, try the Complete Replete Breakfast: honey-cured bacon, tomato relish, poached eggs, roasted field mushrooms, and grilled focaccia. **Known**

for: popular breakfast spot; tasty coffee; New Zealand dishes with an Asian twist. ⑤ *Average main: NZ$16* ✉ *45 Heu Heu St.* ☎ *07/377–3011* ⊕ *www.replete.co.nz* ☾ *No dinner.*

🛏 Hotels

b&b @ number ten

$$ | B&B/INN | The sunny en suite guest rooms at this B&B have panoramic views of Lake Taupo and French doors that let you take full advantage of the views. **Pros:** good location; not far from town; free Wi-Fi. **Cons:** basic amenities; has a suburban feel; no cooking facilities. ⑤ *Rooms from: NZ$160* ✉ *10 Coprosma Crescent, Botanical Heights* ☎ *07/378–6823, 021/237–2405* ⊕ *www.bnbnumberten.co.nz* ⇄ *2 rooms* ♱○♰ *Breakfast.*

Cascades Lakefront Motel

$$ | HOTEL | This lakeside motel offers comfortable rooms with great views. **Pros:** on the lakeside with a safe beach; heated pool; great views. **Cons:** 3 km (2 miles) from town center; units near road may get some traffic noise; uninspiring decor. ⑤ *Rooms from: NZ$145* ✉ *303 Lake Terr., just south of State Hwy. 5 (Napier) turnoff* ☎ *07/378–3774* ⊕ *www.cascades.co.nz* ⇄ *24 units* ♱○♰ *No meals.*

★ Huka Lodge

$$$$ | HOTEL | FAMILY | Set on 17 blissful acres, this riverfront lodge is one of the country's finest and has seen its fair share of prominent guests over the years. **Pros:** one of the world's best lodges with a knowing and established clientele; excellent range of activities; gorgeous setting. **Cons:** perfection does not come cheap; prices are per person per night; fixed dinner times. ⑤ *Rooms from: NZ$2200* ✉ *77–105 Huka Falls Rd.* ☎ *647/378–5791* ⊕ *www.hukalodge.co.nz* ⇄ *25 suites* ♱○♰ *Some meals.*

The Pillars

$$$$ | B&B/INN | This modern, Mediterranean-style country manor features four large en suite rooms, a spacious guest lounge, a conservatory, and patio areas where a complimentary evening drink can be enjoyed. **Pros:** pool and tennis court; free Wi-Fi; delightful, friendly hosts. **Cons:** you need transport to see the sights; encouragement to socialize with other guests isn't for everyone; no restaurant or bar on-site. ⑤ *Rooms from: NZ$395* ✉ *7 Deborah Rise, Bonshaw Park* ☎ *07/378–1512* ⊕ *www.pillarstaupo.co.nz* ⇄ *4 suites* ♱○♰ *Breakfast.*

🏃 Activities

The Central North Island region is an absolute must for anyone keen on hunting, fishing, canoeing, hiking, or just about any other outdoor activity.

BUNGY JUMPING

Taupo Bungy

LOCAL SPORTS | Plunge from a cantilevered platform that projects out from a cliff 150 feet above the Waikato River. You can go for the "water touch" or dry versions. Even if you have no intention of "walking the plank," go and watch the jumpers from the nearby lookout point, 1 km (½ mile) north of town. Jumps cost from NZ$180 a shot and are available daily from 9 to 5. ✉ *202 Spa Rd., off Tongariro St.* ☎ *07/377–1135, 0800/888–408* ⊕ *www.taupobungy.co.nz.*

FISHING

There is some great fishing in the Taupo area and a large number of guides with local expertise who work the Tongariro River and the lake. High season runs from October to April. Costs are usually around NZ$250 for a half day and include all equipment plus a fishing license (note that you need a special license to fish here and in Rotorua). Book at least a day in advance.

Chris Jolly Outdoors

FISHING | Staffed by people with a love of the outdoors, this company can take you mountain biking, hiking, hunting, cruising, and, of course, fishing. Try fly-fishing or cast for trout on a chartered boat trip.

A half-day fly-fishing expedition costs NZ$570 for two people, all equipment included. ✉ *Berth 4, Taupo Boat Harbour, Ferry Rd.* ☎ *07/378–0623, 0800/252–628* ⊕ *chrisjolly.co.nz.*

Mark Aspinall
FISHING | Fly-fish for rainbow and brown trout with Mark Aspinall. He will organize a custom trip to meet your needs and collect you from wherever you are staying, but it's important to book well in advance, especially in summer. A half-day trip, all gear included, will set you back NZ$300; a full-day with lunch costs NZ$550. ✉ *Taupo* ☎ *021/500–384* ⊕ *www.markaspinall.com.*

JET-BOATING
Hukafalls Jet
BOATING | For high-speed thrills on the Waikato River, take a ride with Hukafalls Jet; its jet-boats spin and skip between the Aratiatia Dam and Huka Falls multiple times per day. The 30-minute trip costs NZ$135. ✉ *200 Karetoto Rd.* ☎ *07/374–8572* ⊕ *www.hukafallsjet.com.*

RAFTING
Rafting New Zealand
BOATING | The Wairoa and Mohaka rivers are accessible from Taupo, as are the Rangitaiki and the more family-friendly Tongariro. Rafting New Zealand provides transportation, wet suits, equipment, and much-needed hot showers at the end. Prices start at NZ$119. ✉ *41 Ngawaka Pl.* ☎ *07/386–0352, 0800/865–226* ⊕ *raftingnewzealand.com.*

SKYDIVING
Call at least one day in advance to arrange your jump—weather permitting—and expect to pay NZ$249–NZ$339 per, more if you want to add on a video or other mementos to commemorate your experience.

Skydive Taupo
FLYING/SKYDIVING/SOARING | On a tandem jump you're attached to a professional skydiver for a breathtaking descent. Depending on altitude, free fall can last from a few seconds to close to a minute. Prices start at NZ$359. ✉ *Anzac Memorial Dr.* ☎ *0800/586–766* ⊕ *www. skydivetaupo.co.nz.*

Taupo Tandem Skydiving
FLYING/SKYDIVING/SOARING | For a thrill—along with a bird's eye view of Taupo—try Taupo Tandem Skydiving. Prices start at NZ$279 for a 12,000-foot jump. ✉ *Anzac Memorial Dr.* ☎ *07/377–0428, 0800/826–336* ⊕ *taupotandemskydiving.com.*

Tongariro National Park

110 km (69 miles) southwest of Taupo.

Tongariro offers a spectacular combination of dense forest, wild open countryside, crater lakes, barren lava fields, and rock-strewn mountain slopes. Its rugged beauty and convenient location, almost in the center of the North Island, make it the most popular and accessible of New Zealand's parks.

GETTING HERE AND AROUND
The park is best reached by car. The approach from the north is along Highway 4 on the park's western side; turn off at the village of National Park for Whakapapa. Coming from the south, turn off State Highway 1 at Waiouru for Ohakune. From Taupo to the park, follow State Highway 1 south and turn off at Turangi onto State Highway 47. The roads are generally good; however, snow and ice can be a problem around the park in winter.

It's difficult to reach Tongariro National Park by public transportation, though InterCity does run a daily bus in summer (mid-October–April) between Taupo, Whakapapa, and National Park village; the trip takes around 1½ hours. Numerous local shuttle operators also provide transportation for hikers to and from the park.

Northern Explorer, a scenic train that links Auckland and Wellington, stops at

Tongariro National Park

National Park village and Ohakune; it travels southbound on Monday, Thursday, and Saturday and northbound on Tuesday, Friday, and Sunday.

Whakapapa, on the north side of Ruapehu, is the only settlement within the park with services, and it is the jump-off point for the Whakapapa ski slopes. The second ski area is Turoa, and its closest town is Ohakune, which is just beyond the southern boundary of the park. Both towns keep their doors open for hikers and other travelers when the snow melts. The Tongariro National Park Visitor Centre is the best place to get maps, guides, and, if needed, hut passes. If you want to do some online research, the Department of Conservation's website (⊕ www.doc.govt.nz) is another helpful resource.

TOURS

Tongariro Expeditions

BUS TOURS | This outfit runs a shuttle to Tongariro National Park from the Taupo, Turangi, and Tongariro Base Camp and Ketetahi car park in summer. Only guided trips, which include gear and return transportation, are available in winter. Shuttle prices start at NZ$35. ⊠ *Taupo* ☏ *07/377–0435, 0800/828–763* ⊕ *www. tongariroexpeditions.com.*

VISITOR INFORMATION

CONTACTS Tongariro National Park Visitor Centre. ⊠ *Whakapapa Village, State Hwy. 48, Mt. Ruapehu* ☏ *07/892–3729* ⊕ *www.doc.govt.nz.*

Planning Your Trip to Tongariro

Best Time to Go

Your best window for decent weather is November through March, and the busiest time is between Christmas and New Year. Keep in mind, however, that even during summer you may feel like you're experiencing all four seasons in a single day, with weather ranging from hot and sunny to cool and rainy, and even snowy at higher elevations. In winter, cold alpine conditions are not uncommon. Suitable clothing should always be carried and sensible footwear worn.

Best Activities

Hiking and Tramping. The **Tongariro Alpine Crossing** has been described as the best one-day walk in the world. Approach it with the expectation that sudden changes of weather, even during summer, are always possible. There are numerous other trails covering the area and various types of accommodations, from cheap backpacker campgrounds to lodges and at least one first-class hotel. Most of these will organize transport to get the keen walkers to places where hikes can vary from an hour to several days. The longer trails will have huts to provide basic overnight stopovers.

Skiing. June through October (give or take a week or two, depending on conditions), the slopes of Mt. Ruapehu come to life with hundreds of skiing and snowboarding enthusiasts. On occasion the runs have to be cleared when the mountain's crater lake threatens to overflow, but this hasn't decreased the area's popularity. The combined fields of Turoa and Whakapapa form the largest ski slope in New Zealand and have brought a measure of prosperity to the once sleepy villages of National Park and Ohakune.

Viewing Volcanoes. Massive and downright awesome, Tongariro, Ngauruhoe, and Ruapehu dominate from whichever direction one approaches, and the views from Desert Road are a photographer's dream. If you travel from the south on State Highway 1 on a clear day, the first glimpse of Ruapehu as the road crests will take your breath away. Farther north on the same road, the enormous, almost perfectly truncated, cone-shaped bulk of Ngauruhoe looms alongside a series of hairpin bends.

Sights

Tongariro National Park

NATIONAL/STATE PARK | Tongariro National Park is the oldest national park in New Zealand and the largest on the North Island. Gifted to the nation by the Ngāti Tuwharetoa people in 1887, this stunning mountainous region provided much of the dramatic scenery for the *Lord of the Rings* films. The park has a spectacular combination of dense forest, wild open countryside, crater lakes, barren lava fields, and rock-strewn mountain slopes. Its rugged beauty and convenient location, almost in the center of the North Island, make it the most popular and accessible of New Zealand's parks. Three volcanoes, Tongariro, Ngauruhoe, and Ruapehu, tower above its Central Plateau overlooking miles of untamed country that stretch to the West Coast on one side and the aptly named Desert Road on the other. The volcanoes are no sleeping giants; Tongariro is the least active, but Ngauruhoe and Ruapehu have both erupted in recent years. In 1995, 1996, and again in 2007, Ruapehu spewed ash, created showers of rock, and released lahars (landslides of volcanic debris) that burst through the walls of the crater lake. The park is famed for its hiking trails, but the weather can change very quickly here so be sure to be dressed for the day with good outdoor gear and plenty of food. ⊠ State Hwy. 48 ⊕ www.national-park.co.nz.

🛏 Hotels

Chateau Tongariro

$$ | **HOTEL** | Built in 1929, this French neo-Georgian-style property in Whakapapa hosts everyone from well-heeled movie types to people who tramp and ski by day, then switch their clothing to dress in heels or jacket and tie for the evening. **Pros:** classy, restful place; enormous lounge area has a welcoming open fire and billiard table; superb views. **Cons:** views are often obstructed by mist; long way from the nearest town; may be seen as stuffy. $ Rooms from: NZ$130 ⊠ 99 State Hwy. 48, Mt. Ruapehu 🕾 07/892–3809, 0800/242–832 ⊕ www.chateau. co.nz 🛏 116 rooms ⦿ No meals.

Discovery Lodge

$$ | **HOTEL** | **FAMILY** | The only tourist lodging in the park to give a panoramic view of three active volcanoes is this friendly complex, only minutes from the ski slopes. **Pros:** handy to the village; close to the start of the Tongariro Alpine Crossing and their shuttle gets you there quite early; good food. **Cons:** a long way from shops; breakfast not included; not a good range of shuttle times to the Crossing. $ Rooms from: NZ$145 ⊠ State Hwy. 47, Whakapapa Village 🕾 07/892–2744, 0800/122–122 ⊕ www.discovery.net.nz 🛏 22 rooms ⦿ No meals.

En Route 👁

Straddling State Highway 1 between National Park village and Taupo sits the small town of **Turangi.** A regular stopover for motorists on the main north–south route, its number-one attraction is trout fishing on some of the world's most productive rivers, but there is also great local walking, kayaking, and white-water rafting. Hotpools are also close by. The Turangi i-SITE Visitor Information Centre (🕾 07/386–8999 ⊕ www.greatlaket-aupo.com) is on Ngawhaka Place, Turangi.

🏃 Activities

HIKING

The best one-day itinerary is indisputably the **Tongariro Alpine Crossing.** The 19.4-km (12½-mile) walk starts and finishes in different places, so make arrangements for drop-off and pickup points. Several firms and most lodgings will organize this at a reasonable charge. Check on the condition of the trail before you depart—there have been geological disturbances and, as a result, some parts of the track may not be accessible.

Starting at Mangatepopo, the one-way crossing is a spectacular seven- to nine-hour hike up and over the namesake mountain, passing craters, the evocatively named Emerald Lakes, old lava flows, and hot springs. It's a harsh environment for vegetation, but you'll spot moss and lichens and occasional wetland plants. It's a steep climb to the Mangetepopo Saddle, which lies between Tongariro and Ngauruhoe, but the views on a clear day can seem endless. For the adventurous, an unmarked track leads to the top of Mt. Ngauruhoe (Mount Doom if you're a Lord of the Rings fan). It's very steep and estimated to be a three-hour trip; adding this excursion requires a high level of fitness. The main trail proceeds to the south crater of Tongariro to a ridge leading up Red Crater. Here you can often smell sulfur. Rising 6,120 feet, the Red Crater's summit is the highest point of the Tongariro Alpine Crossing. From here the trail has a lot of loose stones and gravel and is extremely rough underfoot as it descends down to three smaller water-filled craters known as the Emerald Lakes (so named for their brilliant greenish color). The trail then continues across Central Crater to the Blue Lake to lead across the North Crater and downhill all the way to the Ketetahi Hut, where you'll be glad to sit and take a breather. Afterward, hike on to the springs of the same name; these are on private land, which the trail artfully skirts, but their steam cloud is impossible to miss. From here it's pretty much all downhill through tussock slopes to the start of the bush line and a long descent through forest to your pickup at the end.

Although children and school groups commonly do the hike, it is not to be taken lightly. Prepare yourself for rapidly changing weather conditions by bringing warm and waterproof clothing. Wear sturdy footwear, and carry food, plenty of water, sunblock, and sunglasses—and don't forget a hat. Also, be careful not to get too close to steam vents; the area around them can be dangerously hot. From late November to May, you'll be sharing the trail with many other hikers. In the colder months, it's really only for experienced winter hikers who can deal with snow and ice; some transport companies will take you only if you have an ice axe and crampons. It is recommended that you get up-to-date trail and weather conditions from the Department of Conservation's Tongariro National Park Visitor Centre before starting out. A number of trail transport operators provide shuttles to and from the Tongariro Alpine Crossing. Many of the motels and lodges in National Park village can also arrange transport for about NZ$40.

The longest hikes in the park are the three-day **Northern Circuit,** which goes over Tongariro and around Ngauruhoe, and the four-day **Round-the-Mountain Track,** which circles Ruapehu. There are trailside huts throughout the park to use on overnight trips. You'll need to buy a hut pass at the visitor center; it costs NZ$36 from mid-October 19 to late April and NZ$15 the rest of the year. During the "Great Walks Season" (the third week in October to the last week in April), huts musts be booked ahead; otherwise it's first come, first served. Gas cookers are available in the huts. You can also tackle short half-hour to two-hour walks if all you want is a flavor of the region. A 90-minute round-trip trek to the Tawhai Falls via the **Whakapapanui Track** takes you through the forest, and a two-hour round-trip to Taranaki Falls showcases subalpine scenery.

SKIING

Mt. Ruapehu Ski Slopes
SKIING/SNOWBOARDING | Combined, the Mt. Ruapehu ski slopes add up to New Zealand's most extensive skiing and snowboarding area. **Whakapapa,** on the mountain's north side, has more than 30 groomed trails, including beginners' slopes. **Turoa,** on the south side, has a half-pipe. Ski season generally runs from June through October, depending on snow conditions. Expect to pay about NZ$125 for a full day, all-mountain lift pass; lessons and rental equipment are also available. In summer, lifts operate depending on weather for those wanting to enjoy a little alpine sightseeing. ⊠ Taupo ⊕ www.mtruapehu.com.

Sights ▼
1 ASB Bank... **C2**
2 Brookfields Vineyard **D5**
3 Hildebrandt's Building **B2**
4 Market Reserve Building **C2**
5 MTG Hawke's Bay **C1**
6 National Aquarium ... **D5**
7 Rothman's Bulding...... **A1**

Restaurants ▼
1 Mexi Mama **A1**
2 Pacifica Restaurant.. **C3**

Hotels ▼
1 Homestay 157........... **C1**
2 McHardy Lodge........ **A1**
3 Napier Bed and Breakfast - Tequila Sunrise...... **A1**
4 Shoreline Motel........ **D5**

KEY

❶ Sights
❶ Restaurants
❶ Hotels
┅┅ Rail Lines
◉ Tourist Information

Napier

150 km (94 miles) southeast of Taupo, 345 km (215 miles) northeast of Wellington.

The earthquake that struck Napier at 10:46 am on February 3, 1931, was—at 7.8 on the Richter scale—the largest quake ever recorded in New Zealand. The coastline was wrenched upward several feet. Almost all of the town's brick buildings collapsed, and many people were killed on the footpaths as they rushed outside. The quake triggered fires throughout town, and with water mains shattered, little could be done to stop the blazes that devoured the remaining wooden structures. Only a few buildings survived (the Public Service Building with its neoclassical pillars is one), and the death toll was well over 100.

The surviving townspeople set up tents and cookhouses in Nelson Park, and then tackled the city's reconstruction at a remarkable pace. In the rush to rebuild, Napier went mad for art deco, the bold, geometric style that had burst on the global design scene in 1925. Now a walk through the art deco district, concentrated between Emerson, Herschell, Dalton, and Browning streets, is a stylistic immersion. The decorative elements are often above the ground floors, so keep your eyes up.

GETTING HERE AND AROUND

Driving is more relaxed around this region, and you won't experience the traffic problems often found in the larger cities. If you'd rather not take the wheel yourself, InterCity has daily service to Napier from Auckland, Hamilton, Rotorua, Wellington, and other destinations.

Air travelers can catch direct Air New
Zealand flights from Wellington, Auckland, and Christchurch; these arrive daily
at the small Hawke's Bay Airport (NPE).
Direct Jetstar flights from Auckland
land here as well. The airport is 5 km (3
miles) north of Napier. Rental cars are
available at the airport. Taxis and shuttles
also provide transportation into the city:
the former will take you to the center of
Napier for about NZ$28.

AIRPORTS Hawke's Bay Airport. ✉ *111
Main North Rd.* ☎ *06/834–0742* ⊕ *www.
hawkesbay-airport.co.nz.*

BUS CONTACTS Napier Bus Depot. ✉ *12
Carlyle St.*

TOURS

Absolute de Tours

SPECIAL-INTEREST | This company organ-
izes a series of tours, among them art
deco–themed outings in Napier, longer
excursions to scenic points of interest in
the area, and half- or full-day vineyard visits. Custom tours are also available from
Napier, Hastings, and Havelock North.
✉ *112 Avenue Rd., Greenmeadows*
☎ *06/844–8699* ⊕ *www.absolutedetours.
co.nz* ⛴ *From NZ$54.*

Art Deco Trust

SPECIAL-INTEREST | The Trust leads excel-
lent themed tours that highlight Napier's
architectural heritage. A one-hour walk
starts daily at 10 am from the Napier
i-SITE Visitor Information Centre (NZ$24);
a two-hour version, which includes an
audiovisual introduction, starts at 2
pm from the Art Deco Centre (NZ$26).
you can also arrange a private tour in
a vintage car for NZ$185 per hour. DIY
types can pick up the Trust's Art Deco
Tour Map, which plots a self-drive route
through Napier and Hastings. ✉ *Art Deco
Centre, 7 Tennyson St.* ☎ *06/835–0022*
⊕ *www.artdeconapier.com* ⛴ *From
NZ$24.*

**CONTACTS Napier i-SITE Visitor Information
Centre.** ✉ *100 Marine Parade* ☎ *06/834–
1911* ⊕ *www.napiernz.com.*

◉ Sights

ASB Bank

BUILDING | One of Napier's more notable
buildings is at the corner of Hastings and
Emerson streets. The Māori theme on
the lintels is probably the country's finest
example of *kowhaiwhai* (rafter) patterns
decorating a European building. The
traditional red, white, and black pattern is
also continued inside around a coffered
ceiling. ✉ *100 Hastings St.*

Brookfields Vineyard

WINERY/DISTILLERY | One of this region's
most attractive wineries features rose
gardens and a tasting room that over-
looks the vines. The Chardonnay and
Pinot Gris are usually outstanding, but
the showpiece is the reserve Cabernet
Sauvignon–Merlot, a powerful red that
ages well. Syrah grapes are proving
spectacular as is the Brookfields Hillside
Syrah. From Napier take Marine Parade
toward Hastings and turn right on
Awatoto Road. Follow it to Brookfields
Road and turn left. Signs will point to the
winery. ✉ *376 Brookfields Rd.* ☎ *06/834–
4615* ⊕ *www.brookfieldsvineyards.co.nz*
⛴ *Tastings free.*

Hildebrandt's Building

BUILDING | Hildebrandt's has an excel-
lent frieze, which is best viewed from
across Dalton Street. The original owner
was a German who migrated to New
Zealand—hence the German flag at one
end, the New Zealand at the other; the
wavy lines in the middle symbolize the
sea passage between the two countries.
✉ *90 Tennyson St.*

Market Reserve Building

BUILDING | On Tennyson and Hastings,
this was the first building to rise after
the earthquake. Its steel metal frame
was riveted, not welded, so that the

construction noise would give residents the message that the city was being rebuilt. The bronze storefronts with their "crown of thorns" patterned leaded glass are still original. ⊠ *28 Tennyson St.*

★ MTG Hawke's Bay

MUSEUM | This complex, also known as the Hawke's Bay Museum, is home to a museum, a theater, and an art gallery. The museum component's curatorial team is engaged, and the exhibitions ponder a range of local and international issues, so you might see a temporary display devoted to an exploration of memory alongside a cutting-edge digital presentation. There's also a significant collection of newspaper reports, photographs, and audiovisuals that re-create the suffering caused by the 1931 earthquake, plus a unique collection of artifacts—including vessels, decorative work, and statues—relating to the Ngāti Kahungunu Māori people of the East Coast. ⊠ *1 Tennyson St.* ☎ *06/835–7781* ⊕ *www.mtghawkesbay.com* ⊠ *Free.*

★ National Aquarium

ZOO | **FAMILY** | Stand on a moving conveyor that takes you through the world of sharks, rays, and fish. Environmental and ecological displays showcase tropical fish, sea horses, tuatara, and other creatures. For NZ$120—all gear provided—you can even swim with the sharks. There is also a kiwi enclosure where these birds can be seen in ideal viewing conditions. ⊠ *Marine Parade* ☎ *06/834–1404* ⊕ *www.nationalaquarium.co.nz* ⊠ *NZ$22.*

Rothman's Building

BUILDING | A little over a kilometer (½ mile) north of the central core stands one of the area's finest deco edifices. The 1932 structure has been totally renovated and its original name reinstated: the National Tobacco Company Building. It has a rose theme on the stained-glass windows and on a magnificent glass dome over the entrance hall. ⊠ *1 Ossian St.*

🍴 Restaurants

Mexi Mama

$$$ | **MEXICAN** | With its huge wrought-iron chandelier and candlelit shrine to St. Theresa, this cheery Mexican restaurant is a feast for the eyes as well as the stomach. The menu includes many shared plates—the spicy pork tostaditas and *tortitas de pollo* are both recommended. **Known for:** easygoing atmosphere; delicious selection of tapas; margaritas with unique flavors. ⑤ *Average main: NZ$25* ⊠ *58 West Quay* ☎ *027/804–5812* ⊕ *www.meximama.co.nz* ⊗ *No lunch.*

★ Pacifica Restaurant

$$$$ | **NEW ZEALAND** | Enter this weathered blue bungalow to experience the innovative cooking and fresh produce Pacifica brings to the New Zealand dining scene. The five-course degustation menus with matched wine change daily, and reflect the chef's creativity and commitment to using the finest local products. **Known for:** fresh seafood and pasta; two excellent (but pricey) tasting menus; great wines. ⑤ *Average main: NZ$65* ⊠ *209 Marine Parade* ☎ *06/833–6335* ⊕ *www.pacificarestaurant.co.nz* ⊗ *Closed Sun. and Mon. No lunch.*

🛏 Hotels

Homestay 157

$$ | **B&B/INN** | You'll be made to feel very welcome at this luxurious yet comfortable home, which features a lovely en suite bedroom, a private guest lounge, and a covered veranda that provides spectacular views over the ocean to the Mahia Peninsula. **Pros:** genuine and welcoming hosts; free Wi-Fi; incredible views. **Cons:** only one room so close quarters with the hosts; fair distance from town; can only book via phone. ⑤ *Rooms from: NZ$145* ⊠ *157 Thompson Rd.* ☎ *06/835–0117* ⇄ *1 suite* ⑩ *Breakfast* ⊟ *No credit cards.*

McHardy Lodge

$$$$ | B&B/INN | The gardens at this historic mansion, high on Napier Hill, have panoramic views of the Pacific Ocean and the splendid Kaweka Ranges. **Pros:** grand mansion feel; fabulous views; heated pool and full-size billiard table. **Cons:** can be hard to find on a dark night; hard uphill walk from town center; need to book evening meals ahead of time. ⑤ *Rooms from: NZ$595* ✉ *11 Bracken St.* ☎ *06/835–0605* ⊕ *www.mchardylodge. co.nz* ⤴ *6 rooms* ⑩ *Some meals.*

Napier Bed and Breakfast—Tequila Sunrise

$$$ | B&B/INN | This modern hilltop residence with sweeping views over the countryside and ocean was purpose-built as a B&B. **Pros:** quality accommodations; complimentary wine made on premises; quiet atmosphere. **Cons:** 20-minute drive to town; long way from restaurants; decor a little old-fashioned. ⑤ *Rooms from: NZ$249* ✉ *123 Eskridge Dr.* ☎ *06/836–7373* ⊕ *www.napierbandb. co.nz* ⤴ *4 suites* ⑩ *Breakfast.*

Shoreline Motel

$$ | HOTEL | The rooms at this Marine Parade place are well appointed and well equipped; each comes with its own hot tub, a flat-screen TV, and free Wi-Fi. **Pros:** close to town; many rooms have sea views; free off-street parking. **Cons:** often full in the holiday season; two flights of outside stairs to top units; main road can be noisy. ⑤ *Rooms from: NZ$195* ✉ *377 Marine Parade* ☎ *06/835–5222* ⊕ *www. shorelinenapier.co.nz* ⤴ *38 rooms* ⑩ *No meals.*

🛍 Shopping

Art Deco Centre

LOCAL SPECIALTIES | Napier's Art Deco Trust maintains a perfectly laid-out shop that sells everything from table lamps to ceramics, as well as a selection of hats, toys, jewelry, rugs, and wineglasses. ✉ *7 Tennyson St.* ☎ *06/835–0022* ⊕ *www. artdeconapier.com.*

Opossum World

CLOTHING | This fascinating spot sells opossum products and houses a minimuseum about the opossum's effects on New Zealand's environment. Fur items include hats, gloves, and rugs; a soft blend of merino wool and opossum fur is also made into sweaters, scarves, and socks. ✉ *106 Hastings St.* ☎ *06/835– 7697* ⊕ *www.opossumworld.com.*

Hawke's Bay

320 km (205 miles) northeast of Wellington, 165 km (100 miles) southeast of Taupo.

Bounded by the Kaweka and Ruahine ranges, Hawke's Bay is known as the fruit basket of New Zealand. You can't travel far without seeing a vineyard or an orchard, and the region produces some of the country's finest wines. Roughly 25 years ago, a dry, barren area known as the **Gimblett Gravels** was about to be mined for gravel. Then an enterprising vine grower took a gamble and purchased the land. The stony soil turned out to be a boon for grapevines because it retains heat, and now several wineries benefit from its toasty conditions. Chardonnay is the most important white variety here; you'll also find Sauvignon Blanc, Bordeaux varieties, and Syrah.

On the coast east of Hawke's Bay is Cape Kidnappers, a fascinating spot that is home to as many as 20,000 gannets. To the south, you'll find Hastings, which is blessed with art deco buildings, and adorable Havelock North (known locally as "the Village"), with the Te Mata Peak rising dramatically beyond.

Farther south, a hill near Porangahau is the place with **the longest name in the world.** Take a deep breath and say, "Taumatawhakatangihangakoauauotamateaturipukakapikimaungahoronukupokaiwhehuakitanatahu." If that's too difficult to memorize, just remember it as "the place where Tamatea, the man with the big knees who slid, climbed, and swallowed mountains, known as land-eater, played his flute to his loved one," and it should be no problem at all.

GETTING HERE AND AROUND

Distances here are comparatively short: Hastings, for instance, is only 18 km (11 miles) south of Napier, so driving is the optimal way to get around.

TOURS

★ Gannet Beach Adventures

GUIDED TOURS | FAMILY | Make the most of your trip to the Cape Kidnappers gannet colony by boarding a trailer towed by a 1949 Minneapolis-Moline tractor. Along the way, you'll hear commentary about the geological features of this amazing coastline. Tours lasting about four hours run daily, October through late April. They depart approximately two hours before low tide from Clifton Reserve; transport from the Napier or Hastings i-SITE is available. ✉ 475 Clifton Rd., Clifton, Napier ☎ 06/875–0898 ⊕ www.gannets. com ✉ NZ$44.

Gannet Safaris Overland

BUS TOURS | This outfit runs a four-wheel-drive bus to Cape Kidnappers from its base, just past Te Awanga. The three-hour tour includes commentary and stops within a few feet of the gannets—no walking required. Buses leave daily at 9:30 and 1:30, September through April. Advance booking is essential; transportation from Napier or Hastings can be arranged at extra cost. ✉ 396 Clifton Rd., Clifton, Napier ☎ 06/875–0888 ⊕ www. gannetsafaris.co.nz ✉ NZ$88 (4-person minimum).

A gannet comes in for a landing on the rocks of Cape Kidnappers in Hawke's Bay.

VISITOR INFORMATION

CONTACTS Hastings i-SITE Visitor Information Centre. ⊠ *Westerman's Bldg., Russell St. N and Heretaunga St., Hastings* ☎ *0800/429–537* ⊕ *www.visithastings. co.nz.* **Havelock North i-SITE Visitor Information Centre.** ⊠ *Te Aute and Middle Rds., Havelock North* ☎ *06/877–9600* ⊕ *www. havelocknorthnz.com.*

👁 Sights

Cape Kidnappers

LOCAL INTEREST | This outstanding spot is believed to be the only mainland gannet sanctuary in existence. It was named by Captain James Cook after local Māori tried to kidnap the servant of his Tahitian interpreter, Tupaia. Gannets—large white seabirds with black-tipped flight feathers, a golden crown, and a wingspan that can reach 6 feet—generally nest only on remote islands. But between October and April, thousands of them build their nests here, hatch their young, and prepare them for their long migratory flight. Watching them dive for their dinner is particularly impressive; when the birds find a shoal of fish, they fold their wings and plunge straight into the sea at tremendous speed. You can walk to the sanctuary along the beach from Clifton, a community located about 24 km (15 miles) south of Napier—but not at high tide. The 8-km (5-mile) walk must begin no earlier than three hours after the high-tide mark, and the return journey must begin no later than four hours before the next high tide. Tidal information is available at area i-SITE Visitor Information Centres. A rest hut with refreshments is near the colony. ⊠ *Cape Kidnappers, Clifton, Napier* ⊕ *www.doc.govt.nz/parks-and-recreation/places-to-go/hawkes-bay/places/ cape-kidnappers-gannet-reserve.*

★ Craggy Range Winery

WINERY/DISTILLERY | Situated by a small lake with the towering Te Mata Peak beyond, this vineyard has a stellar backdrop. The wines include single-varietal Chardonnay, Merlot, and Syrah; a predominantly Merlot blend called Sophia; and a Pinot Noir dubbed Aroha.

You can sample wines at the cellar door; leave time to linger over a meal at Terroir, a French-inspired restaurant overlooking the lake. ✉ *253 Waimarama Rd., Havelock North* ☎ *06/873–7126* ⊕ *www. craggyrange.com* ✉ *Tastings NZ$10 (refundable with purchase of bottle).*

Elephant Hill Estate & Winery

WINERY/DISTILLERY | Blending contemporary architecture with the traditional aspect of wine making, this stunning estate overlooks jagged rows of vines with expansive views from the terrace taking in the ocean and Cape Kidnappers. Sip a glass of wine in the sunken lounge or enjoy a meal in the ultramodern dining room—it's an unforgettable experience. ✉ *86 Clifton Rd., Te Awanga* ☎ *06/872–6073 winery, 06/872–6073 restaurant* ⊕ *www.elephanthill.co.nz* ✉ *Tastings from $5 (refundable with purchase of bottle).*

Esk Valley Estate Winery

WINERY/DISTILLERY | Winemaker Gordon Russell produces Merlot, Syrah, and blends with Cabernet Sauvignon, Merlot, Cabernet Franc, and Malbec in various combinations, including a rare and expensive red simply called The Terraces. White varieties include Chardonnay, Sauvignon Blanc, Riesling, Verdelho, Chenin Blanc, and Pinot Gris. Look for the Wine-Makers reserve versions of Chardonnay, Syrah, and Merlot-Malbec blend to find out what he has done with the best grapes from given years. The vineyard's position, in a sheltered valley overlooking the Pacific, ensures it captures full sun; it's located 12 km (8 miles) north of Napier, just north of the town of Bay View before Highways 2 and 5 split. ✉ *745 Main Rd., Bay View* ☎ *06/872–7430* ⊕ *www.eskvalley.co.nz.*

Hastings

TOWN | Napier's twin city doesn't have the same concentrated architectural interest as Napier. But the 1931 earthquake also did a great deal of damage here, and buildings in its center exhibit similar art deco flourishes. The Westerman's Building, on the corner of Russell and Heretaunga, is one prime example; it now houses the town's i-SITE center. Hastings is 18 km (11 miles) south of Napier, down Highway 2. ✉ *Hastings.*

Hawke's Bay Farmers' Market

MARKET | For picnic supplies, visit the Hawke's Bay Farmers' Market. It's held at the A&P Showgrounds on Sunday from 8:30 to 12:30. Local products include handmade cheese, breads, ice cream, and fruit. This is also a good place to people-watch. ✉ *Kenilworth Rd., Hastings* ⊕ *hawkesbayfarmersmarket.co.nz.*

★ Mission Estate Winery

RESTAURANT—SIGHT | Surrounded by gardens, this classic winery—the country's oldest—stands in the Taradale hills overlooking Napier. Dating back to 1851, it deserves to be added to your "must-see" list. Award-winning wines, including the Mission Jewelstone range, can be bought or tasted at the cellar door. Learn more about the mission's history by joining one of the twice-daily tours; or order a meal in the on-site restaurant, which serves lunch and dinner daily (take a seat on the terrace for a terrific view of the vineyard and Napier). Also check out the website—the winery occasionally hosts concerts by big-name performers. To get here, leave Napier by Kennedy Road, heading southwest from the city center toward Taradale. Just past Anderson Park, turn right into Avenue Road and continue to its end at Church Road. ✉ *198 Church Rd., Taradale* ☎ *06/845–9350* ⊕ *www. missionestate.co.nz* ✉ *Tastings free.*

Moana Park

WINERY/DISTILLERY | Specific wine styles are selected and handcrafted from each vintage at this small boutique producer, based on its Gimblett Gravels and Dartmoor Valley vineyards. All grapes are grown on either organic or sustainable sites and are vegetarian approved. There's no café here, but platters of local produce are available; you're also welcome to bring along a picnic as there are plenty of tables on the lovely grounds. ✉ *530 Puketapu*

Rd., Taradale ☎ 06/844–8269 ⊕ www. moanapark.co.nz ⌣ Tastings free.

Te Mata Estate

WINERY/DISTILLERY | This is one of New Zealand's oldest and best wineries. Coleraine, a rich but elegant Cabernet–Merlot blend named after the much-photographed home of the owner, John Buck, is considered the archetypal Hawke's Bay red. Bullnose Syrah, Elston Chardonnay, and Cape Crest Sauvignon Blanc show similar restraint and balance. If there's any Zara Viognier open (it's made only in tiny quantities), try it—it's excellent. From Napier head south on Marine Parade through Clive and turn left at the Mangateretere School. Signs will then lead you to Te Mata Road and the estate. ⊠ 349 Te Mata Rd., Havelock North ☎ 06/877–4399 ⊕ www.temata. co.nz ⌣ Tastings NZ$8.

Te Mata Peak

VIEWPOINT | It's possible to gaze across the plains to Napier and the rumpled hills beyond from this famed local viewpoint. The summit is a 15-minute (signposted) drive along Te Mata Peak Road from the village of Havelock North. ⊠ Te Mata Peak Rd., Havelock North.

🍴 Restaurants

Jarks Cityside

$$$ | CONTEMPORARY | On sunny days, you can sit outside on the patio here and enjoy the varied menu. In winter, a large fireplace warms the rustic interior, and candles on the tables enhance the scene. **Known for:** seasonal produce; cheesecake of the day; friendly local vibe. ⑤ Average main: NZ$26 ⊠ 118 Maraekakoho Rd., Hastings ☎ 06/870–8333 ⊕ www.jarks. co.nz ⊗ Closed Sun.

Rose & Shamrock

$$$ | IRISH | This lovely old-world pub in the heart of Havelock North has the largest selection of tap beer in Hawke's Bay. The pints mix with reasonably priced pub fare, including Scotch fillet, Irish sausages, and hearty beef-and-Guinness pie. **Known for:** friendly atmosphere; good standard pub food; fun trivia night. ⑤ Average main: NZ$22 ⊠ Napier Rd. and Porter Dr., Havelock North ☎ 06/877–2999 ⊕ www.roseandshamrock.co.nz.

★ Terroir Restaurant

$$$$ | FRENCH | The massive cedar doors, high circular roof, and open wood fire give this well-regarded restaurant at Craggy Range Winery a rustic character. Although the menu is loosely country French, the "rustic" cuisine here is far from unsophisticated. **Known for:** some of the best wine in the region; twice-baked goat cheese soufflé; gorgeous views from the terrace. ⑤ Average main: NZ$39 ⊠ 253 Waimarama Rd., Havelock North ☎ 06/873–0143 ⊕ www.craggyrange.com ⊗ Closed Mon. and Tues. Apr.–Oct. No dinner Sun.

Hotels

Harvest Lodge

$$ | HOTEL | FAMILY | Close to the center of Havelock North, this up-to-the-minute motel has spacious units with original artwork and comfortable king-size beds. **Pros:** close to town; handy to restaurants and bars; spacious rooms. **Cons:** near busy road; may be some traffic noise; breakfast not included. ⑤ Rooms from: NZ$165 ⊠ 23 Havelock Rd., Havelock North ☎ 06/877–9500 ⊕ www.harvestlodge.co.nz ⥮ 19 units ⧌ No meals.

Mangapapa Hotel

$$$$ | HOTEL | The 1885 grand residence of one of New Zealand's earliest entrepreneurs has been converted into a charming boutique hotel. **Pros:** private and quiet; understated luxury; excellent café. **Cons:** breakfast not included; pricey; grounds could use some maintenance in places. ⑤ Rooms from: NZ$499 ⊠ 466 Napier Rd., Havelock North ☎ 06/878–3234 ⊕ www.mangapapa.co.nz ⥮ 12 suites ⧌ No meals.

Portmans Motor Lodge

$$ | HOTEL | Conveniently located near the center of Hastings, this motel has 20 modern units surrounding a spacious courtyard; 10 have whirlpool baths, and all are comfortably equipped. **Pros:** reasonably priced accommodations; really handy to town; lovely pool. **Cons:** some parking is a little cramped; pool isn't heated; decor not very charming. $ *Rooms from: NZ$165* ✉ *401 Railway Rd., Hastings* ☎ *06/878–8332* ⊕ *www.portmans. co.nz* ↪ *20 rooms* ❍❙ *No meals.*

Gisborne

210 km (130 miles) northeast of Napier, 500 km (310 miles) southeast of Auckland.

The Māori name for the Gisborne district is Tairawhiti (tye-ra- *fee*-tee), "the coast upon which the sun shines across the water," and Gisborne is indeed the first city in New Zealand to see sunrise. With a population of just 30,000, it's hardly large; however, you'll need a day or so to get around properly. The landmark Town Clock stands in the middle of Gladstone Road; nearby, in a house on Grey Street, Kiri Te Kanawa, New Zealand's world-famous opera diva, was born in 1944 (the house is no longer there).

Europeans settled the Gisborne area early in the 19th century. A plaque on the waterfront commemorates the first official sale—of an acre of land—on June 30, 1831. On that site, the first European house and store was reportedly erected (it's long gone, too).

GETTING HERE AND AROUND

Air New Zealand flies daily to Gisborne from Auckland and Wellington. The small Gisborne Airport (GIS) is about 5 km (3 miles) from the city center; you can catch a taxi in for NZ$20. InterCity buses also link Gisborne to Auckland and Wellington once per day.

Motorists should note that Gisborne is a long way from almost anywhere, but the coastal and bush scenery makes the drive wholly worthwhile. Most of the town's historical sights and other attractions are too spread out to explore by foot, and a car is needed for the spectacular countryside. The main driving approach is by State Highway 2, which becomes Gladstone Street as it enters the town.

AIRPORTS Gisborne Airport. ✉ *Aerodrome Rd.* ☎ *06/986–4800* ⊕ *www.eastland. co.nz/gisborne-airport.*

BUS CONTACTS Gisborne Bus Depot. ✉ *Gisborne i-SITE Visitor Information Centre, 209 Grey St.*

VISITOR INFORMATION

CONTACTS Gisborne i-SITE Visitor Information Centre. ✉ *209 Grey St.* ☎ *06/868– 6139* ⊕ *www.gisbornenz.com.*

◉ Sights

Cook Landing Site National Historic Reserve

MEMORIAL | This place has deep historical significance for New Zealanders. A statue of Captain James Cook, who first landed here on October 9, 1769, stands on Kaiti Beach, across the river southeast of the city center. The beach itself attracts interesting birdlife at low tide. ✉ *Esplanade on south end of Turanganui River.*

Eastwoodhill Arboretum

GARDEN | FAMILY | Inspired by the gardens seen on a trip to England in 1910, William Douglas Cook returned home and began planting 160 acres. His brainchild became a stunning collection of more than 600 genera of trees from around the world. In spring and summer daffodils mass yellow, magnolias bloom in clouds of pink and white, and cherries, crab apples, wisteria, and azalea add to the spectacle. The main trails in the park can be walked in about 45 minutes. Maps and self-guided tour booklets are available. Drive west from Gisborne center on State Highway 2 toward Napier, cross the bridge, and

Gisborne is one of the more low-key wine regions in New Zealand, which means its wineries are less crowded.

turn at the rotary onto the Ngatapa–Rere Road. Follow it 35 km (22 miles) to the arboretum. ✉ *2392 Wharekopae Rd., Ngatapa* 🕾 *06/863–9003* ⊕ *www.east-woodhill.org.nz* 🎫 *NZ$15*.

Gisborne–Opotiki Loop

SCENIC DRIVE | Soak in the beauty of Eastland by driving the Provincial Highway 35 loop between Gisborne and Opotiki—it's one of the country's ultimate roads-less-traveled. The 330-km (205-mile) trip takes about five hours without stops. En route, rolling green hills drop into wide crescent beaches or rock-strewn coves; and small towns appear, only to fade into the surrounding landscape. Some scenic highlights are **Anaura Bay,** with rocky headlands, a long beach favored by surfers, and nearby islands; it is between **Tolaga Bay** and **Tokomaru Bay,** two former shipping towns. Tolaga Bay has an incredibly long wharf stretching over a white-sand beach into the sea, and Cooks Cove Walkway is a pleasant amble through the countryside past a rock arch. Farther up the coast in **Tikitiki,** you'll find both a gas station and an Anglican church full of carved Māori panels and beams. East of the small town of **Te Araroa,** which has the oldest *pohutukawa* (po-hoo-too- *ka*-wa) tree in the country, the coast is about as remote as you could imagine. At the tip of the cape, 21 km (13 miles) from Te Araroa, the East Cape Lighthouse promises fantastic views after a long, steep climb from the beach. Back toward Opotiki, **Whanarua** (fahn-ah- *roo*-ah) **Bay** is one of the most gorgeous on the East Cape, with isolated beaches ideal for a picnic and a swim. Farther on, there is an intricately carved Māori marae (meetinghouse) called Tukaki in **Te Kaha.** If you choose to spend a night along the loop, there are motels at various points on the cape and some superbly sited motor camps and backpackers' lodges, though you'll need to be well stocked with foodstuffs before you set off. Gisborne's i-SITE Centre can provide information about lodging.

Millton Vineyard

WINERY/DISTILLERY | The first New Zealand facility to attain organic certification specializes in making fine wine from estate-grown grapes sourced from single vineyards and grown in the traditional manner using biodynamic techniques. It's a great place to sample, sit, and relax. There are no restaurant facilities here, but you're welcome to bring a picnic. The vineyard is signposted off State Highway 2, about 11 km (7 miles) south of Gisborne. ⊠ *119 Papatu Rd., Manutuke* ☎ *06/862–8680* ⊕ *www.millton.co.nz* ⊡ *Tastings free.*

Morere Hot Springs

HOT SPRINGS | FAMILY | Set in 1,000 acres of native bush, this place provides modern bathing facilities in an unusual natural environment. A cold outdoor pool is alongside a warm indoor pool, and in the forest a few minutes' walk away are smaller hot or warm pools with a cold plunge pool. Two private hotpools are also available. Following the walking trails through the forest can take 20 minutes or stretch to two to three hours. Morere is roughly halfway between Wairoa and Gisborne, north of the Mahia turnoff. ⊠ *State Hwy. 2, Morere* ☎ *06/837–8856* ⊕ *www.morerehotsprings.co.nz* ⊡ *From NZ$14.*

Tairawhiti Museum

MUSEUM | FAMILY | With its Māori and *Pākehā* (non-native) artifacts and an extensive photographic collection, this small but interesting museum provides a good introduction to the region's history. A maritime gallery covers seafaring matters, and there are changing exhibits of local and national artists' work. The pottery displays are particularly outstanding. An on-site shop sells locally made items. Check out Wyllie Cottage before leaving the grounds (although it stands outside, it's part of the museum). Built in 1872, this colonial-style house is the oldest in town. ⊠ *Kelvin Park, 10 Stout St.* ☎ *06/867–3832* ⊕ *www.tairawhitimuseum.org.nz* ⊡ *NZ$5 Tues.–Sun.; free Mon.*

Te Poho o Rawiri Meeting House

HISTORIC SITE | One of the largest Māori marae (meetinghouses) in New Zealand has an intriguing interior with complex traditional carvings. One example is the *tekoteko,* a kneeling human figure with the right hand raised to challenge those who enter. There are also unusual alcoves and a stage framed by carvings; it's essentially a meetinghouse within a meetinghouse. Photography is not allowed inside. On the side of the hill stands the 1930s Toko Toro Tapu Church. You'll need permission to explore either site; contact the Gisborne i-SITE Visitor Information Centre. ⊠ *At Ranfurly St. and Queens Dr., Kaiti Hill* ⊡ *Donations requested.*

Titirangi Domain

HISTORIC SITE | This was the site of an extensive pā (fortified village), which can be traced back at least 24 Māori generations. It has excellent views of Gisborne, Poverty Bay, and the surrounding rural areas. **Titirangi Recreational Reserve** is a part of the Domain, and it makes a great place for a picnic or a walk. The Domain is south of Turanganui River. Pass the harbor and turn right onto Esplanade, left onto Crawford Road, then right onto Queens Drive, and follow it to several lookout points in the Domain where the views are extraordinary. ⊠ *Gisborne.*

🍴 Restaurants

The Marina Restaurant & Bar

$$$$ | FRENCH | Originally the ballroom of a stately home, this high-ceilinged restaurant lives up to its pedigree and brings French flair to Gisborne. Attention to detail from start to finish is the hallmark here. **Known for:** modern French fine dining; local ingredients; deck seating with beautiful views. ⑤ *Average main: NZ$43* ⊠ *Marina Park, Vogel St.* ☎ *06/868–5919* ⊕ *www.marinarestaurant.co.nz* ⊗ *Closed Sun. and Mon. No lunch Tues. and Wed.*

The Rivers

$$$ | IRISH | A casual place to hoist a few pints while dining on hearty pub fare, the Rivers is popular with Gisborne locals. Stained-glass partitions separate the dining alcoves, which have brass chandeliers, dark woodwork, and green leather upholstery. **Known for:** friendly atmosphere; great Irish pub food; central location. ⑤ *Average main: NZ$25* ⊠ *At Reads Quay and Gladstone Rd.* ☎ *06/863–3733* ⊕ *www.therivers.co.nz.*

The Works Café & Winery

$$$$ | **NEW ZEALAND** | This eatery in the former Gisborne Freezing Works embraces its industrial roots (note the large drive shaft and pulleys on the brick walls). The menu builds on local products, from cheeses to fruit, scallops to calamari. **Known for:** excellent panfried fish; cool atmosphere; local wine. ⑤ *Average main: NZ$35* ⊠ *41 The Esplanade* ☎ *06/868–9699* ⊕ *www.theworksgisborne.co.nz.*

🛏 Hotels

Linburn Farm Stay

$$ | **B&B/INN** | The 1920s home of Karyn and Mark Watson is situated on a working farm that breeds sheep and cattle. **Pros:** great getaway for peace and quiet; picturesque countryside setting; homey decor. **Cons:** 20-minute drive to the city; location might seem a little isolated; no bar. ⑤ *Rooms from: NZ$130* ⊠ *1279 Waimata Valley Rd.* ☎ *06/867–0375* ⊕ *www. geocities.ws/linburnfarmstay* ▭ *No credit cards* ⤴ *2 rooms* �🍽 *Breakfast.*

Ocean Beach

$$ | **HOTEL** | **FAMILY** | A surfer's paradise, this Mediterranean-looking motel complex is a five-minute drive north of Gisborne, close to Wainui Beach. **Pros:** ideal situation for beach-type holiday; spacious rooms; nice amenities. **Cons:** there may be traffic noise in the busy season; need transport into town; breakfast not included. ⑤ *Rooms from: NZ$140* ⊠ *7 Oneroa Rd., Wainui Beach* ☎ *06/868–6186* ⊕ *www.oceanbeach.co.nz* ⤴ *15 rooms* ⼗🍽 *No meals.*

Senator Motor Inn

$$ | **HOTEL** | Offering comfortable, modern accommodations with lovely views over the marina and inner harbor on one side and main-street shopping on the doorstep, this motel has an ideal location that ticks all the boxes. **Pros:** great views; close to everything; free Wi-Fi and off-street parking. **Cons:** may be full in high season; proximity to street means it may be noisy; breakfast not included. ⑤ *Rooms from: NZ$155* ⊠ *2 Childers Rd.* ☎ *06/868–8877* ⊕ *www.senatormotorinn. co.nz* ⤴ *16 rooms* ⼗🍽 *No meals.*

🏃 Activities

DIVING AND SNORKELING
★ **Dive Tatapouri**

DIVING/SNORKELING | Dean and Chrissie lead an extremely popular snorkeling excursion that lets you swim freely with stingrays, eagle rays, kingfish, crayfish, octopuses, and other ocean creatures. You'll get to observe, touch, and feed them in their natural habitat (NZ$70, wet suits, snorkels, and masks provided). If you'd rather not dive right in, try the Reef Tour. On this one you wade out to spy all manner of marine life. Huge rays slide up the rocks and put their head clear of the water; when you pop a morsel into their mouth, they take it gently, and then glide silently away (NZ$55, waders included). Tours are available year-round but are dependent on tides. Dive Tatapouri is 15 km (9 miles) north of the city, off State Highway 35. ⊠ *Whangara Rd.* ☎ *06/868–5153* ⊕ *www.divetatapouri. com* 💰 *From NZ$55.*

FISHING
Touchwood Fishing Charter

FISHING | Albacore, yellowfin tuna, mako shark, and marlin along with the yellow-tail kingfish are prized catches from January to April (no license required). There are various operators who will help you land one—including Touchwood. Its boat has a full range of safety equipment, plus fish-finding electronics that help it target a number of species from the lesser-known hot spots around Gisborne. Prepare to pay NZ$1,765 per day for a private charter or NZ$150 per person for a party of 10, tackle and bait included. ✉ *37a Massey Rd.* ☎ *06/867–1066* ⊕ *touchwoodfishing-chartersgisborne.co.nz.*

GOLF
Poverty Bay Golf Course
GOLF | This 18-hole championship course ranks among the top five in the country. Established in 1893, the links-style, par 72 course is open for play daily. The greens fee is NZ$30 for nonaffiliated players. ✉ *Lytton and Awapuni Rds., Elgin* ☎ *06/867–4402* ⊕ *www.gisbornegolf.co.nz.*

SURFING
Surfing with Frank
SURFING | **FAMILY** | Gisborne has three good surfing beaches close to town. Waikanae Beach, a short walk from the i-SITE Visitor Information Centre on Grey Street, usually has good learners' surf; the Pipe and the Island are for the more experienced. The former is just south of Waikanae; the latter fronts the Titarangi Domain. You can arrange for lessons at Surfing with Frank. Private lessons are NZ$95 for two hours; group rates start at NZ$65 while surfboard and wet suit hire is NZ$30. ✉ *Gisborne* ☎ *06/867–0823* ⊕ *www.surfingwithfrank.com.*

Te Urewera National Park

163 km (101 miles) west of Gisborne.

New Zealand's fourth-largest national park protects the biggest area of native forest remaining on the North Island. The ancestral home of the Tuhoe people, its main attraction is Lake Waikaremoana, which draws hikers, canoeists, and fishing enthusiasts from around the world.

GETTING HERE AND AROUND
Local bus service is extremely limited, so the best way to get around is by car. Campervans are also popular, as there is plenty of space for the outdoor style of living. Access to the park is from Wairoa, 100 km (62 miles) southwest of Gisborne down Highway 2. It's then another 63 km (39 miles) northwest from Wairoa along Highway 38 to Lake Waikaremoana.

VISITOR INFORMATION
CONTACTS Te Urewera Visitor Centre. ✉ *State Hwy. 38, Aniwaniwa* ☎ *06/837–3803* ⊕ *www.doc.govt.nz.*

⊙ Sights

★ Te Urewera National Park
NATIONAL/STATE PARK | **FAMILY** | Remote Te Urewera National Park is rugged and mountainous. This park's outstanding feature is glorious **Lake Waikaremoana** ("sea of rippling waters"), a forest-girded lake with good swimming, boating, and fishing. The lake is encircled by a 50-km (31-mile) walking trail, which takes three or four days to complete; it's a popular trek, and the lakeside hiking huts are heavily used in the summer months. The Department of Conservation Visitor Centre at Aniwaniwa is stocked with maps and informative leaflets; staff will also give advice about other park walks, like the one to the **Aniwaniwa Falls** (30 minutes round-trip) or to **Lake Waikareiti** (five to six hours round-trip). All trails pass through spectacular countryside of high, misty ridges covered with silver and mountain beech. Waterfalls and streams abound, and on the lower levels the forest giants, *rimu, rata, kamahi, totara,* and *tawa* attract native birds like the New Zealand falcon, North Island brown kiwi, *kaka,* and *kokako.* A motor camp on the lakeshore, not far from the visitor center, has cabins, chalets, and motel units; in summer, a launch operates sightseeing and fishing trips from it. Note that there are areas of private Māori land within the park, so be sure to stay on marked paths. ✉ *Te Urewera National Park, Gisborne* ⊕ *www.doc.govt.nz/parks-and-recreation/places-to-go/east-coast/places/te-urewera.*

NORTH ISLAND'S WEST COAST

7

Updated by
Kathy Ombler

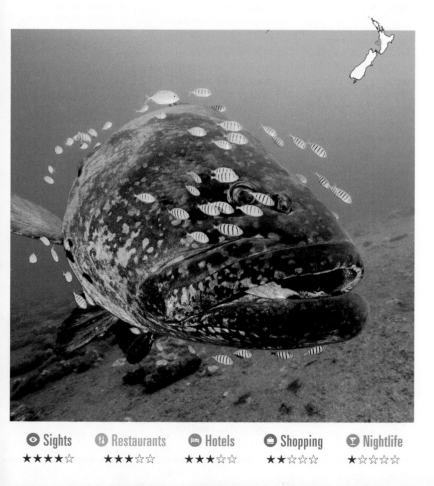

👁 Sights	🍽 Restaurants	🛏 Hotels	🛍 Shopping	🍸 Nightlife
★★★★☆	★★★☆☆	★★★☆☆	★★☆☆☆	★☆☆☆☆

WELCOME TO NORTH ISLAND'S WEST COAST

TOP REASONS TO GO

★ **Caving:** Beneath Waitomo, underground passageways, fossils, limestone formations, and glowworms await. Explore by walking, boating, "black-water" rafting, or rappelling.

★ **Kayaking and Canoeing:** Ideal for beginners, the Whanganui is New Zealand's longest navigable river. Paddling trips promise amazing scenery and historic Māori settlements.

★ **Walking and Hiking:** Take a short walk or multiday trek through the wetlands, alpine fields, and lowland rain forest of Egmont National Park.

★ **Surfing:** The black-sand surfing beaches here are among the world's best. Near Raglan try Whale Bay and Manu Bay; in Taranaki "Surf Highway 45" accesses premier breaks.

★ **Scenic Drives:** Rolling green farmlands, dense forests, mountain ranges, river gorges, and dramatic coastlines—you can see them all from the comfort of your car.

The region's landscape includes the majestic volcano, Mt. Taranaki; the gorges and wilderness of the Whanganui River; the underground wonders of the Waitomo Caves; world-renowned surfing beaches; two national parks; and a host of forest-covered conservation areas, along with highly productive farmland.

In the northwest, surfing town Raglan sits on a sparsely populated coastline, but it's an easy hour's drive from the region's main city, Hamilton. Waitomo is on the westward route to New Plymouth and the Taranaki region. While State Highway 1 traverses the center of the North Island, State Highway 3 travels the West Coast through the Taranaki bight to Whanganui, then meets again with State Highway 1 close to Palmerston North.

1 Raglan. This low-key small town is one of the region's top surfing spots, thanks to Manu Bay and Whale Bay.

2 Waitomo. This small village leads to the area's wondrous underground cave systems and the famed glowworms that live in their ceilings.

3 New Plymouth. The hub for one of the country's largest agricultural regions, New Plymouth also has a great arts scene and some of New Zealand's best gardens.

4 Egmont National Park. The star of New Zealand's second oldest national park is the magnificent Mt. Taranaki.

5 Stratford. This eccentric town serves the surrounding farmland, and features some beautiful gardens.

6 Whanganui. This river city is the main gateway to Whanganui National Park and the multitude of activities found along the Whanganui River.

7 Whanganui National Park. New Zealand's longest navigable river cuts through the single largest tract of lowland forest remaining in the North Island.

8 Palmerston North. This student-friendly city is a center for education and research in the area.

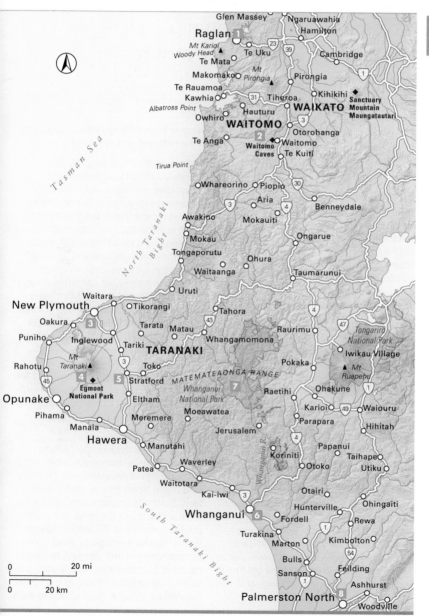

Glen Massey
Ngaruawahia
Raglan 1
Hamilton
Mt Kariol
Woody Head
Te Uku
23
39
Cambridge
Te Mata
Makomako
Mt
Pirongia
Pirongia
1
Te Rauamoa
Kihikihi
Kawhia
31
Tiheroa
WAIKATO
Sanctuary
Mountain
Albatross Point
Owhiro
Hauturu
Maungatautari
WAITOMO
Otorohanga
Te Anga
2
Waitomo
Waitomo
Te Kuiti
Caves

Tirua Point

Whareorino
Piopio
30
Aria
Benneydale
Awakino
3
4
Mokauiti
Mokau
Ongarue
Tongaporutu
Ohura
Waitaanga
Taumarunui
Uruti
Waitara
Tahora
4
New Plymouth
Tikorangi
Raurimu
47
Oakura
3
Tarata
43
Tongariro
National Park
Puniho
Inglewood
Matau
Whangamomona
Iwikau Village
Tariki
TARANAKI
Pokaka
Mt
Rahotu
Mt
3
Toko
MATEMATEAONGA RANGE
Ruapehu
45
Taranaki
4
5
Stratford
Whanganui
7
Ohakune
1
Opunake
Egmont
National Park
Eltham
National Park
Raetihi
Pihama
Meremere
Moeawatea
Karioi
Waiouru
49
Manaia
Jerusalem
Parapara
Hihitah
Hawera
Manutahi
Papanui
Waverley
4
Koriniti
Taihape
Patea
Otoko
Utiku
Waitotara
Otairi
Ohingaiti
Kai-iwi
3
Hunterville
Whanganui
6
Fordell
Rewa
Turakina
1
Kimbolton
Marton
54
Bulls
Feilding
Sanson
1
Ashhurst
Palmerston North
8
Woodville

Tasman Sea

North Taranaki Bight

South Taranaki Bight

Whanganui R.

0   20 mi

0   20 km

The North Island's West Coast is all about landscape diversity: top surfing beaches; world-renowned limestone caves; and two national parks, one centered on a volcanic mountain, the other on a wilderness river.

The land is generally rural, ranging from lifestyle blocks to sheep-and-cattle farms located in remote, rolling hill country and a jumble of forest-covered mountain ranges. The long coastline is captivating; world-class surfing breaks meet sandy swimming beaches and craggy cliffs. Small cities and rural towns throughout the region provide a high level of sophistication for their size; they may have started as service communities, but delve deeper and you'll find galleries, art studios, farmers' markets, designer stores, museums, and funky cafés.

Waikato is a region of surprises. To the west are the famed surfing beaches of Raglan, guarded by ancient forest-covered volcanoes. In the south, 30 million years of Mother Nature's handiwork have created the Waitomo Caves, an underground spectacle that thousands of visitors now explore each year, be it by foot, boat, or rappelling rope.

The Taranaki region sprang from the ocean floor in a series of volcanic blasts, creating that distinctive curve along the West Coast of the North Island. The cone of Mt. Taranaki is the province's dramatic symbol and the backdrop for climbing routes and hiking tracks (trails). Agriculture thrives in the area's fertile volcanic soil, and the gardens around Taranaki and New Plymouth are some of the country's most spectacular. The mythology and historic sites relating to the local people are an integral part of Taranaki, too.

Farther south, the Whanganui River wends its scenic way through the forest-covered ridges and valleys that encompass Whanganui National Park. The river is the first in the world to be given legal personhood status by the government, a designation that recognizes the river's physical and spiritual connection with the local *iwi* (tribe). Steeped in history, for centuries the river formed the "road" for the Māori who lived on its banks, and was later a major route for tourists traveling by steamer. Today the river and surrounding national park draws canoeists, hikers, cyclists, and history buffs. As you veer inland, from river city Whanganui through to the Manawatu region and Palmerston North, the land gives way to prosperous sheep and cattle farms.

MAJOR REGIONS

Waikato. Some think of the Waikato region—a fertile, temperate, agricultural district south of Auckland—as the heartland of the North Island. It's home to New Zealand's largest inland city (Hamilton) and some of the most important pre-European sites. Polynesian sailors first landed on the region's West Coast as early as the mid-14th century; by way of contrast, Europeans (mainly British) didn't settle here until the 1830s. In the 1860s, the Waikato's many tribes united to elect a king in an attempt to resist British encroachment. This King Movement, as it is known, is still a significant cultural and political force within Waikato Māoridom. Other regional attractions are the surfing hot spots and magnificent harbor of Raglan on the West Coast, and the extraordinary cave formations at Waitomo.

New Plymouth and Taranaki. On a clear day, sometimes with a cover of snow, Mt. Taranaki (also known as Mt. Egmont) towers above green flanks of forest and farmland. The nearly perfectly symmetrical volcano forms the basis of Egmont National Park, sitting at the heart of the Taranaki region, and the province has shaped itself around it. Northeast of Taranaki, the provincial city of New Plymouth (known for climbing, hiking, surfing, fishing, and cultural museums) hugs the coast, and smaller rural towns like Stratford dot the roads that circle the mountain's base. Heading seaward, there's some 200 km (124 miles) of shoreline—complete with top surf breaks, beach walks, shipwrecks, seal colonies, small estuaries, and fishing spots—to discover along the Taranaki coast.

Whanganui, the Whanganui River, and Palmerston North. The Whanganui River, flowing through a vast, forest-covered wilderness from the central North Island mountains, is the focus here. At its mouth, Whanganui city was established when river travel was the main form of transport. Today, kayakers and jet-boaters enjoy the scenic, historic, and wilderness experiences of Whanganui National Park. Palmerston North sits in the heart of farming country, an easy one-hour drive southeast of Whanganui. With a population of nearly 90,000, it ranks as New Zealand's seventh largest city. "Palmy," as it's affectionately known, is home to Massey University, and a youthful demographic helps keep it young at heart.

Planning

When to Go

Although the most popular period is from November through mid-April, most attractions can be enjoyed year-round. Spring is garden festival time in Taranaki. Summer is obviously warmer and great for swimming or surfing. However, the weather is often more settled during winter—unlike some South Island regions, it generally has no harsh snow or ice conditions to thwart travel—and there are fewer people.

Planning Your Time

Whether surfing or just enjoying the harbor and bush walks, spare at least a couple of days for Raglan, and another day or two for exploring the Waitomo Caves. From Waitomo travel southwest to Taranaki, where two to three days would allow exploration of the gardens and museums, plus a beach trip and a short walk in Egmont National Park—allow longer for more serious hiking, climbing, or surfing adventures. Whanganui city is worth a day or two. A river jet-boat or road trip provides a quick glimpse of the area; for an in-depth tour try a five-day kayak journey, then take a good day or two to absorb the university town of Palmerston North before heading on south to Wellington.

Getting Here and Around

AIR TRAVEL

Airports serve the main centers but driving or taking a bus is best for other areas. **Air New Zealand** operates flights daily from Auckland and Wellington to Hamilton, New Plymouth, and Palmerston North; and from Christchurch to New Plymouth and Palmerston North. Budget carrier Jetstar also serves New Plymouth and Palmerston North; Originair connects Palmerston North and Nelson; and Air Chathams connects Whanganui with Auckland.

CONTACTS Air Chathams. ☎ *0800 /580–127* ⊕ *www.airchathams.co.nz.* **Air New Zealand.** ☎ *0800/737–000* ⊕ *www.airnewzealand.co.nz.* **Jetstar.** ☎ *0800/800–995* ⊕ *www.jetstar.com.* **Originair.** ☎ *0800/380–380* ⊕ *originair. co.nz.*

BUS TRAVEL

InterCity links all cities and towns throughout the region with regular daily service. Flexible travel passes let passengers stop off as they please along the way. The **Waitomo Wanderer** (now operated by Kiwi Experience) links Rotorua and Taupo with Waitomo, once daily each way. From Otorohanga, the **Waitomo Shuttle** (book in advance) connects with major bus and train arrivals.

CONTACTS InterCity. ☎ *09/583–5780* ⊕ *www.intercity.co.nz.* **Kiwi Experience.** ☎ *0800/364–286* ⊕ *www.kiwiexperience. com.*

CAR TRAVEL

Driving is the most flexible way to travel through this region. Roads are nearly all clearly signposted, and drivers pass through diverse and scenic landscapes of farmland, forest-covered ranges, and rugged coastline.

TRAIN TRAVEL

Northern Explorer, the scenic 10-hour Auckland–Wellington train, stops at Hamilton, National Park, Ohakune, and Palmerston North; it travels southbound on Monday, Thursday, and Saturday and northbound on Tuesday, Friday, and Sunday.

CONTACTS *Northern Explorer.* ☎ *0800/872–467* ⊕ *www.greatjourney-sofnz.co.nz.*

Restaurants

Throughout western North Island, provincial city restaurants and small, tourist-town cafés feature an overall sophistication you might not expect away from major urban centers: think wholesome and hearty fare, local organic produce, good espresso and loose-leaf teas, high-quality New Zealand wines, and local craft beers. Counter food is generally fresh salads, panini, filled rolls, sweet or savory pies, and homemade soups.

Dinner menus in the higher-end restaurants include the chef's latest creations using high-quality New Zealand eye fillet of beef (beef tenderloin), fish, lamb racks, pork fillets, and chicken. The best chefs change menus regularly to focus on fresh regional and seasonal ingredients. You will also find Indian, Thai, Malaysian, Japanese, Mexican, Turkish, and Italian restaurants, even in smaller centers. "Smart-casual" is about as formal as attire gets.

Hotels

Bed-and-breakfasts can be stylishly converted country homesteads; sometimes they're custom built. There are also luxury lodges and a wonderful range of self-catering villas and cottages (some on working farms, others with spectacular coastal locations, and a few deep in the forest-covered hinterland). National parks have mountain lodges, river lodges, basic backcountry huts, and camping spots managed by the Department of Conservation.

In tourist towns and larger cities, there's the full range of options: boutique hotels, standard hotels with basic rooms, motels with full kitchens, holiday parks with RV sites and sometimes apartment units, as well as backpacker hostels. Although hostels are generally budget options with shared facilities, an increasing number are modern and feature private en suite rooms.

Restaurant and hotel reviews have been shortened. For full information, visit Fodors.com. Restaurant prices are the average cost of a main course at dinner or, if dinner is not served, at lunch. Hotel prices are the lowest cost of a standard double room in high season.

What It Costs			
$	$$	$$$	$$$$
RESTAURANTS			
under NZ$15	NZ$15–NZ$20	NZ$21–NZ$30	over NZ$30
HOTELS			
under NZ$125	NZ$125–NZ$200	NZ$201–NZ$300	over NZ$300

Visitor Information

Hamilton and Waikato Regional Tourism
(⊕ www.hamiltonwaikato.com) is a helpful regional resource. The regional tourism organization in Taranaki also maintains a website (⊕ www.taranaki.info/visit) with local listings and event information.

Raglan

176 km (110 miles) south of Auckland, 44 km (27 miles) west of Hamilton.

It's hard to think of a more laid-back, welcoming spot than Raglan. On sheltered Raglan Harbour, and in the lee of the forest-covered volcano, Mt. Karioi, the tiny town owes its easygoing ways to the surfers drawn to the legendary breaks at Manu Bay, 8 km (5 miles) southwest of town, and Whale Bay, just beyond. The Raglan surf is featured in movies and regularly plays host to international competitions. When the surf's up, you can drive out to the parking areas above the sweeping bays to see scores of enthusiasts tackling what's reputed to be the world's longest, most consistent left-hand break.

Surfers have made this seaside village cool, and along the main drag, Bow Street, barefoot dudes in designer shades pad in and out of the hip café-bars or hang in the smattering of craft and surf-wear shops; there is, however, much more to Raglan. The huge harbor, with its long Māori history, sandy beaches, and opportunities for kayaking, fishing, and relaxation, draws vacationers throughout the year.

GETTING HERE AND AROUND

The main road route to Raglan is from Hamilton, an hour's country drive away. Travelers from Auckland can turn off State Highway 1 at Ngaruawahia (10 minutes north of Hamilton) and follow State Highway 39 to Whatawhata to join the road from Hamilton. Turn right to Raglan. Buses to Raglan (NZ$9) run from Hamilton several times daily.

BUS CONTACTS Raglan Bus Depot. ✉ *Waikato District Library Raglan, 7 Bow St.* ⊕ *www.busit.co.nz.*

VISITOR INFORMATION

CONTACTS Raglan i-SITE Visitor Information Centre. ✉ *13 Wainui Rd.* ☎ *07/825–0556* ⊕ *www.raglan.org.nz.*

🍽 Restaurants

Orca Restaurant and Bar
$$$ | NEW ZEALAND | This waterside restaurant has big windows, big views, and big tasty menus. Brunch is served all day, and dinner brings out the chef's creativity. **Known for:** signature braised beef cheek with balsamic pickled onions and garlic mash; best dining views in Raglan (look for the orcas!); excellent food and wine pairings. ⑤ *Average main: NZ$22* ✉ *2 Wallis St.* ☎ *07/825–6543* ⊕ *www.orcarestaurant.co.nz.*

Rock-it Kitchen

$$ | **MODERN NEW ZEALAND** | **FAMILY** | Occupying a 100-year-old shearing shed, the funky, rustic Rock-it serves casual Kiwi fare and local Raglan Roast coffee. The menu is small but wholesome; try the all-day brunch, beef sliders, and soups for lunch or a casual yet classy dinner, either inside or out on the huge deck. **Known for:** country atmosphere; aged prime Scotch fillet with truffle agria mash and smoked vine tomatoes; alternative access (you can paddle a kayak up the Wainui estuary to get there). $ *Average main: NZ$19* ⊠ *248 Wainui Rd.* ☎ *07/825–8233* ⊕ *www.rockitraglan.co.nz.*

★ The Shack

$$ | **CAFÉ** | At this buzzing corner café, surfers—here for the great coffee and organic, free-range food—cram the couches and Formica tables beneath walls decorated with surfboards and Raglan beach scenes. The menu is huge and the meals hearty, starting with breakfast at 8. **Known for:** locally sourced coffee, produce, and beverages; retro, casual beach vibe; gluten-free, paleo, and vegan options all available. $ *Average main: NZ$16* ⊠ *19 Bow St.* ☎ *07/825–0027* ⊕ *www.theshackraglan.com* ⊗ *No dinner Sun.–Wed.*

🛏 Hotels

Raglan Sunset Motel

$$ | **HOTEL** | **FAMILY** | The location (a five-minute walk from town and from the harbor) and family-friendly facilities are key attractions here. **Pros:** lovely barbecue area; quiet yet close to shops and restaurants; free Wi-Fi throughout. **Cons:** grounds not hugely spacious; a bit dated; beware nearby local fire brigade training on Wednesday evening. $ *Rooms from: NZ$180* ⊠ *7 Bankart St.* ☎ *07/825–0050* ⊕ *www.raglansunsetmotel.co.nz* ⇆ *24 studios* ⊗ *No meals.*

★ Waters Edge

$$ | **B&B/INN** | Checking out will be the hardest part when you stay in either the 100-year-old cottage or modern apartment on this waterfront garden property. **Pros:** welcoming hosts; lovely overwater views; quiet, relaxing environment. **Cons:** three-minute drive from town; your visit might not coincide with the orcas; no air-conditioning. $ *Rooms from: NZ$195* ⊠ *100 E. Greenslade Rd.* ☎ *07/825–0567* ⇆ *2 apartments* ⊗ *No meals.*

🏃 Activities

Surfing (with waves to attract both beginners and the world's top surfers), kite surfing, fishing, kayaking, paddle-boarding, and just cruising in the vast harbor are the big water-sport attractions. Coastal walks and forest walks, from one hour to one day, are also popular.

BOATING AND KAYAKING

★ Raglan Boat Charters

BOATING | In Raglan, the harbor is a star attraction, and distinctive harbor cruise experiences operate under the umbrella of Raglan Boat Charters. For a social two-hour sunset cruise, board the Wahine Moe, a 70-person purpose-built catamaran. It runs daily December to April and includes a barbecue dinner (NZ$49). For a quieter, more low-key one-hour cruise, opt for the Harmony III (NZ$30). Long-time skipper Ian Hardie knows his way around the harbor's tidal inlets and bays; you'll see forest reserves, historic habitation sites, isolated beaches, the "pancakes" (limestone outcrops), seabirds, and perhaps the pod of orca that occasionally visits. This tour runs all year, with times based on the tides. Reservations are essential for both cruises. ⊠ *Raglan* ☎ *07/825–7873, 027/488–1215* ⊕ *www.raglanboatcharters.co.nz.*

Raglan surfers head along the beach to catch some waves.

★ Raglan Kayak and Paddleboard

BOATING | There's no better way to explore huge Raglan Harbour than on nature's terms with Steve and Candide Reid and their enthusiastic guides. Local boy Steve searched the world for the perfect place to work on water, then realized it was back home. People of any age and ability are welcome on the daily guided trips, where the focus is on paddling with the tide and wind, swimming on secluded beaches, and great scenery. Trips run for two hours (NZ$79, featuring limestone landscapes) and three hours (NZ$99 includes espresso and home-baked goodies). Kayak and paddleboard lessons and rentals are also offered. Tours are run from October through May. ⊠ *Bow St. Jetty* ☎ *07/825–8862* ⊕ *www.raglankay-ak.co.nz* ⊗ *Closed Easter–Oct.*

SURFING

Raglan Surf Emporium

SURFING | If you're itching to hit the waves, stop by this top surfing store. Once a factory that produced high-performance boards for years, it now stocks homegrown boards as well as the leading brands. The shop also rents surfboards, wet suits, and boogie boards, and staffers pass along helpful tips. ⊠ *3 Wainui Rd.* ☎ *07/282–0018* ⊕ *www.raglansurfemporium.com.*

★ Raglan Surfing School

SURFING | National surfing champions often work as instructors at the RSS. Three-hour group and private lessons are available for beginners (NZ$89 and NZ$149, respectively, board and wet suit included). Other options are multiday adventure packages (daily surf lessons, plus adventures such as rappelling and jet-boating) and "Surf Dame" programs (luxury surfing retreats for women). Rental gear is available from the RSS-operated trailer on Ocean (Ngarunui) Beach in summer or at the school itself year-round. Located a little out of town, transport from Raglan is provided. ⊠ *5b Whaanga Rd., Whale Bay* ☎ *07/825–7873* ⊕ *www. raglansurfingschool.co.nz.*

SWIMMING

Although the surf looks inviting at most of the West Coast beaches, there can be dangerous rips and undertows, so be careful where you take a dip. The safest spots around Raglan are Te Aro Bay (Wallis and Puriri streets), Te Kopua, and at Cox and Lorenzen bays during high tide. Call the Raglan i-SITE Visitor Information Centre (☎ 07/825–0556) for tide times. In summer, lifeguards patrol the beach at Ocean (Ngarunui); to avoid the strong rips, swim between the flags.

WALKING AND HIKING

From Raglan, a number of walks and hikes give you wonderful views of the coastline and take you through splendid native bush. The closest and easiest is from the township itself through Wainui Reserve to gorgeous Ocean (Ngarunui) Beach. You can climb above coastal bluffs to a lookout point and enjoy the drama of the kite surfers at play, or follow the beach for 6 km (4 miles), except during high spring tides. Ask for a brochure at the Raglan i-SITE Visitor Information Centre.

Mt. Karioi

HIKING/WALKING | The trek up Mt. Karioi is steep but rewarding, with great views from the top. The Mt. Karioi Track, from Te Toto Gorge at Whaanga Road, climbs to a lookout and then on to the summit (3–3½ hours one-way). Expect chains and ladders to help you up bluffy bits, but make sure you bring good walking gear, too. Wairake Track, from Karioi Road, is a shorter, and not as challenging, summit option (2–3 hours one way), but the views aren't quite as good. ⊕ www.doc. govt.nz.

★ Waireinga/Bridal Veil Falls

HIKING/WALKING | A 15-minute shaded hike from the parking lot leads through native forest to the spectacle of the falls. Two viewing platforms are poised near the top of the 150-foot drop. This section of trail is wheelchair accessible. Another much steeper track continues to a midway viewing platform; from there a 10-minute trail descends to a bridge and viewing platform at the base of the falls. The tall trees and the sight of the water cascading over the hard basalt cliff justify the effort required for the return climb. The falls are 20 km (12 miles) south of Raglan via the Kawhia road. ⊕ www.doc. govt.nz.

Waitomo

80 km (50 miles) southwest of Hamilton, 65 km (41 miles) southwest of Cambridge, 150 km (95 miles) west of Rotorua.

Waitomo is a busy little village located a short drive from the main highway. Above ground, the surrounding hills are a mix of native bush and verdant farmland. Below ground you'll find the region's famous cave systems, and Waitomo caters to the tourists who come to ogle them. Despite its small size—everything here is within walking distance—the village promises a good selection of cafés, a tavern, plus some 20 different cave tour options ranging from gentle walking on well-lighted pathways to rappelling, tubing, and jumping down dark waterfalls.

The Waitomo Caves are part of an ancient seabed that was lifted and then spectacularly eroded into a surreal subterranean landscape of limestone formations, gushing rivers, and contorted caverns. The name, a combination of *wai* (water) and *tomo* (cave), refers to the Waitomo River that vanishes into the hillside here. Many of the amazing underground passages are still unexplored, but four major cave systems are open for guided tours: Ruakuri, Spellbound, Aranui, and Waitomo Glowworm Cave. Each has its own special characteristics, and you won't be disappointed by any.

After all, notable features include not only stalactites and stalagmites but also glowworms—the 1- to 2-inch larvae of *Arachnocampa luminosa,* which live on cave ceilings. They snare prey by dangling sticky filaments, trapping insects attracted to the light they emit. A single worm produces far less than any firefly, but when massed in great numbers in the dark, it's like looking at the night sky in miniature. The guides who introduce you to all of this below-ground beauty may be descendants of local chief Tane Tinorau (who discovered Waitomo Glowworm Cave); they will certainly be local caving experts who have spent years exploring the amazing network of shafts and passageways around Waitomo.

GETTING HERE AND AROUND

Although it's in the countryside, Waitomo is close to State Highway 3, one of the major highways linking Waikato and Rotorua with Taranaki and Tongariro. The Kiwi Experience Waitomo Wanderer offers daily round-trip bus service from both Rotorua and Taupo, arriving midmorning and departing late afternoon. Day-trippers wishing to see the caves can also take advantage of bus-tour packages offered by InterCity, which travels from Auckland or Rotorua.

If you'd rather ride the rails, the Auckland–Wellington *Northern Explorer* train stops in Otorohanga, 16 km (10 miles) from Waitomo. The Caves Shuttle and Taxi Service (NZ$12 per person) can be booked to meet the train and bring you into town; contact the Waitomo i-SITE Discovery Centre for bookings.

BUS CONTACTS Waitomo Bus Depot. ⊠ *Waitomo i-SITE Discovery Centre, Waitomo Village Rd., 21 Waitomo Caves Village.*

TRAIN CONTACTS Otorohanga Train Station. ⊠ *7 Wahanui Cres., Otorohanga.*

VISITOR INFORMATION
There are two visitor centers in Waitomo village. Waitomo Glowworm Caves Visitor Centre is managed by the company that owns access to the Waitomo Glowworm, Ruakuri, and Aranai caves. The independent Waitomo i-SITE Discovery Centre offers impartial advice to help you decide which tour is most suitable as well as bookings for all cave tours and other regional attractions. Bookings may also be made with the individual tour operators.

CONTACTS Waitomo Glowworm Caves Visitor Centre. ⊠ *39 Waitomo Village Rd.* ☎ *0800/456–922* ⊕ *www.waitomo.com.* **Waitomo i-SITE Discovery Centre.** ⊠ *21 Waitomo Village Rd., Waitomo Caves Village* ☎ *07/878–7640* ⊕ *www.waitomo-caves.com.*

◉ Sights

Aranui Caves
CAVE | This is the smallest yet one of the prettiest of the main Waitomo caves. Eons of dripping water have sculpted a delicate garden of pink-and-white limestone here. Hour-long tours lead along boardwalks into tall, narrow chambers. Keep an eye out for the resident cave wetas; these native insects grow up to 4 inches long, but don't worry—they will most likely hide if they sense you coming. Tours meet in the Ruakuri Reserve car park on Tumutumu Road, 3 km (2 miles) beyond Waitomo Caves Village. Reservations are essential. ⊠ *Cave entrance at Ruakuri Reserve, Tumutumu Rd.* ☎ *0800/456–922* ⊕ *www.waitomo. com* ⊠ *Tours NZ$50; multicave tickets available.*

Ruakuri Cave

CAVE | To enter Ruakuri, visitors descend a dramatic, man-made spiral "drum passage," then go on to explore narrow, low-lit passages. Surrounded by magical limestone formations and the roar of hidden waterfalls, the way follows a dark underground river that twinkles with glowworm reflections. Tours are two-hours (reservations suggested) and limited to 15 people. This is the longest cave-walking tour in Waitomo, but it's easily managed by people of reasonable fitness. All pathways are wheelchair-accessible. Tours meet at the Waitomo Glowworm Caves Visitor Centre or the Long Black Café (585 Waitomo Village Road). ⊠ *39 Waitomo Village Rd.* ☏ *0800/228–464* ⊕ *www.waitomo.com* ⬚ *NZ$74; multicave tickets available.*

Sanctuary Mountain Maungatautari

NATURE PRESERVE | Walk among some of the most ancient forests in the region at the small "mountain" called Maungatautari, where the Maungatautari Ecological Island Trust, in conjunction with the Department of Conservation, is carrying out one of New Zealand's many successful conservation stories. The trust has built a NZ$14 million, 50-km (31-mile) pest-proof fence around 8,400 acres of native forest, creating a refuge for some of New Zealand's rarest native species. Endangered birds, including the kaka bush parrot, kiwi, takahe, and saddleback, have been reintroduced here. The best place to start is at the Manu Tioriori Visitor Centre, which has information and refreshments; it's on the southern side of the mountain at the end of Tari Road in Pukeatua, 32 km (20 miles) outside of Cambridge. From here you can explore on your own or take a short guided walk through the Southern Enclosure (1½-hours, NZ$37). Five kilometers (3 miles) of high-quality trails lead through forest to a 52-foot viewing tower in the treetops, where you can be one with the birds. Another guided walk explores Tautari Wetland (1½ hours, NZ$37).

Keen walkers can tackle the Over the Mountain trail, a full-day walk from one side to the other. It's a good spot to stop if you're driving off the main routes from Rotorua to Waitomo. ⊠ *Tari Rd., Pukeatua, Cambridge* ☏ *07/870–5180* ⊕ *www.sanctuarymountain.co.nz* ⬚ *NZ$20.*

Spellbound Glowworm and Cave Tour

CAVE | This tour offers two different underground experiences: a gentle raft trip and close-up views of glowworms. The short bush walk to the caves is an added bonus. The raft trip, in Spellbound, explores a glowworm chamber that was filmed by Sir David Attenborough for the BBC. Te Ana o te Atua (Cave of the Spirit) features limestone formations, fossils, and bones. Tours take 3½ hours and are limited to 12 people; advanced booking is advised. A specialized tour is also available for photographers, limited to two people per tour. ⊠ *15 Waitomo Village Rd., Waitomo Village* ☏ *0800/773–552* ⊕ *www.glowworm.co.nz* ⬚ *From NZ$75.*

★ Waitomo Glowworm Cave

CAVE | The most "genteel" and perhaps famous of all the caves here was first officially explored in 1887 by local Chief Tane Tinorau and surveyor Fred Mace. They floated on a raft of flax stems, with candles for light, into the cave where the stream goes underground. Now visitors enter via a gentle pathway, explore the limestone cathedral (and, like opera diva Kiri Te Kanawa, are invited to test the amazing acoustics), then board a boat for a magical cruise beneath the "starry" glowworm-lit ceiling, floating out of the cave on the Waitomo River. Tours last 45 minutes and start at the Waitomo Glowworm Cave Visitor Centre. ⊠ *39 Waitomo Village Rd.* ☏ *0800/456–922* ⊕ *www.waitomo.com* ⬚ *Tours NZ$51; multicave tickets available.*

In the Waitomo Caves, you can take a boat ride through these magical formations, where glowworms light up the ceiling and walls like stars.

Waitomo Glowworm Caves Visitor Centre

CAVE | This striking structure has an open design that reflects the drama of the limestone landscape surrounding it and artwork that honors Māori culture. Inside, you can buy tickets to visit the caves, find information about the region, relax in the café and restaurant, or browse the gift shop. ✉ *39 Waitomo Village Rd.* ☎ *0800/456–922* ⊕ *www.waitomo.com.*

Waitomo Walkway

TRAIL | With its limestone features (fluted outcrops, arches, tunnels, and caves), open farmland, and native forest, the 5-km (3-mile) Waitomo Walkway is an interesting short trek. Start at the Waitomo i-SITE Discovery Centre and follow the path beside the Waitomo River. You can return the same way or follow the road (a bit shorter). Alternatively you can drive to Ruakuri Reserve (from the Village take Te Anga Road then Tumutumu Road), and just walk the 30-minute loop through natural rock tunnels, across cantilevered bridges, and beneath limestone bluffs.

The trail is slippery following wet weather, and there are steep sections, so wear good walking shoes. ■ **TIP →** **Many people come after dusk for a free viewing of the local glowworms; bring a flashlight to find your way.** ⊕ *www.doc.govt.nz.*

🍽 Restaurants

★ HUHU Cafe

$$$ | MODERN NEW ZEALAND | This out in the country spot is up there with the best urban-chic cafés. The contemporary New Zealand–style menu runs from lunch through dinner, with a mix of smaller and larger plates that (mostly) stay under NZ$30. **Known for:** traditional rewana (Māori bread); gallery downstairs selling giftware and jewelry; local Te Kuiti slow-cooked lamb shoulder. ⑤ *Average main: NZ$28* ✉ *10 Waitomo Village Rd.* ☎ *07/878–6674* ⊕ *www.huhucafe.co.nz.*

🛏 Hotels

★ Abseil Breakfast Inn

$$ | B&B/INN | Hosts John and Helen treat you like family when you stay in one of the comfortable rooms here; each comes with a local decor theme (bush, cave, farm, and swamp), superqueen bed, and a second deck entrance. **Pros:** quirky, helpful hosts; big and delicious breakfasts; rural views. **Cons:** steep driveway; not for those who like big, impersonal hotels; thin walls. *$ Rooms from: NZ$180 ⊠ 709 Waitomo Village Rd. ☎ 07/878–7815 ⊕ www.abseilinn.co.nz ⇥ 4 rooms ⦿I Breakfast.*

★ Waitomo Top 10 Holiday Park

$$ | HOTEL | FAMILY | Modern, clean, and rated Qualmark four-star-plus, this delightful holiday park in the heart of Waitomo Village offers tents, powered campervan sites, cabins, and a self-contained motel. **Pros:** central location; spacious rural environment with great views of the surrounding forest; friendly hosts. **Cons:** likely to be busy in summer; kid-friendly environment may not suit everyone; by the main road (though it's quiet at night). *$ Rooms from: NZ$190 ⊠ 12 Waitomo Village Rd. ☎ 0508/498–666 ⊕ www. waitomopark.co.nz ⇥ 18 rooms, 70 camper sites ⦿I No meals.*

🏃 Activities

CAVE ADVENTURES

Many of Waitomo's subterranean adventure tours involve black-water rafting—that is, floating through the underground caverns on inflated inner tubes, dressed in wet suits and equipped with cavers' helmets. Be prepared for pitch darkness and freezing cold water. Your reward is an exhilarating trip gliding through vast glowworm-lighted caverns, clambering across rocks, and jumping over waterfalls. There are also dry options. Some tours involve steep rappelling and tight underground squeezes. Each company runs several trips daily.

Kiwi Cave Rafting

WHITE-WATER RAFTING | Thrill-seekers can venture down below on a five-hour combo adventure that includes rappelling, black-water rafting, rock climbing, caving, and checking out the glowworms. *⊠ 95 Waitomo Village Rd. ☎ 07/873–9149 ⊕ www.blackwaterraftingwaitomo.co.nz.*

The Legendary Black Water Rafting Company

WHITE-WATER RAFTING | Most adventurous types can handle the basic, three-hour Black Labyrinth trip, which finishes with a welcome hot shower and mug of soup back at base. Then there's the more intense Black Odyssey, with four hours of twisting and turning via "dry caving" and the five-hour Black Abyss. Although the guides and the underground scenery are great (you'll learn caving techniques from experts), these are staunch physical and emotional challenges and can be scary. Departure times depend on demand. *⊠ 585 Waitomo Village Rd. ☎ 07/878–6219, 0800/456–922 ⊕ www.waitomo.com.*

★ Waitomo Adventures

WHITE-WATER RAFTING | Five different trips with these caving enthusiasts release serious adrenaline. A 328-foot rappel into the famous Lost World cave system is spectacular—not just for a thumping heart, but also for the underground landscape, illuminated by daylight sneaking in through a couple of surface openings. Other tours include Tumu Tumu Toobing (climbing, swimming, tubing, and rafting), Haggas Honking Holes (rappelling, rock climbing, and crawling), and the seven-hour Lost World Epic (rappelling, wading, swimming, and climbing). These caves are a little way out of the main Waitomo tourist center, beneath picturesque farmland. *⊠ Waitomo Adventure Centre, 654 Waitomo Caves Rd. ☎ 07/878-7788, 0800/924–866 ⊕ www. waitomo.co.nz.*

Around Mt. Taranaki

North Taranaki Bight

Waitara

Taranaki-Waitomo Scenic Drive

Urenui

3

Fitzroy

Tikorangi

New Plymouth

Oakura

Lepperton

3A

Egmont Village

3

Inglewood

Tarata

45

Mt Patuha

Pukeiti Gardens

Carrington Rd.

Puniho

Mt Pouakai

Tariki

Te Popo

Pungarehu

North Egmont

Mt Taranaki

East Egmont

Midhirst

Rahotu

Kahui Rd.

Dawson Falls

Stratford

Forgotten Highway

43

Arawhata Rd.

Egmont National Park

Mahoe

Stratford-Taumarumi Scenic Drive

Toko

45

Winemu Rd.

Rowan

Opunake Rd.

Hollard Gardens

Eltham

Oaonui

Kaponge

Hastings Rd.

Opunake

Manaia Rd.

Whanganui National Park

Pihama

Manaia

South Pacific Ocean

Otakeho

45

Tawhiti Museum

Ohawe

Whereroa

Hawera

South Taranaki Bight

3

Kakaramea

Whanganui

Patea

KEY
········· *Walking track*

0 — 8 mi

0 — 8 km

New Plymouth

375 km (235 miles) south of Auckland, 190 km (120 miles) southwest of Waitomo, 163 km (102 miles) northwest of Whanganui.

New Plymouth serves one of New Zealand's most productive dairy regions as well as the gas and oil industries. This natural wealth translates into an optimistic outlook that is reflected in New Plymouth's healthy arts scene, the abundance of cafés and restaurants, and a lifestyle that maximizes the great outdoors.

The area has a strong Māori history and a strong history of Māori–European interaction, not all of it friendly. Before the arrival of Europeans in 1841, *kainga* (villages) and *pā* (fortified villages) spread along the coast. In the mid-1800s, land disputes between Māori and English settlers racked Taranaki. An uneasy formal peace was made between the government and local Māori tribes in 1881, and New Plymouth began to play its current role as a trading port. On the edge of the Tasman Sea, today's city is second to its surroundings, but its few surviving colonial buildings, cafés, stores, galleries, museums, and extensive parklands merit a day's exploration.

Taranaki is a productive agricultural region; layers of volcanic ash have created free-draining topsoil and the western, coastal location ensures abundant rainfall. What serves farmers also serves gardeners. Some of the country's most magnificent gardens, as rated by the New Zealand Gardens Trust, grow in the rich soil. Some, such as Pukekura Park, Pukeiti, and Hollard, are public, but many are private, open only by appointment and during the annual Taranaki Garden Festival and Taranaki Fringe Garden Festival. During these spring events, more than 100 splendid gardens celebrate the area's green-fingered excellence, particularly its rhododendrons.

GETTING HERE AND AROUND

Air New Zealand flies daily to New Plymouth from Auckland, Wellington, and Christchurch, while Jetstar flies direct from Auckland. New Plymouth Airport (NPL) is about 12 km (7½ miles) from the city center; expect to pay about NZ$50 for a taxi to town. Scott's Airport Shuttle runs a door-to-door service from the airport for NZ$24 (first person, plus NZ$4 each additional passenger); book ahead online or by phone.

Coach company InterCity provides a daily service linking New Plymouth, Stratford, and Hawera. Local service provider Citylink runs from New Plymouth to nearby Waitara and the surfing village of Oakura.

Travel by private car, however, is the best option for getting around New Plymouth and Taranaki. The roads are generally paved and in good condition. From the north, State Highway 3 passes through Te Kuiti, near Waitomo, and then heads west to New Plymouth. The highway continues south through Taranaki to Whanganui and onto Bulls, where it connects with State Highway 1. New Plymouth is a six- to seven-hour drive from Auckland and a five-hour drive from Wellington. If you're traveling west on a sunny afternoon, watch out for strong glare from the setting sun.

You can take in most of Taranaki in a couple of days, using New Plymouth as a base, but that would keep you on the run. Ideally, treat yourself to a leisurely week, choosing accommodations from fine lodges, B&Bs, motels, backpacker hostels, and holiday parks spread throughout the region.

AIRPORTS New Plymouth Airport.
✉ *Airport Dr.* ☎ *06/759–6060* ⊕ *www. nplairport.co.nz.*

AIRPORT TRANSFERS Scott's Airport Shuttle. ☎ *06/769–5974, 0800/373–001* ⊕ *www.npairportshuttle.co.nz.*

Did You Know?

Underground streams slowly dissolved limestone to form the Waitomo Caves over thousands of years. The water picked up lime and, as it moved, left deposits that eventually formed intricate, beautiful stalactites and stalagmites.

BUS CONTACTS Ariki Street Bus Station.
✉ *19 Ariki St., City Center* ☎ *0800/872–287* **CityLink.** ☎ *0800/872–287* ⊕ *www.trc.govt.nz/taranaki-bus-information.*

VISITOR INFORMATION

CONTACTS New Plymouth i-SITE Visitor Information Centre. ✉ *Puke Ariki, 65 St. Aubyn St.* ☎ *06/759–0897* ⊕ *www.visit-newplymouth.nz.*

◉ Sights

Govett Brewster Art Gallery and Len Lye Centre

MUSEUM | This stunning architectural drama of twisted towers of glass and steel houses one of the country's leading modern art museums. Collections include New Zealand conceptual, abstract, and contemporary pieces from the 1970s to today, along with visiting international exhibitions. Special features are the experimental film and kinetic art works of New Zealander Len Lye, who is internationally acclaimed for his Modernism and thought-provoking originality. ✉ *42 Queen St.* ☎ *06/759–6060* ⊕ *www.govettbrewster.com* 🎟 *NZ$15.*

New Plymouth Coastal Walkway

TRAIL | **FAMILY** | Step out of the city and onto the coast by taking a stroll or cycle along this gentle coastal path, which meanders for 13 km (8 miles), from Port Taranaki to Hickford Park (a rugby and bike park). It explores beaches and playgrounds, crosses rivers, passes by a golf course, and runs beneath the Wind Wand, a sculpture almost as iconic to New Plymouth residents as the Statue of Liberty is to New Yorkers. Created by the late New Zealand artist Len Lye, the red carbon-fiber tube stands 148 feet high and, like a conductor's baton, dances in the wind as Lye's tribute to what he called "tangible motion." Leaving the city confines the walkway crosses the startling white Te Rewa Rewa Bridge (Mt. Taranaki framed in the bridge's struts

makes a great photo) into farmland and past the Waipu Lagoons, a wetland reserve.

★ Puke Ariki

MUSEUM | The stories of Taranaki's compelling volcanic and cultural history are revealed here, in the region's heritage, research, and information center. From the landscape's violent volcanic formation and the tragic Māori versus English settler/soldier Land Wars to the discovery of natural oil and gas deposits and today's internationally acclaimed surfing culture, it's all here, including interactive science exhibits for children. Located across the road from the beach and popular Wind Wand kinetic sculpture, the in-house Arborio Café is worth a stop, too, as demonstrated by the presence of locals. ✉ *Puke Ariki Landing, 1 Ariki St.* ☎ *06/759–6060* ⊕ *www.pukeariki.com* 🎟 *Free.*

★ Pukeiti Gardens

NATURE PRESERVE | **FAMILY** | Established by the Pukeiti Rhododendron Trust, these 900 acres of lush, native rain forest are surrounded by farmland. The Pukeiti (poo-ke- *ee*-tee) collection of 2,500 varieties of rhododendrons is the largest in New Zealand. Many were first grown here, such as the giant winter-blooming *R. protistum var. giganteum*, collected from seed in 1953 and now standing 15 feet tall, and the delightful Lemon Lodge and Spring Honey hybrids, which bloom in spring. *Kyawi*, a large red "rhodo," is the last to bloom, in April (autumn). Rhododendrons aside, there are many other rare and special plants here. All winter long the Himalayan daphnes fragrance the pathways. Spring-to-summer-growing candelabra primroses reach up to 4 feet; and, for a month around Christmas, spectacular 8-foot Himalayan *cardiocrinum* lilies bear heavenly scented, 12-inch, white trumpet flowers. There's a classy café on-site, and a self-guided Kids Treehouse Trail. Located 20 km (12½ miles) southwest of

New Plymouth's center, Pukeiti is also a wonderful bird habitat. ⊠ *2290 Carrington Rd.* ☎ *06/765–7127* ⊕ *www.trc.govt.nz/ gardens/pukeiti* ⊠ *Free.*

Pukekura Park and Brooklands Park

CITY PARK | FAMILY | Together the lawns, lakes, gardens, and woodlands of these connected parks make up a 128-acre urban oasis. Each summer evening the Festival of Lights transforms the gardens and giant trees of **Pukekura Park** (annually from mid-December through January and during the March WOMAD Festival). Rowboats can be hired to explore the small islands and nooks and crannies of the main lake. The park also has massive botanical display houses and a fernery in caverns carved out of the hillside. The adjoining **Brooklands Park** is known for its ancient rain forest and exotic trees, such as giant copper beeches, pines, walnuts, and oaks. The Monterey pine, magnolia soulangeana, ginkgo, and native karaka and kohekohe here are the largest of their kind in New Zealand. A giant puriri tree is believed to be more than 2,000 years old. Brooklands is also home to the hugely popular Bowl of Brooklands, a natural amphitheater used for concerts and events, including international acts. Brooklands Zoo has farm animals, meerkats, monkeys, and a bird aviary. ⊠ *Park entrances on Brooklands Park Dr. and Liardet, Somerset and Rogan Sts.* ☎ *06/758–6060 for Brooklands Zoo only* ⊠ *Free.*

Taranaki–Waitomo

SCENIC DRIVE | Mt. Taranaki is a receding presence in your rearview mirror as you head northeast up the Taranaki coast from New Plymouth on Highway 3. This is the most direct route to the Waitomo Caves and Hamilton, turning inland at Awakino, 90 km (56 miles) from New Plymouth. The Awakino Gorge, between Mahoenui and the coast, is appealing. Forest-filled scenic reserves are interspersed with stark, limestone outcrops

and lush farmland. Look for well-worn sheep trails traversing the steep-sided hills. At the mouth of the Awakino River, little shacks dot the water's edge. These belong to seasonal fishers of the tiny migrating fish, whitebait. Awakino is worth a stop; the Awakino Hotel (⊕ *www.awakinohotel.co.nz*) offers a friendly country pub experience, or you could turn off the main road by the hotel to find a sheltered picnic spot beneath the summer-flowering *pohutukawa* trees. A little farther along is Mokau. Between September and November, if the whitebait are running, delicious whitebait fritters might be on the menu at the two little cafés nearby. From Awakino to Waitomo, allow about an hour.

⬢ Beaches

Fitzroy Beach

BEACH—SIGHT | A reasonably exposed yet popular and easily accessible beach, Fitzroy is just 1½ km (¾ mile) from the center of New Plymouth. You can even walk or ride there via the New Plymouth Coastal Walkway. Changeable surf makes it a bit wild, so be sure to swim between the patrol flags. There's interesting rock-pool exploring here and at other beaches along this coast, courtesy of the black sand and rocky outcrops. Expect crowds on hot summer days, when *pohutukawa* trees provide shade in some spots. **Amenities:** lifeguards (summer); parking (free); toilets. **Best for:** surfing; swimming; walking. ⊠ *Beach St., Fitzroy.*

🍴 Restaurants

Caffe Windsor

$$ | NEW ZEALAND | Wholesome homemade food attracts both Taranaki locals and travelers to this character-filled village café. Set in a heritage building built in 1878 for the local butcher, the menu runs from breakfast through lunch and dinner on weekends. **Known for:** best

baristas for miles; gourmet burger selection; waffles for breakfast. $ *Average main: NZ$20* ✉ *1 Kelly St., Inglewood* ☎ *06/756–6665* ⊕ *www.caffewindsor. co.nz* ◷ *No dinner Sun.–Wed.*

Social Kitchen

$$$ | CONTEMPORARY | The name says it all: this is the place to socialize with friends while sharing plates from the open kitchen. The food has been fired up with flavor in the South American–styled Mibrasa charcoal oven or slow-cooked to create delicious 12-hour smoked meats. **Known for:** Sunday roasts; lively late dining (go early if you want quiet); charcoal-flavored foods all served with chimichurri. $ *Average main: NZ$30* ✉ *40 Powderham St.* ☎ *06/757–2711* ⊕ *www.social-kitchen. co.nz.*

Snug Lounge

$$ | JAPANESE FUSION | The casual yet stylish setup at this Japanese yakitori grill and cocktail bar is designed to bring people together, and it works. The menu focuses on small plates to share. **Known for:** steamed buns, dumplings with assorted fillings, and spicy meat skewers; deep-fried kusiage delights; alcohol-infused desserts. $ *Average main: NZ$18* ✉ *124 Devon St. W* ☎ *06/757–9130* ⊕ *www.snuglounge. co.nz* ◷ *No lunch Sat.–Thurs.*

🛏 Hotels

★ Ahu Ahu Beach Villas

$$$ | HOTEL | These rustic yet chic studio and one-bedroom villas sit on a clifftop with stunning views of world-famous surf beach Oakura. **Pros:** dramatic coastal views; handsome design; eco-friendly. **Cons:** 15-minute drive to New Plymouth; uphill walk returning from the beach; no shops within walking distance. $ *Rooms from: NZ$260* ✉ *321 Ahu Ahu Rd., Oakura* ☎ *06/752–7370* ⊕ *www.ahu.co.nz* ⇌ *5 villas* ⦿ *No meals.*

Ducks and Drakes Boutique Motel and Backpackers

$ | HOTEL | A place for travelers rather than party animals, Ducks and Drakes offers character, color, and modern accommodations within walking distance of shops, cafés, and Pukekura Park. **Pros:** comfortable lounge; lots of cozy places to relax, indoors and outdoors; friendly hosts. **Cons:** old, steep staircase in main building; parking is tight and only for motel guests; most rooms share bathrooms. $ *Rooms from: NZ$110* ✉ *48 Lemon St.* ☎ *06/758–0404* ⊕ *www.ducksanddrakes. co.nz* ⇌ *18 rooms* ⦿ *No meals.*

Millennium Hotel New Plymouth Waterfront

$$$ | HOTEL | Stylish and modern, New Plymouth's only waterfront lodging is handily placed next to the Puke Ariki Museum. **Pros:** proximity to the beach and Puke Ariki Museum; nice views; excellent hotel restaurant. **Cons:** port traffic rumbles past; not a lot of personality in guest rooms; not all rooms have tubs. $ *Rooms from: NZ$254* ✉ *1 Egmont St.* ☎ *06/769–5301* ⊕ *www.millennium-hotels.com/en/new-plymouth/millennium-hotel-new-plymouth-waterfront* ⇌ *44 rooms* ⦿ *No meals.*

Nice Hotel and Table

$$$ | HOTEL | Personable owner Terry Parkes has transformed this 19th-century heritage building into an opulent city retreat decorated with eclectic furnishings and contemporary art by leading Taranaki artists. **Pros:** boutique character; complimentary Netflix in rooms and port in the library; fine in-house restaurant. **Cons:** reservations a must for hotel and restaurant; parking is difficult to find; next to busy streets so can be noisy. $ *Rooms from: NZ$260* ✉ *71 Brougham St.* ☎ *06/758–6423* ⊕ *www.nicehotel. co.nz* ⇌ *12 rooms* ⦿ *No meals.*

Villa Heights B&B

$$ | B&B/INN | A restored Victorian villa is set in a stunning garden with great views of Mt. Taranaki, surrounding farmland, and the sea. **Pros:** very welcoming hosts;

restful gardens and countryside; spacious en suite rooms. **Cons:** might be too far out of town for some; mountain views are weather dependent; books up quickly. ⑤ *Rooms from: NZ$200* ✉ *333 Upland Rd.* ☎ *06/755–2273* ⊕ *www.villaheights. co.nz* ↪ *3 rooms* ⦿⦿ *Breakfast.*

🛍 Shopping

Devon Street, which runs from Fitzroy in the east to Blagdon in the west, is New Plymouth's main shopping thoroughfare.

Et Vous

CLOTHING | Thanks to leading New Zealand, Australian, French, Italian, Turkish, and Danish labels, this boutique has the best selection of designer clothing in town. It also stocks plus-size items, as well as European shoes. If you work up an appetite browsing, just wander through to the adjoining bakery and cafés. ✉ *118 Devon St. W.* ☎ *06/759–1360* ⊕ *www.etvous.co.nz.*

Kina NZ Design + Art Space

CRAFTS | For magnificent locally made arts and crafts with an edge, visit Kina, which exhibits the works of Taranaki artists and carries contemporary design pieces, from jewelry to sculpture. ✉ *101 Devon St. W* ☎ *06/759–1201* ⊕ *www.kina.co.nz.*

Taranaki Hardcore

SPORTING GOODS | Designer Taranaki-themed clothing and quality surfboards are sold here, plus you can check the shop's webcam to see if the surf's up at nearby Fitzroy Beach. ✉ *454 Devon St. E* ☎ *06/758–1757* ⊕ *www.taranakihardcore. co.nz.*

🏃 Activities

Surfing is the big thing along the Taranaki coast, but the beaches and coastal walkways also draw swimmers, beachcombers, paddleboarders, and kayakers. Fishing, be it surfcasting from the shore, trailing a line from a boat, or netting the delicacy whitebait at stream mouths during the season, is also popular.

BICYCLING

Cycle Inn

BICYCLING | To ride the New Plymouth Coastal Walkway, rent a touring (aka road, not mountain) bike and a helmet at Cycle Inn. Expect to pay NZ$10 for two hours, NZ$20 for a full day. Electric bikes rent for NZ$30 (two hours) and NZ$50 (full day). Lockers are provided. ✉ *133 Devon St.* ☎ *06/758–7418* ⊕ *www.cycleinn. co.nz.*

BOATING AND KAYAKING

★ Chaddy's Charters

BOATING | **FAMILY** | A classic one-hour trip in an old English lifeboat takes you direct from the boat shed into the water and out to Nga Motu–Sugar Loaf Islands, just offshore. You'll probably see seals, sea birds, maybe check lobster pots, and be thoroughly entertained by skipper and former fisherman Happy Chaddy (NZ$40). Rental kayaks and paddleboards are also available here. Note that Chaddy usually takes a break in midwinter. ✉ *Ocean View Parade* ☎ *06/758–9133* ⊕ *www.chaddyscharters.co.nz.*

SURFING

The coastal road between New Plymouth and Hawera is known as the **Surf Highway** for its popular surf beaches. To find the beaches, you'll need to take short detours off the main road and pass through rolling farmland down side roads to the coast. **Oakura,** a village 17 km (10 miles) southwest of New Plymouth, is one of the most popular surf beaches, with the added bonus of good cafés and crafts shops. Closer to New Plymouth, Fitzroy, East End, Back, and Bell Block beaches are all popular with surfers. **Opunake,** in South Taranaki, has an artificial surf reef.

Beach Street Surf Shop

SURFING | Local legend Wayne Arthur has all the equipment surfers need and will give you the lowdown on the hot spots in

Taranaki. ✉ *Fitzroy Beach, 39 Beach St.*
☎ *06/758–0400.*

Vertigo Surf

SURFING | In Oakura, this is the place to
get the latest in surfing gear and advice
on local conditions. A webcam shows
what the Oakura Beach surf is doing at
that moment. ✉ *2 Tasman Parade, Oakura* ☎ *06/752–7363* ⊕ *www.vertigosurf.
com.*

Egmont National Park

*North Egmont Visitor Centre is 26 km (16
miles) south of New Plymouth, Dawson
Falls Visitor Centre is 68 km (42 miles)
southwest of New Plymouth.*

Rising 8,261 feet above sea level, Mt.
Taranaki dominates the landscape of this
national park. It's difficult not to be drawn
toward it. The lower reaches are cloaked
in dense and mossy rain forests; above
the tree line, lower-growing tussocks and
subalpine shrubs cling to spectacularly
steep slopes. Taranaki is the mountain's
Māori name. James Cook gave it its
English name, Egmont, in 1770, to honor
the Earl of Egmont, who supported his
exploration. Both are officially acceptable
today.

Mt. Taranaki is notorious for its changing
weather conditions, and many climbers
and hikers are caught with insufficient
gear. On a clear day, from even the
mountain's lower slopes you can see the
three mountains of Tongariro National
Park in the central North Island—and
sometimes even as far as the South
Island.

GETTING HERE AND AROUND

Three well-marked main roads provide
access up the mountain and to walking trails, lodgings, and visitor centers.
Egmont Road, the first mountain turnoff
as you drive south from New Plymouth
on State Highway 3, leads to the start of
many walking trails and the **North Egmont**

Visitor Centre. Drop in to peruse the excellent displays and grab a bite at the small
café. Pembroke Road, the second road
up the mountain from State Highway 3,
goes to the Ngati Ruanui Stratford Mountain House hotel, a few walking trails,
and, a little farther on, **Stratford Plateau,**
where there are stunning views and
access to the mountain's small ski slope.
A third turnoff (Manaia Road) turns right
off Opunake Road coming from Stratford,
and leads up the south side of the mountain to the **Dawson Falls Visitor Centre.**

You can book a local transport operator
from New Plymouth through the New
Plymouth i-SITE Visitor Information
Centre.

TOURS

Helicopter flights are a quick but spectacular way to enjoy views of Taranaki. Not
surprisingly, the most popular flight is
around the Mt. Taranaki summit.

Beck Helicopters

AIR EXCURSIONS | This outfit flies out of
Eltham in south Taranaki, lifting quickly
above the farmland and heading over the
steep forests, deep ravines, and spectacular volcanic peak of Egmont National
Park. Coastal views are an added bonus.
Flights last 25 to 30 minute, and prices
vary depending on the number of passengers. ✉ *4512 Mountain Rd., Eltham*
☎ *0800/336644* ⊕ *www.heli.co.nz*
🚁 *From NZ$295.*

VISITOR INFORMATION

CONTACTS Dawson Falls Visitor Centre.
✉ *Upper Manaia Rd., RD29, Kaponga*
☎ *027/443–0248* ⊕ *www.doc.govt.nz.*
North Egmont Visitor Centre. ✉ *Egmont Rd.*
☎ *06/756–0990* ⊕ *www.doc.govt.nz.*

⊙ Sights

Egmont National Park

FOREST | Mt. Taranaki (8,261 feet), called
Mt. Egmont by Captain Cook, is a steep,
symmetrically shaped volcanic peak
that dominates the region's landscape

Planning Your Visit to Egmont

Best Time to Go

December through March is the best time for walking, hiking, viewing alpine flowers, and making summit ascents. Experienced or guided mountaineers can snow- and ice-climb in July and August. Skiing is available July through September (depending on snow levels).

Best Ways to Explore

Take a Short Walk. Several gentle, well-signposted walking trails leave from the three main park entrances. Some top examples are Wilkies Pools, which takes in mountain streams, sculpted rocks, and goblin forest (1½-hour round-trip); Patea Loop, encompassing mountain cedar forest and stony riverbeds (two hours); and Potaema, with giant *rimu* and *rata* forest plus a vast wetland (20 minutes).

Take a Scenic Drive. Three main access roads lead into the park, climbing steeply (allow 10 to 20 minutes) up the mountain's forest-lined lower slopes and, in some areas, opening up stunning views. Short strolls along these roads enable you to appreciate the plants, trees, waterfalls, and streams. The interesting displays and photos at the main North Egmont Visitor Centre enhance the experience—as will the taste temptations in the café.

Take a Long Hike. The two- to three-day Pouakai Circuit explores all the park's landscapes: subalpine terrain, lava cliffs and gorges, the vast Ahukawakawa wetland, the tussock tops of the Pouakai Range, and lichen-covered goblin forest. The one-day Pouakai Crossing takes in much of the Pouakai Circuit and descends through forest to the western park boundary (transport shuttles required). Hiking around the mountain (four to five days) is another option, if you're keen to climb in and out of steep gullies and through mud. A second mountain loop above the tree line (three to four days) can be stunning in summer, icy in winter, and exposed to extreme weather at any time.

Climb the Mountain. The steep climb is a serious undertaking, especially with frequent bad weather. The mountain is sacred to the local Māori people, so they ask that climbers respect its spirituality and not clamber over the summit rocks. The main summer route (seven to eight hours round-trip) follows the northeast ridge. When there's no snow, it's all rock underfoot—slippery shingle or big tangled boulders. In winter, climbing is technical, requiring snow- and ice-climbing gear and expertise. Mountain guides can be hired in both winter and summer.

and weather. Egmont National Park was created in 1900 to protect the mountain and its surrounding forests. From a distance the landscape looks simple; a cone-shape mountain draped white with snow in winter and flanked by a near-perfect circle of forest. Look closer, or try walking on the park trails, and a different picture emerges. Thousands of years of volcanic buildup and erosion have crafted steep gullies and rivers, immense lava bluffs, unstable slips, and acres of moss-covered "goblin" trees and tall, ancient forest giants. It's a fascinating place to explore, and thankfully there are many ways of doing this no matter your level of fitness. Try a scenic drive up one of the three access roads, explore the

Did You Know?

Mt. Taranaki is one of the most symmetrical volcanic cones in the world. Its resemblance to Mt. Fuji won it a starring role in *The Last Samurai*.

easy short trails around each of the three park entrances, or take a longer hike, staying in a park hut. The one day Pouakai Crossing or two-to-three day Pouakai Circuit explores all the park's landscapes: lava cliffs, wetlands, tussock tops, and goblin forests. (Check with DOC, some tracks are often temporarily closed due to erosion.) To climb the mountain is a serious undertaking, especially with frequent bad weather. The mountain is sacred to the local Māori people, so they ask that climbers respect this and not clamber over the summit rocks. In winter, climbing is for technically equipped and experienced climbers only. .

🛏 Hotels

Dawson Falls Mountain Lodge and Cafe

$$ | HOTEL | A charming alpine-style building on the southern slopes of Mt. Taranaki, this 1896-built lodge offers stellar views of the coastline and native bush. **Pros:** bush backdrop, waterfalls, and birdsong; superb hosts; quality cuisine. **Cons:** way out in the country; no television; can be cold in rooms. $ *Rooms from: NZ$200 ✉ 1890 Upper Manaia Rd., Kaponga, Dawson Falls ☎ 06/765–5457 ⊕ www.dawsonfalls.co.nz ⤴ 12 rooms ⦿❙ Breakfast.*

Ngati Ruanui Stratford Mountain House

$$ | HOTEL | High on the mountain, this hotel and restaurant has a deserved reputation for its dramatic setting and fine food. **Pros:** dramatic mountain views; owned by local Māori people, Ngati Ruanui; massage treatments available by reservation. **Cons:** can rain often on the mountain; long, steep drive to get there; no Wi-Fi in the rooms. $ *Rooms from: NZ$175 ✉ Pembroke Rd., E. Egmont ☎ 06/765–6100 ⊕ www.stratfordmountainhouse.co.nz ⤴ 10 rooms ⦿❙ No meals.*

🏃 Activities

Whether your thing is climbing sheer rocky crags or taking a 10-minute stroll to a forest waterfall, you'll find something to wow you in this national park. Short walks to natural features, multiday hikes using park huts for accommodation, and the 18 km (11 mile) Pouakai Crossing are all popular. Summit climbs are notoriously dangerous, owing to the changeable weather, the mountain's steepness, and the loose unstable rock that surrounds it. In winter technical expertise is a must. There's also a very basic slope for skiers.

HIKING

Top Guides

HIKING/WALKING | Take a half-day or full-day hiking trip showcasing the finest features of the park, escorted by guides with exceptional local knowledge and mountain experience. They will discuss with you what kind of adventure you would like, although the Pouakai Crossing is their signature day walk. They also offer shuttle transport from New Plymouth for those who want to walk independently on the 18 km (11 mile) trail. ☎ 027/270–2932 ⊕ www.topguides.co.nz.

SKIING

Manganui

SKIING/SNOWBOARDING | Owned by a small club, the sole ski slope on Mt. Taranaki only operates for 10 to 30 days each winter (June–October), based on snow conditions. The terrain is for intermediate and advanced skiers; nonmembers can buy daily tow passes for NZ$50. Note that facilities are limited, and it's a 20-minute walk from the parking lot to the ski area. ✉ Egmont National Park ⊕ www.skitaranaki.co.nz.

Stratford

41 km (27 miles) southeast of New Plymouth.

Sitting under the eastern side of Mt. Taranaki, Stratford is a service town for surrounding farms. Its streets are named after characters from Shakespeare's works, and it has the first glockenspiel in New Zealand, which chimes four times a day. A number of the country's most interesting private gardens, including Hollard, thrive here in the rich volcanic soil. Because the town is at the junction of two highways, you'll likely pass through at some stage if you're exploring Taranaki.

GETTING HERE AND AROUND

Stratford is in central Taranaki, at the junction of State Highway 3, which passes through the region along the eastern side of Mt. Taranaki, and State Highway 43, aka the Forgotten World Highway. The town is just more than a 30-minute drive from New Plymouth. Daily bus service through Stratford, linking New Plymouth and Wanganui, is provided by InterCity; bookings can be made via i-SITE Visitor Information Centres.

BUS CONTACTS Stratford Bus Depot. ⊠ *By Stratford i-SITE Visitor Information Centre, 56 Miranda St.*

VISITOR INFORMATION

CONTACTS Stratford i-SITE Visitor Information Centre. ⊠ *Prospero Pl.* ☎ *06/765–6708, 0800/765–6708* ⊕ *www.stratford. govt.nz.*

◉ Sights

★ Hollard Gardens

GARDEN | A 14-acre horticultural haven 16 km (10 miles) southwest of Stratford, Hollard Gardens encompasses native and exotic trees, rhododendrons, azaleas, camellias, and perennials. The 1920s vision of farmers Bernie and Rose Hollard, the gardens are now managed by the local council for all to enjoy.

Self-contained campervans can stay overnight. ⊠ *1686 Upper Manaia Rd., off Opunake Rd., Kaponga* ☎ *0800/736–222* ⊕ *www.trc.govt.nz/gardens/hollard-gardens* ⊠ *Free.*

Stratford–Taumarunui

SCENIC DRIVE | Known as the Forgotten World Highway, Highway 43, heading northeast from Stratford, takes you on an intriguing, heritage-rich journey back in time as it winds through rolling farmland and dense rain forests to Taumarunui, the northern access point for the Whanganui River. You'll see few cars here, but there's no shortage of scenic sights. Highlights include Mt. Damper Falls (a side trip); spectacular views from three saddles and a lookout point; the steep, forest-filled Tangarakau Gorge; a road tunnel and historic railway; plus Whanganui River views. The 155-km (96-mile) highway is sealed for all but 11 km (7 miles). Allow three hours, and be sure to fill your tank before leaving Stratford. If you need a break, drop into the vintage **Whangamomona Hotel** (*6018 Ohura Rd.*). More than a century old, it's the only place to stop for refreshments along the Forgotten World Highway. Travelers who don't feel like driving a car can sign on with **Forgotten World Adventures** (⊕ *www. forgottenworldadventures.co.nz*), an outfit that lets you "ride the rails"—golf carts mounted on a decommissioned railway line. The self-drive carts reach a top speed of 20 kph (12 mph) as you're led along 140 km (87 miles) of stunning track; guided trips from three hours to two days are available.

Tawhiti Museum

MUSEUM | **FAMILY** | This isn't a boring old museum, but an outstanding presentation of Taranaki's lively history. It's the creation of former schoolteacher-cum-historian Nigel Ogle, who has created life-size fiberglass figures and set them into historic scenes: dioramas depict the huge intertribal wars of the 1830s and European–Māori land wars

Did You Know?

Thomas Dawson was the
first European to discover
this waterfall—when he
almost fell over it. Despite
the inauspicious begin-
ning, he settled nearby
and explored the land.
Dawson Falls still bears
his name.

of the 1860s, for example. More than 800 model warriors, none of them the same, have been created. In "Traders and Whalers," you glide by lantern light on a boat through an eerie world of traders and whalers and witness their first encounters with Māori tribes. Outside, Tawhiti Bush Railway highlights historical logging operations in Taranaki (runs the first Sunday of each month). Mr. Badger's Café, with its Wind in the Willows theme, and a quaint gift shop, can bring you back to the present. To reach the museum, in southern Taranaki, head south on State Highway 3 for 30 km (18 miles). ⊠ *401 Ohangai Rd., Hawera* ☎ *06/278–6837* ⊕ *www.tawhitimuseum.co.nz* ✉ *Museum NZ$15, Traders and Whalers NZ$15, Bush Railway NZ$6* ⊙ *Closed Mon.–Sat. June–Aug.*

🛍 Shopping

Envirofur

CLOTHING | This small but thriving business near Stratford is turning possum, a local environmental pest, into high-end items using all-natural tanning processes. Designer fur and leather products such as hats, rugs, coats, and scarves are sold. ⊠ *1103 Opunake Rd., Mahoe* ☎ *06/764–6133* ⊕ *www.envirofur.co.nz.*

Whanganui

A major gateway to Whanganui National Park, Whanganui is worthy in its own right. Its compact center has lively streets with shops and galleries, plus restored heritage buildings that hark back to colonial times and the busy trading days. The city is home to a vibrant arts community, and locals gather at the River Traders riverside market on Saturday morning for fresh produce and crafts. Restored riverboats cruise the river's lower reaches; gardens, parks, an interesting regional museum, and fine cafés and restaurants complete the picture.

GETTING HERE AND AROUND

Air Chathams flies here from Auckland three times a day (two on the weekend), landing at Whanganui Airport (WAG). The airport is located south of the river, approximately 4 km (2½ miles) from the center of Whanganui; you can catch a taxi in for about NZ$25.

If you're driving, Whanganui is three hours from Wellington; take State Highway 1 north to Sanson and Highway 3 west from there. From New Plymouth drive south on State Highway 3, allowing about 90 minutes for the journey. Access to the lower and middle reaches of the Whanganui River from the city is via the scenic Whanganui River Road—expect it to take two hours to drive from Whanganui to Pipiriki. Remember to keep left on the narrow corners. For a scenic backcountry day trip, drive north up the Whanganui River Road, cut east along the minor road connecting Pipiriki to Raetihi, and then return down Highway 4, a paved though winding route through steep farmland and forest, to Whanganui. To reach the main kayak starting point, take Highway 4 north from Whanganui; it's a three-hour drive to Taumarunui, via Raetihi.

Note that the river is named Whanganui, the traditional spelling. The city can officially be spelled Wanganui or Whanganui, though nearly all businesses, agencies, attractions, and road signs now use the traditionally correct spelling of Whanganui.

AIRPORTS Whanganui Airport. ⊠ *Airport Rd.* ☎ *06/348–0536* ⊕ *www.whanganui-airport.co.nz.*

BUS CONTACTS Whanganui Travel Centre. ⊠ *156 Ridgeway St.*

VISITOR INFORMATION

CONTACTS Whanganui i-SITE Visitor Information Centre. ⊠ *31 Taupo Quay* ☎ *06/349–0508* ⊕ *whanganuinz.com.*

◉ Sights

Durie Hill Lookout

VIEWPOINT | This lookout, Whanganui's most popular attraction, provides spectacular views, but reaching it—via an elevator that runs through the hill—is something else. First, you walk through a 700-foot tunnel to the elevator shaft, and the elevator concierge at the top will see you on camera and lower the elevator for you. Alternatively, you can climb several hundred steps to the lookout, plus another 176 steps up the nearby Durie Hill Memorial Tower. ⊠ *Durie Hill* 🕾 *NZ$2 each way (cash only)*.

New Zealand Glassworks

STORE/MALL | Whanganui is regarded as the country's home for glass artisans; many of them exhibit internationally. This community studio is open for the public to watch some of these artists at work, join workshops, and purchase their own stunning pieces from the retail gallery. ⊠ *2 Rutland St.* ☎ *06/927–6803* ⊕ *www. nzglassworks.com* 🕾 *Free*.

Virginia Lake

BODY OF WATER | The formal gardens here are a delight, and a gentle 25-minute stroll leads around the lake through woodlands and gardens. There's also a small café here. 🕾 *Free*

Waimarie and Waimarie Centre

TRANSPORTATION SITE (AIRPORT/BUS/FERRY/ TRAIN) | The coal-fired paddle steamer, *Waimarie,* is one of the original river boats that operated here. Sunk in 1954, it was salvaged from the river bed and restored in the 1990s. Through summer (Friday to Sunday) you can enjoy a historic, two-hour cruise, just like the old days. The Waimarie Centre displays photographs and related artifacts from the era when riverboats thrived here. Opening hours are variable at this volunteer operation; summer weekends are your best bet. ⊠ *Waimarie Centre, 1A Taupo Quay* ☎ *06/347–1863* ⊕ *www.waimarie.co.nz* 🕾 *Cruise NZ$45, museum by donation.*

Wairua

TOUR—SIGHT | Rescued from the muddy riverbed and restored to first-class order, the classic little riverboat *Wairua* now makes regular two- and three-hour passenger trips upriver. Scheduled cruises depart year-round on Tuesday and Thursday at 11 am. ⊠ *Taupo Quay, opposite Moutoa Gardens* ☎ *0800/924– 782* ⊕ *www.whanganuiriverboat.co.nz* 🕾 *NZ$39.*

★ Whanganui Regional Museum

MUSEUM | This museum offers a superb overview of the region's history and one of the country's best collections of Māori artifacts. It contains *taonga* (Māori ancestral treasures) of the river people and re-creates 19th-century pioneer-town Whanganui. There's also Te Pataka Whakaahua (the Lindauer Gallery), featuring 19th century paintings of Māori leaders by respected artist Gottfried Lindauer. ⊠ *Queens Park, Watt St.* ☎ *06/349–1110* ⊕ *www.wrm.org.nz* 🕾 *Free.*

🍴 Restaurants

Momiji Japanese Restaurant and Cafe

$$ | **JAPANESE** | Traditional Japanese food made with a mix of imported Japanese ingredients and fresh local produce is the star here. There's also a good selection of beer, sake, rice wine, and New Zealand beverages. **Known for:** bento boxes; Kirin beer on tap; sashimi and sushi with locally caught fish. $ *Average main: NZ$20* ⊠ *21 Victoria Ave.* ☎ *06/345–0444* ⊗ *Closed Mon.*

Stellar Restaurant and Bar

$$ | **PIZZA** | This relaxed bar/restaurant specializes in pizzas, burgers, light meals, salads, and meaty main courses. It's also a bar and music venue, with weekly quiz nights. **Known for:** strong Kiwi vibe; late night entertainment; nice craft beer selection. $ *Average main: NZ$19* ⊠ *2 Victoria Ave.* ☎ *06/345–7278* ⊕ *www. stellarbar.co.nz.*

The *Waimarie* paddle steamer plies the Whanganui River.

Yellow House Café

$$ | **CAFÉ** | Join the locals at this cozy café, spread throughout the veranda, garden, and several intimate rooms of an old, mostly yellow, villa. It serves a full breakfast/brunch menu with all the classics as well as wholesome, house-cooked lunches. **Known for:** best brunch menu in town; great tea selection; bright and welcoming atmosphere. ⑤ *Average main: NZ$18* ⊠ *17 Pitt St., at Dublin St.* ☎ *06/345–0083* ⊘ *No dinner.*

Hotels

Anndion Lodge

$$ | **HOTEL** | **FAMILY** | A blend of upmarket "flashpacker" lodge rooms and stylish self-contained suites and apartments give visitors to the Anndion Lodge lots of flexibility. **Pros:** well-equipped kitchen; river and grassy park area just across the road; nice communal layout. **Cons:** short drive from downtown; backpacker area can get rowdy; beside busy main road. ⑤ *Rooms from: NZ$160* ⊠ *143 Anzac Parade* ☎ *06/343–3593, 0800/343–056*

⊕ *www.anndionlodge.co.nz* ⇲ *21 rooms* ⑩ *No meals.*

Aotea Motor Lodge

$$$ | **HOTEL** | Aimed primarily at business travelers, the spacious digs here, with their handsome yet comfy decor and convenient location are popular with tourists, too. **Pros:** amenities include double whirlpool baths; close to supermarkets and fast-food restaurants; spacious rooms. **Cons:** beside busy road; tight car parking spaces; cooked breakfast is not a good value. ⑤ *Rooms from: NZ$210* ⊠ *390 Victoria Ave.* ☎ *06/345–0303* ⊕ *www.aoteamotorlodge.co.nz* ⇲ *28 rooms* ⑩ *No meals.*

151 on London

$$ | **HOTEL** | **FAMILY** | This upmarket motel-style complex comes with a good selection of amenity-packed units. **Pros:** centrally located; high-quality amenities; interesting rustic architectural theme. **Cons:** entrance is off a busy road (but hush glass keeps noise down); breakfast not included in price; no bar or restaurant on-site. ⑤ *Rooms from: NZ$185* ⊠ *151*

London St. ☎ *06/345–8668* ⊕ *ww-w.151onlondon.co.nz* ⇨ *26 units* ¶❍¶ *No meals.*

Rutland Arms

$$ | **B&B/INN** | Elegance and character team with modern amenities in this renovated Edwardian inn in the center of town. **Pros:** central location; old-world elegance; very well heated for an old building. **Cons:** no elevator; on busy main street, so some noise; restaurant can be packed with locals. ⑤ *Rooms from: NZ$160* ⊠ *Victoria Ave. and Ridgeway St.* ☎ *06/347–7677* ⊕ *www.rutlandarms. co.nz* ⇨ *8 suites* ¶❍¶ *Breakfast.*

Whanganui National Park

The Whanganui, the longest continually navigable river in New Zealand, flows through one of the country's largest remaining areas of native lowland forest, much of which is protected in Whanganui National Park. Canoeing, jet-boating, hiking, and mountain biking are the main recreational activities here.

GETTING HERE AND AROUND

Whanganui National Park, through which the eponymous river flows, is in the hinterland of the central North Island. The closest access points are Whanganui in the south and the township of Taumarunui to the north. The latter sits on State Highway 4 and is served by daily InterCity buses from Auckland and Wellington.

Traditional entry points for a Whanganui River journey are Taumarunui and the small settlements of Whakahoro and Pipiriki. To reach Whakahoro, turn off State Highway 4 at Owhango, just south of Taumarunui. Pipiriki is 27 km (17 miles) from Raetihi (also on State Highway 4) and 79 km (49 miles) from Whanganui, via the Whanganui River Road. Shuttle services for kayakers, hikers, mountain-bikers, and

jet-boat travelers are run by tourism operators based in the Whanganui/Ruapehu region, including the towns of Ohakune, National Park, Taumarunui, and Pipiriki.

BUS CONTACTS Taumarunui Bus Depot. ⊠ *Taumarunui i-SITE Visitor Information Centre, 116 Hakiaha St., Taumarunui.*

TOURS

★**Whanganui River Adventures**

ADVENTURE TOURS | Ken and Josephine Haworth, who grew up on the river, run a Pipiriki-based company that offers jet-boat tours to the Bridge to Nowhere, shorter trips to scenic highlights the Drop Scene and Manganui o te Ao River, and jet-boating/canoeing combo trips, plus river shuttle services for mountain bikers, canoeists, and hikers. Tours range from 45 minutes to multiday adventures. They also operate a café and nicely landscaped campground with cabins, tents, and camper van sites on the grounds of the former Pipiriki School. ⊠ *RD 6, Pipiriki, Wanganui* ☎ *06/385–3246, 0800/862–743* ⊕ *www.whanganuiriveradventures.co.nz* ⑤ *Tours from NZ$80.*

Whanganui River Road Mail Tour

ADVENTURE TOURS | Join the rural mail delivery run and enjoy a day of history and scenic splendor along the Whanganui River Road. Highlights include meeting the locals; visiting small Māori settlements with their traditional Māori ceremonial houses; exploring churches, including Jerusalem, where Mother Aubert founded the Home of Compassion; and a journey through steep farmland then the forest-covered hills and valleys of Whanganui National Park. From Pipiriki, a jet-boat tour farther upriver can be arranged at extra cost. Pickups are from city accommodations, and reservations are essential. ☎ *06/345–3475* ⊕ *www.whanganuitours.co.nz* ⑤ *NZ$63.*

Whanganui Scenic Experience Jet

SPECIAL-INTEREST | Mark and Claire Wickham, a pair of knowledgeable locals, offer two- to eight-hour jet-boat tours that can

Planning Your Trip to Whanganui ◉

Best Time to Go

Anytime. Guided river trips generally operate in summer; however, the climate is mild and a winter journey, while a little cooler and possibly wetter, is equally rewarding—and less crowded. The historic Whanganui River Road is open year-round.

Best Ways to Explore

Paddle the River. The Whanganui, New Zealand's most canoed river, is popular both for the terrain it transects and its suitability for beginners. Although the water flows through gorges and forested wilderness, its gradient is gentle and most of its 239 named rapids have little more than a 3-foot fall. The river is suitable for all kinds of craft, from kayaks to open-style Canadian canoes. Department of Conservation huts and campsites provide basic (but very scenic) riverside accommodations. Most people take a three- or five-day trip through the heart of the wilderness to Pipiriki, though paddling the lower reaches past historic Māori settlements is also appealing.

Take a Hike. Two three-day hiking trails (one is also a mountain-bike trail) traverse the park, and each has a distinctive character. Regenerating forests along Mangapurua–Kaiwhakauka Track tell the story of failed farming attempts in these remote valleys. The old farming road was upgraded in 2010 and is now popular with mountain-bikers. In contrast, the Matemateaonga Track passes through the park's most pristine forested areas. Jet-boats can be chartered for access to the river end of each walk.

Take a Drive. The narrow Whanganui River Road follows the water's lower reaches, climbing around bluffs and steep gullies and passing through historic Māori settlements. Heritage stops include an old flour mill, mission settlement, village churches, and traditional Māori *marae* (villages)—check with a local before venturing into these. You can drive yourself, or take the daily mail delivery tour from Wanganui.

Ride a Bike. Much of the Mountains to Sea—Nga Ara Tuhono Cycle Trail passes through Whanganui National Park. Remote, at times challenging, mountain-bike sections traverse the bluff-lined Kaiwhakauka and Mangapurua valleys. The last section follows the narrow, twisting, and very scenic Whanganui River Road before linking with off-road trails through Whanganui city to the sea. Jet-boat shuttles can be booked for the 32-km (20-mile) section of river gorge that links two trail sections. Several companies offer packages including jet-boat shuttles, accommodation, bike rentals, and a guide.

include morning or afternoon tea stops at scenic and historic spots along the river. Trips start from the Wickham family farm, a 30-minute drive from Whanganui. ✉ 1195 Whanganui River Rd., Wanganui ☎ 06/342–5599, 0800/945–335 ⊕ www.whanganuiscenicjet.com ✈ Tours from NZ$80.

VISITOR INFORMATION

CONTACTS Taumarunui i-SITE Visitor Information Centre. ✉ 116 Hakiaha St., Taumarunui ☎ 07/895–7494 ⊕ www.visitruapehu.com. **Whanganui i-SITE Visitor Information Centre.** ✉ 31 Taupo Quay, Wanganui ☎ 06/349–0508 ⊕ whanganu-inz.com.

👁 Sights

Whanganui River and Whanganui National Park

NATIONAL/STATE PARK | The Whanganui River starts high on the volcanic mountains of the central North Island, and travels 329 km (204 miles) to the sea. For several hundred years the tribe Te Atihau nui a Paparangi has lived along the riverbanks; they regard the waterway as their spiritual ancestor. To acknowledge this, the Whanganui became the first river in the world to be accorded legal personhood in 2017. The Whanganui flows through the heart of Whanganui National Park, through steep gorges and huge tracts of forested wilderness. The remoteness and beauty, culture and history, the river's relatively easy navigability, and forest trails and mountain bike tracks are the main draws to this national park. Scenic jet-boat trips operate throughout the year from road access points along the river. Single and multiday kayak trips, both guided and independent, are extremely popular. The Whanganui Journey is, in fact, listed as one of New Zealand's famed Great Walks. Most visitors kayak in summer, but a river trip is feasible at any time. Two multiday walks and many shorter ones explore the lowland forest. Totaling 317 km (197 miles), the Mountains to Sea—Nga Ara Tuhono Cycle Trail traverses remote forest tracks (challenging for mountain bikes) and roads through Tongariro and Whanganui national parks from Mt. Ruapehu to the river's mouth; it can be ridden in stages. The river journey is also part of Te Araroa, the New Zealand Trail. ⊕ www.doc.govt.nz.

Whanganui River Road

SCENIC DRIVE | For a little slice of New Zealand, take a scenic and historic drive along the river's lower reaches by following the Whanganui River Road from the city of Whanganui. Turn left off State Highway 4 15 minutes north of the city. The narrow rural road follows the river for 79 km (49 miles) north, as far as Pipiriki. It passes several small villages and historic sites (ask a local before venturing onto any traditional Māori villages). Be sure to keep left, drive slow, and watch for wandering livestock. ⊠ *Whanganui River Rd., Wanganui.*

🛏 Hotels

Bridge to Nowhere Lodge

$$ | B&B/INN | Roughly 30 miles upriver from Pipiriki, this private farm enclave can only be reached by jet boat or kayak. **Pros:** memorable wilderness experience; range of lodging styles; packages including meals and jet-boat transport available. **Cons:** river access only; remote location; guest rooms quite basic, with shared bathrooms. $ *Rooms from: NZ$160* ⊠ *Whanganui River* 📞 *06/385–4622, 0800/480–308* ⊕ *www.bridgetonowhere.co.nz* ⇨ *8 rooms* ✦ *Some meals.*

The Flying Fox

$$$ | B&B/INN | Even just arriving here is an exceptional experience—whether by boat or the namesake Flying Fox, a cable car that carries you across to the remote, west bank of the Whanganui River. **Pros:** river wilderness; eco-friendly and organic; getting there is an adventure. **Cons:** no cell phone reception; native birdsong will probably wake you early; remote location. $ *Rooms from: NZ$240* ⊠ *Whanganui River Rd., Koriniti* 📞 *06/342–8160* ⊕ *www.theflyingfox.co.nz* ⇨ *6 rooms* ✦ *Some meals.*

★ Frontier Lodge at Blue Duck Station

$$ | B&B/INN | This stylish, purpose-built lodge is set on Blue Duck Station, a multiuse tourism, farming, and conservation venture beside the Whanganui River. **Pros:** stunning New Zealand location; stylish, thoughtful building design; can hear kiwi calling at night. **Cons:** might be too remote for some; nearest shops about an hour drive; birdsong might wake you too early. $ *Rooms from: NZ$195* ⊠ *4265 Oio Rd., Owhango*

Whanganui Eco-stays

The Flying Fox has rustic yet comfortable cottages and glamping sites built from recycled timbers. The property, which is certified organic, is dotted with heritage fruit trees.

Accessible only by river, the **Bridge to Nowhere Lodge** is nestled on a small riverside patch of farmland. There's no electric power, but diesel generators, wood-fueled stoves, and helpful hosts provide all the comforts of home. They also offer jet-boat and canoe trips. **Blue Duck Station** is a multifaceted operation that includes accommodations, a restaurant and café, river trips, and award-winning conservation work protecting endangered kiwi and blue duck species. Frontier Lodge is built to high eco-standards, while other lodges on the property cater for groups. Guests can partake in river, farm, and conservation activities.

All three lodges are set beside the Whanganui River and adjoin Whanganui National Park.

☎ 07/895–6276 ⊕ www.blueduckstation. co.nz ⌑ 3 rooms.

Activities

CANOEING AND KAYAKING

The main season for Whanganui River trips is between October and Easter; the busiest period is during the summer holidays (Christmas–January). Winter trips are also doable; the weather will be slightly colder, but you'll probably have the river to yourself. In summer, although there can be several hundred folks on the water at any one time, they are all moving in one direction, so a group can travel long periods without seeing another soul. The time they do come together is in the evenings, at park huts and campsites.

Travel on the river is generally in open, two-seater canoes or in kayaks. Tour options range from one-day picnic trips to five-day camping expeditions. What's known as the **Whanganui Journey** is regarded as one of nine "Great Walks" in New Zealand's national parks. Most people travel the river from Taumarunui to Pipiriki (a four- to five-day trip) or from Whakahoro to Pipiriki (three to four days).

The latter is a true wilderness experience; there is no road access. A lower-river trip, from Pipiriki to Whanganui, passes through a mix of native forest, farmland, and several small communities and follows a road for much of the way.

To arrange a guided trip, contact a licensed commercial operator or the Whanganui office of the **Department of Conservation** (☎ 06/349–2100 ⊕ www. doc.govt.nz). No experience is necessary as the Whanganui is considered a beginner's river; however, while it's definitely not a white-water adventure, the river should be respected. One or two rapids can play nasty tricks on paddlers, and the river can rise quickly to dangerous flood levels. Operators can supply all equipment, transfers, and the necessary hut and campsite passes, whether the trip is independently undertaken or guided and catered. Prices vary considerably according to the length and style of the journey, but you can expect to pay from about NZ$55 for a simple one-day outing and in the NZ$600 to NZ$800 range for an all-inclusive three-day excursion.

Canoe Safaris

CANOEING/ROWING/SKULLING | One of the most experienced companies with more than three decades running Whanganui River trips, these guides cater to everyone from families to septuagenerians. Their fleet ranges from kayaks to big open Canadian fur trapper-style canoes. Their campsite catering includes three-course dinners with wine; they'll also tell you about the natural fauna and history of the area. Fully guided trips include all equipment, including waterproof gear bags and a Department of Conservation User Pass. Kayak and canoe rentals and combo jet-boat trips are also offered, plus they'll put you up pre- or post-trip nearby in their Ohakune lodge (at extra cost). ☎ *06/385–9237, 0800/272–3353* ⊕ *www.canoesafaris.co.nz.*

Whanganui River Canoes

KAYAKING | Canoe and kayak hire with jet-boat support are offered by this Raetihi-based couple, Ben and Rebecca. Ben is on the river most days in the summer, driving jet boats for his father's Bridge to Nowhere Lodge, so he'll be looking out for you. Rebecca's great-grandad was one of the first to map this river—his maps are still used by river travelers. The couple also owns Raetihi Holiday Park, 27 km (17 miles) from Pipiriki so they can accommodate you pre- or post-trip if required. They'll also organize shuttles for trampers and mountain-bikers. ☎ *0800/408–888, 06/385–4176* ⊕ *www.whanganuirivercanoes.co.nz.*

JET-BOAT TOURS

If you fancy a faster-paced river adventure, consider a jet-boat tour—you'll skim across the rapids, dodge the rocks, and see fantastic scenery. Note that Whanganui River rides are more about grand scenery and cultural history than the short, thrill-seeking ones offered by some southern-based operations. One of the most popular tours is a boat trip from Pipiriki to Mangapurua Landing, followed by a walk to the Bridge to Nowhere in the Mangapurua Valley. The valley was a farming settlement established in 1918 and abandoned in 1942, owing to the impossibly remote and rugged country. The old concrete bridge in the bush is a fascinating reminder. Jet-boat companies also transport hikers to two national park hiking trails: the Matemateonga Track and the Mangapurua Track.

★ Blue Duck Station

BICYCLING | FAMILY | A standout farming, conservation, and tourism operation, you can take your pick here from a slew of activities. Options include jet-boating or kayaking on the river, tramping in the national park, mountain-biking a remote forested section of the Mountains to Sea Heritage Trail, horseback-riding over the farm, taking a Bush Safari to learn about the conservation work protecting the habitats of kiwi and blue duck, or just relaxing by the river. Owner/operator Dan Steele is a Kiwi legend in tourism and conservation circles. ✉ *4265 Oio Rd., Owhango* ☎ *07/895–6276* ⊕ *www.blueduckstation.co.nz.*

Bridge to Nowhere

TOUR—SPORTS | Jet boats make the trip from Pipiriki to the Bridge to Nowhere (NZ$130) as well as to other natural and historic sights. The company also offers a host of additional activities, including canoeing, canoe/jet-boat combos, accommodations at the Bridge to Nowhere Lodge, and transport for mountain bikers tackling the Bridge to Nowhere section of the Mountains to Sea—Nga Ara Tuhono Cycle Trail. ☎ *0800/480–308* ⊕ *www.bridgetonowhere.co.nz.*

★ Forgotten World Adventures

BOATING | These Taumarunui-based jet-boat tours will bounce you over the more shallow rapids of the upper river. Their signature river trip is the eight-hour Bridge to Nowhere Tour; they will also do a shorter, one-hour spin for a minimum of four. You can also check out the company's unique Rail Cart Tours. Self-driving specially adapted golf carts travel on a disused railway line through hinterland forests and farms between the Whanganui River and Taranaki; you can also do a combo of river/rail adventuring. ✉ *9 Hakiaha St., Taumarunui* ☎ *0800/7245–2278* ⊕ *www.forgottenworldadventures.co.nz.*

Palmerston North

145 km (87 miles) northeast of Wellington, 72 km (45 miles) southeast of Whanganui.

Palmerston North—or "Palmy" as the locals call it—is home to several major educational and agricultural research institutes. Thanks to these, students make up one-third of the population. The biggest influence on the city is Massey University, one of the country's leading postsecondary institutions. It is set among huge trees and lovely gardens just across the Manawatu River on Palmerston North's southern edge. The campus includes the Sport and Rugby Institute, which serves as a training facility for players on the All Blacks (New Zealand's revered national rugby team) and other elite athletes.

The city provides services for the surrounding agricultural industry as well. Rolling sheep and cattle farms, stunning gardens, and country homestay retreats are all in close proximity, nestling at the foot of the steep Ruahine Ranges.

GETTING HERE AND AROUND

The Palmerston North Airport (PMR) is 5 km (3 miles) northeast of the city. Air New Zealand serves it with daily direct flights from Auckland, Hamilton, Wellington, and Christchurch; Jetstar flies direct from Auckland; and Originair flies direct from Nelson. Ground transportation options to the city center include Super Shuttle (NZ$20) and Palmerston North Taxis (NZ$28–NZ$30).

The scenic *Northern Explorer* train also stops here as it travels between Auckland and Wellington.

If you're driving, Palmerston North is about two hours north of Wellington (allow more time during busy holiday weekends), and six to seven hours south of Auckland, following State Highway 1 through the central North Island. Whanganui is a one-hour drive to the northwest, and Napier is just under a three-hour drive to the northeast.

InterCity offers daily bus services from all major North Island communities. They arrive and depart from the Palmerston North i-SITE Visitor Information Centre. Activity in the city is centered on the streets around the Square. From there, you can easily explore the cafés, boutiques, art galleries, and museums on foot.

AIRPORTS Palmerston North Airport.
✉ *Airport Dr.* ☎ *06/351–4415* ⊕ *www.pnairport.co.nz.*

AIRPORT TRANSFERS Palmerston North Taxis. ☎ *06/355–5333* ⊕ *www.pntaxis.co.nz.* **Super Shuttle.** ☎ *0800/748–885* ⊕ *www.supershuttle.co.nz.*

BUS CONTACTS Palmerston North Bus Depot. ✉ *Palmerston North i-SITE Visitor Information Centre, The Square.*

TRAIN CONTACTS Palmerston North Train Station. ✉ *Matthew Ave.*

VISITOR INFORMATION

CONTACTS Palmerston North i-SITE Visitor Information Centre. ✉ *The Square* ☎ *06/350–1922, 0800/626–292* ⊕ *www.manawatunz.co.nz.*

◉ Sights

★ Feilding

GARDEN | For a look at an authentic New Zealand farming town visit Feilding, 20 km (12 miles) northwest of Palmerston North. The Feilding Saleyards Guided Tour is a classic experience. One of the largest livestock sale yards in the southern hemisphere, nearly 30,000 sheep and cattle are sold here every week. Every Friday at 11, a retired farmer will guide you (NZ$10, bookings essential) through the sheep pens and computerized cattle auction pavilion, and explain the secrets of a long-time New Zealand farming tradition. After the tour, visit the rustic Saleyards Café, where farmers meet for pie and chips or a toasted steak sandwich. Other local attractions in the Edwardian-style town square include the Friday morning farmers' market and the Coachhouse Museum that displays restored vehicles from the pioneering era (NZ$12). You could also putter about the town's bookshops, art galleries, and boutique movie theater and café. From Feilding, Kimbolton Road passes through prime sheep-farming country to Kimbolton Village, 28 km (17 miles) away. Within a few minutes' drive of it are two outstanding gardens with rhododendrons and myriad other plants: Cross Hills (NZ$10; daily September–May) and Heritage Park Garden (NZ$7; daily year-round). ✉ *Feilding* ☎ *06/323–3318 Feilding & District Information Centre* ⊕ *www.feilding.co.nz.*

New Zealand Rugby Museum

MUSEUM | The only one of its kind in the country, this museum—located upstairs in the Te Manawa complex—is worth a visit whether or not you're a rugby fan because it offers insight into a sport that many New Zealanders treat like a religion. The ever-growing collection of rugby memorabilia dates back to the start of this national game in 1870. Interactive components even let visitors "have a go"; you can kick, tackle, and jump in the lineout, testing your playing skills quite safely. ✉ *326 Main St.* ☎ *06/358–6947* ⊕ *www.rugbymuseum.co.nz* 🎫 *NZ$13.*

Te Manawa

MUSEUM | **FAMILY** | This distinctive complex is divided into three sections that weave together the region's art,

science, and history, including natural history and the history of Rangitane, the local Māori people. For young ones, the Mind Science Centre, with its quirky interactive exhibits, is entertaining and educational. Regular touring exhibitions that visit here are also known for their quality. Te Manawa also houses the New Zealand Rugby Museum. ✉ *326 Main St.* ☎ *06/355–5000* ⊕ *www.temanawa.co.nz* 🎫 *Life and Art galleries free; charges for some exhibitions.*

🍴 Restaurants

Brew Union Brewing Company

$$$ | **MODERN NEW ZEALAND** | **FAMILY** | A buzzy microbrewery, Brew Union serves a flexible menu of small plates, wood-fired pizzas, grills, salads, and burgers. Along with house-brewed beers, there are regular taps serving ales and ciders from craft brewers across New Zealand as well as a full selection of other beverages. **Known for:** fresh house-brewed beers; tasty tapas; lots of different spaces (communal, quiet, indoors, and covered outdoors). 💲 *Average main: NZ$25* ✉ *41 Broadway Ave.* ☎ *06/280–3146* ⊕ *www.brewunion.co.nz.*

Café Cuba

$ | **NEW ZEALAND** | **FAMILY** | Just off the Square, funky Café Cuba is a perennially popular local haunt for breakfast, brunch, lunch, dinner, and after-show mingling. The menu is all classic, wholesome café fare, matched with laid-back background music. **Known for:** student community vibe; modern bubble and squeak (British breakfast) with bacon; sweet treats like cheesecake. 💲 *Average main: NZ$14* ✉ *Cuba and George Sts.* ☎ *06/356–5750* ⊕ *www.cafecuba.co.nz.*

The Herb Farm and Cafe

$$ | **CAFÉ** | **FAMILY** | Wholesome, organic, and scrumptious food is served in a country café that's set in the middle of a 2-acre herb garden. Not only are the herbs served fresh with your food, they are essentially grown to supply the natural healing products manufactured here. **Known for:** spectacular herb garden; generous and fresh Kiwi breakfast and brunch classics; adjacent shop filled with healing herb products made on-site. ⑤ *Average main: NZ$19* ⊠ *88 Grove Rd.* ☎ *06/326–8633* ⊕ *herbfarm.co.nz* ◷ *No dinner.*

★ Nero Restaurant

$$$$ | MODERN NEW ZEALAND | Head to Nero for fine dining in a charming old Victorian-style villa on a quiet inner-city street. Chef and owner Scott Kennedy describes the cuisine as contemporary New Zealand, along with a touch of fusion to celebrate cultural diversity. **Known for:** diverse Asian flavors; 42-day whisky-aged Wagyu beef; quality service. ⑤ *Average main: NZ$37* ⊠ *36 Amesbury St.* ☎ *06/354–0312* ⊕ *www.cafenero. co.nz* ◷ *Closed Sun.*

🛏 Hotels

Distinction Hotel Palmerston North

$$ | HOTEL | The city's largest hotel occupies a 1927 heritage building (check out the cage-style elevator, one of the country's oldest). **Pros:** in central city; good facilities; elevator access. **Cons:** guest rooms lack character; traffic noise; not a lot of personality here. ⑤ *Rooms from: NZ$160* ⊠ *175 Cuba St.* ☎ *06/355–5895, 0800/554–490* ⊕ *www.distinctionho-telspalmerstonnorth.co.nz* ⇌ *85 rooms* ⑪ *No meals.*

Hotel Coachman

$$ | HOTEL | FAMILY | This large, locally owned property comes with a diversity of hotel rooms, motel units, and a luxury villa. **Pros:** close to town; lots of options for types of rooms; peaceful ambience in the garden. **Cons:** by main road so front guest rooms can be noisy; can get busy with business meetings and functions; some decor is dated. ⑤ *Rooms from: NZ$145* ⊠ *140 Fitzherbert Ave.*

☎ *06/356–5065* ⊕ *www.coachman.co.nz* ⇌ *31 rooms.*

🛍 Shopping

Palmerston North's shopping is concentrated around the Square; Broadway Avenue and the Plaza shopping centers are within easy walking distance. George Street, which is also just off the Square, has a number of specialty shops, galleries, and cafés.

Bruce McKenzie Books

BOOKS/STATIONERY | This is considered among New Zealand's leading independent bookstores (and they are becoming a rare breed). ⊠ *37 George St.* ☎ *06/356–9922* ⊕ *www.bmbooks.co.nz.*

Taylor Jensen Fine Arts

CRAFTS | This gallery sells contemporary and traditional New Zealand and international art, sculpture, jewelry, crafts, and furniture, with changing exhibition space. ⊠ *33 George St.* ☎ *06/355–4278* ⊕ *www. finearts.co.nz.*

WELLINGTON AND THE WAIRARAPA

8

Updated by
Mike Stearne

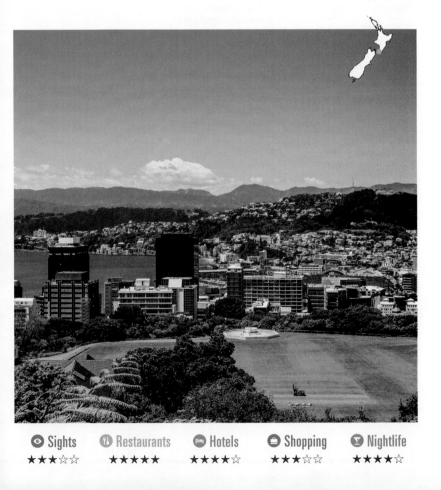

● Sights	⁋ Restaurants	🛏 Hotels	● Shopping	☺ Nightlife
★★★☆☆	★★★★★	★★★★☆	★★★☆☆	★★★★☆

WELCOME TO
WELLINGTON AND THE WAIRARAPA

TOP REASONS TO GO

★ **Arts and Culture:** The national symphony, ballet, and opera are based here. The biennial New Zealand International Arts Festival offers a wide program of drama, music, dance, plus other arts events.

★ **Wineries:** Spend a day or two wine tasting your way through the Wairarapa, home to more than 30 vineyards.

★ **Craft Beer:** With over a dozen local breweries, Wellington has firmly established itself as the home of craft beer in New Zealand.

★ **Eclectic Cuisine:** The great variety of Wellington's restaurants allows you to sample foods from dozens of cultures, while also enjoying plenty of down-to-earth Kiwi fare.

★ **The Waterfront:** Meandering along Wellington's waterfront is a great way to spend a day. You can visit both the Museum of New Zealand Te Papa Tongarewa and the Wellington Museum for free.

1 Wellington. The capital of New Zealand is filled with beaches, good food, and an excellent art scene.

2 Akatarawa Valley. This steep valley is full of hidden gems like the Staglands Wildlife Reserve.

3 Kapiti Coast. This gorgeous coastal area leads you to the arty beach town of Paekakariki.

4 Kapiti Island. One of Wellington's best-kept secrets, this protected island reserve has excellent hiking and nature tours.

5 Martinborough. This low-key town is the center of the Wairarapa wine industry.

6 Palliser Bay and Cape Palliser. The southernmost part of the North Island coast has a seal colony and Putangirua Pinnacles Scenic Reserve.

7 Masterton and Around. Wairarapa's second-biggest city is also a developing wine region.

NORTH
ISLAND

Palmerston North

Ashhurst

Woodville

Tokomaru

RUAHINE RANGE

Pahiatua

Shannon

Levin

Eketahuna

Pongaroa

Alfredton

Waikawa Beach

Otaki Beach

Te Horo Beach

Manakau

Otaki

Mount Bruce

Pukaha Mount Bruce

Dreyers Rock

Kapiti Island

Waikanae

Opaki

TARARUA RANGE

Paraparaumu

Masterton

Castlepoint

Castle
Point

Akatarawa Valley

Upper Hutt

Carterton

Whareama

Porirua

Featherston

Greytown

Riversdale

Lower Hutt

Fell Locomotive Museum

Uruti Point

WELLINGTON

WAIRARAPA

Lake
Wairarapa

Martinborough

RIMUTAKA RANGE

Baring Head

Lake Ferry

Flat Point

Turakirae Head

Palliser
Bay

AORANGI RANGE

Action Point

Cape
Palliser

0   20 mi

0   20 km

Amid a gorgeous backdrop fittingly used as the setting to many a Lord of the Rings scene, Wellington has developed the lively, friendly, and infectious spirit of a city coming into its own.

From the windswept green heights overlooking New Zealand's capital, a crystal-clear winter morning reveals stunning views over the deceptively quiet waters of Cook Strait stretching to the snow-capped mountains of the South Island; and it's sheer heaven on a mild summer night when a silver medallion of moon tops mysterious misty hillsides. People are making their way to Wellington, and not merely because it's the sailing point for ferries heading south. You might find yourself content to laze around the harbor, perhaps sipping a chilled glass of Chardonnay from a nearby vineyard. The burgeoning film industry—thanks to the *Lord of the Rings (LOTR)* and *The Hobbit* extravaganzas—has injected life into the local arts scene. Ardent film fans can still visit the many *LOTR* sites around the region via tours, but everyone benefits from the lively cafés and the rapidly expanding restaurant culture. On the waterfront the first-class Museum of New Zealand Te Papa Tongarewa has many hands-on exhibits equally fascinating for children and adults, while the Wellington Museum is dedicated to the city's history.

Wellington and the adjacent Hutt Valley are the southern gateway to the Wairarapa, a region whose name has become synonymous with wine. Journey over the hills and meander along quiet byways from vineyard to vineyard for a day—or two, or three—of wine tasting. If wine isn't your thing, the Wairarapa is still worth an excursion for its gardens,

walking trails, and fishing opportunities. Head for the coast, too, where waves crash against craggy beaches, and the dramatic sunsets intoxicate you with their beauty.

GETTING ORIENTED

All main roads from Wellington and the adjacent Wairarapa head north, as these regions are at the North Island's southern point where the sometimes-stormy waters of Cook Strait divide the country's two major islands. Separated by mountain ranges that virtually tumble into the Strait, road travel between the two regions is via the Hutt Valley and the winding Rimutaka Hill road. Expect peaceful river scenery, a green and pleasant outlook, and spectacular views.

MAJOR REGIONS

Greater Wellington. Right outside of Wellington, you'll find a lovely variety of day trips, from exploring the rugged Akatarawa Valley to enjoying the nature and beaches of the Kapiti Coast and Kapiti Island.

The Wairarapa. In the eastern Wairarapa, windswept cliffs form a boundary against the vast Pacific; on the western side the rugged Rimutaka and Tararua ranges outline a massive division from the capital city and coastal region beyond. Spreading north from the cold deep waters of Palliser Bay, a rural panorama of fields and quiet vineyards stretches north as far as the eye can see. For some years, the rather daunting access road gave a sense of isolation to the Wairarapa, which was essentially a farming area. But the emergence of the wine industry has triggered a tourism boom in the region. Red grape varieties flourish in the local soil (the Pinot Noir is particularly notable), and Wairarapa wines, produced in small quantities, are sought after in New Zealand and overseas. These days, vineyards, wine tastings, olive farms, and the twice-yearly Martinborough Fair are firmly established attractions. Sea-and-freshwater fishing, walking, the "Golden Shears" shearing competition, and other outdoor activities have also brought visitors over "The Hill." Towns like Martinborough and Masterton are good bases for exploring the region's wineries, while areas around them like Pallister Bay and Cape Pallister showcase the region's rugged beauty.

Planning

In Wellington make time to enjoy a relaxing day on the waterfront; it's a stone's throw from the city center. This area is mainly flat, easy walking with interesting shopping and numerous cafés and restaurants. You don't need a car in the city, but to explore the Wairarapa and its vineyard-rich countryside, it's best to make a day trip of it and drive. You also need to drive to go north to the long sweeping beaches of the Kapiti Coast.

When to Go

November to mid-April is the best time weather-wise in the Wellington area. Most establishments are open (apart from Christmas Day, New Year's Day, and Good Friday). In Wairarapa book well ahead if you're traveling during summer school holidays from mid-December to the end of January. From February to April, you can expect fewer crowds and many brilliant, warm days. Winters bring more rain, but they're rarely bitterly cold. Be prepared for unpredictable weather,

though; rain and southerly gales are possible even during the summer.

FESTIVALS
Matariki
CULTURAL FESTIVALS | FAMILY | One of the key Māori occasions in Wellington is Matariki, the North Island Māori New Year in late May–early June, which begins with the first new moon after the appearance of Matariki (Pleiades). The Museum of New Zealand Te Papa Tongarewa hosts nearly two weeks of music, storytelling, and dance performances; events kick off with a ceremony at dawn. Brochures, available at the museum, have details. ✉ Museum of New Zealand Te Papa Tongarewa, 55 Cable St., Wellington ⊕ www.tepapa.govt.nz/visit/events.

The New Zealand Festival
ARTS FESTIVALS | The country's major arts event is held February through March on even-numbered years at venues across the city. A huge array of international talent in music, drama, dance, the visual arts, and media descends upon Wellington. Events fill up quickly; check online for program information, and book a month in ahead if you can. ✉ Wellington ☎ 04/473–0149 ⊕ www.festival.co.nz.

Summer City
FESTIVALS | FAMILY | One of the largest summer fests spans three months and hosts more than 90 events throughout the city. ✉ Wellington ⊕ wellington.govt.nz/events/annual-events/summer-city.

Wellington On a Plate
FESTIVALS | Wellington's annual food festival hosts over 100 events, with local and visiting chefs creating special menus and experiences. New Zealand's largest beer festival, Beervana kicks off the two-week festival in early August. Burger Wellington sees more than 200 eateries competing to be ruled the Best Burger. ✉ Wellington ☎ 04/473–8044 ⊕ www.visawoap.com.

Getting Here and Around

AIR TRAVEL

Wellington International Airport (WLG) lies about 8 km (5 miles) from the city. Domestic carriers serving Wellington include **Air New Zealand, Qantas, Jetstar,** and **Sounds Air.** You can rent a car on-site or catch a shuttle into town; a taxi from the airport to central Wellington costs about NZ$35.

AIRPORTS Wellington Airport. ⊠ *Stewart Duff Dr., Rongotai* ☎ *04/385–5100* ⊕ *www.wellingtonairport.co.nz.*

AIRLINE CONTACTS Air New Zealand. ☎ *0800/737–000* ⊕ *www.airnewzealand. co.nz.* **Jetstar.** ☎ *0800/800–995* ⊕ *www. jetstar.com.* **Qantas.** ☎ *0800/808–767* ⊕ *www.qantas.com.* **Sounds Air.** ☎ *0800/505–005* ⊕ *www.soundsair.com.*

AIRPORT TRANSFERS Airport Flyer. ☎ *0800/801–7000* ⊕ *www.airportflyer. co.nz.* **Super Shuttle.** ☎ *0800/748–885* ⊕ *www.supershuttle.co.nz.*

BOAT AND FERRY TRAVEL

The **Interislander** runs a ferry service between Wellington and Picton; the boats take three hours. Fares vary by time of year, ranging from NZ$56 to NZ$75 one-way per person; for a car and driver, fares are NZ$176 to NZ$330. You can book up to six months in advance. A free bus leaves Platform 9 at the Wellington Railway Station for the ferry terminal 50 minutes before sailings.

Bluebridge Cook Strait Ferry vessels, *The Strait Feronia* and *The Straitsman,* sail up to four times per day between Wellington and Picton. Fares are NZ$53 to NZ$89 one-way per person, and NZ$173 to NZ$189 for a driver with car up to 20 feet long. Most car-rental agencies offer North Island–South Island transfer programs.

BOAT AND FERRY CONTACTS Bluebridge Cook Strait Ferry. ☎ *0800/844–844* ⊕ *www.bluebridge.co.nz.* **Interislander.**

☎ *0800/802–802* ⊕ *www.greatjourneysofnz.co.nz/interislander.*

BUS TRAVEL

InterCity operates daily long-distance bus services, connecting Wellington to most other cities and major towns in New Zealand.

BUS CONTACTS InterCity. ☎ *04/385–0520* ⊕ *www.intercity.co.nz .* **Wellington Bus Depot.** ⊠ *Wellington Railway Station, Bunny St. and Waterloo Quay, Wellington.*

CAR TRAVEL

The main access to the city is via the Wellington Urban Motorway, which starts just after Highways 1 and 2 merge, a few miles north of the city center. The motorway links the city center with all towns and cities to the north.

Outside of the city, transportation options are very limited, so you'll need a car to properly explore the area. State Highway 2 runs north–south through the region between Napier and Wellington. From Wellington you drive through Upper Hutt (the River Road bypasses the town), over the hills into the gateway town of Featherston. Highway 53 takes you to Martinborough; turn southwest here on Lake Ferry Road for Lake Ferry and Cape Palliser. Masterton is farther north along State Highway 2, roughly a 30-minute drive from Martinborough. The journey from Wellington to Martinborough takes about 75 minutes; Masterton is another 15. From Napier, Masterton is about three hours.

TRAIN TRAVEL

Metlink operates trains connecting the Wellington Railway Station with the Hutt Valley and Masterton. If you're a fan of scenic train trips, try the *Northern Explorer;* linking Wellington and Auckland, it stops in Paraparaumu, Palmerston North, Ohakune, National Park, Otorohanga (near Waitomo), Hamilton, and Papakura. The train travels southbound on Monday, Thursday, and Saturday and northbound on Wednesday, Friday, and Sunday.

TRAIN CONTACTS Metlink. ☎ *0800/801–700* ⊕ *www.metlink.org.nz.* **Northern Explorer.** ☎ *0800/872–467* ⊕ *www.great-journeysofnz.co.nz/northern-explorer .* **Wellington Railway Station.** ✉ *Bunny St. and Waterloo Quay, Wellington.*

Restaurants

In Wellington, restaurants, cafés, bars, and breweries spring up overnight like mushrooms. Although you'll never be without the classic meal of steak, fries, and ale, chefs returning from stints abroad have also embraced more adventurous fare. Chinese, Thai, Japanese, Malaysian, Mexican, and Italian cuisines are all easy to find. Locally sourced food is also appearing in restaurants around the city—native plants might be paired with traditional seafood or made into sauces to accompany meat or sweet-potato dishes.

In rural areas outside Wellington, the wine industry has revolutionized local tables, with excellent dining and wine-tasting spots. In the Wairarapa, restaurants are winning a reputation for creative cuisine.

Generally, lunch runs from noon until 2, and most restaurants close for a few hours before opening for dinner around 6. On Monday, many restaurants are shuttered. Dress codes are still really relaxed; jeans would rarely be frowned upon even at the top restaurants.

Hotels

Accommodations in Wellington range from no-frills backpacker hostels and motel units to sleek central hotels and classic bed-and-breakfasts in colonial-era villas.

As more people move into the city, serviced-apartment hotels are also gaining steam. Rates are significantly more expensive than those of the average motel, but they're a good option if you're planning to stay a while. Most of these apartment-hotel hybrids have weekend or long-term specials.

Lodgings generally do not have air-conditioning, but the temperate weather in Wellington rarely warrants it.

Restaurant and hotel reviews have been shortened. For full information, visit Fodors.com. Restaurant prices are the average cost of a main course at dinner or, if dinner is not served, at lunch. Hotel prices are the lowest cost of a standard double room in high season.

What It Costs			
$	$$	$$$	$$$$
RESTAURANTS			
under NZ$15	NZ$15–NZ$20	NZ$21–NZ$30	over NZ$30
HOTELS			
under NZ$125	NZ$125–NZ$200	NZ$201–NZ$300	over NZ$300

Visitor Information

There is a comprehensive information service for the city and surrounding districts—⊕ *WellingtonNZ.com*—which covers everything you need to know. The Wellington i-SITE Visitor Information Centre, on Wakefield Street, can provide you with brochures, tour bookings, theater tickets, and more.

CONTACTS WellingtonNZ.com. ☎ *04/916–1205* ⊕ *www.WellingtonNZ.com.* **Wellington i-SITE Visitor Information Centre.** ✉ *111 Wakefield St., Wellington* ☎ *04/802–4860* ⊕ *www.wellingtonNZ.com.*

Wellington

Wellington, the seat of government since 1865, is between the sea and towering hillsides that form a natural arena with the harbor as the stage. Ferries carve patterns on the green water while preening seabirds survey the scene. Houses cascade down the steep hills, creating a vibrant collage of colorful rooftops against a spectacular green backdrop. An old brick monastery peers down on the marina—a jigsaw of masts and sails bobbing alongside the impressive Museum of New Zealand Te Papa Tongarewa. Modern high-rises gaze over Port Nicholson, one of the finest natural anchorages in the world. Known to local Māori as the Great Harbor of Tara, its two massive arms form the "jaws of the fish of Maui" (Maui being the name of a god from Māori legend).

Civic Square represents the heart of the city and forms a busy shopping area with Willis and Cuba streets. The entertainment district is centered on Courtenay Place, south of Civic Square. Thorndon, the oldest part of the city, is notable for its many historic wooden houses just north of the Parliamentary district, which includes the distinctive (some might say bizarre) "Beehive" government building.

At the northern end of the waterfront, the Westpac Trust Stadium, home to rugby matches, soccer games, and rock concerts, dominates the skyline, and Lambton Quay is part of a seafront constructed on reclaimed land. At the southern end of the harbor, Norfolk pines line the broad sweep of Oriental Bay, a suburb with a small beach and a wide promenade, backed by art deco buildings and Wellington's most expensive real estate.

GETTING HERE AND AROUND
Wellington is a great walking city. The compact area around Lambton Quay and on Cuba Street is flat. A stroll along the waterfront around Oriental Bay provides outstanding sea views. If you head for the hills, take the cable car, and see the sights before walking down.

For cyclists, designated bike lanes in and around Wellington are marked with a continuous white line and a white bike image on the pavement. More details about urban cycling are on the city's website, ⊕ www.wcc.govt.nz.

Buses are a great way to navigate the city, though service outside the city center is sporadic. In Wellington, buses are operated by several companies; for information on all routes and fares contact Metlink (☎ 0800/801–700 ⊕ www.metlink.org.nz). The main terminals are at the Wellington Railway Station (Bunny Street and Waterloo Quay) and at Courtenay Place. For all inner-city trips, pay when you board the bus. Bus stops are marked with red-and-white signs. A Metlink Explorer day pass starts at NZ$10, but does not include the Airport Flyer. For longer stays, a Snapper card costs NZ$10, and offers good discounts and convenience.

You don't need a car to get around central Wellington—and you probably don't want one as its many one-way streets can frustrate drivers. Having one, however, is essential if you hope to fully explore the outlying regions.

Taxi ride rates are NZ$3.50 on entry, then NZ$2.95 per 1 km (½ mile). Taxis idle outside the railway station, on Dixon Street, and along Courtenay Place and Lambton Quay.

TOURS
BOAT TOURS
★ East by West Ferry
BOAT TOURS | East by West Ferries runs a commuter service between the city and Days Bay, on the east side of Port Nicholson; it's one of the best value tours around. On the 10 am sailing, you can stop at Matiu/Somes Island; this former quarantine station makes a unique picnic spot on a warm afternoon. Just be sure to confirm your return pick-up time with the crew. Days Bay itself has seaside village character, a lovely swimming beach, local craft shops, and great views of Wellington. Weekdays the catamaran regularly departs Queens Wharf between

6:20 am and 7:05 pm. The return boats leave Days Bay roughly 30 minutes later. The sailing schedule is cut back on weekends and holidays, but additional Harbour Explorer Tours visit Seatoun Wharf. You can pick up tickets at the ferry terminal between 8 and 5; otherwise, tickets can be bought on board. All sailings may be canceled in stormy weather. ✉ *Queens Wharf* ☎ *04/499–1282, 04/494–3339* ⊕ *www.eastbywest.co.nz* ✉ *From NZ$12.*

BUS TOURS
Hop On Hop Off
BUS TOURS | While central Wellington is wonderfully walkable, many of the attractions, such as Wellington Zoo and Zealandia Eco-Sanctuary, are tucked away in the suburbs or on large hills. Ninety-minute hop-on/hop-off tours depart the Wellington i-SITE Visitor Information Centre daily from 9:30 am, making 11 stops around the city. The buses depart every 30 minutes between October and late April, and every 90 minutes between late April and September. ✉ *111 Wakefield St.* ☎ *0800/246–877* ⊕ *www.hoponhopoff. co.nz* ✉ *NZ$45.*

Rover Rings Tours
SPECIAL-INTEREST | As the base of production for the *Lord of the Rings* and *The Hobbit* films, there are many famous filming locations in and around Wellington. Rover Rings Tours offers half-day and full-day *Lord of the Rings* film location tours, with the full-day option including a picnic lunch and a tour of Weta Workshop. All leave from the i-SITE Visitor Information Centre, and advanced reservations are essential. ✉ *Wellington* ☎ *04/471–0044* ⊕ *www.roverringstours. co.nz* ✉ *From NZ$95.*

PRIVATE GUIDES
Black Cars
PERSONAL GUIDES | With an emphasis on luxury, these all-inclusive, upmarket tours are offered in chauffeur-driven vehicles. Tours range from four to eight hours, and can follow a set itinerary or a tailor-made

experience. Private transfers and driver services are also available. ☎ *022/588–0085* ⊕ *www.blackcars.co* ✉ *From NZ$450 for two people.*

VISITOR INFORMATION
CONTACTS Wellington i-SITE Visitor Information Centre. ✉ *111 Wakefield St.* ☎ *04/802–4860* ⊕ *www.wellingtonnz. com.*

◉ Sights

Archives New Zealand
MUSEUM | History buffs should make a beeline here, as the national archives are a gold mine of documents, photographs, and maps. Records of New Zealand ancestry from as far back as the early 1800s trace the country's development, making this a great place for New Zealanders to research their family history. ✉ *10 Mulgrave St., Thorndon* ☎ *04/499–5595* ⊕ *www.archives.govt.nz* ✉ *Free.*

Ascot Street
NEIGHBORHOOD | Built in the 1870s, the little doll-like cottages along Ascot remain the finest example of a 19th-century streetscape in Wellington. A bench at the top has been thoughtfully provided in the shady courtyard should you need to catch your breath. ✉ *Off Glenmore St. and Tinakori Rd., northeast of Wellington Botanic Garden, Thorndon.*

City Gallery Wellington
MUSEUM | This gallery offers world-class exhibitions of contemporary New Zealand and international art with specific programs dedicated to local artists, Māori and Pacific arts, and the City Art Collection. Visitors can view sometimes challenging but always captivating work. ✉ *Civic Sq., Wakefield St.* ☎ *04/913–9032* ⊕ *www.citygallery.org.nz* ✉ *Most exhibitions free; charges for special exhibits vary.*

Civic Square
PLAZA | Wellington's Civic Square is reminiscent of an Italian piazza; its artwork,

benches, lawns, and harbor viewpoints make it both a social hub and a delightful sanctuary from traffic. The City Gallery, the library, and the Town Hall concert venue are just steps apart. Architect Ian Athfield's steel sculptures of *nikau* palms are a marvel, and Māori artist Para Matchitt contributed the impressionistic sculptures flanking the wide wooden bridge that connects the square to the harbor. With its sweeping water views, this bridge is a popular place to enjoy a picnic or just sit down and dream. ⊠ *Wakefield, Victoria, and Harris Sts.*

Katherine Mansfield House & Garden

HOUSE | The writer, born in 1888, lived the first five years of her life here. Katherine Mansfield (née Kathleen Beauchamp) left to pursue her career in Europe when she was only 20, but many of her short stories take place in Wellington. A year before her death in 1923, she wrote, "New Zealand is in my very bones. What wouldn't I give to have a look at it!" The house, which has been restored as a typical Victorian family home, contains furnishings, photographs, and videos that elucidate Mansfield's life and times. ⊠ *25 Tinakori Rd., Thorndon* ☎ *04/473–7268* ⊕ *www.katherinemansfield.com* ⊡ *NZ$8.*

Lady Norwood Rose Garden

GARDEN | On a fine summer day you couldn't find a better place to enjoy the fragrance of magnificent flowers. This rose garden is the most popular part of the **Wellington Botanic Garden.** Situated on a plateau, the formal circular layout consists of 110 beds, each planted with a single variety of modern and traditional shrubs. Climbing roses cover a brick-and-timber colonnade on the perimeter. Adjacent to the rose beds, the Begonia House conservatory is filled with delicate plants. ⊠ *North end of Wellington Botanic Garden* ☎ *04/499–1400* ⊡ *Free.*

★ Museum of New Zealand Te Papa Tongarewa

MUSEUM | FAMILY | Te Papa Tongarewa (the Māori translation is "container of treasures") provides an essential introduction to the country's people, cultures, landforms, flora, and fauna. Bringing together the latest technology, interactive exhibits, and storytelling, it shares New Zealand's past and present. Whether you want to enter a carved *marae* (Māori meetinghouse), walk through living native bush, be shaken in the Earthquake House, or see a colossal squid, there's inspiration for everyone. Don't miss the Toi Art gallery; spanning two floors, it features New Zealand, Pacific, and international works. ⊠ *55 Cable St.* ☎ *04/381–7000* ⊕ *www.tepapa.govt.nz* ⊡ *Free; guided tours from NZ$20; some exhibitions from NZ$15.*

Nairn Street Cottage

HOUSE | Built in 1858 as a family home by immigrant carpenter William Wallis, this cottage is Wellington's oldest remaining building. With its steep shingled roof and matchboard ceilings, kauri wood paneling, and somber Victorian wallpapers, the house has been kept almost completely in its original state. The spinning wheel, smoke-blackened cooking pot, hand-pegged rugs, and oil lamps re-create the feeling of those pioneer days. Outside, a garden of flowers and herbs blooms in a riot of color during the summer. ⊠ *68 Nairn St.* ☎ *04/384–9122* ⊕ *www.museumswellington.org.nz* ⊡ *NZ$8* ⊙ *Closed weekdays in winter.*

★ National Library

LIBRARY | Opposite the Parliament Buildings is the country's national library. The Alexander Turnbull Library, a "library within a library," specializes in archival materials about New Zealand and the Pacific. Its books, manuscripts, photographs, newspapers, maps, and oral history tapes are available for research. One special highlight, *He Tohu*, is an exhibition housing *Te Tiriti o Waitangi*, the Treaty of

Wellington

Wellington-Picton Ferry Terminal

TO PICTON →

Wellington Harbor

THORNDON

Stellin Memorial Park

U.S. Embassy

Westpac Trust Stadium

Railway Station

Bus Terminal

KELBURN

Kelburn Park

Queens Wharf

TO DAYS BAY →

Lambton Harbor

HIGHBURY

MT. VICTORIA

TO WELLINGTON AIRPORT

| 0 | 400 yards |
| 0 | 400 meters |

KEY

1 Sights
1 Restaurants
1 Hotels
⊢—⊢ Rail line
•—• Cable car
– – – Ferry lines
······· Path lines
◉ Tourist information

Waitangi. This controversial 1840 agreement between the British crown and more than 500 Māori chiefs is considered the founding document of modern New Zealand. The oldest document on display is the Declaration of Independence of the Northern Chiefs, signed by more than 30 northern Māori chiefs on October 28, 1835, a confederation agreement that led up to the Waitangi treaty. Also on view is the 1893 Women's Suffrage Petition, which led to New Zealand becoming the world's first nation to grant women the vote. ✉ 58 Molesworth St., Thorndon ☎ 04/474–3000 ⊕ www.natlib. govt.nz 🖾 Free.

Old Government Buildings

COLLEGE | The largest wooden structure in New Zealand is now home to Victoria University's law faculty. Constructed in 1876, the original plans called for concrete and timber construction. Due to the high price of concrete at the time, plans were modified and it was ultimately fashioned entirely from timber, including a considerable amount of native kauri. Inside are historic exhibits and an information center, but it's the exterior that most captivates visitors. ✉ 55 Lambton Quay 🖾 Free.

Old St. Paul's Cathedral

BUILDING | Consecrated in 1866 in a style dubbed Colonial Gothic, the church is a splendid example of the English Gothic Revival style executed entirely in native timbers. Even the trusses supporting the roof transcend their mundane function with splendid craftsmanship. ✉ 34 Mulgrave St., Thorndon ☎ 04/473–6722 ⊕ www.oldstpauls.co.nz 🖾 Free.

Otari-Wilton's Bush

GARDEN | Devoted to gathering and preserving indigenous plants, Otari's collection is the largest of its kind. With clearly marked bushwalks and landscape demonstration gardens, it aims to educate the public and ensure the survival of New Zealand's unique plant life. While in the garden, you'll learn to identify forest plants, from the various *blechnum* ferns underfoot to the tallest trees overhead. An aerial walkway crosses high above the bush, giving an unusual vantage point over the gardens. Look and listen for the native birds that flock to this haven: the bellbird (*korimako*), New Zealand wood pigeon (*kereru*), and parson bird (*tūī*) among others. Take the No. 14 Wilton bus from downtown (20 minutes) and ask the driver to let you off at the gardens. ✉ 160 Wilton Rd., Wilton ☎ 04/475–3245 🖾 Free.

The Parliament Buildings

GOVERNMENT BUILDING | These buildings include **Parliament House** with its **Debating Chamber,** a copy of the one in the British House of Commons right down to the Speakers Mace. Here legislation is presented, debated, and voted on. There is fine Māori artwork in the **Māori Affairs Select Committee Room.** The adjoining building is the **Parliamentary Library.** The neighboring **Executive Wing** is known for architectural reasons as **The Beehive**; it's where the Prime Minister and Cabinet Ministers of the elected Government have their offices and hold Cabinet meetings. Across the road at the corner of Bowen Street and Lambton Quay, **Bowen House** is also part of the complex. Tours start in The Beehive, and a guide explains the Parliamentary process in detail. ✉ Molesworth St. ☎ 04/817–9503 ⊕ www.parliament.nz 🖾 Free.

Space Place At Carter Observatory

OBSERVATORY | **FAMILY** | Lie back and watch an almost limitless range of virtual space journeys in the planetarium; or, on a clear night, view the heavens through the observatory telescope. Such experiences—plus state-of-the-art displays and a remarkable collection of artifacts that includes the oldest working telescope of its kind in the country—make this a popular stop. The observatory is only a two-minute walk from the top of the Kelburn Cable Car, and you can also wander up from the botanical gardens. ✉ 40

Performers welcome visitors to the marae (meetinghouse) at the Museum of New Zealand Te Papa Tongarewa.

Salamanca Rd. ☎ *04/910–3140* ⊕ *www. museumswellington.org.nz* ✉ *NZ$13* ⊘ *Closed Mon., Wed., and Thurs.*

Tinakori Road
NEIGHBORHOOD | The lack of suitable local stone, combined with the collapse of most of Wellington's brick buildings in the earthquake of 1848, ensured the almost-exclusive use of timber for building here in the second half of the 19th century. Most carpenters of the period had learned their skills as cabinetmakers and shipwrights in Europe, and the sturdy houses on this street are a tribute to their craftsmanship. Two notables are the tall and narrow **No. 306** and **Premier House.** ✉ *Wellington.*

Wellington Botanic Garden
GARDEN | In the hills overlooking downtown is a concentration of splendidly varied terrain. Woodland gardens under native and exotic trees fill the valleys, water-loving plants line a pond and mountain streams, and lawns spread over flatter sections with beds of bright seasonal bulbs and annuals. The lovely

Lady Norwood Rose Garden is in the northeast part of the garden. If you don't want to walk up the hill, the **Kelburn Cable Car** can take you. Or catch the No. 2 bus (direction: Karori) from Lambton Quay to the main (Glenmore Street) entrance. ✉ *Upland Rd. and Glenmore St., parking lot on Tinakori Rd.* ☎ *04/499–1400 gardens* ✉ *Free.*

Wellington Cable Car
TRANSPORTATION SITE (AIRPORT/BUS/FERRY/ TRAIN) | The Swiss-built funicular railway makes a short-but-sharp climb from among the shops on Lambton Quay to the highest point in the Wellington Botanic Gardens, the Kelburn Terminal. Once up there, you get great views across parks and city buildings to Port Nicholson. Sit on the left side during the six-minute journey for the best scenery. At the top, a small Cable Car Museum in the old winding house has a free display of restored cable cars. ✉ *280 Lambton Quay, at Grey St. and Upland Rd.* ☎ *04/472–2199* ⊕ *www.wellingtoncablecar.co.nz* ✉ *From NZ$5.*

Wellington Museum

MUSEUM | FAMILY | Smell the burlap sacks, hear the gulls, and see the (mechanical) rats scuttling around in this refurbished 1892 bond store, now a museum that portrays the history of the original Māori tribes and the European settlers who arrived around 1840. The displays cover work, leisure, crime, and education in Wellington. A steampunk-themed fourth floor attic is cluttered with weird and wonderful exhibits. ✉ *The Bond Store, 3 Jervois Quay, Queens Wharf* ☎ *04/472–8904* ⊕ *www.museumswellington.org. nz* ✉ *Free.*

Zealandia

NATURE PRESERVE | FAMILY | Just minutes from downtown Wellington, more than 500 acres of regenerating forest and wetland have been turned into a unique safe haven for some of New Zealand's most-endangered native animals. A specially designed fence creates a cage-free ecosanctuary for species that had disappeared from the mainland. Tuatara, New Zealand's unique "living fossil," are breeding, as are takahe and saddleback, which have both been brought back from the brink of extinction. Pick up a map and explore at your leisure, or join a two-hour guided tour. The flashlight-led nighttime tour is also very popular; departing about 30 minutes before sunset, it provides a glimpse into the nocturnal world—you might even spy a little spotted kiwi. ✉ *53 Waiapu Rd., Karori* ☎ *04/920–9213* ⊕ *www.visitzealandia.com* ✉ *NZ$20; tours from NZ$55.*

GREATER WELLINGTON

The Dowse Art Museum

MUSEUM | Near Petone, this museum stages a changing array of exhibitions—including ones focused on extraordinary jewelry, fashion, photography, and ceramics—that showcase the creativity of New Zealand's artisans. ✉ *45 Laings Rd., Lower Hutt* ☎ *04/570–6500* ⊕ *www. dowse.org.nz* ✉ *Free.*

Eastbourne

NEIGHBORHOOD | From Petone, a winding road leads south about 10 km (6 miles) to the suburb of Eastbourne. Have an alfresco bite in its tiny shopping area before driving on to where the road eventually transforms into a 4-km (2½-mile) walking trail, following the coast to Pencarrow Head and its lighthouse, with views across the strait. (There's a kiosk where you can rent a bike if you wish.) ✉ *Lower Hutt.*

Hutt River Trail

TRAIL | Starting at Hikoikoi Reserve on Petone Marine Parade, near the Hutt River mouth, this scenic trail follows the river for more than 32 km (20 miles) to Upper Hutt. Intended specifically for walkers and cyclists, it links up with the Remutaka Rail Trial to the Wairarapa for those looking for a longer hike or bike ride. ✉ *Petone Marine Parade, Lower Hutt.*

Kaitoke Regional Park

FOREST | From Upper Hutt, continuing north on State Highway 2 takes you to the Wairarapa region. But if you have time to spare, stop into Kaitoke Regional Park. Just beyond Upper Hutt, it's a great camping and picnic spot with pleasant walks by the river. *LOTR* lovers can check out the corner of forest that stood in for Rivendell, the great homeland of the elves. Pause by the crystal-clear river, flanked by towering trees and native bush, and listen to the birdsong. ✉ *Waterworks Rd., off State Hwy. 2, Upper Hutt* ☎ *0800/496–734 for rangers* ⊕ *www.gw.govt.nz/kaitoke.*

Petone

MUSEUM | A 15-minute drive north of Wellington on State Highway 2—with magnificent harbor views all the way—leads you to the Hutt Valley and its namesake river. Start exploring it by paying a visit to pretty Petone. The Petone Esplanade, on the eastern side of the harbor, has good fishing from the wharf and is overlooked by houses clinging to steep bush-clad

Visitors dine alfresco in Courtenay Place, Wellington's entertainment center.

hills. While on the waterfront, visit the small but interesting Petone Settlers Museum; it's open Wednesday through Sunday from 10 to 4. Housed in the historic Wellington Provincial Centennial Memorial building, the free museum stands near the 1840 landing site of New Zealand's first organized European settlement. Nearby Jackson Street is home to many boutique shops and eateries. ✉ *Lower Hutt* ☎ *04/568–8373 museum* ⊕ *www.petonesettlers.org. nz* ✉ *Free* ⊙ *Museum closed Mon. and Tues. Apr.–Nov.*

★ Weta Cave & Workshop

MUSEUM | The innovative designers and effects wizards at Weta have brought many high-profile movies to life, so it's no surprise that their home turf is nirvana for cinephiles. At Weta Cave, you get a fascinating "behind the scenes look" at a compact but comprehensive display detailing the characters and equipment used in special effects for *The Lord of the Rings, The Hobbit, Avatar, King Kong,* and many other award–winning films.

There's a free documentary showcasing Weta's history, technical departments, and achievements playing every 30 minutes. Memorabilia (think models, limited-edition sculptures, books, posters, and T-shirts) are sold at the on-site shop. Standing alongside the Cave, the Workshop Tour has a larger display of props and costumes; you might even see Weta artists and technicians at work. Daily tours run half hourly from 9:30 to 5; an extended version departs from Wellington's i-SITE Visitor Information Centre, taking in filming locations along the way. ✉ *Corner of Weka St. and Camperdown Rd.* ☎ *04/909–4100* ⊕ *www.wetaNZ. com* ✉ *Cave free; workshop tours from NZ$25.*

🍴 Restaurants

The Backbencher Gastropub

$$$ | **NEW ZEALAND** | Right across the way from the Parliament buildings sits this landmark watering hole where politicians grab a cold beer after a hot debate. The walls have become a gallery of political cartoons and caricature puppets of government characters and well-known sports figures, while menu items are named after notable politicians. **Known for:** quirky decor; rubbing elbows with politicians; upscale pub cuisine. $ *Average main: NZ$28* ⊠ *34 Molesworth St.* ☎ *04/472–3065* ⊕ *www.backbencher. co.nz.*

★ Boulcott Street Bistro
$$$$ | **BISTRO** | A well-respected institution on the Wellington dining scene, this old colonial-style house conveys tradition and class. The delightful bistro menu features long standing dishes like the aged beef fillet with béarnaise sauce. **Known for:** excellent wine selection; cozy intimate setting; simple yet well-rounded menu. $ *Average main: NZ$35* ⊠ *99 Boulcott St.* ☎ *04/499–4199* ⊕ *www.boulcottstreet-bistro.co.nz* ⊗ *No lunch Sat.*

The Crab Shack
$$$ | **SEAFOOD** | **FAMILY** | Set on the waterfront, with crab-pots and ropes hanging from the ceiling and walls bedecked in old-world maps and colorful recycled timber, the Crab Shack is an American-style diner with a Kiwi twist. Strong Cajun flavors and massive crab dishes are the order of the day, but there are plenty of land-based options if you don't feel like seafood. **Known for:** engaging and fun staff; broad menu options but a big focus on seafood; dishes for sharing. $ *Average main: NZ$25* ⊠ *Queens Wharf* ☎ *04/916–4250* ⊕ *www.crabshack.co.nz.*

Dockside Restaurant & Bar
$$$$ | **NEW ZEALAND** | A wood-beam roof and oiled floorboards enhance the nautical vibe at this former warehouse on the wharf, and you can get close to the water on the large harborfront deck. Inside or out, it's a lively spot, particularly on Friday nights, and as expected, the menu features a broad range of fresh seafood. **Known for:** five-course degustation menu (book well in advance); prime waterfront location; busy weekend nights. $ *Average main: NZ$35* ⊠ *Shed 3, Queens*

Wharf, Jervois Quay ☎ *04/499–9900* ⊕ *www.docksidenz.com.*

Dragonfly
$$$ | **ASIAN** | Cylindrical orange shades hovering over polished wood tables give this modern Asian eatery a warm, intimate atmosphere. A scattershot approach of ordering multiple small plates ensures the most fun and variety of flavors before finishing with Dragonfly's mini-tasting dessert: four tiny delights that are perfect for sharing. **Known for:** cool, chic decor; cocktails with an Asian twist; lively outdoor dining in the back. $ *Average main: NZ$29* ⊠ *70 Courtenay Pl.* ☎ *04/803–3995* ⊕ *www. dragon-fly.co.nz* ⊗ *Closed Sun. No lunch.*

Grill Meats Beer
$$$ | **BURGER** | A relaxed and fun place to enjoy conversation, the focus here is on the casual beer drinker rather than the aficionado. Each dish has a recommended beer to go with it; if you want to try something out of your comfort zone, staff are trained to help you expand your palate. **Known for:** local sustainable produce; excellent beer pairings; chipotle-braised brisket fries. $ *Average main: NZ$25* ⊠ *227 Cuba St.* ☎ *04/801–8787* ⊕ *www. grillmeatsbeer.co.nz.*

La Bella Italia
$$$ | **ITALIAN** | **FAMILY** | Within sight of Petone Wharf, this old warehouse has been transformed into a vibrant Italian restaurant and delicatessen; in-your-face murals, photographs, and posters with an Italian theme cover the walls. Savor the vibe while enjoying dishes from the ever-changing menu of authentic Italian cuisine. **Known for:** plenty of locals; traditional Italian menu; large vibrant space. $ *Average main: NZ$26* ⊠ *10 Nevis St., Petone* ☎ *04/566–9303* ⊕ *www.labellaitalia.co.nz* ⊗ *No dinner Mon. and Tues.*

★ Logan Brown
$$$$ | **NEW ZEALAND** | The imposing exterior and classical interior of this former bank building showcase the fact that this

Wellington stalwart delivers exceptional dining in an unpretentious way. The menu highlights New Zealand's produce and exemplary wines; knowledgeable and friendly staff talk you through each dish, and there's an early bistro menu, or a longer degustation menu if you want to make a night of it. **Known for:** paua (abalone) ravioli; seven-course menu on Saturday; local and sustainable ingredients. ⑤ *Average main: NZ$40* ✉ *192 Cuba St.* ☎ *04/801–5114* ⊕ *www.loganbrown.co.nz* ⊘ *Closed Mon. No lunch Sun.–Tues.*

Pravda

$$$$ | **EUROPEAN** | Three king-size chandeliers dominate the high ceilings in this classic, old Wellington building; the café area has half-paneled walls and a matching bar that gives a touch of understated class. The menu changes regularly to capture the best of the season's produce and if you're passing by during the day, their cheese scones are much loved by locals. **Known for:** Soviet-kitsch decor; great wine list; excellent steak. ⑤ *Average main: NZ$35* ✉ *107 Custom House Quay, Wellington Central* ☎ *04/801–8858* ⊕ *www.pravdacafe.co.nz* ⊘ *Closed Sun.*

Shed 5

$$$$ | **ECLECTIC** | Huge windows facing the harbor disguise the fact that this historic building on the wharf was once a woolshed. On the menu, seafood stands out; the daily fish selection is sourced and filleted on-site by Shed 5's fishmonger, and the seafood risotto changes daily depending on what the tide brings in. **Known for:** lovely window seating; huge range of local and international wine; vegetarian options. ⑤ *Average main: NZ$33* ✉ *Queens Wharf, Jervois Quay* ☎ *04/499–9069* ⊕ *www.shed5.co.nz.*

Victoria St Cafe

$$ | **CAFÉ** | One of the few establishments in town open from 6:30 am, this centrally located place delivers delicious breakfast and brunch every day of the week. It's a great place to start your day, but be aware that things get very busy with the work crowd from 7:30 am to 9 am on weekdays. **Known for:** all-day breakfast; signature black pudding; lamb meatballs for lunch. ⑤ *Average main: NZ$20* ✉ *98 Victoria St.* ☎ *04/470–7752* ⊕ *www. victoria-st-cafe.co.nz.*

🛏 Hotels

Bolton Hotel

$$$ | **HOTEL** | Well known to upmarket business travelers, this independently owned hotel is great for extended stays, with some rooms containing full kitchen facilities and washer/dryers. **Pros:** lovely decor; quiet location; large suites. **Cons:** some rooms overlook an old cemetery; limited parking; no harbor views from most rooms. ⑤ *Rooms from: NZ$239* ✉ *12 Bolton St.* ☎ *04/472–9966* ⊕ *www. boltonhotel.co.nz* ⇄ *139 rooms* ⦿ *No meals.*

Booklovers B&B

$$$ | **B&B/INN** | Local author Jane Tolerton has set up house in a Victorian villa in sunny Mount Victoria and, true to her passion, has lined the hallway with books. **Pros:** walkable to virtually all the city attractions; free off-street parking and Wi-Fi; comfortable homey vibe. **Cons:** due to Jane's writing commitments personal service may not always be available; decor is a bit tired; lots of street noise. ⑤ *Rooms from: NZ$260* ✉ *123 Pirie St.* ☎ *04/384–2714* ⊕ *www. booklovers.co.nz* ⊘ *Closed May–Aug.* ⇄ *3 rooms* ⦿ *Breakfast.*

CityLife Wellington

$$$ | **HOTEL** | **FAMILY** | This apartment-style hotel is smack-dab in the middle of the city—and if you can snag a suite at a weekend or special summer rate, it's one of the best-value lodgings in town. **Pros:** in the heart of the city; just an elevator ride to Lambton Quay; good for families or large groups. **Cons:** more suited to a longer stay; parking can be difficult; no views. ⑤ *Rooms from: NZ$239* ✉ *14 Gilmer Terr.* ☎ *04/922–2800, 0800/368–888*

⊕ www.heritagehotels.co.nz/citylife-wellington ⌷ 70 rooms |○| No meals.

★ Edgewater Lodge

$$$ | B&B/INN | By the water's edge with stunning harbor views from every room, this place exudes class. **Pros:** superbly comfortable accommodation; amazing views; excellent food. **Cons:** 15-minute ride into the city; parking can be tight; less mobile guests may struggle with the stairs. $ *Rooms from: NZ$270* ⌷ *423 Karaka Bay Rd.* ☎ *04/388–4446* ⊕ *www.edgewaterwellington.co.nz* ⌷ *3 suites* |○| *Breakfast.*

★ InterContinental Wellington

$$$$ | HOTEL | In the heart of the business district and a stone's throw from the waterfront, this landmark high-rise gets the details right. **Pros:** comfortable lobby bar with around 100 whiskies; central location; extra amenities like yoga classes. **Cons:** can get booked up with corporate functions; gets expensive around events; some rooms have views of office buildings. $ *Rooms from: NZ$359* ⌷ *2 Grey St.* ☎ *04/472–2722* ⊕ *www.intercontinental.com* ⌷ *236 rooms* |○| *No meals.*

QT Wellington

$$$ | HOTEL | With bold art on display everywhere you look, this hotel is for the hip and trendy. **Pros:** wonderfully walkable location; one of the best restaurants in the city; well-appointed rooms. **Cons:** can be affected by loud street noise; some guests will be put off by the choice of art; city-side rooms lack views. $ *Rooms from: NZ$249* ⌷ *90 Cable St.* ☎ *04/802–8900* ⊕ *www.qthotelsandresorts.com* ⌷ *179 rooms* |○| *No meals.*

Rydges Wellington

$$$ | HOTEL | Situated near several major Wellington landmarks, including the waterfront, this hotel makes navigating the city a breeze. **Pros:** indoor heated lap pool; complimentary tasters served between 5 pm and 6 pm; upper level suites enjoy beautiful harbor views.

Cons: street front is a wind tunnel in bad weather; foyer bar can be crowded with locals; poor views from many rooms. $ *Rooms from: NZ$229* ⌷ *75 Featherston St.* ☎ *04/499–8686* ⊕ *www.rydges.com* ⌷ *280 rooms* |○| *No meals.*

Sofitel Wellington

$$$ | HOTEL | In celebration of its proximity to the Wellington Botanic Garden, this sophisticated hotel has a strong but subtle floral theme throughout the rooms and shared spaces. **Pros:** lovely modern decor; excellent gym; large rooms with comfortable beds. **Cons:** some rooms face an old cemetery; limited parking; no pool. $ *Rooms from: NZ$259* ⌷ *11 Bolton St.* ☎ *04/472–2001* ⊕ *www.sofitel-wellington.com* ⌷ *129 rooms* |○| *No meals.*

☖ Nightlife

Wellington's after-dark scene splits between several main areas. The "alternative" set spends its time at Cuba Street's funky cafés, bars, and clubs, which stay open until around 1 am during the week and about 3 am or later on weekends; cocktails are innovative, and the music is not top-20 radio.

Courtenay Place is home to the traditional drinking action with a selection of pubs, sports bars, and a few upscale establishments. It's packed on Friday and Saturday nights, especially when a rugby game is on, and the streets fill with beery couples in their late teens and early twenties lining up to get plastered (New Zealand's legal drinking age is 18).

In the downtown business district—between Lambton Quay and Manners Street—a couple of brewpubs and a few taverns cater to the after-work mob. Down by the harbor, a flashy corporate crowd hangs out in several warehouse-style bars, sipping martinis on weeknights and filling the dance floor on weekends.

Did You Know?

Matiu/Somes Island in Wellington Harbour was a human and livestock quarantine station until 1980 and served as an internment camp during both world wars. Today it is a tranquil wildlife preserve with native birds, reptiles, and plants.

BARS

Dockside

BARS/PUBS | This restaurant and bar has a pleasant nautical theme with antique boats hanging from the ceiling. It's a popular watering hole with the locals. In good weather, everyone spills outside for the best close-up harbor views in Wellington. ⊠ *Shed 3, Queens Wharf, Jervois Quay* ☎ *04/499–9900* ⊕ *www. docksidenz.com.*

Golding's Free Dive

BARS/PUBS | With a comfortable speakeasy atmosphere and excellent beer selection, Golding's is a great place to spend an hour or two. There is Star Wars memorabilia on every wall, and it's especially nice for solo travelers, whether you want to mingle or sit quietly and read. There's no food menu, but you can get some of the best pizza in town delivered from the pizza parlor next door. ⊠ *14 Leeds St.* ☎ *04/381–3616* ⊕ *www. goldingsfreedive.co.nz.*

The Grand

BARS/PUBS | This well-lived-in spot, once a brewery and then a distillery, has exposed brick walls, timber floors, and four levels with everything from a 400-person main bar to a garden bar, plus a couple of pool tables. ⊠ *69 Courtenay Pl.* ☎ *04/801–7800* ⊕ *www.thegrandwellington.com.*

Green Man Pub

BARS/PUBS | In the heart of Wellington's central business district, this pub is a little bit Kiwi and a little bit Irish. The atmosphere is warm and friendly, the service excellent. Expect it to be packed on weekends. ⊠ *25 Victoria St.* ☎ *04/499–5440* ⊕ *www.thegreenmanpub.co.nz.*

The Library

PIANO BARS/LOUNGES | On Courtenay Place, you'll find this speakeasy bar hidden within a nondescript doorway between an ATM and Burger King. If you're brave enough to venture in, you'll find a warm, dark lounge with walls covered in old books. If you're dining out in Wellington, you may want to skip dessert and come here for sweets and a cocktail. ⊠ *53 Courtenay Pl.* ☎ *04/382–8593* ⊕ *www.thelibrary.co.nz.*

Malthouse

BREWPUBS/BEER GARDENS | Modern with polished wood and plate glass aplenty, Malthouse's long bar with illuminated lettering is an attractive place to drink a pint. With 29 taps, the only problem is deciding where to start. ⊠ *48 Courtenay Pl.* ☎ *04/802–5484* ⊕ *www. themalthouse.co.nz.*

Mishmosh

BARS/PUBS | Look for the bright cluster of lights on the overhead awning of this gastropub. It's a popular venue with a lively atmosphere. ⊠ *36 Courtenay Pl.* ☎ *04/384-8015* ⊕ *www.mishmosh.co.nz.*

LIVE MUSIC AND DANCE CLUBS

TSB Arena

THEMED ENTERTAINMENT | Headlining tours head to this large indoor venue on the waterfront. ⊠ *Queen's Wharf, Jervois Quay* ☎ *04/801–4207* ⊕ *www.venueswellington.com.*

Valhalla

BARS/PUBS | One of the best places to catch live local rock, Valhalla is a classic hole-in-the-wall dive: small, dark, and a little seedy, with concrete floors and a surprisingly good beer selection. ⊠ *154 Vivian St.* ☎ *04/385–4361* ⊕ *www.valhallatavern.com.*

⭐ Performing Arts

For current event listings in Wellington, check the entertainment section of the *Dominion Post,* Wellington's daily newspaper. The website for Positively Wellington Tourism (⊕ *www.WellingtonNZ. com*) also has up-to-date entertainment listings, covering everything from movies to theater and music.

Bats Theatre

THEATER | Wellington's long-standing source for experimental, sometimes off-the-wall theater hosts a range of performances throughout the year, including stand up, dance, and theater. There are three performance spaces and a small bar on-site. ⊠ *1 Kent Terr., Te Aro* ☎ *04/802–4175* ⊕ *www.bats.co.nz.*

Circa Theatre

THEATER | Catch contemporary New Zealand pieces along with established masterworks from Harold Pinter to Oscar Wilde. It's on the wharf next to the Museum of New Zealand Te Papa Tongarewa. ⊠ *1 Taranaki St.* ☎ *04/801–7992* ⊕ *www.circa.co.nz.*

Michael Fowler Centre

ARTS CENTERS | Named after a former long-standing mayor, this venue regularly hosts shows ranging from the New Zealand Ballet to orchestral and pop concerts. ⊠ *111 Wakefield St.* ☎ *04/801–4207* ⊕ *www.venueswellington.com.*

Opera House

CONCERTS | The century-old Opera House, with its plush carpets and tiered seating, has a similar line-up to the St. James Theatre. Because both are under the same ownership, the NBR New Zealand Opera and the Royal New Zealand Ballet use either venue as schedules allow. ⊠ *111–113 Manners St.* ☎ *04/801–4231* ⊕ *www.venueswellington.com.*

St. James Theatre

DANCE | The ornate, turn-of-the-20th-century St. James Theatre hosts dance performances, musicals, and opera. This is the official home of the Royal New Zealand Ballet and the New Zealand Opera. ⊠ *77–83 Courtenay Pl.* ☎ *04/801–4231* ⊕ *www.venueswellington.com.*

Ticketek

TICKETS | Buy tickets for local performances at this spot between the Michael Fowler Center and the Town Hall. ⊠ *Wellington i-SITE Visitor Information Centre, 111 Wakefield St.* ☎ *04/384–3840* ⊕ *www.ticketek.co.nz.*

🛍 Shopping

The main downtown shopping area, for department stores, clothes, shoes, books, outdoor gear, and souvenirs, is the so-called Golden Mile—from Lambton Quay, up Willis, Victoria, and Manners streets. For smaller, funkier boutiques, visit Cuba Street.

DEPARTMENT STORE AND MALLS

David Jones

DEPARTMENT STORES | Locals were initially resistant to the arrival of this Australian giant, but they quickly came around when exposed to its range of high-end brands previously unavailable in Wellington. Featuring a lovely early-19th-century facade, this three-level department store is an absolute must for the discriminating shopper. There is a wide range of women's and men's fashion clothing, household goods, china, and more. The extensive perfume department is an olfactory delight with fine fragrances from around the world. ⊠ *165 Lambton Quay* ☎ *04/912–0700* ⊕ *www.davidjones.com.*

Old Bank Arcade

SHOPPING CENTERS/MALLS | A couple of indoor malls are on upper Lambton Quay: **Harbour City** and **Capital on the Quay** have a decent range of jewelry, lingerie, housewares, and clothing shops. A better mall is **The Old Bank Arcade** in the old-fashioned former Bank of New Zealand building, which is becoming something of a fashion enclave. The Arcade contains a slew of well-known boutiques, including New Zealand designers Taylor, Ricochet, and Ruby. There is classic jewelry at The Gold Exchange and de Spa Chocolatier sells delicious handmade sweets. ⊠ *233–237 Lambton Quay, at Customhouse Quay and Willis St.* ☎ *04/922–0600* ⊕ *www.oldbank.co.nz.*

BOOKS

Arty Bee's Books

BOOKS/STATIONERY | This friendly and locally owned store sells new and secondhand books as well as sheet music, with a strong focus on New Zealand fiction and nonfiction. ⊠ *The Oaks, 106 Manners St.* ☎ *04/384–5339* ⊕ *www. artybees.co.nz.*

Unity Books

BOOKS/STATIONERY | Find a generous supply of New Zealand and Māori literature in this bright and spacious independent store. ⊠ *57 Willis St.* ☎ *04/499–4245* ⊕ *www.unitybooks.nz.*

CLOTHING AND ACCESSORIES

Area 51

CLOTHING | Street-savvy clothing brands like Adidas and Herschel Supply Co. fill the shelves here, but the real reason to come in is to check out the popular, local Huffer label. ⊠ *Cuba and Dixon Sts.* ☎ *0508/273–251* ⊕ *www.area51store. co.nz.*

Deadly Ponies

JEWELRY/ACCESSORIES | Based on the gorgeous decor alone, this store focused on leather accessories is well worth a visit. The leather in their products is all ethically and locally sourced. ⊠ *28 Ghuznee St.* ☎ *03/802–5511* ⊕ *www.deadlyponies. com.*

Jane Daniels

CLOTHING | A comprehensive range of Jane Daniels's New Zealand ladies fashions are offered here, all locally manufactured from European fabrics. ⊠ *97c Customhouse Quay* ☎ *04/473–7400* ⊕ *www.janedaniels.co.nz.*

Karen Walker

CLOTHING | The eponymous owner has made a name for herself overseas. This Wellington store carries her own clothing, accessories, and fragrances. ⊠ *126 Wakefield St.* ☎ *04/499–3558* ⊕ *www. karenwalker.com.*

Zambesi

CLOTHING | Well-established New Zealand designer Elisabeth Findlay of Zambesi whips up innovative and extremely wearable clothes. ⊠ *103 Customhouse Quay* ☎ *04/472–3638* ⊕ *www.zambesi.co.nz.*

MARKETS

★ Harbourside Market

OUTDOOR/FLEA/GREEN MARKETS | **FAMILY** | On Sunday, between 7:30 am and 1 pm, folks flock to this outdoor food market on the waterfront. Organic produce, cheese, and fresh fish and meats are the main draws. There's also a plethora of food trucks serving coffee and international street food. ⊠ *At Cable and Barnett Sts.* ⊕ *www.harboursidemarket.co.nz.*

Wellington Night Market

OUTDOOR/FLEA/GREEN MARKETS | **FAMILY** | Two outdoor markets—one Friday night at Left Bank, Cuba Mall, and the other Saturday night on lower Cuba Street—lure crowds with a variety of international foods and entertainment from local performers. They're open from 5 pm to 11 pm. ⊠ *Cuba St.* ⊕ *www.wellington-nightmarket.co.nz.*

OUTDOOR EQUIPMENT

Gordons

SPORTING GOODS | This spot sells camping gear and outdoor clothing from international brands as well as footwear. ⊠ *Cuba and Wakefield Sts.* ☎ *04/499–8894.*

Kathmandu

SPORTING GOODS | Wellington is a fine place to stock up on camping supplies before hitting the great outdoors. Kathmandu carries its house brand of clothing and equipment. ⊠ *1 Willis St.* ☎ *04/472–0113* ⊕ *www.kathmandu.co.nz.*

SOUVENIRS

Kura Gallery

GIFTS/SOUVENIRS | Part gallery, part gift store, this establishment has a strong contemporary Māori current running through the work. Some of the smaller, less-expensive items make unique souvenirs. ✉ *19 Allen St.* ☎ *04/802–4934* ⊕ *www.kuragallery.co.nz.*

Simply New Zealand
GIFTS/SOUVENIRS | As its name suggests, this store focuses on New Zealand-made handicrafts, including ceramics, wooden items, jewelry, knitwear, and accessories. ✉ *Lambton House, 160 Lambton Quay* ☎ *04/470–7868* ⊕ *www.simplynz.co.nz.*

Akatarawa Valley

40 km (25 miles) northeast of Wellington.

Winding through the steep bush-clad hills north of Wellington, the narrow road to the Akatarawa Valley (in the Māori language, Akatarawa means "place of tangled vines") requires a degree of driving care, but it leads to a number of hidden gems. About 35 minutes north of Wellington on State Highway 2, turn left at the clearly marked Brown Owl turnoff north of Upper Hutt. About two minutes after the turnoff, look for **Harcourt Park,** where a number of scenes in the *Lord of the Rings* movies were filmed.

A kilometer (½ mile) farther on, a bridge spanning the junction of the Hutt and Akatarawa rivers leads into the Akatarawa Valley proper. Drive over the bridge, go past the cemetery, and then on the left, look for the Blueberry Farm and nearby Bluebank Blueberry and Emu Farm. After picking to your heart's content, continue uphill on the very winding road. On the right is the Staglands Wildlife Reserve. It's around 7 km (4½ miles) to the summit, then the narrow road winds downhill. Look for the tiny wooden Church of St. Andrews nearby and turn right immediately for the Reikorangi Potteries. The road continues for about 3 km (2 miles) to join State Highway 1 at the Waikanae traffic lights, where you can head back to Wellington; from here, you're about 45 minutes north of the city.

CONTACTS Upper Hutt i-SITE Visitor Information Centre. ✉ *836 Fergusson Dr., Upper Hutt* ☎ *04/527–2168* ⊕ *www.visit. upperhuttcity.com.*

⊙ Sights

Bluebank Blueberry and Emu Farm
FARM/RANCH | This property produces delicious blueberries and is home to several emus, a large flightless bird. ✉ *1301 Akatarawa Rd., Upper Hutt* ☎ *04/526–9540* ⊕ *www.bluebank.co.nz.*

★ Staglands Wildlife Reserve
NATURE PRESERVE | FAMILY | Staglands offers visitors the opportunity to feed and freely interact with wildlife in a beautiful natural environment. As you wander around its 25 peaceful acres, you can walk through aviaries to ogle kea, kaka, and many more brilliantly colored birds. At the stables you'll meet a native *kune kune* pig and impressive Clydesdale horse. Watch rainbow and brown trout fighting over their dinner at the Trout and Eel Pool. Have fun exploring the nooks and crannies of the re-created Old Bush Settlement. Climb to the Deer Park lookout for stunning views; then enjoy a picnic on the banks of the beautiful Akatarawa River, or dig into the scrumptious food served at the log cabin café. ✉ *2362 Akatarawa Rd., Upper Hutt* ☎ *04/526–7529* ⊕ *www.staglands.co.nz* 🎫 *NZ$24.*

Kapiti Coast

50 km (31 miles) north of Wellington.

A drive up the West Coast from Wellington is not to be missed. State Highway 1 leads you north, and about a half hour out of the city you hit the water at Paremata. From here you can take State Highway 1 straight up the Kapiti Coast, so called for the view of Kapiti Island. Alternatively, you can take the longer—but infinitely more scenic—drive around the Pauata-hanui Inlet, following the road along the ridge of the rugged, winding, and windy Paekakariki Hill, where stunning views of the coastline and Kapiti Island await. Both routes lead to **Paekakariki** (pie-*kahk*-a-reeky), a small, artsy beach town.

VISITOR INFORMATION

CONTACTS Paraparaumu i-SITE Visitor Information Centre. ⊠ *Coastlands Shoppingtown, Main Rd., Paraparaumu* ☎ *04/298–8195* ⊕ *www.kapiticoast.govt. nz.*

Sights

Queen Elizabeth Park

BEACH—SIGHT | FAMILY | Paekakariki's draw is the shore, but it's also the main entry point for Queen Elizabeth Park. Covering more than 1,600 acres, the park is edged by sand dunes and swimmable beaches. Walking, horseback riding, and cycling are popular activities here. Of special interest is the WWII U.S. Marines memorial and display. ⊠ *State Hwy. 1, Paraparaumu* ⊕ *www.gw.govt.nz/QEP.*

★ Southward Car Museum

MUSEUM | FAMILY | Housing the southern hemisphere's largest private car collection, this museum has more than 400 automobiles and 140 motorcycles, plus aircraft, bicycles, vintage tools, and an old fire engine. Among the most popular are Marlene Dietrich's 1934 Cadillac Town Cabriolet, a 1915 Stutz Indianapolis race car, a gull-winged Mercedes-Benz, a 1950 Cadillac "Gangster Special" that had belonged to gangster Mickey Cohen, and an 1895 Benz Velo. ⊠ *Otaihanga Rd., Paraparaumu* ☎ *04/297–1221* ⊕ *www. southwardcarmuseum.co.nz* ⊠ *NZ$18.*

Kapiti Island

50 km (31 miles) north of Wellington and 5 km (3 miles) off the coast of Paraparaumu.

Paraparaumu is the departure point for one of Wellington's best-kept secrets: Kapiti Island. A protected reserve since 1897, the island is a fantastic place to hike. All pests have been eliminated from it, and birdlife—including saddlebacks, stitchbirds, and colonies of little spotted and South Island brown kiwi—is abundant. Don't be surprised if a curious and fearless weka bird investigates your day pack or unties your shoelaces. Climb to the Tuteremoana lookout point, which is more than 1,700-feet high, for stellar views.

The island's most famous inhabitant was the Ngati Toa chief Te Rauparaha, who took the island by ruse in 1822. From this stronghold, he launched bloodthirsty raids before he was captured in 1846. He died in 1849, but his burial place is a mystery. Old tri-pots (used for melting down whale blubber) on the island bear testimony to the fact that Kapiti was also used as a whaling station in the late 19th century.

The reserve is 5 km (3 miles) from the mainland. Sign on with a tour operator for the boat trip out; all depart from the Kapiti Boating Club, Paraparaumu Beach. Crossings are weather-dependent.

TOURS
Kapiti Explorer

GUIDED TOURS | This outfit offers scenic cruises to Kapiti and guided walks around the island. Part of your admission fee goes to keeping Kapiti Island predator-free. ⊠ *Kapiti Boating Club, Kapiti Rd., Paraparaumu* ☎ *0800/433–779* ⊕ *www. kapitiislandeco.co.nz* ⊠ *Scenic cruise NZ$80; guided walk NZ$15.*

Greater Wellington and the Wairarapa

Kapiti Island Nature Tours

GUIDED TOURS | Sample genuine Māori hospitality with Kapiti Island Nature Tours. Options range from a day trip with an introductory talk, lunch, and a guided walk to an overnight stay with accommodations, three meals, and a kiwi-spotting night walk. Passage to the island and Department of Conservation park permits are included. ⊠ *Kapiti Boating Club, Kapiti Rd., Paraparaumu* ☎ *0800/527–484* ⊕ *www.kapitiisland.com* ✉ *From NZ$184.*

Martinborough

70 km (44 miles) north of Wellington.

The pleasant town of Martinborough embodies the changes that have taken place in the Wairarapa as a result of the burgeoning wine industry. The town gets its name from its founder, John Martin, who, in 1881, laid out the streets in a union jack pattern, radiating from the square that forms the hub. Most restaurants and shops are on or close to the square.

To tap into the Wairarapa wine world, Martinborough is the place to come. More than 20 vineyards are within a few miles of it—an easy walk or bike ride to some and a pleasant drive to most.

GETTING HERE AND AROUND
During weekdays the roads are mostly quiet, ideal for cycling and relaxed motoring; however, driving on rural roads can be deceptive. Keep a sharp eye out for livestock movement—large herds of cattle or sheep can be just around that bend.

Weekends at virtually any time of the year can bring a flood of visitors. The first Saturday in February and March, the two Martinborough Fair Days, can see traffic jams for miles. On a good, sunny winter weekend, Wellington people regularly pop "over the hill" to sample a vineyard meal and a glass of vino. Plan your visit if you want to avoid the crowds.

VISITOR INFORMATION

CONTACTS Martinborough i-SITE Visitor Information Centre. ⊠ *18 Kitchener St.* ☎ *06/306–5010* ⊕ *www.wairarapanz.com.*

Sights

Ata Rangi Vineyard

WINERY/DISTILLERY | This family-owned and family-managed winery makes exceptional Chardonnay, Sauvignon Blanc, Pinot Noir, and Célèbre (a Cabernet-Merlot-Shiraz blend) in small quantities. Tastings are free and must be booked in advance through their website. ⊠ *14 Puruatanga Rd.* ☎ *06/306–9570* ⊕ *www.atarangi. co.nz.*

Coney Wines

WINERY/DISTILLERY | Have lunch here for a view over vines that produce a terrific Pinot Noir and Pinot Gris plus a rosé you can get only on-site. ⊠ *107 Dry River Rd.* ☎ *06/306–8345* ⊕ *www.coneywines. co.nz* 🍽 *Tastings NZ$5 (refundable with purchase)* ⊗ *Closed Mon.–Thurs., Aug., and Sept.*

Luna Estate

WINERY/DISTILLERY | This winery is set on a beautiful property towards the end of Puruatanga Road, and it's worth a cycle or drive past several other wineries to enjoy some of its lovely Pinot Noir. If you're hungry, you can pair the wines with an Asian-inspired lunch menu. ⊠ *133 Puratanga Rd.* ☎ *06/306–9360* ⊕ *www.lunaestate.co.nz.*

Martinborough Fair

FESTIVAL | The town's signature event, held in the Square on the first Saturday of February and March, draws thousands of people and packs the place with crafts stalls. ⊠ *Martinborough* ☎ *021/0891– 5860* ⊕ *www.martinboroughfair.org.nz.*

Martinborough Vineyard

WINERY/DISTILLERY | With their first Pinot Noir grapes planted in 1980, this fine regional winery was the first to convince the world of the Wairarapa's wine potential. Their Chardonnay is also exceptional. ⊠ *57 Princess St.* ☎ *06/306–9955* ⊕ *www.martinborough-vineyard.co.nz* 🍽 *Tastings NZ$5.*

Martinborough Wine Merchants

STORE/MALL | For an overview of area wines, take an oenophile's shortcut and hit Martinborough Wine Merchants. The shop stocks a thorough selection of local vintages and wine accessories. Arrangements can be made to have your purchases shipped home. ⊠ *6 Kitchener St.* ☎ *06/306–9040* ⊕ *www.martinboroughwinemerchants.com.*

Olivo

FARM/RANCH | For a taste-bud-tickling exercise that doesn't involve grapes, head to Helen and John Meehan's olive grove, 3 km (2 miles) north of Martinborough. You can visit the grove and its 5 acres of gardens to learn how oils are produced. Tastings (and sales) of their extra-virgin and infused olive oils are encouraged. ⊠ *136 Hinakura Rd.* ☎ *06/306–9074* ⊕ *www.olivo.co.nz* 🍽 *Tours NZ$15* ⊗ *Closed weekdays Feb.–Dec.*

Palliser Estate

WINERY/DISTILLERY | Don't miss the whites here—they're some of the best around. Of particular note is the Sauvignon Blanc, which is renowned for its intense ripe flavors, and the Pinot Noir, which is made in an elegant classic style. ⊠ *96 Kitchener St.* ☎ *06/306–9019* ⊕ *www.palliser.co.nz* 🍽 *Tastings NZ$5.*

Toast Martinborough Wine, Food & Music Festival

FESTIVAL | Devoted to the hedonist's holy trinity, this festival occurs on the third Sunday of November. Tickets cost NZ$85, and thousands of them are typically sold within hours—you can get yours online through Ticketek (*www.ticketek.co.nz*). ⊠ *Martinborough* ☎ *06/306–9183* ⊕ *www.toastmartinborough.co.nz.*

🍴 Restaurants

Tirohana Estate and Cellars Restaurant

$$$$ | **EUROPEAN** | The dark-tiled floor and white tablecloths put this classy dining area way above the usual winery restaurant, and a wrought-iron door, black leather chairs, and polished-brass ceiling fan add to the aura. It's a prix-fixe dinner menu, and there is usually a lamb and a beef dish among their offerings. **Known for:** bread and butter pudding; complimentary transfers from local accommodation; excellent wines to go with your meal. ⑤ *Average main: NZ$32* ⊠ *42 Puruatanga Rd.* ☎ *06/306–9933* ⊕ *www.tirohanaestate.com* ◷ *Closed Mon. No lunch Tues.*

Union Square Bistro and Bar

$$$$ | **BISTRO** | Located and independently operated within the historic Martinborough Hotel, the decor here is understated yet comfortable. The classic bistro menu offers European favorites for lunch and dinner, with brunch on weekends. **Known for:** Michelin-starred chef; town center location; great gin menu. ⑤ *Average main: NZ$32* ⊠ *Martinborough Hotel, Union Sq.* ☎ *06/306–8350* ⊕ *www.unionsquare.co.nz.*

The Village Café

$$ | **NEW ZEALAND** | At this rustic barnlike café with a sunny outdoor courtyard, all the food is made from local ingredients. The cooks even smoke their own salmon and stuff their own sausages. **Known for:** hearty brunches; huge and varied menu; plenty of space. ⑤ *Average main: NZ$17* ⊠ *6 Kitchener St.* ☎ *06/306–8814* ◷ *No dinner.*

🛏 Hotels

The Claremont

$$ | **HOTEL** | In a quiet rural area just outside the village center, this motel complex has a variety of stylishly modern units to suit a range of budgets. **Pros:** quiet location out of the town center; good modern lodgings; spacious rooms. **Cons:** no swimming pool or activities; you need to go into town for a restaurant; no air-conditioning. ⑤ *Rooms from: NZ$150* ⊠ *38 Regent St.* ☎ *06/306–9162* ⊕ *www.theclaremont.co.nz* ⇘ *23 rooms* ⊙ *No meals.*

The Martinborough Hotel

$$$ | **HOTEL** | Sitting on a corner of the Martinborough Square, this vintage hotel was built in 1882 and has rooms that open onto either the veranda or the garden. **Pros:** colonial charm; handy to everything; lovely restaurant downstairs. **Cons:** books up fast at peak times; no air-conditioning; some rooms affected by street noise. ⑤ *Rooms from: NZ$239* ⊠ *The Square* ☎ *06/306–9350* ⊕ *www.martinboroughhotel.co.nz* ⇘ *20 rooms.*

Peppers Parehua

$$$ | **RESORT** | Located next to a vineyard, luxurious Peppers Parehua enjoys a park-like setting. **Pros:** modern luxury lodgings; outdoor pool; tennis court. **Cons:** a long way from the bright lights; no air-conditioning; underwhelming breakfast. ⑤ *Rooms from: NZ$270* ⊠ *New York St. W.* ☎ *06/306–8405* ⊕ *www.peppers.co.nz* ⇘ *28 cottages* ⊙ *Breakfast.*

Palliser Bay and Cape Palliser

Southwest of Martinborough: 25 km (16 miles) to Lake Ferry, 40 km (25 miles) to Putangirua Pinnacles, 65 km (40 miles) to Cape Palliser.

This, the most southerly part of the North Island's coast, can be a wild and desolate

8

Wellington and the Wairarapa PALLISER BAY AND CAPE PALLISER

Matiu/Somes Island

A wonderful place to spend a day walking and exploring, the Matiu/Somes Island Scientific and Historic Reserve lies in Wellington Harbour approximately 8 km (5 miles) from the city. The island has lots of walking trails, great beaches for swimming, good picnic spots, and opportunities to see whales, dolphins, penguins, and other birds (sharp eyes may also pick out assorted small lizards on the paths). Because the boats carry a limited number of passengers to the island at a time, it's never crowded.

Although the 62-acre island was opened as a DOC reserve in 1995, it has an interesting history. From the early 1880s until 1980 it was used as a quarantine station for both humans and animals—including dogs, cattle, sheep, llamas, and other livestock—on their way into the country. During the world wars, it was also used as a place of internment for immigrants considered a security threat.

In 1981, Matiu/Somes Island became a project of the Royal Forest and Bird Protection Society. Volunteers began planting trees that year to replace vegetation that had previously been cleared to allow grazing for quarantined animals. Many other native plants that flourished before the arrival of Europeans have also been replanted, and native insects (such as the giant, wingless wetas) reintroduced. The island is now a breeding ground for a variety of seabirds.

This is strictly a place to enjoy natural beauty. The few man-made structures on it today include the old quarantine station and gun emplacements from World War II—which were never used, and which remain on the southernmost summit of the island. An automated lighthouse built in 1900 to replace the original structure from 1866 also still sends out its southward beacon to ships traveling from Wellington Harbour.

The island can be reached by the *Eatsby West* ferry service; multiple round-trip runs are made from Wellington Harbour per day.

area in winter. But the lighthouse and seal colony at Cape Palliser are well worth seeing, as are the eerie rock formations in Putangirua Pinnacles Scenic Reserve. Wedged between the bay and a lagoon, Lake Ferry is a great spot to enjoy rugged scenery on a good day.

◉ Sights

Cape Palliser

LIGHTHOUSE | Named by Captain Cook, Cape Palliser marks the eastern end of Palliser Bay. You can't miss its lighthouse, a candy-striped classic erected in 1897. Climb the 250 (the sign says 258) wooden steps for terrific views up and down the wild coastline. Below the lighthouse, splashing in the surf and basking on the rocks, are members of the North Island's only resident fur seal colony. Don't get too close for photos though; these animals are fiercely protective of their young. Department of Conservation rules require you keep 20 meters from seals, so don't get between seals and pups, or seals and the ocean. To reach it from Martinborough, start at Memorial Square and turn left into Jellicoe Street, this becomes Lake Ferry Road. After 30 km (18½ miles) turn left at the Cape Palliser road sign; from there it's another 35 km (21½ miles) to the cape itself. You'll pass The Pinnacles on your left; after this

Continued on page 295

SEARCHING FOR MIDDLE-EARTH

With the Oscar-winning Lord of the Rings trilogy, Peter Jackson secured his place among great location directors like John Ford and Martin Scorsese. He also sealed New Zealand's reputation for otherworldly beauty, putting the country on the map by celebrating it on screen.

The sets have long been struck, but New Zealand's vistas will inspire your imagination to fill in the castles, coombs, and creatures. It seems as if half the country was involved in filming, so you can always ask a local to tell a tale of Middle-earth. Or take a tour—elf ears are optional!

The Lord of the Rings marked New Zealand scenery's star turn, but, like an aspiring actor, it has worked its way up, often as a stand-in for better-known, bigger names. Mountain peaks outside of Queenstown double for the Rockies in advertisements, and Mt. Taranaki on the North Island played Japan's Mt. Fuji alongside Tom Cruise in The Last Samurai.

Now, thanks to generous incentives and a favorable exchange rate, New Zealand has lured other large international productions such as The Chronicles of Narnia. And Jackson has given Tolkien fans three more reasons to celebrate with The Hobbit trilogy.

Above: Scene from The Lord of the Rings: The Two Towers

MIDDLE-EARTH

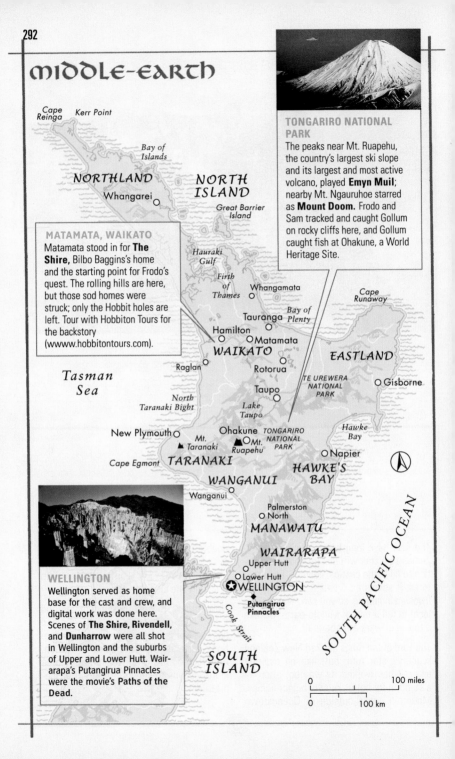

Cape
Reinga   Kerr Point

Bay of
Islands

NORTHLAND

Whangarei

**NORTH
ISLAND**

Great Barrier
Island

Hauraki
Gulf

Firth
of
Thames   Whangamata

Cape
Runaway

Bay of
Plenty

Tauranga

Hamilton
Matamata

WAIKATO

Raglan

Rotorua

EASTLAND

Gisborne

TE UREWERA
NATIONAL
PARK

**Tasman
Sea**

North
Taranaki Bight

Taupo

Lake
Taupo

Ohakune   TONGARIRO
NATIONAL
PARK

Hawke
Bay

New Plymouth   Mt.
Taranaki   Mt.
Ruapehu

Napier

Cape Egmont   **TARANAKI**

**HAWKE'S
BAY**

WANGANUI

Wanganui

Palmerston
North

MANAWATU

WAIRARAPA

Upper Hutt

Lower Hutt

WELLINGTON

Putangirua
Pinnacles

Cook
Strait

**SOUTH
ISLAND**

SOUTH PACIFIC OCEAN

TONGARIRO NATIONAL PARK

The peaks near Mt. Ruapehu, the country's largest ski slope and its largest and most active volcano, played **Emyn Muil**; nearby Mt. Ngauruhoe starred as **Mount Doom.** Frodo and Sam tracked and caught Gollum on rocky cliffs here, and Gollum caught fish at Ohakune, a World Heritage Site.

MATAMATA, WAIKATO

Matamata stood in for **The Shire,** Bilbo Baggins's home and the starting point for Frodo's quest. The rolling hills are here, but those sod homes were struck; only the Hobbit holes are left. Tour with Hobbiton Tours for the backstory (wwww.hobbitontours.com).

WELLINGTON

Wellington served as home base for the cast and crew, and digital work was done here. Scenes of **The Shire, Rivendell,** and **Dunharrow** were all shot in Wellington and the suburbs of Upper and Lower Hutt. Wairarapa's Putangirua Pinnacles were the movie's **Paths of the Dead.**

0   100 miles

0   100 km

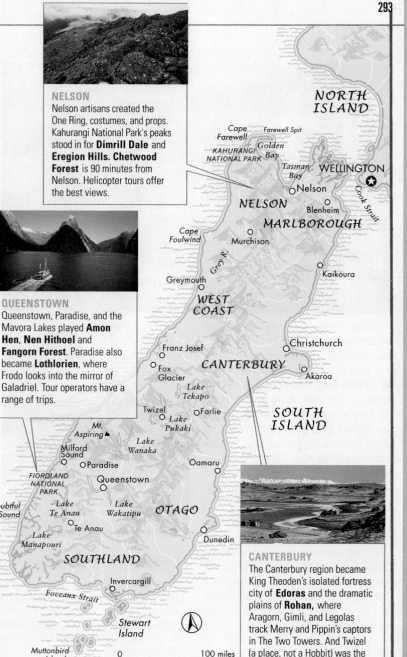

NELSON
Nelson artisans created the One Ring, costumes, and props. Kahurangi National Park's peaks stood in for **Dimrill Dale** and **Eregion Hills. Chetwood Forest** is 90 minutes from Nelson. Helicopter tours offer the best views.

QUEENSTOWN
Queenstown, Paradise, and the Mavora Lakes played **Amon Hen**, **Nen Hithoel** and **Fangorn Forest**. Paradise also became **Lothlorien**, where Frodo looks into the mirror of Galadriel. Tour operators have a range of trips.

CANTERBURY
The Canterbury region became King Theoden's isolated fortress city of **Edoras** and the dramatic plains of **Rohan,** where Aragorn, Gimli, and Legolas track Merry and Pippin's captors in The Two Towers. And Twizel (a place, not a Hobbit) was the site of the winged-beast battle of **Pelennor Fields.**

NORTH ISLAND

Cape Farewell
Farewell Spit
KAHURANGI NATIONAL PARK
Golden Bay
Tasman Bay
WELLINGTON
Nelson

NELSON
Blenheim
MARLBOROUGH
Cook Strait

Cape Foulwind
Murchison

Grey R.

Kaikoura

Greymouth

WEST COAST

Franz Josef
Christchurch

Fox Glacier
CANTERBURY
Akaroa

Lake Tekapo

Twizel
Lake Pukaki
Farlie

SOUTH ISLAND

Mt. Aspiring ▲
Lake Wanaka

Milford Sound
Paradise
Oamaru

FIORDLAND NATIONAL PARK
Queenstown

Doubtful Sound
Lake Te Anau
Lake Wakatipu
OTAGO

Te Anau

Lake Manapouri
Dunedin

SOUTHLAND

Invercargill

Foveaux Strait

Stewart Island

Muttonbird Islands

0   100 miles

0   100 km

TOURS OF THE RINGS

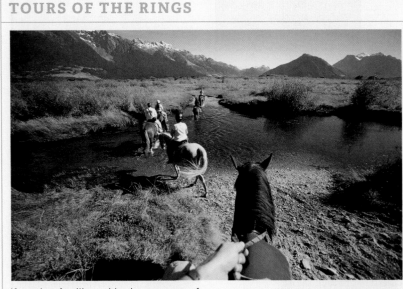

If you're familiar with the concept of "second breakfast," and know the difference between a smaug and a warg, you may want to break the bank for Glenorchy Air's **Three Ring Trilogy Tour,** an all-day adventure, including flying to and touching down at three filming locations on the South Island, or try their shorter **Two Ring** option for half a day. You can drive to some locations outside major cities on your own, but without a guide it may be difficult to "see" where the films were made (⊕ www.trilogytrail.com).

Hobbitontours (⊕ www.hobbitontours.com) offers guided tours of the Hobbiton Movie Set. Explore Hobbit Holes, the Green Dragon Inn, The Mill, and other structures from The Hobbit and Lord of the Rings sets that have been meticulously rebuilt. Based on a private farmland, The Hobbiton Movie Set is truly a journey into the Shire.

PRECIOUS MOMENTS

Many LOTR tours feature capes, swords, and flag replicas in the famous settings. Be sure to check out the Weta Cave in Wellington, the museum of the movies' special-effects team (⊕ www.wetanz.com).

(top) The leisurely two-hour ride across the river flats at Glenorchy. (bottom) Mount Aspiring National Park the road deteriorates and is unpaved in places. It is a bleak and dramatic drive, though not particularly hard if you take care. The travel time from Martinborough is approximately 80 minutes. ⊠ *Cape Palliser.*

Lake Ferry
TOWN | The tiny settlement of Lake Ferry sits beside Palliser Bay, 40 km (25 miles) northwest of Cape Palliser. The lake in question, called Onoke, is actually a salt lagoon formed by the long sandbank here. Vacation homes, fishing spots, and remarkable sunsets bring in the weekend Wellingtonian crowd. If you're coming from Martinborough, expect a 25-km (16-mile) drive through rolling sheep country. ⊠ *Lake Ferry.*

Putangirua Pinnacles Scenic Reserve
NATURE SITE | Just before Lake Ferry, turn left (coming from Martinborough) at the sign for Cape Palliser and drive another 15 km (9 miles) around Palliser Bay to Te Kopi, where the Putangirua Pinnacles Scenic Reserve is protected from the hordes by its relative isolation. The spectacular rocks have been formed over the last 120,000 years as rains have washed away an ancient gravel deposit, and pinnacles and towers now soar hundreds of feet into the air on both sides of a stony riverbank. An hour-long round-trip walk from the parking area takes you along the riverbank and close to the base of the pinnacles. If you're feeling adventurous, a three- to four-hour bushwalk involves some steep climbs and wonderful vistas of the coast—as far off as the South Island on a clear day. Stout footwear and warm clothing are essential. The Pinnacles are an hour's drive from Martinborough. ⊠ *Palliser Bay, Featherston.*

🛏 Hotels

Kawakawa Station
$$ | RENTAL | On 5,000-acres of rolling hills with sheep, cattle, horses, and dogs is a cozy, self-contained hillside cottage that welcomes guests. **Pros:** a real Kiwi farm experience; not too far from the sea; glamping option available. **Cons:** no restaurant on-site; the silence might keep you awake at night; an hour from all services. $ *Rooms from: NZ$135* ⊠ *2631 Cape Palliser Rd., Cape Palliser* ☎ *06/307–8989* ⊕ *www.kawakawasta-tion.co.nz* ▭ *No credit cards* ⤳ *3 cottages* ¶◎¶ *No meals.*

Lake Ferry Hotel
$ | HOTEL | This waterfront hotel is home to the North Island's southernmost pub, with breathtaking views across Cape Palliser to the South Island's Kaikoura Ranges. **Pros:** if you like the feeling of being at the end of the Earth, this is for you; great food; genuine local experience. **Cons:** don't expect the Ritz; only one room is en suite; can get crowded because it's the only place to stay in town. $ *Rooms from: NZ$75* ⊠ *2 Lake Ferry Rd., Lake Ferry* ☎ *06/307–7831* ⊕ *www.lakeferry-hotel.co.nz* ⤳ *10 rooms* ¶◎¶ *Breakfast.*

★ Wharekauhau
$$$$ | HOTEL | A working sheep station meets bygone-era elegance at this unique coastal getaway, 90 minutes from Wellington; the 3,200-acre estate comes complete with an Edwardian-style main lodge surrounded by 16 guest cottages, each with king-size bed, small patio, and open fireplace. **Pros:** on-site working farm; breakfast and dinner included in beautiful dining area; luxurious spa using organic New Zealand products. **Cons:** steep price; you won't want to move far from the fireplaces in rough weather; don't expect the nightlife to set you alight. $ *Rooms from: NZ$2254* ⊠ *Wharekauhau Rd., Featherston* ☎ *06/307–7581* ⊕ *www.wharekauhau. co.nz* ⤳ *16 cottages* ¶◎¶ *Free Breakfast.*

Masterton and Environs

Masterton is 40 km (25 miles) northeast of Martinborough.

Masterton is Wairarapa's major population center, and, like Martinborough to the south, it's in a developing wine region. There's not much to do in the town, but it's a handy gateway for hiking in the nearby parks and on the coast. Popular annual events include the Hot Air Balloon Festival in early April and the Golden Shears sheep-shearing competition, usually held the first weekend in March.

State Highway 2 strings together a handful of eye-catching small towns on its way north past the Rimutakas. Farther north on the arrow-straight highway is **Greytown,** where well-preserved Victorian buildings now filled with cafés and boutiques line the main street. After a few miles more you'll reach **Carterton,** another small town with a handful of tempting stores—especially Paua World.

GETTING HERE AND AROUND

Approached on State Highway 2, Masterton is about a 90-minute drive from Wellington. Trains operated by Metlink come here from Wellington via the Hutt Valley, making the trip up to six times per day. Metlink buses also provide a very limited local bus service, but you need a car to explore the outlying areas.

BUS CONTACTS Masterton Bus Depot. ⊠ *316 Queen St., Masterton.*

TRAIN CONTACTS Masterton Railway Station. ⊠ *Perry St., Masterton.*

VISITOR INFORMATION

CONTACTS Masterton i-SITE Visitor Information Centre. ⊠ *10 Dixon St., Masterton* ☎ *06/370–0900* ⊕ *www.wairarapanz. com.*

👁 Sights

Castlepoint

VIEWPOINT | An hour's drive east of Masterton along Te Ore-ore Road (which turns into the Masterton–Castlepoint Road), Castlepoint is perhaps the most spectacular site on the entire Wairarapa coast. Castle Rock rises a sheer 500 feet out of the sea; below, in **Deliverance Cove,** seals sometimes play. ⊠ *Masterton.*

Fell Locomotive Museum

MUSEUM | The tiny town of Featherston is worth a stop for the Fell Locomotive Museum. Along with photos, models, and memorabilia, it has the last remaining Fell locomotive in the world; built in 1875 and expertly restored, the engine is one of only six that clawed their way up the notorious Rimutaka Incline on the way to Wellington. ⊠ *Lyon and Fitzherbert Sts., behind Information Center on State Hwy. 2, Featherston* ☎ *06/308–9379* ⊕ *www.fellmuseum.org. nz* ⊠ *NZ$6.*

★ Pukaha Mount Bruce

NATURE PRESERVE | Head 30 km (19 miles) north of Masterton for a fine introduction to the country's wildlife—particularly its endangered birds. An easy trail through the bush (one hour, round-trip) takes you past aviaries containing rare, endangered, or vulnerable birds, including the takahē, a flightless species thought to be extinct until it was rediscovered in 1948. The real highlight, though, is the nocturnal habitat containing foraging kiwis, endearing little bundles of energy that are the national symbol. Here you can also view the only white kiwi in captivity; she glows in the dark, so you won't have to wait for your eyes to adjust to the gloom to see her. Indigenous parrots are fed daily at 3, and the reserve's stream writhes when the long-finned eels are fed at 1:30. ⊠ *85379 State Hwy. 2, Masterton* ☎ *06/375–8004* ⊕ *www.pukaha.org.nz* ⊠ *NZ$20.*

Tararua Forest Park

FOREST | For enjoyable bushwalks in gorgeous forests laced with streams, come to Tararua Forest Park. The Mt. Holdsworth area at the east end of the park is popular for tramping. If you're in the mood for an alfresco lunch, the park also has picnic facilities. To get here turn off State Highway 2 onto Norfolk Road, 2 km (1 miles) south of Masterton. ⊠ *Masterton* ☏ *06/377–0700 DOC office.*

🍴 Restaurants

The Farriers Bar & Eatery

$$$ | **MODERN NEW ZEALAND** | At The Farriers, you can watch the chefs in the open kitchen while waiting for your order to arrive. Much of the large menu is devoted to pub fare and wood-fired pizzas, all made from scratch, but interesting main courses tempt those with more ambitious appetites. **Known for:** popular with locals; basic, well-executed menu; courtyard for summer seating. ⑤ *Average main: NZ$28* ⊠ *4 Queen St. N, Masterton* ☏ *06/377–1107* ⊕ *www.thefarriers. co.nz.*

The White Swan Country Hotel

$$$ | **NEW ZEALAND** | This former railway administration building was chopped in to several pieces and relocated before being reimagined as this grand country hotel. The menu changes seasonally and incorporates locally sourced meat and vegetables. **Known for:** warm fire in winter; excellent veranda seating; good local wine selection. ⑤ *Average main: NZ$29* ⊠ *109 Main St., Greytown* ☏ *06/304–8894* ⊕ *www.whiteswangreytown.com.*

🛏 Hotels

Copthorne Resort Solway Park Wairarapa

$$ | **HOTEL** | **FAMILY** | With 24 acres of landscaped grounds and gardens, this spot on the southern outskirts of Masterton is a large resort for a small town. **Pros:** delicious restaurant; indoor pool, squash court, and golf driving range; good off-road parking. **Cons:** weekdays popular for corporate conferences; can get crowded on weekends with special family rates; dated decor. ⑤ *Rooms from: NZ$145* ⊠ *High St. S, Masterton* ☏ *06/370–0500* ⊕ *www.solway.co.nz* ↪ *102 rooms* ❍| *No meals.*

🛍 Shopping

Paua World

GIFTS/SOUVENIRS | Just off the main highway in Carterton, Paua World is an interesting diversion. Akin to abalone, *paua* has been collected by the Māori since ancient times (they used it to represent eyes in their statues). The highly prized, rainbow-color shell interiors are polished, processed, then turned into jewelry and the like. ⊠ *54 Kent St., Carterton* ☏ *06/379–4247* ⊕ *www.pauaworld.com.*

Chapter 9

UPPER SOUTH ISLAND AND THE WEST COAST

Updated by
Kathy Ombler

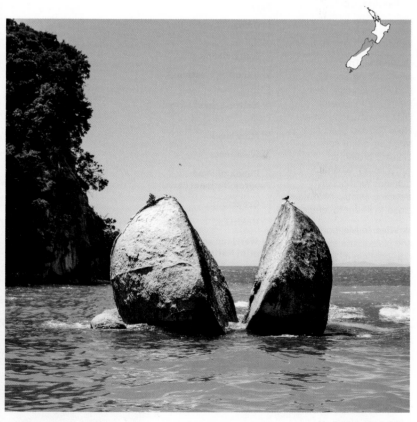

👁 **Sights**
★★★★★

🍴 **Restaurants**
★★★☆☆

🛏 **Hotels**
★★★☆☆

🛍 **Shopping**
★☆☆☆☆

🍸 **Nightlife**
★★☆☆☆

WELCOME TO UPPER SOUTH ISLAND AND THE WEST COAST

TOP REASONS TO GO

★ **Mountains, Glaciers, and Rain Forests:** Hiking, climbing, short rain forest and coastal walks, glacier walks, and scenic flights are all popular West Coast activities.

★ **Beaches:** Golden beaches and forest-fringed bays ring Upper South Island.

★ **Wildlife:** The Marlborough Sounds and Abel Tasman coast are home to several island sanctuaries where New Zealand seals and rare native bird species are protected. At Kaikoura, whales, dolphins, and ocean-traveling albatross come close to shore to feed.

★ **Wine:** In Marlborough and Nelson the sunny-day–cool-night climate and diverse soil types mean grapes come off the vines plump with flavor.

★ **Mining Legacy:** Nelson, Marlborough, Murchison, Reefton, and the West Coast all have a strong legacy of mining, for gold and coal. This rich history comes alive in such places as the Denniston Mine near Westport.

1 **Kaikoura.**

2 **Blenheim.**

3 **Picton.**

4 **Havelock.**

5 **Nelson.**

6 **Around Nelson.**

7 **Motueka.**

8 **Abel Tasman National Park.**

9 **Golden Bay and Takaka.**

10 **Farewell Spit.**

11 **Kahurangi National Park.**

12 **Nelson Lakes National Park.**

13 **Murchison.**

14 **Westport.**

15 **Punakaiki and Paparoa National Park.**

16 **Greymouth.**

17 **Hokitika.**

18 **Westland and Tai Poutini National Park.**

Tasman Sea

Paparoa National Park

Punakai

Greymouth 16

Kumara Junction

Hokitika 17

Ross

Kakapotahi

SOUTHERN ALPS

Westland/ Tai Poutini National Park

Harihari 6

Whataroa

Franz Josef Glacier

Fox Glacier

Aoraki/ Mount Cook

The South Island has been carved by ice, water, and tectonic uplift, and all these processes are still rapidly occurring today. Here, the mellow farmland greens and jumbled forest-covered ranges of the North Island are replaced by snowcapped mountains, glaciers, rivers that sprawl across wide-shingle beds and, along the northern coastlines, drowned river valleys, and golden beaches.

Marlborough occupies the northeast corner of the South Island. The bays and inlets of the Marlborough Sounds (these are the drowned river valleys) wash around bush-covered peninsulas and sandy coves. Marlborough is also the largest wine-growing region in New Zealand, with more than 27,000 acres of vineyards. It's a relatively dry and sunny area, and on a hazy summer day the inland plains can resemble the American West, with mountains rising beyond the arid flats.

The northwest corner of the island is the sun-drenched Nelson region, which enjoys a relatively mild climate that allows a year-round array of outdoor activities. Nelson city is a lively place to visit, with fine restaurants and a vibrant network of artists and craftspeople. It's also the gateway to three national parks, an internationally recognized wetland, beaches, hiking tracks, and boating opportunities. Abel Tasman National Park, to the west of the city, is ringed with spectacularly blue-green waters studded with golden beaches and craggy rocks, and it's home to the popular Abel Tasman Coast Track. To the southwest is Kahurangi National Park, with unique karst marble mountains and the popular Heaphy Track. Farther to the south Nelson Lakes National Park, with its glacial lakes, bushwalks, longer hiking trails, alpine passes, and snowcapped peaks, is a popular holiday spot for both Kiwi folk and overseas visitors.

After the gentler climes of Marlborough and Nelson, the wild grandeur of the West Coast is a dramatic contrast. This is Mother Nature with her hair down, flaying the coastline with huge seas and drenching rains and littering its beaches with tons of bleached driftwood. When it rains, you feel like you're inside a fishbowl; then the sun bursts out, and you swear you're in paradise. (Always check local conditions before taking an excursion.) This region has a rich heritage of mining for gold and coal, and milling, a legacy that has created a special breed of rough-hewn and powerfully independent locals—known to the rest of the country as Coasters—who occupy a special place in New Zealand folklore.

GETTING ORIENTED

In the northeast are the myriad waterways of the Marlborough Sounds. Heading south a tad, you come to sunny Marlborough wine country. From Blenheim, the main town here, State Highway 1 travels south along the eastern coast, a narrow stretch between mountains and ocean to Kaikoura, then continues south through Canterbury farmland to Christchurch. The rebuilding of this highway, which was severely damaged in the Kaikoura earthquake in 2016, has been an engineering triumph. Heading west, a series of forest-covered ranges separates Blenheim and Nelson. West of Nelson you'll pass through Motueka to Abel Tasman National Park and Golden Bay. Heading southwest on State Highway 6 brings you to big mountain country—Nelson Lakes and Kahurangi national parks—then through the Buller Gorge to the West Coast. Head north to the coastal towns of Westport and Karamea, then south towards the highest peaks of the Southern Alps. The highway follows the plains between the alps and Tasman Sea, passing settlements of Greymouth and Hokitika before reaching glacier and world heritage country: Franz Josef and Fox glaciers in Westland/Tai Poutini National Park.

MAJOR REGIONS

Marlborough. This region is a contrast of two delights; all about vineyards covering, wide open river valleys shingle riverbeds, and the sheltered, forest-lined waterways of the Marlborough Sounds. The Marlborough Sounds were first settled 700 to 900 years ago by the seafaring Māori people who named the area Te Tau Ihu O Te Waka a Māui ("the prow of Maui's canoe"). As legend has it, the legendary Maui fished up the North Island from his canoe via a jawbone hook with special powers. Consequently, the North Island is called Te Ika a Māui—"the fish of Maui." European settlers arrived in the early 1800s, mostly to hunt whales and seals. By the 1830s the whale and

seal population had dropped drastically, so the settlers looked inland, to farm the fertile river plains of the Wairau Valley, where Blenheim now stands. While surveyors were pressured to open territory for farming, local Māori were reluctant to part with more of their land and responded by sabotaging the surveyors' work and equipment.

Captain Arthur Wakefield, founder of an English settlement in Nelson, arrived to confront the two Māori chiefs leading the protests. A fracas flared up beside the Tuamarina River (now marked by a memorial on the roadside between Picton and Blenheim), resulting in several deaths, both Māori and European, including Captain Wakefield and the daughter of noted chief, Te Rauparaha. New Zealand's Governor Fitzroy later upbraided the English for their "impudent behavior" in what is now referred to as the "Wairau Affray." The land was later sold reluctantly by the Māori tribes, and by 1850 the new settlers began farming.

Thirty years later, the unwittingly prescient Charles Empson and David Herd began planting red muscatel grapes among local sheep and grain farms. Their modest viticultural torch was rekindled in the next century by the Freeth family, and by the 1940s Marlborough wineries were successfully producing port, sherry, and Madeira. In 1973 New Zealand's largest wine company, Montana, planted vines in Marlborough to increase the supply of New Zealand grapes. This was the beginning of the region's success with Sauvignon Blanc. Other vintners followed suit, and within a decade today's major players—such as Hunter's and Cloudy Bay—had established the region's international reputation. Marlborough now glories in being New Zealand's single largest area under vine, and many local growers sell grapes to winemakers outside the area. Blenheim, Picton, and Havelock are popular towns in the region to base yourself for wineries and outdoor adventures.

The Northwest. The northern coast encompasses the massive sand spit, Farewell Spit, the sheltered, golden-sand bays of the Abel Tasman National Park, and the wide expanse of Tasman Bay. On the broad curve of Tasman Bay and backed by mountains, Nelson is a top area for year-round adventure. To the west beckon the forested bays and golden beaches of Abel Tasman and Golden Bay. To the south, the high peaks and glacial lakes and valleys of Nelson Lakes National Park draw hikers, climbers, fishers, kayakers, and sightseers. In the west are the tussock and karst rock mountains of Kahurangi, New Zealand's second largest national park. There's a climatic allure here as well; Nelson usually has more hours of sunlight than any other city in the country. New Zealanders are well aware of these attractions, and in December and January the region is swamped with vacationers. Apart from this brief burst of activity, you can expect the roads and beaches to be relatively quiet.

First settled by Māori hundreds of years ago, and originally named Whakatu, the area that is now Nelson city was chosen for its extremely sheltered harbor, good climate, and plentiful *kaimoana* (seafood). These enticements later caught the eye of the entrepreneurial London-based New Zealand Company, and Nelson became the second town developed by that organization, with British immigrants arriving in the 1840s. These days Nelson is one of the country's chief fishing ports and a key forestry, orchard, hop-growing, wine-producing, and olive-growing area. This setting has long attracted creatively minded people, and a significant community of artists, craftspeople, and writers is settled in the countryside around Nelson. Westport and Murchison are other popular small towns in the area.

The West Coast. The Coast is a long narrow strip of land hemmed between the Tasman Sea and the Southern Alps. Landscapes encompass subtropical rain forests in the north and icy, steep glaciers in the south, and Westland/Tai Poutini National Park is a part of the massive Te Wahipounamu/South West New Zealand World Heritage Area.

Māori, the first inhabitants, knew this area to be rich in *pounamu* (greenstone or jade). The Māori name for the South Island, Te Wai Pounamu, reflects this treasure. For hundreds of years the riverbeds, beaches, and mountain passes served as walking trails to access pounamu for intertribal trade, and you'll still hear references to "greenstone trails" throughout the area. Today, the rights to gather, craft, and sell pounamu sit exclusively with the South Island *iwi* (tribe) of Ngai Tahu. West Coast galleries sell their traditional and contemporary greenstone carvings. Early *Pākehā* (European) settlers carved out a hardscrabble life during the 1860s, digging for gold while constantly lashed by the West Coast rains. After the gold rushes, waves of settlers arrived to mine the vast coal reserves in the surrounding hills. Farmers and loggers followed; although the gold has mostly gone and magnificent native forests are now protected from milling, the coal mining (to a lesser extent than before) and farming remain. The towns along this stretch of coastline are generally no-frills rural service centers, and make good bases for exploring the primeval landscape. These communities have also known mining tragedy: the most recent was at Pike River in late 2010, when 29 miners lost their lives in an underground explosion.

Near the southern glacier towns of Franz Josef and Fox, nature's spectacles are the high mountains, voluminous precipitation, and massive valleys of ice descending straight into rain forests (a combination also present on the southwest coast of South America). South of the glaciers, the road follows the coast, where majestic *kahikatea* rain forest grows closer to the ocean than anywhere else in New Zealand. On sunny days the Tasman Sea can take on an almost transcendent shade of blue.

In 2000, New Zealand's Labour-led government legislated to end commercial logging of the West Coast's native forests; since then the local communities have been in flux, as residents turn to tourism, farming, and a now struggling coal mining industry to sustain their livelihoods. But it's the environment that continues to determine the lifestyle here. Locals pride themselves on their ability to coexist with the wild landscape and weather. As a visitor, you may need a sense of adventure—be prepared for rain, swirling mist, and cold winter winds alternating with warm, clear days. "The Barber," Greymouth's infamous winter wind, blasts down the Grey River valley to the sea. The meteorological mix can mean that the glacier flight you planned at Franz Josef or Fox won't fly that day. So plan to stay an extra day, or more, as there are plenty of other things to do while you wait on the weather. Although the coast is well known for its rain, it also has clear, bright days when the mountains shine above the green coastal plains and the surf pounds onto sunny, sandy beaches; often the best, most settled weather is in winter.

Planning

When to Go

Nelson and Marlborough are delightful year-round, but beach activities are best from December to mid-March if you plan to be in or on the water. From Christmas through January some places can be busy with New Zealanders on their own vacations so book ahead; international tourists flock to the West Coast and glacier region throughout the summer. Snow generally covers the mountains from June through October. Don't let this stop you from driving through these regions; scenically they will look even more stunning. Sperm whales and dolphins live year-round off the coast of Kaikoura. Humpback whales visit in early winter. The pleasures of winter weather around the West Coast glaciers—clear skies and no snow at sea level—are a well-kept local secret. Look into local festival schedules; they occur year-round.

Planning Your Time

Anything less than three or four days through Nelson and Marlborough and an additional three to four days on the West Coast will be too few. Don't be deceived by the maps; steep, winding roads slow down the drive times. Campervans proliferate these roads in summer, and tend to move slowly so be patient and wait for a clear place to pass.

Getting Here and Around

AIR TRAVEL

Several daily Air New Zealand flights operate from Auckland and Wellington to Blenheim and Nelson, and from Christchurch to Nelson. Sounds Air flies smaller planes daily between Wellington and Blenheim, Picton, Nelson, and Westport. Origin Air flies from Nelson to Palmerston North and New Plymouth. Jetstar flies between Nelson and Wellington and Auckland. Hokitika is also serviced by Air New Zealand flights from Christchurch. Picton and Golden Bay are serviced by smaller commuter aircraft.

CONTACTS Origin Air. ☎ *0800/380–380* ⊕ *originair.co.nz.* **Sounds Air.** ☎ *0800/505–005* ⊕ *www.soundsair.com.*

BUS TRAVEL

InterCity runs daily between Christchurch and Kaikoura, Picton, Blenheim, and Nelson a couple of times a day. Atomic Shuttles operates coaches between Christchurch, Blenheim, Picton, and Nelson and has a seat-booking arrangement with InterCity for the West Coast. Bus tickets can be booked directly or at information centers.

CAR TRAVEL

Roads through this region's mountain ranges and gorges can be narrow and winding, and a 160-km (100-mile) drive might take more than three hours. However, the roads are generally good, and there's always something to look at. There are a number of one-way bridges along the way. Check the road sign with two colorful arrows: if the arrow is red for your side of the road, that means you give way if traffic is coming the other way. Remember always to keep left. It can also be a long way between gas stations, so fill up when you can.

Nelson is about a two-hour drive from Picton. From Nelson, State Highway 6 runs southwest to the West Coast, then north to Westport, and south down the coast to the glaciers. At Haast, south of the glaciers, the road turns inland, and crosses the Haast Pass and leads to highways to Wanaka, Queenstown, and Central Otago. For the West Coast, count on at least seven hours solid driving (and photo stops) for the 458-km (284-mile) journey from Nelson to Franz Josef. (But seriously, don't even think about doing this in one haul. Take a few days.) For Nelson to Christchurch, allow up to five hours, whether you go through the mountains of the Lewis Pass or take the coastal route via Blenheim and Kaikoura. Heading direct west from Nelson, Highway 60 splits from State Highway 6 about 13 km (8 miles) out of the city, near Richmond, and continues to Motueka, Abel Tasman National Park, and Golden Bay.

Westport, gateway to the northern West Coast, is roughly a three-hour trip from Nelson on State Highway 6 or a five- to six-hour drive over Arthur's Pass on Highway 7 from Christchurch. State Highway 7 climbs from Arthur's Pass and across the backbone of the Southern Alps before winding steeply down through rain forest to the tiny town of Otira and on to the coastal river plains of the mid–West Coast.

Some car rental agencies have North Island–South Island transfer programs for their vehicles: you leave one car in Wellington, travel as a foot passenger, and pick another car up in Picton on the same contract. Others let you keep one car that you drive on and off the ferry; check first.

FERRY TRAVEL

Visitors traveling from the North Island can take either the Interislander or Bluebridge ferry from Wellington to Picton, the northern entrance to the South Island. The trip is scenic, especially through sheltered Tory Channel in the Marlborough Sounds, though Cook Strait itself can be rough at times. The one-way adult fare ranges from NZ$59 to NZ$80. Ferries dock in Picton, right beside the township.

CONTACT Bluebridge. ☎ *0800/844–844* ⊕ *www.bluebridge.co.nz.* **Interislander.** ☎ *0800/802–802 New Zealand only* ⊕ *www.greatjourneysofnz.co.nz.*

TRAIN TRAVEL

Two of New Zealand's three scenic rail journeys serve these regions. The West Coast is connected with Christchurch by the **TranzAlpine Express,** which ranks as one of the world's great rail journeys. The train crosses the Southern Alps between Christchurch and Greymouth, winding through southern beech forests and snow-covered mountains. In summer, the **Coastal Pacific** meets some Cook Strait ferry sailings and travels through Marlborough and along the scenic Kaikoura coast to Christchurch. Both trains are modern and comfortable, with panoramic windows and a no-frills dining and bar service.

CONTACTS The Coastal Pacific Train. ☎ *0800/872–467* ⊕ *www.greatjourneysofnz.co.nz.* **The TranzAlpine Train.** ☎ *0800/872–467 New Zealand only* ⊕ *www.greatjourneysofnz.co.nz.*

Restaurants

In Marlborough, visit a winery restaurant—there's no better way to ensure that your meal suits what you're drinking. Cloudy Bay clams are harvested here, salmon and Greenshell mussels are farmed in the Marlborough Sounds, and local crops—besides grapes—include cherries and garlic. In Kaikoura try crayfish. The region is named after this delicacy (in Māori, *kai* means "food" and *koura* means "lobster"). Nelson is also famous for seafood, in particular scallops, and for fresh produce and, yes, for wine. On the West Coast, try the local delicacy whitebait fritters—a sort of omelet filled with the whitebait—tiny, young eel-like fish netted at river mouths as they migrate upstream in late spring.

Some restaurants in more remote tourist regions close in winter (June through August); others may curtail their hours. In summer, all doors are open and it's best to make reservations. If a restaurant is open on a major holiday, it may add a surcharge to your bill.

Year-round, the restaurants and cafés around the glaciers and other remote spots can be quick to close their doors at night. Arrive by 8:30 (it's sometimes even earlier in winter) or you might go hungry. Some of the smallest towns, including Punakaiki, settlements in the Marlborough Sounds, and parts of Golden Bay, have few cafés and no general stores, so bring your own supplies.

Hotels

Bed-and-breakfasts, farm stays, and homestays, all a variation on the same theme, abound in the South Island, many in some spectacular coastal and mountain environments. Your hosts will generally feed you great breakfasts and advise on where to eat and what to do locally. Other choices include boutique luxury lodges and hotels, or less expensive but well-equipped motel rooms and backpacker lodges.

Locals generally take vacations from Christmas through January, so book early at these times. From April through November everything settles down, and in most towns you can book at short notice. Heating is standard in virtually every room, especially in cooler southern regions, and most places around Nelson and Marlborough, which can be hot in summer, provide air-conditioning.

Restaurant and hotel reviews have been shortened. For full information, visit Fodors.com. Restaurant prices are the average cost of a main course at dinner or, if dinner is not served, at lunch. Hotel prices are the lowest cost of a standard double room in high season.

What It Costs			
$	$$	$$$	$$$$
RESTAURANTS			
under NZ$15	NZ$15–NZ$20	NZ$21–NZ$30	over NZ$30
HOTELS			
under NZ$125	NZ$125–NZ$200	NZ$201–NZ$300	over NZ$300

Visitor Information

Every large, and most small, town has an information center or i-SITE office; watch for the blue-and-white "i" sign showing their location.

Several regional tourism organizations maintain helpful websites: Destination Marlborough (⊕ *www.marlboroughnz.com*), Nelson Tasman Tourism (⊕ *www.nelsonnz.com*), Tourism West Coast (⊕ *www.west-coast.co.nz*), and Glacier Country Tourism Group (⊕ *www.glaciercountry.co.nz*). The Department of Conservation (⊕ *www.doc.govt.nz*) is the best source for national parks, forest parks, and scenic reserves.

Kaikoura

129 km (81 miles) south of Blenheim, 182 km (114 miles) north of Christchurch.

With its marine wildlife and spectacular coastal location, the town of Kaikoura sits at the base of a peninsula that juts into the ocean from the east coast, and is backed by the steep Kaikoura mountain range. In addition to its spectacular scenery, Kaikoura is famous for the abundant marine life that gathers here because of offshore sea canyons and the meeting of subtropical and cold southern sea currents, which support a rich and complex underwater food chain. Sperm whales feed closer to shore at Kaikoura than anywhere else in the world. Humpbacks, pilot whales, and orca join them during seasonal migrations. You are most likely to see the whales between October and August, though the sperm whale lives here year-round. Joining the marine melee are dolphins and seals, and the birdlife is equally prolific. On a good day, Kaikoura is considered one of the world's best places for watching pelagic (oceangoing) birds, such as albatross, while Hutton's Shearwaters, also oceanic travelers, nest only here, high in the craggy peaks of the Seaward Kaikoura Range. Ecotourism, whale-watching, bird-watching cruises, and swimming with dolphins and seals have become the backbone of Kaikoura's economy, attracting thousands of visitors each year. There has also been a whole new perspective to a Kaikoura

visit since November 2016, when a 7.8 magnitude earthquake struck the region, thrusting the seabed upward 5 meters, and causing massive slips and landfalls along the coast. Seeing the physical changes and hearing the stories of the resilient locals are all now as much of the experience as watching whales and dolphins.

Kaikoura's main street runs close to the coast, behind a high, stony bank, protected from stormy swells. On the southern shoreline of the peninsula, a few minutes' drive away, is South Bay, the boarding point for whale-watching and dolphin-swimming operators.

GETTING HERE AND AROUND
Kaikoura township sits on State Highway 1, between Picton and Christchurch and the coastal route between Nelson and Christchurch. It's a 2½-hour drive south from Kaikoura to Christchurch and 2 hours north to Blenheim. The highway has reopened after suffering significant damage caused by the 2016 earthquake, but it's still currently subject to occasional closures and delays, especially in stormy weather.

InterCity runs daily buses between Christchurch, Kaikoura, Blenheim, Picton, and Nelson.

In summer, the Coastal Pacific train follows the coast from Christchurch to Picton, meeting with the Cook Strait ferries. It stops at Kaikoura both ways.

VISITOR INFORMATION
CONTACTS Kaikoura i-SITE Visitor Centre.
✉ *West End* ☎ *03/319–5641* ⊕ *www.kaikoura.co.nz.*

◉ Sights

Fyffe House
BUILDING | Kaikoura's oldest building, erected soon after Robert Fyffe's whaling station was established in 1842, is now a small museum. Partly built on whalebone piles on a grassy rise overlooking

the sea, the house provides a look at what life was like when people aimed at whales with harpoons rather than cameras. ⊠ *62 Avoca St.* ☏ *03/319–5835* ⊕ *www.heritage.org.nz* ⊠ *NZ$10.*

Kaikoura Lavender Farm

GARDEN | Visitors are welcome to wander this working 5-acre farm, where rows of heavenly scented lavender stretch out against the stunning backdrop of the Seaward Kaikoura Range (catch the harvest from December to February). In the shop, lavender hangs from the ceiling and lavender mustards, chutneys, soaps, oils, and salves line the shelves. There's a café serving tea and coffee, ice creams, cold drinks, and a few lavender-flavor treats. They also have two rustic self-contained B&B cottages in the garden, which is just 15 minutes' drive north of Kaikoura. ⊠ *268 Postmans Rd.* ☏ *03/319–5473* ⊕ *www.lavenderfarm. co.nz* ⊠ *NZ$2* ⊙ *Closed Aug. and Sept.*

Kaikoura Short Walk

GUIDED TOURS | This is a great one-hour guided walk looking at heritage and cultural highlights of the town. These include the Memorial Gardens, Takahanga *Marae* (traditional home for the local *iwi* [tribe]), and a look at the incredible landscape changes and seabed lift that occurred as a result of the 2016 earthquake. Meet and book at the Kaikoura i-SITE Visitor Centre. ⊠ *West End, Kaikoura* ☏ *027/435–3905* ⊠ *NZ$20.*

🍴 Restaurants

For a small place Kaikoura has an excellent choice of restaurants. But for a taste of the local crayfish visit one of the roadside caravans; on the coast north of town Nin's Bin at Rakautara has a strong fan base. Crays come cooked or uncooked, or you may prefer to get your crayfish fix at a local café, though they are expensive even at a casual place. Also try the whitefish-like *groper* (grouper) and *terakihi,* or

the shellfish, for example abalone, known here as *paua.*

Café Encounter

$ | **CAFÉ** | Here's a bright outdoor eatery sharing space with the Dolphin and Albatross Encounter operations and a gallery/shop. Food is available off the menu or from the cabinet; breakfasts and light lunches are appealing; and their range of cakes and slices are always tempting. **Known for:** waterfront views; homemade baking; big breakfasts before you hit the sea in pursuit of dolphins and seabirds. ⑤ *Average main: NZ$14* ⊠ *96 The Esplanade* ☏ *03/319–6777* ⊙ *No dinner.*

The Craypot

$$ | **SEAFOOD** | **FAMILY** | Sustainably caught seafood is the star at this casual, friendly café, but other menu offerings are equally appealing. Meals range from eggs, pancakes, and toasties for breakfast and brunch to lunch steaks, soups, and salads. **Known for:** seafood chowder; Kiwi craft beer menu; board games to keep diners entertained. ⑤ *Average main: NZ$18* ⊠ *70 West End Rd.* ☏ *03/319–6027.*

★ Hislops Café

$$$ | **CAFÉ** | This wholesome foodie café is a local institution, a few minutes' walk north of town and worth the trip. In the morning you'll find tasty free-range eggs and bacon, plus freshly baked, genuinely stone-ground whole-grain bread served with marmalade or their own honey. **Known for:** house-made bircher and organic muesli bowls for breakfast; open fish sandwiches; mountain and ocean views. ⑤ *Average main: NZ$26* ⊠ *33 Beach Rd.* ☏ *03/319–6971* ⊕ *www.hislops-whole-foods.co.nz* ⊙ *Closed Mon. and Tues. No dinner.*

The Pier Hotel

$$$$ | **NEW ZEALAND** | In a two-story Victorian waterfront hotel overlooking Ingles Bay, one of Kaikoura's most dependable eateries serves traditional New Zealand pub fare with a bit of a makeover. The bar

serves cheaper lunches and pub snacks if you're just looking to graze. **Known for:** vintage pub ambience; focus on seafood like chowders, lobster, and line-caught fish; mountain views. $ *Average main: NZ$34* ✉ *1 Avoca St.* ☎ *03/319–5037* ⊕ *www.thepierhotel.co.nz.*

★ The Store at Kekerengu

$$ | **CAFÉ** | This big, indoor/outdoor café/restaurant overlooking a rolling surf beach on State Highway 1 makes one of the best road stops in the area (maybe even the whole country). You can choose lunch from a selection of prepared dishes or order from the menu. **Known for:** location with wild coastal views and sprawling gardens and lawns; classic fish-and-chips; outdoor deck to enjoy the view while eating. $ *Average main: NZ$18* ✉ *5748 State Hwy. 1, Kekerengu* ⊹ *64 km (40 miles) south of Blenheim* ☎ *03/575–8600* ⊕ *www.thestore.kiwi* ⊘ *No dinner.*

 Hotels

Accommodations in Kaikoura are a mix of country lodge and motels, apartments, and holiday parks in town.

Alpine-Pacific Holiday Park

$$ | **HOTEL** | **FAMILY** | Just outside town, this nicely laid-out site has cabins, studios, and full motel units, plus powered campervan sites and campsites. **Pros:** incredibly clean, tidy outfit layered down a terraced slope; hot tubs and heated pool; bikes for rent. **Cons:** small site can be crowded when full; by main road so busy entrance/exit; no ocean views. $ *Rooms from: NZ$135* ✉ *69 Beach Rd.* ☎ *03/319–6275, 0800/692–322 free in New Zealand* ⊕ *alpine-pacific.co.nz* ⇆ *8 cabins, 4 studio units, 8 en suite studio units, 2 2-bedroom units, 50 campsites* ⏹ *No meals.*

★ Hapuku Lodge and Tree Houses

$$$$ | **HOTEL** | Luxurious tree houses are the star accommodations here, but there's also a main lodge with restaurant

and hotel-style rooms, plus the salubrious "Olive House Suite," featuring spacious dining, lounge, and bedroom areas and 360-degree views. **Pros:** unique luxury accommodations; surf out the back window and snow out the front; gourmet meals. **Cons:** stay in the main lodge if you can't manage stairs; out of town; tree house life not for everyone. $ *Rooms from: NZ$1150* ✉ *State Hwy. 1 at 1 Station Rd., 12 km (8 miles) north of Kaikoura* ☎ *03/319–6559, 0800/524–56872* ⊕ *www.hapukulodge.com* ⇆ *10 rooms* ⏹ *All-inclusive* ⊆ *Children not allowed in main lodge.*

Surfwatch Getaway Cottages

$$$ | **B&B/INN** | Perched high on the cliffs overlooking Mangamaunu Beach and just two minutes north of town, a private en suite room attached to the main house and a character-filled, self-contained garden cottage stand true to the name of this homey property. **Pros:** views from the B&B suite are exceptional; 5-acre property is also a small farm; lots of handcrafted furniture and wood detail. **Cons:** really steep access road; opens off a fast stretch of coastal highway so take care crossing the road; out of town. $ *Rooms from: NZ$230* ✉ *1137 State Hwy. 1, Mangamaunu* ☎ *03/319–6611* ⊕ *surf-watch.co.nz* ⇆ *2 rooms* ⏹ *Breakfast.*

The White Morph Heritage Collection

$$$ | **HOTEL** | **FAMILY** | A waterfront view is hard to ignore—even more so on the rugged Kaikoura coast—and this rather fancy apartment-style lodge is just across the road from the beach and a few minutes' walk from the town center. **Pros:** well-designed, comfortable units with a taste of luxury; breakfast available in the neighboring Encounter Café; great location on Esplanade close to cafés and shops. **Cons:** not all units have sea views; on a busy road; no elevator. $ *Rooms from: NZ$230* ✉ *92 The Esplanade* ☎ *03/319–5014* ⊕ *www.whitemorph. co.nz* ⇆ *50 rooms* ⏹ *No meals.*

Whale-watchers delight in spotting a whale in the waters near Kaikoura.

🏃 Activities

December to March are the most popular months for whale-watching and swimming with dolphins or seals. Book well in advance.

BIRD-WATCHING

⭐ Albatross Encounter

BIRD WATCHING | Kaikoura is one of the leading pelagic (oceangoing) bird-watching destinations in the world. It's also one of the most accessible, as the birds come close to shore to feed. These boat tours provide an intimate encounter with several albatross species and the Hutton's shearwater, which disperses all around the world yet breeds only in the Seaward Kaikoura Range. Tours last 2½ hours. Longer specialist tours are available by arrangement. ✉ *96 The Esplanade* 🕾 *03/319–6777, 0800/733–365* ⊕ *www. albatrossencounter.co.nz* ✍ *NZ$125.*

HIKING

Kaikoura Coast Track

HIKING/WALKING | This two-day walk provides uncrowded, unguided hiking

and two nights in rustic yet comfortable accommodations along spectacular coastal farmland. You'll explore high cliffs, sandy beaches, an ancient buried forest, forested valleys, open tussock country, and farmland. Take binoculars to search out seals and seabirds. Expect about 13 km (8 miles) of walking each day. Bags are transferred so you only need to carry a day pack. The walks operate between October and April, and reservations are essential. The start point is a ¾-hour drive south of Kaikoura; public transport can drop you at the gate. ✉ *356 Conway Flat Rd., Cheviot* 🕾 *03/319–2715* ⊕ *www.kaikouratrack.co.nz* ✍ *NZ$210 per person, including bag transfers. Inquire about all-inclusive meal prices.*

Kaikoura Peninsula Walkway

HIKING/WALKING | **FAMILY** | Here great coastal scenery from the cliff tops is mixed with likely close encounters with seal and seabird colonies. The southern entry point is at South Bay, while the first section to Limestone Bay is wheelchair accessible. The northern access point, by the Point Kean parking lot, is where you are most likely to encounter seals; they can move fast so keep a safe distance. There are short (five-minute) walks to lookout points, or you can walk one long circuit from town, right around the coastline (up to three hours). ☒ *Penisula Walkway* ⊕ *www.doc.govt.nz.*

RAFTING

Clarence River Rafting

WHITE-WATER RAFTING | The Clarence is one of New Zealand's most geologically interesting and beautiful wilderness rivers. It follows a fault line between the Inland and Seaward Kaikoura ranges, through tussock-covered hills covering ancient limestone. The 2016 earthquake actually reshaped the valley, forming new lakes and rapids, and adding huge interest to a river trip. This experienced local company is a good, safe option for you to explore these changes. They will organize the entire expedition, including gear, food, and access to the remote upper reaches. Half-day to multiday trips are offered. The rapids are "bouncy" up to grade two, and suitable for families. ☒ *3802 State Hwy. 1* ☎ *03/319–6993* ⊕ *www.clarenceriverrafting.co.nz* ⊘ *Closed May–Sept.*

SWIMMING WITH DOLPHINS AND SEALS

The dolphin- and seal-spotting opportunities are fantastic here. Although operators have led visitors to view and swim with dolphins and seals off the Kaikoura coast for years, and the animals may be familiar with boats, they are not tame. New Zealand fur seals are also common along this coast and, if you get into the water around the rock pools, you might spot crayfish. Pods of Dusky dolphins stay in the area year-round; you may even see them doing aerial jumps and flips.

Options to engage with seals and dolphins vary and operators will explain these before you book. These creatures live in the wild and all tours adhere strictly to Department of Conservation wildlife watching regulations. Some boat operators go quite a ways offshore, whereas others hug the coast. If you have any questions about the suitability of a trip, pipe up; these guys are happy to help. Guides can prime you with information on the local species and will be in the water with you. Wet suits and other gear are provided.

Dolphin Encounter

WILDLIFE-WATCHING | Swim with, or just watch from the boat, the Dusky dolphins that live around here. You'll be out in the deep ocean so you'll need to be confident in the water, and ideally have some snorkeling experience. All tours adhere strictly to marine mammal watching regulations. Tours operate three times a day through summer and twice a day in winter, but can be canceled due to bad weather so prepare to be flexible. There is heavy demand so book well ahead. ☒ *96 The Esplanade* ☎ *03/319–6777, 0800/733–365* ⊕ *www.dolphinencounter. co.nz* ☒ *From NZ$95.*

Point Kean Sea Colony

WILDLIFE-WATCHING | To see seals you can drive to this seal colony just outside of town on the northern side of the Kaikoura Peninsula. Watch the seals in their natural habitat, lying in the sun or playing in the kelp-filled shallows. These are wild animals and can move fast, so don't approach closer than 30 feet. With seabirds wheeling above and waves breaking along the shore, this is a powerful place just minutes from the main street. Follow Fyffe Quay to the colony at the end of the road. ☒ *Pt. Kean.*

★ Seal Swim Kaikoura

SWIMMING | New Zealand's original seal-swimming experience has both boat- and shore-based tours running daily from October to May. The swims (wetsuits and snorkels are provided) are in shallow, sheltered waters. You're virtually guaranteed to see New Zealand fur seals up close and your guides will tell you lots of interesting facts about them. If the seals don't want get off the rocks to play in the water with you, the guides won't disturb them, but will give you a 50% refund. ✉ *58 West End* ☎ *03/319–6182, 0800/732–579* ⊕ *www.sealswimkaikoura.co.nz* ✍ *From NZ$60.*

WHALE-WATCHING
★ **Whale Watch Kaikoura**
WHALE-WATCHING | Sperm whales feed closer to shore at Kaikoura than anywhere else in the world. Humpbacks, pilot whales, and orcas pass by on annual migrations. See these marine giants on specialist whale-watching cruises operated by local iwi (tribe) Ngai Tahu. All interactions with whales adhere strictly to marine mammal protection laws. Allow 3½ hours for the whole experience, 2¼ hours on the water. Check in at the Whaleway Station to be transported to your boat. Book well in advance. Should your tour miss seeing a whale, which is rare, you will get an 80% refund. No children under three are allowed.
■TIP➜ **Take motion-sickness pills if you suspect you'll need them; even in calm weather the sea around Kaikoura often has a sizable swell. Trips are subject to cancellation if the weather is particularly bad.** ✉ *Whaleway Station Rd.* ☎ *03/319–6767, 0800/655–121* ⊕ *www.whalewatch.co.nz* ✍ *NZ$150.*

Wings over Whales
WHALE-WATCHING | If you're in a hurry, take a half-hour whale-viewing flight with a guaranteed 95% success rate of spotting giant sperm whales and others that pass by. Your small, fixed-wing aircraft will drop to 450 feet for a closer view and your pilots will give an informative commentary. The scenic coastal flight is a bonus, and, of course, you won't get seasick. Also, the planes can often fly when it's too rough for the boats to go out. ✉ *Kaikoura Airfield, State Hwy. 1* ☎ *03/319–6580, 0800/226–629* ⊕ *www.whales.co.nz* ✍ *NZ$180; shuttle to airfield NZ$10 if required.*

Blenheim

29 km (18 miles) south of Picton, 120 km (73 miles) southeast of Nelson, 129 km (80 miles) north of Kaikoura.

Many people come to Blenheim (pronounced *bleh*-num by the locals) for the wine. There are dozens of wineries in the area, some with stylish cellar doors and restaurants, and Blenheim township is developing fast, though it still has a small-town veneer.

In 1973 the Montana (pronounced Mon-*taa*-na here) company paid two Californian wine authorities to investigate local grape-growing potential on a commercial scale. Both were impressed with what they found. It was the locals who were skeptical—until they tasted the first wines produced. After that, Montana opened the first modern winery in Marlborough in 1977, although there had been fledgling efforts over the past 100 years by pioneering wine growers. The region now has more than 100 vineyards and wineries. The Marlborough Wine and Food Festival held in mid-February each year celebrates the region's success in suitable style.

Don't bury your nose in a tasting glass entirely, though; the landscape shouldn't be overlooked. The vineyards sprawl across the large alluvial plains of the Wairau River, backed by mountains. From many points you can see Mt. Tapuae-o-Uenuku, which, at 9,465 feet, is the highest South Island mountain outside the Southern Alps. Blenheim is a 30-minute drive from the Marlborough Sounds to the north, and 90 minutes from the Nelson Lakes National Park to the west. Looking closer, you can walk off your winery excesses in the Wither Hills Farm Park on the southern side of town, where you can climb through open farmland for a wide view across the Wairau Plains.

GETTING HERE AND AROUND

Marlborough Airport (BHE), near Blenheim, is served by Air New Zealand, with several return flights daily from Wellington and Auckland. Local airline Sounds Air flies daily to and from Wellington to Marlborough Airport and to Picton's small Koromiko Airport (PCN).

InterCity runs daily between Christchurch, Picton, Blenheim, and Nelson. The ride between Christchurch and Blenheim takes about 4 to 5 hours, from Christchurch to Picton 5 to 6 hours, and from Picton to Nelson, about 2½ hours. At Blenheim, buses stop at the train station; at Picton, they use the ferry terminal. Once in Marlborough, if you're looking to explore the wineries you'll find them easily, on roads laid out more or less in a grid that extends from close to Blenheim and across the Wairau Plains. Rapaura Road is the central artery route for vineyard visits; wineries cluster around Jeffries and Jacksons roads, Fairhall, the area around Renwick village, the lower Wairau Valley, and State Highway 1 south of Blenheim. To access the Marlborough Sounds, take either the road to Picton, or head west on the main road to Nelson and turn off at Havelock. The main road inland from Renwick, that heads toward the West Coast, accesses Nelson Lakes National Park. ■TIP→ **Pick up a map of the Marlborough wine region at the Marlborough i-SITE Visitor Centre.**

FESTIVALS AND EVENTS

Garden Marlborough

FESTIVALS | Marlborough's climate and soils encourage great gardens and this is one of the country's most popular garden festivals. For five days in November you can wander through inspiring and beautifully kept gardens, and partake in workshops and social events. Watch the website for bookings; tickets go on sale at least a couple of months ahead. ☎ 03/577–5500, 0800/627–527 ⊕ www. gardenmarlborough.co.nz.

TOURS

Bubbly Grape Wine Tours

SPECIAL-INTEREST | With a choice of times, wineries, and lunch stops, these tours are about as flexible as you can get. There's no minimum number of people required, and if you're into chocolate, owner Kerry will take you to a boutique chocolatier as well. Options include the Sauvignon Blanc Blended Tour (half day), Special Reserve Tour (full day), and Gourmet Lunch Wine Tour (full day). Tour prices include wine tastings. Pickup from your accommodations can be arranged. ☎ 0800/228–2253 New Zealand only, 027/672–2195 ⊕ www.bubblygrape.co.nz ✉ From NZ$115.

Molesworth Tour Company

SPECIAL-INTEREST | Molesworth Station is the largest high-country farm in the country, covering almost 450,000 acres behind the Kaikoura Mountains, south of Blenheim, extending through remote and beautiful country. Tours are one to four days, traversing Molesworth and the neighboring Rainbow Station by luxury 4WD vehicle. Meet the farming families and share a meal, with optional stays at Hanmer Springs or a high-country homestead. There's also a four-day cycle tour, if you're feeling active. Pickups from Marlborough lodgings can be arranged. ✉ 50 State Hwy. 63, Renwick ☎ 03/572–8025, 027/435–1955 ⊕ www.molesworthtours. co.nz ✉ From NZ$500.

VISITOR INFORMATION

CONTACTS Blenheim i-SITE Visitor Centre. ✉ Blenheim Railway Station, 8 Sinclair St. ✛ Beside State Hwy. 1 ☎ 03/577–8080, 0800/777–181 ⊕ marlboroughnz.com.

 Sights

Marlborough is the flagship wine-growing region of New Zealand. Most famous for its Sauvignon Blancs, the region also produces top Chardonnays, Rieslings, and Pinot Noirs. Throughout Marlborough there are over 70 vineyards, many of

Around Blenheim

TO PICTON
& FERRY

0   1 miles
0   1 kilometers

TO NELSON
& HAVELOCK

Wairau River

Hunter's
Wines

Rapaura Rd.

Wairau
River Wines

Jeffries Rd.

The Vines
Village

Allan
Scott
Family
Winemakers

Cloudy Bay
Vineyards

Hammerichs Rd.

O'Dwyers Rd.

Grove Rd.

Opawa River

Bedford Rd.

Jackson's Rd.

Old Renwick   Rd.

RENWICK

Fromm
Winery

Middle Renwick Rd.

Boyce St.   High St.

Godfrey
Rd.

Highfield Estate

Bells Rd.

Batty Rd.

BLENHEIM

Main St.

Brancott Estate
Heritage Center

New Renwick Rd.
Aerodrome
Rd.

Wither Hills Winery & Restaurant

Omaka Aviation
Heritage Center

Brookby Rd.

Brancott Rd.

Maxwell Rd.

Redwood St.

TO
CHRISTCHURCH

which are open to the public and also offer fine cuisine. Wine buffs can also take a guided tour through the wineries, pick up a Wine Marlborough map (updated each year) from the i-SITE Visitor Centre, or visit Wine Marlborough (⊕ *www.wine-marlborough.co.nz*) for more information.

Allan Scott Family Winemakers

WINERY/DISTILLERY | One of the most respected Marlborough winemakers, Allen Scott launched his own company in 1990 and his whole family is now involved in the business. They make well-respected Sauvignon Blancs, Chardonnays, Pinot Gris, Pinot Noirs, methode traditionelle (try the Blanc de Blancs), Gewürztraminers, and Rieslings (the last two are particularly good). The cellar door adjoins the indoor-outdoor Twelve Trees Restaurant, which opens

out to a delightful herb garden. Marlborough salmon fillet and seafood chowder are menu classics (open for lunch only). ✉ *Jackson's Rd.* ☎ *03/572–9054* ⊕ *www. allanscott.com.*

Brancott Estate Heritage Centre

WINERY/DISTILLERY | This estate is worth a visit not only for its history (the region's first Sauvignon Blanc grapes were planted here), but also for the striking views across Wairau Valley, the excellent restaurant (lunch only), and, of course, the wines. Both the Sauvignon Blanc and Pinot Noir have merit. Brancott also supports preservation of the rare New Zealand falcon (which helps vineyards by keeping the mice at bay). A "Living Land Falcon Encounter" is offered here. You can also take a guided cycle tour through the vineyard. ✉ *180 Brancott Rd.,* *off New Renwick Rd.* ☎ *03/520–6975* ⊕ *www.brancottestate.com.*

Cloudy Bay Vineyards

WINERY/DISTILLERY | Since its first vintage in 1985, Cloudy Bay has produced first-class Sauvignon Blanc, along with a range that includes an equally impressive Pelorus sparkling, Chardonnays, Pinot Noirs, Rieslings, Pinot Gris, Gewürztraminers, and its unique barrel-aged Sauvignon Te Koko. Various tasting options are available, as are small plates of seasonal cuisine. Relax in the restful courtyard or dine alfresco at Jack's Raw Bar, which offers clams and oysters matched with house wines. ⊠ *230 Jackson's Rd.* ☎ *03/520–9147* ⊕ *www. cloudybay.co.nz.*

Fromm Winery

WINERY/DISTILLERY | Terroir over technology is the mantra at Fromm, one of Marlborough's smaller wineries known for its organic, sustainable growing principles. All grapes are handpicked. Fromm pioneered the local use of Pinot Noir and is also known for Syrah, Malbec, and Merlot reserves. Visitors can enjoy cheese and meat platters with their tastings while full lunch or dinner is available for groups by reservation. ⊠ *Godfrey Rd., Renwick* ☎ *03/572–9355* ⊕ *www. frommwinery.co.nz.*

Highfield Estate

WINERY/DISTILLERY | Sitting high on the Brookby Ridge, with spectacular views over the Wairau Plains, this winery is signposted by a Tuscany-inspired tower that visitors are welcome to climb. Highfield produces first-class Sauvignon Blanc, Pinot Noir, Chardonnay, and Riesling; their best, however, is a sparkling Elstree Cuvée Brut. You can relax and enjoy this magnificent setting in the Mediterranean-style Highfield Terra Vin Vineyard Restaurant, which opens for lunch daily. ⊠ *27 Brookby Rd., RD 2* ☎ *03/572–9244* ⊕ *www.highfield.co.nz.*

★ Hunter's Wines

GARDEN | Jane Hunter is an internationally respected winemaker and a pioneer of wine making in Marlborough. A visit to her wine cellar, a restored old farm house, is a delight. You can also savor a wine and artisan cheese and meat board in the 5-acre garden, an environmental showpiece for the rare native plants it protects. There's also a regular artist-in-residence on-site. Famous Hunter wines include the Kaho Roa (oak-aged Sauvignon Blanc), Pinot Noir, and the Miru Miru (Māori for bubbles). ⊠ *603 Rapaura Rd.* ☎ *03/572–8489, 0800/486–837 New Zealand only* ⊕ *www.hunters. co.nz.*

★ Omaka Aviation Heritage Centre

MUSEUM | FAMILY | War stories are brought to life with actual historic planes placed in settings dramatized by New Zealand's Oscar-winning special-effects teams Weta Digital and Wingnut Films. The planes are from famed director Sir Peter Jackson's collection. World War I–era planes, and the stories of their pilots, are showcased in the Knights of the Sky exhibition. Dangerous Skies focuses on aviation development during World War II. There's also a café and shop. ⊠ *Omaka Aerodrome, 79 Aerodrome Rd., off New Renwick Rd.* ☎ *03/579–1305* ⊕ *www. omaka.org.nz* ⊠ *Exhibitions from $20.*

The Vines Village

GARDEN | FAMILY | Artisan food and craft products are as classy as the local wines in these artisan shops that showcase wines alongside olive oils, fudge, homeware, quilts, ceramics, glassware, jewelry, and recipe books. Let the kids loose in the playground, or you can all just relax in the tranquil lakeside grounds. ⊠ *193 Rapaura Rd.* ☎ *03/579–5424* ⊕ *www. thevinesvillage.co.nz.*

Wairau River Wines

WINERY/DISTILLERY | Another Marlborough family institution, Phil and Chris Rose were among the first contract grape growers here. Now the family helps produce award-winning Sauvignon Blanc and other excellent varietals under their own label. The winery building is made from mud bricks and has two log-fires in winter; in summer you can relax on the sun-drenched lawns. Local produce features in the lunch restaurant adjacent to the cellar door. It's popular with the locals so reservations are recommended. ⊠ *Rapaura Rd. and State Hwy. 6* ☎ *03/572–9800* ⊕ *www. wairauriverwines.com.*

Wither Hills Winery & Restaurant
WINERY/DISTILLERY | From this impressive, three-story edifice of river rock, tiles, concrete, and wood, there's a commanding view across the Wairau Valley and the Wither Hills. Tastings include award-winning Sauvignon Blancs and Rieslings. At the popular winery restaurant, guests can relax at alfresco tables, lounge on beanbags on the lawn, or opt for more formal seating inside. A "wine library" consists of vines of wine grape varieties grown in New Zealand—30 of them lined up across the front of the winery. ⊠ *211 New Renwick Rd.* ☎ *03/520–8284* ⊕ *www.witherhills.co.nz.*

 Restaurants

Arbour
$$$$ | MODERN NEW ZEALAND | A friendly and very stylish eatery, Arbour is innovative and critically acclaimed yet so laid-back and hospitable. The quality produce is matched with quality local wine. **Known for:** degustation-style option for chef to create entire menu for you; dining in the kitchen alongside the chef; great desserts. $ *Average main: NZ$79* ⊠ *36 Godfrey Rd., Renwick* ☎ *03/572–7898* ⊕ *www.arbour.co.nz.*

Cafe Home
$ | CAFÉ | Every town needs a darn good café and this one is Blenheim's. The breakfast menu runs all day on the weekends, with all the standard Kiwi options like hotcakes, eggs, and muesli. **Known for:** big hot chocolates, fresh smoothies,

and great coffee; homemade cranberry and orange muesli; vegetarian breakfasts. $ *Average main: NZ$14* ⊠ *1C Main St.* ☎ *03/579–5040* ⊗ *No dinner.*

Dodson Street Beer Garden
$$ | NEW ZEALAND | In this cheery beer garden/restaurant, hearty ales and craft brews are matched with traditional German cuisine, pizzas, and Kiwi fare. If beer is your focus, you can also get a beer tasting tray. **Known for:** pork knuckles, goulash soup, strudels, and other German classics; huge tap beer selection; busy crowds. $ *Average main: NZ$19* ⊠ *1 Dodson St.* ☎ *03/577–8348* ⊕ *www. dodsonstreet.co.nz* ⊗ *Closed Mon.*

Saveur Cafe, Bistro and Patisserie
$$$ | NEW ZEALAND | Be it coffee and French pastries, mussels and clams, or wine for lunch and a full à la carte dinner, the European chef and owners at Saveur will treat you. Meals, from breakfast to dinner, are light, healthy, organic, and locally sourced when possible. **Known for:** riverside dining; patisserie on-site; French influence on top local produce. $ *Average main: NZ$28* ⊠ *6 Symons St.* ☎ *03/577–8822* ⊕ *www.saveur.co.nz.*

Scotch Wine Bar
$$$ | ECLECTIC | This contemporary-style wine bar offers evening dining with tapas plates and some larger main courses. The menu changes weekly to enable the freshest and most seasonal produce. **Known for:** cool black booths and brick decor; shared plates; 500-plus wines offered from temperature-controlled cellar. $ *Average main: NZ$21* ⊠ *26 Maxwell Rd.* ☎ *03/579–1176* ⊕ *www. scotchbar.co.nz* ⊗ *Closed Sun.*

🛏 Hotels

Chateau Marlborough
$$$ | HOTEL | The region's only Qualmark-rated five-star hotel offers a mix of suites, apartments, and studios, all luxuriously appointed, some with full

Continued on page 326

In recent decades New Zealand has emerged as a significant presence on the international wine stage. The country's cool, maritime climate has proven favorable for growing high-quality grapes, and winemakers now produce some of the world's best Sauvignon Blancs and Pinot Noirs, as well as excellent Chardonnays and Merlots.

Touring wineries in New Zealand is easy, as vineyards stretch virtually the entire length of the country, and most properties have tasting rooms with regular hours. Even if you just sample wines at a shop in Auckland, here's how to get the most out of your sipping experience.

(top) Pinot Noir grapes on a vine
(right) Rippon Vineyard, Lake Wanaka, Otago

Wines of
New Zealand

NEW ZEALAND WINES: THEN AND NOW

(top left) Nikola Nobilo was a New Zealand wine pioneer (right) Central Otago vineyard
(bottom left) Ripe Cabernet Sauvignon grapes

A BRIEF HISTORY

The first grapes were planted by missionaries on the North Island of New Zealand in 1819, and a British official (and hobbyist viticulturist) **James Busby** was the first to make wine almost 20 years later. For the next 150 years, the country's vineyards faced the significant challenges of powdery mildew and phylloxera, a root-killing louse.

New Zealand's modern-day wine production started in the 1970s, as European varietals were planted and started to show promise. Pioneers like Lebanese immigrant **Assid Corban** of Corbans Wines, and Croatian immigrants **Nikola Nobilo** of Nobilo and **Josip Babich** of Babich Wines settled in Henderson Valley, near Auckland, and helped shape the future of New Zealand wine production, innovating with cultured yeast, stainless steel tanks, and temperature-controlled fermentation, which have become widespread practices in many of the world's wine regions.

TODAY'S WINE SCENE

Ever since the country's Sauvignon Blancs captured the imagination of British wine critics at a major international tasting in 1985, wine drinkers worldwide have clamored for this crisp, fruity wine. New Zealand wines are now exported to 80 countries, with Australia biting a 20 percent chunk out of the export share, followed by the U.K. and the United States.

New Zealand is a long, narrow country of 1,000 miles between the north and south islands, with numerous microclimates and soil types, each suited to different varietals. Sauvignon Blanc is eminently well matched to the South Island, particularly Marlborough, while Chardonnay and Pinot Gris conveniently grow in most areas. Pinot Noir—NZ's most-planted red grape—and Riesling do best in Martinborough and on the South Island, with high-quality bottles coming from Marlborough, Nelson, Waipara, and Central Otago, the country's southernmost winegrowing area. Heavy-bodied red grapes like Cabernet Sauvignon, Merlot,

Grapevines at Fairmont Estate, a winery and vineyard in Gladstone, Wairarapa

Malbec, and Syrah excel in warmer Hawke's Bay and Auckland on the North Island.

As for the future, many winegrowers are playing around with new varieties, hoping to find the "next big thing." Gewürztraminer and Viognier are already well established, while varieties like Arneis and Grüner Veltliner are still rare. For red grapes, Sangiovese and Montepulciano show great promise, while Zinfandel and Tempranillo are making inroads.

Neudorf Vineyards, Nelson, produces several well-regarded wines

WHY DID NZ SWITCH FROM CORK?

The New Zealand Screwcap Initiative was formed in 2001 by the country's top producers who were concerned that their wines were being compromised by cork taint and premature oxidation. Even though the public eschewed the screwcap 10 years previously, the winemakers regarded the closure as an evolution in quality packaging. Now, more than 90 percent of New Zealand wines sport screwcaps, and customers worldwide are becoming accustomed to this type of bottle closure.

NZ SAUVIGNON BLANC

Sauvignon Blanc grapes

New Zealand is best known for its celebrated Sauvignon Blanc wines, but the varietal wasn't planted in the country until the 1970s.

In recent years, Sauvignon Blancs from Marlborough have become the worldwide benchmark for the varietal, with concentrated grassy, herbal, and floral notes. Compared to the Sauvignon Blancs of France, New Zealand's wines are more intensely perfumed, with fruitier flavors.

NEW ZEALAND'S WINE REGIONS

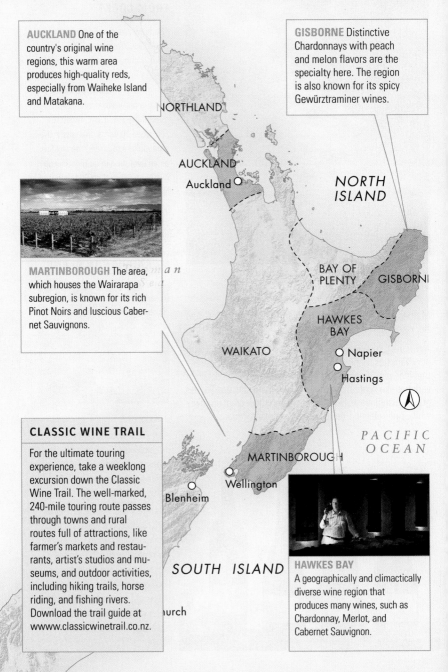

AUCKLAND One of the country's original wine regions, this warm area produces high-quality reds, especially from Waiheke Island and Matakana.

GISBORNE Distinctive Chardonnays with peach and melon flavors are the specialty here. The region is also known for its spicy Gewürztraminer wines.

NORTHLAND

AUCKLAND

Auckland

NORTH ISLAND

MARTINBOROUGH The area, which houses the Wairarapa subregion, is known for its rich Pinot Noirs and luscious Cabernet Sauvignons.

Tasman Sea

BAY OF PLENTY

GISBORNE

HAWKES BAY

WAIKATO

Napier

Hastings

CLASSIC WINE TRAIL

For the ultimate touring experience, take a weeklong excursion down the Classic Wine Trail. The well-marked, 240-mile touring route passes through towns and rural routes full of attractions, like farmer's markets and restaurants, artist's studios and museums, and outdoor activities, including hiking trails, horse riding, and fishing rivers. Download the trail guide at wwww.classicwinetrail.co.nz.

PACIFIC OCEAN

MARTINBOROUGH

Wellington

Blenheim

SOUTH ISLAND

urch

HAWKES BAY
A geographically and climactically diverse wine region that produces many wines, such as Chardonnay, Merlot, and Cabernet Sauvignon.

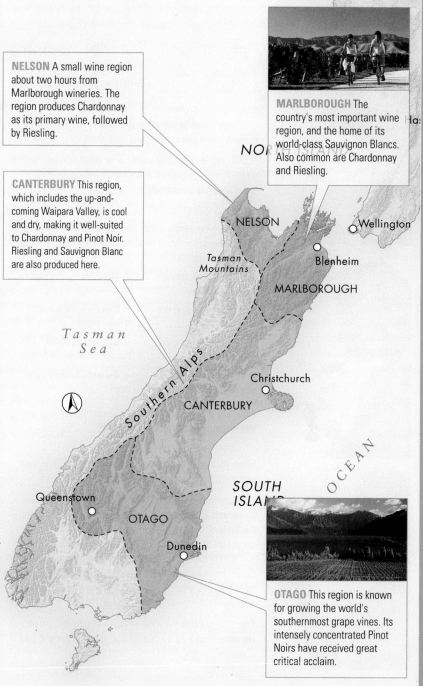

NELSON A small wine region about two hours from Marlborough wineries. The region produces Chardonnay as its primary wine, followed by Riesling.

MARLBOROUGH The country's most important wine region, and the home of its world-class Sauvignon Blancs. Also common are Chardonnay and Riesling.

CANTERBURY This region, which includes the up-and-coming Waipara Valley, is cool and dry, making it well-suited to Chardonnay and Pinot Noir. Riesling and Sauvignon Blanc are also produced here.

OTAGO This region is known for growing the world's southernmost grape vines. Its intensely concentrated Pinot Noirs have received great critical acclaim.

NORTH ISLAND

Ha

NELSON

Wellington

Tasman Mountains

Blenheim

MARLBOROUGH

Tasman Sea

Southern Alps

Christchurch

CANTERBURY

SOUTH ISLAND

OCEAN

Queenstown

OTAGO

Dunedin

WINE-TASTING PRIMER

Ordering and tasting wine—whether at a winery, bar, or restaurant—is easy once you master a few simple steps.

LOOK AND NOTE

Hold your glass by the stem and look at the wine in the glass. Note its color, depth, and clarity.

For whites, is it greenish, yellow, or gold? For reds, is it purplish, ruby, or garnet? Is the wine's color pale or deep? Is the liquid clear or cloudy?

SWIRL AND SNIFF

Swirl the wine gently in the glass to intensify the scents, then sniff over the rim of the glass. What do you smell? Try to identify aromas like:

- **Fruits**—citrus, peaches, berries, figs, melon

- **Flowers**—orange blossoms, honey, perfume

- **Spices**—baking spices, pungent, herbal notes

- **Vegetables**—fresh or cooked, herbal notes

- **Minerals**—earth, steely notes, wet stones

- **Dairy**—butter, cream, cheese, yogurt

- **Oak**—toast, vanilla, coconut, tobacco

- **Animal**—leathery, meaty notes

Are there any unpleasant notes, like mildew or wet dog, that might indicate that the wine is "off"?

SIP AND SAVOR

Prime your palate with a sip, swishing the wine in your mouth. Then spit in a bucket or swallow.

Take another sip and think about the wine's attributes. Sweetness is detected on the tip of the tongue, acidity on the sides of the tongue, and tannins (a mouth-drying sensation) on the gums. Consider the body—does the wine feel light in the mouth, or is there a rich sensation? Are the flavors consistent with the aromas? If you like the wine, try to pinpoint what you like about it, and vice versa if you don't like it.

Take time to savor the wine as you're sipping it—the tasting experience may seem a bit scientific, but the end goal is your enjoyment.

WINE & FOOD PAIRING

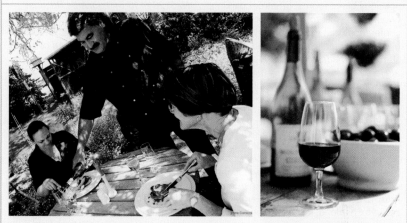

Hospitality is a core value in Maori society, something you'll encounter in wineries and eateries

New Zealand cuisine is influenced by Pacific Rim, Asian, and European flavors and traditions. The diversity of the cuisine and its wide variety of ingredients—beef, lamb, venison, pork, poultry, and seafood—makes for a number of interesting food and wine pairings.

Sauvignon Blanc is delicious with shellfish and seafood, summer herbs, feta cheese, and salad greens.

Pinot Noir complements mushroom-based dishes. Lighter wines are best paired with tuna and salmon, while heavier wines suit lamb, duck, venison, and game.

Cabernet Sauvignon and **Merlot** work well with steaks and minted lamb.

Chardonnay goes well with rock lobster.

Pinot Gris matches beautifully with fresh salmon.

Riesling suits South Pacific-influenced dishes, such as seafood with coconut and lime.

Gewürztraminer is especially suited to lightly spiced Asian cuisine.

THE VISITING EXPERIENCE

Many wineries have tasting rooms where wines can be sampled for free or for a nominal fee. Facilities vary from grandiose buildings to rustic barns. Most larger wineries are open daily, all year round, while boutique vintners may close from Easter until Labour Weekend (end of October). If a winery is closed, you may still be able to make an appointment. Regional winegrower associations publish wine trail guides detailing opening hours and other attractions, such as tours, dining options, and vineyard accommodations. Pick up a guide at a visitors center or local wine shop.

(Left) A tour of Marlborough vineyards could last for three hours to three days, depending on your stamina kitchens, dining areas, and laundry. **Pros:** spacious guest rooms; off-street parking; two-minute walk to town center. **Cons:** conferences can make it a busy spot; big complex; feels a bit jammed into the site. ⓢ *Rooms from: NZ$230* ⊠ *High St. at Henry St.* ☎ *03/578–0064* ⊕ *www. marlboroughnz.co.nz* ⤳ *80 rooms* ⏺ *No meals.*

The Marlborough Lodge

$$$$ | **ALL-INCLUSIVE** | Drive the lavender-lined driveway and you'll come to this 1901-built Victorian convent, now a luxury boutique lodge, with beautifully decorated suites, rambling lawns, and gardens. **Pros:** 16 acres of vineyard and rambling, beautiful gardens; located in the heart of Marlborough wine country; handmade truffles on turn-down, muffins to take at check-out. **Cons:** only downstairs rooms are easily accessible to guests with limited mobility; out in the country; beverage list could be more varied. ⓢ *Rooms from: NZ$1500* ⊠ *776 Rapaura Rd., RD 3* ☎ *03/570–5700* ⊕ *www.themarlborough-lodge.co.nz* ⤳ *10 suites* ⏺ *All-inclusive.*

Marlborough Vintners Hotel

$$ | **HOTEL** | Nestled on 6 acres of landscaped grounds, each of the 16 suites in the contemporary Tuscan-style villas enjoys views of the vineyards and gardens. **Pros:** delightful vineyard and Wither Hills views; self-contained restaurant on-site; good gym. **Cons:** country location not for everyone; weddings and small conferences can bring a crowd; no shops handy. ⓢ *Rooms from: NZ$185* ⊠ *190 Raupara Rd.* ☎ *03/572–5094* ⊕ *www. mvh.co.nz* ⤳ *16 suites* ⏺ *No meals.*

St. Leonards Vineyard Cottages

$$$ | **HOTEL** | **FAMILY** | This rural retreat comes with five self-contained cottages dotted around an expansive rambling garden and surrounded by vineyards. **Pros:** sheep, deer, and chickens to amuse the kids; each accommodation is in a private setting; tennis and petanque courts. **Cons:** have to drive to get to area restaurants; no shops nearby; might be too rural for some. ⓢ *Rooms from: NZ$220* ⊠ *18 St. Leonards Rd., just off State Hwy. 6, 3 km (2 miles) from Blenheim* ☎ *03/577–8328* ⊕ *www.stleonards.co.nz* ⤳ *5 self-contained cottages* ⏺ *Breakfast.*

Picton

29 km (18 miles) north of Blenheim, 110 km (69 miles) east of Nelson.

The maritime township of Picton (population 4,000) is a popular boating spot and has two sizable marinas, the smaller at Picton Harbour and the much larger at nearby Waikawa Bay. There's plenty to do in town, with crafts markets in summer, cafés and bars, historical sites, and museums (including one on a boat), and walking tracks through bushy scenic reserves to beaches and gorgeous lookouts over the Sounds. The Picton foreshore is a delightful parklike area looking up into Queen Charlotte Sound. It's a nice spot to wait for your ferry to the North Island, and to watch the comings and goings of smaller pleasure craft and water taxis.

GETTING HERE AND AROUND

Picton lies at the head of Queen Charlotte Sound and is the arrival point for ferries from the North Island, and summer-visiting international cruise ships. The town is the base for services and transport by water taxi to the popular Queen Charlotte Track, and to remote communities in the vast area of islands, inlets, and peninsulas of Queen Charlotte Sound.

Visitors from the North Island can take the Interislander or Bluebridge ferry from Wellington to Picton. Ferries dock in Picton wharf.

TOURS

Beachcomber Cruises

BOAT TOURS | Scheduled daily scenic and eco-cruises run throughout Queen

Many of New Zealand's wineries also come with picturesque scenery.

Charlotte Sound and include the Mail Boat cruise, which explores all the way to the outer reaches. Help deliver mail and supplies to families living in these wild, remote spots. They can also take you to the Queen Charlotte Walkway for one-day or longer unguided walks and bike rides. Boats depart from the Picton waterfront throughout the day (tours, times, and prices vary according to the time of year; check the website). ☒ *London Quay, The Waterfront* ☎ *03/573–6175, 0800/624–526* ⊕ *www.beachcombercruises.co.nz* ⬚ *From NZ$81.*

Cougar Line

BOAT TOURS | Several water taxi trips operate daily through the Queen Charlotte Sound, dropping passengers (sightseers included) at accommodations and private homes. Scenic cruises range from three-hour morning and afternoon cruises to shorter trips for passengers in a hurry. Also on offer are walking/cruise combos, an early bird eco-cruise to Motuara Island bird sanctuary, and transport for Queen Charlotte Track walkers. Recommended

is the Twilight Fish and Chips cruise. Reservations for all trips are essential at peak times and recommended at others. ☒ *The Waterfront* ☎ *03/573–7925, 0800/504–090* ⊕ *www.cougarline.co.nz* ⬚ *From NZ$85.*

★ Seafood Odyssea Cruise

BOAT TOURS | Cruise to a salmon farm on Queen Charlotte Sound on board the Marlborough Tour Company's 65-foot catamaran MV *Odyssea*. Enjoy a taste of smoked salmon and locally farmed oysters, washed down with a top Sauvignon Blanc. Three-and-a-half-hour afternoon cruises depart daily at 1:30 (October to April, otherwise four days a week), from Picton Marina. ☒ *London Quay* ☎ *03/577–9997, 0800/990–800 New Zealand only* ⊕ *www.marlborough-tourcompany.co.nz* ⬚ *NZ$155.*

Sounds Connection

SPECIAL-INTEREST | If you like drinking wine and/or catching fish, let these folks guide you. Full-day and half-day tours are offered to Marlborough's most renowned wineries—and others less well known.

The Gourmet Experience tour (November through April) combines a wine-and-food appreciation tour with behind-the-scenes glimpses and a four-course, wine-matched lunch. They also offer half-day and longer fishing charters in the Sounds with third-generation fishing guides. ✉ *94 Wellington St.* ☎ *03/573–8843, 0800/742–866* ⊕ *www.soundsconnection.com* ✉ *From NZ$85.*

CONTACTS Picton i-SITE Visitor Centre. ✉ *Picton Foreshore* ☎ *03/520–3113* ⊕ *marlboroughnz.com.*

 # Sights

Edwin Fox Maritime Museum

HISTORIC SITE | The preserved hulk of the *Edwin Fox* demonstrates just how young New Zealand's European settlement is. The ship was used in the Crimean War, transported convicts to Australia, and brought settlers to New Zealand. Now dry-docked, it serves as a museum, bringing to life the conditions the early immigrants faced. ✉ *Dunbar Wharf* ☎ *03/573–6868* ⊕ *www.edwinfoxsociety.com* ✉ *NZ$15.*

Lochmara

LOCAL INTEREST | **FAMILY** | Take the short boat ride out to explore this delightful café, lodge, wildlife refuge, and art studio on the shore of Lochmara Bay. Follow the bushwalks to see native gecko and the *kakariki* (a native parrot) being nurtured here as part of the Lodge's wildlife recovery program. There's a pampering spa room and bathhouse above the beach, galleries of local art, and a sculpture trail. Artists-in-residence sometimes work here. Four-star chalets are suitable for couples and families, if you plan to stay longer. ✉ *Lochmara Bay, Queen Charlotte Sound* ☎ *03/573–4554* ⊕ *www.lochmara.co.nz.*

Picton Heritage and Whaling Museum

MUSEUM | Picton's seafaring history is captured with a wealth of memorabilia showcased in this quaint and worthy museum. The area was first a key Māori settlement called Waitohi, then an important whaling and sealing location for European immigrants in the early 19th century. Until 1860, all trade and travel was done by sea. ✉ *London Quay* ☎ *03/573–8283* ⊕ *www.pictonmuseum-newzealand.com* ✉ *NZ$5.*

Queen Charlotte Drive

SCENIC DRIVE | The main road out of Picton, State Highway 1, heads directly to Blenheim. If you're heading west toward Havelock and Nelson, and don't mind a slower, though much more scenic, route, Queen Charlotte Drive is for you. From Picton the drive climbs the hill to the west of the town, then winds in and out of bays along the edge of Queen Charlotte Sound. Governor's, Momorangi, and Ngakuta bays are gorgeous spots for a picnic. The drive then cuts across to Pelorus and Keneperu sounds, and follows the water's edge to Havelock township. Cullen Point, a short walk near the Havelock end of the drive, leads to a good lookout point across Pelorus Sound. From Havelock you join State Highway 6, which leads to Nelson.

Pelorus Bridge Scenic Reserve

BODY OF WATER | Halfway between both Picton and Nelson, and Blenheim and Nelson, on State Highway 6 is this remnant of the native lowland forests that once covered this whole region. Easy walking trails explore the beech, *podocarp* (a species of evergreen), and broadleaf trees. In summer the river is warm enough (just) for swimming (watch for the sand flies). There's also a rare colony of endangered long-tailed native bats that come to play round the streetlight at the bridge at night. This is an utterly delightful place to take a pause, especially with a campground and café both in

A launch cuts a swathe through the calm waters of Queen Charlotte Sound.

the vicinity. ⊠ *Pelorus Bridge, State Hwy. 6, Havelock* ⊕ *www.doc.govt.nz.*

 Restaurants

Le Café

$$$ | **CAFÉ** | Sitting outside Le Café on the waterfront you can look right down Queen Charlotte Sound and watch the local boats and the big Cook Strait ferries coming and going. Staff source organic, local, and free-range foods wherever possible—your fish was probably landed on the wharf at the end of the street and, if it's beef, they reckon they know the farmer. **Known for:** great coffee; edgy vibe; Continental European classics at dinner. ⑤ *Average main: NZ$26* ⊠ *London Quay* ☎ *03/573–5588* ⊕ *www. lecafepicton.co.nz.*

Cafe Cortado

$$$ | **CAFÉ** | A blend of South American and Mediterranean influences are paired with top Marlborough wines and craft range beers at this prime waterfront spot. The fresh breakfasts will sufficiently fuel you up for a day out on the Sounds. **Known for:** good selection of tapas; pizzas and breakfast burritos; sustainable sourcing. ⑤ *Average main: NZ$28* ⊠ *Corner of High St. and London Quay* ☎ *03/573– 5630* ⊕ *cafecortado.co.nz.*

Seumus' Irish Picton

$$$ | **IRISH** | This place definitely has the classic Irish bar vibe. Irish locals confirm they pour a good Guinness, plus there's lots of live music; it's not all Celtic, but it will get your toes tapping regardless. **Known for:** classic Irish pub menu; beef burgers and fries; Sunday roasts. ⑤ *Average main: NZ$25* ⊠ *25 Wellington St.* ☎ *03/573–5050* ⊕ *www.seumusirishbar. co.nz* ⊗ *Closed Mon. and Tues.*

Hotels

Bay of Many Coves

$$$$ | **RESORT** | A contemporary-designed luxury waterfront lodge built to complement the surrounding native bush and seascape. **Pros:** idyllic spot in a sheltered, iconic Marlborough Sounds

location; great views from every unit; health spa on-site. **Cons:** boat or foot access only; minimum stay requirement for two weeks over Christmas; built on a hillside so steepish paths (guests can request a golf cart); dining shared with day visitors. ⑤ *Rooms from: NZ$900* ✉ *Bay of Many Coves, Queen Charlotte Sound* ☎ *03/579–9771, 0800/579–9771* ⊕ *www.bayofmanycoves.co.nz* ⤳ *11 1–3 bedroom apartments* ⑪ *No meals.*

Jasmine Court Travellers Inn

$$ | HOTEL | Stylish, well-sized guest rooms, with kitchenettes and en suite bathrooms, overlook the town to the main harbor. **Pros:** bike and luggage storage if you're off to walk the Queen Charlotte Track; handy for an early morning ferry sailing; parking outside your door. **Cons:** often full in summer; kids by arrangement only; units a bit jammed into a small area. ⑤ *Rooms from: NZ$185* ✉ *78 Wellington St.* ☎ *03/573–7110, 0800/421–999* ⊕ *www.jasminecourt. co.nz* ⤳ *19 rooms* ⑪ *No meals.*

Sennen House

$$$$ | B&B/INN | Private, boutique accommodation in an 1886 Victorian villa, this is one of Picton's most historic homes. **Pros:** two apartments have full kitchens and three have kitchenettes; sense of history; understated luxury. **Cons:** ask for the downstairs rooms if you have limited mobility; short winter close-down that varies year to year; no children under 13. ⑤ *Rooms from: NZ$370* ✉ *9 Oxford St.* ⊕ *Follow western part of Oxford St. from Nelson Sq., crossing 2 roads, to reach property* ☎ *03/573–5216* ⊕ *www.sennen-house.co.nz* ⤳ *4 suites and apartments* ⑪ *Breakfast.*

Whatamonga Homestay

$$$$ | B&B/INN | These are purpose-built guest apartments. **Pros:** quiet and private; magnificent Marlborough Sounds environment with great views; friendly hosts share their kayaks and barbecue, for example. **Cons:** minimum two-night stay; particularly steep driveway with

concealed exit; away from township, need a vehicle. ⑤ *Rooms from: NZ$390* ✉ *425 Port Underwood Rd., Waikawa Bay* ☎ *03/573–7193* ⊕ *www.whsl.co.nz* ⤳ *2 apartments, 2 rooms* ⑪ *Breakfast.*

🏃 Activities

★ E-Ko Tours

WILDLIFE-WATCHING | Swim with or watch dolphins with this knowledgeable Department of Conservation permitted company. Rare Hector dolphins, plus bottlenose, Dusky, and common dolphins all frequent the Sounds. Orcas sometimes visit. Or engage with the prolific birdlife on Motuara Island, an island wildlife reserve and home to rare and endangered species. Walk to the top of the island for a great view of the Sounds. Tour options include Dolphin Swim and View, Motuara Island Bird Sanctuary and Dolphin Cruise, and Bird Watchers Expedition, including close-up encounters with King Shags. ✉ *The Waterfront, Picton Foreshore* ☎ *03/573–8040, 0800/9453–5433* ⊕ *www.e-ko.nz* ✉ *From NZ$99.*

★ Marlborough Sounds Adventure Company

SPECIAL-INTEREST | Kayaking, walking, biking, or all three, guided or independent, half-day or multiday trip—it's your choice with this local company of soft adventure pioneers. Their signature fully guided three-day trip combines walking, biking, and kayaking with meals and high-quality lodging taken care of, and your luggage ferried ahead each day. The trip kicks off weekly from November through April. Other guided and independent options are available with all logistics taken care of, some including an ecotour of Motuara Island en route to the Queen Charlotte Track. ✉ *The Waterfront* ☎ *03/573–6078* ⊕ *www.marlboroughsounds.co.nz* ✉ *From NZ$995 for 3-day trip.*

HIKING

★ Queen Charlotte Track

TRAIL | Picton is the entryway to the Queen Charlotte Track, which stretches 70 km (44 miles) along peninsulas, around inlets, and on ridgetops, playing hide-and-seek with the Marlborough Sounds along the way. The Department of Conservation provides a few camping areas, but there is also a variety of other accommodations, including backpacker hostels, lodges, and plush resorts. (Booking ahead is advised.) Boat companies Cougar Line or Beachcomber Cruises can drop you at various places for one- to four-day walks (guided or unguided). You can also mountain-bike on this track—it's the longest single track ride in New Zealand. (The outermost section, Ship Cove to Keneperu Sound, is closed to bikes from December 1 to February 28.) The boat companies can deliver and retrieve you and your bike to points along the track. For walkers and bikers they'll also carry your luggage between overnight stops. Some of the track passes through private land. Track users must buy a Queen Charlotte Track Pass, which contributes toward track maintenance. ■TIP→ **Though it's relatively easy to access, the track shouldn't be taken lightly.** It has steep inclines and long drop-offs, and the weather can be unpredictable. The track gets busy in summer, it is also part of Te Araroa, the Long Pathway walking trail that runs the length of New Zealand. ⊕ *www.qctrack.co.nz.*

KAYAKING

A great way to experience the Marlborough Sounds is by sea kayak—and the mostly sheltered waters of Queen Charlotte Sound are perfect for it.

★ Wilderness Guides

KAYAKING | These local experts offer guided walking, kayaking, and mountain-biking trips exploring the glorious Marlborough Sounds. Day and multiday trips are available, including fully catered and guided inn-to-inn walking or biking on the Queen Charlotte Track. (Booking ahead is essential.) Alternatively, they'll set you off to walk independently, organizing your accommodation and water taxi transport; the price varies depending on the standard of accommodation you choose. Or you can just hire their guiding expertise for a day walk, half-day kayak, or combinations of walking, kayaking, and biking. ✉ *Picton Waterfront* ☎ *03/573–5432, 0800/266–266 toll-free in New Zealand* ⊕ *www.wildernessguidesnz.com* ☞ *From NZ$99 for ½-day guided kayak tour of Queen Charlotte Sound.*

Havelock

35 km (22 miles) west of Picton.

Known as the Greenshell mussel capital of the world (Greenshells are a variety of green-lipped mussel), Havelock is at the head of Pelorus and Keneperu sounds, and trips on the Pelorus Sound mail boat, *Pelorus Express,* depart from here. Pelorus Sound is larger than Queen Charlotte Sound but less accessible by commercial craft. Small, waterside Havelock (population 400) is a pretty place to stroll; check out the busy little marina, shop in the few arts and crafts shops, and enjoy those mussels.

TOURS

Greenshell Mussel Cruise

BOAT TOURS | **FAMILY** | This cruise takes you into the largely untouched Kenepuru and Pelorus sounds, home of the world's largest Greenshell mussel farms. Your skipper will cruise to the black buoys that mark the farms, pull up ropes covered in great swathes of clinging mussels, and harvest them for your gourmet delight. You can enjoy the mussels onboard, steamed gently and washed down with a Marlborough Sauvignon Blanc. You'll also hear about the pioneering history of the region. Transfers are available from Blenheim and Picton. ☎ *03/577–9997, 0800/990–800 New Zealand only*

⊕ *www.marlboroughtourcompany.co.nz* ✉ *NZ$135.*

Pelorus Mail Boat

BOAT TOURS | The Pelorus Express is a sturdy launch that makes a daylong trip around Pelorus Sound, delivering mail and supplies to residents, as it has since 1918. This is an excellent way to discover the waterway and meet the locals. You might also see dolphins, King shags, and a mussel farm. The boat leaves from Havelock daily November through April and on Monday, Wednesday, and Friday from May through October. Reservations advised in summer. Bring your lunch; there is tea and coffee onboard. ✉ *Havelock Marina 1* ☎ *03/574–1088* ⊕ *www. themailboat.co.nz* ✉ *NZ$132.*

🍴 Restaurants

The Mussel Pot

$$ | **SEAFOOD** | **FAMILY** | The locally farmed mussels are the star in this quirky café although the other meals like fish, burgers, pastas, and salads, all served with local wines and craft beers, are also good. As for the mussels, you can order them steamed or grilled with amazing flavors and toppings. **Known for:** steamed mussels; mussel chowder; fish-and-chips. ⑤ *Average main: NZ$20* ✉ *73 Main Rd.* ☎ *03/574–2824* ⊕ *www.themussel-pot.co.nz.*

★ Pelorus Bridge Café

$ | **CAFÉ** | This is one of the better on-the-road cafés in the area. Friendly locals serve great breakfasts and wholesome, homemade lunches to both passersby and the campers in the adjacent DOC Campsite. **Known for:** homemade pies; alfresco tables in beautiful bush setting; busy crowds in summer. ⑤ *Average main: NZ$9* ✉ *State Hwy. 6, by Pelorus Bridge* ☎ *03/571–6019* ⊕ *www.doc.govt. nz.*

Slip Inn

$$$ | **CAFÉ** | An all-day café down at the marina, Slip Inn comes with a large deck overlooking the main boat ramp and working port area. The menu is all about local produce; mussels and salmon are sourced from the Sounds, along with breakfasts, antipasto, and a comprehensive dinner selection. **Known for:** mussel platters; waterfront views and ambience; big, wholesome breakfasts. ⑤ *Average main: NZ$25* ✉ *Havelock Marina* ☎ *03/574–2345* ⊕ *www.slipinn.co.nz.*

🛏 Hotels

Raetihi Lodge

$$$$ | **HOTEL** | This grand old lodge has been given a thorough overhaul and overlooks the forest-covered hills and waterfront. **Pros:** absolute peace, quiet, and tranquility; in-house massage therapist; boating, country golf, or walking on nearby tracks all leisure options. **Cons:** not easy to access in a hurry; hotel dining is your only option here; birdsong might wake you early. ⑤ *Rooms from: NZ$330* ✉ *7124 Keneperu Rd., Keneperu Sound* ☎ *03/573–4300* ⊕ *raetihilodge.co.nz* ⊙ *Closed Apr.–Oct.* ⟿ *14 rooms.*

Nelson

116 km (73 miles) west of Blenheim.

Relaxed, hospitable, and easy to explore on foot, Nelson has a way of always making you feel as though you should stay longer. You can make your way around the mostly two-story city in a day, poking into craft galleries and stopping at cafés, but two days is a practical minimum. You can also use Nelson as a base for a variety of activities within an hour's drive of the city itself.

GETTING HERE AND AROUND

Nelson Airport (NSN) is a small regional airport 10 km (6 miles) south of the city center. **Air New Zealand** links Nelson with Christchurch, Auckland, and Wellington a number of times each day. **Sounds Air** flies to and from Wellington three

Greenshell mussels are Havelock's specialty.

times a day with a scenic, low-level flight over the Marlborough Sounds, weather permitting. **Origin Air** connects Nelson with Palmerston North, Napier, and New Plymouth. **Jetstar** links Nelson with Wellington and Auckland.

Geographically Nelson is quite isolated, and you'll climb a range of hills to approach from any direction. It's a 2½-hour drive from Westport, 5½ hours from Christchurch via the Lewis Pass, and 2 hours from Blenheim. From Nelson, head west to Motueka and on to reach Abel Tasman Park, Golden Bay, and Kahurangi National Park. There is a big hill to climb to reach Golden Bay but the road is good, and it's well worth the trip.

InterCity buses run daily services between Christchurch, Blenheim, Nelson, and the West Coast.

ScenicNZ Abel Tasman runs from Nelson to Motueka and to Kaiteriteri and Marahau, gateways to Abel Tasman National Park. **Golden Bay Coachlines** run from Nelson and Motueka to Golden Bay

townships, and provide access to Abel Tasman National Park and Kahurangi National Park.

Many of the smaller routes cut their service frequency in winter, so double-check the schedules.

AIRPORT Nelson Airport. ✉ *Trent Dr.* ☎ *03/547–3199* ⊕ *www.nelsonairport. co.nz.*

AIRPORT TRANSFERS Super Shuttle. ☎ *03/547–5782, 0800/748–885* ⊕ *www. supershuttle.co.nz.*

BUS CONTACTS Golden Bay Coachlines. ☎ *03/525–8352* ⊕ *www.goldenbaycoa-chlines.co.nz.* **ScenicNZ Abel Tasman.** ☎ *03/548–0285* ⊕ *www.scenicnzabeltas-man.co.nz.*

BUS DEPOT Bus Depot Nelson. ✉ *27 Bridge St.* ☎ *03/548–3290.*

TOURS
Bay Tours Nelson
SPECIAL-INTEREST | Local, knowledgeable guides run daily half- and full-day tours of wine trails, craft breweries,

arts-and-crafts tours, plus scenic adventure and custom-designed tours by arrangement. Wine tours can include tastings and platters or full lunches, depending on your preference. ☎ *03/540–3873, 0800/229–868* ⊕ *www.baytours-nelson.co.nz* ✉ *From NZ$120, including wine tastings.*

Nelson Tours & Travel

DRIVING TOURS | Learn about the region's wines, winemakers, and artisan food producers with local guide (and fledgling winemaker) CJ. He offers a five-hour tour of selected local wineries. He'll also take you to the Marlborough vineyards, combine both regions into one tour, or customize tours to suit any special interests you might have. ☎ *0800/222–373 New Zealand only, 027/237–5007* ⊕ *www.nelsontoursandtravel.co.nz* ✉ *From NZ$120.*

Wine Art and Wilderness

GUIDED TOURS | Premium, fully catered gourmet tours explore the Nelson region's wine, art, and wilderness. Your host Noel is a true wine buff, plus he knows several local artists, and will take you into their homes and studios. He once worked for the Department of Conservation and is licensed to guide in all three of the region's national parks. Whatever your interest, he has many options for full day tours—check the website for the full line-up. ☎ *0800/326–868* ⊕ *www.wineartandwilderness.co.nz* ✉ *From $325.*

VISITOR INFORMATION

CONTACTS Nelson i-SITE Visitor Centre.
✉ *77 Trafalgar St. at Halifax St.* ☎ *03/548–2304* ⊕ *www.nelsonnz.com.*

⊙ Sights

Once you arrive in Nelson get your bearings at the visitor center on the corner of Trafalgar and Halifax streets. The heart of town is farther up **Trafalgar Street,** between Bridge Street and the cathedral steps, also home to the region's museum. This area is lined with shops, and

the block between Hardy Street and the cathedral steps is a sunny spot to enjoy a coffee. Lively Nelson Markets (produce and arts) are held at the Montgomery parking lot on weekend mornings (used goods and crafts) and on Wednesday you'll find the Nelson Farmers Market selling fresh produce in Morrison Square. There are a few art stores and galleries on Nile Street, too. For a dose of greenery, the **Queens Gardens** are on Bridge Street between Collingwood and Tasman. You will find yourself, literally, in the center of New Zealand in this park.

A five-minute drive around the waterfront from town, Tahunanui Beach offers some of the safest swimming in the country. This long, open beach is perfect for watching the sky change during the sunset and is a favorite spot for paddleboarders and kite-boarders, with its rollicking summer sea breeze. There are also several bars and cafés here, and one of the country's largest campgrounds.

Seventy years ago the first potters were drawn by the abundant clays in the hills of the hinterlands. Over the decades not only potters, but painters, ceramicists, glass artists, and mixed-media practitioners have continued to enjoy the climate, colors, and inspiring light of the region. Many artists continue to work in Nelson and Golden Bay and the locally published *Nelson Arts Guide* is at local visitor centers, bookshops, some hotels and cafés, and online. See ⊕ *www.nelsonartsguide.co.nz.*

Boulder Bank

NATURE SITE | A defining Nelson landscape feature is the 13-km (8-mile) natural stone bank, built from eroding cliffs farther north along the coast. The sheltered harbor the bank created is essentially the reason the region was first settled by Māori. Later an entry was cut through the boulders to allow larger ships into the harbor. A lighthouse on the Boulder Bank guided ships from the 1860s until the 1980s. As you look across from the

KEY

- ❶ Sights
- ❶ Restaurants
- ❶ Hotels

Nelson waterfront consider that for 27 years a lighthouse keeper, his wife, and 10 children lived there on the isolated bank. ⊠ Boulder Bank Dr.

The Suter Art Gallery Te Aratoi o Whakatu

MUSEUM | An impressive gallery for its size, Suter was bequeathed to the city of Nelson by Bishop Suter in 1899. In 1916 the gallery was significantly redeveloped and expanded. Collections include the watercolors of 19th-century artist John Gully; works of local Sir Toss Woollaston, a Nelson and New Zealand pioneer of modern art; British Modernism works by various artists; and ceramic pieces from local, nationally renowned artists. Visiting exhibitions change regularly. The gallery's popular café looks out over neighboring Queen's Gardens. ⊠ 208 Bridge St. ☎ 03/548–4699 ⊕ www.thesuter.org.nz.

Te Pupuri Taonga O Te Tai Ao (Nelson Provincial Museum)

MUSEUM | On the site of New Zealand's first museum, the city's provincial museum explores the first Māori residents and early European settlements, the city's development as a port, and general events that shaped the region. Exhibits include a rare collection of Māori musical instruments. There are heritage pieces donated from private collections, and regular visiting exhibitions. ⊠ Hardy St. and Trafalgar St. ☎ 03/548–9588 ⊕ www. nelsonmuseum.co.nz ⊠ NZ$5.

★ World of WearableArt & Classic Car Museum (WOW)

MUSEUM | Wacky and wonderful, this museum displays garments from the World of WearableArt Awards Show, an event pioneered in Nelson but now presented in Wellington, exhibiting international designers. Here you get to see up close the amazing details of the wearable art. Exhibits change every six months. There's also a superb collection of classic cars, ranging from a pink Cadillac to Aston Martin and more. ⊠ *Cadillac Way off Quarantine Rd., Annesbrook* ☎ *03/547–4573* ⊕ *www.wowcars.co.nz* ⊠ *NZ$24.*

Restaurants

★ Hopgoods

$$$$ | MODERN NEW ZEALAND | Chef/owner Kevin Hopgood focuses on using regional produce and regularly wins national restaurant awards for this small, eponymously named bistro-restaurant. Along with the à la carte menu, Hopgoods offers a five-course degustation tasting spectacle, plus an ever-changing two or three course bistro-style menu on Monday and Tuesday. **Known for:** angus beef fillet; duck confit; big crowds so reservations are a good idea. $ *Average main: NZ$40* ⊠ *284 Trafalgar St.* ☎ *03/545–7191* ⊕ *www.hopgoods.co.nz* ⊗ *Closed Sun. No lunch.*

Morri Street

$$$ | ECLECTIC | FAMILY | Regional, artisanal produce is showcased at this upbeat, all-day café that's been around for more than 20 years. Wholesome breakfasts, lots of home baking, and a tasty lunch menu are the stars here. **Known for:** Moroccan eggs for breakfast; Atomic coffee matched with locally produced Oakland milk; tasty, innovative children's menu. $ *Average main: NZ$21* ⊠ *244 Hardy St.* ☎ *03/548–8110* ⊕ *www.morrisonstreetcafe.co.nz* ⊗ *No dinner.*

Hotels

Cambria House

$$$$ | B&B/INN | Built for a sea captain, this restored 1880s Victorian villa pairs antiques with modern fabrics and conveniences, so each bedroom has an en suite bathroom with shower; the three luxury rooms also have a separate bathtub. **Pros:** elegant old house in leafy surroundings; close to the Maitai River and riverside walkway; hospitable, helpful hosts. **Cons:** tight off-street parking when at capacity (but plenty of street parking); 10-minute walk to town and restaurants; decor a bit old-fashioned. $ *Rooms from: NZ$325* ⊠ *7 Cambria St.* ☎ *03/548–4681* ⊕ *www.cambria.co.nz* ⊷ *6 rooms* ⦿ *Breakfast.*

Delorenzo's Studio Apartments

$$$ | HOTEL | These spacious and stylish studio apartments have plenty of conveniences, including washer-dryers and very comfy leather lounger chairs. **Pros:** walking distance to restaurants, the cinema, and the riverside walk; lots of flashy appliances; great pool. **Cons:** roadside units have some street noise; a bit jammed into a small site; dinner and breakfast not included with the price. $ *Rooms from: NZ$225* ⊠ *43–55 Trafalgar St.* ☎ *03/548–9774, 0800/468–357* ⊕ *delorenzos.co.nz* ⊷ *25 suites* ⦿ *No meals.*

Joya

$$$ | B&B/INN | This heavenly spot encapsulates what Nelson is all about, with a focus on eco-values in its B&B room, a studio unit in the main house, and a delightful studio cottage in the garden with its own water garden and turf roof. **Pros:** patios with garden and city views; natural, organic ethos throughout; multilingual and friendly host. **Cons:** extremely steep driveway, need to park on the street; steep walk back from town; some rooms have shared bathrooms. $ *Rooms from: NZ$210* ⊠ *49 Brougham St.* ☎ *03/539–1350* ⊕ *www.joya.co.nz* ⊷ *3 rooms* ⦿ *Breakfast.*

Wakefield Quay House

$$$$ | B&B/INN | This graceful villa has one of the best waterfront locations in town. **Pros:** 180-degree views of mountains, sea, and sunsets; easy walk to good waterfront restaurants; evening drinks on the veranda with host. **Cons:** some road noise; limited off-street parking; minimum two-night stay. $ *Rooms from: NZ$380* ✉ *385 Wakefield Quay* ☎ *03/546–7275, 027/265–7547* ⊕ *www. wakefieldquay.co.nz* ⊘ *Closed June–Aug.* ⥀ *2 rooms* ⑩ *Breakfast.*

🌃 Nightlife

Nelson is known for its craft beers, so be sure to check out the local bars and their expensive beer menus. For the latest in music and performing arts events, check out ⊕ *www.itson.co.nz.*

The Free House

BARS/PUBS | FAMILY | Sorry, the ale isn't actually free here—the name means that this place isn't tied to any particular brewery, so you can try a range of craft beers from this very crafty beer region. Light meals are served from a food caravan or you can bring your own food along (the one rule is no global branded fast food). Eat with the locals in the garden—plates and blankets are provided. Oh, and it's in a former church, which adds another touch of uniqueness. ✉ *95 Collingwood St.* ☎ *03/548–9391* ⊕ *www.thefree-house.co.nz.*

⭐ Sprig & Fern

BARS/PUBS | This locale is one of nine Sprig & Fern outlets throughout the Nelson region and Wellington, pouring 100% natural beers and ciders from the Nelson-based brewery. At the flagship bar, there is indoor and courtyard seating, a good bistro menu, and often live music on Saturday night. If you're looking for an even more casual tipple, the Sprig & Fern at nearby Milton Street is a true neighborhood bar set in an old villa. ✉ *280 Hardy St.* ☎ *03/548–1154* ⊕ *www. sprigandfern.co.nz.*

🆕 Performing Arts

Nelson Arts Festival

FESTIVALS | A top music and performance event is the Nelson Arts Festival,

usually held in October. It's a magnet for top-notch Kiwi and international acts. ⊕ *www.nelsonartsfestival.co.nz.*

Nelson Centre of Musical Arts

MUSIC | New Zealand's oldest music school is known for its excellent acoustics. Each year it hosts musical performances, local productions, and top national and international tours. Check the website for upcoming events that coincide with your visit. ✉ *48 Nile St.* ☎ *03/548–9477* ⊕ *www.ncma.nz.*

🛍 Shopping

Talented artists live throughout the Nelson region, working full- or part-time in various media: ceramics, glassblowing, wood turning, fiber, sculpture, and painting. Not surprisingly there are many arts-and-crafts trails to follow, for which there is a brochure at the i-SITE Visitor Centre. There is also a colorful Monty's Sunday Market in the central city, where you'll find both new and preloved crafts and goods.

⭐ Jens Hansen Contemporary Gold & Silversmith

JEWELRY/ACCESSORIES | Jens Hansen craftspeople have long been known for their skilled gold and silver jewelry creations. Contemporary pieces are handmade at the workshop/showroom, and many are set with precious stones or local pounamu (jade). The focus here changed when Jens crafted the precious "One Ring" of *Lord of the Rings* film trilogy fame. The original prototype is on display, and this is now the only place where an officially authorized replica ring can be purchased. ✉ *320 Trafalgar Sq.* ☎ *03/548–0640* ⊕ *www.jenshansen.com.*

Nelson Markets

OUTDOOR/FLEA/GREEN MARKETS | Nelson is a market town, and Saturday morning's Nelson Market, in Montgomery Square, is one of the oldest in the country. It showcases the region's wealth of artists, craftspeople, and artisan food producers.

There's only one place to get an authentic replica of the One Ring; Jens Hansen Contemporary Gold & Silversmith in Nelson.

Vintage items, recyclables, and collectibles feature at Monty's Sunday Market, also in Montgomery Square. On Wednesday it's the local foodies' turn, selling their produce at the Nelson Farmers Market in Morrison Square (⊕ *www.nelsonfarmersmarket.org.nz*). ⊠ *Montgomery Sq.* ⊕ *www.nelsonmarket.co.nz.*

🏃 Activities

BIKING

The Tasman Great Taste Trail, one of the Nga Herenga New Zealand Cycle Trail rides, offers rides on largely flat terrain, exploring the vineyards, orchards, cafés, and coastal areas from Nelson to Kaiteriteri and along the Motueka River valley. You can ride it independently or with a guide, in sections or in a multiday package that includes all accommodations, bike rentals, and baggage-carrying services, with add-on options to walk or kayak in Abel Tasman National Park. You can also stop at the many cafés, wineries, craft beer breweries, beaches, orchards, and art galleries along the way; in fact, many cycling companies incorporate tastings into their tour packages. You can even be met at the airport, your luggage swapped for a bike, and off you pedal. For more information, visit ⊕ *www. nzcycletrail.com.*

The Gentle Cycling Company

BICYCLING | A range of guided rides and themed rides (options include Great Taste Beer and Great Taste Wine, for example), independent bike and e-bike hire, and multiday packages including accommodation from these experienced local biking hosts. They provide all that you need: bikes, helmets, high-visibility vests, maps, and advice. They'll shuttle you and your bike to and from anywhere on the trail, pick you up from your accommodations, and carry your purchases (wine or crafts) home for you. ■ TIP→ **They're based at Stoke, just around the corner from McCashins Brewery and Café, so plan your ride to finish there.** ⊠ *411 Nayland Rd., Stoke* ☎ *03/929–5652, 0800/932–453 in NZ* ⊕ *www.gentlecycling.co.nz* 🚲 *Bike rentals from NZ$30 full-day.*

Trail Journeys Nelson

BICYCLING | Bike rentals, day and multiday tour packages, and Mapua Ferry crossings (a vital link in the Great Taste Trail) are all provided by this highly experienced company. In addition to rides in the Mapua area, they also offer bike rentals from Nelson and Kaiteriteri Beach. ⊠ *Mapua Wharf, 10 Aranui Rd.* ☎ *03/540–3095, 0800/292–538* ⊕ *trail-journeysnelson.co.nz* ⊠ *From NZ$45 full-day rental.*

Wheelie Fantastic

BICYCLING | Bike hire, single-day and multiday rides, and luxury packages are all on offer from this experienced and knowledgeable outfit. They're based at Mapua but will deliver bikes and luggage wherever they're needed. ⊠ *8 Aranui Rd., Shed 6, Mapua Wharf* ☎ *03/543–2255, 0800/229–253 New Zealand only* ⊕ *wheeliefantastic.co.nz* ⊠ *From NZ$45 full-day rental.*

Around Nelson

Though Nelson's a bustling city, it retains a rural quality. Overlooking Tasman Bay and the foothills of the Bryant and Richmond ranges behind, open farmland, national parks, and vineyards are within easy reach. State Highway 6 winds southwest from the city through the outlying suburb of Stoke and through to Richmond, a good-size neighboring town. The commercial and civic center of the Tasman District, Richmond, has a good library and a modest shopping mall.

Just beyond Richmond, State Highway 60 branches northwest off State Highway 6, heading coastward to Mapua, Motueka, and Golden Bay. There's a wealth of vineyards along the strip toward Motueka, plus small farm and coastal communities with craft galleries and serious art studios tucked into valleys that run inland. If on a day drive, detour back along the inland route through historic Upper Moutere, with its blackcurrant and hop gardens. If you carry on south without turning to Motueka, look out for the birthplace of scientist Ernest Rutherford, on the right as you're leaving the small town of Brightwater. Five minutes south of Richmond the elaborate, atom-shape monument remembers this local boy's contribution to the world of nuclear science.

◉ Sights

Hoglund Art Glass

MUSEUM | One of New Zealand's longest-standing glass galleries is known internationally for its iconic collectible family of penguins as well as bold platters and vases. Their work creates a kaleidoscope of bright saturated colors and smooth curves. The gallery is open seven days; if the glassblowers are working during your visit, you can watch them at their craft. They don't do this every day, so call ahead to check. ⊠ *52 Lansdowne Rd., Richmond* ☎ *03/544–6500* ⊕ *www.hoglundartglass.com* ⊠ *Free.*

Isel House

GARDEN | This grand house, in the delightful tree-filled Isel Park in Stoke, was built for Thomas Marsden, one of the region's prosperous pioneers. It was Marsden who laid out the magnificent gardens surrounding the house, which include several towering California redwoods. The well-preserved stone house has had several rooms restored to their former glory, and contains stories of Isel and its surroundings, interpreted in part by local artists. You'll also find on-site original anecdotal material, family items, and a herbarium. For some visitors, the sprawling woodland gardens are the highlight of a visit here. ⊠ *16 Hilliard St., Isel Park, Stoke* ☎ *03/547–1347* ⊕ *www.nelsontasman.nz* ⊠ *By donation.*

Kahurangi Estate

WINERY/DISTILLERY | This boutique winery, in the small village of Upper Moutere, was one of the region's first, developed by Hermann Seifried in the 1970s. Greg and Amanda Day now produce a good range of Riesling, Pinot Gris, Pinot Noir, Montepulciano, Sauvignon Blanc, Chardonnay, and a fine Gewürztraminer. A new cellar door and restaurant serves wine tastings and delicious, locally produced artisan foods. There is also a luxurious vineyard cottage accommodation on the property. ⊠ *At Main and Sunrise Rds., Upper Moutere* ☎ *03/543–2980* ⊕ *www.kahurangiwine.com.*

Neudorf Vineyard

WINERY/DISTILLERY | Despite its tiny size, Neudorf has established an international reputation for its Pinot Noir and Chardonnay. Riesling, Pinot Gris, and Sauvignon Blanc are also highly regarded. The top wines wear the Moutere designation on the label, as the winery is in the Moutere Valley surrounded by acres of vineyards and hop gardens. The Moutere Chardonnay is regarded as the vineyard's signature wine. Artisan cheeses are served in summer, and they also stock olives, cheese, and oat crackers in the small deli to enjoy in the lovely grounds. ⊠ *138 Neudorf Rd., Upper Moutere* ☎ *03/543–2643* ⊕ *www.neudorf.co.nz* ☽ *Closed July and Aug.*

🍴 Restaurants

Richmond is a larger service town with some good cafés. While exploring craft galleries at Mapua, check out **Mapua Wharf** for its smokehouse, craft brewery, and café overlooking the estuary that serves some great fish-and-chips.

The Apple Shed Cafe

$$$$ | **MODERN NEW ZEALAND** | The Mapua Wharf setting complements the food, and you can watch the boats go by while dining on quality produce (organic when possible) washed down with Nelson wines, ciders, and craft beers. All bread is baked in-house, the coffee is great, and the menu serves a mix of small and large plates. **Known for:** dining overlooking the water; Golden Beer craft beer from the brewery next door; local fish and shellfish dishes. ⑤ *Average main: NZ$31* ⊠ *Shed 3, Mapua Wharf* ☎ *03/540–3381* ⊕ *www.appleshed.co.nz.*

🛏 Hotels

Throughout the Moutere, Mapua, and Motueka region there are a number of delightful B&Bs and boutique lodges for staying the night.

The Applepickers Cottages

$$$ | **B&B/INN** | Three self-contained cottages on the shoreline of the Waimea Estuary began life as apple pickers' cottages and have been refurbished in a pleasing rustic style. **Pros:** intimate waterfront setting and views; fresh farm eggs and fruit when available; coastal reserve and bird habitat restoration project out your door. **Cons:** minimum two-night stay; could feel a bit isolated; books up quickly. ⑤ *Rooms from: NZ$250* ⊠ *Apple Valley Rd. E, Mapua* ☎ *03/540–2214* ⊕ *www.applepickers.nz* ⤵ *3 cottages* ⌖ *No children under 12.*

Te Koi the Lodge at Bronte

$$$$ | **HOTEL** | Nestled beside an estuary this estate features pure, simple luxury. **Pros:** excellent hosts with wide local knowledge; bird-watching opportunities on the sand flats; right in the heart of wine country. **Cons:** out in the country; might be too buttoned up for some; very expensive. ⑤ *Rooms from: NZ$960* ⊠ *133 Bronte Rd. E, off State Hwy. 60, Mapua* ☎ *03/540–2422* ⊕ *www.tekoithelodge.com* ☽ *Closed June–Sept.* ⤵ *5 suites* ⑩ *Breakfast.*

🛍 Shopping

Down at the Mapua Wharf you'll find an aquarium, an ice-cream store, a gardening store, ceramics and craft stores, a few restaurant-bars, and a microbrewery.

Cape Soucis

Whangamoa Head

TO FRENCH PASS
& D'URVILLE ISLAND →

Delaware Bay

PEPIN
ISLAND

Cable Bay

Cable Bay
Adventure Park

6

BRYANT RANGE

Rai
Valley

6

TO PICTON →
& BLENHEIM

Pelorus Bridge
Reserve

Mount Richmond
Forest Park

Pelorus River

5 mi

5 km

0

The Glen

Atawhai

Boulder Bank

Nelson
see detail
map

6

Stoke

Isel House

Main Rd.

Richmond

Queen
St.

T a s m a n   B a y

Ruby Bay

RABBIT
ISLAND

Hoglund
Art Glass

Appleby

Hope

Brightwater

Wakefield

Nelson Lakes
National Park

Marahau

Kaiteriteri

Riwaka

Motueka

Port Motueka

JACKETT ISLAND

60

Tasman

Harakeke

Mapua

Redwood Rd.

Moutere Hwy.

Neudorf
Vineyard

Upper Moutere

Kahurangi
Estate

Motueka
Valley

Motueka River

ARTHUR RANGE

60

Abel Tasman N.P.
see detail map

TO
GOLDEN BAY
& TAKAKA →

Kahurangi
National
Park

61

Waimea River

6

Kohatu Junction

Around Nelson

Murchison →

Cool Store Gallery

CRAFTS | In an old apple cool store (where apples were stored at cool temperatures after being picked), this gallery is filled with well-priced, New Zealand-made art and craft work. The work, produced by artists from the Nelson and West Coast regions, includes paintings, sculpture, textiles, paua-shell items, ceramics, glasswork, and jewelry. They can arrange to ship your hard-to-travel-with purchases home in one piece. ⊠ *10 Aranui Rd., Mapua* ☎ *03/540–3778* ⊕ *www. coolstoregallery.co.nz.*

🏃 Activities

Cable Bay Adventure Park

ZIP LINING | FAMILY | There's a ton of fun on this 1,600-acre farm a 10-minute drive from Nelson. The Skywire is a mile-long zip line (reportedly the world's longest) that zooms across a forest-filled gully. Quad bikes climb a bush-lined track for 14 exciting km (8½ miles) before reaching a grand, hilltop ocean view. Horse treks explore the entire farm taking in steep trails and stunning views; they can be tailored depending on your riding ability. Then there's paintball, rides in the argo, all-terrain vehicle rides, and Base Café to replenish at the end of it all. ⊠ *194 Cable Bay Rd., 10-min drive north of Nelson, Nelson* ☎ *03/545–0304* ⊕ *www.cablebayadventurepark.com.*

Motueka

50 km (31 miles) west of Nelson.

Motueka (mo-too- *eh*-ka) is a horticultural center—hops, kiwifruit, and apples are among its staples. As a major gateway to two national parks, Kahurangi and Abel Tasman, Motueka also attracts kayakers, hikers, and holidaymakers. The town sits at the seaward end of the Motueka Valley, close to the mountains of Kahurangi National Park. Like Golden Bay, Motueka is popular with the "alternative"

communities around Nelson, and a few artisans and erstwhile hippies live alongside more traditional farming and orchard families. The hinterland is now also laced with vineyards, olive groves, and small, well-to-do farms often owned by absentee overseas owners. Many good cafés and places to stay are outside the town center, either in the sheltered inland valleys or out along the Abel Tasman coast and nearby bays, just north of town. South of town, the Motueka River is internationally known for its trout fishing, and the Great Taste Cycle Trail passes through the town.

GETTING HERE AND AROUND

Motueka is a 50-minute drive west of Nelson, on State Highway 60. You can also arrive from the south along the Motueka Valley Highway, which leaves State Highway 6 at Kohatu, 50 minutes north of Murchison. From Motueka it's a one-hour drive over the Takaka Hill to Golden Bay.

ScenicNZ runs coaches from Nelson to Motueka, Kaiteriteri, and Marahau. Golden Bay Coachlines travel from Nelson to Motueka and on to Takaka, in Golden Bay.

VISITOR INFORMATION

CONTACTS **Motueka i-SITE Visitor Centre.** ⊠ *20 Wallace St.* ☎ *03/528–6543* ⊕ *www. motuekaisite.co.nz.*

👁 Sights

Motueka Valley

SCENIC DRIVE | If you are headed for the West Coast from Motueka, turn south onto Highway 61 at the very obvious Motueka Clock Tower, following the sign to Murchison. The road snakes through the Motueka Valley alongside the Motueka River, with the green valley walls pressing close alongside. If this river could talk, it would probably scream, "Trout!" After the town of Tapawera, turn south on State Highway 6 at Kohatu and continue to the West Coast.

🍴 Restaurants

Jester House Cafe
$$$ | CAFÉ | FAMILY | The locally sourced, mainly organic food at this funky place includes a raft of home baking, chutneys and dressings, and hearty country fare like chowders and salads. There's cozy indoor seating, and tables dotted throughout the garden and veranda. **Known for:** family-friendly atmosphere; tame eels (to feed, not eat); twice-baked three-cheese soufflé. $ *Average main: NZ$21* ✉ *320 Aporo Rd.* ⟴ *Follow Ruby Bay Scenic Dr.* ☎ *03/526–6742* ⊕ *www. jesterhouse.co.nz.*

Riverside Café
$$ | ECLECTIC | FAMILY | In this rambling old colonial cottage, the menus are largely built around produce sourced from the gardens and farm of the Riverside Community based here, which focus on organic, natural food, including raw milk from their own cows. Menu choices range from stylish restaurant fare to casual pizzas and fries. **Known for:** breakfast until 3 pm; country ambience; outdoor seating. $ *Average main: NZ$20* ✉ *289 Main Rd., Inland Hwy., Lower Moutere* ⟴ *South of Motueka toward Upper Moutere* ☎ *03/526–7447* ⊕ *www.riverside.org.nz/cafe* ⊗ *No dinner Sun.–Thurs.*

★ T.O.A.D. Hall
$$ | CAFÉ | At this café, shop, and produce market in a former church, enjoy breakfast like pancakes, salmon rosti, and free-range eggs cooked heaps of ways, then stock up for your holiday travels. Or you can just chill over a wholesome lunch like the excellent slow-roast lamb burger. **Known for:** fresh, wholesome local foods; wooden toys and furniture for sale made by the owners; Townshend Brewery beers. $ *Average main: NZ$19* ✉ *502 High St.* ☎ *03/528–6456* ⊕ *www. toadhallmotueka.co.nz* ⊗ *No dinner except in summer on Fri. and Sat.*

🛏 Hotels

Kairuru Farmstay Cottages
$$ | B&B/INN | FAMILY | Halfway up the Takaka Hill from Motueka, these homey cottages with timber interiors and verandas have all you need for a comfortable stay in the country. **Pros:** fantastic country base for area exploration; a real Kiwi sheep and cattle farm, with tame animals for the kids to pat; gorgeous views. **Cons:** steep 15-minute drive up the Takaka Hill from Riwaka; long, narrow driveway onto the farm; a few gates to open and close as you drive in. $ *Rooms from: NZ$150* ✉ *1014 State Hwy. 60, Takaka Hill* ☎ *03/528–8091, 0800/524–787 New Zealand only* ⊕ *www.kairurufarmstay. co.nz* 🛏 *2 cottages* ⦿ *No meals.*

Motueka River Lodge
$$$$ | B&B/INN | Tranquility, marvelous mountain views, and a superb standard of comfort are the hallmarks of this rustic lodge on 35 acres overlooking the Motueka River. **Pros:** all meals can be arranged, and they are superb; fishing rivers all around; Kiwi hosts who know and understand this part of the world. **Cons:** out in the countryside; 50-minute drive from Nelson airport; closed June through August. $ *Rooms from: NZ$1200* ✉ *Motueka Valley Hwy. (State Hwy. 61)* ☎ *03/526–8668* ⊕ *www.motuekalodge. com* 🛏 *5 suites* ⦿ *Some meals.*

Motueka Top Ten Holiday Park
$$ | RESORT | FAMILY | A typical Kiwi holiday park, this one comes with top facilities and hosts. **Pros:** pool and hot tub; parklike setting; pizza truck on-site. **Cons:** can get crowded; no views; not many options for food on-site. $ *Rooms from: NZ$200* ✉ *10 Fearon St., Motueka* ☎ *03/528–7189, 0800/668–835* ⊕ *www.motuekat-op10.co.nz* 🛏 *35 units.*

⚡ Activities

FISHING

You won't lack for places to land some whopping brown trout in this region. Fishing season here runs from October to April. Fly-fishing excursions to local rivers and remote backcountry areas, for example, Kahurangi National Park, involve hiking or helicopter trips and give plenty of excitement to visiting anglers. Daily guiding rates are generally around NZ$900 and include lunches, drinks, and 4WD transportation. (Helicopter access is additional.) Best areas to base yourself for trout fishing are: St. Arnaud, Motueka, Murchison, or at one of the dedicated though pricey fly-fishing lodges close to these towns.

Strike Adventure Fishing

FISHING | Zane Mirfin is a very experienced fly-fishing guide, with huge local knowledge. His company takes clients to the best spots throughout Nelson and Marlborough, as well as the West Coast and North Canterbury. (He'll also take you sea fishing, if that's your preference.) ☎ *03/544–2100* ⊕ *www.strikeadventure. com.*

Abel Tasman National Park

77 km (48 miles) northwest of Motueka, 110 km (69 miles) northwest of Nelson.

Abel Tasman National Park is a stunning-yet-accessible swath of idyllic golden beaches and estuaries backed by a hinterland of native beech forests, granite gorges, and waterfalls. Unlike many of New Zealand's national parks, Abel Tasman has few serious challenges in its climate or terrain, making it a perfect place for a hiking, kayaking, or just cruising day trip.

GETTING HERE AND AROUND

From Motueka, the drive to the two southern entry points of Abel Tasman National Park is about 20 minutes. Tour boats leave from Kaiteriteri and Marahau—turn hard right off State Highway 60 just after the little townships of Riwaka to reach Kaiteriteri. Keep left at the same intersection to reach Marahau, but then take an immediate right for a road that leads over the Marahau Hill to Marahau. This is where the popular Abel Tasman Coast Track begins, although you can also get access to the track via water taxis at Kaiteriteri. ScenicNZ coaches service Abel Tasman National Park from Nelson and Motueka to Kaiteriteri and Marahau, the southern entry points. Golden Bay Coachlines travel to Totaranui, the Golden Bay entry point to the park. Many tour operators provide transfers as well.

Four companies provide boat transport to the coastal areas of the park, including day cruises, cruise/walk/kayak combos, and water taxi services for hikers and kayakers. These are Wilsons Abel Tasman, Abel Tasman Sea Shuttles, Marahau Water Taxis, and Abel Tasman Aqua Taxi.

Abel Tasman National Park information is available from the Motueka i-SITE Visitor Centre in Motueka.

BOAT TRANSPORTATION Abel Tasman Aqua Taxi. ✉ *275 Sandy Bay Rd., Marahau, Motueka* ☎ *0800/278–282 New Zealand only* ⊕ *www.aquataxi.co.nz.* **Abel Tasman Sea Shuttles.** ✉ *Kaiteriteri Beach* ☎ *03/527–8688, 0800/732–748 New Zealand only* ⊕ *www.abeltasmanseashuttles. co.nz.* **Marahau Water Taxis.** ✉ *8 Franklin St., Marahau* ☎ *03/527–8176, 0800/808– 018 New Zealand only* ⊕ *www.marahau-watertaxis.co.nz.* **Wilsons Abel Tasman.** ✉ *2 Inlet Rd., Kaiteriteri* ☎ *03/528–2027, 0800/223–582 New Zealand only* ⊕ *www.abeltasman.co.nz.*

Planning Your Trip to Abel Tasman ◉

9

Best Time to Go

Anytime, but be wary during the peak summer holiday period, from Christmas to mid-January, when the locals flock here in great numbers. Most people prefer to visit in summer, November through April, but don't let winter put you off, especially if you prefer your solitude. Though colder, winter weather can be very settled and sunny.

Best Activities

Cruise or Water Taxi. In midsummer the coastline buzzes with little water taxis and bigger cruising catamarans delivering people to various parts of the track, picking up those who have walked or kayaked a section or two, and dropping off supplies and even kayaks. And if you just want to sit back and enjoy the scenery then join a cruise up the coast and back.

Kayak. Sea kayaking is popular, and several companies offer packages, often combining paddling and walking. These can be from half-day to multiday trips, freedom or fully guided and catered, with optional accommodations arranged. Water taxis can also be arranged to deliver your packs to your next stopover point. It's a pleasant, possibly invigorating trip, especially if the wind is going your way.

Sail. Almost without fail a healthy sea breeze comes up along the coast every summer afternoon. With this in mind catch a sailboat cruise out of Kaiteriteri in the morning. It's a slow gentle way to interact with the park. Then hang on as the skipper hooks the boat into that sea breeze on the way home behind a fully set spinnaker.

Walk. The entire 60 km (37 miles) Abel Tasman Coast Track, from Wainui Bay in the north to Marahau in the south, can be walked in three to five days, depending on your pace and how many swims you want along the way. This designated Great Walk is well formed and easy to follow. Alternatively you can walk short sections by arranging a drop-off and pickup by water taxi. Bark Bay to Torrent Bay and Awaroa to Torrent Bay are ideal for this. There are a few tidal crossings along the track that can only be crossed at mid- to low tides. Each of these has a longer all-tide alternative, but plan ahead and remember to allow for this if you are meeting a water taxi. The park's inland tracks explore more rugged, forest-covered areas— best tackled by more experienced trampers.

VISITOR INFORMATION

CONTACTS Abel Tasman Centre. ✉ 229 Sandy Bay–Marahau Beach Rd., Marahau ☎ 03/527–8176 ⊕ www.abeltasmancentre.co.nz. **Motueka i-SITE Visitor Centre.** ✉ 20 Wallace St., Motueka ☎ 03/528–6543 ⊕ www.motuekaisite.co.nz.

◉ Sights

★ **Abel Tasman National Park**
BEACH—SIGHT | One of New Zealand's most easily accessible parks is also one of the most visited, thanks to its golden sand beaches, sculptured granite headlands, and forest-lined tidal inlets and islands. Unlike other South Island parks, Abel Tasman has few extremes in weather and its coastal track, one of the

KEY

········· *Walking track*

 Ferry route

Abel Tasman National Park

Taupo Point

Mutton Cove

Abel Tasman Memorial

Wharawharangi Hut

TO COLLINGWOOD
Farewell Spit

Golden Bay

Lookout Rock

Totaranui

Tarakohe

Pohara

Awaroa Bay

Centre Peak

Takaka

Abel Tasman Road

Awaroa Inlet

Tonga Island Marine Reserve

Inland Track

East Takaka Road

Wainui Track

60

Tonga Quarry

Tonga Island

Tasman Bay

West Road

Rameka Track

Wainui Saddle

Abel Tasman National Park

Coast Track

Bark Bay

Harwoods Hole

Inland Track

Torrent Bay

Te Puketea Bay

Castle Rocks

Adele Island

Motueka Forest

Fishermans Island

0 ____ 4 mi

TO UPPER TAKAKA & MOTUEKA

TO RIWAKA & MOTUEKA

Sandy Bay

Marahau

FERRY TO KAITERITERI

0 ____ 4 km

Great Walks, is an ideal place to explore without the need of serious technical equipment or experience. Day and multi-day trips, walking, sea-kayaking, sailing, and scenic cruises, and combos of all of these, are popular ways to explore the area. Keep in mind in the peak summer holiday season (Christmas to late January) this area is very busy and you will rarely be on that dream beach alone. Any time of the year, however, is perfectly suitable for an Abel Tasman trip. The small settlements of **Kaiteriteri** and **Marahau** are the main gateways to the national park, both at the southern end and 20- to 40-minutes' drive from Motueka. Stop first at the Nelson or Motueka i-SITE Visitor Centre for maps and information. If you're planning to stop overnight at a Department of Conservation campsite or hut, along the Abel Tasman Coast Track, you need to book ahead. You can do this online or at the Nelson or Motueka i-SITE. It pays to book well ahead, especially in summer. Water taxis service the coastline, and they drop-off or pick-up at many points along the way. At the northern end of the park, a road leads from Golden Bay through the park to Totaranui, where there is a large DOC campground and long, beautiful beach. This is a popular start/finish point for those walking the Abel Tasman Coast Track. ⊠ *Abel Tasman National Park* ⊕ *www.doc.govt.nz.*

🏖 Beaches

Kaiteriteri Beach

BEACH—SIGHT | The approach to Kaiteriteri Beach, through orchards then forest-lined coast, is lovely, and the beach is one of the area's prettiest, with its curve of golden sand, rocky islets offshore, and deep clear water. This place is packed

One-Day Itinerary in Abel Tasman 👁

Try a walking/boat trip combo on the beautiful coastal track. Pack a picnic, your sunblock, and walking shoes and, if leaving from Nelson, hit the road by 8 am. Most operators will pick you up from accommodations; if you're driving, there's parking available at Kaiteriteri and Marahau beaches, the departure points for boat tours and water taxis. The drive across to the park takes around 80 minutes from Nelson, and around 30 minutes from Motueka.

Midmorning, catch a big, modern catamaran or small, fast-water taxi along the coast to Bark Bay. On the way, if you've left from Kaiteriteri, you will pass Split Apple Rock, a giant granite marble in the sea that looks just like ... a giant split apple. Farther up the coast you'll pass sandy beaches like Apple Tree Bay and Coquille Bay before cruising past birdlife sanctuary, Adele Island. Then, the boat hits open water for a short stretch before rounding Pitt Head and calling into Anchorage, a beautiful sheltered bay with a DOC hut and campsite that looks across to neighboring Torrent Bay, with its few private holiday

homes. Your boat will most likely drop off and pick up walkers, kayakers, and supplies here, then continue to Bark Bay, a little farther up the coast. Here is where you disembark. You'll walk off the boat ramp onto the beach and be shown where to join the Abel Tasman Coastal Track for your afternoon's walk back to Anchorage.

By now you'll be ready for lunch. There are few more idyllic spots than the forest-lined beach and estuary of Bark Bay for a picnic. From here it's an easy and scenic three-hour walk to Torrent Bay. The track climbs steeply at first, before ambling around several hillsides with pleasant outlooks through gaps in the trees. In summer you'll meet plenty of other walkers. Follow the track as it descends to Torrent Bay, then continue on to Anchorage, which you can now see across the bay. Depending on the tide you can either cross the estuary or walk around the all-tide track to Anchorage. Pass through the DOC campground and relax on the beach until your boat arrives to return you to Kaiteriteri or Marahau, all in good time for a well-earned sundowner.

---

in midsummer, but once the four-week post-Christmas rush is over, the area returns to its usual less frenzied pace. Many water-taxi and scenic cruises leave from here for Abel Tasman National Park. The Great Taste Trail cycle trail, which starts in Nelson, ends here, at the Kaiteriteri Mountain Bike Park. There is a popular campground and a few cafés in the village, although all prune their hours or close in winter. A number of private holiday homes are also located here. **Amenities:** accommodation; cruise- and water-taxi services; food and drink; parking (free); toilets; tour booking offices.

Best for: swimming; walking. ✉ *Kaiteriteri–Sandy Bay Rd., Motueka.*

🛏 Hotels

⭐ Abel Tasman Lodge

$$ | **HOTEL** | Spacious chalets and studios, with native gardens between them, are nestled between Abel Tasman National Park and Marahau Beach. **Pros:** close to everything in Marahau; travelers share tales in the communal kitchen; stylish, homey accommodations overlook the hills of Abel Tasman National Park. **Cons:** no breakfast in the room rate; studios

Overnight in Abel Tasman

Plan ahead if you want to stay in the park overnight, at either a Department of Conservation (DOC) campground or hut, like those at Anchorage, a four-hour, 12.4-km (7-mile) walk from the start of the track at Marahau. These huts and campsites are on the Abel Tasman Coast Track, which is a part of the national Great Walks system. Tickets (NZ$75 per night for huts and NZ$30 per night for campsites, or NZ$32 and NZ$15, respectively, for New Zealanders) must be bought beforehand, either at the Nelson or Motueka i-SITE Visitor Centre, DOC visitor centers throughout the country, or on the DOC website (⊕ *booking.doc. govt.nz*). Huts are basic, with cooking, shower and toilet facilities, filtered water, and sleeping bunks. There are four huts and 18 campsites (some accessible by sea, for kayakers) plus Totaranui Campground. You will need to bring all your food (water taxis can be arranged to deliver fresh supplies, at a cost). You will also be expected to pack out all your rubbish. There are more salubrious park accommodations, like the lodges at Awaroa and Torrent bays, should comfort be your thing. From Torrent Bay, near Anchorage, there's a lovely short walk from the bridge over the Torrent River inland a short distance to Cleopatra's Pool. This rugged rock pool sits in between huge granite boulders and is surrounded by bush. But it's a frosty swim, even in summer.

don't have kitchen facilities; need to remember to stock up with groceries before getting here. ⑤ *Rooms from: NZ$195* ⊠ *295 Sandy Bay–Marahau Rd., Marahau* ☎ *03/527–8250* ⊕ *www. abeltasmanlodge.co.nz* ⤴ *12 rooms* ⍾ *No meals.*

Kimi Ora Spa Resort
$$$ | **RESORT** | The cozy wood walls and simple furnishings of the guest quarters are part of the philosophy here: Kimi Ora means "seek health" in Māori, and this aims to be an environmentally friendly, health-oriented resort. **Pros:** bordered by a mix of exotic forest and regenerating native bush; all the rooms have distant sea views; geared toward healthy living. **Cons:** 10-minute walk to Kaiteriteri Beach; native birdsong will wake you early; healthy lifestyle isn't for everyone. ⑤ *Rooms from: NZ$219* ⊠ *Martins Farm Rd., Kaiteriteri* ☎ *03/527–8027, 0508/5464–672* ⊕ *www.kimiora.com* ⤴ *22 units* ⍾ *Breakfast.*

The Resurgence
$$$$ | **B&B/INN** | Free-standing chalets and villas, and four lodge rooms in the main house, are surrounded by native forest and stunning scenery and offer every luxury. **Pros:** gorgeous scenery and terrific hosts; massage and therapeutic treatments available; walking tracks through the property. **Cons:** long, winding driveway is quite narrow and steep in places; villas and chalets are away from the main house, with gravel walks between; two-night minimum stay. ⑤ *Rooms from: NZ$695* ⊠ *574 Riwaka Valley Rd., Motueka* ☎ *03/528–4664* ⊕ *www.resurgence. co.nz* ⊗ *Closed May–Sept.* ⤴ *10 rooms* ⍾ *Breakfast* ⌖ *No children age 1–18.*

🏃 Activities

HIKING
Abel Tasman Coast Track
HIKING/WALKING | One of the most popular multiday hikes in any New Zealand national park is the three- to five-day Abel

Tasman Coast Track. From beach to golden beach, over gentle forest-covered hills and across tidal inlets, this is gourmet hiking. One of the premier-rated Great Walks, and traversed year-round, the track is popular because of its relatively easy terrain, short distances between huts and campsites, and the stunning landscapes. Water taxis can be booked to drop off and pick up hikers from several points along the track, allowing flexible options for walks of anything from one hour to five days. There are four huts and 19 campsites, and spaces in both must be booked year-round. Bookings can be made online, through DOC visitor centers anywhere, and i-SITES in the Nelson region. ⌗ *Abel Tasman Coast Track* ☎ *03/546–7393 Nelson i-SITE Visitor Centre, 03/546–8210 DOC Great Walk Bookings Helpdesk* ⊕ *www.doc.govt.nz.*

MULTISPORT ADVENTURES AND TOURS

Wilsons Abel Tasman

HIKING/WALKING | One of the original operators of excursions to this beautiful park, the Wilson family now offers a whole gamut of scenic cruises and single- and-multiday walking, running, and kayaking combos that include accommodation in their stylish family lodges at Torrent Bay and Awaroa. Their multipurpose fleet cruises every day from Kaiteriteri—with several departures a day in summer, including an evening barbecue cruise. They'll also link with riders on the Great Taste Trail. ⌗ *409 High St., Motueka* ☎ *03/528–2027, 0800/223–582 New Zealand only* ⊕ *www.abeltasman.co.nz.*

SAILING AND KAYAKING

Abel Tasman Sailing Adventures

SAILING | If you'd like a day in the park without breaking a sweat, call up the sailing gurus. Their large catamarans set sail daily from Kaiteriteri. Along the way you might call for a photo at Split Apple Rock, stop for a swim at a golden sand beach, or check out the seals around Motuareronui/Adele Island. The most popular trip

is a full-day sail that includes lunch. You can also arrange overnight trips, walking/sailing combos, and exclusive charters. ☎ *03/527–8375, 0800/467–245 New Zealand only* ⊕ *www.sailingadventures.co.nz* ⊠ *Full-day sail NZ$190, with lunch.*

Kaiteriteri Kayaks

KAYAKING | One of the long-standing operators here offers the whole gamut of guided half-day, full-day, and multiday kayak trips, plus walk/kayak combos and kayak rentals. They work with partner company Sea Shuttle Cruises to get you quickly into the best spots along this incredible coast—for example, to Tonga Island Marine Reserve, a trip that encompasses golden beaches, seals for company, a sheltered lagoon, and amazing rock formations. ⌗ *Kaiteriteri-Sandy Bay Rd., Kaiteriteri* ☎ *03/527–8383, 0800/252–925 New Zealand only* ⊕ *www.seakayak.co.nz* ⊠ *NZ$205 for full-day catered paddle.*

The Sea Kayak Company

KAYAKING | Check out this little local company's guided kayaking trips, including stops on beaches and campsites that simply can't be reached by hikers. Popular options include the "Ab-Fab" Marine Reserve one-day paddle and walk and a two-day "More than Beaches" tour. All multiday tours are fully catered and all equipment is supplied. Reservations are recommended. They'll also rent kayaks and gear for independent travel, and give you a heap of advice to help make your trip a happy and safe one. ⌗ *506 High St., Motueka* ☎ *03/528–7251, 0508/252–925 New Zealand only* ⊕ *www.seakayak-nz.co.nz* ⊠ *From NZ$85.*

Golden Bay and Takaka

55 km (35 miles) northwest of Motueka, 110 km (70 miles) west of Nelson.

The gorgeous stretch of coastline that begins at Separation Point, in Abel Tasman National Park, and runs westward

Did You Know?

Abel Tasman National Park is New Zealand's smallest, and arguably most popular, national park. The forest-lined golden sand beaches, estuaries, islands, and fascinating, weathered granite rock are the big attractions.

past Takaka to Farewell Spit is known as **Golden Bay,** named for the gold discovered there in the 1850s. It's a 40-km (25-mile) crescent of beaches, farms, and orchards. Alternating sandy and rocky shores curve up to the sands of Farewell Spit, the arcing prong that encloses the bay. A 19th-century lighthouse station near its tip, here to warn shipping of the low-lying sandy spit, is the only man-made intrusion. Dutch navigator Abel Tasman anchored briefly in Golden Bay a few days before Christmas 1642. His visit ended abruptly when four of his crew were killed in an altercation with local Māori iwi (tribe), Ngāti Tūmatakōkiri. Tasman named the place Moordenaers Baij, or Murderers' Bay, and sailed away without ever setting foot on New Zealand soil. Today a relaxed crew of locals firmly believe they live in paradise, and a huge annual influx of summertime holidaymakers agrees with them. The only road to Golden Bay climbs over the steep Takaka Hill from Motueka. You need to be determined to get here; it's not a place you pass on the way to somewhere else.

The Golden Bay lifestyle has for some years been considered "alternative"—a hideout for hippies, musicians, and artists. It's also the center of a rich dairy farming area, and its warm, sheltered climate nurtures crops such as citrus, avocados, and kiwifruit that struggle on the colder, Nelson side of "the hill."

GETTING HERE AND AROUND

Golden Bay Air flies scheduled flights from Wellington to Takaka, and offers shuttle connections to both ends of the Heaphy Track (a Great Walk) and the Abel Tasman National Park.

The road into Golden Bay, over the Takaka Hill on State Highway 60, rises up 2,500 feet before plunging again to sea level to the tiny township of Takaka, a jumping-off point for Farewell Spit, Kahurangi National Park, and the Heaphy Track. This road is a 40-minute climb of twisting corners, steep drop-offs, and occasional passing

bays. Don't be tempted to check the views while you're driving; wait until you reach Bob's Lookout, on the Nelson side of the hill, and Harwood Lookout, on the Takaka side, for safe viewing.

AIRLINE CONTACTS Golden Bay Air.
☎ *03/525–8725, 0800/588–885 New Zealand only ⊕ www.goldenbayair.co.nz.*

BUS CONTACTS Golden Bay Coachlines.
☎ *03/525–8352 ⊕ www.goldenbaycoachlines.co.nz.*

VISITOR INFORMATION
CONTACTS Golden Bay Visitor Centre.
✉ *16 Willow St., Takaka ☎ 03/525–9136 ⊕ www.goldenbaynz.co.nz.*

◉ Sights

Golden Bay begs to be explored, so if you take the trouble to cross the Takaka Hill into this spectacular area, plan to stay at least two nights or you'll spend your whole time driving and none enjoying the rewards of your travels. Golden Bay Coachlines runs daily services to Takaka, the Heaphy Track, and Totaranui (check times in winter).

Collingwood
TOWN | After winding past several small farming districts and close to beach communities such as Paton's Rock, Onekaka, and Tukurua, State Highway 60 arrives at Collingwood, a small seaside village at the mouth of the giant Aorere River, 26 km (16 miles) west of Takaka. The earliest European settlers came here in the 1840s to build small ships from the timber lining the beaches and to farm the fertile river plains that spill out of the surrounding mountains. In the 1850s, gold was discovered nearby and Collingwood became a thriving port-of-entry town; at one time it was even under consideration to be the country's capital. Collingwood is a bit out on a limb from the main roads, but nevertheless has much to offer. It's the northern access point for the Heaphy Track Great Walk and the

main base for trips to internationally recognized bird-watching site Farewell Spit and to the wild, remote coastline of the northernmost West Coast. The town's rich heritage is well documented, in both the small Collingwood Museum and the neighboring Aorere Centre. ⊠ *Collingwood.*

Totaranui

TOWN | From Takaka the coast road heading northeast leads to Totaranui, the northern entry for Abel Tasman National Park. This scenic road passes through Pohara Beach, which has a few cafés and a holiday park, before winding around to Wainui Bay with its alternative Tūi community (a residential community that welcomes visitors) and cascading waterfall (a slightly rough 75-minute return walk from the road). From Wainui Bay, the road over the Totaranui Hill is a gravel surface. Take it slowly: it's a gorgeous drive through dense native bush to the coast. Totaranui Beach is a long golden-sand beach that is safe for swimming. This area can also be reached by boat from Kaiteriteri and Marahau, on the Motueka side of the Takaka Hill. It's a slice of pure beach bliss, and there's an unpowered campground with basic facilities. There's generally a wait-list to camp here for the first few weeks after Christmas, large though it is. Otherwise you should be fine—however, reservations are required no matter what time of year. ⊠ *Totaranui.*

Waikoropupu Springs

BODY OF WATER | The water in these springs is reportedly some of the clearest ever measured, anywhere. Six kilometers (4 miles) west of Takaka is the largest cold-water spring system in the southern hemisphere, and clear cold water bubbles into the Waikoropupu Valley after traveling underground from its source at the nearby Takaka Hill. Swimming or touching the water is not allowed, to prevent the introduction of weeds and damage to the delicate flora within the

springs; so leave your swimsuits and dive gear in the car. Instead, take a leisurely stroll around the valley on the 40-minute, top-quality walk to the main spring, Dancing Sand Spring and Fish Creek Springs. Go quietly—the better to spot *tūī*, bellbirds, wood pigeons, and other birdlife. The turnoff from State Highway 60 to Pupu Springs Road is signposted, on the western side of the Takaka River bridge. ⊠ *Pupu Springs Rd., Takaka* ⊕ *www.doc. govt.nz.*

🏖 Beaches

Golden Bay has miles of swimming beaches and small bays. Popular with families for its safe, shallow water is **Ligar Bay,** while **Tata Beach** is deeper—these are two of the best spots near Takaka.

Whariki Beach

BEACH—SIGHT | A must-see for its dramatic landscapes is Whariki Beach, out beyond the road to Farewell Spit. To get there, drive past Collingwood to Pakawau and follow the signs. Go as far as the road will take you, and then walk over farmland on a well-defined track for 20 minutes. Allow at least an hour for the return circuit, along the beach and back via another well-marked track. Be wary though; it's too rough for swimming and very easy to get caught by the incoming tide. Remember, this dramatic coast is quite remote, with few people (certainly no lifeguards) and tides change very quickly. Don't be one of those who get trapped by the sea walking out to the offshore rocks. Also, among the massive sand dunes you're likely to come across fur seals. Keep at least a 30-foot distance, as they can move quickly and do bite, and never get between a seal and the sea. It can be very windy here, at which times the sand will whip you like in a Sahara storm. But don't let any of that put you off this great place. **Amenities:** none. **Best for:** solitude; walking. ⊠ *Takaka* ⊕ *Drive past Collingwood to Pakawau and follow signs.*

Restaurants

The Brigand

$$$ | NEW ZEALAND | This bar and café is located in a lovely old house on Takaka's main street and has a sunny courtyard, cool handmade furniture, plenty of indoor seating, and roaring fires (indoor and out) for cozy nights. The menu consistently provides New Zealand classics, from light snacks and daily specials to full dinners. **Known for:** sea-run salmon; nice garden; sticky pork spare ribs. $ *Average main: NZ$29* ⊠ *90 Commercial St., Takaka* ☎ *03/525–9636.*

Courthouse Cafe

$$ | NEW ZEALAND | In the lovely old former Collingwood Courthouse, on the main crossroads into town, this laid-back and popular café makes good use of local produce. Their breakfast "stacks" (rosti, bacon, egg, avocado) will set you up for a trip to the beach or Farewell Spit or Heaphy Track. **Known for:** lots of gluten-free and vegan options; breakfast tortillas; house-made pies. $ *Average main: NZ$18* ⊠ *At Gibbs and Elizabeth St., Collingwood* ☎ *03/524–8194* ⊕ *www.thecourthousecafecollingwood.com.*

★ Mussel Inn

$$$ | NEW ZEALAND | FAMILY | Swing by the Mussel Inn for a quintessential slice of Golden Bay life: music, craft beer, and darn good pub food. Locals come for the live music (most evenings in summer), mussel chowder, steamed mussels, or local Anatoki salmon, washed down with house-brewed beer and ciders. **Known for:** craft beers and ciders; rustic, country ambience; live music. $ *Average main: NZ$27* ⊠ *State Hwy. 60, Onekaka* ☎ *03/525–9241* ⊕ *www.musselinn.co.nz* ⊗ *Closed Aug.*

Wholemeal Cafe

$$$ | CAFÉ | Set in the old Takaka theater, this place is synonymous with the alternative feel that is Golden Bay. The breakfast and lunch menus are substantial and wholesome, or you can catch an early

dinner on Friday when they are open until 8 pm. **Known for:** funky vibe; amazing baked goods; coffee sourced direct from farmers in Timor Leste. $ *Average main: NZ$23* ⊠ *60 Commercial St., Takaka* ☎ *03/525–9426* ⊕ *www.wholemealcafe.co.nz* ⊗ *No dinner Sat.–Thurs.*

🛏 Hotels

Adrift In Golden Bay

$$$$ | HOTEL | Here, a short walk across soft grass from your luxurious, fully self-contained cottage or studio unit gets you to your own quiet beach. **Pros:** calm, thoughtful atmosphere; Jacuzzi-style hot tubs; sundecks out front and private rear courtyards. **Cons:** a long driveway through farmland; minimum night stays enforced (up to four nights in peak summer); expensive. $ *Rooms from: NZ$529* ⊠ *52 Tukurua Rd., 18 km (11 miles) north of Takaka* ☎ *03/525–8353* ⊕ *www.adrift.co.nz* ⊗ *Closed July* ⊅ *6 units* ❖ *Breakfast* ⌂ *No children under 12.*

Pohara Top 10 Holiday Park

$$ | HOTEL | Well-appointed cabins and motel units, with various bedding configurations and some with full kitchens,

---

Enchanted Forest 👁

The Grove Scenic Reserve is a small patch of native forest at Rocklands that escaped development when the area was cleared for farming. It's an enchanting collection of giant *rata*, elegant *nikau* palms, and trailing vines that grow between and over gnarly limestone outcrops and gulches. In early summer the rata wear a cloak of bright scarlet flowers. Heading toward Pohara from Takaka, turn right off Abel Tasman Drive at Clifton and follow the signs.

are set on 5 beachfront acres with plenty of trees for shelter. **Pros:** beachfront property; good casual dining options nearby; helpful, professional hosts. **Cons:** some units have shared bathroom facilities; might be lots of kids making noise; cabins are quite small. $ *Rooms from: NZ$135* ✉ *808 Abel Tasman Dr., Pohara* ☎ *03/525–9500, 0800/764–272 New Zealand only* ⊕ *www.poharabeach.com* ⇌ *24 units.*

Sans Souci Inn

$$ | **B&B/INN** | **FAMILY** | Just a two-minute walk from Pohara Beach, this inn has striking adobe and tile construction, wide verandas, a turf roof, and a touch of Mediterranean decor. **Pros:** self-contained family unit sleeps up to four; you can cook in the restaurant kitchen for yourself; friendly, thoughtful hosts. **Cons:** restaurant is only open late October to Easter; shared bathrooms; shared kitchen. $ *Rooms from: NZ$140* ✉ *11 Richmond Rd., Pohara* ☎ *03/525–8663* ⊕ *www. sanssouciinn.co.nz* ⊘ *Closed winter (exact dates flexible)* ⇌ *7 units* ⦿ *No meals.*

Twin Waters Lodge

$$$ | **B&B/INN** | A small but stunning lodge nestled on a small peninsula beside the Pakawau Estuary, Twin Waters overlooks the surrounding hills and wetlands. **Pros:** interesting tidal estuary out the door; good location to explore Farewell Spit and Wharariki Beach; thoughtful and friendly hosts. **Cons:** limited evening dining options in shoulder seasons; remote from town and shops; probably not the best spot as sea levels rise. $ *Rooms from: NZ$280* ✉ *30 Totara Ave., Pakawau, 9 km (5½ miles) past Collingwood on road to Farewell Spit, Collingwood* ☎ *03/524–8014* ⊕ *www.twinwaters.co.nz* ⊘ *Closed June–mid-Oct.* ⇌ *4 rooms* ⦿ *Free Breakfast.*

🏃 Activities

FISHING

Anatoki Salmon

FISHING | **FAMILY** | At this salmon farm, on the banks of Anatoki River, you can fish for salmon then have your catch prepared for your lunch while you wait. Or they will smoke it for you, or package it to take away and prepare at your leisure. Entry is free; just pay for what you catch. Fishing gear is provided, and experience is not necessary. You can also feed eels here, and there's a petting farm for kids—and a café in case the fish didn't bite. ✉ *230 McCallum Rd., Anatoki Valley* ☎ *03/525– 7251, 0800/262–865 New Zealand only* ⊕ *www.anatokisalmon.co.nz.*

HORSE TREKKING

Cape Farewell Horse Treks

HORSEBACK RIDING | **FAMILY** | Saddle up at Cape Farewell and ride off into the sunset, or to the beach. This outfit provides some of the best horse trekking in the country, on possibly the most spectacular beaches. For the best views, ride the combined Triangle and Old Man Range treks, or try the Puponga Beach ride for something more tranquil; it's also suitable for kids age five and up. If you're into wild beach gallops then join the Wharariki Beach Trek. ✉ *23 McGowan St., Puponga* ☎ *03/524–8031* ⊕ *www.horsetreksnz. co.nz* 🎫 *From NZ$80.*

Farewell Spit

A 35-km (22-mile) sandspit that expands 10-fold when the tide goes out, Farewell Spit is the home of tens of thousands of seabirds, many of them migrants from the northern hemisphere, and is an internationally recognized bird sanctuary. The landscape is wild.

GETTING HERE AND AROUND

The nearest town to Farewell Spit is Collingwood, 2½ hours from Nelson on SH60. The road continues 30 km (19 miles) from Collingwood to Puponga Farm Park, where the public road ends at the base of the Spit. Golden Bay Coachlines runs a daily service from Nelson to Takaka, which includes a connection 23 km (14 miles) farther to Collingwood. Golden Bay Air flies from Wellington to Takaka. If you fly, rental vehicles can be hired in Takaka.

Access onto the Spit itself is only possible with the licensed tour operator Farewell Spit Eco Tours, based in Collingwood. Tours run daily, times depending on the tides.

TOURS

★ Farewell Spit Eco Tours

SPECIAL-INTEREST | This is one of the premier bird-watching tours of New Zealand and even if you're not an avid bird-watcher, traversing this vast, windblown, sandy landscape is a must. (Sliding down the massive sand dunes is optional.) Most popular is the 6½-hour Eco Tour, driving all-terrain vehicles on the sand to a lighthouse near the tip of the Spit. The Gannet Tour travels farther to a hardy gannet colony, or there's the two-hour Wader Watch Tour. A shorter, 4½-hour Eco Tour onto the Spit is also offered. This company has been running tours for generations, and is the only one licensed to travel on the Spit (which is closed to public access). Reservations are essential. Times vary with the tides. ⊠ 6 Tasman St., Collingwood ☎ 03/524–8257, 0800/808–257 New Zealand only ⊕ www.farewellspit.com ⊠ From NZ$155.

Kahurangi National Park

35 km (21 miles) west of Takaka.

New Zealand's second-largest national park, Kahurangi is 1.1 million acres of marbled mountains with fluted rock forms, arches, shafts, and sinkholes (featured in the *Lord of the Rings* films), remote river gorges, alpine tops, beech

forests, and coastal rain forests, plus designated wilderness areas where no development or helicopter access is allowed. There are more than 350 miles of hiking tracks of various levels of difficulty, including the longest Great Walk, the Heaphy Track. Beneath the park are the deepest caving systems in the southern hemisphere, which are meant for serious cavers only. The Golden Bay Visitor Centre (⊕ www.doc.govt.nz) provides local trail maps.

GETTING HERE AND AROUND

There are two main entry points to the park from Takaka. One is at the northern end of the Heaphy Track, south of Collingwood. Most people walk the four- to five-day track one-way, and arrange a bus pickup or drop-off. The second entry point is up the Cobb Valley: turn left at East Takaka, at the base of the Takaka Hill on its western side. The Cobb Valley road ends approximately 22 km (15 miles) farther in. You'll find camping areas and short walks, plus the starting points to several park hiking trails in this valley. Golden Bay Coachlines also runs daily connections to the northern end of the Heaphy Track in summer.

◉ Sights

★ Kahurangi National Park

NATIONAL/STATE PARK | Kahurangi is a vast wilderness of marbled karst mountains, glaciated landforms, alpine tablelands, rivers, alpine tarns and beech, podocarp, and coastal rain forests. Underground are the country's longest, deepest, and oldest cave systems. Multiday hikes, short walks, caving, extreme rafting, fly-fishing, and hunting are what people like to do here. Kahurangi National Park spans 1.1 million acres, much of it untamed, yet crisscrossed by 570 km (353 miles) of hiking tracks of various levels. Most well known is the four- to five-day Heaphy Track, one of New Zealand's Great Walks. Probably the most popular road access from Nelson is the steep,

Planning Your Trip to Kahurangi

Best Time to Go

Kahurangi can be visited any time of the year, although snow in winter will inhibit access to the higher areas like Mt. Arthur and the Mt. Owen massif. The Heaphy Track is generally passable year-round. It's particularly popular with walkers in summer, and mountain bikers are permitted on the track in winter (May to September).

Best Activities

Caving and Cave Diving. There is a spectacular network of caves beneath the park, in particular under "the mountains with plumbing," as Mt. Arthur and Mt. Owen are known. New passages are still being discovered and the cave systems at the northern end of Kahurangi join up with those under Abel Tasman. Local guides are essential if you want to explore these. The Pearce and Riwaka rivers, on the eastern side of Mt. Arthur, are both well-known cave-diving spots with well-defined resurgence caves. The Riwaka resurgence is popular with scuba enthusiasts. A local guide is essential.

Helicopter or Fixed Wing Plane. In some areas of the vast Kahurangi there's absolutely no development permitted, and the only way to get there is to walk. In other areas, however, helicopters can be chartered to ferry hikers and rafters to remote rivers and tracks, to get trout fishermen to favored spots, and for general sightseeing. A helicopter flight to *Lord of the Rings* film locations on spectacular Mt. Owen and Mt. Olympus has also become popular.

Tramp. The five-day Heaphy Track is one of the country's Great Walks, traversing tussock-covered tablelands and remote, wild West Coast beaches in the northwest corner of the park, between Collingwood and Karamea. Other challenging and less-walked walks are available; while shorter, easier and popular tracks leave from the Flora Carpark (accessed from Motueka and Nelson) and the Cobb Valley (south of Takaka).

White-Water Rafting and Kayaking. The Grade V Karamea River offers some of the country's most remote white-water rafting and kayaking. Access is generally by helicopter and rafting trips last up to a week, thus involving overnight camping. There is also great white water on the Buller River near Murchison, which runs along part of the park's southern boundary. Local knowledge is essential on these trips so use a local guiding company of good repute.

slightly scary climb to Flora Carpark on Mt. Arthur, and from Golden Bay its into the Cobb Valley. The main West Coast access is through Karamea; this is also the southwestern entry to the Heaphy Track. Helicopters regularly transport fishing fans to secret river spots, though large areas of the park are designated wilderness, where no development or helicopter transport is permitted. ⊕ *www.doc.govt.nz/parks-and-recreation/* *places-to-go/nelson-tasman/places/ kahurangi-national-park.*

Oparara Cave System

CAVE | Magical rain forests and sculpted landforms here are encompassed in the Honeycomb Hill Caves Specially Protected Area, within Kahurangi National Park. Spectacular features at Oparara include a series of huge limestone arches (including the largest in the southern hemisphere, at

470 feet), passages, and caverns. Several short walks explore the caves, which are about a 45-minute drive northeast of Karamea. The Oparara Valley Project Trust, a community project, has enhanced visitor facilities, and offers guided tours that can include both walks and kayaking explorations. Also in this cave system is Honeycomb Hill, featuring underground passages of more than 13 km (8 miles) in length that contain the largest collection of subfossil bird bones found in New Zealand; many of them are extinct, including nine moa species and the giant NZ eagle. The caves are protected, and access is by guided tour only. ⊠ *Karamea* ☎ *03/782–6652* ⊕ *www.oparara.co.nz* ✉ *Guided tours from NZ$95.*

 ## 🏃 Activities

HIKING

Bush & Beyond Guided Walks

HIKING/WALKING | Walk with the locals on guided day walks or multiday hikes throughout Kahurangi National Park. Trips are tailored to your level of fitness and interests. They can be self-catering (still guided) or fully catered, where your accommodations, food, and transfers are all taken care of. These guys operate year-round and know the Kahurangi area and beyond. They are also ardent conservationists, volunteering with predator pest control groups aimed to restore the wildlife in the park. ☎ *03/543–3742, 21/0270–8209* ⊕ *www.heaphytrackguidedwalks.co.nz.*

Heaphy Track

HIKING/WALKING | The 78-km (49-mile), five-day Heaphy Track is a Great Walk, one of New Zealand's premier multiday trails. It traverses a grand landscape mix of beech, rata, nikau, and coastal rain forests along with tussock-covered table lands, as it crosses Kahurangi National Park from Golden Bay to the West Coast. The track can be approached from Karamea or Collingwood. Kiwi are often heard at night. There are seven huts and nine

campsites, and spots in both must be booked year-round. Bookings can be made online or through DOC offices or the Nelson, Motueka, or Golden Bay i-SITE Visitor Centre. Each end of this track is a drive of several hours apart; shuttle transport (by coach or air) can be arranged. Mountain bikers are permitted on the track in winter (from May 1 to November 30). Several companies offer guided options. ⊠ *Kahurangi National Park* ☎ *03/546–8210 Great Walks Help Desk, Nelson DOC office* ⊕ *www.doc.govt.nz.*

Kahurangi Guided Walks

HIKING/WALKING | If you'd like some expert company on hikes around the national park, these specialists run half- and one-day treks on the best routes, as well as the full five-day Heaphy Track hike. More strenuous, multiday walks explore The Matiri Tops, Wangapeka Track, and remote, rarely visited spots such as Boulder Lake. Prices vary for each customized trip; these folks also run guided walks in Abel Tasman National Park and around Golden Bay. ☎ *03/391–4120* ⊕ *www.kahurangiwalks.co.nz.*

Nelson Lakes National Park

100 km (62 miles) south of Nelson.

Spread around mountains and two spectacular glacial lakes, Rotoroa and Rotoiti, Nelson Lakes National Park also extends to high alpine passes and rocky peaks, clear-running rivers, and bush-lined trails. The native beech forests pour down to the lakeshore. On cloudy days, mist swirls through the trees, wetting the draping mosses. On sunny days the intense green shines through and the birdsong resounds. Lake Rotoiti is also one site of the Rotoiti Nature Recovery Project, through which long-term intensive pest control has helped the recovery of native

Planning Your Trip to Nelson Lakes

Best Time to Go

Summer is the most popular time of year to visit as the weather is warm (for an alpine region), the lakes are swimmable (barely), and, for climbers, the high-alpine passes are usually free of snow and avalanche risk. Voracious sand flies, however, are a problem at any time. Bring your repellent.

Best Activities

Climb. Experienced alpinists enjoy the challenges of the high passes and summit ridgelines that lead to the highest peaks of the park. Experience is vital; some of this climbing is technical and subject to severe and changeable weather.

Kayak. Both Rotoroa and Rotoiti are excellent places to kayak. Although both lakes can attract high winds, summer conditions are usually favorable. Pick your day, pack a lunch, and leave from the jetty at the head of either lake. At St. Arnaud in summer, kayaks can be hired from the Rotoiti lakeshore. Pull up to a quiet stretch of pebble beach, where all you will hear are the birds and the breeze singing through the trees. Don't forget your sand-fly repellent.

Ski. In winter a small club ski field welcomes visitors. Rainbow Ski Area is an hour's drive from St. Arnaud.

It has basic facilities (rope tows and a café) and access is via a steepish mountain road (open June to October). There is also ski hire at Rainbow.

Walk. The park is laced with walking tracks, which center on the two lakes and range from easy 30-minute wanders to serious multiday treks deep into the mountains. In summer the longer walks are usually passable, although a cold snap can bring snow at any time to the passes between valleys. Day walks include the climb up Mt. Robert on the zigzagging Pinchgut Track, the climb to Parachute Rocks, and the lakeside walk around Rotoiti. Popular longer hikes are overnight to Lake Angelus Hut (often crowded in summer) and the three- to four-day Travers-Sabine circuit, which leads up the Travers, crosses an alpine pass, and returns down the Sabine. You camp or stay in park huts along the way.

Water Taxi. During summer water taxis work on both lakes. They save a half-day walk at the start of some longer trails, such as the Travers/Sabine circuit, and give nonwalkers quick access into the park. Remember to take everything you need with you as there are no shops, cafés, or amenities away from St. Arnaud.

birds and the reintroduction of others, including great spotted kiwi.

GETTING HERE AND AROUND

It's a 100-km (65-mile) drive south from Nelson to St. Arnaud, the hub of the park. Head south on State Highway 6; at Wai-iti, just south of Wakefield, veer left off the highway and follow the Golden Downs Road through to St. Arnaud. If coming up from the West Coast, pass through Murchison then after 35 km (21 miles), turn right at Kawatiri Junction. It's a further 30 minutes from here to St. Arnaud. From the East Coast, drive up the Wairau Valley from Blenheim, heading left (west) off State Highway 6 at Renwick.

Shuttle transport to the park is available through Nelson Lakes Shuttles; they will deliver to most track terminus points and

There are numerous hiking tracks through the vast tracts of forest, deep river valleys, tussock tablelands, and mountain ridges of Kahurangi National Park.

the main stops as well. They can also link you between the various local national parks and track entry points.

BUS CONTACTS Nelson Lakes Shuttles.
☎ 03/540–2042 ⊕ www.nelsonlakesshuttles.co.nz.

CONTACTS DOC Nelson Lakes Visitor Centre. ✉ View Rd., St. Arnaud ☎ 03/521–1806 ⊕ www.doc.govt.nz.

Sights

Nelson Lakes National Park
NATIONAL/STATE PARK | Snow-covered peaks and alpine passes sit between two deep brooding, forest-surrounded lakes. Dense native forest, swampy wetlands, and tumbling rivers line the valleys, and birdlife join in a resounding dawn chorus. It's an exhilarating environment. Two stunningly scenic glacial-formed lakes, Rotoroa and Rotoiti, are the central focus of Nelson Lakes National Park. Also in the park are rocky peaks and tussock-covered tops, glacier-gouged river valleys, and bush-lined trails. Native beech forest pours down to the lakeshores. On cloudy days, mist swirls through the trees, wetting the draping mosses. On sunny days the intense greens shine through and the birds' chorus resounds. Of the two lakes, Rotoroa is less developed, with just a few fishing cottages and a campsite on its northern shore. The village of St. Arnaud, at the northern end of Lake Rotoiti, is the main gateway to the park. An accommodation lodge, a handful of B&Bs, a general store, a café, the DOC Nelson Lakes Visitor Centre, and a host of private holiday homes are located here. Each year in late February or early March, the Antique and Classic Boat Show is held at Lake Rotoiti with close to 200 antique boats congregating for several days of boat racing and boat talk. The DOC Visitor Centre is particularly good, with information on the area's geology, ecology, and human history. Maps and details and advice on the hiking trails are available, and a mountain weather forecast is issued daily. DOC also

administers two excellent campgrounds near the lake frontage. Bookings for these, at Kerr Bay and West Bay, can be made online or at the visitor center. ⊕ *www.doc.govt.nz/parks-and-recrea-tion/places-to-go/nelson-tasman/places/ nelson-lakes-national-park.*

Hotels

Alpine Lodge

$$ | HOTEL | This might be a European alpine-inspired lodge, but the view out the window is all Kiwi—wetlands, forest, and mountains. **Pros:** nice backcountry lodge ambience; the bushwalks are beautiful; varied, wholesome menu selection. **Cons:** bring repellent for the sand flies; restaurant closed July through October; a bit of a long walk to some rooms. $ *Rooms from: NZ$185* ✉ *Main Rd., St. Arnaud* ☎ *03/521–1869* ⊕ *www. alpinelodge.co.nz* ➽ *32 rooms* ⚭ *No meals.*

Activities

Nelson Lakes has a number of half-, full-, and multiday trails that leave from the area around St. Aranud. The **Lake Rotoiti Circuit** gets you around the lake in an easy daylong walk. The rather steep **Mt. Robert Track** zigzags up the face of Mt. Robert, giving you a superb view back across Lake Rotoiti toward St. Arnaud village. The return walk (fitness and good weather required) can be done in a loop by descending a marked track down Mt. Robert's eastern slopes to meet up with the Lake Rotoiti Circuit Track. Other tracks lead off these into the higher and more remote mountain areas and river valleys. Hut accommodations are available on a "first-in, first-served" basis. Backcountry experience (or traveling with someone who has this) and quality out-door equipment are necessary on these longer tracks. Walkers on the Te Araroa Trail (which consists of walking the

length of New Zealand) tend to crowd into the huts here in late summer.

Murchison

125 km (78 miles) south of Nelson, 63 km (40 miles) west of Lake Rotoiti.

Surrounded by high mountains and roaring rivers, this small town is in some big country. With Nelson Lakes National Park to the east, Kahurangi National Park to the north, and the Matakitaki, Buller, Matiri, and Mangles rivers all converging on its doorstep, Murchison has gained the reputation as New Zealand's "white-water capital," and boasts the most-kayaked stretches of white water in the southern hemisphere. There are 13 rivers within 20 km (12½ miles) of town and white-water kayakers and rafters turn up every year to enjoy the sport these rivers offer. In particular, the first weekend in March brings more than 500 devotees to Murchison for Bullerfest, a churning gathering of white-water junkies. These local rivers are also teeming with trout and fly-fishing enthusiasts from all over the world who converge to test their skills in one of the world's top fishing regions. Murchison residents still consider their landmark historic event "the earthquake," a major quake that hit in June 1929. The epicenter was nearby in the Buller Gorge, and the quake drastically altered the landscape. A second in 1968 (centered on nearby Inangahua) also rearranged the landscape considerably but was less destructive in loss of life. Although most operators now accept credit cards, the only ATM in town accepts New Zealand cards only; so if yours is from elsewhere, make sure you have some cash on you.

If you're driving to the West Coast from Nelson or Motueka, State Highway 6 passes through Murchison before turning right, crossing the **Buller River** 12 km (7 miles) farther south then heading through the Buller Gorge toward the West Coast.

This twisting, narrow road follows the Buller as it carves a deep gorge below the jagged, earthquake-rocked mountain bluffs. Not far from here is New Zealand's longest swaying footbridge, the **Buller Gorge Swing Bridge** and the departure point for the **Buller Canyon Jet,** should you want to ride a few rapids. The upper gorge is tight and hilly, but once past the township of Inangahua the lower gorge is easier to navigate. This is all forested country, so you'll have to use your imagination to reconstruct the days when places such as Lyell, 34 km (21 miles) west of Murchison, were bustling gold mining towns. There's now only a peaceful, Department of Conservation campsite at Lyell, also the trailhead for The Old Ghost Road and a multiday mountain biking and walking route to the West Coast. As you drive, you'll pass high forest-clad mountains, narrow single-lane bridges, and the village of Inangahua.

GETTING HERE AND AROUND

Although it's 100 km (62 miles) from the nearest town, Murchison is easy to access by road, sitting right on State Highway 6. It's a 1¾-hour drive south of Nelson, 4¼ hours north of Christchurch, and 1½ hours east of Westport (without scenic stops). It is also one of only a couple of comfort and fuel stops on these long stretches so if you are only passing through, take advantage of its conveniences.

InterCity buses pass through daily on its services between Nelson and Christchurch and Nelson and the West Coast.

VISITOR INFORMATION

CONTACTS Murchison Information Centre. ✉ *47 Waller St.* 🕾 *03/523–9350* ⊕ *www. visitmurchison.nz.*

👁 Sights

Murchison District Museum

MUSEUM | For a small-town operation this local, community-run museum has a lot to look at. The rustic little building features an exhibit and memorial for the 1929 earthquake here, in which several locals died. There's also a good collection of farming and agricultural machinery from the town's colonial era, plus displays on the region's gold and coal mining history. The museum is run by a few volunteers, who make a valiant attempt to open regularly. ✉ *60 Fairfax St.* 🕾 *03/523–9392.*

The Natural Flames Experience

LOCAL INTEREST | There are few places in the world where you can find a natural gas flame, but this is one. In an ancient forest setting near Murchison, there's been one quietly glowing since the 1920s, and this tour company has sole access rights. The four-hour tour involves a short, scenic drive, education about oil drilling and farming, a one-hour backcountry walk (you might get wet feet) through farmland and forest to the flame, and a hot brew cooked up on the natural fire. Tour groups are restricted to eight people. Booking ahead is essential. ✉ *47 Waller St.* 🕾 *0800/687–244 New Zealand only* ⊕ *www.naturalflames.co.nz* 💲 *NZ$95.*

Restaurants

Murchison has a great selection of casual cafés serving fresh, wholesome fare, just what you need after a day playing in white water.

Beechwoods Cafe

$$ | CAFÉ | Lots of wholesome breakfast and lunch options, hot snacks, and sweet treats are offered here. Some popular choices include the snapper (fish) sandwich, Beechwood burgers, and real fruit ice cream. **Known for:** popular stop for bus passengers so gets crowded; classic highway café; nice selection of to-go foods. 💲 *Average main: NZ$16* ✉ *32 Waller St.* 🕾 *03/523–9571.*

Rivers Café

$$$ | CAFÉ | Good food and good coffee is served every day in a welcoming, rustic setting. It's hard to find, tucked around a corner, so it's mostly frequented by locals and those in the know. **Known for:** family-friendly atmosphere; big helpings; lamb shank. $ *Average main: NZ$23* ✉ *51 Fairfax St.* ☎ *03/523–9009* ⊕ *www. visitmurchison.nz/rivers-cafe.html.*

🛏 Hotels

★ Murchison Lodge

$$$ | **B&B/INN** | Tucked in a quiet back-street of Murchison, these comfortably countrified guest rooms, with strong colors and lots of wood in a beautiful old villa, are within easy walking distance of the mighty Buller River. **Pros:** private access to the Buller River through a grassy field; welcoming hosts; incredible breakfast included. **Cons:** a few stairs to climb; lounge (albeit beautiful) is shared with other guests; bathrooms on the small side. $ *Rooms from: NZ$240* ✉ *15 Grey St.* ☎ *03/523–9196* ⊕ *www. murchisonlodge.co.nz* ⊘ *Closed July and Aug.; exact dates vary* ⇥ *6 rooms* ⦿| *Breakfast* ⌕ *No children under 12.*

Owen River Lodge

$$$$ | **HOTEL** | One of the classiest of several fully inclusive luxury fly-fishing lodges in this region, Owen River has six beautifully appointed cottages overlooking the Owen River Valley. **Pros:** large garden; fully equipped tackle room and fly-making table; beautiful views. **Cons:** the last mile or two to the lodge is not paved but is easy enough to drive; quite remote; if you're not into fishing, you might feel out of it. $ *Rooms from: NZ$845* ✉ *Owen Valley East Rd., 15 min north of Murchison* ☎ *03/523–9075* ⊕ *www.owenriverlodge.co.nz* ⊘ *Closed May–Sept.* ⇥ *6 suites* ⦿| *All-inclusive.*

🏃 Activities

Murchison's claim as a white-water destination is not to be ignored. They have some of the best white water anywhere.

RAFTING

Buller Gorge Swingbridge and Buller Canyon Jet Boat Ride

BOATING | A bit of an oddity in seemingly the middle of nowhere, you can cross what is reportedly New Zealand's longest bridge (NZ$10), then, instead of walking back, for a further NZ$30 you can zip-line back across the river. Jet-boat trips (NZ$105) through the Buller Gorge also leave from here; the 80-minute rides depart hourly throughout the summer, 10 to 4, and by arrangement in winter. You can also try your luck panning for gold or simply read about the massive earthquake that shook the land around here in 1968. ✉ *Upper Buller Gorge, State Hwy. 6* ☎ *03/523–9809, 0800/285–537 New Zealand only* ⊕ *www.bullergorge.co.nz.*

★ Ultimate Descents New Zealand

WHITE-WATER RAFTING | **FAMILY** | Highly experienced guides run rafting trips on the Maruia (Grade III), Clarence (Grade II), Buller (Grade II–IV), Mokihinui (Grade IV), and Karamea (Grade V) rivers. All half-day and day trips include a light snack, and the multiday trips are fully catered. They also run family trips, day trips on a gentle section of the Buller, and overnights on the Maruia River. They've been doing this for years and know the water well. ✉ *38 Waller St.* ☎ *03/523–9899, 0800/748–377 New Zealand only* ⊕ *www.rivers.co.nz* ✉ *From NZ$160.*

Wild Rivers Rafting

WHITE-WATER RAFTING | Qualified guides introduce even first-time rafters to one of the premium white-water rafting experiences in the country, the legendary "Earthquake Rapids" on the Buller River. These are Grade III and IV rapids. The 25-foot cliff jump into the river is optional. River time is two hours; allow four hours total. Pickup is at the Iron Bridge on State Highway 6, 37 km (23 miles) from Murchison. ✉ *Iron Bridge, Upper Buller Gorge Rd., State Hwy. 6* ☎ *0508/467–238 in New Zealand,*

03/789–8953 ⊕ *www.wildriversrafting. co.nz* ✉ *NZ$160 for 4-hr trip.*

Westport

230 km (144 miles) southeast of Nelson.

One of New Zealand's oldest ports sits at the mouth of the mighty Buller River. Once a boomtown for two separate gold rushes, it's now a quiet little hub (population 3,100) for the local farming and coal industries, plus the rapidly expanding adventure-tourism niche. It's an interesting place to stop before heading south toward Punakaiki and the glaciers or north to remote Karamea and the Heaphy Track; the best of Westport is out of town, either on the coast or up the rivers. The classic sights of the Westport region are breaking white-capped waves, blue sea, seals, rocky outcrops, and acres of flax and wetlands. In the town itself, several striking art deco buildings line the main street. Stop by the little **Coaltown Museum** at the i-SITE Visitor Centre on Palmerston Street to learn about the town's coal mining history. Or treat yourself to a drive to the **Denniston Plateau,** 18 km (11 miles) northeast of town and high on a mountain plateau. Information panels and actual machinery detail life in this lonely outpost from the late 1800s through the early 1900s. Carving a living from the rich seams of coal in the surrounding tussock-covered hills, the miners and their families had to struggle with wild weather, isolation, and primitive conditions. A popular historical novel about these coal mining pioneers and their families, *The Denniston Rose,* by New Zealand writer Jenny Pattrick, details the area and the harsh colonial lifestyle.

The **Westport i-SITE Visitor Centre** can also provide information on Karamea township and Kahurangi National Park.

GETTING HERE AND AROUND

It's a 3-hour drive to Westport from Nelson to the north, or a 1½-hour drive south to Greymouth. Either way you'll pass along incredibly scenic coastlines or river gorges surrounded by thick native bush and high ranges. InterCity buses travel to Westport daily, en route between Nelson and the glaciers.

TOURS
OutWest Tours
GUIDED TOURS | Four-wheel drive tours take you through private farmland and forest, with interesting limestone landscapes, rivers and waterfalls, historic mining trails, and local characters to meet along the way. They'll also take you onto the Denniston Plateau, and explain the history of the mining village that struggled to survive on this remote, mist-clad mountain. Three day-long tours are also offered. ☎ *027/641–8267, 0800/688–937 New Zealand only* ⊕ *www.outwest. co.nz* ✉ *From NZ$160.*

★ Underworld Adventures
ADVENTURE TOURS | **FAMILY** | Near the small town of Charleston, you'll find several gentle adventures leading into the nearby rain forest and then beneath it. Ride an open-sided bush-train through the forest, take a cave walk into a limestone mountain in the Nile Valley (the glowworm grotto is the highlight), and drift slowly by raft through the glowworm caves before breaking out to the river. For a bigger challenge, try the full day caving adventure; it includes a 154-foot abseil (rappel), then crawling, swimming, and climbing your way back to the surface. The guides are great. Reservations are essential. ✉ *Charleston Hotel, State Hwy. 6, Charleston* ☎ *03/788–8168* ⊕ *www. caverafting.com* ✉ *Train ride NZ$25, activities from NZ$120.*

VISITOR INFORMATION
CONTACTS Westport i-SITE Visitor Centre and Coaltown Museum. ✉ *123 Palmerston St.* ☎ *03/789–6658* ⊕ *www.westport.nz.*

◉ Sights

Coaltown Museum
MUSEUM | Westport is a town based around coal, and the stories, challenges,

and hardships of mining on (and under) the high plateau behind the town are related in this interactive museum. Hogging the limelight is the 8-ton coal wagon, perched on the 45-degree angle just as it would have been when descending the famous incline, off the Denniston Plateau. Museum entry is through the Westport i-SITE Visitor Centre. ⊠ *123 Palmerston St.* ☎ *03/789–8204* ⌑ *NZ$10.*

 ## Restaurants

Denniston Dog

$$$ | CAFÉ | FAMILY | This old bank building is loaded with local character in its current guise as a cheerful pub and gathering spot. If the coal mining heritage of this town interests you, you will enjoy the memorabilia and photos on display. **Known for:** traditional New Zealand food; big breakfasts; stone-grilled meats and seafood. ⑤ *Average main: NZ$30* ⊠ *18 Wakefield St.* ☎ *03/789–5030* ⊕ *www. dennistondog.co.nz.*

PortSide Bistro & Bar

$$$$ | MODERN NEW ZEALAND | There's a huge range of fare on the menu here, be it for breakfast, lunch, or dinner. Breakfasts are served until 3 pm, and coffee and cake are always ready on the go. **Known for:** fresh market fish, delivered directly from the boats; bistro burgers; local atmosphere. ⑤ *Average main: NZ$34* ⊠ *13 Cobden St.* ☎ *03/789–7133* ⊕ *www. portsidebistro.co.nz* ⊘ *Closed Mon.*

Hotels

Archer House

$$$ | B&B/INN | Rooms are spacious, linens are fine, and the art collection is impressive at this villa that was built in the late 1800s. **Pros:** sunny conservatory for coffee; short walk to Westport restaurants; gracious old home with beautiful garden. **Cons:** no modern heating; patchy Wi-Fi; decor not for everyone. ⑤ *Rooms from: NZ$245* ⊠ *75 Queen St.* ☎ *03/789–8778, 0800/789–877 New Zealand only*

⊕ *www.archerhouse.co.nz* ⌑ *3 rooms* ⎮⊙⎮ *Breakfast.*

★ Birds Ferry Lodge

$$$$ | B&B/INN | Named for the ferry that crossed the local river during the gold rush, this lodge and self-contained cottage is set on 50 acres. **Pros:** lots of good walks; home-baked bread and organic produce from the garden; outdoor bath. **Cons:** hard to find in the dark (watch closely for signs off the highway); entry road is rough gravel; no shops nearby. ⑤ *Rooms from: NZ$420* ⊠ *Birds Ferry Rd., Charleston* ☎ *03/429–1604, 0800/212–207* ⊕ *www.birdsferrylodge. co.nz* ⌑ *3 rooms* ⎮⊙⎮ *Breakfast.*

The Steeples Cottage, Studio & B&B

$ | B&B/INN | Perched on the cliff top overlooking the Steeples rocks offshore, this self-contained cottage (with sea views) along with the rooms in the main house are all great value. **Pros:** stunning coast views; safe swimming at nearby beach; charming, helpful hosts. **Cons:** parking can be a bit tight; can be hard to find; out of town so need to stock up before you go. ⑤ *Rooms from: NZ$120* ⊠ *48 Lighthouse Rd., Cape Foulwind* ☎ *03/789–7876* ⊕ *www.steeplescottage. co.nz* ⌑ *4 rooms* ⎮⊙⎮ *Breakfast.*

Punakaiki and Paparoa National Park

269 km (168 miles) southwest of Nelson.

Paparoa National Park extends from the mountainous Paparoa Range inland, to the coast. With steep bluffs, limestone basins, canyons, caves, and fluted rock, it's a formidable environment. The cliffs, flood-prone rivers, dense rain forest, and extensive cave systems in this park draw hikers, cavers, and, of course, photographers. The major track entry points—Bullock Creek, Fox River, and Pororari River on the coast, and Blackball township on the eastern side of the park—open onto an otherworldly zone of jungle green, striking *nikau* palms, rain forest, beech forest, and rushing streams. A purpose-built Great Walk, the Paparoa Track, is a two- or three-day walk or bike ride that crosses the park from east to west. Along the Punakai coastal road, there is much to do, like day hikes into the park, canoeing on the Pororari River, coastal tracks to collapsed sea caverns, horse treks, and entry-level cave experiences. Call into the Paparoa National Park i-SITE Visitors Centre for maps and information.

One of the stars of the West Coast is the walk to the **Pancake Rocks & Blowholes,** one of New Zealand's most popular short walks. The huge swells that batter this coast have eroded the limestone cliffs, carving them into fantastical shapes. A paved walkway leads you past the curious pancake-stacked rocks and through the windswept cover of tenacious New Zealand flax and *nikau* palms to the most dramatic viewpoints, including the broiling cauldron called the Surge Pool (once a sea cavern before the roof collapsed) and the pumping fissure of the Chimney Pot. In the right conditions, these blowholes can spout a thundering geyser of spray. To add to the drama, New Zealand's highest mountain, Aoraki/Mt. Cook, is sometimes visible across the sea to the south. To reach the rocks from the highway, cross the road from the visitor center and follow the clearly signed, easy 20-minute walk. Keep turning left along the path so you don't miss the best bits out around the Surge Pool. Look for the white-fronted terns, who nest on the spray-soaked rock stacks here.

GETTING HERE AND AROUND
At first glance, Punakaiki looks like nothing more than a small cluster of beach houses and shops—a blip on the radar without even a gas station or ATM. It's worth stopping, though, for its famous Pancake Rocks—a maze of limestone stacked high above the sea, and an easy walk from the road. Punakaiki is also the main entry point to the Paparoa National Park tracks and river activities. Punakaiki is roughly halfway along the coast between Greymouth and Westport on State Highway 6; 40 minutes north of Greymouth; and one hour south of Westport. The road is winding and steep in places, with high drop-offs to the coast on the stretch north of Punakaiki. InterCity buses pass through daily. Accommodations range from a holiday park to holiday homes, B&Bs, and a resort-style hotel.

If you have a spare half-hour, follow the Truman Track, 3 km (2 miles) north of the village down to the coast. It's a delightful walk through native bush to a dramatic coastal bay. There's also easy access to the coast from the beach in front of the Punakaiki Resort just south of the Pancake Rocks.

The Paparoa National Park i-SITE Visitors Centre, across the road from the track to the Pancake Rocks, is a handy place to learn more about the rock formations and the park.

VISITOR INFORMATION
CONTACTS Paparoa National Park Visitors Centre. ✉ *4294 Main Rd., State Hwy. 6, Punakaiki* ☎ *03/731–1895* ⊕ *www.doc. govt.nz.*

🍴 Restaurants

Eating options are limited in tiny Punakaiki, with just a pub and couple of daytime cafés open to the public. The oceanfront restaurant at Punakaiki Resort is a slightly higher-priced option. If you decide to stay in a self-catering unit, you'll need to bring in all your food, as there are no general stores in town.

Pancake Rocks Cafe
$$ | CAFÉ | A little café open daily, Pancake Rocks serves a full breakfast, lunch, and (in summer) dinner menu (the burgers will set you right for beach-walking). There's also a small gallery/shop here, selling quality New Zealand souvenirs,

including jewelry. **Known for:** pancake stack with maple syrup and bacon; quirky decor; stone-oven pizzas. $ *Average main: NZ$27* ✉ *Coast Rd., Punakaiki* ☎ *03/731–1122* ⊕ *www.pancakerockscafe.com.*

🛏 Hotels

Although tiny, Punakaiki is a popular tourist spot and therefore has some good accommodations available, including a sizable hotel and self-catering cottages with friendly hosts.

Hydrangea Cottages

$$$ | **B&B/INN** | You'll be lulled by the constant roar of the ocean in these brightly colored apartments with recycled native timbers and contemporary furniture; there's also a rustic studio cottage and a large cottage with sea views and a bath on the deck. **Pros:** ocean views; relaxing atmosphere; close to Pancake Rocks. **Cons:** steep driveway; turns onto a very busy main road, especially in summer; native birds pūkeko and weka will grab scraps off the decks if you're not careful. $ *Rooms from: NZ$275* ✉ *Main Rd., Punakaiki* ☎ *03/731–1839* ⊕ *www.pancake-rocks.co.nz* ⇆ *6 cottages* ⦿ *No meals.*

Punakaiki Resort

$$$ | **HOTEL** | The modern beach house design at this resort blends well with the dynamic coastal site; the front steps almost reach to the beach. **Pros:** prime seafront location; spectacular views from rooms and oceanfront restaurant and bar; restaurant dinner menu is very good. **Cons:** traffic noise in some units; guest rooms quite basic; not all rooms have a balcony. $ *Rooms from: NZ$300* ✉ *State Hwy. 6, 1 km (½ mile) south of Pancake Rocks, Punakaiki* ☎ *03/731–1168, 0800/706–707 New Zealand only* ⊕ *www.punakaiki-resort.co.nz* ⇆ *61 rooms* ⦿ *No meals.*

🏃 Activities

★ Punakaiki Canoes

CANOEING/ROWING/SKULLING | FAMILY | The essence of this region is best understood by a paddle up the Pororari River, on the northern edge of Punakaiki. Glide the dark yet clear waters between sheer limestone cliffs, nikau palms, and giant rata trees. Pretend you're in the movies—*The Hobbit* cliff scenes were actually filmed here. Or head to the estuary, where the water opens out into a more playful area. These trips are suitable for all abilities and ages, but are dependent on the weather and the river level. All gear is provided. ✉ *State Hwy. 6, by bridge, Punakaiki* ☎ *03/731–1870* ⊕ *www.riverkayaking.co.nz* ⛏ *From NZ$45.*

Punakaiki Horse Treks

HORSEBACK RIDING | One of the most scenic horse riding options in the country includes riding on the beach through the forest beside huge limestone bluffs, and a river crossing. Treks run daily during summer months. The horses are good, and you will get some riding instruction should you need it. ✉ *4224 Main Rd., Punakaiki* ☎ *03/731–1839* ⊕ *www.pancake-rocks.co.nz* ⛏ *From NZ$190 (minimum 2 people).*

Greymouth

44 km (28 miles) south of Punakaiki, 258 km (160 miles) west of Christchurch.

The town of Greymouth sits, as the name suggests, at the mouth of the Grey River. But gold and green (as in pounamu, or jade) were initially the colors of note in this settlement, thanks to its strong mining history. It's the biggest town on the West Coast, and today many travelers arrive here on the TranzAlpine train from Christchurch. Instead of being captivated by the area's stunning coastal drives, train-goers will

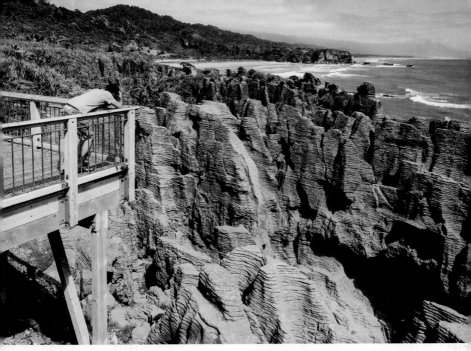

Paparoa National Park's eroded coastline includes the amazing Pancake Rocks.

enjoy a breathtaking ride on viaducts high above riverbeds, beneath steep peaks, and through dripping rain forest. If you're arriving and returning by train, take an extra day or two for a trip up to Punakaiki or down to the glaciers, to grasp the scope of the landscape in these parts.

GETTING HERE AND AROUND

Drive from Nelson or Westport in the north, from the glaciers to the south, or from Christchurch in the east, over Arthur's Pass. Be on your guard around Greymouth and Hokitika as there are a number of one-way bridges and unalarmed rail crossings. InterCity buses arrive in Greymouth daily.

The TranzAlpine train departs Christchurch daily at 8:15 am and arrives in Greymouth at 1:05 pm; the return train departs Greymouth at 2:05 pm and arrives at Christchurch at 6:31 pm. One-way fare options range NZ$139–NZ$219.

BUS DEPOT Greymouth InterCity. ✉ Railway Station, 164 Mackay St. ⊕ www.intercity.co.nz.

TRAIN CONTACTS TranzAlpine Express.
☎ 04/495–0775, 0800/872–467 New Zealand only ⊕ www.greatjourneysofnz.co.nz/tranzalpine.

VISITOR INFORMATION

CONTACTS Greymouth i-SITE Visitor Centre.
✉ Old Railway Station, 164 Mackay St. ☎ 03/768–7080 ⊕ www.westcoasttravel.co.nz.

◉ Sights

The land around Greymouth (like Hokitika to the south) is particularly rich in pounamu, the greenstone (New Zealand jade) highly prized by Māori. This is all Ngai Tahu iwi (tribe) area, and as part of the 1997 Ngai Tahu Settlement between the tribe and the Crown, the government recognized Ngai Tahu as having sole rights to collect and sell the precious pounamu in its natural form. If you want the authentic product, when buying greenstone on the West Coast, make sure it is local greenstone and not imported jade. All genuine greenstone found by iwi in local waters is identified with a unique traceability code.

Left Bank Art Gallery

MUSEUM | This is a top spot to see and purchase a range of artworks, including contemporary pounamu (greenstone or jade) carvings. Housed in the old Greymouth branch of the Bank of New Zealand, this progressive little gallery supports local artists and holds regularly changing exhibitions. Displays in the old vault include a collection of older pounamu artworks. ✉ 1 Tainui St. ☎ 03/768–0038 ⊕ www. leftbankarts.org.nz.

Shades of Jade

MUSEUM | Come here to find quality greenstone sourced from West Coast rivers from Punakaiki to Haast. Be sure to check out the unique flower jade, with gold or white markings found in rivers close to Greymouth. Pendants, sculptures, and a variety of jade types are on display. The gallery's principal carver, Jeremy Dalzell, can often be seen at work here. ✉ 22 Tainui St. ☎ 03/768–0794 ⊕ www.shadesofjade.co.nz.

Shantytown Heritage Park

MINE | FAMILY | A hands-on reenactment of an 1880s industrial town, Shantytown will show you it was all about steam in those days. Most of the buildings are reproductions, including a jail, a blacksmith shop, a railway station, and Chinatown. Gold-digging displays include a giant water jet for blasting the gold-bearing rock and soil from the hillside, water races, and a stamper—battery-powered by a 30-foot waterwheel—for crushing the ore. You can pan for gold, ride an old bush tramline, take a break in the café, or share a picnic on the lawns then go back for more. ✉ 310 Rutherglen Rd. ☎ 03/762–6634, 0800/742–689 New Zealand only ⊕ www.shantytown.co.nz ≊ NZ$34, tram ride included.

🍴 Restaurants

DP1 Cafe

$$ | CAFÉ | Homey hospitality in this colorful, retro-style spot comes with house-cooked breakfasts (scrambled eggs are as good as you'll find anywhere), lunches, and baked goods. Plus, the outlook over the Grey River is great. **Known for:** local art on display; hip, funky vibe; tasty coffee and breakfasts. Ⓢ Average main: NZ$17 ✉ 104–108 Mawhera Quay ☎ 03/768–4005 ⊗ No dinner ▭ No credit cards.

★ Monteiths Brewing Company

$$$ | MODERN NEW ZEALAND | They started brewing beer on the West Coast right here in 1868, and now the modern version of the brewery offers a full restaurant, a brewing museum, brewery tours and, of course, lots of fresh brews. The restaurant serves standard Kiwi fare, along with tapas and platters to match the beers. **Known for:** historic brewery tours; antipasto platters; great local brews. Ⓢ Average main: NZ$23 ✉ 60 Herbert St. ☎ 03/768–4149 ⊕ www. monteiths.co.nz.

Speight's Ale House

$$$ | NEW ZEALAND | The bistro-style menu here includes the signature whitebait (seasonal in September) and blue cod, along with the usual steaks, lamb, salmon, and mussels. In addition, the ales of the famous southern brand, Speights, flow in the stylishly restored interior with shiny, bold copper vents contrasting against the wood and brick decor. **Known for:** local beer selections; pot pies; historic building. Ⓢ Average main: NZ$30 ✉ 130 Mawhera Quay ☎ 03/768–0667 ⊕ www.speightsale-housegreymouth.co.nz.

Stationhouse Café

$$$ | ECLECTIC | The café is in an old railway house with a superb view across Lake Brunner and the forests and wetlands beyond. Lunch options include chowders, salads, homemade pies with mashed potatoes and peas, blue cod, and chips. **Known for:** handy stop for train travelers;

The
West Coast

Kahurangi National Park
Heaphy Track
Oparara Cave System
Karamea

Te Namu

Tasman Sea

Karamea Bight

Mokihinui
Hector
Granity

Westport 67 Waimangaroa

Cape Foulwind

Inangahua

6

69

**Paparoa
National Park**

Punakaiki 65

Reefton

7

Ikamatua

Springs
Junction

Ahaura

TO →
HANMER SPRINGS
& CHRISTCHURCH

Greymouth Ngahere

Taylorville

Moana

Kumara Junction

Jackson

Hokitika

Kumara

Otira

*Arthur's
Pass
National
Park*

Ross 6

Arthur's
Pass

Kakapotahi

73

Okarito

*Lake
Coleridge*

Harihari

Whataroa

*Mount
Hutt*

Darfield

**Westland/
Tai Poutini
National Park** 6

Fox
Glacier

Franz Josef
Glacier

Lake Matheson

Mt Tasman
Aoraki/
Mount Cook

77

Mount
Hutt

Karangarua

Aoraki/
Mount Cook

*Mount Cook
National Park*

*Lake
Tekapo*

80

*Lake
Pukaki*

Ashburton

0 ————— 20 mi
0 ————— 20 km

S O U T H E R N   A L P S

PAPAROA RANGE

VICTORIA RANGE

Hokitika R.

whitebait fritters (in season); family-friendly atmosphere. $ *Average main: NZ$28 ⊠ Koe St., Moana ☎ 03/738–0158 ⊕ www.lakebrunner.net ⊙ Sometimes closed for dinner in winter.*

🛏 Hotels

★ Breakers

$$$$ | B&B/INN | At this welcoming B&B between Greymouth and Punakaiki, two rooms in the main house and two suites in the garden overlook spectacular coastline, with penguins on the beach, native bush surroundings, and welcoming hosts. **Pros:** dinner by arrangement to save a late drive into Greymouth; scenic coastal views; brilliantly friendly and helpful hosts. **Cons:** 15-minute drive from Greymouth; by the main road; can get cold at night. $ *Rooms from: NZ$330 ⊠ 1367 State Hwy. 6, 14 km (9 miles) north of Greymouth ☎ 03/762–7743, 0800/350–590 New Zealand only ⊕ www.breakers.co.nz ⇆ 4 rooms ○ Breakfast.*

Rosewood

$$$ | B&B/INN | Friendly hosts run this traditional-style B&B in a restored 1920s home, with original oak paneling, leadlight windows, and cozy seats in the bay windows. **Pros:** good off-street parking; near the town center; generous cooked breakfast included. **Cons:** busy main street position; upstairs with no elevator; not all rooms have en suite bathrooms. $ *Rooms from: NZ$250 ⊠ 20 High St. ☎ 03/768–4674 ⊕ www.rosewoodnz. co.nz ⇆ 4 rooms ○ Breakfast.*

🏃 Activities

On Yer Bike!

ADVENTURE TOURS | FAMILY | If it's raining, your outdoor options just got a lot more exciting. On Yer Bike! makes the most of rain and mud with some wild fun. The two-hour Bush 'N' Bog tour and the one-hour Enchanted Forest tour will both take you through beautiful native forest, streams, mud, and puddles on an easy-to-ride 4WD buggy. ⊠ *511 State Hwy. 6 ✛ 5 km (3 miles) north of Greymouth ☎ 03/762–7438, 0800/669–372 New Zealand only ⊕ www.onyerbike.co.nz ⊠ From NZ$145.*

Hokitika

41 km (26 miles) south of Greymouth.

Hokitika is one of the larger towns along the West Coast, nestled between the pounding ocean and farms and bush-covered hills. It's a place of simple pleasures: scouting the craft galleries, taking a bushwalk, enjoying the seafood, and looking for evocatively shaped driftwood on the often stormy beach. Hokitika is central enough to take a day trip to Punakaiki or Arthur's Pass. During the height of the gold rushes in the 1860s, Hokitika was New Zealand's busiest port, and had more than 100 hotels. Pick up a Hokitika Heritage Walk brochure (50 cents) from the i-SITE Visitor Centre and explore this rich heritage, along with more recent colonial history. Start with a walk along the Quayside Heritage Area at the southern end of Tancred and Revell streets, and walk along to Sunset Point Lookout. See the old Custom House and river mouth; on a clear day you'll see Aoraki/Mt. Cook across the sea. West Coast rivers are the source of pounamu (jade), which has long been a precious resource for the South Island Māori people, Ngai Tahu. Hokitika is recognized as the center for artists and carvers who create stunning jewelry, from pounamu and other mediums. The town is filled with studios and galleries where you can watch the artists at work, and perhaps take home something special. Wood carvings, pottery, textiles, and photography are also showcased in the galleries, mostly found along Tancred and Weld streets.

Okarito Lagoon

Don't miss a visit to beautiful, coastal Okarito Lagoon, just a 13-km (8-mile) detour off the highway, 15 km (9.3 miles) north of Franz Josef township. An immense forest-fringed coastal lagoon, nestled in scenic splendor beneath the Southern Alps, Okarito is arguably one of the largest, most pristine wetlands remaining in New Zealand. It is home to thousands of sea and wading birds and is backed by the Okarito Kiwi Sanctuary, 27,000 acres of lowland forest and home of the Rowi, a rare species of kiwi. Back in 1866 Okarito was a thriving town of more than 1,200 people, with three theaters and 25 hotels. People came for the gold and for many years there was a working port inside the bar at the entrance to the lagoon. Things have changed dramatically and Okarito is now known for its natural values. A tiny settlement remains, most people just visit to kayak or cruise on the lagoon, watch the birds, walk the short forest and coastal trails, or head out at night for a kiwi-spotting expedition.

Okarito Boat Tours. Your open air, shallow-draft boat glides across the lagoon, nosing into narrow channels lined with ancient rain forest. Watch the feeding birds, possibly a white heron visiting from its nearby breeding colony, or a godwit, one of thousands that fly here each summer from Arctic Siberia. Look up to the majestic backdrop of Aoraki/Mt. Cook and Franz Josef Glacier. Your host Swade runs three daily tours. Trips leave from Okarito Wharf; booking ahead is recommended. ⊠ *Okarito Wharf, Okarito* ☎ *03/753–4223* ⊕ *okaritoboattours.co.nz* ⊠ *From NZ$75.*

Okarito Kiwi Tours. Rowi, or Okarito brown kiwi, live only in this forest and this company holds the only license to guide people to them in their natural habitat. You'll walk softly through the bush, listening for their scuffles and calls before most likely catching a glimpse. They say there's a 98% chance of seeing one on a night tour; all you need is patience and warm, quiet clothes (no nylon windbreakers). Tours last three to five hours, depending on how shy the kiwi are. ⊠ *53 The Strand, Okarito* ☎ *03/753–4330* ⊕ *www.okaritokiwitours.co.nz* ⊠ *NZ$75.*

Okarito Nature Tours. Explore the largest and possibly least modified coastal wetland in New Zealand by kayak, either on a guided tour or by paddling independently. The lagoon is renowned for its birdlife; plucky godwits and other migrants fly here all the way from Siberia each spring (and back in autumn). It's also a great spot to see white herons, who fly here to feed from their sole New Zealand nesting ground in the Waitangiroto River nearby. Enjoy the views—dense rain forest backed by the Southern Alps. ⊠ *1 The Strand, Okarito* ☎ *03/753–4014* ⊕ *www.okarito.co.nz* ⊕ *www.birdingwestcoast.co.nz* ⊠ *From NZ$60.*

GETTING HERE AND AROUND

There are daily flights to Hokitika from Christchurch with Air New Zealand. Arrive by road from Christchurch or Greymouth to the north, or from the glaciers to the south (via State Highway 6). Either way you will enjoy a spectacular drive through mountainous country, national parks, and scenic reserves. InterCity buses arrive in Hokitika daily and stop in front of the National Kiwi Center on Tancred Street.

VISITOR INFORMATION

CONTACTS Hokitika i-SITE Visitor Centre. ✉ *36 Weld St.* ☎ *03/755–6166* ⊕ *www. hokitika.org.*

Sights

Mountain Jade

STORE/MALL | The largest outlet in New Zealand to showcase pounamu has greenstone cutting and carving areas, and an extensive shop. Two or more artists are usually at work, plus they offer two tours each day that relate the history of pounamu, its significance to the Māori people, and its uses. ✉ *41 Weld St.* ☎ *03/755– 8007* ⊕ *www.mountainjade.co.nz.*

Traditional Jade

STORE/MALL | This small family business creates carvings and sculptures, and has a collection of raw jade for you to admire. Visit in the mornings for the best chance of seeing one of the family artists at work. ✉ *2 Tancred St.* ☎ *03/755–5233* ⊕ *www.traditionaljade.co.nz.*

Waewae Pounamu

LOCAL INTEREST | Ngati Waewae is the iwi (tribe) of this area, a subtribe of the South Island Ngai Tahu. The iwi owns and carves all the pounamu at this center. The artists will reveal how every stone has a story. If you buy a piece, they will give you its unique code, which you can use to trace the story of your stone on the center's website. ✉ *39 Weld St.* ☎ *03/755–8304* ⊕ *www.waewae-pounamu.co.nz.*

West Coast Treetop Walk and Cafe

FOREST | You can wander the tops of the ancient trees in the West Coast rain forest on this 1,500-foot long, 66-foot-high walkway through the canopy. You can go even higher on the Hokitika Tower, 130 feet above the forest floor. Views extend over the rain forest to dark, glacial Lake Mahinapua and beyond to the Southern Alps. The walkway is fully wheelchair-accessible. A café and gift shop are also on-site. ✉ *1128 Woodstock Rimu Rd.*

☎ *03/755–5052, 0508/873–38677 New Zealand only* ⊕ *www.treetopsnz.com* 💰 *NZ$32.*

★ West Coast Wilderness Trail

BICYCLING | Hokitika is at about the half-way point of the West Coast Wilderness Trail, one of the Nga Haerenga, New Zealand Cycle Trails. This three-to-four-day purpose-built trail explores the mountains, rivers, rural countryside, and mining history here, and this local company is your best friend to help you with logistics so that you can simply enjoy yourself. They'll rent you bikes, shuttle you to wherever you need, deliver your luggage to your accommodations, and organize day trips that focus on the best trail sections. ✉ *216 Revell St.* ☎ *03/755–5042* ⊕ *wildernesstrailshuttle.co.nz.*

Wildfoods Festival

FESTIVAL | This annual event celebrates bush tucker (food from the bush) from the West Coast's natural food sources. Bite into such delectables as *huhu* grubs, grasshoppers, beetles, whitebait patties (far more mainstream), and wild pork (as in from pigs running wild in the bush, not farmed—or angry), and follow it all with gorse wine, elderflower champagne, or Monteith's bitter beer. It's usually held in the second weekend of March. Book well ahead, as there's a cap of 10,000 participants and usually sells out. ⊕ *www.wildfoods.co.nz.*

Restaurants

Stations Inn - Waterwheel Restaurant and Bar

$$$$ | NEW ZEALAND | Experience quality, classic New Zealand fare in a setting with grand views of the Southern Alps and Tasman Sea. Whether its meat, fish, shell-fish, or vegetables, this place delivers, and also matches its food with the local West Coast brew, Monteith's. **Known for:** special occasion dining; stunning views; excellent beef and lamb dishes. 💲 *Average main: NZ$34* ✉ *Blue Spur Rd., RD 2*

☎ *03/755–5499* ⊕ *www.stationsinnhoki-tika.co.nz* ⊗ *Closed Sun. and Mon. No lunch.*

Stella Cafe and Cheesery

$$ | CAFÉ | At this quirky café and delicatessen, the honey comes directly from the in-house beehive. A breakfast menu, baked goods (try the cheese scones), and lunch dishes that change with the seasons are on offer. **Known for:** cheese tasting menus; in-house beehive; wholesome to-go food. ⑤ *Average main: NZ$15* ✉ *84 Revell St.* ☎ *03/755–5432.*

★ Theatre Royal Hotel Kumara

$$$ | MODERN NEW ZEALAND | The owners spent years restoring this old pub, and now the place hums with activity and tasty food. Locally cured bacon, venison patties, wild (bush) pork sliders, house-made pies, and salads all vie for attention on the breakfast/brunch/lunch menus. **Known for:** the community's local pub; history (ambience) meets modernity (food); classic miner's breakfast. ⑤ *Average main: NZ$30* ✉ *81 Seddon St., Kumara* ☎ *03/736–9277* ⊕ *www.theatreroyalhotel.co.nz.*

 Hotels

Rimu Lodge

$$$$ | B&B/INN | This two-story luxury lodge sits in the country, high above the Hokitika River Valley. **Pros:** bird-watchers' delight; good local walks and heritage walks nearby; warm hosts who make a great breakfast. **Cons:** bit hard to find at night; 10 minutes out of town and away from shops; cave wetas in house might not be for everyone (although they are harmless). ⑤ *Rooms from: NZ$345* ✉ *33 Seddons Terrace Rd., Rimu* ☎ *03/755–5255* ⊕ *www.rimulodge.co.nz* ⌁ *4 rooms* ⦿ *Breakfast.*

Shining Star

$$ | HOTEL | FAMILY | These stylish oceanfront wooden cabins, chalets, and motels are as close to the beach as you'll get. **Pros:** facing wild surf beach; very peaceful; pet animals and playground to amuse kids. **Cons:** on the edge of town; long walk to restaurants; need to book well ahead in summer. ⑤ *Rooms from: NZ$180* ✉ *16 Richards Dr.* ☎ *03/755–8921, 0800/744–646 New Zealand only* ⊕ *www.accommodationwestcoast.co.nz* ⌁ *23 suites* ⦿ *No meals.*

Teichelmann's Bed & Breakfast

$$$ | B&B/INN | At this friendly, traditional B&B in the center of town, accommodation is in five rooms in the house (upstairs and downstairs) and in a cute, stand-alone cottage set in a delightful "miner's garden" behind the house. **Pros:** one of the West Coast's most historic accommodations; gracious hosts who are history buffs; location right in town. **Cons:** no ocean or mountain views; smallish en suites in some rooms; some rooms have a shared bathroom. ⑤ *Rooms from: NZ$260* ✉ *20 Hamilton St.* ☎ *03/755–8232* ⊕ *www.teichel-manns.nz* ⌁ *6 rooms* ⦿ *Breakfast.*

Westland/Tai Poutini National Park

North end 146 km (91 miles) south of Hokitika.

Westland/Tai Poutini is a place of extremes, from the highest mountains to most ancient rain forest, and certainly extreme precipitation.

Try to allow more than a day in the region to increase your chance of clear weather. Otherwise, put your rain gear on and get out in it: walking in the rain forest, or in those massive glacial valleys with waterfalls roaring down the sheer sides, is a special experience. Annual rainfall here ranges from more than 120 inches at the coast to an incredible 16 feet on the alpine summits. Huge volumes of snow are dumped each year, feeding the 140 glaciers. The snow is compressed into ice on the névé, or head, of the glaciers (New Zealanders say "glassy-urs"), then moves steadily downhill under its own weight. The best known and most visited glaciers are Franz Josef and Fox. If, however, you're driving through on a cloudy or wet day—quite likely—you will get no idea of the size of the mountain ranges looming beside you. The main stopping places are townships near these glaciers, named simply **Fox Glacier** and **Franz Josef,** the latter slightly larger. Both towns have solid tourist infrastructures. The summer tourist rush means you should make reservations well in advance for lodgings and restaurants, or plan to travel in the shoulder seasons. In winter some places close so be sure to check ahead.

GETTING HERE AND AROUND

State Highway 6 passes through this region and is the only road access in and out. Drive in from Hokitika in the north or Wanaka and Haast to the south. There are only a few fuel stops between Hokitika and Haast so plan ahead. InterCity buses travel daily from the north and the south, stopping at both glacier villages.

BUS DEPOTS Fox Glacier. ✉ *Northbound: Fox Glacier Guiding, Main Rd.; Southbound: opposite Fox Glacier Guiding, Main Rd., Westland National Park.* **Franz Josef.** ✉ *Franz Josef Bus Stop, Main Rd.; Franz Josef YHA, 2–4 Cron St., Westland National Park.*

VISITOR INFORMATION

CONTACTS Franz Josef i-SITE Visitor Information Centre. ✉ *63 Cron St., Franz Josef* ☎ *0800/354–748* ⊕ *www.glaciercountry. co.nz.* **Westland/Tai Poutini National Park Visitor Centre.** ✉ *69 Cron St., Franz Josef* ☎ *03/752–0360* ⊕ *www.doc.govt.nz.*

👁 Sights

Glacier Hot Pools

SPA—SIGHT | After your day touring and hiking, fall into these pools nestled in a bewitching area of rain forest right in Franz Josef village. The three public pools range from family-friendly to completely relaxing. There is also a massage therapy room,

and three private hot tubs with their own shower, changing areas, and towels. This is a great stop if the weather just won't cooperate, but the compact complex may fill up on such days. ✉ *63 Cron St., Franz Josef* ☎ *03/752–0099, 0800/044–044 New Zealand only* ⊕ *www.glacierhotpools.co.nz* 🖼 *Pools from NZ$28.*

★ West Coast Wildlife Centre

NATURE PRESERVE | **FAMILY** | Here you can see firsthand the Department of Conservation's successful breeding program of the rare kiwi species, Rowi. You can see a few Rowi in the Nocturnal House, but by far the best option is to witness the incubation and rearing program in the Kiwi Backstage Tour. If your timing is lucky, perhaps you'll see a hatching chick. Other displays here include the West Coast storytelling hut, where you can learn from the "old-timers" and a quite lifelike glacial exploration. ✉ *At Cron and Cowan Sts., Franz Josef* ☎ *03/752–0600* ⊕ *www.wildkiwi.co.nz* 🖼 *From NZ$38.*

Westland/Tai Poutini National Park

NATIONAL/STATE PARK | The glaciers are the main attractions here, yet there are many other beautiful places to explore in this magnificent national park and World Heritage region, which encompasses everything from New Zealand's highest mountains to glaciers, rain forests, hidden lakes, and coastal wetlands. Scenic drives and a couple of walks in the glacial valleys bring you to viewpoints within 500 feet or so of the glaciers. Alternatively, from Fox township, drive about 4 km (2½ miles) toward the coast on Cook Flat Road for a roadside view of Fox Glacier (weather permitting). Because of glacial recession access onto the actual glaciers is no longer possible by foot, but by helicopter only. There are many guided heli/hike options, as well as scenic flights for both glaciers. Flights are generally best early in the morning, when visibility tends to be clearest. Summer may be warmer, but there is more rain and fog

Upper South Island and the West Coast   WESTLAND/TAI POUTINI NATIONAL PARK

that can scuttle flightseeing and hiking plans. In winter, there are fewer people and the skies are clearer, which means fewer canceled flights and more spectacular views. In fact, in winter this area can be a lot warmer than the snow resort towns east of the Southern Alps. Note that the glaciers are currently receding fast, and with less ice to bind their rocks, the mountains and valleys are increasingly prone to slips and landslides. Accordingly, access roads and trails change regularly for safety reasons; do check with the Department of Conservation or i-SITE Visitor Informtion Centre about current conditions and be sure to heed all DOC warning signs. Away from the ice, just a five-minute drive west of Fox Glacier township is the walk around Lake Matheson, leading to one of the country's most famous views. A trail winds by the lakeshore to where (weather permitting) the snowcapped peaks of Aoraki/Mt. Cook and Mt. Tasman are reflected in the water. It's an easy 2.6-km (1-mile) walk right around the lake. The best times to visit are sunrise and sunset, when the mirror-like reflections are less likely to be fractured by the wind. Other beautiful park walks are on the coast; at Gillespies Beach (coastal wetlands and forests and wild surf), and at Okarito, where your choices are the wetland boardwalk (20 minutes), Okarito Trig for an amazing viewpoint of Okarito Lagoon and Aoraki/Mt. Cook (1½ hour round-trip), and the Three Mile Pack Track, where you can return along the beach if you get the tide right. ⊠ Fox Glacier Hwy., Westland National Park ⊕ www.doc.govt.nz.

🍴 Restaurants

There are several dining options in the glacier villages. Remember these places shut early in winter, so get in soon after the sun goes down.

★ The Alice May
$$$ | NEW ZEALAND | One of those cozy, buzzing places so prevalent on the West Coast, The Alice May serves country fare that is good and plentiful, with a welcome range of light meals (fish-and-chips, curries, venison burgers) and more substantial main courses (slow roasted pork belly, beef cheeks, and good vegetarian options). The wine and beer lists are stacked with mainstream NZ favorites. **Known for:** full of character and ambience; great service even when packed; interesting à la carte menu. ⑤ Average main: NZ$28 ⊠ Cowan and Cron Sts., Franz Josef ☎ 03/752–0740.

Blue Ice Café
$$$$ | NEW ZEALAND | Head here for quality New Zealand dishes, and a bar that can carry you to the wee small hours of the morning. This place can become a late-night party spot during the tourist season. **Known for:** lamb shanks; huge salads; party hotspot. ⑤ Average main: NZ$32 ⊠ 5 Main Rd., Franz Josef ☎ 03/752–0707 ⊗ No lunch May–Oct.

Café Neve
$$$ | NEW ZEALAND | This standout along Fox Glacier's main street sparks up no-nonsense options with fresh local flavors, such as the pizza topped with locally made Blackball salami, field mushrooms, spinach, rosemary, and tomato. From breakfast through to lunch and dinner the menu is big and varied, taking you through eggs Benedict, BLT sandwiches, soups and chowders, burgers, chicken, pizzas, and fillet steak—just what you need after a day exploring or driving. **Known for:** New Zealand–focused wine list; veranda dining to watch the tourists; varied menu of NZ classics. ⑤ Average main: NZ$22 ⊠ 21 Main Rd., Fox Glacier ☎ 03/751–0110.

★ Matheson Cafe
$$$$ | CAFÉ | The food at this all-day café is great (a huge breakfast menu, burgers at lunch, beef rib eye, and lamb cutlets for dinner) but the scenery steals the show. If the weather plays ball you'll be able to enjoy a memorably stunning view: an amphitheater of mountains (Aoraki/Mt.

Known for: incredible view (weather permitting); classy evening menu worthy of special occasion dining; outside seating. $ *Average main: NZ$32 ⊠ Lake Matheson Rd., Fox Glacier ☎ 03/751–0878 ⊕ www.lakematheson.com ♥ No dinner Apr.–Oct.*

 Hotels

As major tourist destinations both Fox and Franz Josef townships, and nearby areas, are well serviced with campsite, backpacker motel, B&Bs, hotels, and lodge accommodations.

58 On Cron Motel

$$$ | **HOTEL** | Cook for yourself if you wish at this modern motel-style accommodation that offers great value, with well-appointed studios and apartments, excellent facilities, and a sunny environment. **Pros:** parking is right outside your door; property is well-managed; location close to attractions and cafés but off the noisy main road. **Cons:** the units are a bit crowded and on the small side; birdsong might wake you early; slow Wi-Fi. $ *Rooms from: NZ$220 ⊠ 58 Cron St., Franz Josef ☎ 03/752–0627, 0800/662–766 New Zealand only ⊕ 58oncron.co.nz ⤴ 16 rooms.*

Glenfern Villas

$$$ | **B&B/INN** | **FAMILY** | A short drive north of Franz Josef village, these stylish, well equipped one- and two-bedroom villas are in a quiet rural location away from the tourist bustle and helicopters. **Pros:** home-away-from-home in size and feel; rural and mountain views; villas are luxuriously appointed and very well-equipped. **Cons:** some road noise from the highway; a bit out of town for handy shopping or dining; not all villas face the mountains. $ *Rooms from: NZ$260 ⊠ State Hwy. 6, Franz Josef ⊹ 3½ km (2 miles) north of Franz Josef village ☎ 03/752–0054, 0800/453–633 New Zealand only ⊕ www.glenfern.co.nz ⤴ 18 suites ☉ No meals.*

Te Waonui Forest Retreat

$$$$ | **HOTEL** | Here you'll feel enfolded not only in luxury but also the rain forest, as the hotel has been built to fit in and not intrude on the trees—from concrete jungle to real jungle, as their mantra states. **Pros:** quiet atmosphere; surrounded by rain forest; walking distance to village. **Cons:** subdued guest room lighting for ambience makes reading difficult; no room-only rate; closed for winter. $ *Rooms from: NZ$827 ⊠ 3 Wallace St., Franz Josef ☎ 03/752–0555 ⊕ www.tewaonui.co.nz ♥ Closed May–Aug. ⤴ 100 rooms ☉ Some meals.*

Westwood Lodge

$$$$ | **B&B/INN** | For unpretentious luxury near the glaciers, turn into this spacious, modern lodge-style B&B just a few minutes' drive from Franz Josef village. **Pros:** large dining and lounge conservatory area with pool table; alpine gardens; some private decks with mountain views. **Cons:** a bit away from town and its restaurants; in-house labradoodles won't be for everyone; on the pricey side. $ *Rooms from: NZ$410 ⊠ 2796 State Hwy. 6, Franz Josef ☎ 03/752–0112, 0800/200–209 New Zealand only ⊕ www.westwoodlodge.co.nz ⤴ 9 rooms ☉ Breakfast.*

★ Wilderness Lodge Lake Moeraki

$$$$ | **HOTEL** | In World Heritage rain forest, with luxury food and accommodations and the attention of passionate, knowledgeable eco-guides, this lodge is a stunning spot in which to relax and learn about your natural surroundings. **Pros:** a top eco-experience; guides have licenses to visit hidden tawaki (rare penguin) sites; pure luxury, in both facilities and specialist knowledge. **Cons:** remote location; minimum two-night stay in high season; lunch not included in all-inclusive plan. $ *Rooms from: NZ$520 ⊠ State Hwy. 6, Westland National Park ⊹ 90 km (56 miles) south of Fox Glacier ☎ 03/750–0881 ⊕ www.wildernesslodge.co.nz ♥ Closed June and July ⤴ 28 rooms ☉ All-inclusive ⌖ Rates also include 2 short guided activities daily.*

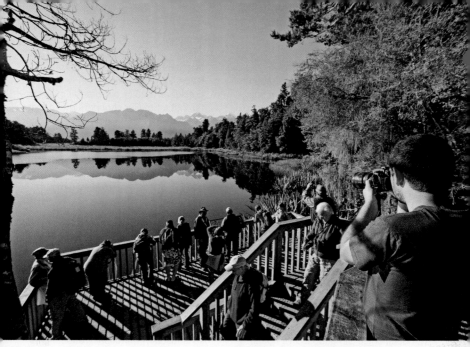

The Southern Alps are reflected in Lake Matheson's calm waters in Westland/Tai Poutini National Park.

🏃 Activities

BIRD-WATCHING

★ White Heron Sanctuary Tours

BIRD WATCHING | FAMILY | For more than 30 years, the local Arnold family have taken exclusive tours to the rare (in New Zealand) kotuku (white heron) colony, hidden in the wetlands and rain forest of Waitangiroto Nature Reserve and reached by a gentle jet-boat trip along the Waitangiroto River. You'll see other wetland birds and walk a boardwalk through the rain forest to the hide, just meters from the colony. Trips last 2½ hours and run four times daily, from mid-September to early March. In winter they offer a gorgeous Rainforest Nature Tour. Reservations are essential. ✉ *State Hwy. 6, Whataroa* ☎ *03/753–4120, 0800/523–456 NZ only* ⊕ *www.whiteherontours.co.nz* 📷 *NZ$150.*

GLACIER TOURS

The walks to the Fox Glacier viewpoint and Franz Josef Glacier viewpoint are the easiest and cheapest ways to see the ice of a glacier. Landing on a glacier by helicopter and perhaps joining a guided walk on the ice is unforgettable. All the helicopter companies listed here offer similar tours and prices, as well as similarly stunning spectacles.

Fox and Franz Heliservices

FLYING/SKYDIVING/SOARING | This company has been operating since 1986. If your time is limited, try a 20-minute spin with a landing on either Fox or Franz Josef glacier. Longer flights also include glacier landings, exploring close to Mt. Aoraki/Mt. Cook and Mt. Tasman, and, weather permitting, across the Main Divide. Departures are from both Franz Josef and Fox Glacier townships. ✉ *Alpine Adventure Centre, 29 Main Rd., Fox Glacier* ☎ *03/752–0793, 0800/800–793 New Zealand only* ⊕ *www.heliservices.nz.*

★ Fox Glacier Guiding

TOUR—SPORTS | FAMILY | This pioneering guiding company offers glacier heli-hikes and climbs to suit all fitness levels. They start from the most popular four-hour round-trip, where your guide will escort you from your helicopter high on the glacier, fit you with crampons, and then show you the amazing crevices and tunnels. There's also an "Extreme Fox" all-day heli-hike, and a heli-ice climbing trip, plus an amazing day heli/guided/climb of Chancellor Dome located high above the glacier or overnight option to stay in a historic alpine hut. Reservations are recommended for all trips, which are highly weather dependent. ⊠ *Fox Glacier Guiding Bldg., 44 Main Rd., Fox Glacier* ☎ *03/751–0825, 0800/111–600 New Zealand only* ⊕ *www.foxguides.co.nz* ⊠ *From NZ$469.*

Franz Josef Glacier Guides

TOUR—SPORTS | With these guides, you'll be helicoptered high up onto the Franz Josef glacier and guided on an amazing icy adventure, either a glacier walk (four hours) or ice climb (up to five hours). The company also offers a guided glacier valley walk up the canyon-like floor where the glacier once ground its icy way before retreating. You won't get to stand on the ice on this trip, but you'll learn about its awesome power. Booking ahead is essential for all tours, which are highly weather dependent. ⊠ *63 Cron St., Franz Josef* ☎ *03/752–0763, 0800/484–337 New Zealand only* ⊕ *www.franzjosefglacier. com* ⊠ *From NZ$79.*

Glacier Country Scenic Flights

FLYING/SKYDIVING/SOARING | Scenic flights leave from Whataroa Valley, just a 30-minute drive north of Franz Josef township. The advantage is you get to see more mountains en route to the glaciers, and the weather can be more settled in the open valley, away from the glaciers. Transfers are available from Franz Josef or Fox township. This company will also book heli-hikes for you with the local companies. ⊠ *Main Rd., Whataroa* ☎ *03/753–4096, 0800/423–463 New Zealand only* ⊕ *glacieradventures.co.nz* ⊠ *From NZ$235.*

Mountain Helicopters

FLYING/SKYDIVING/SOARING | Fly out of Fox Glacier on a quick but dramatic helicopter flight. Smaller choppers mean that everyone gets a window seat, and the experience is more intimate than it can be with the bigger operators. Options range from 10-, 20-, and 30-minute flights, taking in glacier, mountain, and rain-forest scenery, plus a 40-minute flight that includes a quick snow landing. Reservations are required and all trips are weather dependent. ⊠ *Next to Snakebite Restaurant, State Hwy. 6, Franz Josef* ☎ *03/751–0045, 0800/369–423 New Zealand only* ⊕ *www.mountainhelicopters. co.nz* ⊠ *From NZ$129.*

KAYAKING AND RAFTING

Glacier Country Kayaks

KAYAKING | **FAMILY** | Glacial Lake Mapourika is (usually) mirror-still, reflecting its rain forest and mountain surroundings. Kayaking is the way to explore it, and you'll navigate your kayak into an estuary that backs onto protected forest where rare Rowi kiwi live—on a sunset paddle you might hear them calling. Lots of options are offered: kayak-only trips, kayak-and-walk combos, paddle boarding, and even combinations with sky diving and glacier heli-hikes. Reservations are essential. ■ TIP➜ **The best views are likely to be in winter, when the weather is clearer and calmer.** ⊠ *64 Cron St., Franz Josef* ☎ *03/752–0230, 0800/423–262 South Island only* ⊕ *www.glacierkayaks.com* ⊠ *From NZ$85.*

Chapter 10

CHRISTCHURCH AND CANTERBURY

10

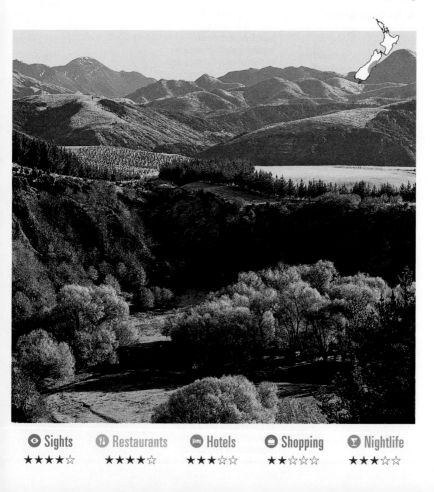

👁 **Sights**
★★★★☆

🍽 **Restaurants**
★★★★☆

🛏 **Hotels**
★★★☆☆

🛍 **Shopping**
★★☆☆☆

🍸 **Nightlife**
★★★☆☆

WELCOME TO CHRISTCHURCH AND CANTERBURY

TOP REASONS TO GO

★ **The Arts:** Christchurch's galleries, museums, and cultural activities highlight the city's heritage and its bright future; thought-provoking art projects are dotted around the city.

★ **The Great Outdoors:** You don't have to go far to be among mountains, forests, rivers, and beaches. There is an abundance of places to hike, trek, cycle, mountain-bike, boat, and ski; and it's easy to hire any gear you need.

★ **Parks and Gardens:** The Botanic Gardens and Hagley Park are Christchurch's green living rooms. Riverside promenades and landscaped squares line the city center. In spring and summer, several public and private gardens are open for viewing.

★ **Superb Skiing:** Christchurch has 12 ski areas all within a few hours' drive. The season usually runs from June until early October.

★ **Fantastic Festivals:** Festivals celebrate the arts, music, seasons, heritage, wine, and food.

1 Christchurch. New Zealand's second largest and newest city, Christchurch has survived many earthquakes to become a place filled with art, adventure, and unbridled optimism.

2 Arthur's Pass National Park. In the heart of the Southern Alps, this national park offers richly diverse landscapes, from beech forests and snowcapped mountains to dense rain forests and beautiful wildflower fields.

3 Lyttelton. This small, quiet town was where many settlers first arrived in Canterbury and today attracts artists.

4 Akaroa and the Banks Peninsula. The fishing village of Akaroa and its surrounding coastline is a lovely day trip from Christchurch.

5 Waipara Valley. This low-key valley is filled with excellent wineries.

6 Hanmer Springs. This spa town still offers hot springs for soaking as well as plenty of outdoor adventures.

7 Methven. One hour from Canterbury, this is a great base for skiing in the area.

8 Geraldine. This charming town makes a great stop while traveling to Aoraki and Mt. Cook.

↑ TO NELSON

Greymouth

Hanmer Springs

Waiau

Rotherham

CANTERBURY

Culverden Cheviot

Arthur's Pass

Huruni

TO KAIKOURA

Arthur's Pass National Park

Waipara

PUKETERAKI RANGE

Amberley

Oxford Cust Rangiora

Sefton

Springfield

Southbrook Woodend

WAIPARA VALLEY

Kaiapoi

Darfield

Belfast

Christchurch

Templeton

Rolleston

Halswell

Lyttelton Harbour

Pegasus Bay

Hakatere

Lyttelton

BANKS PENINSULA

Methven

Dunsandel

Taitapu

Mount Somers

Doyleston

Little River

Akaroa

Rakaia

Leeston

Akaroa Head

Southbridge

Ashburton

Pendarves

Lake Ellesmere

Akaroa Harbour

ndel Hinds

Hakatere

Canterbury Bight

Geraldine

Orari

Coldstream

South Pacific Ocean

Winchester

Temuka

Pleasant Point

0   20 mi

0   20 km

Timaru

With its vast food basket, water, and natural resources, Canterbury could be its own country. The expansive coast, fertile plains, and snow-lined Alps not only define the region's beauty, they also sustain a thriving agricultural industry.

The province is served by a major international airport, several ports, and an excellent road network. The dynamic city of Christchurch (Otautahi in Māori) with its growing immigrant population, has become known as the southern gateway to Antarctica, and has a keen arts community and a vibrant culinary scene.

Captain Cook sailed right past the Canterbury coast in 1770 and thought Banks Peninsula was an island. The Māori knew better: they were already well established (by some 500 years) around Te Waihora and Waiwera—lakes Ellesmere and Forsyth today. In 1850 the English were back to colonize the land. John Robert Godley had been sent by the Canterbury Association to prepare for the arrival of settlers for a planned Church of England community. That year, four settler ships arrived bearing roughly 800 pioneers, and their new town was named for Godley's college at Oxford.

Built in a Gothic Revival style of dark gray stone, civic buildings such as the Arts Center (originally Canterbury University) and Canterbury Museum give the city an English quality. This style, plus elements such as punting and cricket, often pegs Christchurch as a little slice of England. Though the city may have a conservative exterior, it has been a nursery for social change. It was here that Kate Sheppard began organizing a campaign that led to New Zealand being the first country in the world to grant women the vote.

Beyond Christchurch the wide-open Canterbury Plains sweep to the north, west, and south of the city. This is some of New Zealand's finest pastureland, and the higher reaches are sheep stations where life and lore mingle in the South Island's cowboy country. This is where young Samuel Butler dreamed up the satirical *Erewhon*—the word is an anagram of *nowhere*. But the towns here are no longer considered the back of beyond; communities such as Hanmer Springs, Akaroa, and Geraldine are now favorite day-trip destinations. Arthur's Pass is probably the best place for a one-day-wonder experience of the Southern Alps while the Waipara Valley is now an established vineyard area, highly regarded for its Pinot Noir, Chardonnay, and aromatics.

GETTING ORIENTED

Canterbury is the South Island's largest geographical region, with a natural boundary formed by the Main Divide (the peaks of the Southern Alps) in the west and stretching from Kaikoura in the north down to the Waitaki River in the south. The region's main city is Christchurch and the area also includes Banks Peninsula, the Waipara wine country, the ski town of Methven, and the alpine resort town of Hanmer Springs, north and west of the city. Arthur's Pass National Park is a

Christchurch Earthquakes

The first earthquake was early in the morning of September 4, 2010, magnitude 7.1, centered beneath farmland on the Canterbury Plains. It caused considerable damage in the city but no loss of life. Collectively, Cantabrians believed they had been spared. But not so. At lunchtime, on February 22, 2011, a magnitude 6.3 aftershock, centered directly beneath the city, caused massive damage, injured several thousand people, and resulted in the loss of 185 lives. Many of the city's heritage buildings crumbled, suburban streets were swamped with liquefaction (a black silty deposit from underground), and even modern, inner-city buildings rocked and rolled on their foundations as the earth heaved. The central business district was cordoned off for more than two years afterward and more than half of the buildings there had to be demolished. The Canterbury Earthquake

National Memorial on the banks of the Avon River is a now place to reflect on the events that changed Canterbury forever. It combines a riverside garden on the north bank and a memorial wall on the south bank, designed by Slovenian architect Grega Vezjak.

Christchurch is now focused on the future, with much of the central city rebuilt or currently in the process of rebuilding. It is achieving international acclaim for creative and clever urban design, evidenced by inspiring street art, cycle and pedestrian-friendly streets, world-class hospitality and shopping precincts, and a "cardboard" cathedral awarded the world's top architecture prize. The city's focal point is the Avon/Otakaro River, and an attractive promenade now follows the river through the city, lined with gardens, artworks, access points to the water, seating, and restaurants.

few hours northwest of Christchurch by car or train and a great mountain day trip from the city.

MAJOR REGIONS

Christchurch. The city spreads out from the Port Hills, with stand-out contemporary buildings sitting alongside restored heritage properties. To the west Christchurch's leafy suburbs are reminders of a genteel history. To the east, exciting projects like the Otakaro Avon River Corridor are meant to regenerate the area following severe earthquake damage in 2011.

Arthur's Pass and Canterbury. East of the city, you can explore the wonderful coastline of Banks Peninsula. The peninsula's two harbors, Lyttelton and Akaroa, were formed from the remnants of two ancient volcanoes; their steep grassy

walls drop dramatically to the sea. Looking north, consider stopping in Waipara and its wineries if you're en route to or from Kaikoura or Hanmer Springs. Hanmer Springs' thermal baths are good for a relaxing soak, or you can ride the white water on the river, ski, or mountain bike. Head south or west of town into the Canterbury Plains countryside, and you can ski at Mt. Hutt (in winter) or drive the scenic inland highway to Geraldine and Timaru. Where once only sheep and cattle grazed, you're now just as likely to spot alpacas, deer, and ostriches. If you're heading to the West Coast by road or rail, then Arthur's Pass is worth investigating. You should set an entire day aside for any of these side trips, or, better still, stay overnight.

Planning

When to Go

Christchurch is a city of four distinct seasons and generally low rainfall. Spring brings cherry blossoms and daffodils while summer days are often hot and windy. Winter's weather is crisp and cool, but this is the perfect time to come for skiing and snowboarding. From late June through early October you can be assured of snow at Mt. Hutt (remember seasons are switched from the northern hemisphere). Snow on the ground in Christchurch is a rarity.

November's New Zealand Cup and Show Week is a wacky time, when locals kick their heels up at Riccarton Park and Addington Raceway for horse racing and the country's largest agricultural and pastoral show where "country comes to town." If you've organized your accommodation well in advance it can be good fun but very busy. Wine and beer festivals follow over summer and the Garden City Summer Times festival runs from New Year's until late February, while mid-January brings the World Buskers Festival; the Electric Avenue Music Festival is in February. In winter the Christchurch Arts Festival is held biennially. Every second August, the Botanic Gardens and the Arts Centre are lit up with an interactive lighting and projection event called Botanic D'Lights.

Planning Your Time

Take at least four days to explore the Canterbury region. A full day in the city only skims the surface. An overnight trip to Hanmer, Arthur's Pass, or to Akaroa gives you a taste of the hinterland. Waipara and Hanmer Springs can be visited when heading north to Kaikoura or Nelson. Arthur's Pass is on the main road to the West Coast, and Geraldine is on the main route south to Dunedin and Queenstown.

FESTIVALS
Christchurch Arts Festival
ARTS FESTIVALS | In odd-numbered years, the city hosts a late-winter, month-long Arts Festival, featuring everything from dance and theater to comedy, visual art, and cabaret. ⊕ www.artsfestival.co.nz.

Getting Here and Around

AIR TRAVEL
Direct flights arrive into Christchurch from the major New Zealand cities, the larger Australian cities, Singapore, China, and the Pacific Islands. There are no direct flights from North America, but easy daily connections can be found through Auckland. **Air New Zealand** connects Christchurch to most New Zealand centers. Jetstar has flights to all New Zealand's main centers, and several regional centers. For access to the Chatham Islands there's Air Chathams. Air New Zealand, Qantas, Jetstar, Virgin Australia, and Emirates fly direct from Australia. A private jet terminal is operated by Garden City Aviation at Christchurch Airport, with charter helicopters connecting to high country and remote lodges.

AIRPORTS Christchurch International Airport. ⊠ 30 Durey Rd., Harewood ☎ 03/358–5029 ⊕ www.christchurchairport.co.nz.

CONTACTS Air Chathams. ☎ 0800/580–127 ⊕ www.airchathams.co.nz **Air New Zealand.** ☎ 0800/737–000 NZ only ⊕ www.airnewzealand.co.nz. **Jetstar.** ☎ 0800/80–0995 ⊕ www.jetstar.com. **Virgin Australia.** ☎ 0800/67–0000 ⊕ www.virginaustralia.com.

BUS TRAVEL
InterCity bus service connects Christchurch with major towns and cities in the South Island.

CONTACTS Great Journeys of NZ.
☎ 0800/872–467 ⊕ www.greatjour-neysofnz.co.nz. **InterCity Coachlines.**
☎ 03/365–1113 ⊕ www.intercity.co.nz.
Interlslander. ☎ 0800/802–802 ⊕ www.greatjourneysofnz.co.nz/interislander.

CAR TRAVEL

Outside the city the best way to explore the region is by car. Roads across the Canterbury Plains tend to be straight and flat with good signage and low traffic volume. State Highway 1 runs the length of the region's coast, linking all the major towns. State Highway 72 follows the contours of the hills, farther inland, beneath the Alps. State Highway 7 leaves the main road at Waipara and heads inland to Hanmer Springs before heading north to Nelson, and State Highway 73 heads west across the plains before leaping into the Southern Alps on its way to the West Coast.

TRAIN TRAVEL

The **Coastal Pacific** train runs from Christchurch to Blenheim and Picton at the top of the South Island and connects with the **Interlslander Ferry** to the North Island. The **TranzAlpine** train is one of the Great Train Journeys of the World and departs Christchurch daily. Christchurch has a good metropolitan bus service.

Restaurants

Christchurch has an exciting foodie scene, and many new restaurants, cafés, and bars have opened in recent years. Restaurants are usually open every day; if they do close, it's either Sunday or Monday. Outside Christchurch, restaurants are more likely to close on Monday and Tuesday and during the winter.

The Waipara Valley wine region is seeing a surge in exotic food production. North Canterbury is now a key producer in the country's fledgling black truffle industry. Locally sourced saffron, hazelnuts, *manuka* (an indigenous kind of tea tree) honey,

and olive oil are also making their way onto area menus.

Hotels

There's an extraordinary array of lodging in Christchurch to suit all tastes and budgets—from backpackers lodges to gorgeous boutique B&Bs, from modern multilevel contemporary hotels within the city center to plenty of motels heading out west and toward the airport. The more substantial lodges tend to be out in the hinterland. Many accommodations do not include breakfast in their room rates. Reservations are most necessary in summer, on public holidays, during rugby tests, and at festival times.

Outside Christchurch, it can be hard to find a place to stay in summer, especially over the holidays. If you're planning on going to Akaroa, Hanmer Springs, or Waipara during peak season, be sure to reserve well in advance. Bookings can also be heavy in winter around the ski areas and during school holidays.

Restaurant and hotel reviews have been shortened. For full information, visit Fodors.com. Restaurant prices are the average cost of a main course at dinner or, if dinner is not served, at lunch. Hotel prices are the lowest cost of a standard double room in high season.

What It Costs			
$	$$	$$$	$$$$
RESTAURANTS			
under NZ$15	NZ$15–NZ$20	NZ$21–NZ$30	over NZ$30
HOTELS			
under NZ$125	NZ$125–NZ$200	NZ$201–NZ$300	over NZ$300

Visitor Information

The **Christchurch i-SITE Visitor Information Centre** is open daily from 8:30 to 5 (later in summer) and is located in the Arts Center on Worcester Boulevard. The knowledgeable and friendly staff can help you learn about possible activities and book everything from lodging to bike rentals. Here you will also find the Department of Conservation's visitor center, with information and bookings for all of New Zealand's national parks and Great Walks. *Cityscape,* a local magazine and website with events listings and reviews, is also worth a browse (⊕ *www. cityscape-christchurch.co.nz*).

CONTACTS ChristchurchNZ. ⊕ *www. christchurchnz.com/city-events* .
Christchurch i-SITE Visitor Information Centre. ⊠ *Old Boys High Bldg., Arts Center, 28 Worcester Blvd.* ☎ *03/379–9629* ⊕ *www.christchurchnz.com.*

Christchurch

Earthquakes aside, the face of Christchurch is changing, fueled by both New Zealand residents drawn from other centers as well as immigrants, attracted by rebuild opportunities. The Māori community, although still below the national average in size, is growing. Ngai Tahu, the main South Island Māori tribe, settled Treaty of Waitangi claims in 1997 and has invested in many high-profile property and tourism ventures. There is a growing Asian population, reflected in the number of restaurants and stores catering to their preferences. Christchurch's population is rising, the arts scene is flourishing, and the city continues to attract cutting-edge technology companies.

Christchurch is also the forward supply depot for the main U.S. Antarctic base at McMurdo Sound, and if you come in by plane in summer, you are likely to see the giant U.S. Air Force transport planes of Operation Deep Freeze parked on the tarmac at Christchurch International Airport.

GETTING HERE AND AROUND
The inner city is compact and easiest to explore on foot or by bicycle; the central sights can be reached during an afternoon's walk. Beyond this core are a number of special-interest museums and activities, about 20 minutes away by car.

Outside the central city, the best way to get around is to use the network of buses. There is an indoor Bus Interxchange on the corner of Lichfield and Colombo streets, and Metro has a great website (⊕ *www.metroinfo.co.nz*) that helps plan your route. Once in Christchurch you can purchase a Metrocard from the exchange or a Metro Agent (their website provides a list); a Metrocard is a preloaded card that will give cheaper fares. You can also top-up these cards once you've used the initial funds. A number of tourist attractions, like the Antarctic Centre, Orana Park, and the Gondola provide shuttle services from the city; some trips are included in the entry price; just check when you book.

BUS CONTACTS Christchurch Bus Interchange. ⊠ *Corner of Lichfield and Colombo Sts.* ☎ *03/366–8855* ⊕ *www. metroinfo.co.nz.*

TRAIN CONTACTS Christchurch Railway Station. ⊠ *Troup Dr., Addington* ☎ *03/341–2588.*

TOURS
BICYCLE TOURS
Christchurch Segway Tours
GUIDED TOURS | FAMILY | Informative and fun Segway tours with a knowledgeable local guide are popular with visitors to Christchurch. You can book a two-hour guided tour with three different route options. Full training and helmets are provided. Tours meet in South Hagley Park off Hagley Avenue. ⊠ *Hagley Ave.* ☎ *027/542–1887* ⊕ *www.urbanwheels. co.nz* 🖃 *From NZ$109.*

SIGHTSEEING TOURS
★ Soaring Kiwi Tours
BUS TOURS | Hop-on, hop-off Christchurch City tours depart from outside the Canterbury Museum aboard classic London double-decker buses, with open tops in summer. One-hour tours of the central city with an expert guide are offered, as well as a further two hours on the Discover Christchurch tour, which includes Sumner Beach and the Port Hills. There are regular departures from 10 am until 2 pm daily. The same company runs Hassle-free Tours with four-wheel-drives to the Canterbury high country, including guided *Lord of The Rings* tours, alpine safaris, and jet-boat river tours, all with regular departures and hotel pick-ups in Christchurch. Private and specialized tours can also be arranged. ⊠ *Rolleston Ave.* ☎ *03/385–5775* ⊕ *www.soaringkiwi. co.nz* ⊠ *From NZ$35.*

★ Wildsouth Discovery
GUIDED TOURS | Small, stylish, and customized tours are offered by this Christchurch couple who have lots of experience in hospitality and tourism. They'll take you off-the-beaten track, where you'll discover little known secrets not crowded with tourists. With picnics loaded in the trunk you won't go hungry, and they might even take you to their own holiday home for wine and cheese. Paula and Brian run day tours from Christchurch and multiday itineraries exploring the South Island, or they can make a bespoke itinerary just for you and your interests. Tours are best suited to just one or two couples traveling together. ⊠ *Christchurch* ☎ *03/332–3665* ⊕ *www.wildsouth.com* ⊠ *Tours from NZ$580.*

WALKING TOURS
Botanic Gardens Tour
GUIDED TOURS | **FAMILY** | Take the hard work out of walking round the 52-acre Botanic Gardens on this hop-on, hop-off tour. The vehicles are environmentally powered (electric and solar) and a ticket lasts two days. You can buy tickets ahead online or give them a call. The full circuit with commentary from an expert guide takes approximately one hour. ⊠ *9 Rolleston Ave.* ☎ *03/366–7830* ⊕ *www.christchurchattractions.nz* ⊠ *From NZ$20.*

Canterbury Horticultural Society - Garden Tours
GUIDED TOURS | The Canterbury Horticultural Society began with the colonization of Canterbury in the 1850s, and continues to provide inspiration to gardeners throughout the region today. The Society runs seasonal tours of gardens and are happy to have nonmembers join in. Their Ramblers walks start at 9:45 am every second and fourth Tuesday of the month. Check the website for details of upcoming dates, and for a list of gardens that are open to view. ⊠ *Canterbury Horticultural Society, Botanic Gardens* ☎ *03/366–6937* ⊕ *www.chsgardens. co.nz* ⊠ *Free.*

⊙ Sights
CENTRAL CHRISTCHURCH
Antigua Boat Sheds & Cafe
MARINA | **FAMILY** | Built for the Christchurch Boating Club in 1882, this green-and-white wooden structure is the last shed standing of a half dozen that once lined the Avon. On sunny days, punts, canoes, and paddleboats take to the river paddled by visitors and families alike. Join them by renting a boat and taking a champagne picnic into the Botanic Gardens or farther up into the woodlands of Hagley Park. After exploring the waterway you can hire a bike for more action or rest a while at the boat shed's licensed café (open for breakfast and lunch) with a deck overlooking the Avon. ⊠ *2 Cambridge Terr.* ☎ *03/366–5885 boat shed, 03/366–6768 café* ⊕ *www.boatsheds. co.nz* ⊠ *From NZ$12 per hr.*

★ Arts Centre
BUILDING | After major restoration, a large section of the historic Arts Centre, once

Christchurch

KEY

- **1** Sights
- **1** Restaurants
- **1** Hotels
- Tourist Information
- Tramway

a popular cultural venue, has reopened with galleries, theaters, boutique shopping, and dining. Further careful restoration and strengthening is still underway on this fine collection of Gothic Revival stone buildings that were originally built as Canterbury's University. ⊠ *Worcester Blvd. between Montreal St. and Rolleston Ave.* ⊕ *www.artscentre.org.nz.*

Bridge of Remembrance and Triumphal Arch
MEMORIAL | Arching over Cashel Street, this Oamaru limestone memorial arch and Avon River bridge was built in memory of the soldiers who crossed the river here from King Edward Barracks on their way to the battlefields of Europe during World War I. ⊠ *76 Cashel St. at Avon River.*

★ **Canterbury Museum**
MUSEUM | FAMILY | When this museum was founded in 1867, its trading power with national and international museums was in moa bones (these Jurassic birds roamed the plains of Canterbury and are believed to have been hunted to extinction by early Māori). The museum still houses one of the largest collections of artifacts from the moa hunting period. You'll also find an interactive natural-history center, called Discovery, where kids can dig for fossils. The Hall of Antarctic Discovery charts the links between the city and Antarctica, from the days when Captain Cook's ship skirted the continent in a small wooden ship. Among the 20th-century explorers celebrated here are the Norwegian Roald Amundsen, who was first to visit the South Pole, and Captain Robert Falcon Scott, who died returning from the continent. *Fred & Myrtle's Paua Shell House* tells the story of an iconic Kiwi couple and recreates their *paua* (abalone) shell–covered living room. The café looks out over the Botanic Gardens. ⊠ *11 Rolleston Ave.* ☎ *03/366–5000* ⊕ *www.canterburymuseum.com* 🎫 *Free admission, donations appreciated; Discovery, NZ$2.*

Captain Robert Falcon Scott Statue
PUBLIC ART | The captain known as Scott of the Antarctic (1868–1912), who stayed in Christchurch while preparing for his two Antarctic expeditions, is memorialized by this unfinished white marble statue sculpted by his widow, Kathleen. It's inscribed "Do not regret this journey, which shows that Englishmen can endure hardships, help one another and meet death with as great fortitude as ever in the past." Scott wrote these words in his diary as he and his party lay dying in a blizzard on their return journey from the South Pole—a story of endurance taught to all New Zealand schoolkids. Scott's marble statue was toppled and broken in the earthquakes, but has now been restored. ⊠ *Worcester Blvd. and Oxford Terr.*

Chalice
PUBLIC ART | FAMILY | An artwork created by internationally acclaimed Christchurch sculptor Neil Dawson, this giant steel vessel was installed in Cathedral Square in 2001 to celebrate the 150th anniversary of the founding of Christchurch and Canterbury. It survived the earthquakes and is now a major city landmark. ⊠ *Cathedral Sq.* ⊕ *www.ccc.govt.nz.*

★ **Christchurch Art Gallery—Te Puna O Waiwhetu**
MUSEUM | The city's stunning art gallery wows visitors as much for its architecture as for its artwork. Its tall, wavy glass facade was inspired by Christchurch's Avon River and the shape of the native *koru* fern. The museum's Māori name refers to an artesian spring on-site and means "the wellspring of star-reflecting waters." Free guided tours, entertaining events, and family activities make the gallery a must-see. Shop for a great selection of gifts, or relax at the brasserie and café. Check the website for updates on the gallery program. ⊠ *Worcester Blvd. and Montreal St.* ☎ *03/941–7300* ⊕ *www.christchurchartgallery.org.nz* 🎫 *Free.*

Christchurch Botanic Gardens

GARDEN | FAMILY | One of the largest city parks in the world, these superb gardens are known for the magnificent trees planted here in the 19th century. Pick up the Historic Tree Walk brochure from the information center for a self-guided Who's Who tour of the tree world. Spend time in the conservatories and the award-winning Visitor Centre and ilex Cafe to discover tropical plants, cacti, and ferns on days when you'd rather not be outside. Go to the New Zealand plants area at any time of the year; the modern and heritage rose gardens are also quite lovely. ⊠ *Rolleston Ave.* ☎ *03/366–1701* ✉ *Free*.

★ Christchurch Tram

TRANSPORTATION SITE (AIRPORT/BUS/FERRY/TRAIN) | FAMILY | There's something nostalgic and reassuring about the *ding-ding* of these heritage trams. All-day tickets allow you to hop on and off and explore the inner city with fascinating commentary by the conductors. The Tramway Restaurant departs daily at 7 pm. The Tramway ticket office is in Cathedral Junction, but you can buy tickets at other places en route and onboard. Tickets can also be bought in a combination pass that includes the Punting, Gondola, and the Botanic Gardens Tour. ⊠ *Cathedral Junction* ☎ *03/366–7830* ⊕ *www. christchurchattractions.nz* ✉ *NZ$25*.

Christ's College

COLLEGE | FAMILY | Founded in 1850, Christ's College is New Zealand's most well-known private school for boys. It is housed in a magnificent precinct of buildings designed by the city's leading architects over a period of 165 years. Set around an open quadrangle neighboring Hagley Park and the Botanic Gardens, the school's many heritage buildings are undergoing extensive repair and strengthening following the earthquakes. Guided tours of the school are available during summer from mid-October to late April, at 10 am for 80 minutes on Monday,

Wednesday, and Friday. ⊠ *Rolleston Ave.* ⊕ *www.christscollege.com* ✉ *NZ$10*.

★ CoCA - Centre of Contemporary Art

ART GALLERIES—ARTS | Christchurch's leading contemporary art home was built in 1968, and has since been restored and remodeled as a modern and stylish gallery space. Formed in 1880 as the Canterbury Society of Arts, CoCA is a not-for-profit art gallery run by a trust whose members include several of New Zealand's leading contemporary artists. The gallery commissions, produces, and collaborates with top artists to present an ever-changing set of exhibitions. ⊠ *66 Gloucester St.* ☎ *03/366–7261* ⊕ *www. coca.org.nz*.

Hagley Park

CITY PARK | FAMILY | Hagley Park was developed by European settlers in the mid-1800s with imported plants given trial runs in what would become the Botanic Gardens. Now the 407-acre park includes a golf course, sports fields, world-class cricket oval, netball and tennis courts, cycling paths, walking and jogging tracks, and a 17-station fitness circuit. In spring you'll be treated to a magnificent blossom display from the flowering cherry trees and a host of golden daffodils. You can access the park from most of its perimeter. The Botanic Gardens are near the middle, closest to the city center. Every Saturday morning at 8 am, hundreds join in the Hagley Parkrun, a free timed 3-mile run. ⊠ *8 Riccarton Ave.* ⊕ *www.ccc.govt.nz*.

Peacock Fountain

FOUNTAIN | This colorful sight at the entrance to the Botanic Gardens is a fine and rare example of Edwardian ornamental cast ironwork, set in a large circular pool. It was made in Shropshire, England, funded by a bequest to the city from politician and philanthropist John Peacock in 1911. ⊠ *Rolleston Ave.*

St. Michael and All Angels Anglican Church
RELIGIOUS SITE | The bell in this church's belfry came out with the Canterbury Pilgrims on one of the first four ships and was rung hourly to indicate time for early settlers; it is still rung every day. The original building was the first church to be built in Christchurch. The current white-timber church was built in 1872, entirely of *matai*, a native black pine, and has 26 English-made stained-glass windows dating back as far as 1858. It's one of the largest timber Victorian Gothic churches in Australasia. The building stood up to the 2010–11 earthquakes, apart from its 1872 Bevington pipe organ, which was badly damaged but has been beautifully restored. ⊠ *At Oxford Terr. and Durham St.* ☎ *03/379–5236.*

★ Transitional "Cardboard" Cathedral
BUILDING | After the famed Christchurch Cathedral was severely damaged from the 2010-11 earthquakes, the Anglican church's Transitional Cathedral opened to help fill a little of the enormous gap left by the loss. Locals call it the Cardboard Cathedral because it is built largely from 98 cardboard tubes, covered in plastic. It can seat 700 and is the largest "emergency structure" to be designed by award-winning Japanese architect Shigeru Ban, who gifted the design (right down to its unusual chairs) to Christchurch. The large triangular window at the front contains images from Christchurch Cathedral's original rose window. Built to last at least 50 years, it has been named by *Architectural Digest* magazine as one of the world's 10 daring buildings. The striking venue is also used for functions and community events outside of church hours. ⊠ *234 Hereford St.* ⊕ *www.cardboardcathedral.org.nz.*

Victoria Square
HISTORIC SITE | FAMILY | This central square was named for Queen Victoria in her jubilee year, and has recently been restored, keeping its character and heritage. A *poupou*, a tall, carved, wood column in the square, acknowledges the site's history as a significant trading point between Māori and the European settlers. It is home to Christchurch's oldest iron bridge, a floral clock, two fountains, and statues of Queen Victoria and Captain Cook. ⊠ *Armagh and Colombo Sts.*

Women's Suffrage Memorial
PUBLIC ART | This bronze memorial wall, unveiled in 1993, commemorates 100 years of votes for women. New Zealand was the first country in the world to grant women the vote, and Christchurch resident Kate Sheppard played a key role in petitioning Parliament for this essential right. The vote for all women over 21, including Māori women, was granted on September 19, 1893; the work of Sheppard and other activists is celebrated each year on that date at the memorial. ⊠ *Oxford Terr. and Worcester Blvd.*

SOUTH OF CHRISTCHURCH

Air Force Museum of New Zealand
MUSEUM | FAMILY | Starting in 1916, New Zealand pilots learned how to fly at Wigram Airfield. The Air Force's old hangars plus a state-of-the-art aircraft hall now hold exhibits on aviation history, including the Royal New Zealand Air Force, flight simulators, and 30 classic aircraft. Take the behind-the-scenes guided tour to see aircraft restoration projects in action in other hangars. ⊠ *45 Harvard Ave., Wigram* ✛ *By bus, take No. 5, 81, or Metro Star and walk from Main South Rd., just south of Sockburn Overbridge* ☎ *03/343–9532* ⊕ *www.airforcemuseum. co.nz* ✍ *Free.*

EAST OF CHRISTCHURCH

★ Christchurch Gondola
VIEWPOINT | FAMILY | For one of the best vantage points to view Christchurch, the Canterbury Plains, and Lyttelton Harbour head to Christchurch Gondola. At the top, you can journey through the **Time Tunnel** to experience the history and geological evolution of the Canterbury region. Afterward, sit with a glass of local wine at the Red Rock Café. Ride the gondola

Youngsters press in close to see penguins at the International Antarctic Centre.

with your back to the Port Hills for the best views of the Southern Alps. The adventurous can walk or mountain-bike back down (your bike can be transported to the top); it's steep in parts so watch your footing. If you don't have a car, hop on a No. 28 bus from the city center or take a Gondola shuttle from the i-SITE next to the Canterbury Museum. ⊠ *10 Bridle Path Rd., Heathcote* ☎ *03/384–0310* ⊕ *www.christchurchattractions.nz* 🖃 *NZ$28.*

Ferrymead Heritage Park
HISTORIC SITE | FAMILY | Ferrymead is the site of the country's first railway (built in 1863) and is now home to a replica Edwardian township and museum area. While exploring the shops and cottages, you can taste homemade scones or an old-fashioned *lamington* (chocolate-covered sponge cake dipped in coconut). You can watch an old-time movie at the Arcadia, see some knees-up dancing, or check out displays of fire engines, farming tools, and printing equipment. The park is home to 19 societies, particularly

train and tram enthusiasts, who maintain their collections here, so trams and trains run on weekends and public holidays. A steam train operates on the second Sunday of each month. ⊠ *50 Ferrymead Park Dr., Harewood* ☎ *03/384–1970* ⊕ *www.ferrymead.org.nz* 🖃 *NZ$13.*

★ Riccarton House and Bush
HOUSE | The Deans, a Scottish family, beat even the Canterbury Association settlers to this region. Riccarton Bush, their home, is now run by a trust. You can view the small wooden cottage (built 1843) that was their first house. The larger Victorian/Edwardian wooden house, built between 1856 and 1900, now houses a café called Local. Guided heritage tours are available; check the website for details. You can also amble through the last remnant of the original native floodplain forest still standing in Christchurch, with its 600-year-old *kahikatea* trees. The **Christchurch Farmers' Market** is held in the grounds of Riccarton House each Saturday morning from 9 to 1. ⊠ *16 Kahu Rd., Riccarton* ☎ *03/341–1018* ⊕ *www.*

riccartonhouse.co.nz ✉ *Free entry to gardens.*

WEST OF CHRISTCHURCH

International Antarctic Centre

MUSEUM | FAMILY | Ever since Scott wintered his dogs at nearby Quail Island in preparation for his ill-fated South Pole expedition of 1912, Christchurch has maintained a close connection with the frozen continent. You can experience a small taste of the modern polar experience here. Bundle up in extra clothing (provided) and brave a simulated storm with temperatures of minus 25 degrees Fahrenheit for a few minutes. Or take a ride on the Hägglund vehicle used to get around the ice. The 4D extreme theater show of life at New Zealand's Scott Base is superb, and the Penguin Encounter lets you get up close with some blue penguins, the smallest penguin species. ■TIP➜ **There's a free shuttle service that leaves on the hour from outside the Canterbury Museum.** ✉ *38 Orchard Rd., Harewood* ☎ *03/357–0519* ⊕ *www. iceberg.co.nz* ✉ *NZ$59.*

★ Mona Vale Gardens & Homestead

HOUSE | Visit this beautifully restored Arts & Crafts movement home, enjoy tea or lunch in the Mona Vale Pantry, and stroll or punt along the Avon River and through the well-tended perennial gardens. Built in 1899, the house and 13½-acre gardens were almost lost to the city in the 1960s when the estate was in danger of being subdivided. A public campaign saw the homestead "sold" to individual Christchurch residents for NZ$10 per square foot. To get here, you can catch a Purple Line bus from the city. ✉ *40 Mona Vale Ave., Fendalton* ✛ *2 km (1 mile) from city center* ☎ *03/341–7450* ⊕ *www. monavale.nz* ✉ *Free.*

Orana Wildlife Park

ZOO | FAMILY | New Zealand's only open-range zoo is now home to its only Great Ape Center for gorillas and orangutans, making it the place to come to glimpse these endangered animals. You will also see both native (kiwi and *tuatara*) and exotic (tigers, wild dogs, cheetah, zebras, and white rhinos) animals. Orana is world-renowned for its conservation work and breeding programs for endangered native and exotic species. Check out the different animal feeding times; hand-feeding the giraffes is a real highlight and even small kids manage with a bit of help. For a seriously close-up view of the lions being fed, join the Lion Encounter, where you can watch from inside a specially modified vehicle. A zebra-striped Safari Shuttle with commentary loops around the park, or you can join a guided walk. It's about a 15-minute drive from Christchurch airport; there's also a door-to-door shuttle for an additional cost. ✉ *Orana Park, McLeans Island Rd., Harewood* ☎ *03/359–7109* ⊕ *www.oranawild- lifepark.co.nz* ✉ *NZ$35.*

Willowbank Wildlife Reserve

NATURE PRESERVE | FAMILY | In addition to familiar farm animals and other zoo regulars, Willowbank has a section devoted to New Zealand's unique wildlife, from the national symbol, the kiwi, to the *tuatara*—the world's only living dinosaur. There's the cheeky mountain parrot, *kea*; the bush parrot, *kaka*; and the very rare but majestic *takahe*. To have all five of these iconic creatures in one place is a rarity. Willowbank is also home to *Ko Tane,* a fun, interactive Māori cultural experience followed by a traditional meal with a *hāngi* main course. You'll be greeted with a *powhiri*, a welcome ceremony, and you can try your hand at swinging the *poi*, flaxen balls on long strings used in traditional Māori dances (it's not as easy as it looks), or the famous *haka*. ✉ *60 Hussey Rd., Harewood* ☎ *03/359–6226* ⊕ *www.willowbank.co.nz* ✉ *NZ$30; Ko Tane and dinner, NZ$135.*

⚓ Beaches

New Brighton Beach

BEACH—SIGHT | About 8 km (5 miles) from the city center, this beach is popular with surfers. The long pier that goes well out into the surf is a great place to stroll when the sea is calm, but even better when it's rough. Yellow Line buses go here. **Amenities:** food and drink. **Best for:** surfing; walking. ✉ *8 km (5 miles) east of city center.*

Sumner Beach

BEACH—SIGHT | This is a popular swimming and surfing spot. The sandy beach and the beach promenade are great for walking, and there are some excellent ice cream parlors nearby. You can catch a Purple Line bus if you don't have a car. **Amenities:** food and drink; lifeguards. **Best For:** swimming; walking. ✉ *12 km (7 miles) southeast of city center.*

Taylor's Mistake

BEACH—SIGHT | Experienced surfers prefer Taylor's Mistake to Sumner Beach because the waves are often higher. This area is also poular for hikers, bikers, and runners thanks to the spectacular clifftop views. You can catch the Purple Line bus to Sumner and then walk the Flower Track in Scarborough down to the beach. If you're lucky, you'll see tiny, rare Hector's dolphins playing off Sumner Head on your way out. **Amenities:** none. **Best for:** surfing. ✉ *16 km (10 miles) southeast of city center.*

🍴 Restaurants

Cuisine hubs are now dotted throughout the central city, in areas like The Terrace, High Street, Lichfield Street, and New Regent Street. **St. Asaph Street** hosts an array of international cuisines. You can kick on into the night here, too, with live music and dancing. **Victoria Street,** near the city center, is packed with easygoing bars, top restaurants, and cafés. **Papanui Road,** starting across Bealey Avenue from Victoria Street and going all the way up to Merivale Mall, has several popular bars, cafés, and restaurants, while **Addington** also has a lively café and restaurant scene, plus bars and live music along Lincoln Road.

CENTRAL CHRISTCHURCH

Amazonita

$$$$ | **MEDITERRANEAN** | Set in the heart of Christchuch's new dining haven The Terrace, this rain-forest-inspired restaurant combines delicious food with friendly service. Behind the busy bar is an opulent dining area with an open kitchen where you can watch the talented chefs create Mediterranean-style dishes. **Known for:** wood-fired grill; impressive interior design; chefs willing to cook to order if you have special requirements. ⑤ *Average main: NZ$32* ✉ *126 Oxford Terr.* ☎ *03/377–4144* ⊕ *www.amazonita. co.nz.*

Curator's House

$$$$ | **SPANISH** | Here you can dine in a 1920s Tudor-style house, looking out on the Botanic Gardens and the Peacock Fountain, or take a garden table and be part of it. The menu has tapas selections and a good variety of seafood, with owner/chef Javier Garcia producing authentic Spanish cuisine evoking an old-world atmosphere. **Known for:** excellent paella; impressive kitchen garden supplying herbs and vegetables all year-round; alfresco dining in summer, and cozy fireside dining in winter. ⑤ *Average main: NZ$39* ✉ *7 Rolleston Ave.* ☎ *03/379–2252* ⊕ *www.curatorshouse.co.nz.*

★ Dux Central

$$$ | **MODERN NEW ZEALAND** | **FAMILY** | This restaurant's laneway setting and beautifully restored two-level building gives it a London pub feel. With food and drinks to suit all tastes, it is a popular hangout for locals day and night. **Known for:** nearly 200 beers, including their own brews, and an extensive wine list; great options for vegans, seafood lovers, and meat-eaters alike; DJs and live bands late night.

Average main: NZ$25 ✉ *10 Poplar St.* ☎ *03/366–6919* ⊕ *www.duxdine.co.nz.*

ilex Cafe

$$$ | CAFÉ | One of the city's most beautiful pieces of architecture also houses one its most popular cafés. Christchurch Botanic Gardens' rare plants and nurseries sit alongside a busy dining room in this modern take on a glass conservatory. **Known for:** fresh produce from local suppliers and the kitchen garden; creative brunch fare; clever kids' menu. *Average main: NZ$22* ✉ *Christchurch Botanic Gardens, Armagh St.* ⊕ *Entrance off Armagh St., walk across bridge from parking lot* ☎ *03/941–5556* ⊕ *www. goodcompany.nz/ilex.*

★ King of Snake

$$$$ | MODERN ASIAN | Don't be fooled by the unassuming alleyway outside, this chic restaurant and bar delivers fine Asian fusion cuisine on all levels. It's hard to recommend particular dishes because they are all exquisitely prepared and taste so good, served in a striking, seductive setting. **Known for:** signature King of Snake cocktail with potent kick of chili and ginger; delicious snack menu at the bar; exotic dishes designed to share. *Average main: NZ$35* ✉ *145 Victoria St.* ☎ *03/365–7363* ⊕ *www.kingofsnake. co.nz* ☾ *No lunch weekends.*

Pescatore

$$$$ | NEW ZEALAND | This predominantly seafood restaurant is renowned for its creative, conceptual New Zealand cuisine. From the moment you set foot into the white space-age foyer at the George Hotel, taste buds are tantalized with local, seasonally influenced and sustainably sourced ingredients. **Known for:** artfully prepared degustation menus matched with an extensive wine list; superb service and attention to detail; great views over Hagley Park. *Average main: NZ$44* ✉ *The George, 50 Park Terr.* ☎ *03/371–0257* ⊕ *www.thegeorge.com* ☾ *Closed Sun. and Mon. No lunch.*

Supreme Supreme

$$ | CAFÉ | More than just a great coffee fix, this hip café is styled with a utilitarian look based on a distinctive red-and-white grid pattern. Careful attention to detail is evident on the food side, too, with simple homemade, organic, and locally sourced breakfast and lunch dishes. **Known for:** trendy ex-garage location on Christchurch's coolest street; great coffee and can't miss milkshakes; Supreme hash for breakfast, mac and cheese for lunch. *Average main: NZ$15* ✉ *10 Welles St.* ☎ *03/365–0445* ⊕ *www. coffeesupreme.com* ☾ *No dinner.*

★ Twenty Seven Steps

$$$$ | BISTRO | It's worth the climb 27 steps to this stylish bistro on New Regent Street's heritage row, consistently named as one of New Zealand's best. The welcoming staff deliver standout dishes from a wide variety of fresh local produce, including Canterbury beef, lamb, venison, Akaroa salmon, and several excellent vegan options. **Known for:** contemporary bistro-style in a beautiful heritage space; stellar service from the owners and staff, who really know their food; top local wines and beers in a cute little bar. *Average main: NZ$37* ✉ *16 New Regent St.* ☎ *03/366–2727* ⊕ *www. twentysevensteps.co.nz* ☾ *No lunch.*

Welles Street

$$$ | MODERN NEW ZEALAND | FAMILY | This inner city pub anchors the emerging South Town neighborhood of the CBD, and the big indoor-outdoor space has plenty of atmosphere. Menu flavors range from contemporary pub food to Mediterranean cuisine, all using local produce. **Known for:** amazing free-range rotisserie chicken; 18 beers on tap and massive wine list; outdoor seating year-round. *Average main: NZ$25* ✉ *44 Welles St.* ☎ *03/366–0172* ⊕ *www. wellesstreet.co.nz.*

Hotels

Staying in the central city is a good choice, with most hotels either relatively new or recently refurbished. All the city sights, shopping, restaurants, and bars are within easy walking distance of central city hotels. There are also some lovely boutique B&Bs that offer more personal accommodation around the arts district.

CENTRAL CHRISTCHURCH

Crowne Plaza

$$$ | HOTEL | FAMILY | As Christchurch's tallest central city building (once an office tower), this is a prime location with spectacular views overlooking historic Victoria Square and the Avon River. **Pros:** latest technology including smart TVs with device mirroring; three in-house dining options; luxurious tiled bathrooms. **Cons:** large tour groups can often take over the lobby; long-term building work surrounds the hotel site; rooms are compact. $ *Rooms from: NZ$225* ✉ *764 Colombo St.* ☎ *03/741–2800* ⊕ *www.christchurch. crowneplaza.com* ⇨ *204 rooms* ☉ *No meals.*

Distinction Hotel

$$$ | HOTEL | FAMILY | This 11-floor upscale hotel is a postearthquake renovation with a contemporary design. **Pros:** great soaking bathtubs; plush slippers, toothbrush, and bathrobes; valet parking at reasonable rates. **Cons:** conference hotel, so can be busy; overlooks the earthquake damaged Christchurch Cathedral; room lighting needs dimmer options. $ *Rooms from: NZ$275* ✉ *14 Cathedral Sq.* ☎ *03/377–7000* ⊕ *www.distinctionhotels. co.nz* ⇨ *179 rooms* ☉ *No meals.*

★ The George

$$$$ | HOTEL | Overlooking the Avon River and Hagley Park, this small luxury hotel has spacious, modern guest rooms. **Pros:** consistently voted one of the country's best small hotels; free parking and free Wi-Fi; two excellent in-house restaurants and bar. **Cons:** can get busy in the public areas; no gym or pool, but you can use gym facilities at Hotel Montreal; the room lighting is high-tech and takes some practice. $ *Rooms from: NZ$555* ✉ *50 Park Terr.* ☎ *03/379–4560* ⊕ *www. thegeorge.com* ⇨ *53 rooms* ☉ *No meals.*

Heritage Christchurch

$$$$ | HOTEL | Inside the beautifully restored Old Government Building built in 1913, with its sweeping central staircase and high ceilings, the Heritage has suites in an Italian Renaissance style complete with stained-glass windows and darkwood paneling. **Pros:** self-contained with kitchen and laundry; decent spa and lap pool; extremely comfortable beds. **Cons:** short-term parking can be difficult; O.G.B. bar is always busy and can be noisy outside, especially in summer; Christchurch Cathedral and the square surrounding are under long-term restoration. $ *Rooms from: NZ$385* ✉ *28–30 Cathedral Sq.* ☎ *03/983–4800, 0800/368–888* ⊕ *www. heritagehotels.co.nz/christchurch* ⇨ *42 suites* ☉ *No meals.*

Novotel Christchurch Cathedral Square

$$$ | HOTEL | From the moment you walk in to the futuristic lobby you will receive a warm welcome from staff who know the city well and can help with directions and recommendations. **Pros:** right in the heart of the city; stunning views of the Southern Alps from executive rooms; comfortable contemporary bar open till late. **Cons:** bathroom sink is set outside the bathroom door in the living areas; quake-damaged Cathedral is right next door, and building work surrounds it; valet parking is expensive (better to use public carpark nearby). $ *Rooms from: NZ$206* ✉ *52 Cathedral Sq.* ☎ *03/372– 2111* ⊕ *www.accorhotels.com* ⇨ *154 rooms* ☉ *No meals.*

★ Orari Bed & Breakfast

$$$ | B&B/INN | Hidden behind an ivy-clad wall and pretty gardens, this lovely heritage villa boasts modern spacious rooms. **Pros:** no need for a car with so much nearby; the apartments are ideal for longer stays, and good for families who need adjoining rooms; extremely helpful and friendly hosts. **Cons:** two of the rooms have separate bathrooms, not en suites; you will need to book well ahead to get a room in peak summer season; some uneven, squeaky floorboards. ⑤ *Rooms from: NZ$225* ✉ *42 Gloucester St.* ☎ *03/365–6569, 0800/267–274 NZ only* ⊕ *www.orari.co.nz* ⇗ *15 rooms* ⦿ *Breakfast.*

Rendezvous Hotel Christchurch
$$$ | **HOTEL** | **FAMILY** | Hard to miss, this city landmark has expansive central city, Port Hills, and mountain views. **Pros:** valet parking in a clever car-stacker inside the building; across the road from the Isaac Theatre Royal and New Regent Street; small well-equipped gym and sauna. **Cons:** some rooms are on the small side and corridors are narrow; at busy times there can be a long wait for the elevators; pillow and blanket choice is limited. ⑤ *Rooms from: NZ$224* ✉ *166 Gloucester St.* ☎ *03/943–3888* ⊕ *www.tfehotels.com* ⇗ *171 rooms* ⦿ *No meals.*

Rydges Latimer Christchurch
$$$ | **HOTEL** | **FAMILY** | Set on leafy Latimer Square, this newly built low-rise hotel is just a few minutes' walk from the central city, but far enough away to be quiet and relaxed. **Pros:** free Wi-Fi throughout the hotel; free parking on-site; excellent in-house dining options. **Cons:** big conference hotel often busy with large groups; just a little too far to walk into the central city on cold days; traffic on the one-way roads surrounding the hotel. ⑤ *Rooms from: NZ$234* ✉ *30 Latimer Sq.* ☎ *0800/176–176 NZ only* ⊕ *www.rydges.com* ⇗ *138 rooms* ⦿ *No meals.*

WEST OF CENTRAL CHRISTCHURCH

Commodore Hotel Christchurch Airport
$$$ | **HOTEL** | **FAMILY** | Just minutes from the airport and 10 minutes from central Christchurch, this family-owned, resort-style accommodation includes a heated indoor pool, sauna, spa, fitness center, and tennis court. **Pros:** free 24-hour shuttle service to and from the airport; free Wi-Fi throughout the hotel; plenty of outdoor space and gardens. **Cons:** there can be big functions here, keeping the lobby and the car park full; no other amenities nearby; longish walk to get from one end of the property to the other. ⑤ *Rooms from: NZ$228* ✉ *449 Memorial Ave.* ☎ *03/358–8129* ⊕ *www.commodorehotel.co.nz* ⇗ *157 rooms* ⦿ *No meals.*

Sudima Hotel Christchurch Airport
$$ | **HOTEL** | Within walking distance of the airport but far enough to be quiet, this modern hotel has a wonderful lobby and executive accommodation tower. **Pros:** free 24-hour shuttle service to and from the airport whenever required; green-lawned garden courtyard; close to the International Antarctic Centre and a shopping center next door. **Cons:** also a conference hotel so can be busy; older parts of the hotel need upgrading; free Wi-Fi is limited to 1GB. ⑤ *Rooms from: NZ$180* ✉ *550 Memorial Ave.* ☎ *03/358–3028* ⊕ *www.sudimahotels.com/en/our-hotels/christchurch-airport* ⇗ *246 rooms* ⦿ *No meals.*

SOUTH OF CENTRAL CHRISTCHURCH

Otahuna Lodge
$$$$ | **HOTEL** | Just 20 minutes from Christchurch and almost hidden by glorious century-old gardens is one of New Zealand's most important historic homes, now an award-winning luxury retreat. **Pros:** memorable five-course degustation dinner included; lots of fresh homegrown fruits and vegetables and cooking classes are available; exceptional hosts with special touches at every turn. **Cons:** not for the budget-minded; TV only available by request; you will need a car if you want to visit the city. ⑤ *Rooms from: NZ$2800* ✉ *224 Rhodes Rd., 17 km (10 miles) from Christchurch, Tai Tapu*

☎ *03/329–6333* ⊕ *www.otahuna.co.nz* ⇨ *7 suites* ❍ *Some meals.*

☻ Nightlife

BARS AND PUBS

Baretta Bar & Restaurant

DANCE CLUBS | Step into another world at this most Italian of nightspots, but it's good Kiwi live music you'll hear in the evening or on a Sunday afternoon. With its fabulous turquoise walls and ornate, carved wooden bar, first impressions are of Milan. Second impressions are that these people know their Italian food. A great place to go for lunch and dinner or tasty pizza and then stay on as it starts to rock as a bar. There's a big piazza-style courtyard and another bar out the back, complete with heaters to warm the evening chill. Later on the live entertainment changes from acoustic duos to DJs and a separate dance floor. ✉ *174 St. Asaph St.* ☎ *03/260–2600* ⊕ *www. baretta.co.nz.*

Boo Radley's Food and Liquor

MUSIC CLUBS | Hip music and top-notch craft beers go nicely together in this cozy southern USA-themed bar. Add great food and a heady cocktail list for a memorable night out. There's a good sharing plate selection, a huge range of bourbons, and excellent craft beers and wines. Don't expect to talk too much when the live music starts, as it can get pretty loud here. Open-mike comedy nights are fun, too. ✉ *Level 1, 98 Victoria St.* ☎ *03/366–9906* ⊕ *www.booradleys. co.nz.*

Fat Eddie's

MUSIC CLUBS | Christchurch's most popular jazz club is in a prime position on the corner of Oxford Terrace and Hereford Street. It boasts a big dance floor and top local and visiting artists every night of the week, from 6:30 pm and until late on weekends. This place is packed from around 9 pm later in the week, so it's worth coming early to get a booth and some of their tasty pizzas and New Orleans–inspired snacks. Make the most of the big beer selection, too. ✉ *Corner of Hereford St. and Oxford Terr.* ☎ *03/595–5332* ⊕ *www.fateddiesbar. co.nz.*

The Last Word

WINE BARS—NIGHTLIFE | Time for a wee dram anyone? Far from being a den for older whisky drinkers, The Last Word is, just as its name suggests, the ultimate place to go if you are an up-and-coming discerning drinker looking for something different. Christchurch's character-filled heritage row, New Regent Street, is the perfect location for this intimate whisky-and-cocktail lounge. There are dozens of hand-picked whiskies to choose from and some excellent cocktails, local wines, and beers on the menu, too. ✉ *Christchurch* ☎ *022/0947–445* ⊕ *www. lastword.co.nz.*

O.G.B. Bar and Cocktail Lounge

WINE BARS—NIGHTLIFE | Consistently named Christchurch's best bar, this 1920s speakeasy set in the Old Government Building has an atmosphere that's hard to beat. Live music in the outside courtyard and superb drinks served in beautiful glassware add up to a classy night out. Next door there's also a cleverly concealed cocktail and champagne bar called Parlour; an old-fashioned barber shop is also part of the mix. ✉ *28 Cathedral Sq.* ☎ *03/377–4336* ⊕ *www. ogb.co.nz.*

Strange and Co

NIGHTLIFE OVERVIEW | Join the throngs heading for the cocktails, chargrilled steaks, and live music in this architecturally stunning building set in a quirky passageway. They host DJs, open-mike comedy nights, and big screen sports matches, too. The party really starts going around 11 pm on weekends. Check their website or Facebook page for upcoming events. ✉ *89 Lichfield St.* ☎ *03/365–7018* ⊕ *www.strangeand.co.*

CASINOS

Christchurch Casino

CASINOS | When all else has closed, make your way to the Christchurch Casino for blackjack, American roulette, baccarat, and gaming machines. Open 24 hours over the weekend and until 3 am Monday to Thursday, there are four restaurant and bar areas. Places to dine and relax in the casino are the Grand Cafe, Chi Kitchen, and the Monza Sports Bar. The latter has TV monitors at every vantage point plus one huge screen for watching live sports. The casino is strict on its dress code; if you're unsure on what to wear, check their website for details. ■ TIP→ **Free shuttles go to and from some local hotels and motels daily from 6 pm to 2 am—book through the casino reception.** ✉ *30 Victoria St.* ☎ *03/365–9999* ⊕ *www.chchcasino. co.nz.*

🎭 Performing Arts

Christchurch has a strong arts scene, with impressive orchestras, choirs, and theaters. The Isaac Theatre Royal has been restored to its former glory, adding a grand venue for performances and film. Christchurch Town Hall is curently underway with a major restoration project. To find out what's on when you're visiting, check out ⊕ *www.christchurchnz.com* and ⊕ *eventfinda.co.nz.* Cityscape magazine also has an excellent website and app ⊕ *www.cityscape-christchurch.co.nz* with information about the city's events.

Ticketek

TICKETS | Tickets for many performance venues and concerts are sold through Ticketek online. ☎ *0800/842–538 NZ only* ⊕ *www.ticketek.co.nz.*

ART GALLERIES

Although the Christchurch Art Gallery Te Puna O Waiwhetu is the city's visual arts mother ship, there are many smaller galleries and plenty of street art to check out. For more information, check the Canterbury Art Trails website.

SCAPE Public Art

ARTS CENTERS | SCAPE public art installs free-to-view contemporary art all year round in Christchurch, with a focus on its Public Art Annual Seasons between September and November. The works, many of which are now permanent, are urban and alternative arts such as conceptual architecture, sculpture, and city murals. Check the website for details. ⊕ *www. scapepublicart.org.nz.*

THEATER

★ Isaac Theatre Royal

THEATER | The grand lady of Christchurch's theater scene, dating back to 1908, was fully restored in 2014. This opulent setting, complete with an intricate painted ceiling dome and marble staircase, hosts some of New Zealand's best touring shows including ballet and music. It is also home to a giant screen for the New Zealand International Film Festival, held every July. Get dressed up and enjoy the glamour of a bygone era, in the comfort of today's plushest seating. There are stylish bars on every level for a drink before the show or during intermission. ✉ *145 Gloucester St.* ☎ *03/366–6326* ⊕ *www.isaactheatreroyal.co.nz.*

🛍 Shopping

SHOPPING STREETS AND CENTERS

ANZ Centre

SHOPPING CENTERS/MALLS | This retail precinct offers standout local designer brands, including Macpac, Partridge Jewellers, Superette, Glassons, Hallensteins Brothers, and Merchant. There's also a Mecca Maxima cosmetics store, the ANZ bank, and an excellent café, Arbo. ✉ *Junction of Colombo, High, and Cashel Sts.* ⊕ *www.anzcentre.co.nz.*

★ Ballantynes

DEPARTMENT STORES | Established in 1854 as New Zealand's first department store, Ballantynes is an institution in the South Island. Far from allowing its traditions to slow it down, it has morphed into a world-class shopping experience with some of the best New Zealand and international designer brand names all under one roof. Allow plenty of time to browse the racks and shelves, where you will find everything from the latest trends in designer concept stores to New Zealand gifts and wine and the very best crystal and china. When you need a break there are three cafés and a wine bar. They also have a store at Christchurch Airport, where you can pick up your purchases and take advantage of tax-exempt shopping. ⊠ *Cashel St.* ☎ *03/379–7400* ⊕ *www.ballantynes.co.nz.*

The Crossing

SHOPPING CENTERS/MALLS | Dubbed Christchurch's new retail heart, the Crossing is an artfully designed precinct boasting top international and local brands. Walking through the outdoor courtyards and laneways lined with impressive contemporary sculptures, you will find designer clothes and shoes, along with a florist, cafés, beauty salons, and a gourmet supermarket. ⊠ *166 Cashel St.* ☎ *027/506–8149* ⊕ *www. thecrossing.co.nz.*

The Colombo

SHOPPING CENTERS/MALLS | A new take on a neighborhood mall, this haven for food and fashion fans includes a stylish mix of designer clothes, eats, and gifts. Shops to spend time browsing include Bolt of Cloth for homewares, Annah Stretton for designer frocks, and the Beer Library, which has the largest craft beer selection in the region. It's located just outside the central city, in Sydenham. ⊠ *363 Colombo St.* ☎ *03/365–5091* ⊕ *www. thecolombo.co.nz.*

The Tannery

SHOPPING CENTERS/MALLS | It is one of those unlikely projects that would probably never have got off the ground in Christchurch before the earthquakes: turning an old former industrial tannery into a Victorian shopping mall. Not only

that but the developer had each brick removed, cleaned, and put back, once the buildings were reinforced. The Tannery's now an interesting place to head, with quirky shops, fashion, deluxe cinemas, and a fabulous cake shop and deli. Try Mitchelli's Cafe Rinato for tasty food in a friendly atmosphere or The Brewery for craft beers and superb wood-fired pizza. ⊠ *3 Garlands Rd.* ⊕ *www.thetannery. co.nz.*

SPECIALTY STORES
de Spa Chocolatier

FOOD/CANDY | The delicious sweets at de Spa Chocolatier's pair Belgian chocolate with Kiwi ingredients and fruit fillings (among other delectable things). Here you can watch the chocolatiers at work through a glass-walled kitchen, and they conduct factory tours. They also make a special line of sugar-free chocolate. The factory and showroom are on the way to Ferrymead Heritage Park and Sumner. ⊠ *1013 Ferry Rd., Ferrymead* ☎ *03/384–5285* ⊕ *www.despa.co.nz.*

Dunsandel Store

FOOD/CANDY | FAMILY | If you've left Christchurch a bit late for breakfast, about 30 minutes south in Selwyn district, stop at the Dunsandel Store. It's a fascinating mix of local store, deli, and café with excellent food. The cabinets are stuffed with tasty sandwiches and baked goods. They have a good range of breakfasts and all-day treats made from mostly local and organic produce. There are tables indoors and out, surrounded by a courtyard full of fruit trees and vegetables. ⊠ *3414 Main South Rd., Dunsandel* ☎ *03/325–4037* ⊕ *www.dunsandelstore. co.nz.*

Kathmandu

CLOTHING | This store sells a colorful range of outdoor clothing, backpacks, accessories, and tents. This chain is found throughout New Zealand and has particularly good reductions at sale times. It has several stores throughout the city and a clearance outlet at 124 Riccarton

Road. ✉ *201 Madras St.* ☎ *03/343–4634* ⊕ *www.kathmandu.co.nz.*

Macpac

SPORTING GOODS | Founded in Christchurch in 1973, Macpac sells good-quality outdoor (and merino) clothing, backpacks, accessories, sleeping bags, and tents. The store is now found at locations across New Zealand, with five outlets in Christchurch including the central city flagship store. It also frequently has great sale prices, but if you're not here at the right time, you can hunt for a bargain in its biggest clearance area—upstairs at Tower Junction off Mandeville Street, Riccarton. ✉ *Tower Junction, 7a Mandeville St.* ☎ *03/371–9342* ⊕ *www.macpac. co.nz.*

★ Scorpio Bookshop

BOOKS/STATIONERY | This independent bookstore started in the early 1970s and has gathered a cult following over the years. The shop stocks a wide range of fiction, cooking, and history books as well as design studies, philosophy tomes, and travelogues. ✉ *120 Hereford St.* ☎ *03/379–2882* ⊕ *www.scorpio-books.co.nz.*

Untouched World

CLOTHING | New Zealand's leading sustainable lifestyle fashion brand was established in Christchurch, and has a real designer edge. The stylish lifestyle clothing is easy on the Earth too, with signature fabrics including organic cotton, Ecopossum (a mixture of possum fur and merino wool), and Mountainsilk (silky-fine machine-washable organic merino). Their flagship store has a licensed café serving fresh food, organic when possible, in its native garden environment. ✉ *155 Roydvale Ave., Burnside* ☎ *03/357–9399* ⊕ *www.untouchedworld.com.*

🏃 Activities

BALLOONING
★ Ballooning Canterbury

BALLOONING | Here's an activity worth getting up early for: Ballooning Canterbury picks you up from most central city places and takes you to Darfield, where you help set up the mighty balloon. Then you're away, floating above river gorges, the Canterbury Plains, and the foothills of the Southern Alps. You may see as far south as Aoraki/Mt. Cook, north up to the Kaikouras, and the ocean all the way down the coast to Timaru—much of the South Island in just an hour's flight. A glass of bubbly is the perfect finish. It's very weather dependent so don't leave it to the last minute to organize. You must be at least 4½ feet tall to ride. ✉ *2136 Bealey Rd., Darfield* ☎ *03/318–0860* ⊕ *www.ballooningcanterbury.com* 🎫 *NZ$395 per person.*

BICYCLING

Christchurch's relative flatness makes for easy biking, and the city has cultivated excellent resources for cyclists. A network of well-marked and well-designed Major Cycle Routes connects the central city with local attractions. The award-winning Uni-Cycle runs 3½ miles from the city center through Hagley Park and leafy suburbs to the University of Canterbury. Other popular cycle trails include the Rail Trail at Little River and the spectacular trails around the Port Hills.

You can pick up a route map from the city council or visit their cycling website, which shows cycleways and recreational routes ⊕ *www.ccc.govt.nz/transport/cycling.*

★ Christchurch Adventure Park

BICYCLING | Christchurch's Port Hills are home to New Zealand's longest chairlift as well as the country's longest and highest zip line; both are found within the 900-acre Christchurch Adventure Park. Just 17 minutes by bike from the central city, you can be on the downhill mountain biking trails via chairlifts (for you and your bike) or experiencing dual zip line tours and incredible sightseeing. Bikes and protective gear are available for hire. There's an excellent café here too. ✉ *225 Worsleys Rd.* ☎ *0508/247–478* ⊕ *www. christchurchadventurepark.com.*

City Cycle Hire

BICYCLING | FAMILY | Here you can hire mountain, touring, and tandem bikes. Rentals include helmets, locks, and cycle map; and they'll deliver your bike to your accommodation. ✉ *20 Raymond Rd., Ferrymead* ☎ *03/377–5952, 0800/343–848 NZ only* ⊕ *www.cyclehire-tours.co.nz* 🎫 *From NZ$25.*

Cyclone Cycles

BICYCLING | Cycles can be rented from Cyclone Cycles for a flat fee of NZ$45 per hire bike. Special rates are available for groups or longer periods. Book online. ✉ *245 Colombo St.* ☎ *03/332–9588* ⊕ *www.cyclone.net.nz.*

Mountain Bike Adventure Company

BICYCLING | The Mountain Bike Adventure Company offers a NZ$70 package including a ride up on the Christchurch Gondola to the summit station. Then there's the choice of either an off-road mountain-bike trail or a scenic-road route down to the beach and back to the Gondola base—cycle distance is approximately 16 km (10 miles). ☎ *03/377–5952, 0800/424–534 NZ only* ⊕ *www.cyclehire-tours.co.nz.*

BOATING

Punting on the Avon

SCENIC DRIVE | Sit back and enjoy the changing face of the central city from water level, framed by weeping willows, tranquil parks, and ornate bridges. Replicating English punting at Oxford and Cambridge, the boat tours leave from the Antigua Boat Sheds, near the hospital, or the Worcester Street Bridge daily from 9 to 6 in summer and from 10 to 4 the rest of the year. A 30-minute trip costs NZ$28. Call ahead to book a time. ✉ *2 Cambridge Terr.* ☎ *03/366–0337* ⊕ *www. christchurchattractions.nz.*

HIKING

Godley Head—Taylors Mistake Walkway

HIKING/WALKING | To reach this scenic track take the coast road through Sumner then take a left turn at the summit intersection. The road climbs and winds for several kilometers before breaking out above Lyttelton Harbour with startling views to the hills of Banks Peninsula. You'll see some of the World War II coastal defense battery built in 1939; rated one of the country's significant defense-heritage sites. There's also a 1½-hour walking track from here back to Taylors Mistake near Sumner (although you'll need to arrange a pickup at the other end, or plan on a three-hour round-trip). The Godley Head lookout is particularly exciting in a strong southerly wind. ⊕ *www.ccc.govt. nz.*

Port Hills Walks

HIKING/WALKING | FAMILY | Christchurch's Port Hills are worth climbing for spectacular views of the city, the Southern Alps, and Banks Peninsula. This is the route the first settlers took when they arrived at the port of Lyttelton. Well-marked tracks include the Bridle Path, Rapaki Track, and the Bowenvale-Sugarloaf Circuit. ⊕ *www. christchurchnz.com.*

RUGBY

Canterbury fans are as rugby-mad as the rest of the country. In fact the first match ever played in New Zealand took place in 1862 in Cranmer Square, in central Christchurch. This is the home of the Crusaders, and the breeding ground for many famous All Blacks. Every Saturday in winter you can catch little All-Blacks-in-the-making playing games in Hagley Park and suburban parks.

Christchurch Stadium

RUGBY | Canterbury's professional rugby union team, the Crusaders, have won the most titles in the history of the Super Rugby competition, played between

Best Trails in Christchurch

Enterprising local tourist offices have sketched out thematically linked, self-guided sightseeing routes throughout the region. You can pick up maps at the Christchurch i-SITE Visitor Information Centre, at visitor centers along the way, or online. The following are the best of the bunch:

Alpine Pacific Touring Route. This links three of the most popular getaways in Canterbury: Waipara, Hanmer Springs, and Kaikoura (⊕ www.alpinepacific.nz).

Selwyn Food and Wine Trail. Pick up a brochure from the i-SITE Visitor Center and follow the trail that starts 20 minutes west of the city to discover wineries, cheesemakers, farmers' markets, and country stores (⊕ www. sensationalselwyn.co.nz).

Pioneer Trail. Connecting several historic sights between Timaru and Geraldine, this route includes the Richard Pearse Memorial, dedicated to a local aviation innovator.

Inland Scenic Route 72. Scenic Highway 72 runs from Amberley, north of Christchurch, along the foothills of the Southern Alps through two spectacular gorges, past Geraldine to Winchester. You can join up with it at various points along the way (⊕ www.scenicroute72.nz).

teams from South Africa, Australia, and NZ. So they're not a bad team to watch if you get the chance to cheer them on at their home turf. The season goes from February through September. ✉ *95 Jack Hinton Dr., Addington* ☎ *03/379–1765* ⊕ *crusaders.co.nz.*

Arthur's Pass National Park

153 km (96 miles) northwest of Christchurch.

Established in 1929, Arthur's Pass was the South Island's first national park. Follow in the footsteps of ancient Māori hunters, 1860s gold rushers, and 1990s road workers who constructed the 1,444-foot Otira Viaduct. Each of the many twists and turns reveals another photo op: waterfalls, fields of wildflowers, dizzying drops. And it's all easily accessible from Christchurch.

GETTING HERE AND AROUND
For any confident driver the road through Arthur's Pass is a glorious drive—paved all the way, but with a few steep, gnarly sections in the middle. The train and bus tours are also good options, but you lose the flexibility to stop and do a walk or follow a waterfall track, or to just admire the breathtaking scenery if you're stuck on a tour.

To drive there from Christchurch head out on the West Coast Road—it is particularly well signposted from town. The turnoff is near the airport. There is only one road over the Alps within 100 km (62 miles) either way, so you can't go wrong. The road heads out through the small town of Springfield then heads up toward Porter's Pass and Cass before hitting the real stuff at Arthur's Pass.

Information on the park is available on the **Department of Conservation's** website and at the DOC-run **Arthur's Pass Visitor Center.** The **Arthur's Pass Mountaineering** site is another good source for information on local mountaineering conditions.

East and West
of Christchurch

CONTACTS Arthur's Pass Mountaineering.
⊕ *www.arthurspass.com* . **Department
of Conservation Arthur's Pass Visitor
Centre.** ✉ *State Hwy. 73, Arthur's Pass*
☎ *03/318–9211* ⊕ *www.doc.govt.nz.*

👁 Sights

Arthur's Pass National Park

NATIONAL/STATE PARK | This spectacular
alpine region is a favorite hiking destination. Initially hacked through as a direct
route to the West Coast gold fields in
1865, the road over Arthur's Pass was
a tortuous, dangerous track. When the
railway arrived, in 1923, the pass's skiing
and hiking opportunities came to the
fore, and the TranzAlpine train service
now offers a supreme way to see this
rugged area without getting your shoes
dirty. On the way to the pass, along

State Highway 73 from Christchurch,
you'll pass the **Castle Hill Conservation
Area,** which is filled with interesting rock
formations. Nearby **Craigieburn Conservation Park** has wonderful beech and fern
forests and some great mountain-biking
trails—take the road leading to Broken
River Ski Field. Above the tree line you'll
find ski slopes and, between November and March, masses of wildflowers,
including giant buttercups. Around the
summit you'll also have a good chance of
seeing *kea,* the South Island's particularly
intelligent and curious mountain parrots.
Arthur's Pass Village, at 2,395 feet, is a
true alpine village, so pack a jacket even
in summer. A couple of restaurants and
a store provide basic food supplies,
and there are several places to stay,
including an excellent wilderness lodge
near Bealey. There's also a Department of
Conservation visitor center to help with

Planning Your Trip to Arthur's Pass ⊙

Best Time to Go

November through March brings gorgeous wildflowers to the park. Ski at Temple Basin from late June to early October. Remember: with 6,562-foot peaks, the weather in the park can change for the worse *anytime* at this altitude.

Best Ways to Explore

By Car. Driving offers the flexibility to stop for hikes and sightseeing when you please. The road, extensively revamped in the 1990s, is a feat of engineering, particularly the Otira Viaduct. Five thousand cubic meters (176,573 cubic feet) of concrete were used to create the viaduct on a steep unstable foundation in an area prone to flash floods and earthquakes. As you navigate the turns, spare some thoughts for the men who spent backbreaking years creating it.

By Foot. Everything from 10-minute strolls to multiday hikes are available in the park. We recommend the Punchbowl Falls Track (one-hour return from Arthur's Pass Village) and Dobson Nature Walk (30-minute return), which follows a lovely loop at the summit of Arthur's Pass. Marvel at brilliantly colored alpine lichen splashed across boulders and cliff faces. Kea, wrybill (with bent beaks), and green bellbirds populate the park. Lucky visitors will spot the roroa—or great-spotted kiwi—that roam the steep terrain.

By Mountain Climbing. There are plenty of ways up the peaks of Arthur's Pass. Mountain climbing in the area is prone to changeable weather and many routes involve river crossings, so check in with the Department of Conservation before any endeavor and make sure you are well equipped and up to the challenge.

By Train. Take to the tracks and relax on board the TranzAlpine Scenic Journey. It takes you from Christchurch ("ChCh" to locals) to Greymouth in 4½ hours, through 16 tunnels and over 5 viaducts. The train has an open-air carriage, which provides breathtaking views of the plains, gorges, valleys, and beech forests.

enjoying the vast selection of mountains and rivers in the area. Both the Devil's Punchbowl and Bridal Veil Falls are worth the short walk. The tracks are in good condition and, although they're a bit steep and rocky in places, no serious hiking experience is required. ☎ *03/318–9211* ⊕ *www.doc.govt.nz.*

🍴 Restaurants

The Wobbly Kea Café and Bar

$$$ | NEW ZEALAND | This pleasant place is named for the cheeky mountain parrots that circle above it day after day. It's open daily from 10 am to 8 pm, serving a wide menu selection that includes great pizza. **Known for:** bratwurst bangers and mash; great breakfasts; classic pub atmosphere. ⑤ *Average main: NZ$25* ⊠ *108 Main Rd., Arthur's Pass* ☎ *03/318–9101* ⊕ *www.wobblykea.co.nz.*

🛏 Hotels

⭐ **Arthur's Pass Wilderness Lodge**

$$$$ | B&B/INN | Surrounded by spectacular peaks, beech forests, and serene lakes, this sophisticated back-to-nature lodge shares 6,000 acres with its own high-country merino sheep station and nature reserve in a valley called Te Ko

Awa a Aniwaniwa (Valley of the Mother of Rainbows). **Pros:** on alternate days, you can muster sheep with border collies and help blade-shear sheep the old-fashioned way; great wine and food with a view; rates include breakfast, dinner, and guided activities. **Cons:** quite remote if you like shopping; closed in the off-season; surcharge on New Zealand holidays. $ *Rooms from: NZ$960* ⊠ *State Hwy. 73, Arthur's Pass* ☎ *03/318–9246* ⊕ *www.wildernesslodge.co.nz* ⊘ *Closed June and July* ⇆ *24 rooms* |O| *Some meals.*

Mountain House Arthur's Pass YHA

$ | B&B/INN | This is the biggest spot in town with a main lodge that has private and shared rooms; there are also two separate cottages, two motel units, and backpacker dorms in the old YHA lodge. **Pros:** wing of newer facilities and private rooms that are clean and tidy; YHA members get discounts and free Wi-Fi; spectacular walking tracks start right next to the front door. **Cons:** whole complex is spread over about a kilometer; no en suite bathrooms; more expensive than most hostels because it's so remote. $ *Rooms from: NZ$94* ⊠ *84 West Coast Rd., Arthur's Pass* ☎ *03/318–9258* ⊕ *www.trampers.co.nz* ⇆ *27 rooms* |O| *No meals.*

⚷ Activities

HIKING AND WALKING

There are plenty of half- and full-day hikes and 10 backcountry trails with overnight huts for backpacking. A popular walk near Arthur's Pass Village is the short Punchbowl Falls Track, which passes through diverse subalpine forest to a 450-foot-high waterfall. It takes roughly one hour to do the track. For a full-day hike, trails leading to the summits of various mountains are all along State Highway 73. Be prepared for variable weather conditions. Two of the most popular and challenging overnight treks are the Cass/Lagoon Saddle trip and the Avalanche-Crow route

over Avalanche Peak. For these, you'll need an experienced leader and full gear. The Department of Conservation Visitor Centre has up-to-date information on weather and trail conditions. Before you go into the outdoors, tell someone your plans and leave a date to raise the alarm if you haven't returned.

Lyttelton

12 km (7½ miles) east of Christchurch.

Lyttelton, a sleepy port town, was the arrival point for many of the early Canterbury settlers. The Canterbury Pilgrims' landing place is marked by a rock near the road entrance to the port. A mix of renovated wooden villas and contemporary homes now rises halfway up what was once a volcanic crater. Today, although only a 20-minute drive from Christchurch, Lyttelton has developed its own distinctive quality, with a funky, hipster vibe created by a strong-knit local community that was attracted here by the wonderful harbor views and abundant creative energy. Saturday is a good day to come, with a farmers' market from 10 to 1, then you can explore the boutique shops known for handmade crafts, gourmet foods, and art. Governors Bay and farther round to Diamond Harbour makes a nice half-day drive from the city.

GETTING HERE AND AROUND

Lyttelton can be reached by driving down Ferry Road from Christchurch, heading toward Sumner, and then taking the road tunnel. Another scenic route is to follow the main street, Colombo, east out of the city, up the Port Hills, and over Dyers Pass to Governors Bay. Then turn left and head back along the harbor edge to Lyttelton. If you don't have a car, you can catch Bus 28 from Christchurch.

Lyttelton stretches along a terrace above the port. Norwich Quay runs along the waterfront, but the main street, London

Did You Know?

Arthur's Pass National Park forms the South Island's "backbone" between Canterbury and the West Coast. The park is a study in contrasts, with dry beech forests to the east and dense rain forests to the west.

Street, runs parallel a block higher up the hill. London Street joins the road back over to Sumner, and in the other direction back past the tunnel entrance along Simeon Quay toward Governors Bay. Call the Lyttelton Harbor Information Center at 20 Oxford Street for maps and brochures.

VISITOR INFORMATION

CONTACTS Lyttelton Harbour Information Centre. ✉ *20 Oxford St.* ☎ *03/328–9093* ⊕ *www.lytteltonharbour.info.*

Sights

Diamond Harbour

TOWN | Diamond Harbour is the largest township on the far side of Lyttelton Harbour. You can drive to Diamond Harbour (around 40 minutes from Christchurch) or take a 10-minute journey on the Black Diamond ferry from Jetty B at Norwich Quay. Sailings are frequent. There's a small farmers' market once a fortnight over summer, excellent cafés and restaurants, some great walks, and the beautiful Charteris Bay Golf Club. ✉ *"B" Jetty, 17 Norwich Quay* ☎ *03/328–9078, 0800/436–574* ⊕ *www.diamondharbour. info* ☎ *NZ$13 return.*

★ Ohinetahi

GARDEN | Sir Miles Warren is one of New Zealand's foremost architects with a pedigree as large as his garden. Ohinetahi, which is also the Māori name for the area, features not only his large, stone, colonial villa, but also his immaculate garden—considered one of the best formal gardens in the country. Blending Sir Miles's eye for detail and design with a stunning situation this garden maximizes the use of "garden rooms"—the red room being particularly memorable—hedging, and color. ✉ *Governors Bay-Teddington Rd.* ☎ *03/329–9852* ⊕ *www. ohinetahi.co.nz* ☎ *NZ$15* ⊙ *Closed Apr.–Aug.*

Quail Island

ISLAND | Located in Lyttelton Harbour, Quail Island was used by the early European settlers as a quarantine zone and leper colony and was named after the now-extinct native quail. It was once a significant area for collecting birds' eggs by local Māori. These days Quail Island, also known as Otamahua, is being restored as an ecological reserve, and is home to many native birds including kingfisher, fantail, *silvereye* (a small bird common in New Zealand), and various seabirds. The *Black Cat* ferry from Lyttelton can zip you out here for a hike or a picnic. ✉ *"B" Jetty, 17 Norwich Quay* ☎ *03/328–9078* ⊕ *www.blackcat.co.nz* ☎ *NZ$30.*

🍴 Restaurants

Civil and Naval

$$ | **TAPAS** | This cozy haunt is packed with locals who come for tasty tapas-style food produced in a tiny kitchen, and the excellent cocktails. There's an eclectic selection of international and New Zealand wines, spirits, and craft beers. **Known for:** green courtyard on sunny days and cozy log fires in winter; inventive cocktails created by a master barman; beautifully executed and affordable food. $ *Average main: NZ$15* ✉ *16 London St.* ☎ *03/328–7206* ⊕ *www.civilandnaval.nz.*

Lyttelton Coffee Company

$$ | **CAFÉ** | Well-known for its excellent coffee available in many Christchurch cafés, this is the home of the legendary roastery and plenty of hearty fare to match. Great service and an arty atmosphere mean this heritage building is buzzing from early morning until late afternoon every day. **Known for:** some of the best coffee in the region; outdoor deck with fabulous views over the harbor; freshly baked muffins big enough for two. $ *Average main: $18* ✉ *29 London St.* ⊙ *No dinner.*

★ Roots

$$$$ | **MODERN NEW ZEALAND** | It's well worth making the journey to this award-winning haven for honest food, made from scratch by passionate people, using local organic and biodynamic ingredients. The philosophy here is all about bringing high-quality produce to the table, from the owners' garden, preserve cellar, and foraged nature. **Known for:** eight-course degustation menu of seasonal and local products that changes every three months; wonderful wine pairings; open-kitchen setting. $ *Average main: NZ$90* ⊠ *8 London St.* ☎ *03/328–7658* ⊕ *www.rootsrestaurant.co.nz.*

Super

$$ | **ASIAN FUSION** | This eatery's clever take on Asian fusion has rave reviews from locals thanks to its selection of carefully crafted dishes that are perfect for sharing. Set in the beautiful Old Royal Hotel Building on the waterfront, the atmosphere is stylish and relaxed. **Known for:** tasty okonomiyaka (Japanese pancakes with a twist); locally sourced, organic produce with lots of vegan options; intriguing desserts. $ *Average main: NZ$20* ⊠ *5 Norwich Quay* ☎ *021/0862–2632* ⊕ *www.super. restaurant.*

 Nightlife

Wunderbar

BARS/PUBS | Not your average bar, this Lyttelton institution prides itself on being different. Dolls' heads as lamp shades, a supersize Madonna, and 1950s newspapers on the bathroom walls give you an idea of the fun to be had here. There's live music just about every night. Pool and foosball tables will also keep you entertained as will the great views over Lyttelton port. ⊠ *19 London St.* ☎ *03/328–8818* ⊕ *www.wunderbar.co.nz.*

 Activities

HIKING

Bridle Path

HIKING/WALKING | Quail Island is a good option, but if you'd rather stay on the mainland, you could instead follow in the

trail of the early settlers by taking the Bridle Path. The steep zigzag track goes from Cunningham Street up to the crater rim. You can walk to the Gondola Summit Station, a few minutes' farther, to see the Canterbury Plains from the site of the memorial to the pioneer women, or walk down the rest of the trail to finish near the Christchurch Gondola base station. A No. 28 bus will take you to Lyttelton, and the same bus will pick you up on the other side. Allow 1½ hours for the walk—some of which is quite steep. ⊠ *Bridal Path at Cunningham Terr.*

Akaroa and the Banks Peninsula

82 km (50 miles) east of Christchurch.

Sheep graze almost to the water's edge in the many small bays indenting the coastline of Banks Peninsula, the nub that juts into the Pacific east of Christchurch. On the southern side of the peninsula, in a harbor created when the crater wall of an extinct volcano collapsed into the sea, nestles the fishing village of Akaroa (Māori for "long harbor"). The port is a favorite day trip for Christchurch residents on Sunday drives, and on weekends and over the summer holidays (December to February) it can be extremely busy. If you're planning to stay the night during the busy times (summer and weekends), book a room and dinner before you leave Christchurch.

Although Akaroa was chosen as the site for a French colony in 1838, the first French settlers arrived in 1840 only to find that the British had already established sovereignty over New Zealand by the Treaty of Waitangi. Less than 10 years later, the French abandoned their attempt at colonization, but the settlers remained and gradually intermarried with the local English community. Apart from the *rue* (street) names, a few family surnames, and architectural touches, there is little sign of a French connection anymore, but the village has splendid surroundings. A day trip from Christchurch will get you to and from Akaroa, including a drive along the Summit Road on the edge of the former volcanic dome, but take an overnight trip if you want to explore the peninsula bays as well as the town. It's an easy drive most of the way but the last hill over to Akaroa is narrow and winding with few passing areas. By the time you've taken a harbor cruise, driven around a few bays, and stopped for a meal, you'll be right in the mood to kick back overnight in this quiet spot.

GETTING HERE AND AROUND

The main route to Akaroa is State Highway 75, which leaves the southwest corner of Christchurch as Lincoln Road. The 82-km (50-mile) drive takes about 90 minutes. You can also head out through Lyttelton and Teddington, then over the hill to Little River for a really scenic but slightly longer trip.

If you'd rather not drive, the Akaroa Shuttle has a daily service between Christchurch and Akaroa from October to April for NZ$55 per person return, or NZ$35 one-way. Direct shuttles run from Rolleston Avenue in Christchurch and from outside the Akaroa Adventure Centre, and there is also a free pickup service from central city hotels.

BUS CONTACTS Akaroa Shuttle.
☎ *0800/500–929 NZ only ⊕ www. akaroashuttle.co.nz.*

TOURS

Akaroa Harbour is home to the world's smallest and rarest dolphins. The Akaroa Marine Reserve is a fully protected area, similar to a national park. White flippered penguins, the smallest penguins in the world, also frequent the harbor. To get up-close to the wildlife you can take a swimming with dolphins tour, hire a kayak, or book a scenic nature safari to see the penguin colony.

VISITOR INFORMATION

CONTACTS Akaroa Information Centre.
✉ *74a Rue Lavaud, Akaroa* ☎ *03/304–7784* ⊕ *www.visitakaroa.com.*

◉ Sights

Akaroa Walks

TRAIL | Take the village walk, where you amble along the narrow streets past old-fashioned little cottages and historic buildings that reflect the area's multicultural background. If you are feeling more ambitious try the country walks on routes ranging from two hours to all day. For hikers, there are also 20 km (12.5 miles) of well-mapped tracks from summit to sea level. Start at the Akaroa Information Centre and choose from a range of free brochures and maps to enhance your experience. ✉ *74a Rue Lavaud, Akaroa* ⊕ *www.visitakaroa.com.*

Akaroa Museum

MUSEUM | The focus of historic interest is the Akaroa Museum, which has a display of Māori *pounamu* (greenstone) as well as alternating exhibits on the area's multicultural past. The peninsula supported a significant Māori population and the collections and displays tell some of the exciting stories of Kai Tahu, the people of the land. The building is currently being strengthened for earthquakes but the museum is still open. The Old Courthouse, the old Custom House, and Langlois-Eteveneaux House, the two-room cottage of an early French settler, are also part of the museum. ✉ *71 Rue Lavaud at Rue Balguerie, Akaroa* ☎ *03/304–1013* ⊕ *www.akaroamuseum. org.nz* ⌦ *Free.*

Okains Bay

BEACH—SIGHT | The contrast of the rim of the old volcanic cone and the coves below is striking—and when you drop into one of the coves, you'll probably feel like you've found your own little corner of the world. One of the easiest bays to access is Okains Bay. Take the Summit

Road at Hilltop if approaching from Christchurch, or Ngaio Point Road behind Duvauchelle if approaching from Akaroa. It's about 24 km (15 miles) from Akaroa and takes about a half hour to drive. The small settlement lies at the bottom of Okains Bay Road, which ends at a beach sheltered by tall headlands. ⊠ *Okains Bay, Akaroa.*

Okains Bay Māori and Colonial Museum

MUSEUM | This collection of buildings contains 20,000 Māori and 19th-century colonial artifacts, including *waka* (canoes) used in Waitangi Day celebrations and displays such as a smithy and print shop. There are also a *wharenui* (Māori meetinghouse), colonial homes, including a *totara* slab cottage, and a saddlery and harness shop. If you happen to be in the area on Waitangi Day (February 6), New Zealand's national day, the museum marks it in style. ⊠ *1146 Okains Bay Rd., Okains Bay* ☎ *03/304–8611* ⊕ *www.okainsbaymuseum.co.nz* ☞ *NZ$10.*

State Highway 75

SCENIC DRIVE | State Highway 75 leads from Christchurch out onto the peninsula, curving along the southern portion past Lake Ellesmere. There are interesting stops on your way out to Akaroa. The small town of **Little River** used to be the end of the line for a now-defunct railway line from Christchurch; the route is now a walkway and bicycle trail. The old, wooden train station houses a crafts gallery and information office, and a café is next door in the grocery store. Look out for Silo Stay, where grain silos have been cleverly transformed into eco-accommodation units called Silococoons. When you reach **Hilltop,** pause for your first glimpse of Akaroa Harbour; on a sunny day it's magnificent. (At Hilltop the highway crosses the Summit Road, the other major route through the peninsula.) ⊠ *State Hwy. 75, Christchurch* ⊕ *www.visitakaroa.com.*

🍴 Restaurants

Bully Hayes Restaurant & Bar

$$$$ | NEW ZEALAND | Named after a notorious American pirate, this modern restaurant occupies a great site overlooking the yachts moored in the harbor. New Zealand cuisine is highlighted and there are light and full-size main courses for breakfast, lunch, and dinner, all year-round. **Known for:** spectacular views of Akaroa harbor; craft beers and a great wine list; home-cured Akaroa salmon gravlax. ⑤ *Average main: NZ$35* ⊠ *57 Beach Rd., Akaroa* ☎ *03/304–7533* ⊕ *www.bullyhayes.co.nz.*

Murphy's Seafoods

$ | CAFÉ | Acclaimed around the country as having some of the best fish-and-chips available, this take-out–style eatery often has queues out the door. The deep-fried fish is served with a big side of perfectly cooked chips and a big chunk of lemon or try the ciabatta fish sandwich from the wharfside caravan. **Known for:** classic and delicious fish-and-chips; Murphy himself spending most days filleting his morning catch; Akaroa salmon cooked to perfection. ⑤ *Average main: NZ$12* ⊠ *Akaroa Main Wharf, Akaroa* ☎ *03/304–7464.*

The Trading Rooms Restaurant & Bar

$$$$ | NEW ZEALAND | European spins on local produce, meat, and seafood, along with a seaside location, make for sought-after reservations here. Dark wooden floors, white tablecloths, and leather chairs lend a seaside chic quality and on a nice day you can sit outside. **Known for:** excellent seafood, particularly Akaroa salmon and groper; boutique Banks Peninsula wines; signature dish of Canterbury lamb. ⑤ *Average main: NZ$39* ⊠ *71 Beach Rd., Akaroa* ☎ *03/304–7656* ⊕ *www.thetradingrooms.co.nz* ⊙ *Closed every June but may vary; check website.*

Hotels

Annandale

$$$$ | **ALL-INCLUSIVE** | **FAMILY** | This gem set on a private farm at Pigeon Bay is made up of four secluded villas, including an ultramodern waterfront home and a magnificent Victorian homestead surrounded by expansive heritage gardens with an impressive pool and spa facilities. **Pros:** amazing views amid complete privacy; superb farm-to-table cuisine; working farm and garden you can explore. **Cons:** expensive; rather difficult to get to; minimum two-night stay. ⑤ *Rooms from: NZ$1200* ✉ *130 Wharf Rd., Pigeon Bay, Akaroa* ☎ *03/304–6841* ⊕ *www.annandale.com* 🛏 *12 rooms* ⑩ *All-inclusive.*

The Giant's House

$$$$ | **B&B/INN** | Named so because it looked like a giant's house to a visiting child, this grand old 1880 villa is full of art in unexpected places. **Pros:** fabulous, crazy mosaic artwork; pleasant garden and leafy outlook; contemporary art gallery. **Cons:** very steep driveway; garden tour visitors wander through in the afternoon; mosaic paths can be slippery after rain. ⑤ *Rooms from: NZ$400* ✉ *68 Rue Balguerie, Akaroa* ☎ *03/304–7501* ⊕ *www.thegiantshouse.co.nz* 🛏 *3 rooms* ⑩ *Breakfast.*

Oinako Bed and Breakfast

$$$$ | **B&B/INN** | Surrounded by a tranquil garden, just a two-minute walk from town and a few steps from Akaroa Harbour, this character Victorian manor house has its original, ornate plaster ceilings and marble fireplaces. **Pros:** old-fashioned leafy garden overlooking the harbor; tea, coffee, wine, cookies, feather pillows, and duvets add a luxurious touch; beautifully restored homestead. **Cons:** no televisions in rooms; no fridges in rooms; no desks or chairs in rooms, but they can be provided on request. ⑤ *Rooms from: NZ$325* ✉ *99 Beach Rd., Akaroa* ☎ *03/304–8787* ⊕ *www.oinako.co.nz* ⊗ *Closed June–Aug.* 🛏 *6 rooms* ⑩ *Breakfast.*

⚲ Activities

Akaroa Dolphins

WILDLIFE-WATCHING | **FAMILY** | With these nature cruises aboard a luxury vessel on Akaroa Harbour, a portion of your fare goes to the Department of Conservation for further research into the Hector's dolphin, which is threatened with extinction. Cruises are two hours and depart three times daily in summer, and once a day in winter for two hours, from the main wharf. Informed guides give you insight into the marine life found here, and a beverage and home-baked snacks are also included as part of the ticket price. ✉ *65 Beach Rd., Akaroa* ☎ *03/304–7866* ⊕ *www.akaroadolphins. co.nz* 💲 *NZ$80.*

Akaroa Harbour Nature Cruises & Swimming With Dolphins

TOUR—SPORTS | The *Black Cat* catamaran runs Akaroa Harbour Nature Cruises and Swimming with Dolphins (two different trips). On the Nature Cruise, you'll pull in beside huge volcanic cliffs and caves and bob around in the harbor entrance while tiny Hector's dolphins—an endangered and adorable species of dolphin with rounded dorsal fins that look like Mickey Mouse ears stuck on their backs—play in the wake of the boat. Trips leave daily and cost NZ$79. Or take your swimsuit and get in the water for the Swimming with Dolphins cruise, the only place in the world you can do so. Dolphin swim trips cost NZ$160 (NZ$89 to watch). Wet suits are provided and advance reservations are essential. ✉ *Main Wharf, Akaroa* ☎ *03/304–7641, 0800/436–574* ⊕ *www. blackcat.co.nz* ⊗ *Swimming with Dolphins not available in winter.*

Banks Track

HIKING/WALKING | **FAMILY** | The 35-km (22-mile) Banks Track crosses spectacular coastal terrain. From Akaroa hike over headlands and past several bays, waterfalls, and seal and penguin colonies, and you might even see Hector's dolphins at sea. Two-day and three-day self-guided hikes are available from October to April. The tracks follow the same route, so if you're a novice hiker or have plenty of time, take the longer option. You will stay overnight in cozy cabins with fully equipped kitchens and a bath under the stars. Rates include lodging, transport from Akaroa to the first hut, landowners' fees, and a booklet describing the features of the trail. No fear of overcrowding here—the track is limited to up to only six people at a time. ⊠ *Banks Track, Akaroa* ☎ *03/304–7612* ⊕ *www. bankstrack.co.nz* ✉ *NZ$260 for three days* ⊙ *Closed May–Sept.*

Pohatu Penguins Nature & Sea Kayaking Safaris

TOUR—SPORTS | Pohatu Marine Reserve is a key breeding area for the Little Penguin (*korora*), which are endemic to the Canterbury region. Best time for viewing is during the breeding season, September to January. You may also see the yellow-eyed penguin (*hoiho*), which also breed in the bay. Options range from day and evening penguin or nature tours (from NZ$75 per person) and 4WD sea-kayaking safari trips (from NZ$95). Price includes a scenic drive to Pohatu with photo stops along the way and there are several other tour options as well. An accommodation package is also available in a self-catering cottage inside the penguin colony—a rare opportunity—(from NZ$135 per person for 24-hour stay). All trips leave from Akaroa. ⊠ *Unit 2, 8 Rue Balguerie, Akaroa* ☎ *03/304–8542, 021/246–9556* ⊕ *www.pohatu.co.nz.*

Waipara Valley

65 km (40 miles) north of Christchurch.

Once known for its hot, dry summers and sheep farms, the Waipara Valley is now an established vineyard area. The local Riesling, Chardonnay, and Pinot Noir are particularly good. Sheltered from the cool easterly wind by the Teviotdale Hills, the valley records hotter temperatures than the rest of Canterbury, and warm dry autumns ensure a longer time for the grapes to mature. Winemakers are also exploiting the area's limestone soil to grow Pinots—Pinot Noir, Pinot Gris, and *Pinotage*. There are 80 vineyards in the valley, producing around 100,000 cases of wine a year.

GETTING HERE AND AROUND

To reach Waipara from Christchurch, take State Highway 1 north. Waipara's about 45 minutes away, north of Amberley, where State Highway 7 turns left off the main road. You can head from here to Hanmer Springs and Nelson on State Highway 7 and other northern towns along State Highway 1. The Hanmer Connection runs a daily service between Hanmer Springs and Christchurch, stopping in Waipara and elsewhere en route in the Waipara Valley. You can also join a wine tour from Christchurch.

BUS CONTACTS Hanmer Connection.

⊠ *Canterbury Museum, 11 Rolleston Ave., Christchurch* ☎ *0800/242–663, 03/382–2952* ⊕ *www.hanmerconnection. co.nz.*

 Sights

Pick up a copy of the North Canterbury Food and Wine Trail guide and map from the Christchurch i-SITE Visitor Centre or visit the website (⊕ *www.foodandwinetrail.co.nz*) to locate all the wineries, eateries, and activities in the region. Waipara's wines are celebrated each year at the North Canterbury Wine and Food

Festival held in March on the grounds of the local Glenmark Church. The oak-tree-lined gardens are filled with music, local produce like cheese, nuts, and breads, and, of course, plenty of wine from dozens of local vineyards.

★ Black Estate

WINERY/DISTILLERY | With its distinctive black barn tasting room and restaurant on the warm, sunny slopes of the Omihi Hills, this family-run vineyard has become a local landmark. The award-winning architecture perfectly complements the acclaimed Pinot Noir, Chardonnay, and Riesling vintages hand-harvested and made on-site. Add to this a delicious lunch and tasting menu, focusing on the best local produce and superb service to match the wine. Enjoy a beautiful view while you dine and sip, overlooking the vineyards and west to the Main Divide. ⊠ *614 Omihi Rd., Waipara Valley, Amberley* ☎ *03/314–6085* ⊕ *www.blackestate. co.nz.*

Pegasus Bay

WINERY/DISTILLERY | Family-run Pegasus Bay has one of the region's best reputations for wine and food in Canterbury, and the helicopters lined up on the lawn at lunchtime will confirm that. Taste the award-winning Rieslings, Chardonnay, and Pinot Noir while you look through a window at floor-to-ceiling stacks of oak aging casks. It has been ranked among the top five wine producers nationally by Robert Parker's buyer's guide and it's been named Best Winery Restaurant in NZ by *Cuisine* magazine nine times. In good weather, dine outdoors in the garden or picnic in a natural amphitheater by a small man-made lake. It's best to book ahead if visiting for a meal or large group tastings. ⊠ *263 Stockgrove Rd., Waipara* ☎ *03/314–6869* ⊕ *www.pegasusbay.com.*

Torlesse Wines

WINERY/DISTILLERY | Kym and Ben Rayner are consummate winemakers, and Kym is one of the pioneers of Waipara winemaking. At Torlesse Wines they use grapes from several vineyards around Waipara and farther afield, and Riesling is their biggest seller. Sauvignon Blanc, Gewürztraminer, Chardonnay, Pinot Gris, Pinot Noir, and Rosé are also produced, as are the Omihi Road reserve wines and Old Reserve Port, made in the same barrels since 1992. While you're there you can also check out the local arts and crafts for sale. ⊠ *10 Loffhagen Dr., off State Hwy. 1, Waipara* ☎ *03/314–6929* ⊕ *www.torlesse.co.nz.*

Waipara Hills

WINERY/DISTILLERY | The huge, cathedral-like European castle rock-and-timber building at Waipara Hills, although just more than 20 years old, looks somewhat medieval. The Waipara Hills Riesling, Pinot Gris, Rosé, and Pinot Noir are all worth trying. The label uses grapes from Marlborough, Otago, and Waipara so there's a lot happening in a bottle. The café in the Cloisters, the high ceiling–medieval style section of the building, is open for lunch and afternoon coffee. There's a cellar door across the entrance hall for tastings. ⊠ *780 Glasnevin Rd. (part of State Hwy. 1), Waipara* ☎ *03/314–6900* ⊕ *www.waiparahills.co.nz.*

🍴 Restaurants

Little Vintage Espresso

$$ | **CAFÉ** | **FAMILY** | Tucked away down a side street off the main road, this cute little café with a red door is packed with country locals, and is fast becoming a popular visitor stop, too. Besides the great coffee, there's also an excellent selection of well-priced baked goods including delicious muffins, and a tasty brunch menu to suit all appetites. **Known for:** cinnamon scrolls; delicious gluten-free cakes and slices; power-packed salads. **⑤** *Average main: NZ$15* ⊠ *20 Markham St., Amberley* ☎ *03/314–9580* ⊗ *Closed Sun.*

🛏️ Hotels

Black Estate B & B

$$$$ | **B&B/INN** | The highly rated accommodations located right at Black Estate's award-winning winery/restaurant is a perfect escape for couples. **Pros:** sunny terrace with vast vineyard and mountain views; exceptionally knowledgeable and friendly hosts; gorgeous decor and architecture. **Cons:** only room for two people; need to book well ahead; apartment is downstairs below the winery, which is busy most days until 5 pm. ⑤ *Rooms from: NZ$325* ✉ *614 Omihi Rd., Waipara* ☎ *03/314–6085* ⊕ *www.blackestate.co.nz* ⇨ *1 room* ❣️ *Free Breakfast.*

Greystone PurePod

$$$$ | **HOTEL** | Set high above the award-winning, organic Greystone Vineyard, you will find a beautiful setting for a private lodging experience under the stars with glass floors, walls, and ceilings. **Pros:** complete immersion in nature; dinner and breakfast packages available; optional guided tour of the vineyard and winery that includes tasting and lunch. **Cons:** no power plugs or Wi-Fi (USB device charger available); can get pretty hot in summer, so remember to pull the shades down; ½-mile walk from the parking lot with no lighting. ⑤ *Rooms from: NZ$590* ✉ *376 Omihi Rd., Waipara* ⊕ *www.purepods. com* ⇨ *1 room* ❣️ *No meals.*

Old Glenmark Vicarage

$$$ | **B&B/INN** | Once a real vicarage, Old Glenmark is now a funky barn lodging suitable for families, with lots of rough-sawn timber and colonial trimmings that provides a very comfortable base while touring the area. **Pros:** central to most Waipara wineries and restaurants; on-site boutique vineyard and vegetable garden; large well-equipped kitchen and BBQ area for self-catering. **Cons:** close to busy State Highway 1; rustic style may be too eclectic for some; popular in summer. ⑤ *Rooms from: NZ$210* ✉ *161 Church Rd., Waipara* ☎ *03/314–6775* ⊕ *www.*

glenmarkvicarage.co.nz ⇨ *3 rooms* ❣️ *No meals.*

Waipara Sleepers

$ | **B&B/INN** | Wake up to fresh-baked bread and newly laid eggs every morning at this basic-but-rather-quirky backpackers lodge housed in old railway carriages and huts. **Pros:** very rustic and rural; complete with all the sounds and smells of the country; good stop for anyone cycle-touring. **Cons:** some of the accommodations and services are quite basic; often cold at night; cramped parking if its busy. ⑤ *Rooms from: NZ$70* ✉ *10–12 Glenmark Dr., Waipara* ☎ *03/314–6003* ⊕ *www.waiparasleepers.co.nz* ⇨ *6 rooms* ❣️ *No meals.*

🏃 Activities

Mt. Cass Walkway

HIKING/WALKING | Here's a moderately strenuous way to wear off some of those wine- and lunch-induced calories. This three-hour return climb up Mt. Cass produces a spectacular view over the surrounding countryside of the Waipara Valley. As it crosses through working farmland on the Tiromoana Station, be careful to leave gates and marker posts as you find them. Use the stiles provided for crossing fence lines and wear strong walking shoes. The track is closed each year in spring while the sheep are lambing. ✉ *Mt. Cass Rd., Waipara* ⊕ *www. visithurunui.co.nz.*

Hanmer Springs

120 km (75 miles) northwest of Christchurch.

People used to come to Hanmer Springs to chill out with quiet soaks in the hot-pools and to take gentle forest walks, but things have been changing fast. The number of boutique stores and restaurants has doubled, and an increasing number of off-road and backcountry activities are turning Hanmer Springs into Canterbury's adventure-sports hub. It is also a spa town in the true sense of the word, with relaxing and indulgent spa facilities available at the Hanmer Springs Thermal Pools and Spa and in the village. On holidays and weekends the springs can be busy. The Amuri Ski Field, a small ski area in the mountains behind town, attracts a dedicated following of local skiers in winter. Mountain biking is especially big, and Hanmer Springs is now the end point for several long-distance mountain-bike and endurance races through the backcountry. During the summer months Hanmer Springs is also the southern terminus of the drive along the Acheron road through the Molesworth Station, which runs through from the Awatere Valley in Marlborough. This backcountry trail is open for only a few months a year and is a solid six-hour drive on an unpaved road through some spectacular country. Go to the **Department of Conservation** website and search for Molesworth for more information.

GETTING HERE AND AROUND

The Hanmer Connection runs a daily service between Hanmer Springs and Christchurch. Service goes through Waipara on the way. By car, take State Highway 1 north out of Christchurch. About 45 minutes north, State Highway 7 turns left off the main highway toward Nelson. From here drive through the small town of Culverden and the foothills for another 45 minutes on State Highway 7, before turning onto Highway 7A toward Hanmer Springs (this is well signposted).

Navigation around Hanmer Springs is easy, as it's a really small place. The main road into town, Amuri Drive, is a wide tree-lined road, with the thermal resort and visitor center opening off it. Conical Hill Road carries on up the hill and has most of the stores and cafés along its lower portion. Jacks Pass Road to the left and Jollies Pass Road to the right lead

to the great outdoors and many of the adventure activities.

BUS CONTACTS Hanmer Connection.
☎ 0800/242–663 NZ only, 03/382–2952 ⊕ www.hanmerconnection.co.nz.

VISITOR INFORMATION Department of Conservation. ⊕ www.doc.govt.nz . **Hanmer Springs i-SITE Visitor Centre.** ✉ 40 Amuri Ave. ☎ 03/315–0020, 0800/442–663 NZ only ⊕ www.visithurunui.co.nz.

◉ Sights

Hanmer Springs Thermal Pools & Spa
HOT SPRINGS | FAMILY | The Hanmer Springs Thermal Pools & Spa consists of 15 outdoor thermal pools of varying temperatures, a heated freshwater pool with lazy river, a family activity pool, and three waterslides. There are also six private mineral-rich thermal pools, as well as adults-only aquatherapy pools, private sauna, and steam rooms. Massage and beauty treatments are available at the on-site spa. The Greenhouse Cafe, a beautifully renovated 1904 building, has bar facilities, and there's a picnic area, too. The heated changing rooms are a real treat. ✉ 42 Amuri Ave. ☎ 03/315–0000, 0800/442–663 NZ only ⊕ www.hanmersprings.co.nz ◉ From NZ$24.

Jacks Pass
SCENIC DRIVE | The scenic gravel drive along Jacks Pass, to the north of the village, crosses the lower slopes of Mt. Isobel before dropping into the upper Clarence River valley, an alpine area 15 minutes from Hanmer Springs. This is the beginning of some serious backcountry. The tiny stream trickling past the road at the end of the pass eventually reaches the coast north of Kaikoura at the rough and rumbling Clarence River—a favorite for rafters and kayakers. This is also the southern end of the Acheron Road through the Molesworth Station and the 4WD Rainbow Road through to St. Arnaud and the Nelson Lakes. There's restricted access at certain times of the

year and the roads can be impassable during winter so before you go check with the Hanmer Springs i-SITE Visitor Centre.

🍽 Restaurants

Malabar Restaurant

$$$ | ASIAN | Looking out toward Conical Hill, this modern restaurant has a fine reputation for its Asian-fusion food presented with Kiwi flair. Dinner favorites are the lamb shank rogan josh, crispy duck, and ginger stir-fry along with a selection of traditionally cooked Indian curries. **Known for:** southern Indian cuisine, including clay oven tikkas; delicious citrus crème brûlée; tasty Malaysian roti served with all mains. ⑤ *Average main: NZ$28* ✉ *Alpine Pacific Centre, 5 Conical Hill Rd.* ☎ *03/315–7745* ⊗ *No lunch Sun.–Fri.*

No. 31 Restaurant & Bar

$$$$ | MODERN NEW ZEALAND | In a renovated villa on the main road into Hanmer, No. 31 serves exceptional food. Its well-established local chef specializes in modern NZ cuisine, using the best local produce, offered with a selection of wines from the Waipara/Hanmer area. **Known for:** award-winning beef, lamb, and venison dishes; great craft beer selection; romantic atmosphere. ⑤ *Average main: NZ$39* ✉ *31 Amuri Ave.* ☎ *03/315–7031* ⊗ *Closed Mon. and 2 wks in winter (dates vary).*

Powerhouse Cafe and Restaurant

$$$ | CAFÉ | Now a popular café for locals, the Powerhouse building used to contain a small hydroelectric generator that supplied power to the old Queen Mary Hospital and a few streetlights. Today, it opens at 8 am with a great brunch menu to suit all tastes using local and free-range ingredients to create dishes that are all homemade. **Known for:** hearty high-country breakfasts; lots of gluten-free options; wonderful fresh salads for lunch. ⑤ *Average main: NZ$26* ✉ *8*

Jacks Pass Rd. ☎ *03/315–5252* ⊕ *www.powerhousecafe.co.nz* ⊗ *No dinner Sun.–Fri.*

Hotels

Braemar Lodge & Spa

$$$ | HOTEL | Part lodge, part boutique hotel, these accommodations were built around all that remained of the original Braemar Lodge—an impressive two-story-high river stone fireplace. **Pros:** on-site day spa; packages available with outdoor activities included; large rooms with great views. **Cons:** 10-minute drive from Hanmer; access is by several kilometers of gravel road with a steep but paved driveway; some parts need an upgrade. ⑤ *Rooms from: NZ$270* ✉ *283 Medway Rd.* ☎ *03/315–7555* ⊕ *www.selectbraemarlodge.com* ⬚ *24 suites* ⦿ *Breakfast.*

Heritage Hanmer Springs

$$$ | HOTEL | Set in beautifully landscaped gardens, this hotel is just a short walk from the thermal pools, and staying here will remind you of the grand, genteel era in which it was built. **Pros:** lovely old Spanish Mission–style building; in the middle of town within easy walk of most things; very comfortable beds. **Cons:** during NZ school holidays it can get busy; renovations underway, but some rooms still need upgrades; no elevator. ⑤ *Rooms from: NZ$268* ✉ *1 Conical Hill Rd.* ☎ *03/315–0060* ⊕ *www.heritagehotels.co.nz* ⬚ *65 rooms* ⦿ *No meals.*

Settlers Motel

$$ | HOTEL | This property has peaceful apartments and studios set off Amuri Avenue, the main street into Hanmer. **Pros:** quiet, friendly motel-style establishment; short walk to town; flexible check-in and check-out times. **Cons:** units all open onto central courtyard and parking lot; reservations are essential over weekends and holiday periods; popular with families and can be busy. ⑤ *Rooms from: NZ$200* ✉ *6 Leamington St.*

The central Canterbury Plains area is the premier hot-air ballooning spot.

☎ 03/315–7343, 0800/587–873 ⊕ www.
settlershanmer.co.nz ⊃ 14 rooms ❄ No
meals.

Tussock Peak Motor Lodge

$$ | B&B/INN | FAMILY | Adjacent to the thermal pools, this stylish eco-friendly 14-unit complex offers a choice of spacious one- and two-bedroom units. **Pros:** Netflix on demand with smart TVs in every room; free Wi-Fi; excellent power steam showers. **Cons:** can be busy with lots of families during NZ school holidays; no air-conditioning in summer; basic kitchen facilities in units. ⑤ Rooms from: NZ$175 ⊠ Corner Amuri Ave. and Leamington St. ☎ 03/315–5191 ⊕ www.tussockpeak.co.nz ⊃ 14 units ❄ No meals.

▶ Nightlife

Saints Pizzeria and Bar

BARS/PUBS | Saints Pizzeria and Bar is probably the closest thing to a nightclub in Hanmer Springs. It's open until 1 am Friday and Saturday, but closes around 11 other nights. It has a dance floor and pool table and features a DJ some Saturday nights. They do brunch and lunch, too, but not always during the week when it's quiet. Service can be a bit slow if they're really busy, but the wait is usually worth it. ⊠ 6 Jacks Pass Rd. ☎ 03/315–5262 ⊕ www.saintshanmer.co.nz.

⚡ Activities

ADVENTURE SPORTS

Hanmer Springs Adventure Centre

TOUR—SPORTS | Hanmer Springs Adventure Centre runs quad-bike tours, clay-bird shooting, mountain biking, and archery in the backcountry behind Hanmer Springs. Quad-bike tours leave at 10, 1:30, and 4 each day, bouncing through some spectacular hill country, native bush, river crossings, hill climbs, and stunning scenery over their 15,000-acre Woodbank Station. ⊠ 20 Conical Hill Rd. ☎ 03/315–7233, 0800/368–7386 NZ only ⊕ www.hanmeradventure.co.nz ⊃ From NZ$139.

Hanmer Springs Attractions
TOUR—SPORTS | FAMILY | This adventure company offers it all, including 115-foot bungy jumps off the 19th-century Ferry Bridge. You can also choose to raft or ride on a jet-boat through the scenic gorge or let the kids do a quad-bike safari. Try clay-bird shooting or paintball, or just peer off the 100-foot balcony and watch the bungy jumpers and jet-boats in the canyon below. ⊠ *839 Hanmer Springs Rd.* ☎ *03/315–7046, 0800/661–538 NZ only* ⊕ *www.hanmersspringsattractions.nz* ⊠ *From NZ$149.*

Methven

95 km (59 miles) southwest of Christchurch.

Methven's main claim to fame is as a ski town. It's a one-hour drive from Christchurch and the closest town to Mt. Hutt, which has New Zealand's longest ski season from June to October. You can't stay on the mountain, so Methven is après-ski central. It's also a great base to stay if you are skiing at the five boutique club fields within the region. The small boutique ski club fields are also open to the public—the accommodation is members-only during peak season but you can stay in Methven and go to these club fields for the day. They have basic facilities and are suited to more experienced skiers. Tow prices are cheaper if you are a member. An hour away is Canterbury's other major ski area, Porters. Some of New Zealand's best heli-skiing is available from Methven, too. In late September the famous Peak to Pub race challenges competitors to skiing, biking, and running across snow, dirt, and pavement from the top of the mountain to the famous Blue Pub. If you are here in summer, you will get a feel for the area's strong mountain bike culture. There's a range of established mountain bike trails and many more in

the works, while uncrowded country roads provide great flat riding for road cyclists. You can also enjoy horse riding, hiking, salmon fishing, jet-boating, tandem skydiving, and hot-air ballooning.

GETTING HERE AND AROUND
The best way to get to Methven by car is the quiet Scenic Highway 72, which you can join near Darfield, or via Hororata (but be wary of icy spots in the shade and hidden speed cameras on these straight roads). You could also travel down the busy State Highway 1 to Rakaia and take Thompson's Track (clearly signposted and paved) to Methven. Or join it from the north at Amberley, passing through Oxford and Sheffield. This stretch of highway, known as the **Inland Scenic Route,** makes a nice day drive from Christchurch, taking in the upper Rakaia and Rangitata River gorges, the small towns of Darfield, Methven, and Geraldine, scenic views of the Southern Alps, and the wide-open farmlands of the plains.

There are plenty of buses from Christchurch to Methven and Mt. Hutt in ski season, but the options drop off in summer. Mt. Hutt SNOWBUS runs daily in winter, and Methven Travel runs a daily bus in winter and four times a week in summer.

BUS CONTACTS Methven Travel. ☎ *03/302–8106, 0800/684–888* ⊕ *www. methventravel.co.nz.* **Snowman Shuttles.** ☎ *03/337–5750, 0800/766–928 NZ only* ⊕ *www.snowmanshuttles.co.nz.*

VISITOR INFORMATION Methven i-SITE Visitor Centre. ⊠ *160 Main St.* ☎ *03/302–8955* ⊕ *www.methvenmthutt.co.nz.*

 Sights

New Zealand Alpine and Agriculture Encounter
MUSEUM | FAMILY | This purpose-built attraction brings to life the stories of the mountains, plains, and people who live

there with multimedia and interactive displays. Get on board a huge combine harvester, operate a digger, explore a snow cave, view a ski film, and learn about Mid-Canterbury's dairying and seed growing. ⊠ *Methven Heritage Centre, 160 Main St.* ☎ *03/302–9666* ⊕ *www. methvenheritagecentre.co.nz* ⊠ *NZ$10.*

🍽 Restaurants

Methven isn't a culinary hotbed, but it has several good casual places and is known for its two famous watering holes: the Blue Pub and the Brown Pub on opposite corners in the middle of town. Both have reasonably priced bistro-style meals and a courtyard where you can sit and have a beer. For a quintessential New Zealand café experience head to Cafe Primo set in a retro-vintage shop on MacMillan Street, where you'll find treasures along with their legendary bacon-and-egg sandwiches and excellent coffee. Grab a granola breakfast here and pack a muffin for later.

🛏 Hotels

Alpenhorn Chalet

$ | **B&B/INN** | **FAMILY** | This wonderfully pleasant backpacker lodge is in an old wooden villa built in the early 1900s, very typical of small-town Victorian architecture in New Zealand at the time. **Pros:** homey feel is far removed from the usual backpackers-hostel vibe; wonderful conservatory garden; superb free espresso coffee. **Cons:** short walk from the center of Methven; no credit cards; spa open in winter only. **$** *Rooms from: NZ$60* ⊠ *44 Allen St.* ☎ *03/302–8779* ⊕ *www. alpenhorn.co.nz* ⊟ *No credit cards* ⊅ *5 rooms* ⊖ *No meals.*

Brinkley Resort

$$ | **RESORT** | **FAMILY** | These one- and two-bedroom apartment-style units are just a two minute walk from the center of town, surrounded by landscaped gardens. **Pros:** tennis court, hot tub,

children's playground, and putting green; plenty of off-street parking and a helipad; 12 ski areas within easy range, including Mt. Hutt. **Cons:** convention center on-site, so sometimes it can be busy; rooms overlooking the parking lot are noisy; some rooms are compact. **$** *Rooms from: NZ$165* ⊠ *43 Barkers Rd.* ☎ *03/302–8855* ⊕ *www.brinkleyresort.co.nz* ⊅ *80 rooms* ⊖ *No meals.*

Central Luxury Apartments

$$$ | **RENTAL** | **FAMILY** | These modern apartments just off the main street of Methven offer all the amenities, and they're built to display the best of the Southern Alps' views. **Pros:** drying room downstairs for the skis and ski gear, and laundry in each apartment; good parking; very quiet. **Cons:** style is neutral with minimal decoration; parts are in need of a revamp; Wi-Fi can be intermittent and charges apply. **$** *Rooms from: NZ$240* ⊠ *7 Methven Chertsey Rd.* ☎ *03/302– 8829, 0800/128–829 NZ only* ⊕ *www. centralapartmentsmethven.co.nz* ⊅ *6 apartments* ⊖ *No meals.*

Methven Motels and Apartments

$$ | **B&B/INN** | **FAMILY** | This modern accommodation complex has both motel rooms and apartments for small or large groups. **Pros:** drying cupboard for ski clothing and short-term gear storage; electric blankets; upstairs rooms have views of Mt. Hutt. **Cons:** road outside can be busy; free Wi-Fi only if you book directly with the hotel; TVs could do with an upgrade. **$** *Rooms from: NZ$140* ⊠ *197 Main St.* ☎ *03/302–9200* ⊕ *www.methvenmotels. co.nz* ⊅ *8 units* ⊖ *No meals.*

Mt. Hutt Lodge

$$ | **B&B/INN** | If you've come south for the views and outdoor activities then the Mt. Hutt Lodge delivers. **Pros:** close to great fishing spots, skiing, golf, and tramping; amazing views of the mountain; restaurant on-site with beef steak specialty. **Cons:** building is very 1970s and needs an upgrade; 15-minute drive from Methven, so you'll need a car to get here; no washer in room, but there's a communal laundry. $ *Rooms from: NZ$140* ✉ *45 Zig Zag Rd.* ☎ *03/318–6898* ⊕ *www.mthuttlodge.co.nz* 🛏 *14 rooms* ⦿ *No meals.*

Terrace Downs

$$$$ | HOTEL | Considered a top golf resort in NZ, Terrace Downs is a good place to base yourself for a vacation away from the crowds. **Pros:** 18-hole championship golf course on-site; day spa and extended list of on- and off-site activities; kid's club and babysitting available. **Cons:** you'll need two nights if you want to really appreciate the surroundings and venue; high winds in this exposed area; the hotel has been through a series of management changes, and service can be varied. $ *Rooms from: NZ$310* ✉ *Coleridge Rd., Rakaia Gorge* ☎ *03/318–6943* ⊕ *www.terracedowns.co.nz* 🛏 *19 villas* ⦿ *No meals.*

Nightlife

Black Beech Wine Bar

WINE BARS—NIGHTLIFE | This sophisticated meeting place in Oxford offers a vast selection of wines and craft beers served alongside excellent pizzas and live music. ✉ *Unit 1, 46 Main St., Canterbury* ☎ *03/312–3338* ⊕ *www.blackbeechbar.com.*

Activities

BOATING

Discovery Jet

BOATING | FAMILY | Zoom along the glacier-fed Rakaia River with Discovery Jet as you journey through the deep canyon and braided courses of the river. The Rakaia's jewel-like aqua water contrasts wonderfully with the white limestone cliffs and views of Mt. Hutt ski field. Fishing and scenic tours are options or catch a ride up to the Rakaia Gorge Walkway. Tours vary from 15 to 45 minutes and are suitable for all ages. ☎ *0800/538–2628 NZ only, 021/538–386*

⊕ *www.discoveryjet.co.nz* 🛏 *From NZ$45 for 15 mins.*

HIKING

Mt. Somers Track

HIKING/WALKING | One of New Zealand's top 10 walkways, the Mt. Somers Track is a great way to get a taste of the subalpine New Zealand bush. Start at the Mt. Somers–Woolshed Creek end and hike downhill to the Staveley end and Sharplin Falls. The 16-km (10-mile) walk will take one to two days, and there are two huts to stay in along the way—or do it in reverse. Call the Staveley Village Store, which also has a great café, before you start your trip (☎ *03/303–0859*) for information on transport to the end of the trail; there are a number of small guiding companies. There are excellent self-contained accommodations at Red Cottages Staveley, too. ⊕ *www.doc.govt.nz.*

Rakaia Gorge Walkway

HIKING/WALKING | Leaving from just below the Rakaia River gorge bridge, the Rakaia Gorge Walkway provides upstream access to the northern bank of the river and offers easy walking, taking in some beautiful scenery. You can also take a jet-boat upriver and walk back—just name your distance. ✉ *State Hwy. 72* ⊕ *www.methvenmthutt.co.nz.*

MULTISPORT OUTFITTERS

Big Al's Snowsports

BICYCLING | In summer Big Al's Snowsports turns into a cycling center for those keen to don Lycra and head to the trails. Al and his team have decades of experience and really know what they're talking about with trail maps, and the best riding tips for the region. You can rent full-suspension cross-country bikes and 29r xc hardtails from them, too. ✉ *The Square* ☎ *03/302–8003* ⊕ *www.bigals.co.nz* 🛏 *Ski hire NZ$38 per day; bike hire from NZ$15 per hr.*

South of
Christchurch

SKIING

Methven Heliski

SKIING/SNOWBOARDING | Methven has access to some of New Zealand's best backcountry helicopter-accessed terrain and hundreds of square miles of pristine snow. You don't have to be an advanced skier to enjoy it—there is something for every range of ability here, including long runs in deep powder, gentle glaciers, plus a fabulous day out soaring over the Alps with a friendly team. Methven Heliski is located at Glenfalloch Station and there's excellent accommodations available here too, with superb meals and drinks included. They fly every fine day from July 1 through September 30. ⊠ *114 Main St.* ☎ *03/302–8108* ⊕ *www.methvenheli. co.nz* ⊠ *NZ$1085 per person for full day.*

Mt. Hutt Ski Area

SKIING/SNOWBOARDING | **FAMILY** | The views across the Canterbury Plains are amazing from this high-country ski area. It has one of the longest vertical drops in the South Island and a complete terrain mix for all skiers and boarders. A great family ski spot, there is a beginner's area with a 140-meter-long enclosed Magic Carpet, and modern chairlifts. For advanced skiers and snowboarders there's plenty of off-piste action, too. ⊠ *Mt. Hutt Ski Area* ☎ *03/308–5074* ⊕ *www.mthutt.co.nz* ⊠ *From NZ$79.*

Porters

SKIING/SNOWBOARDING | **FAMILY** | Take the drive from Methven along the Great Alpine Highway to the Porters ski area, with some spectacular views along the way. The access road is one of the shortest and least intimidating in the

The Chatham Islands

Although officially part of New Zealand, the Chatham Islands, 800 km (500 miles) east of the South Island, are a land apart. Bearing the full force of the open Southern Ocean, the islands are wild and weather-beaten. The air has a salty taste to it, the colors of the landscapes are muted by salt spray, and the vegetation is stunted and gnarly. Many unusual plants and birds are about—including the extremely rare black robin—and the empty beaches invite fishing and diving (although the presence of sharks makes the latter unadvised).

Locals here refer to the mainland as New Zealand, as though it were an entirely separate country. Just 2 of the 10 islands are inhabited—the main island and tiny, neighboring Pitt Island, which is well known for its extensive conservation programs. Most of the 600 residents are either farmers or fishermen, but tourism is increasing. The Chathams were first settled by the Moriori, a race of Polynesian descent, about 800–1,000 years ago, although there are now no full-blooded Moriori left. Māori and

Europeans followed, and conflicts broke out between the separate populations throughout the 1800s. By the end of the 19th century, however, tensions had died down after the Native Land Court intervened in key disputes, and the new settlers established the strong maritime culture that still prevails on the islands.

When booking to fly to the Chathams, it's imperative that you make lodging reservations in advance. There is only one round-trip flight a week from Christchurch on Tuesday, but you can return earlier through Auckland or Wellington, and **Air Chathams** (☎ 09/257–0261, ⊕ www.airchathams. co.nz) is the only carrier. The islands are 45 minutes ahead of NZ time and, therefore, the first place on Earth to see the sun each day. Check out the Air Chathams website for more details on the islands, their natural history, accommodation, and activities. Allow at least three days to visit—you'll rarely get the chance to visit anywhere this remote. And don't forget to try the crayfish and blue cod.

region, too. There are excellent learner facilities here, as well as a terrain park for boarders. An Easyrider chairlift connects the base with the upper mountain. Two of New Zealand's legendary runs are here—Bluff Face and Big Mama. If you need a break, the café has great views over the Torlesse Range. ✉ Porters Ski Area ☎ 03/318–4731 ⊕ www.skiporters. co.nz ✉ From NZ$79.

Geraldine

138 km (85½ miles) southwest of Christchurch.

For years, this lovely town has been a favorite stop on the road to Aoraki/ Mt. Cook; these days, it's becoming a magnet in southern Canterbury for art mavens and foodies.

GETTING HERE AND AROUND

State Highway 1 is the fastest route here from Christchurch; just after crossing the Rangitata River, turn inland for about 10 minutes on State Highway 79. State

Highway 72—known as the Inland Scenic Route—gives you closer views of the mountains and river gorges but takes a bit longer. The rolling downs around Geraldine are especially breathtaking in the late afternoon, when the sun turns them golden.

Geraldine is three hours from Christchurch by bus, and even faster by car. It is served by InterCity buses.

BUS CONTACTS InterCity Coachlines.
☎ 03/365–1113 ⊕ www.intercity.co.nz.

👁 Sights

You know you're in small-town New Zealand when the biggest store on the main street is the rural merchandiser. Luckily, along Geraldine's main drag, Talbot Street, you'll find other stores and galleries to browse as well. Or stop in at Barker's of Geraldine for their legendary fruit preserves and Talbot Forest Cheese for some delicious locally made cheeses, ice creams, fudge, and other tasty delights. Head farther to the Rangitata Valley and visit Peel Forest, the ancient podocarp remnant of the vast forest expanse that once covered much of Mid- and South Canterbury. The area is now a haven for birdlife and there are many trails for hikers and bikers.

Geraldine Vintage Car and Machinery Museum

MUSEUM | At the Geraldine Vintage Car and Machinery Museum, there's some good rural stuff with more than 100 tractors (some dating back to 1912) and other farm machinery sharing space with vintage cars. ✉ 178 Talbot St. ☎ 03/693–8756 ⧉ NZ$15.

🛏 Hotels

Peel Forest Lodge

$$$$ | B&B/INN | Tucked in among giant *kahikatea* trees and native forest, and overlooking Little Mt. Peel (which isn't so little), this comfortable oregon log lodge

provides a haven of peace and quiet.
Pros: café and bar just down the road at Peel Forest village; full kitchen for your use; big schist fireplace in the lounge.
Cons: a few trophy heads on the walls, which might not be for everyone; can sometimes be booked out for weddings; you will need a car to get here.
⑤ *Rooms from: NZ$400* ✉ *Brake Rd., off Dennistoun Rd., Peel Forest* ✛ *Don't drive into Peel Forest Estate, take a right at their gate and continue another mile or so along gravel road* ☎ 03/696–3703 ⊕ www.peelforestlodge.co.nz ⧉ 4 rooms ⧉ No meals.

🛍 Shopping

Barker's

FOOD/CANDY | For foodie treats, stop by Barker's in the Four Peaks Plaza to try fruit chutneys, fruit syrups, sauces, spreads, and tasty jams. They do good gift boxes and they'll ship overseas for you, too. ✉ 76B Talbot St. ☎ 0508/227–537 NZ only, 03/693–9727 ⊕ www.barkers.co.nz.

Louk NZ Clothing

CLOTHING | Stop off at Louk NZ Clothing for a big range of designer merino wear and cool outdoor gear, for both males and females. They also have the biggest Swazi range (another hip outdoor label) in the South Island. They're in the old post office on the main street. ✉ 47 Talbot St. ☎ 03/693–9070 ⊕ www.louknzclothing.co.nz.

The Tin Shed

GIFTS/SOUVENIRS | Looking more like a shearing shed than a store, The Tin Shed is exactly that. Surrounded by farmland and animals, it is an authentic piece of rural New Zealand architecture being put to good use. Inside is a selection of lifestyle and handmade clothing. There's a good range of merino and possum fur knits and shawls, knitwear, and thermals, oilskins, sheepskin footwear, and locally produced skin-care items. This is a great spot to stock up with gifts before leaving the country, and they can arrange postage. Watch the turn-in off the main road as traffic moves fast here. ⊠ *State Hwy. 79, just off State Hwy. 1 south of Rangitata* ☎ *03/693–9416* ⊕ *www. thetinshed.co.nz.*

Activities

Rangitata Rafts
WHITE-WATER RAFTING | Rangitata Rafts runs white-water rafting trips on the Grade V Rangitata River starting at 11:30 most days from October through May. The river grades build as you drop lower so if you can't face the Grade V section (the last part of the trip), you can walk around with the photographer then rejoin the raft. Rates include an early lunch, hot showers, spectacular scenery, a barbecue, and 2½ hours of rafting. Reservations are essential. They also do a more gentle Grade II trip that's suitable for anyone eight years or older; it's good fun and a nice introduction to white-water rafting. Nonrafters can relax at the lodge. ☎ *03/696–3534, 0800/251–251 NZ only* ⊕ *www.rafts.co.nz* ⊠ *From NZ$215* ☺ *Closed June–Sept.*

THE SOUTHERN ALPS AND FIORDLAND

11

Updated by
Mike Stearne

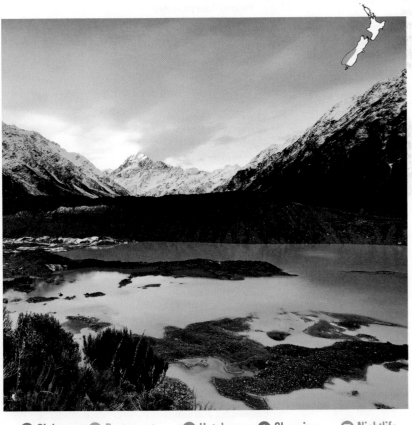

👁 Sights	🍴 Restaurants	🛏 Hotels	🛍 Shopping	🍸 Nightlife
★★★★★	★★★☆☆	★★★☆☆	★★☆☆☆	★★☆☆☆

WELCOME TO THE SOUTHERN ALPS AND FIORDLAND

TOP REASONS TO GO

★ **Adventure Sports:** Jump, fly, splash, or swing; your inner daredevil will find its voice in Queenstown's multitude of adventurous activities.

★ **Star-Gazing:** Everything is clearer here. Filmmakers comment on the quality of the light and you will see an extraordinary number of stars. This is where the world's largest International Dark Sky Reserve was declared in 2012.

★ **Fly-Fishing:** The crystal-clear lakes and rivers of the Southern Alps are some of the world's best fly-fishing spots.

★ **Hiking:** Tramping doesn't get any better than the Milford, the Kepler, the Routeburn, and the Hollyford tracks. Because trail traffic is carefully managed, you'll feel wonderfully alone in the wilderness.

★ **Scenery:** The landscape here is breathtaking: peaks, fjords, lakes, forest, and tussock lands lie in close proximity. A scenic flight to take it all in is money well spent.

1 Mackenzie Country and Lake Tekapo. The country's highest lake and some of the world's best star-gazing.

2 Aoraki/Mount Cook National Park. New Zealand's tallest mountain at the center of a park filled with hikers and mountain-climbers.

3 Twizel. A service town that's a good base for visiting Aoraki.

4 Mount Aspiring National Park. The country's third-largest national park, full of geological wonders.

5 Wanaka. A quieter alternative to Queenstown and a good base for Mt. Aspiring.

6 Queenstown. The extreme sports capital of the world.

7 Arrowtown. A quaint village with a glimpse into the region's gold rush history.

8 Te Anau and Fiordland National Park. A good base for Fiordland.

9 Milford Sound. The most popular part of Fiordland with dramatic views of breathtaking fjords.

10 Lake Manapouri and Doubtful Sound. A lovely lake with access to less traveled but still beautiful fjords.

Tasman Sea

Sutherland Sound
Bligh Sound
George Sound

Charles Sound

Thompson Sound

Doubtful Sound

MURCHISON MT

Fiordland National Park

FIORDLAND

Lake Maiapou

Breaksea Sound

Resolution Island

TAKITIMU MTS

Dusky Sound

CAMERON MTS

Lake Hourako

Cape Providence

Preservation Inlet

Puysegur Point

Foveaux Strait

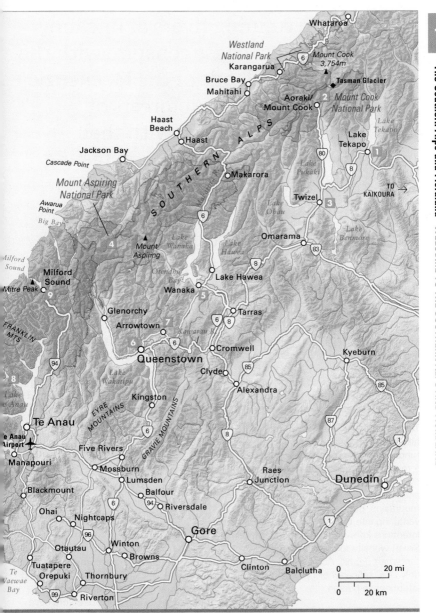

There are hundreds of glaciers locked in the Southern Alps, slowly grinding their way down to lower altitudes and melting into running rivers of uncanny blue-green hues. These conspire with the vast brown grasslands of the Mackenzie Basin and ancient green forests of Fiordland to humble you with their imposing presence, leaving you feeling very small and temporary. Nothing is permanent though—the freeze-thaw cycle constantly refreshes this mighty landscape making it feel absolutely alive.

Aoraki, or Mt. Cook, at 12,218 feet, is New Zealand's highest mountain, and 22 other peaks in this alpine chain are higher than 10,000 feet. Aoraki/Mount Cook National Park is a UNESCO World Heritage Area, and the alpine region around it contains the Tasman Glacier, at 27 km (17 miles), New Zealand's longest.

The Southern Alps region is great for hiking. Terrain varies from high alpine tundra to snow-covered peaks, heavily forested mountains, and wide, braided river valleys. A good network of trails and marked routes are throughout the mountains, but be well informed before venturing into them. Always make your intentions known: go to the Adventure Smart website for details (⊕ *www.adventuresmart.org.nz*); Aoraki/Mt. Cook is the only DOC office where you still sign your intentions in person.

There are many easier options for exploring the foothills and less arduous parts of the Southern Alps. On the southwest corner of the island, glaciers over millennia have cut the Alps into stone walls dropping into fjords, and walking trails take you into the heart of the wild Fiordland National Park. The Milford Track is the best known—it has been called the finest walk in the world since a headline to that effect appeared in the London *Spectator* in 1908. If you're not keen on walking to Milford Sound, hop on a boat and take in the sights from on deck. Most river valleys with road access have well-marked walking trails leading to scenic waterfalls, gorges, and lookout points.

Floods of tourists have come to see the otherworldly landscape used in shooting *The Hobbit* and *Lord of the Rings* film trilogies, and Hollywood directors have been drawn to the area for the magnificent backdrops that depicted Tolkien's Middle Earth. The vastness of the region keeps it from feeling crowded, even with all the new visitors. Queenstown, often billed as an adventure-sports hot spot, is perhaps the best-known destination in the Southern Lakes district. It and the nearby town of Wanaka are steeped in gold-rush history and surrounded by stunning mountain scenery.

GETTING ORIENTED

The Southern Alps start in the northern end of the South Island around Kaikoura and stretch through the provinces of Canterbury, inland Otago, Westland, and Southland. These are serious mountains, with jagged 9,000-feet-plus peaks. The Mt. Cook area is the heart of Kiwi mountaineering. These majestic formations take center stage, and amazing landscapes unfurl at their feet—green rivers braided with white stone banks, acres of lupines, and lakes hued with indescribable blues. From Lake Tekapo, you finally come to "rest" at the adventure-friendly cities of Queenstown and Wanaka, historic Arrowtown, and the truly restful aura of the Otago vineyards. To the west, magnificent Milford Sound dominates Fiordland.

MAJOR REGIONS

The Southern Alps. In Mount Cook National Park, activities naturally revolve around the mountain—climbing, hiking, skiing, and scenic flights. But as you travel down into the foothills and valleys, the choices for adventure multiply. Stargaze at Lake Tekapo in Mackenzie Country, or explore Mount Aspiring National Park. Places like Twizel and Wanaka make good bases for these outdoor activities. Enjoy the miles of hills and farmland as you travel through Lindis Pass; soon the uninhabited country will give way to the bustle of Queenstown, which provides dozens of ways to get your adrenaline pumping. A handful of notable vineyards calms the nerves post-extreme-sport experience

while Arrowtown will give you an intriguing glimpse into the area's history.

Fiordland. On the southwest of the South Island, this is a majestic wilderness of rocks, ice, and beech forest, where glaciers have carved mile-deep notches into the coast. Most of this terrain is officially designated Fiordland National Park, and in conjunction with South Westland National Park, is a designated UNESCO Te Wahipounamu World Heritage Area. Parts of the park are so remote that they have never been explored, and visitor activities are mostly confined to a few of the sounds and the walking trails. Te Anau serves as the base, with lodgings, a supermarket, cafés/restaurants, and sports outfitters. The most accessible scenic highlight of this area—and perhaps of the whole country—is Milford Sound, where trees cling to tremendous rock faces that plunge into the sea, and rare species of coral wait just below the water's surface. Doubtful Sound is also a beautiful area and is actually closer to Te Anau than Milford but involves crossing Lake Manapouri and an alpine pass to get there.

Planning

Making the Most of Your Time

Give yourself two to three days to explore the Aoraki/Mt. Cook area; two days is a good idea at Mt. Cook in case the namesake peak is hiding behind clouds, and you'll want to allow for an evening at the space observatory in Tekapo. Once you head south you can use Queenstown or Wanaka as a base from which you can visit Mount Aspiring National Park, wine country, and take on some exciting adrenaline-fueled activities around Queenstown—three days should be sufficient to pack it all in. Then head to

Te Anau, which is a perfect base for seeing Fiordland National Park. An overnight on Milford or Doubtful Sound is recommended for unwinding and reflecting after the road-tripping, bungy-jumping excitement of the past week.

When to Go

Although the Southern Alps and Fiordland have four distinct seasons, it's not unusual for the mountains to get snow even in summer. If you're traveling in winter, check the weather forecasts and road conditions regularly. The road into Milford Sound can close for days at a time because of snow or avalanche risk and you must carry chains.

For winter sports, from July through September you can be assured of snow around Queenstown and Wanaka, where the ski scene is ushered in by the Queenstown Winter Festival. In the height of summer—from January to March—both resort towns have a lot of Kiwi holidaymakers. If you're planning on hiking one of the major trails, such as the Milford Track, summer and early autumn are the best times, but you'll need to book well ahead.

Getting Here and Around

AIR TRAVEL

Air New Zealand flies from Auckland, Wellington, and Christchurch into Queenstown, the main hub. Jetstar flies in from Auckland and Wellington. Air NZ, Jetstar, Virgin Australia, and Qantas provide trans-Tasman flights (Brisbane, Sydney, and Melbourne). Tourist enterprises operate helicopters and fixed-wing planes, which buzz between Queenstown, Wanaka, Milford Sound, Franz Josef, and Mt. Cook. You can do fly-cruise-fly packages from Queenstown to Milford, although the flight from Wanaka to Milford is the most spectacular.

BUS TRAVEL

It may take a full day, but you can take buses to and from the major towns in the Southern Alps and Fiordland area. InterCity operates a daily bus service between Christchurch and Queenstown down the South Island's eastern flank via Dunedin or the longer, more scenic route via Mount Cook Village, with a one-hour stop at the Hermitage Hotel for lunch. Their coaches also make daily trips from the Franz Josef and Fox glaciers through Wanaka to Queenstown. InterCity also has a daily bus round-trip route from Queenstown and Te Anau to Milford Sound. Alpine ConneXions sends buses between Wanaka and Queenstown several times a day. They also run to Cardrona, Clyde, Cromwell, Dunedin, Ranfurly, Alexandra, and pickup and drop-off to various walking tracks and rail trails.

CONTACTS Alpine Connexions. ☎ 03/443–9120 ⊕ www.alpineconnexions.co.nz. **InterCity Coachlines.** ☎ 03/442–4922 ⊕ www.intercity.co.nz.

CAR TRAVEL

Exploring is best done by car on the state highways that weave through the vast mountain ranges, skirting several major lakes and rivers. Be prepared for rugged, quickly changing terrain, ice in winter, and frequent downpours, particularly around Milford Sound. Rental-car companies may discourage driving on some of the smaller, unpaved roads, so it is best to avoid them. That said, an ideal way to see the Alps is to "tiki-tour" (wander around) by car, as the main network of roads is paved and easy to negotiate.

Restaurants

Queenstown, as the main regional resort, has the widest range of restaurants. Throughout the area, menus focus on local produce, seafood, lamb, and venison. Wine lists often highlight South Island wines, especially those from Central Otago and Gibbston Valley. Cafés and restaurants driven by the summer tourist trade shorten their hours in winter. Dress standards are generally relaxed, with jeans or khakis acceptable almost everywhere. At high-end places, particularly in Queenstown, you'll need to reserve a table at least a day in advance.

Outside of Queenstown and Wanaka dining options can be limited. In summer, meals of some sort are available almost everywhere, but outside the high season, there are fewer options in the smaller settlements and they don't tend to stay open late.

Hotels

Lodgings in the Southern Alps and Fiordland milk the fantastic views for all they're worth. You can almost always find a room that looks out on a lake, river, or rugged mountain range. Queenstown and Wanaka are busy in summer (January through March) and winter (July through September), so you should reserve in advance. Luxury options are plentiful in Queenstown, and costs are correspondingly high. Other towns, such as Aoraki/Mount Cook Village, have extremely limited options, so you should plan ahead there, too. Air-conditioning is rare because it's rarely needed. Heating, though, is standard, and essential in winter.

Restaurant and hotel reviews have been shortened. For full information, visit Fodors.com. Restaurant prices are the average cost of a main course at dinner or, if dinner is not served, at lunch. Hotel prices are the lowest cost of a standard double room in high season.

What It Costs

	$	$$	$$$	$$$$
RESTAURANTS				
	under NZ$15	NZ$15–NZ$20	NZ$21–NZ$30	over NZ$30
HOTELS				
	under NZ$125	NZ$125–NZ$200	NZ$201–NZ$300	over NZ$300

Visitor Information

The regional visitor bureaus are open daily year-round, with slightly longer hours in summer. These local tourism organizations have helpful websites, including **Destination Fiordland, Destination Queenstown,** and **Aoraki/Mount Cook Mackenzie Region Tourism.**

CONTACTS Aoraki/Mount Cook Mackenzie Region Tourism. ⊕ *www.mackenzienz. com.* **Destination Fiordland.** ⊕ *www. fiordland.org.nz.* **Destination Queenstown.** ⊕ *www.queenstownnz.co.nz.*

Mackenzie Country and Lake Tekapo

227 km (141 miles) west of Christchurch.

You will know you have reached the **Mackenzie Country** after you cross Burkes Pass and the woodland is suddenly replaced by high-country tussock grassland, which is full of lupines in the summer months. The area is named for James ("Jock") McKenzie, one of the most intriguing and enigmatic figures in New Zealand history. McKenzie was a Scot who may or may not have stolen the thousand sheep found with him in these secluded upland pastures in 1855. Arrested, tried, and convicted, he made several escapes from jail before he was granted a pardon nine months after his trial—and disappeared from the pages of history. Regardless of his innocence or guilt, McKenzie was a master bushman and herdsman. A commemorative obelisk marks Mackenzie Pass, 30 km (18 miles) off the main highway if you turn off at Burkes Pass.

GETTING HERE AND AROUND
From Christchurch take Highway 1 south. At the tiny town of Rangitata turn right onto Highway 79 to Lake Tekapo. Bus companies that serve Lake Tekapo include InterCity Coach, The Cook Connection (summer only), and several tour operators. Check ⊕ *www.mtcooknz.com* for a complete list.

VISITOR INFORMATION
CONTACTS Lake Tekapo New Zealand. ⊕ *www.laketekaponz.co.nz* . **Tekapo Springs Information Centre.** ✉ *State Hwy. 8, Village Center* ☎ *03/680–6579* ⊕ *www. mackenzienz.com.*

 ## Sights

Bullock Wagon Trail
HISTORIC SITE | This 268-km (167-mile) heritage highway, which stretches from Timaru to Twizel via Mt. Cook, recognizes the long, arduous journeys early settlers in the region made by bullock wagon. Leaving the Canterbury Plains at Geraldine or Pleasant Point (depending on whether you are coming directly from Christchurch or through from Timaru), the highways join at Fairlie and quickly climb toward the first of the alpine passes—Burkes Pass—along the Bullock Wagon Trail. The Burkes Pass monument marks the division between the high and low country, and from there the country immediately dries out and takes on the look of high-country tussock lands. To learn more about the trail and the history of the region, stop in at one of two information centers along the way.

Church of the Good Shepherd
RELIGIOUS SITE | On the east side of the township, the tiny Church of the Good Shepherd is one of the most photographed buildings in New Zealand. This beautifully simple stone interdenominational church has sat on the shore of Lake Tekapo since 1935. There's no need for stained glass as the view through the window is the lake's brilliant blue. A victim of its own popularity, the church has restricted parking and no longer allows photography inside the building. Right next to the church is a lovely bronze statue dedicated to the working sheep dogs of the area. ✉ *Pioneer Dr., Lake Tekapo* ☎ *03/685–8389* ⊕ *www.churchofthe-goodshepherd.org.nz.*

Earth and Sky
OBSERVATORY | FAMILY | If you're extremely lucky, you'll see the southern lights in this area. Even if you don't, you're still at one of the best stargazing sites in the world. Earth and Sky operates from the Mt. John Observatory and studies the skies above Lake Tekapo. The Astro Café has ham-off-the-bone sandwiches, telescopes, and dizzying views. Stargazing trips leave from the town office in the evening, and reservations are essential. Earth and Sky also offers a shorter one-hour tour of the Cowan's Observatory, which is more suitable for those with younger children. ✉ *Main St., State Hwy. 8, Lake Tekapo* ☎ *03/680–6960* ⊕ *www. earthandsky.co.nz* 🎟 *From NZ$99.*

Lake Tekapo
TOWN | The long, narrow expanse of Lake Tekapo anchors the area. Its extraordinary milky-turquoise color comes from rock flour, rock ground by glacial action and held in a soupy suspension. Tekapo, the country's highest large lake, has good fly-fishing in the lake and in the surrounding rivers and canals. As you drive into the small town, you'll notice a knot of restaurants with tour buses parked outside. It's a rather off-putting image, but it's relatively easy to keep the township at your back and your eyes on the lake and mountains. If you're not planning to stay at Mt. Cook, then Tekapo is the best place in the Mackenzie Basin to stop for the night. And once the buses

have passed through for the day, it's a quiet spot—at least until the hordes of Cantabrians arrive for the summer break. A pleasant lakefront recreation area separates the town retail area from the lakeshore. ⊠ *Lake Tekapo.*

Tekapo Springs

HOT SPRINGS | FAMILY | If you've taken advantage of the walks around Tekapo then you'll really appreciate this day spa and hot-pool complex with its beautiful views. There's a sauna, steam room, and traditional plunge pool at lake temperature. In winter there's a skating rink and tube park. ⊠ *6 Lakeside Dr., Lake Tekapo* ☎ *03/680–6550* ⊕ *www.tekaposprings. co.nz* ⚞ *From NZ$27.*

🍴 Restaurants

Kohan Japanese Restaurant

$$$ | JAPANESE | FAMILY | For more than 25 years, Masato Itoh has run the only Japanese restaurant in town, combining fresh local ingredients with imported spices and seasoning to produce a traditional Japanese menu. The food is a refreshing change from the more traditional offerings in town; any salmon dish is a winner, but the Bento Box is especially good value. **Known for:** great lake views; big crowds; lots of locals. ⑤ *Average main: NZ$25* ⊠ *State Hwy. 8, Village Center* ☎ *03/680–6688* ⊕ *www.kohannz. com* ☉ *No dinner Sun.*

Hotels

The Chalet

$$$ | HOTEL | The Chalet's seven fully self-contained apartments stretch beside the turquoise waters of Lake Tekapo, with units ranging from studio size to a two-bedroom cottage apartment. **Pros:** superb views; host is an experienced local guide; extremely comfortable rooms. **Cons:** it's difficult to book a single night stay; garden rooms lack lake views; subtle clown theme not for everyone. ⑤ *Rooms from: NZ$230* ✉ *14 Pioneer Dr., Lake Tekapo* ☎ *03/680–6774* ⊕ *www. thechalet.co.nz* ⤳ *7 units* ⦿ *No meals.*

★ Lake Tekapo Lodge

$$$$ | B&B/INN | The large picture windows offer spectacular lake views, providing a blend of natural beauty and modern sophistication. **Pros:** the most luxurious stay in Lake Tekapo; dinner available by arrangement; wonderful personal attention. **Cons:** book well in advance; some buildings in the foreground of lake and mountain views; no pool. ⑤ *Rooms from: NZ$450* ✉ *25 Aorangi Cres, Lake Tekapo* ☎ *03/680–6566* ⊕ *laketekapolodge.co.nz* ⤳ *3 rooms* ⦿ *Breakfast* ⌁ *No children allowed.*

Lake Tekapo Village Motel

$$$ | HOTEL | FAMILY | A nice midrange alternative with good family-style facilities, this resort is in the center of town. **Pros:** good value; huge bathrooms; right next to restaurants. **Cons:** lake views obstructed by buildings in front; many rooms face parking lot; adjoins backpacker accommodation. ⑤ *Rooms from: NZ$255* ✉ *Village Centre, State Hwy. 8, Lake Tekapo* ☎ *03/680–6808, 0800/118–666* ⊕ *www.laketekapo.com* ⤳ *19 rooms* ⦿ *No meals.*

⛷ Activities

If you're not up for tourist adventures on a particular day, a nice walk around Tekapo may suffice, which will lead you to spectacular views, and there's always the hotpools at Tekapo Springs to relax in afterward.

HIKING

Domain to Mt. John Lookout Track

HIKING/WALKING | At the **Tekapo Information Centre** you can pick up a walking-trail map and then take off to hike the Domain to Mt. John Lookout Track. In a couple of hours you can be well above the township, enjoying extensive views of the Mackenzie Basin, Southern Alps, and Lake Tekapo.

Aoraki/Mount Cook National Park

99 km (62 miles) from Lake Tekapo.

If you think you've experienced all the grandeur of New Zealand, just wait until you visit Aoraki/Mount Cook National Park. A few things about Aoraki/Mt. Cook: it's dually named with Māori and Anglo titles. Second, you may never see New Zealand's tallest mountain, as weather can shroud the peaks for days. Plan to stay in the park overnight in case your arrival coincides with curtains of clouds. Note that shopping in Aoraki/Mount Cook Village is very limited. If you don't intend to eat every meal in a restaurant, purchase food and necessary supplies in Twizel or Lake Tekapo. The ice cornices and granite faces are the realm of serious mountain climbers. Nonclimbers can still get a strong sense of the place with hikes, scenic flights, glacier ski trips, and a visit to the excellent Sir Edmund Hillary Alpine Centre at the Hermitage Hotel. And, finally, be prepared to be awed by these majestic peaks and the stunning immensity of Tasman Glacier.

WHEN TO GO

For driving to and hiking in the park unhampered by bad weather, visit in the summer. Book accommodations and activities well in advance for November to March. If your trip revolves around skiing or snowboarding, then winter is a wonderland here, albeit a somewhat inaccessible one during snow storms.

GETTING HERE AND AROUND

The 330-km (205-mile) drive from Christchurch straight through to Aoraki/Mount Cook Village takes four hours. Take Highway 1 south out of Christchurch. At the tiny town of Rangitata turn right onto Highway 79 to Lake Tekapo. Pass through Lake Tekapo and look on the right for Highway 80 to Aoraki/Mount Cook Village. InterCity buses make daily stops at Mount Cook Village. The village itself is small and manageable on foot.

BUS COMPANY InterCity Coachlines.
☎ 03/365–1113 ⊕ www.intercity.co.nz.

TOURS

Alpine Guides Ltd.
GUIDED TOURS | Alpine Guides is NZ's longest-established mountain and ski guiding company. In summer they offer guided ascents and climbing instruction—trips are 6–10 days. In winter they have two heli-ski operations at Mount Cook and Methven, Ski the Tasman, and ski touring. ✉ 98 Bowen Dr., Aoraki Mount Cook ☎ 03/435–1834 ⊕ www.alpineguides.co.nz ✆ From NZ$1425.

Glacier Explorers
BOAT TOURS | Take a spectacular, almost surreal, boat trip on the terminal lake of New Zealand's largest and longest glacier, the Tasman Glacier. The lake formed in the mid-1980s, and every now and then icebergs calve and increase its size. It's the only place in the country where you can do a trip like this. The season starts once the lake has thawed, but generally runs from mid-September to late May. It's a good idea to book ahead, and bring a warm jacket. ✉ Aoraki Mount Cook ☎ 03/435–1641, 0800/686–800 ⊕ www.glacierexplorers.com ✆ NZ$170.

VISITOR INFORMATION

CONTACTS Aoraki/Mount Cook National Park Visitor Centre. ✉ Aoraki/Mount Cook Village, 1 Larch Grove, Aoraki Mount Cook ☎ 03/435–1186 ⊕ www.doc.govt.nz.

◉ Sights

★ Aoraki/Mount Cook National Park
MOUNTAIN—SIGHT | Aoraki/Mt. Cook is New Zealand's highest peak at approximately 12,218 feet. There are 22 peaks over 10,000 feet in Aoraki/Mount Cook National Park. According to Māori legend, Aoraki was one of three sons of Rakinui, the sky father. Their canoe caught on a reef and froze, forming the South Island. South Island's oldest name to local Māori is Te Waka O Aoraki (Aoraki's canoe) and the highest peak is their ancestor Aoraki, frozen by the south wind, and turned to stone. The officially recognized names of this mountain and the national park were changed to their original Māori names of Aoraki (Aorangi to North Island Māori) as part of a 1998 settlement between the government and the major South Island Māori tribe, Ngai Tahu. The Māori and Anglo names are used interchangeably or together. The 273-square-mile national park surrounds tiny **Aoraki/Mount Cook Village**, which consists of a visitor center, an airfield, a pub, a little school, and a range of accommodation providers. Walking is always an option, and in winter there's heli-skiing. If the weather is clear, a scenic flight can be the highlight of your stay in New Zealand. Contact the Aoraki/Mount Cook National Park Visitor Centre or the weather phone to check conditions before setting out on an unguided excursion. Hiking trails radiate from the visitor center, providing everything from easy walking paths to full-day challenges. Be sure to fill your car's gas tank and purchase essentials before leaving Twizel or Tekapo as services are very limited in the village. For a unique hands-on educational experience take a half-hour hike to the

Did You Know?

Practice makes perfect at Aoraki/Mt. Cook. Sir Edmund Hillary honed his climbing skills here to prepare for his historic ascent of Mt. Everest.

Safety in the High Country

The Fiordland region's remoteness and changeable weather make it necessary to take some sensible precautions. So, before you head out on that trek or boat trip, keep the following in mind:

Be sure to wear the right protective clothing: sturdy hiking boots, a waterproof jacket, and a warm layer such as a fleece or wool pullover. Weather in this region, especially at high altitude, can change dramatically in a short time.

Watch out for sunburn—take sunscreen and a hat with you. Also bring bug repellent for sand flies, which are impossible to avoid in this region unless you're traveling offshore by boat.

If you're heading off without a guide for more than an hour or two, let someone know where and when you're going and when you've returned. See the Adventure Smart website for advice (⊕ www.adventuresmart.org. nz). DOC visitor centers issue regular weather and trail updates.

Use extreme caution when crossing rivers. Especially after rain, mountain runoff can quickly turn a gentle stream into an angry torrent, and drowning is a major hazard. If you do get trapped on one side of a quickly rising river, wait for the water to recede rather than risk crossing.

For longer treks into serious country always carry a map and compass, first-aid gear, bottled water, high-energy foods, warm clothes and tent, and a mountain radio or EPIRB (locator beacon—these can be rented locally). Cell phones don't work in the mountains.

fast-growing 2-km (1-mile) **Terminus Lake of the Tasman Glacier.** Fed by the retreating glacier and the Murchison River, the lake was formed only in the past couple of decades. From Terminus Lake you can examine up close the terminal face of the glacier, which is 3 km (2 miles) wide. A trip with Glacier Explorers takes you by boat to explore some of the large floating icebergs that have calved (fallen away) from the glacier. It's an eerie experience skimming across the milky-white water and closing in on icebergs. From the airfield at Mount Cook Village, helicopters and fixed-wing aircraft make spectacular scenic flights across the Southern Alps. One of the most exciting is the one-hour trip aboard the ski planes that touch down on the **Tasman Glacier** after a gorgeous scenic flight. The 10-minute stop on the glacier doesn't allow time for much more than a snapshot, but the sensation is tremendous. The moving tongue of ice beneath your feet—one of the largest glaciers outside the Himalayas—is 27 km (17 miles) long and up to 2,000 feet thick in places. The intensity of light on the glacier can be dazzling, and sunglasses are a must. ⊠ *Aoraki Mount Cook.*

🍴 Restaurants

The Old Mountaineers Cafe, Bar & Restaurant

$$$ | CAFÉ | This cozy, very personable café/restaurant has big picture windows for grand views of the outside and all sorts of interesting mountaineering memorabilia and photos to peruse inside. The meals are flavorful, hearty, and wholesome and they source a lot of organic produce, including organic wines and coffee (if you take it with milk, that's organic, too). **Known for:** spectacular views; organic produce; huge

Mountaineers Breakfast served all day. $ *Average main: NZ$30* ✉ *Larch Grove Rd., Aoraki Mount Cook* ☎ *03/435–1890* ⊕ *www.mtcook.com.*

🛏 Hotels

Aoraki Court Motel

$$$$ | **HOTEL** | **FAMILY** | Being fully self-catering is a huge plus with the lack of shopping in Mount Cook Village, and Aoraki Court Motel has 25 modern studio or two-bedroom units, all of which have kitchenettes. **Pros:** removed from the hordes of bus groups; great walks right out the door; option to cook your own meals. **Cons:** free Wi-Fi is patchy due to the remote location; expensive for what you get; books up months in advance. $ *Rooms from: NZ$375* ✉ *26 Bowen Dr., Aoraki Mount Cook* ☎ *03/435–1111* ⊕ *www.aorakicourt.co.nz* ↻ *25 rooms* ⦿ *No meals.*

Aoraki/Mt. Cook Alpine Lodge

$$ | **HOTEL** | **FAMILY** | This lodge, run by a young local family, has twin, triple, and family rooms, all with private bathrooms and two have kitchenettes. **Pros:** great guest lounge with fireplace; nice views from rooms; bikes for hire. **Cons:** not many meal options, so be prepared to buy groceries and cook; thin walls; lots of stairs to climb. $ *Rooms from: NZ$179* ✉ *Bowen Dr., Aoraki Mount Cook* ☎ *03/435–1860* ⊕ *www.aorakialpinelodge.co.nz* ↻ *16 rooms* ⦿ *No meals.*

Hermitage Hotel

$$$$ | **HOTEL** | Famed for its stupendous mountain vistas from most rooms, the Hermitage is also home to the Sir Edmund Hillary Alpine Centre, a tribute to one of the most famous New Zealanders. **Pros:** unbeatable mountain views; most local activities are operated by the hotel; excellent in-house dining. **Cons:** no gym, pool, or spa; lots of tour groups in summer; sprawling layout. $ *Rooms from: NZ$310* ✉ *Terrace Rd., Aoraki*

Mount Cook ☎ *03/435–1809* ⊕ *www.hermitage.co.nz* ↻ *183 rooms* ⦿ *No meals.*

🏃 Activities

You don't want to miss the chance to see Sir Edmund Hillary's playground or the backdrop of *Lord of the Rings*. Climbing the icy slopes yourself will provide a day full of exercise and an unforgettable experience.

CLIMBING AND MOUNTAINEERING

Adventure Consultants

CLIMBING/MOUNTAINEERING | Summer is the best climbing season in the Aoraki/Mount Cook National Park area. Adventure Consultants, a group specializing in the world's top peaks, guides ascents of Aoraki, Mt. Tasman, and throughout the Southern Alps. They also give private multiday mountaineering, alpine-climbing, and ice-climbing courses. The company is based in Wanaka and has a full range of equipment. ✉ *20 Brownston St., Wanaka* ☎ *03/443–8711, 866/757–8722 toll-free in U.S* ⊕ *www.adventureconsultants.com* 🖩 *From NZ$550 per day.*

FLIGHTSEEING

Flightseeing gives you an unparalleled view of the mountains, with the added thrill of landing on a glacier for a short walk. The light can be intensely bright in such dazzlingly white surroundings, so be sure to bring sunglasses. Generally, the best time for flights is early morning.

Air Safaris

FLYING/SKYDIVING/SOARING | Take a breathtaking 50-minute scenic flight over the two longest glaciers in New Zealand, the Tasman and the Murchison, as well as the Fox and Franz Josef glaciers. You'll pass high-country sheep farms and see Aoraki/Mt. Cook and the rain forests on the west side of the Main Divide. There are helicopter charter options, too. ✉ *253 Tekapo-Twizel Rd., Tekapo* ☎ *03/680–6880* ⊕ *www.airsafaris.co.nz*

Flights NZ$395 per person; helicopter from NZ$199 per person.

Helicopter Line
FLYING/SKYDIVING/SOARING | The Helicopter Line runs flights from 20 to 50 minutes, all of which include a remote landing, from Glentanner Park, about 20 km (12 miles) toward Pukaki from the Hermitage. You can land on the glaciers or high ski slopes, depending on the weather. ⊠ *Glentanner Park, State Hwy. 80, Aoraki Mount Cook* ☎ *03/435–1801* ⊕ *www.helicopter.co.nz* ⓢ *From NZ$270 per person.*

Mount Cook Ski Planes
FLYING/SKYDIVING/SOARING | Choose between a ski plane or helicopter; it's the way to go for a bird's-eye view of the stunning Mt. Cook. Flightseeing options include a 25-minute flight to the bottom of the Tasman Glacier or a 40-minute flight with a glacier landing. ⊠ *Mount Cook Airport, State Hwy. 80, Aoraki Mount Cook* ☎ *03/430–8034, 0800/800–702* ⊕ *www.mtcookskiplanes.com* ⓢ *From NZ$249 per person.*

HIKING

The hiking trails spooling out from the visitor center range in difficulty and length, from the 10-minute Bowen Track to the 5½-hour climb to the 4,818-foot summit of Mt. Sebastopol. Several tracks can be done in running shoes and don't require hiking experience; the rest of the park's trails require some hiking experience, and the higher routes require serious mountaineering experience. The Mueller Hut route is a popular climb, taking three to four hours; a 28-bunk hut provides overnight accommodation (book and pay at the visitor center). The rewarding Hooker Valley walk, a four-hour round-trip, will take you across a couple of swingbridges to the Hooker Glacier terminus lake, and the Tasman Glacier Lake walk gives an intimate view of New Zealand's longest glacier.

Twizel

65 km (40 miles) from Lake Tekapo, 40 km (25 miles) from Aoraki/Mt. Cook.

A service town to its core, Twizel was built in 1968 as a base for workers constructing a major hydroelectric power plant. When the hydroelectric scheme wrapped up, the residents fought to keep their town intact. Now it's a handy place for tourist overflow in the Aoraki/Mt. Cook area. There's good fishing to be done in its rivers and those hydro canals (a 45-pound brown trout was landed there in 2013). Birders should check with the visitor center about tours to the *kakī* aviary to see these striking endangered red-legged birds.

Twizel is close to five good-size boating and leisure lakes and has a couple of good places to eat. Having already passed Tekapo and Pukaki, you'll find Lake Ruataniwha a little tame. Lake Ohau is off the main road, but is another high-country fishing gem. A ski slope, Ohau Snow Fields, opens in July each winter, and a number of walks are in the nearby Ohau Forest Range.

GETTING HERE AND AROUND

Twizel is on State Highway 8. If you're driving south from Christchurch on Highway 1, turn onto Highway 8 at Fairlie. If you're coming north from Queenstown, follow Highway 6 to Cromwell, then turn onto Highway 8 and continue over the Lindis Pass to Twizel. InterCity Coachlines serve Twizel.

BUS INFORMATION InterCity Coachlines. ☎ *03/365–1113* ⊕ *www.intercity.co.nz.*

VISITOR INFORMATION

CONTACTS Twizel Information Centre. ⊠ *Market Pl.* ☎ *03/435–3124* ⊕ *www.twizel.info.*

🍴 Restaurants

Poppies Cafe

$$$$ | **CAFÉ** | **FAMILY** | For years Poppies has been a great place to eat, drink, socialize, and bask in the sun. Meat, seafood, pizza, and pasta are complemented by organic produce from the garden along with fresh-baked bread and pizzas. **Known for:** summer alfresco dining; popularity with locals; lovely wine list. ⑤ *Average main: NZ$32* ✉ *1 Benmore Pl.* ☎ *03/435–0848* ⊕ *www.poppiescafe.com.*

🛏 Hotels

MacKenzie Country Hotel

$$ | **HOTEL** | The imposing stone-and-timber buildings here make an impression in this otherwise nondescript town. **Pros:** reasonably priced; great location; friendly staff. **Cons:** food isn't great; tired decor; can be noisy. ⑤ *Rooms from: NZ$160* ✉ *2 Wairepo Rd.* ☎ *03/435–0869, 0800/500–869* ⊕ *www.mackenzie.co.nz* 🛏 *108 rooms* ❏ *No meals.*

Matuka Lodge

$$$$ | **B&B/INN** | This lodge is ideal for anyone wanting to enjoy the hikes and activities of the Mt. Cook area, and is particularly nice for fly fishermen. **Pros:** endearing hosts; rooms have verandas with mountain views; incredible night sky. **Cons:** 50-minute drive to Mt. Cook; you have to drive to the nearest restaurant; books up quickly. ⑤ *Rooms from: NZ$450* ✉ *395 Glen Lyon Rd.* ☎ *03/435–0144* ⊕ *www.matukaluxurylodge.com* ⊘ *Closed June and July* 🛏 *4 rooms* ❏ *Breakfast.*

Mount Aspiring National Park

Roads only skirt the edge of this huge park, which compels you to hike, boat, and fly to see it. Only a winged, hoofed supercreature could possibly see the majority of Aspiring's wilderness. Daunting yet tantalizing: that's the magic draw of this unspoiled landscape.

At 877,224 acres, Mount Aspiring is the country's third-largest national park. The park's namesake mountain is only one of numerous geological wonders. The area has yielded much *pounamu* or greenstone, and the famous Otago schist featured in the architecture of the gateway communities. One unusual stretch of peaks is known as the Red Hills, where the toxic minerals in the soil rendered the landscape barren (and a deep rusty red). Most of the park is marked by beech forest and wildflower-filled valleys, with snow tussock grasslands and alpine herb fields above the snowline. The park is home to the famous Routeburn Track, a three-day Great Walk, and dozens of shorter hikes. Gateway communities include lively Wanaka, which offers a multitude of choices for lodging, dining, shopping, and those rewarding posthike pints.

GETTING HERE AND AROUND

Gateway communities to the park are Wanaka, Makarora, Queenstown, Glenorchy, and Te Anau. These towns are all served by bus companies, and you can fly into Wanaka, Queenstown, and Te Anau. Major thoroughfares lead to them and driving to any of these locations is a treat—the scenery in this part of the country is dramatic and roadside attractions include gorgeous vineyards, fresh fruit stands, mountain passes, white-water rivers, and if you're en route to Wanaka from Queenstown you can stop and bungy jump.

For maps, information on local walks, and information on the three campgrounds and 20 backcountry huts in the park, contact the DOC. Many tours to the park leave from Wanaka.

VISITOR INFORMATION

CONTACTS Department of Conservation.
✉ *Ardmore St. and Ballantyne Rd., Wanaka* ☎ *03/443–7660* ⊕ *www.doc.govt.nz.*

 # Activities

Siberia Experience

FLYING/SKYDIVING/SOARING | Siberia Experience has one of the area's best adventure packages. The journey begins with a funky little yellow plane in a paddock-cum-airstrip. After a breathtaking 25-minute journey from Makarora, the pilot drops you off in the pristine wilderness of Mount Aspiring National Park's Siberia Valley, and points you to a trailhead. From there, embark on a magnificent three-hour hike on a well-marked, relatively easy trail. Finally, a jet-boat meets you at the Wilkin River and returns you to Makarora. There is a hut out there if you'd like to arrange overnight stays. ✉ *5944 Haast Pass-Makarora Rd., Makarora* ☎ *0800/345–666, 03/443–4385* ⊕ *www.siberiaexperience.co.nz* 🎫 *NZ$415.*

Wanaka

70 km (44 miles) northeast of Queenstown, 140 km (87 miles) southwest of Twizel.

On the southern shore of Lake Wanaka, with some of New Zealand's most striking mountains behind it, Wanaka is the welcome mat for Mount Aspiring National Park. It has labeled itself the world's first "Lifestyle Reserve" and is a favorite of Kiwis on vacation, a smaller, quieter alternative to Queenstown. The region has two ski resorts, numerous trekking and river-sports opportunities, and if you

arrive on a rainy day, you can hit a couple of unusual cultural attractions. These good points have not gone unnoticed, and Wanaka is one of the fastest-growing towns in New Zealand, with new housing popping up in record time.

GETTING HERE AND AROUND

If you're coming from Queenstown, you have two choices for getting to Wanaka: go over the Crown Range for stunning views (not recommended in snow) or take the winding road along the Kawarau River through wine and fruit country. From Christchurch, drive south through Geraldine and Twizel. Once in Wanaka it's easy to park and walk around town, and a taxi service can get you back to your accommodations if you take advantage of the nightlife. A short but pleasant drive to the western side of the lake brings you to Glendhu Bay. With nothing here but a campground and fabulous mountain and lake views, the real beauty in this drive lies in the unspoiled calm and surreal quiet (except in midsummer, when it is packed full of vacationing locals). This road also leads to the Aspiring region and the Treble Cone ski area. Several bus companies serve Wanaka.

BUS COMPANIES Alpine Connexions.
⊕ *www.alpineconnexions.co.nz.*

TOURS

Deep Canyon

GUIDED TOURS | With the steep rugged waterways of the Matukituki and Wilkin valleys within easy reach, Wanaka is a key spot in the country for canyoning. Deep Canyon leads expeditions down the Niger Stream, Wai Rata Canyon, the Leaping Burn, and others. No experience is necessary but the minimum age is 12. ✉ *100 Ardmore St.* ☎ *03/443–7922* ⊕ *www.deepcanyon.co.nz* 🎫 *From NZ$260.*

★ Eco Wanaka

GUIDED TOURS | **FAMILY** | Visit the lake that's on top of an island that's on top of the lake. Riddles aside, this is a journey to

the Mou Waho Island Nature Reserve in the middle of Lake Wanaka; a guided nature walk to the summit reveals the lake on top and hopefully you'll hear or catch a glimpse of rare native birds along the way. On every trip, guests plant a native tree. The guides are all locals, incredibly knowledgeable, and guide walks all over this World Heritage Area, including the Rob Roy Glacier. ☒ *Lake Wanaka i-SITE, 103 Ardmore St.* ☏ *03/443–2869* ⊕ *www.ecowanaka.co.nz* 🎫 *From NZ$245.*

VISITOR INFORMATION

CONTACTS Lake Wanaka i-SITE Visitor Information Centre. ☒ *103 Ardmore St.* ☏ *03/443–1233* ⊕ *www.lakewanaka. co.nz.*

Sights

Cardrona Distillery

WINERY/DISTILLERY | Although it will be years until their first batch of single malt whisky is ready, Cardrona Distillery has a lovely range of spirits ready to go right now, including vodka and gin. The setting in the Cardrona Valley is beautiful and they offer tours departing hourly 10–3 every day. ☒ *2125 Cardrona Valley Rd.* ☏ *03/443–1393* ⊕ *www.cardronadistillery.com* 🎫 *Tours NZ$25.*

Crossfire

AMUSEMENT PARK/WATER PARK | **FAMILY** | At this excellent facility, you can have a hand at clay bird or rifle shooting, archery, or get a basket of golf balls and swing away. It's fun for experts, and you get full instruction if you're a novice. There's an activity for everyone including the kids at the minigolf course. This is a great option if the weather's misbehaving. ☒ *9 Mt. Barker Rd., opposite Wanaka Airport* ☏ *03/443–5995* ⊕ *www.crossfirewanaka. co.nz* 🎫 *From NZ$13.*

Puzzling World

AMUSEMENT PARK/WATER PARK | **FAMILY** | The cartoonlike houses built at funny angles with the *Leaning Tower of Wanaka* is just

the start. Turn off here for a number of puzzling life-size brainteasers, including the amazing Tumbling Towers, Hologram Halls, and Tilted House, which is on a 15-degree angle (is the water really running uphill?). There's a "3-D" Great Maze to get lost in and a *Sculptillusion* gallery. For a break, head to the café, take on the puzzle of your choice, order a cup of coffee, and work yourself into a puzzled frenzy. ☒ *Hwy. 84, 188 Wanaka Luggate Hwy.* ☏ *03/443–7489* ⊕ *www.puzzlingworld.co.nz* 🎫 *NZ$23.*

Rippon Vineyard

WINERY/DISTILLERY | Lying spectacularly by the shores of Lake Wanaka, Rippon is one of the most photographed vineyards in the country. The vineyard's portfolio includes Riesling, Gewürztraminer, Chardonnay, Sauvignon Blanc, and fine Pinot Noir. Head west from Wanaka along the lake on Mt. Aspiring Road for 4 km (2½ miles). ☒ *246 Mt. Aspiring Rd.* ☏ *03/443–8084* ⊕ *www.rippon.co.nz.*

Wanaka National Transport and Toy Museum

MUSEUM | **FAMILY** | Lying somewhere between a treasure trove and a junkyard, the National Transport and Toy Museum is both compelling and a little disorienting. One man's hoard featuring hundreds of vehicles, from cars and motorcycles to fire engines and aircraft, is almost overwhelming in its abundance. It can feel like there is just *too much stuff*. The toy collection is also enormous, and includes display cabinets overflowing with Star Wars collectibles and many other well-known brands. ☒ *891 State Hwy. 6* ⊹ *Beside Wanaka Airport* ☏ *03/443–8765* ⊕ *www.nttmuseumwanaka.co.nz* 🎫 *NZ$18.*

Warbirds & Wheels

MUSEUM | There are around 35 privately owned classic cars on display here. Their 1934 Duesenberg is the star of the show, with Packards, Lincolns, and Fords among the mix. You may have heard of the NZ Fighter Pilots Museum—it's long gone but you can still see some of the planes here, including a WWI SE5A, Hawker Hurricane, Vampire, Strikemaster, and impressive Skyhawk fighter jet. This is also home of New Zealand's largest contemporary touring art collection; at least half the collection stays here. There's also a retro diner serving breakfast and lunch daily. ✉ *11 Lloyd Dunn Ave., Wanaka Airport* ☎ *03/443–7010* ⊕ *www.warbirdsandwheels.co.nz* ☞ *NZ$20.*

🍴 Restaurants

★ Bistro Gentil

$$$$ | FRENCH | Indulge with a modern fine French meal in a quiet setting with lake and mountain views on the outskirts of Wanaka. The menu changes regularly, but the local Cardrona merino lamb is always there in one form or another, accompanied by heirloom vegetables and herbs from the kitchen garden. **Known for:** provincial olive oils; self-dispensed wine tastings; multicourse tasting menus. ⓢ *Average main: NZ$38* ✉ *76a Golf Course Rd.* ☎ *03/443–2299* ⊕ *www.bistrogentil.co.nz* ☾ *Closed Sun. and Mon.*

Kai Whakapai

$$ | ECLECTIC | Just across the road from the lake, this is a great place to sit shoulder to shoulder with the locals for breakfast outside on a crisp sunny morning. The menu ranges from simple breakfast and lunch choices (coffee and croissants, salads, nachos, and kebabs), to beef ribs and rump roast for dinner. **Known for:** bustling crowds; live music; local beers on tap. ⓢ *Average main: NZ$20* ✉ *121 Ardmore St.* ☎ *03/443–7795.*

Relishes Café

$$$$ | NEW ZEALAND | You could hit this lakeside spot for every meal of the day, starting with the bacon or salmon eggs Benedict or check the counter food for something homemade and delicious, like their cinnamon sticky buns. They focus on local, seasonal fare and cater to all dietary needs. **Known for:** best coffee in town; local Pinot of the week; lake views. ⓢ *Average main: NZ$32* ✉ *99 Ardmore St.* ☎ *03/443–9018* ⊕ *www.relishescafe.co.nz.*

🛏 Hotels

Cardrona Hotel

$$ | HOTEL | This classic old-country hotel and pub, 20 minutes from Wanaka on the Crown Range Road, is the Cardrona après-ski spot for mulled wine in front of the outdoor fireplace. **Pros:** genuinely historic property; hearty dinner and drinks; crowds leave after dinner. **Cons:** squeaky floorboards; no air-conditioning; basic rooms. ⓢ *Rooms from: NZ$195* ✉ *Cardrona Valley Rd.* ☎ *03/443–8153* ⊕ *www.cardronahotel.co.nz* ☞ *16 rooms* ⓞ *No meals.*

Edgewater

$$$$ | HOTEL | On the lakefront in a quiet area away from town, this property is great for a longer stay in Wanaka. **Pros:** free shuttle to town; good on-site café; washer/dryer in some rooms. **Cons:** ½-hour walk from the middle of town; no air-conditioning; sprawling property. ⓢ *Rooms from: NZ$315* ✉ *54 Sargood Dr.* ☎ *03/443–0011* ⊕ *www.edgewater.co.nz* ☞ *103 rooms* ⓞ *No meals.*

Lakeside Apartments

$$$$ | RENTAL | FAMILY | These modern apartments provide nice family-size accommodation in a particularly central location. **Pros:** great location; lovely pool; use of a barbecue. **Cons:** books up quickly; pool area can get noisy; only penthouse has air-conditioning. ⓢ *Rooms from: NZ$349* ✉ *9 Lakeside Rd.* ☎ *03/443–0188* ⊕ *www.lakesidewanaka.co.nz* ☞ *23 rooms* ⓞ *No meals.*

★ Waiorau Homestead

$$$ | B&B/INN | From the peaceful rural setting and exceptionally good food to the warmth of the hospitality and finest linen on your bed, this is a memorable place to stay. **Pros:** lovely guest lounge;

outdoor hot tub; owner is a fantastic chef. **Cons:** 20-minute drive from Wanaka; very limited availability; one room isn't en suite. $ *Rooms from: NZ$270* ✉ *2127B Cardrona Valley Rd.* ☎ *03/443–2225* ⊕ *www.waiorauhomestead.co.nz* ⮧ *3 rooms* ⦿ *Breakfast.*

Wanaka Alpine Lodge

$$$ | **B&B/INN** | This B&B is in a large house, and the hosts are so warm and friendly, it always feels like you're staying with friends. **Pros:** large, modern rooms; lovely breakfast; freshly baked treats. **Cons:** quite far from town; some noise; some uphill walking to get to town. $ *Rooms from: NZ$269* ✉ *114 Albert Town-Lake Hawea Rd.* ☎ *03/443–5355* ⊕ *www.wanakaalpinelodge.co.nz* ⮧ *5 rooms* ⦿ *Free Breakfast* ☞ *No children under 13.*

Wanaka Homestead Lodge and Cottages

$$$ | **B&B/INN** | The owners used local schist and timber from the farm buildings that once stood here to build their fine solar-powered lakeshore lodge. **Pros:** outdoor fireplace; hot tub; free bike hire. **Cons:** occasional noise from the road disrupts tranquility; no air-conditioning; large communal breakfast table not for everyone. $ *Rooms from: NZ$240* ✉ *1 Homestead Close* ☎ *03/443–5022* ⊕ *www.wanakahomestead.co.nz* ⮧ *7 rooms* ⦿ *Breakfast.*

▼ Nightlife

Cinema Paradiso

FILM | **FAMILY** | The local institution Cinema Paradiso is not your usual movie house— its seating includes couches, recliners, pillows, and even a yellow Morris Minor car. During intermission you can snack on homemade ice cream and warm cookies (straight out of the oven) or even have dinner with a glass of wine. Check the local paper or website for film details and make sure you book ahead. ✉ *72 Brownston St.* ☎ *03/443–1505* ⊕ *www. paradiso.net.nz* ⮧ *NZ$15.*

The Cow

BARS/PUBS | If you want a late bite and a good bottle of wine, pop into The Cow on Post Office Lane for good garlic bread and pizza. It's a very comfortable place, modeled in local stone and heavy timber, just like the original Cow in nearby Queenstown. In winter the open fireplace does an incredible job of warming the bones (and the wine). Feel free to add commentary to their restroom chalkboard walls. ✉ *Post Office La., 33 Ardmore St.* ☎ *03/443–4269* ⊕ *www. thecowpizza.co.nz.*

Lake Bar

BARS/PUBS | This bar's in an iconic spot at the top of Ardmore Street. Sit inside or out and soak up the amazing views of the lake and mountains; if you get hungry they turn out pub-style tapas and lunch, as well as dinner with a separate kids' menu. If you just want a pint in the sun, or after dark, the Lake Bar is a great place for visitors and locals alike. ✉ *155 Ardmore St.* ☎ *03/443–2920* ⊕ *www. lakebar.co.nz.*

Water Bar

BARS/PUBS | This is a very popular upmarket bar with a deck on the lakefront, and an outdoor fire in winter. Head here for late-night entertainment. It has an attractive food menu, and often hosts live music acts. ✉ *145 Ardmore St.* ☎ *03/443–4345* ⊕ *www.waterbarwanaka.co.nz.*

⚐ Activities

With the base of Mount Aspiring National Park on Wanaka's doorstep, renting a bicycle isn't such a bad idea. Soon mountains will surround you and then swingbridges will connect you to the trails, where you'll embark on foot.

BICYCLING

Rent a bicycle and explore along the shores of Lake Wanaka, and out along the Clutha River toward Albert Town. There are many places to rent bikes and get trail maps including Outside Sports (✉ *23 Dunmore St.*) or Thunderbikes (✉ *16 Helwick St.*). Both the Deans Bank Track near Albert Town, a scenic 11½ km (7 miles) intermediate-level loop track, and the Plantation or "Sticky Forest," as locals call it, have good networks of mountain bike trails for all abilities.

FISHING

Locals will tell you that fishing on Lake Wanaka and nearby Lake Hawea is better than at the more famed Taupo area. You won't want to enter that argument, but chances are good you'll catch fish if you have the right guide. Fishing is year-round.

If you're not keen on hiring a guide, you can rent fly-fishing gear and buy your fishing license at **Southern Wild** (✉ *10 Helwick St.*) or **Lakeland Adventures** in the Log Cabin on Ardmore Street.

Hatch Fly Fishing Wanaka

FISHING | If you've always loved the idea of fly-fishing but wouldn't know where to start, Craig Smith is a superb guide and a really nice guy who's happy to teach the basics. You can opt to get dropped in to your fishing spot by helicopter or jet-boat, and there are even overnight campouts available. Rates include lunch and all equipment, as well as pickup and drop-off. ✉ *9 Flora Dora Parade, Lake Hawea* ☎ *03/443–8446* ⊕ *www.hatchfishing. co.nz* ⊠ *From NZ$270.*

Lake Hawea Fishing & Farmstay

FISHING | Harry Urquhart has trolling excursions for rainbow trout, brown trout, and quinnat salmon on Lake Hawea. He's been doing it for 25 years and knows his stuff. He even offers a money-back guarantee: if you don't catch any fish you don't have to pay. He also has self-contained accommodation. ✉ *33 Nook Rd.* ☎ *03/443–1535, 027/440–3070* ⊠ *NZ$350.*

Telford Fishing and Hunting Services

FISHING | Fishing and hunting guide Gerald Telford will tailor an experience just for you, whether you're fly-fishing, including night-fishing and multiday fishing expeditions, or hunting for trophy red stag. Hunting is free range, and you can choose rifle or bowhunting. Gerald has been doing this for more than 30 years and will show you the very best spots. ✉ *Wanaka* ☎ *027/517–4006* ⊕ *www. flyfishhunt.co.nz* ⊠ *From NZ$750.*

RAFTING

Pioneer Rafting

WHITE-WATER RAFTING | At Pioneer Rafting you can do some white-water rafting at a calmer pace. Lewis Verduyn is New Zealand's leading eco-rafting specialist. His highly informative eco-rafting adventure, suitable for most ages, retraces a historic pioneer log-raft route. Both full-day and half-day trips are available, and leave from the Visitor Information Centre in Wanaka. It's closed May through August. ✉ *Lake Wanaka i-SITE Visitor Centre, 103 Ardmore St.* ☎ *03/443–1246* ⊕ *www. ecoraft.co.nz* ⊠ *From NZ$150.*

SCENIC FLIGHTS

The weather around Wanaka is clear much of the time, which has allowed it to become a scenic-flight base for fixed-wing planes and helicopters. Flights take in Mt. Cook and the West Coast glaciers, the Mt. Aspiring area, Queenstown, and Fiordland.

Aspiring Helicopters

FLYING/SKYDIVING/SOARING | It may be hard to believe the scenery can get any better but fasten your seat belt and prepare to be enthralled. Aspiring Helicopters does scenic and adventure trips ranging from a 20-minute local flight to a three-hour trip to Milford Sound. If you can, the longer flight to Milford goes via Mt. Aspiring and includes a landing at a high alpine lake and on a glacier. If you're after the serious wilderness spots to climb, ski, bike, fish, or even get married—they'll take you there, too. ✉ *2211 Wanaka-Mount Aspiring Rd.* ☎ *03/443–7152* ⊕ *www. aspiringhelicopters.co.nz* ⊠ *From NZ$210 per person.*

Wanaka Flightseeing

FLYING/SKYDIVING/SOARING | Wanaka Flightseeing runs small Cessna aircraft to Mt. Cook, Mt. Aspiring, and Milford Sound. They also do private charters to create an itinerary of your choice. ☒ *Wanaka Airport, 10 Lloyd Dunn Ave.* ☎ *03/443–8787* ⊕ *www.flightseeing.co.nz* ☒ *From NZ$225.*

SKIING

With reliable snow and dry powder, Wanaka has some of the best skiing and snowboarding in New Zealand. Cardrona and Treble Cone are the two biggest winter-sports resorts, and Snow Farm specializes in cross-country skiing. For more information about skiing and snowboarding in the area, check out ⊕ *www. lakewanaka.co.nz.*

Cardrona Alpine Resort

SKIING/SNOWBOARDING | Cardrona, 34 km (21 miles) southwest of Wanaka, is great for families with its wide open trails, a kids' ski school and activity center, plus kid- and beginner-friendly lifts, and food outlets. A special "heavy metal" trail pours on the rails and jumps and there are two half pipes that are well used by international snowboarding teams (American snowboard star Shaun White landed his first back-to-back cork 10-80 in competition on one of them). The season is roughly mid-June–early October. A bonus at Cardrona is the 15 apartments up on the mountain, but you'll need to book early to get in. Daily shuttles are available from Wanaka, Queenstown, and Cromwell. ☒ *Cardrona Valley Rd., Cardrona* ⊕ *www.cardrona.com* ☒ *1-day lift pass NZ$115.*

Treble Cone

SKIING/SNOWBOARDING | Treble Cone, 19 km (11½ miles) west of Wanaka, is the South Island's largest ski area, with lots of advanced trails and off-piste skiing. You can purchase a single-day lift pass, or if you're planning to ski a few days you can buy a Flexi pass, which makes it a bit cheaper. You can call their Snow Phone to get up-to-date snow reports or check their website. If you're not a skier it's still worth getting a scenic chairlift ride on the home basin chairlift; the view is sensational. ☒ *Wanaka-Mount Aspiring Rd.* ☎ *03/443–1406* ⊕ *www.treblecone. com* ☒ *Single-day lift pass NZ$135.*

SKYDIVING

Skydive Wanaka

FLYING/SKYDIVING/SOARING | Wanaka Airport is a hub for all kinds of aviation adventures. Perhaps the most exciting of these is skydiving. If you've considered skydiving, this is a spectacular place to do it. You can jump from 9,000, 12,000, and 15,000 feet, with photos and video of your jump available for an extra fee. ☒ *Wanaka Airport, Mustang La.* ☎ *03/443–7207* ⊕ *www.skydivewanaka. com* ☒ *From NZ$299.*

WALKING AND TREKKING

The Mount Aspiring National Park provides serious hiking and mountaineering opportunities, including Wilkins Valley, Makarora River, and Mt. Aspiring tracks and trails.

Diamond Lake Track

HIKING/WALKING | The complete Diamond Lake Track takes three hours and starts 25 km (15½ miles) west of Wanaka, also on the Glendhu Bay–Mt. Aspiring road. The track rises to 2,518 feet at Rocky Peak, passing Diamond Lake along the way. If you've got time for only a short walk, take the one that heads to the lake; it takes only 20 minutes. The Diamond Lake area is also popular with mountain bikers and rock climbers. ☒ *Matukituki Valley Rd.* ☎ *03/443–7660* ⊕ *www.doc. govt.nz.*

Lake Wanaka Outlet Track

HIKING/WALKING | **FAMILY** | You get maximum views for minimal challenge on one of the prettiest local trails, which meanders along the Clutha River from the Lake Wanaka Outlet to Albert Town. This is a kid-friendly route, and also fly-fisherman-, bicyclist-, and picnicker-friendly. It takes about an hour one way. ✉ *Outlet Track.*

Mt. Iron

HIKING/WALKING | If you have time for only one walk, Mt. Iron, rising 780 feet above the lake, is relatively short and rewarding. The access track begins 2 km (1 mile) from Wanaka, and the walk to the top takes 45 minutes. You can descend on the alternative route down the steep eastern face. ✉ *124 Wanaka-Luggate Hwy.*

Queenstown

103 km (64 miles) southeast of Wanaka, 480 km (300 miles) southwest of Christchurch.

Set on the edge of the glacial Lake Wakatipu, with stunning views of the sawtooth peaks of the Remarkables mountain range, Queenstown is the most popular tourist stop in the South Island. Once prized by the Māori as a source of greenstone, the town boomed when gold was discovered in the Shotover River during the 1860s; the Shotover quickly became famous as "the richest river in the world." By the 1950s Queenstown had become the center of a substantial farming area, and with ready access to mountains, lakes, and rivers, the town has since become the adventure capital of New Zealand. Today, New Zealanders' penchant for bizarre adventure sports culminates in Queenstown; it was here that the sport of leaping off a bridge with a giant rubber band wrapped around the ankles—bungy-jumping—took root as a commercial enterprise. On a short walk along Shotover and Camp streets you can sign up for anything from white-water rafting and jet-boating to heli-skiing, parachuting, and ATV adventures. Queenstown unabashedly caters to adrenaline junkies, so height, G-force, and thrill factor are emphasized. Want to go on a nice rope swing? Queenstown

has the world's biggest—120 meters (394 feet) long—in the Nevis Canyon; the ride is 120 kph (75 mph). In late June, the Queenstown Winter Festival brings the winter-sport frenzy to a climax, with musical performers, ski-slope antics and races, and serious partying.

If you're not an extreme adventure enthusiast, you might recoil a bit and view the city with a cynical eye. Luckily there's a side to Queenstown that doesn't run on pure adrenaline: a large network of peaceful walks, several world-class golf courses, and you can always find a nice café, have wine by the lake, and sample the cuisine.

GETTING HERE AND AROUND

Highway 6 enters Queenstown from the West Coast; driving time for the 400-km (250-mile) journey from Franz Josef is eight hours. It takes approximately 1½ hours to drive between Queenstown and Wanaka; the drive between Queenstown and Te Anau generally lasts a little over two hours. Bus and airplane service are also available between Christchurch and Queenstown. The town is small and fun for seeing on foot. If you're out and about at night, there are several taxi services available.

AIRPORTS Queenstown Airport. ✉ *Sir Henry Wigley Dr.* ☎ *03/450–9031* ⊕ *www. queenstownairport.com.*

AIRPORT TRANSFERS Super Shuttle Queenstown. ☎ *09/522–5100, 0800/748–885 toll-free in NZ* ⊕ *www.supershuttle. co.nz.*

BUS CONTACTS Frankton Bus Shelter. ✉ *Kawarau Rd., Frankton* **InterCity Coachlines.** ☎ *03/442–4922 in Queenstown* ⊕ *www.intercity.co.nz .* **The Station - Queenstown.** ✉ *At Camp and Shotover Sts.*

RENTAL CARS Apex. ✉ *26 Shotover St.* ☎ *03/442–8040* ⊕ *www.apexrentals.co.nz.* **GO Rentals.** ✉ *20 Lucas Pl.* ☎ *03/441–4340* ⊕ *www.gorentals.co.nz.*

TOURS

COMBINATION TRIPS

Nomad Safaris

DRIVING TOURS | FAMILY | Nomad Safaris runs half-day 4WD trips to the old gold-rush settlements (or their remains), Skippers Canyon and Macetown. Try your hand at gold panning—they don't plant gold so any success or disappointment is genuine. Another off-roading trip takes you to see some of the areas filmed for the *Lord of the Rings* trilogy, and there's also the option of booking a combo tour that includes Shotover Jet. All tours include a tea/coffee stop. ✉ *37 Shotover St.* ☎ *03/442–6699, 0800/688–222* ⊕ *www.nomadsafaris.co.nz* 🖂 *From NZ$195.*

Queenstown Heritage Tours

GUIDED TOURS | Take a historical tour to Skippers Canyon in Queenstown Heritage's comfortable air-conditioned vehicles with delicious snacks. They also run separate wine-lovers tours in Gibbston Valley in the afternoon. If you book both as a combo it's cheaper, and includes lunch and tastings at three wineries. ✉ *Unit 10, 174 Glenda Dr.* ☎ *03/409–0949* ⊕ *www.queenstown-heritage.co.nz* 🖂 *From NZ$140.*

Real Journeys

SPECIAL-INTEREST | For a wide choice of fly-drive-cruise tour options to Milford and Doubtful sounds from Queenstown, Te Anau, and Milford, check out Real Journeys. ■TIP→ **Do the overnight cruise if you really want to experience both sounds at their best; early in the morning and in the evening.** The Doubtful Sound cruise is longer and more remote. The boat's engines are cut for a moment of silence, and what a moment it is—makes you realize how little true silence most of us have in our lives. The food's superb, too, and is all-inclusive. ✉ *Steamer Wharf, Beach St.* ☎ *0800/656–501 within NZ, 03/442–7500* ⊕ *www.realjourneys.co.nz.*

VISITOR INFORMATION

CONTACTS Queenstown i-SITE Visitor Information Centre. ✉ *Clocktower Bldg., 22 Shotover St., and Camp St.* ☎ *03/442–4100* ⊕ *www.queenstownisite.com.*

◉ Sights

The vineyards across Central Otago and into the Queenstown and Wanaka areas constitute the world's southernmost wine region, and the country's highest, and are particularly noted for producing outstanding Pinot Noir. Specifically, Bannockburn, Gibbston Valley, and Lowburn are home to big plantings. There are more than 90 wineries in the region with more than 4,774 acres planted in vines.

Amisfield Winery & Bistro

WINERY/DISTILLERY | Step into this expansive winery and bistro and enjoy stunning lake and mountain views. Both the wines and the restaurant have earned accolades over the years. Go for a memorable "Trust the Chef" lunch or dinner. Wine-tastings are available at the cellar door; the Pinot Noir, aromatic whites such as Riesling and Pinot Gris, and the Methode Traditionelle are all worth sampling. ✉ *10 Lake Hayes Rd.* ☎ *03/442–0556* ⊕ *www.amisfield.co.nz* 🖂 *Tasting NZ$10, refunded with purchase of bottle.*

Chard Farm

WINERY/DISTILLERY | The Chard Farm vineyard perches on a rare flat spot on the edge of the Kawarau Gorge, not far from Gibbston Valley and opposite AJ Hackett Bungy. Its location and access road are beautiful and you'll find an excellent portfolio of wines to taste including Pinot Noir, Chardonnay, Gewürztraminer, Pinot Grigio, and Riesling. ✉ *Chard Rd., RD 1* ☎ *03/442–6110* ⊕ *www.chardfarm.co.nz.*

Fear Factory

LOCAL INTEREST | A scary addition to the adventure scene in Queenstown, Fear Factory challenges you to walk through their haunted house in the center of town. Not for kids—thousands of people

Queenstown

| A | B | C | D | E |

Sights ▼

1 Amisfield
  Winery & Bistro..........**E1**
2 Chard Farm..............**E4**
3 Fear Factory.............**C2**
4 Gibbston Valley
  Wines.....................**E1**
5 Mt. Difficulty.............**E4**
6 Queenstown Gardens...**C5**
7 Skippers Canyon........**D1**
8 Skyline Gondola.........**B1**
9 T.S.S *Earnslaw*...........**E5**

Restaurants ▼

1 The Bathhouse...........**C4**
2 The Bunker...............**C3**
3 Fergburger................**C2**
4 Ivy & Lola's
  Kitchen & Bar...........**B3**
5 Jervois Steak House....**C2**
6 Vudu Cafe and Larder...**C3**
7 Winnie's...................**C3**
8 Yonder....................**C3**

Hotels ▼

1 Blanket Bay **A4**
2 Camp Glenorchy
  Eco Retreat..............**A4**
3 Eichardt's
  Private Hotel **C3**
4 Heritage
  Queenstown.............**A4**
5 QT Queenstown.........**A3**
6 Queenstown Park
  Boutique Hotel..........**C1**
7 The Rees..................**E4**
8 The Sherwood **E4**

have chickened out (just yell chicken and you don't have to continue). It's best to do this half-hour activity with friends. Under 15 must be accompanied by an adult. ⊠ *54 Shotover St.* ⊕ *www.fearfactory.co.nz* ✉ *NZ$40.*

★ Gibbston Valley Wines

WINERY/DISTILLERY | The wine-making industry in Central Otago began with the vines that were first planted here. The best-known vineyard in Central Otago, Gibbston Valley Wines is a beautiful spot for lunch and wine tasting. There are cheese platters and tasty sandwiches through to a full à la carte menu with wine recommendations. You can even taste wines in a cool, barrel-lined cave with cave tours on the hour. If you can't get out to the winery, Gibbston Valley also has a café in Arrowtown, where you'll get hint of what you've missed. ⊠ *1820 State Hwy. 6, RD1, Gibbston* ⊹ *20-min drive east of Queenstown on State Hwy. 6* ☎ *03/442–6910* ⊕ *www.gibbstonvalley.com* ✉ *Wine-cave tour and tasting NZ$19.*

Mt. Difficulty

WINERY/DISTILLERY | You could spend a lot of time in the tasting room with the large range of good wines on offer here, or you can keep it simple and grab one of their tasting trays, featuring a selection complete with notes. There are some sweet dessert wines that can only be bought at the cellar door to consider as well. Make sure you stay for lunch. Staff are friendly and know their stuff, and the view is pure Central Otago. ⊠ *73 Felton Rd., Cromwell* ☎ *03/445–3445* ⊕ *www.mtdifficulty.nz.*

Queenstown Gardens

GARDEN | The public Queenstown Gardens on the waterfront peninsula are always worth a quiet stroll. It's one of the few places in Queenstown that hasn't changed. There's an easy path to wander along to wear off some of those calories you've consumed during your stay. Bring a disc and have a toss at the country's first Frisbee golf course. ⊠ *Park St.*

Skippers Canyon

CANYON | One of the enduring attractions in the area is the drive up Skippers Canyon. Harking back to the days when the hills were filled with gold diggers, the Skippers Road was hand carved out of rock, and it reaches into the deep recesses of the Shotover Valley. It's breathtakingly gorgeous but you could also be breathtakingly scared: there's a good reason that rental car companies don't insure you if you drive on this twisty, narrow, unpaved road fraught with slips and vertical drops. It's usually best to visit this place on a tour. ⊠ *Skippers Rd.*

Skyline Gondola

VIEWPOINT | Get the lay of the land by taking the Skyline Gondola up to the heights of Bob's Peak, 1,425 feet above the lake, for a smashing panoramic view of the town and the Remarkables. You can also get there by walking the One Mile Creek Trail. Once there, watch the paragliders jump off the summit for their slow cruise back down to lake level. There are restaurants at the summit (there's a great buffet) plus a *Kiwi Haka, or* Māori song-and-dance show, in the evening. For something a little faster, there's a luge ride, weather permitting. If even that isn't exciting enough, you can bungy jump from the summit terminal. ⊠ *Brecon St.* ☎ *03/441–0101* ⊕ *www.skyline.co.nz* ✉ *From NZ$35.*

★ T.S.S. *Earnslaw*

FARM/RANCH | **FAMILY** | This lovely old ship is more than 100 years old, and one of the world's few coal-fired steamships still operating. It's in superb condition partly because it's only been on this lake and the water's so pure. T.S.S. (Twin Screw Steamer) *Earnslaw* runs across to Walter Peak and back on a 1½-hour cruise. You can do a stopover at **Walter Peak High Country Farm** and watch a sheep shearing and farm dog demonstration. But the best trip is to go to the Colonel's

Homestead Restaurant for dinner (or lunch); it's an exceptional buffet—make sure you leave room for the sumptuous selection of desserts. The cruise back into Queenstown's particularly beautiful when the sun's going down. ⊠ *Steamer Wharf, Beach St.* ☎ *03/442–7500, 0800/656–501 NZ only* ⊕ *www.realjourneys.co.nz* ⚓ *Cruises from NZ$72.*

🍴 Restaurants

At first glance Queenstown's little side streets seem full of party bars and pizza joints, but that's because all the really great spots are hidden away or down at Steamer Wharf, which juts out into Lake Wakatipu. Some places aren't easy to find, so ask if you can't find what you're looking for.

The Bathhouse

$$$ | ECLECTIC | Built to commemorate the coronation of King George V, this early 1900s bathhouse on the beach now turns out breakfast, lunch, fresh scones, tapas, and dinner from its tiny kitchen. Many people find it by accident as they walk to the Queenstown Gardens, but it's worth seeking out deliberately. **Known for:** unbeatable location; log fire in winter; some of the best staff in town. ⑤ *Average main: NZ$30* ⊠ *38 Marine Parade* ☎ *03/442–5625* ⊕ *www.bathhouse.co.nz.*

The Bunker

$$$$ | ECLECTIC | A loungy vibe with log fires, leather armchairs, and an impressive wine list make the Bunker a particularly cozy dining location. Dinner is an all-night affair, especially if you continue with drinks in their upstairs bar; there's even a special "Taste of the South" degustation menu if you really want to indulge. **Known for:** late night hotspot; excellent wine pairings; James Bond-esque vibe. ⑤ *Average main: NZ$44* ⊠ *14 Cow La.* ☎ *03/441–8030* ⊕ *www.thebunker.co.nz.*

Fergburger

$$ | BURGER | A Queenstown institution, the famous Fergburger gets mentioned in media around the world. It began life as a burger bar serving from a hole in the wall and kept growing; now there's a permanent queue stretching outside. **Known for:** enormous and legendary burgers; late night dining; long lines at lunch. ⑤ *Average main: NZ$15* ⊠ *42 Shotover St.* ☎ *03/441–1232* ⊕ *www.fergburger.com.*

Ivy & Lola's Kitchen & Bar

$$$$ | ECLECTIC | Feast your eyes on a collection of relics from the 1940s to '60s, right down to the mismatched crockery and enjoy good food, great service, and a lovely atmosphere. The cuisine here is a delightfully eclectic mix, with flavors from NZ and around the world. **Known for:** excellent lamb of the day; generous portions; lakeside dining. ⑤ *Average main: NZ$35* ⊠ *Steamer Wharf, 88 Beech St.* ☎ *03/441–8572* ⊕ *www.ivyandlolas.com.*

★ Jervois Steak House

$$$$ | STEAKHOUSE | Dine here and find out why New Zealand is so proud of its beef and lamb: you could take it to the next level with the Wagyu beef, but honestly it's hard to beat the standard Jervois fillet, with onion rings on the side and delicious sauces. Steak is the undisputed hero here, but like the great American steak houses on which Jervois models itself, there's fabulous seafood too, and even a quality vegetarian menu. **Known for:** pricey cuts of beef; extremely knowledgeable staff; elegant steak-house atmosphere. ⑤ *Average main: NZ$45* ⊠ *Sofitel Complex, 8 Duke St.* ☎ *03/442–6263* ⊕ *www.jervoissteakhouse.co.nz.*

Vudu Cafe and Larder

$$ | CAFÉ | You'll be fighting the locals for a breakfast seat at this Queenstown institution, thanks to its lakefront seating and delicious array of counter food. Eggs Benedict with a classic coffee is probably the most common breakfast order in New Zealand, and this is perhaps the best in the area. **Known for:** big breakfast crowds; coffee to go (and enjoy by the lake); healthy options. ⑤ *Average main:*

NZ$20 ✉ *16 Rees St.* ☎ *03/441–8370* ⊕ *www.vudu.co.nz* ⊘ *No dinner.*

Winnie's

$$$ | **PIZZA** | A long-serving local favorite restaurant and bar with the winning combination of excellent pizza, pool tables, and beer. At night this place transforms into a happening spot extremely popular with backpackers. **Known for:** late night parties; retractable roof; warm winter hideout. $ *Average main: NZ$28* ✉ *7 The Mall, Mall St.* ☎ *03/442–8635* ⊕ *www. winnies.co.nz.*

Yonder

$$$ | **INTERNATIONAL** | In a lovely old cottage in the middle of town, Yonder comes with outdoor seating in front, a café-style area in the middle, and finally a restaurant, bar, and live venue in the rear. Their menu is inspired by the countries of origin of the chefs, and changes to match the seasons and what's fresh. **Known for:** eclectic global menu; friendly to those with dietary restrictions; bright, welcoming atmosphere. $ *Average main: NZ$28* ✉ *14 Church St.* ☎ *03/409–0994* ⊕ *www.yonderqt.co.nz* ⊘ *No dinner Mon. and Tues.*

Hotels

Blanket Bay

$$$$ | **B&B/INN** | Near the end of a long road, this imposing schist lodge is surrounded by thousands of acres of sheep-station land. **Pros:** spectacular property; unbeatable views; celebrity hideaway. **Cons:** 40-minute drive to Queenstown; dining area outdated; very expensive. $ *Rooms from: NZ$1750* ✉ *4191 Glenorchy-Queenstown Rd.* ☎ *03/441–0115* ⊕ *www.blanketbay.com* ⇗ *12 rooms* ⦿ *Some meals.*

★ Camp Glenorchy Eco Retreat

$$$$ | **RENTAL** | **FAMILY** | Built to the exacting standards of the Living Building Challenge, Camp Glenorchy is an inspiration to those with an interest in sustainable building and living. **Pros:**

huge outdoor fireplace; inspirational and educational ethos; beautiful decor, art, and furniture throughout. **Cons:** 45-minutes from Queenstown; shower time is limited to save energy; eco-living comes with a price tag. $ *Rooms from: NZ$395* ✉ *34 Oban St., Glenorchy* ☎ *03/409–0401* ⊕ *www.theheadwaters.co.nz* ⇗ *14 rooms* ⦿ *No meals.*

Eichardt's Private Hotel

$$$$ | **HOTEL** | Once patronized by gold miners during the 1860s, Eichardt's is now an elite boutique resort hotel. **Pros:** centrally located; great service; exceptional house bar. **Cons:** breakfast restaurant is small and open to public; can get some noise from neighbors; busy street front, especially at sunset. $ *Rooms from: NZ$1500* ✉ *2 Marine Parade* ☎ *03/441–0450* ⊕ *www.eichardts. com* ⇗ *10 rooms* ⦿ *Breakfast.*

Heritage Queenstown

$$$$ | **HOTEL** | Situated at the bottom of Fernhill, the Heritage is quieter than other local hotels and has panoramic views of the Remarkables and Lake Wakatipu. **Pros:** great service; pleasant rooms; very comfortable beds. **Cons:** 10-plus minute walk to downtown; due for a refurbishment; some rooms lack views. $ *Rooms from: NZ$354* ✉ *91 Fernhill Rd.* ☎ *03/450–1500* ⊕ *www.heritagehotels. co.nz* ⇗ *175 rooms* ⦿ *No meals.*

★ QT Queenstown

$$$$ | **HOTEL** | This genuinely fun and quirky hotel with countless small touches ensures a memorable stay. **Pros:** very close to town; large rooms and bathrooms; fun and fanciful decor. **Cons:** not all rooms offer lake views; no gym; limited parking. $ *Rooms from: NZ$485* ✉ *30 Brunswick St.* ☎ *03/450–3450* ⊕ *www. qthotelsandresorts.com* ⇗ *69 rooms* ⦿ *No meals.*

Queenstown Park Boutique Hotel

$$$$ | **HOTEL** | This plush hotel is located in the center of town and you can walk to the lake, shopping, dining, and tour departure points in just five minutes. **Pros:** great location; tasty predinner drinks and canapes; amazing hospitality. **Cons:** street-view rooms can be noisy; limited parking; no gym or pool. ⑤ *Rooms from: NZ$530* ✉ *21 Robins Rd.* ☎ *03/441–8441* ⊕ *www.queens-townparkhotel.co.nz* ⊋ *19 rooms* |◯| *No meals.*

The Rees

$$$$ | **HOTEL** | Named for Queenstown's first European settler who oversaw the birth of the town during the 1860s gold rush, accommodations here range from hotel rooms, and apartments, to multibedroom lakeside residences. **Pros:** exceptional restaurant and wine selection; hourly shuttles to town; amazing wine lounge. **Cons:** quite far from the town center; no pool; no air-conditioning. ⑤ *Rooms from: NZ$355* ✉ *377 Frankton Rd.* ☎ *03/450–1100* ⊕ *www.therees.co.nz* ⊋ *155 rooms* |◯| *No meals.*

The Sherwood

$$ | **HOTEL** | Built on the bones of an older motor inn, this hotel has reinvented itself as an eco-conscious alternative to the standard hotel experience. **Pros:** great lake views (on request); wonderfully repurposed property; focus on relaxation and recharging. **Cons:** rooms are quite dark; far from town center; can be noisy when there's live music. ⑤ *Rooms from: NZ$200* ✉ *554 Frankton Rd.* ☎ *03/450–1090* ⊕ *sherwoodqueenstown.nz* ⊋ *78 rooms* |◯| *No meals.*

♥ Nightlife

After days spent testing limits, visitors cram Queenstown's clubs and bars, and often end up mingling with the friendly locals next to fireplaces, and catching up again as they walk between the popular venues, which are all close together. Grab a copy of the free weekly paper the *MountainScene* or check out the *Source* magazine, a monthly gig guide available in most cafés and bars or on Facebook.

Bardeaux

WINE BARS—NIGHTLIFE | In winter Bardeaux has that upmarket mountain-après-ski atmosphere; even in summer there's a fair chance the fire will be roaring. There's a wide selection of whiskey and wine. They know how to fix you up a cocktail at this pleasing bar that's good for a quiet, intimate evening. ✉ *Eureka Arcade off The Mall* ☎ *03/442–8284* ⊕ *www.good-group.co.nz.*

Minus 5° Ice Bar

BARS/PUBS | Ice bars have become popular over the past few years, and it's great fun if you've never tried one—even just for the beautiful ice sculptures alone. They deck you out in jackets and gloves prior to entering. In summer it's a good reminder of how close to Antarctica you are, and in winter it just adds to that alpine resort experience. It costs NZ$30 to get in, but that includes a cocktail. ✉ *Steamer Wharf, 88 Beach St.* ☎ *03/442–6050* ⊕ *www.minus5icebar.com.*

Searle Lane

BARS/PUBS | With its roaring fire, good food, and quirky decor, Searle Lane is a popular Queenstown spot. There's plenty of beer on tap and a good selection of wine by the glass. They do a mean cocktail, too. The food is made for sharing with hearty choices; their specialty is rotisserie chicken, which is seriously good. ✉ *15 Church St.* ☎ *03/441–3934* ⊕ *www.searlelane.co.nz.*

Smiths Craft Beer House

BREWPUBS/BEER GARDENS | This bar offers the best range of New Zealand and international beer in town, including the stand-out local beer, Queenstown's own Altitude Brewing. There's a great pub food menu of burgers and sandwiches, and a nice balcony from which to enjoy the hustle and bustle of Queenstown. ✉ *53 Shotover St.* ☎ *03/409–2337.*

The World Bar

BARS/PUBS | This is a great place for drinks in the sun or inside by the huge open fire on colder days. Later in the evening, it turns into a rowdy venue, with DJs playing 6 nights a week, and an acoustic open mic on Sunday nights. The famed cocktails are served in teapots, and you can get good gastro pub food throughout the day and early evening. ⊠ *12 Church St.* ☎ *03/450–0008* ⊕ *www.theworldbar. co.nz.*

🏃 Activities

You'll find many people raving about their bungy-jumping experience or their jet-boat tour from the day before. Any activity you choose around Queenstown will bring you deep into the scenery that you can only ogle from the wharf.

BUNGY JUMPING

AJ Hackett Bungy

FLYING/SKYDIVING/SOARING | This is where bungy began in New Zealand, at the original jump site: Kawarau Bridge, 20 minutes from Queenstown on State Highway 6. Even if you don't plan on taking the leap it's worth heading there to watch from the viewing decks. There's a zipride, too, that's way easier on the nerves but still gives something to write home about. Those who graduate from the 142-foot plunge might like to test themselves on the Nevis Bungy, suspended 440 feet above the Nevis River, or try out what they claim is the world's biggest swing. If you're short on time, there's always the *Ledge* by the Skyline Gondola where you can also jump or swing. Be sure to check age, height, and weight requirements. ⊠ *The Station, Camp and Shotover Sts.* ☎ *0800/286–4958 NZ only, 03/450–1300* ⊕ *www.bungy.co.nz* ⊠ *From NZ$205.*

Shotover Canyon Swing

LOCAL SPORTS | For those who think bungy jumping doesn't keep the adrenaline pumping long enough, the Shotover Canyon Swing gives a terrifying jump with an added scenic boost. Choose your jump style—go forward, backward, or tied to a chair—and leave the edge of a cliff 358 feet above the Shotover Canyon. Price includes transfers to/from town, and age, height, and weight requirements apply. ⊠ *34 Shotover St.* ☎ *03/442–6990* ⊕ *www.canyonswing.co.nz* ⊠ *NZ$249.*

HIKING

Several scenic walks branch out from town. For a history lesson with your ramble, head to the **Time Walk,** entering through an iron gateway on the Queenstown Hill trail. Narrative panels line the route; it takes about two hours, and you'll feel good when you see the view at the top. The **Ben Lomond Track** takes you to one of the highest peaks in the basin. Take the gondola to the Bob's Peak summit, then follow signs to the saddle and the steep climb to the peak (5,730 feet). You'll need to be reasonably fit and this can be a full-day walk, so make sure you bring all the necessary supplies.

★ Queenstown Trail

BICYCLING | For a wonderful journey around the Queenstown area, take a look at the trail map (see website) of this 120-km (74.5-mile) walking and cycling trail and start planning. The trail is well built and there are plenty of places to hire all the biking equipment you need (also on its website). The trail takes you over to Arrowtown and the wineries of Gibbston, past two lakes and three rivers, over some interesting bridges, and always through stunning scenery. You can do it all or just parts of it. Queenstown is the lowest point on the trail so if you want to make it a little easier for yourself, start your trip in Arrowtown. ⊕ *www.queenstowntrail.co.nz.*

HORSE TREKKING

High Country Horses

HORSEBACK RIDING | Glenorchy is already an incredibly peaceful and beautiful place, and it's even better when enjoyed from horseback. High Country Horses offers half-day, full-day, and overnight tours, including a *Lord of the Rings* filming location tour that wanders through native beech forest where climactic battle scenes from *The Lord of the Rings: The Fellowship of the Ring* were shot. They cater to all riding abilities and offer transfers from Queenstown. Maximum rider weight applies. Rides start at NZ$175. ⊠ *243 Priory Rd., Glenorchy* ☎ *03/442–9915* ⊕ *www.highcountryhorses.nz.*

Moonlight Stables

HORSEBACK RIDING | Moonlight Stables offers a 1½-hour ride with spectacular views of the mountains and rivers around the Wakatipu–Arrow Basin. Ride across an 800-acre deer farm in Australian stock saddles and western saddles. Both novice and experienced riders are welcome, and private rides can be arranged. Transportation from Queenstown is provided; allow 2½ hours return. ⊠ *69 Morven Ferry Rd., Arrow Junction* ☎ *03/442–1229* ⊕ *www.moonlightstables.co.nz* 🖭 *From NZ$120.*

JET-BOAT RIDES

★ Dart River Wilderness Jet

BOATING | **FAMILY** | With Dart River you can get an unrivaled look at rugged Mount Aspiring National Park, one of the most spectacular parts of South Island. Their route includes jet-boating on the upper and lower Dart River, along with a bit of walking and a back-road tour of the "Paradise" area. The Funyak option takes you upstream by jet-boat, then you paddle gently downstream, exploring the Rockburn Chasm on the way. Start your adventure from their office in Glenorchy, or catch a shuttle bus, departing daily from Queenstown for the 45-minute ride to the boats. Rates include transfer. ⊠ *45 Mull St., Glenorchy* ☎ *0800/327–853 NZ only, 03/442–9992* ⊕ *www.dartriver.co.nz* 🖭 *NZ$269.*

Hydro Attack

BOATING | Strap into the F-16–style cockpit of this watercraft styled to look like a shark and fly across and under Lake Wakatipu. This is the world's first commercial operation using the Seabreacher X watercraft, and your expert pilot will tailor your trip to suit your comfort levels, from scenic cruise to wild ride. Riders are restricted by height and weight and you need to be somewhat flexible to board the craft. Not recommended if you are subject to seasickness. ⊠ *Lapsley Butson Wharf, Beach St.* ☎ *027/477–9074* ⊕ *www.hydroattack.co.nz* 🖭 *NZ$149.*

KJet

BOATING | With the sun sparkling off the lake, wind whistling past, and traveling way faster than you had imagined, this is good holiday fun. KJet takes you 42 km (27 miles) on Lake Wakatipu and down two rivers, the Kawarau and Shotover, with some exciting spins along the way. Boats leave from the Main Town Pier where there's also an interesting underwater observatory. Reservations recommended. ⊠ *Main Town Pier, Marine Parade* ☎ *03/442–6142* ⊕ *www.kjet.co.nz* 🖭 *NZ$135.*

Shotover Jet

BOATING | Shotover Jet's famous red boats lead high-speed, heart-stopping rides in the Shotover River canyons; it's got exclusive rights to operate in these waters. The boat pirouettes within inches of canyon walls. The boats are based at the Shotover Jet Beach beneath the historic Edith Cavell Bridge, a 10-minute drive from Queenstown. If you don't have transport, a free shuttle makes frequent daily runs. Reservations are essential. ⊠ *Gorge Rd., over Edith Cavell Bridge at Arthur's Point* ☎ *03/442–8570, 0800/746-868 NZ only* ⊕ *www.shotoverjet.com* 🖭 *From NZ$155.*

MOTORSPORTS

Highlands Motorsport Park

AUTO RACING | Fulfill your dream of being a race car driver at Highlands. There's a range of activities including go-kart racing, self-drive hot laps, and ride-along hot laps. The Highlands Taxi is a Porsche Cayenne Turbo driven by a professional

Jet-boats offer a thrillingly wet way to enjoy the Queenstown area's natural beauty.

racer. The first lap is taken slowly and the driver talks about the facility, the second lap is full speed ahead. If you want to go faster, there is also a supercar option, and a range of purpose-built race cars. Located in Cromwell, Highlands Motorsport Park is a 45-minute drive from Queenstown on State Highway 6, and you can call Highlands to arrange a free shuttle from Queenstown. The Highlands National Motorsport Museum is here, too. ⊠ *Corner State Hwy. 6 and Sandflat Rd., Cromwell* ☎ *03/445-4052* ⊕ *www. highlands.co.nz* ⌨ *From NZ$129.*

RAFTING

Rafting is generally an adult thrill, with age restrictions for children. You'll need your swimsuit and a towel, but all other gear, including wet suit, life jacket, helmet, and wet-suit booties, are provided by the rafting companies. Instructors spend quite a bit of time on safety issues and paddling techniques before you launch.

★ **Go Orange Rafting**

WHITE-WATER RAFTING | This company runs white-water rafting in the Queenstown area year-round, with trips on the Shotover (grade 3–5) and Kawarau (grade 2–3) rivers. You can double the action with either a helicopter or jet-boat combo and save on the individual price of both tours. Prices start at NZ$199. ⊠ *35 Shotover St.* ☎ *03/442-7340* ⊕ *www. goorange.co.nz.*

Serious Fun River Surfing

WATER SPORTS | This is serious—for the adventurous and those with surfing or water experience. You'll get kitted out in a full wet suit, helmet, life jacket, and fins. There's an introduction to river surfing on calm water first. Then grab your bodyboard and prepare to surf the waves of Queenstown's stunning Kawarau River. Where your guide ends up taking you will depend on the conditions but the Kawarau River has plenty of white water. They'll pick you up from town. ⊠ *37 Shotover St.* ☎ *03/442-5262* ⊕ *www. riverboarding.co.nz* ⌨ *NZ$225.*

SCENIC FLIGHTS
Over the Top Helicopters
FLYING/SKYDIVING/SOARING | Over the Top Helicopters runs a diverse selection of flights in their executive-style helicopters, including glacier and alpine ski slope landings, and scenic tours above Queenstown, the Remarkables, Fiordland, and Milford and Doubtful sounds. They'll also deliver you to fly-fishing spots absolutely miles from anywhere, or take you heli-skiing or on ecotours as far away as Stewart Island. ✉ *Blue Hangar, 10 Tex Smith La.* ☎ *03/442–2233, 0800/123–359* ⊕ *www. flynz.co.nz* ✉ *From NZ$290 per person.*

SKIING
Coronet Peak
SKIING/SNOWBOARDING | Queenstown's original ski resort, 20 minutes from town, rocks day and night to a ski and snowboard crowd that returns year after year. Not only is it accessible, but it also has a veritable army of ski guns to keep the snow topped up. It has a skiable area of 700 acres, a vertical drop of 1,360 feet, a high-speed six-seater, two express quads, and a T-bar, as well as four learner conveyor lifts in the learners area. The season usually runs June to October. Night skiing is available on Wednesday, Friday, and Saturday night from late June to early September. Ski shuttles depart regularly from Queenstown Snow Centre. ✉ *Coronet Peak Station Rd.* ☎ *03/441–1516* ⊕ *www.coronetpeak. co.nz* ✉ *Day pass NZ$119.*

The Remarkables
SKIING/SNOWBOARDING | FAMILY | Just across the valley, the Remarkables is a higher ski area that's a bit more of a drive but has something to suit all abilities, from seven terrain parks to wide sunny slopes to serious black runs. The vertical drop here is 1,160 feet and it has a fast-speed six-seater, and three quads. It's a great place to take kids with good vantage points to watch them on the learners slopes. It's a 45-minute drive from Queenstown or you can catch the Ski Shuttle from the Queenstown Snow Centre in town. ✉ *The Remarkables Ski Area* ☎ *03/441–1456* ⊕ *www.theremarkables.co.nz* ✉ *NZ$119.*

SKYDIVING
NZONE Skydive
FLYING/SKYDIVING/SOARING | Here's a different way of taking in the view of Queenstown—from a tandem skydive. At 15,000 feet the Earth is already taking on that round from-out-of-space look about it that says you're a long way up. You don't have to jump from that high: there are 12,000- and 9,000-feet options. Either way it's an unforgettable experience, helped by Jumpmasters who make you feel at ease (relatively speaking). Weight restrictions apply. ✉ *35 Shotover St.* ☎ *03/442–5867* ⊕ *www.nzoneskydive. co.nz* ✉ *From NZ$299.*

ZIP-LINING
Ziptrek Ecotours
ZIP LINING | With Ziptrek you can zip every which way (upside down if you want) among the trees on the hills above Queenstown. It's a very scenic adventure and as each zip line stops at a tree platform, you learn about the ecology of the area. Most of all, it's good fun; but not for anyone who's scared of heights. Not suitable for children under six. ✉ *45 Camp St.* ☎ *03/441–2102, 0800/947–873 NZ only* ⊕ *www.ziptrek.com* ✉ *From NZ$145.*

Arrowtown

22 km (14 miles) northeast of Queenstown, 105 km (66 miles) south of Wanaka.

Arrowtown is tucked into a corner at the foot of the steep Crown Range. It's a quaint village that takes pride in the history of the area, with around 70 buildings from the original gold rush, a partially restored Chinese village from the 1880s, and a small but fantastic museum. Jack Tewa, or Māori Jack, as he was known,

A former gold-rush town, Arrowtown now only sees gold in the autumn leaves.

found gold along the Arrow River in 1861, and when William Fox, an American, was seen selling large quantities of the precious metal in nearby Clyde shortly afterward, the hunt was on. Eventually a large party of prospectors stumbled on Fox and his team of 40 miners. The secret was out, miners rushed to stake their claims, and Arrowtown was born. On the first gold escort in January 1863 a whopping 12,000 ounces of gold were carried out. At the height of the rush there were more than 30,000 hardy souls in this tiny settlement. After the gold rush ended in 1865, the place became another sleepy rural town until tourism created a second boom.

Each April, Arrowtown celebrates the Autumn Festival when the trees are at their most spectacular, and includes the NZ Gold Panning championships. On a stroll along **Buckingham Street,** you can stop in the old post and telegraph office, still open for business. Take time to explore some of the lanes and arcades, filled with cafés and boutique shops,

drop in to the Jade & Opal Factory shop to see hand carving done on-site and to Patagonia chocolates to see chocolate being made; as if that's not enough the ice-cream there's delicious, too (below Buckingham Street on Ramshaw Lane).

GETTING HERE AND AROUND
Arrowtown is a 20-minute drive from Queenstown, and you can take a bus there. Exploring the town is easily and enjoyably done on foot. If you'd like to venture out toward the old gold-mining settlement Macetown, you can walk or bike if you're a hearty sort (it's 16 km [10 miles] and entails 22 river crossings). A great way to explore the region is in a 4WD vehicle. Nomad Safaris provides a number of 4WD tour options. For a beautiful start to the day go up in a balloon and see Arrowtown and the Wakatipu Basin from the air.

The local bus network, Orbus, is NZ$10 per trip from the airport, NZ$5 for other trips, or NZ$2 per trip with a GoCard. The card costs NZ$5 and has a minimum top up of NZ$10. It's definitely worth getting the card if you plan on riding the bus more than once or twice. Depending on your destination, you may need to switch buses at the Frankton hub.

BUS COMPANIES Orbus Queenstown.
☎ *0800/672–8778* ⊕ *www.orc.govt.nz.*

VISITOR INFORMATION

CONTACTS Arrowtown Visitor Information Centre. ✉ *Lakes District Museum, 49 Buckingham St.* ☎ *03/442–1824* ⊕ *www. arrowtown.com.*

◉ Sights

Chinese Settlement

HISTORIC SITE | FAMILY | In a less-visited part of the town is the former Chinese settlement. Chinese miners were common on the goldfields, brought in to raise a flagging local economy after the gold rush abated, but local prejudice from resident Europeans forced them to live in their own separate enclave. Some of their tiny 19th-century buildings, which have been restored, were built of sod, which endures well in the dry climate; others were built of layered schist stone, with roofs of corrugated iron or tussock thatch. Ah Lum's store (also restored) was built in a style typical of the Canton Delta region of China and operated until 1972. The settlement is a worthwhile part of any day-walk in the area. ✉ *Bush Creek, west end of town* ☞ *Free.*

★ Lakes District Museum

MUSEUM | FAMILY | Don't leave Arrowtown without dropping in to this small but very cleverly constructed museum. It gives a great insight into the history of the area, with artifacts of the gold-rush days, and even a whole streetscape underground, complete with Victorian schoolroom, bakery, and blacksmith. There's also an information center, small bookstore, and gallery. You can even rent a pan for NZ$3 and get gold-panning tips to try your luck in the nearby Arrow River. When your patience frays and your hands go icy, keep in mind that a hobby prospector

found a 10 oz. nugget in this very river in 2006. (He sold it on eBay for NZ$15,000.) ✉ *49 Buckingham St.* ☎ *03/442–1824* ⊕ *www.museumqueenstown.com* ☞ *NZ$10.*

🍴 Restaurants

The Chop Shop Food Merchants

$$$ | INTERNATIONAL | Tucked away in a back alley, locals don't want you to know about the Chop Shop for fear they won't get a seat for themselves. They serve an eclectic mix of international dishes for breakfast and lunch, including some good spicy options. **Known for:** strong coffee; Turkish eggs; very busy so waits are common. ⑤ *Average main: NZ$25* ✉ *Arrow La.* ☎ *03/442–1116.*

★ La Rumbla

$$$ | TAPAS | With the owners either cooking in the kitchen or out front making sure this is the best experience it can be, this is one of those rare places that's got all the elements right: food, service, and atmosphere. It's a tapas restaurant, but with generous servings; the food is a mixture of Spanish and all sorts of interesting savory influences. **Known for:** great cocktails; good vegan options; reservations usually necessary. ⑤ *Average main: NZ$30* ✉ *54 Buckingham St.* ☎ *03/442–0509* ⊕ *www.larumbla.co.nz* ☉ *Closed Mon.*

Patagonia Chocolates

$ | SOUTH AMERICAN | FAMILY | Owned by a local Argentine couple who missed the desserts of their homeland, Patagonia is the best place around to buy ice cream, chocolates, cakes, and other sweets. They have locations in Queenstown and Wanaka, too. **Known for:** specialty chocolates; South American confections; chili hot chocolate. ⑤ *Average main: NZ$8* ✉ *31 Ramshaw La.* ☎ *03/409–8636* ⊕ *www.patagoniachocolates.co.nz.*

Provisions of Arrowtown

$$ | CAFÉ | Set in a historic cottage, Provisions gets its name from the range

Fiordland

Tasman Sea

Poison Bay
Mitre Peak ▲
Sutherland Sound
Bligh Sound
Milford Sound
Milford Rd.
Hollyford Track ◆
Routeburn Track ◆
Milford Track
Glenorchy
Fiordland National Park
George Sound
FRANKLIN MTS
Cascade Creek
Queenstown
Caswell Sound
Charles Sound
Knobs Flat
STUART MTS
Nancy Sound
SECRETARY ISLAND
MURCHISON MTS
Lake Te Anau
Te Anau Downs
94
Lake Wakatipu
6
Doubtful Sound
Dragg Head
Dagg Sound
Kepler Track
Te Anau
Punanga Mau o Te Anau/
Te Anau Bird Sanctuary
Garston
Breaksea Sound
RESOLUTION ISLAND
Lake Manapouri
Manapouri
94
Five Fingers Point
Anchor Is
Fiordland National Park
HUNTER MTS
TAKITIMU MTS
Mossburn
Lumsden
Dusky Sound
South Point
West Cape
Lake Monowai
Blackmount
Avondale
94
Balfour
Cape Providence
Chalky Is
CAMERON MTS
Lake Hauroko
Ohai
Nightcaps
Wreys Bush
6
0 — 18 mi
Coal Is
Clifden
Otautau
Winton
0 — 18 km
Lake Poteriteri
Tuatapere
Te Waewae
99
Orepuki
Thornbury
96
Te Waewae Bay

---

of gourmet preserves they make. The welcoming atmosphere and lovely garden make it a delightful place to have breakfast or lunch. **Known for:** pretty garden setting; breakfast supplies to go; legendary sticky buns. ⑤ *Average main: NZ$20* ✉ *65 Buckingham St.* ☎ *03/442–0714* ⊕ *www.provisionsofarrowtown. co.nz.*

🛏 Hotels

★ Arrowtown House Boutique Hotel

$$$$ | B&B/INN | Somewhere between a boutique hotel and a bed-and-breakfast, Arrowtown House offers arguably the best service in Arrowtown. **Pros:** lovely mountain views; quiet, central location; great hosts. **Cons:** hard to get a booking in peak season; quite expensive; style is slightly dated. ⑤ *Rooms from: NZ$530* ✉ *10 Caernarvon St.* ☎ *03/441–6008*

⊕ *www.arrowtownhouse.co.nz* ⤺ *5 rooms* ❙❀❙ *Breakfast.*

Millbrook Resort

$$$$ | RESORT | A 20-minute drive from Queenstown, this glamorous resort has a special appeal for golfers: a 27-hole course first designed by New Zealand professional Sir Bob Charles. **Pros:** terrific golf course; plenty of amenities; several great restaurants. **Cons:** sprawling and somewhat impersonal; hotel rooms are dated; no air-conditioning. ⑤ *Rooms from: NZ$385* ✉ *1124 Malaghans Rd.* ☎ *0800/800–604, 03/441–7000* ⊕ *www. millbrook.co.nz* ⤺ *160 rooms* ❙❀❙ *No meals.*

🍸 Nightlife

The Blue Door

WINE BARS—NIGHTLIFE | What goes on behind the Blue Door? Whiskey, wine, and cocktails, served by knowledgeable and chatty (when it's quiet) staff. Sit in a dark corner near the fire, or at the bar. Set in a beautiful old stone building with candles burning around the room, it's the perfect place for a nightcap before walking back to your accommodation. ✉ *18 Buckingham St.* ☎ *03/442–0415* ⊕ *www. bluedoorbar.co.nz.*

Dorothy Brown's Boutique Cinema and Bar

FILM | It may not have a flashy marquee, but Dorothy Brown's Boutique Cinema and Bar is a memorable movie house. The theater doesn't seat many people, but the chairs are cushy and have plenty of legroom. Better yet, you can get a glass of wine at the fireplace bar and bring it with you, along with a cheeseboard to nibble from, and if you run out, all screenings have an intermission. The schedule mixes Hollywood releases with art and international films and they have 3D screenings here, too. Book ahead—it's popular. ✉ *18 Buckingham St.* ☎ *03/442–1964* ⊕ *www.dorothybrowns. com* 🎫 *NZ$19.*

The Fork and Tap

BARS/PUBS | In this cozy historic building, there are 14 beers and ciders on tap, a great selection of local Central Otago wine, and a hearty pub-style menu for lunch and dinner. If you're looking for a lively spot to enjoy a beer and share stories after a big day of skiing or sightseeing, this is it. Don't sit too close to the fire if you can help it, it can get very hot. ✉ *51 Buckingham St.* ☎ *03/442–1860* ⊕ *www.theforkandtap.co.nz.*

🏃 Activities

There are several spectacular walks—**Tobin's Track, Sawpit Gully,** and the **Lake Hayes Walk**—to raise the fitness levels

and give you a feeling for where you are. You can get details on all of them from the Lakes District Museum Information Centre. For easier ambles take the Arrow River Trail or the Bush Creek Trail. And if you want a real challenge tackle the hike out to the old gold settlement Macetown. Make sure you take your own picnic: although you might hear the Macetown Bakehouse mentioned, be aware the place is a ghost town now and there are only remnants of the settlement.

You can hire a bike from places like Arrowtown Bike Hire or Queenstown Bike Tours. Grab a map or check out ⊕ *www.queenstowntrail.co.nz* and head to Gibbston Valley for lunch or some wine tasting; the trail is well maintained and there are several interesting bridges to cross.

There are also three quite distinct golf courses within a 10-minute drive of Arrowtown that offer some of the most scenic golf holes you'll ever play; the most accessible is the Arrowtown Golf Course, but there's also Millbrook, and the Hills, which need booking well in advance.

Te Anau and Fiordland National Park

175 km (109 miles) southwest of Queenstown.

Lake Te Anau (tay- *ah*-no), which is 53 km (33 miles) long and up to 10 km (6 miles) wide, is the largest lake in New Zealand after Lake Taupo. The town of Te Anau, on the southern shores, serves as a base for Fiordland National Park. From Te Anau, you can set out on sightseeing trips by bus, boat, or plane to Milford and Doubtful sounds, or take off on one of the park's superb hiking trails. Of these, the most accessible to town is the Kepler Track. The town itself is very quiet and

Planning Your Trip to Fiordland

Best Time to Go
Spring and summer (October through April) are the best, but busiest, times to go. Still there are many opportunities to commune quietly with the park, such as kayaking, scuba diving, or hiking. If you only have time for a cruise, it is still well worth the trip; even the drive into Milford in itself is well worth the trip.

Best Ways to Explore
Cruise the sound. Milford and Doubtful sound cruises run all day and include scenic, nature, and overnight trips. Most of Milford's day trips get you close to a waterfall. Kayak on Milford Sound (guided or not) for eye-level views of New Zealand fur seals, penguins, and dolphins. For high-seas adventure, charter a fishing trip in the Tasman Sea.

Walk the Finest Walk. New Zealand's most famous walk, the Milford Track, has been called the "Finest Walk in the World." Take the guided walk option if you want to stay warm and dry and have your meals cooked for you; otherwise it requires a bit of gumption and organization—and boat transport from either end—to complete the four-day track. The experience,

which includes rain forest, glacial lakes, mountains, and several massive waterfalls, like Sutherland Falls (1,904 feet), is worth the effort. There are other wonderful walks, including the 60-km (37-mile) Kepler Track, which is accessible from Te Anau. Sights along this four-day walk include the Luxmore Cave, beech forests, mountains, and rivers.

Scuba. The thick layer of rainwater, pigmented by forest tannins, that sits atop the sounds' saltwater filters the sunlight and simulates deep-sea darkness. This means creatures of the deep in shallow waters. Scuba divers come here for uncommonly accessible glimpses of spiny sea dragons, sea pens, and black coral. If you don't want to suit up, visit the Milford Discovery Centre & Underwater Observatory.

Drive Milford Road. Most visitors drive to the park themselves, traveling the scenic Milford Road. Places to stop and enjoy short walks include Mirror Lake, which lives up to its name on calm days, and the Avenue of the Disappearing Mountain. And don't drive past the Chasm walk in your haste to get to Milford Sound; it's worth the short walk (20-minute round-trip).

rural, but it does have its attractions and is very picturesque. It's busiest in summer; in winter, some cafés and shops close or reduce their hours.

GETTING HERE AND AROUND
BUS CONTACTS InterCity Coachlines.
☎ 03/442–4922 ⊕ www.intercity.co.nz . **Te Anau.** ✉ 2 Miro St.

VISITOR INFORMATION
Fiordland National Park Visitor Centre
✉ Lakefront Dr. ☎ 03/249–7924 ⊕ www. doc.govt.nz.

◉ Sights

★ **Fiordland National Park**
NATIONAL/STATE PARK | Encompassing more than 2 million acres of wilderness, Fiordland is the country's biggest national park. Nearly a million people visit each

year to see playful dolphins and rain forest–coated mountains, but most converge on Milford and Doubtful sounds, the park's stars. Don't worry—the park is massive enough to easily absorb the crowds. The scenery actually quiets them, too: entire boatloads of visitors have been known to just *hush* out on the water. Sand flies and rain (along with your job, breaking news, and the rest of the world) will seem like tiny nuisances when you behold Milford Sound, with Mitre Peak rising along the coast and waterfalls tumbling into the sea. *I see the falls,* said one returning visitor, *and everything just falls away.* ⊕ *www.fiordland.org.nz/about-fiordland/fiordland-national-park.*

Milford Road

SCENIC DRIVE | If there was nothing to see at the end of this road it would still be worth the journey. It's a spectacular route, on one of the highest highways in New Zealand, traveling through mossy beech forests, past waterfalls and grand sweeping valleys. The road is narrow and winding at times, so allow at least 2½ hours. Stop for some great photo ops at Mirror Lakes, Knobs Flat, and Lake Gunn before reaching the Divide, a watershed between rivers flowing both east and west and the starting point for the Routeburn Track. When you reach the **Homer Tunnel** think of the unemployed workers who began building it as a relief project in 1935 using picks and shovels. Before making the trip, check the transit website ⊕ *www.milfordroad.co.nz* or phone ☎ *0800/444–449* for avalanche warnings (snow and trees) and between May and November come equipped with tire chains, which you can rent in any Te Anau service station. ⚠ **There have been a number of accidents on this stretch of road caused by overseas drivers unfamiliar with the conditions driving too fast or on the wrong side of the road.** Take care and drive to the conditions, and if you're just not comfortable, you can always take a bus from Te Anau or Queenstown.

Punanga Manu o Te Anau/Te Anau Bird Sanctuary

NATURE PRESERVE | The lakeshore Te Anau Bird Sanctuary gives you the chance to preview some of the wildlife you're likely to encounter when hiking in Fiordland. The center houses one of New Zealand's rare flightless birds, the takahe, which was once thought to be extinct. The lakeside walk to the center makes for a pleasant one-hour stroll. The birds here have either been injured or involved in captive rearing programs. The injured birds are rehabilitated and sent back to the wild if they're strong enough. Entry's free, but if you have a NZ$1 or NZ$2 coin to donate it helps with the upkeep. ✉ *Manapouri Rd., 1 km (½ mile) west of Te Anau* ☎ *03/249–0200* 💲 *Donation requested.*

Te Anau Glowworm Caves

BODY OF WATER | **FAMILY** | Boats and walkways take you through a maze of caves containing underground whirlpools, waterfalls, and gushing streams. Then you'll reach the inner, quieter part and on the cave walls glowworms shine like constellations in a clear night sky. It's a surreal experience. The caves can only be reached by water. This is a lovely family trip that takes around 2½ hours. Don't miss it if you're going through Te Anau; if you're short on time you can do it in the evening. ✉ *Real Journeys, 85 Lakefront Dr.* ☎ *03/249–6000, 0800/656–501* ⊕ *www.realjourneys.co.nz* 💲 *NZ$98.*

🍴 Restaurants

★ Redcliff Café & Bar

$$$$ | **NEW ZEALAND** | Don't let the modest, homey exterior and laid-back attitude of the staff fool you, these guys produce the best meals in Te Anau (it was a favorite hangout spot for the cast and crew of *The Lord of the Rings* during local filming). The menu is strong on wild game and seafood, and if you stay after dinner, you might get to enjoy live music at the bar. **Known for:** local venison and hare;

lively, cozy, and comfortable atmosphere; can get booked up so smart to reserve ahead. $ *Average main: NZ$35* ✉ *12 Mokonui St.* ☎ *03/249–7431* ⊕ *www. theredcliff.co.nz.*

Sandfly Cafe

$$ | **CAFÉ** | This is the perfect place to load up on coffee and a hearty breakfast before hitting the road to Milford Sound or Queenstown. It's a simple menu, but the homemade counter food is well-presented and delicious. **Known for:** best coffee in town; friendly and fast service; outdoor seating. $ *Average main: NZ$16* ✉ *9 The Lane* ☎ *03/249–9529* ⊗ *No dinner.*

 Hotels

Blue Thistle Cottages

$$$ | **RENTAL** | A five-minute drive past town on the road to Milford, these four cozy and comfortable cottages make a good base for local exploration, and an early start if you're driving to Milford Sound. **Pros:** outdoor seating areas; beautiful views; cottage kitchens have fridges and microwaves. **Cons:** outside of walking distance to Te Anau; slow Wi-Fi; a little dated. $ *Rooms from: NZ$235* ✉ *168 Te Anau Milford Hwy.* ☎ *03/249–8338* ⊕ *www.bluethistlecottages.com* ⊗ *Closed June–Aug.* ➪ *4 cottages* ⦿ *No meals.*

Cinema Suites

$$$$ | **RENTAL** | This one-of-a-kind, loft-style accommodation sitting above the boutique Fiordland Cinema and Black Dog Bar includes a welcome bottle of wine and tickets to a screening of Ata Whenua Fiordland Experience downstairs. **Pros:** in the heart of everything; full air-conditioning; quiet. **Cons:** only one room; quite expensive; requires good mobility. $ *Rooms from: NZ$750* ✉ *7 The Lane* ☎ *03/249–8551* ⊕ *www.thecinemasuites. co.nz* ➪ *1 room* ⦿ *Free Breakfast.*

Fiordland Lodge

$$$$ | **B&B/INN** | A few kilometers out of Te Anau on the road to Milford Sound, glass, stone, and timber blend together to make a stylish place to spend a few days. **Pros:** cabins offer great privacy; outstanding meals; views are incredible. **Cons:** it's 5 km (3 miles) out of town; some noise possible between interconnecting rooms; Wi-Fi slows when busy. $ *Rooms from: NZ$900* ✉ *472 Te Anau–Milford Hwy.* ☎ *03/249–7832* ⊕ *www.fiordlandlodge. co.nz* ➪ *12 rooms* ⦿ *Some meals.*

Murrell's Grand View House

$$$ | **B&B/INN** | Twenty minutes south of Te Anau, this B&B sits on one of New Zealand's prettiest and most pristine lakes—Lake Manapouri. **Pros:** leave your car here while on the overnight cruise in Doubtful Sound; peaceful hideaway; uninterrupted lake views. **Cons:** it's a bit of a detour from the usual tourist circuit; Wi-Fi is patchy; basic for the price. $ *Rooms from: NZ$280* ✉ *Murrell Ave., Manapouri* ☎ *03/249–6642* ⊕ *www.murrells. co.nz* ⊗ *Closed May–Sept.* ➪ *4 rooms* ⦿ *Breakfast.*

Radfords on the Lake

$$$$ | **RENTAL** | Fabulous lake views and the personal touches make this lakefront motel a great place to stay; it also has spacious, modern rooms and is a few minutes' walk from town. **Pros:** great location; incredible service; nice BBQ area. **Cons:** popular over summer so need to book in early; there's a road between the units and the lake; ground floor faces car park. $ *Rooms from: NZ$334* ✉ *56 Lakefront Dr.* ☎ *03/249–9186* ⊕ *www. radfordsonthelake.co.nz* ➪ *14 rooms* ⦿ *No meals.*

🏃 Activities

Although Te Anau seems small, its lake serves as a larger and beautiful landmark. Trails around Fiordland reveal the natural blue color of the park's water with looming mountains in the distance.

Staying the Night at Fiordland

Overnight cruises are a leisurely, thorough way to experience the sounds. If you choose Doubtful Sound, your tour company will provide a boat across Lake Manapouri and a bus ride to your cruise vessel. Drive to Lake Manapouri, or, for an extra fee, arrange for a coach transfer from Te Anau or Queenstown. Sleeping quarters aboard the vessel range from bunking with three others to a private cabin and bathroom. Dinner and breakfast are included, and you can arrange for a picnic lunch. The park's deepest sound, Doubtful, has three distinct arms and features the 619-meter (2,031-foot) Browne Falls. If you are lucky, you will see Fiordland crested penguins on the rocks or bottlenose dolphins swimming at the bow. Cliffs rise from the sea to 900 meters (2,953 feet), often disappearing in a mist. You can explore the sound in kayaks once you anchor at the evening's mooring. Or you can sit on a viewing deck, sip a beverage from the bar, and take in the sights from your floating hotel. Milford overnight cruises generally leave around 4:30 pm and return around 9 the following morning; Doubtful cruises generally leave around noon and return around noon the next day.

HIKING

Fiordland National Park Visitor Centre
HIKING/WALKING | Information, transport options, and maps for the plethora of hikes near Te Anau, including the Kepler Track, can be obtained from the Fiordland National Park Visitor Centre. ⊠ *Lakefront Dr.* ☎ *03/249–7924* ⊕ *www.doc.govt.nz.*

Kepler Track
HIKING/WALKING | The 60-km (37-mile) Kepler Track loops from the south end of Lake Te Anau and takes three to four days to complete. It goes through extensive beech forest, past limestone bluffs, and provides incredible views of the South Fiord and Te Anau Basin. It's a moderate walking trail but there are a number of hills to climb and a steep zigzag downhill section that takes a couple of hours and can be hard on the knees. It also includes an alpine crossing and hikers should beware of high wind gusts while crossing the exposed saddle above the bush line. If you're on a tight schedule take a day hike to the Luxmore and Moturau huts. Huts cost NZ$65 per person in summer and you need to book; check online or call the Great Walks booking office for advice and conditions. ⊠ *Te Anau* ☎ *03/249–8514 Great Walks booking* ⊕ *www.doc.govt.nz.*

Fiordland Jet
BOATING | Fiordland Jet zips you up the Upper Waiau River, where the forest comes down to the river's edge. Once on lovely Lake Manapouri, you'll stop to experience the serene quiet. The company also pairs its jet-boat rides with helicopter flights, including an alpine landing in the Kepler Mountain Range. Once you reach Manapouri, you could take off on a floatplane to see Doubtful Sound or Lake Te Anau by air, or be whisked back to base by helicopter. ⊠ *84 Lakefront Dr.* ☎ *0800/253–826 NZ only* ⊕ *www.fjet.nz* ⊠ *From NZ$139.*

KAYAKING

Go Orange Kayaks
CAMPING—SPORTS-OUTDOORS | If you're an intrepid adventurer at heart, love camping and the great outdoors, and you're pretty active, then you'll find Go Orange Kayaks' overnight Doubtful Sound trip an incredibly rewarding experience. It's not

for the fainthearted; you can get wet and cold and the sand flies can be bad. But you'll be in a World Heritage area and you'll meet some wonderful like-minded people. If you're not keen on the overnight, go sea kayaking in Milford Sound for a day or half a day to gain the unique perspective on the fiord that being on the water gives you. Trips operate from September to May, with some differences according to location, so call ahead. ⊠ *21 Town Centre* ☏ *03/442–7340, 0800/505–504 NZ only* ⊕ *www.goorange.co.nz* ✉ *From NZ$120.*

SCENIC FLIGHTS

Fly Fiordland

FLYING/SKYDIVING/SOARING | Fly Fiordland provides a range of scenic flights in its three Cessna fixed-wing aircraft; including to Milford and Doubtful sounds, and on the rare occasion that weather permits, an overfly of the most remote place in New Zealand, Dusky Sound. Prices don't include a cruise in Milford Sound, but you can add this as an option. Prices start at NZ$335. ⊠ *4/52 Town Centre* ☏ *03/249–4352, 0800/359–346 NZ only* ⊕ *www.flyfiordland.com.*

★ Southern Lakes Helicopters

FLYING/SKYDIVING/SOARING | Once you've seen the movie *Ata Whenua* at Fiordland Cinema you'll want to take to the air and see some of this scenery for yourself (or do the flight first and see the movie after). Either way this helicopter company, privately owned by renowned helicopter pioneer Sir Richard "Hannibal" Hayes, has operated successfully here for more than 35 years. The Southern Lakes pilots have a wealth of knowledge and experience flying in this World Heritage area and offer a range of airborne services. ⊠ *79 Lakefront Dr.* ☏ *03/249–7167, 0508/249–7167* ⊕ *www.southernlakeshelicopters.co.nz* ✉ *From NZ$230.*

Wings and Water Te Anau

FLYING/SKYDIVING/SOARING | Wings and Water Te Anau operates scenic flights with a floatplane that takes travelers to some of the region's most inaccessible areas, including a 10-minute trip over Lake Te Anau, Lake Manapouri, and the Kepler Track, and longer flights over Doubtful, Dusky, and Milford sounds. ⊠ *65 Lakefront Dr.* ☏ *03/249–7405* ⊕ *www.wingsandwater.co.nz* ✉ *From NZ$150.*

Milford Sound

120 km (75 miles) northwest of Te Anau, 290 km (180 miles) west of Queenstown.

Fiordland National Park's most accessible and busiest attraction is Milford Sound; in some ways it's also the most dramatic. Hemmed in by walls of rock that rise straight and sheer from the waterline up thousands of feet, the 13-km-long (18-mile-long) fjord was carved by a succession of glaciers as they gouged a track to the sea. Its dominant feature is the 5,560-foot pinnacle of Mitre Peak, which is capped with snow for all but the warmest months of the year. Opposite the peak, Bowen Falls tumbles 520 feet before exploding into the fjord. You'll often see seals on rocks soaking up the sun and dolphins sometimes flirt with the boats. Milford Sound is also spectacularly wet: The average annual rainfall is around 20 feet, and it rains an average of 200 days a year. In addition to a raincoat you'll need insect repellent—the sand flies can be voracious.

GETTING HERE AND AROUND

Highway 94 North out of Te Anau to Milford Sound is only 118 km (73 miles), but between the weather, the views, and the winding, hilly nature of the road, it's best to allow at least 2½ hours to get there safely. Most day tours in Milford Sound offer transport from Te Anau or Queenstown, and InterCity Coachlines run a daily service from Te Anau. If the weather is clear, there is an airport open to scenic fixed-wing and helicopter landings.

◉ Sights

Milford Sound does not have a surrounding town. Here you'll fill your days with wondrous exploration. Because of excessive rain, make sure you come prepared with extra clothing and rain gear.

Milford Discovery Centre & Underwater Observatory

TOUR—SIGHT | Even in heavy rain and storms Milford Sound is magical. Rainfall is so excessive that a coat of up to 20 feet of fresh water floats on the surface of the saltwater fjord. Lightly stained with tannins from the plants and soil, it creates a unique underwater environment similar to that found at a much greater depth in the open ocean. Head downstairs at the Milford Underwater Observatory, and you can see rare black coral (that looks white) as well as anemones, starfish, octopus, and any number of fish swimming by. The Discovery Centre and Observatory is operated by Southern Discoveries and is only accessible by boat; you can add it on to most Milford Sound cruises. ⊠ *Milford Sound* ☎ *03/441–1137, 0800/264–536 NZ only* ⊕ *www.milforddiscoverycentre. co.nz* 🎫 *NZ$15.*

🍴 Restaurants

Accommodations are scant at Milford Sound; pack your lunch in Te Anau before coming, or preorder the lunch box included on some boat tours. If you're staying overnight, be aware there is no shopping. You can buy dinner at Milford Sound Lodge, whether you are a guest or not.

Discover Milford Information Centre

$$ | **CAFÉ** | Situated at the main public car park, the Discover Milford Information Centre offers coffee, snacks, and counter food. The view out the front window, across Milford Sound to Mitre Peak and the mountains beyond, is amazing. **Known for:** only dining option in Milford Sound; high prices for simple food; impressive views. ⑤ *Average main: NZ$15* ⊠ *Milford Sound* ☎ *03/249–7931* ◔ *No dinner.*

🛏 Hotels

★ Milford Sound Lodge

$$$$ | **HOTEL** | Just 1 km (½ mile) out of the Milford settlement, on the banks of the Cleddau River, this lodge provides Riverside Chalets with either one super-king or twin bed, kitchenette, and spectacular mountain and river views. **Pros:** beautiful chalets; only place to stay in Milford Sound; otherworldly views. **Cons:** very expensive; limited Internet; shares location with campervans and hostel. ⑤ *Rooms from: NZ$515* ⊠ *Milford Sound* ☎ *03/249–8071* ⊕ *www.milfordlodge. com* ⤳ *14 chalets* ❍| *Free Breakfast.*

🏃 Activities

CRUISING

The gorgeous views from the water account for the popularity of cruising here. It's essential to book ahead between mid-December and March. All boats leave from the Milford wharf area. Avoid the midday sailings, as they link with tour buses and are the most crowded. Southern Discoveries and Real Journeys run more than a dozen cruises a day between them, with extra options in summer.

Real Journeys

BOATING | The most satisfying way to experience Milford (or Doubtful) Sound is to do an overnight cruise, giving you time in the fjord when it's at its best—first thing in the morning and early evening. There are two overnight boats: the *Milford Mariner*'s the more luxurious cruise with roomier bunks (with en suites), but the *Milford Wanderer*'s not too far behind. Fewer passengers and shared facilities make it a very friendly boat. An overnight cruise includes a superb dinner and breakfast. If you want to do a day cruise, go for the Nature Cruise over the

Scenic Cruise. It's more personal, longer (2½ hours), and it's on a boat with more character and a nature guide you can ask questions. Both trips cruise the full length of Milford Sound to the Tasman Sea and have the same extraordinary views of waterfalls, rain forest, mountains, and wildlife. ✉ *85 Lakefront Dr., Te Anau* ☎ *03/249–6000, 0800/656–501* ⊕ *www.realjourneys.co.nz* ✉ *From NZ$441 per person overnight; NZ$82 for day trip* ⊗ *Overnight cruises don't operate through winter (mid-May–Sept.).*

★ **Southern Discoveries**

BOATING | You can't miss Southern Discoveries' big red boats in Milford Sound. If you're only here for the day the Cruise/Kayak option is great for getting close to the shore and seeing the edges of the fjord in all its lush detail—right down to its damp, green, earthy smell. It's an easy paddle on calm water so no experience is necessary. Kayaking starts at the Discovery Centre and Underwater Observatory, which is also included in the price and is well worth a visit. ✉ *Milford Sound Wharf* ☎ *03/441–1137* ⊕ *www.southerndiscoveries.co.nz* ✉ *From NZ$79.*

HIKING

Fiordland National Park Visitor Centre

HIKING/WALKING | To hike independently of a tour group for either the Milford, Kepler, or Routeburn Track, call the **Great Walks Booking Office** at the Fiordland National Park Visitor Centre or book online through the website. Reservations for the coming season can be made starting on the first of July every year. Book well in advance—especially if you plan to go in December or January. Independent walking, without a guide, requires that you bring your own food, utensils, bedding, and other equipment. You stay in clean, basic Department of Conservation huts. ✉ *Lakefront Dr., Te Anau* ☎ *03/249–8514* ⊕ *www.doc.govt.nz.*

Hollyford Track

HIKING/WALKING | If you're itching to see some coastline during your hike, and you are fit, consider the Hollyford Track. At 56 km (35 miles), it's usually a four-day endeavor, taking you from the Hollyford Road down to Martins Bay by roughly following the Hollyford River. You'll pass a couple of lakes and waterfalls on your way; at the coastline you'll likely spy seals and penguins. Be particularly careful of flooded creek crossings. Make sure you buy your hut tickets, but you can't book in advance. It's a good idea to drop in to the Fiordland National Park Visitor Centre to check on conditions before you head off. ✉ *Lakefront Dr., Te Anau* ☎ *03/249–7924* ⊕ *www.doc.govt.nz.*

★ **Milford Track**

HIKING/WALKING | If you plan to walk the Milford Track—a rewarding four-day bushwalk through Fiordland National Park—understand that it is one of New Zealand's most popular hikes. The 53½-km (33-mile) track is strictly one-way, and because park authorities control access, you can feel as though you have the wilderness more or less to yourself. The trail ends for the track are remote. Independent and guided groups stay in different overnight huts. Guided and unguided walks begin with a 1½-hour ferry ride to Glade Wharf on Lake Te Anau and end with a 20-minute ferry taking you from Sandfly Point over to the Milford Sound wharf. The track's well maintained during the restricted hiking season, which runs from late October to April (because of the risk of avalanche). For seasonal reservations, visit a Department of Conservation office or book online. Make sure you book well in advance. ✉ *Fiordland National Park* ⊕ *www.greatwalks.co.nz.*

Real Journeys

HIKING/WALKING | If you don't have enough time for the whole Milford Track, you can still experience a good slice of what makes it New Zealand's most famous walk on a guided day-walk with Real Journeys. It includes a cruise across Lake Te Anau. You'll hike about 11 km (7 miles), lunch is included, and the good thing is there are no big hills. No children under 10. ✉ *Lakefront Dr., Te Anau* ☎ *03/249–6000, 0800/656–501* ⊕ *www. realjourneys.co.nz* ✈ *NZ$201.*

Routeburn Track

HIKING/WALKING | The 33-km (20.5-mile) Routeburn Track, like the Milford Track, is designated one of the country's Great Walks, so you need to book in season. The Routeburn goes between Lake Wakatipu, near Glenorchy, and the road between Milford and Te Anau; it takes about three days to hike. The alpine landscape is stunning, and once you're above the tree line, the sand flies back off. It's a linear track so make sure you organize your transport home. The track's well maintained but be prepared for rain and mud. Tramping out of season is not advised for most people as there's avalanche risk. ✉ *Milford Sound* ⊕ *www. doc.govt.nz.*

Ultimate Hikes

HIKING/WALKING | If you want to do the Milford Track but don't like the idea of hauling a heavy backpack for 34 miles with all your food and gear, then Ultimate Hikes is the rather wonderful alternative. All your meals are provided, you'll have a comfortable bed and hot showers, and you can wash and dry your gear if it rains. They'll organize your transport and provide backpacks. Their Milford Track journey includes a cruise on Milford Sound and transport to and from Queenstown; the Routeburn Track is a bit less expensive. If you're not up for a multiday trek, you can take a single-day "encounter" hike on either the Milford or Routeburn Track. ✉ *The Station Bldg., Duke St. entrance, Queenstown* ☎ *03/450–1940, 0800/659–255* ⊕ *www.ultimatehikes. co.nz* ✈ *From NZ$1375 (in multishare accommodation).*

KAYAKING

Rosco's Milford Kayaks

KAYAKING | If you like immersing yourself in nature then sea kayaking's a lovely way to see this extraordinary part of

New Zealand and the creatures (seals, penguins, or dolphins if you're lucky) that live here. Rosco's Milford Kayaks leads a number of different guided kayaking options on Milford Sound that can even include a hike along part of the famous Milford Track. You can get picked up and dropped off from Te Anau. No children under 14. ✉ *Milford Sound* ☎ *03/249–8500, 0800/476–726 in New Zealand* ⊕ *www.roscosmilfordkayaks. com* ✈ *From NZ$115.*

SCENIC FLIGHTS

Glacier Southern Lakes Helicopters

FLYING/SKYDIVING/SOARING | You're in good hands flying with this company, which has highly sought-after helicopter pilots with a wealth of knowledge about the area. Helicopters are easily the best way to see this part of the country and even a short flight up the Remarkables or over the Skippers Canyon is an incredible experience. Flying to Milford Sound, the West Coast, and Mount Aspiring National Park, landing on a glacier on the way, could be life changing. There's a Middle-earth flight to some of *The Lord of the Rings* and *The Hobbit* locations— about as authentic as you can get as one of this company's pilots, Alfie Speight, was the principal aerial photography pilot for the movies. ✉ *35 Lucas Pl., Queenstown* ☎ *03/442–3016* ⊕ *www.glacier-southernlakes.co.nz* ✈ *From NZ$255 per person.*

Lake Manapouri and Doubtful Sound

Just 20 minutes south of Te Anau, Lake Manapouri has long had the reputation as one of New Zealand's prettiest lakes. The lake is hemmed by high mountains and studded by many bush-covered islands; it's 1,457 feet deep in parts. Cruises run several times a day to the head of the lake, where you can join a tour of the West Arm hydro-station, deep underground. West Arm is also the departure point for those traveling on to Doubtful Sound, a stunning stretch of water, largely untouched by visitors. A connecting bus crosses you over the 2,177-foot Wilmot Pass before dropping steeply down to sea level at Deep Arm, the head of Doubtful Sound.

GETTING HERE AND AROUND

To get to Lake Manapouri, head south of the Te Anau center onto Highway 95 to drive the 20 minutes to Manapouri township. Doubtful Sound is not accessible by car. Book a day trip or overnight tour and your tour will include a boat ride across Lake Manapouri and a bus ride across Wilmot Pass. You can park you car near the wharf at Pearl Harbour, which is the end of the road. Most tours will have the option to depart on a bus from Te Anau, allowing you to leave your car in town.

Activities

Fiordland Expeditions

BOAT TOURS | Fiordland Expeditions provides a very Kiwi overnight experience on their two boats, *Tutuko* and *Tutoko II*. With a maximum of 14 passengers, these are relaxed and personal trips and great if you want to do a bit of fishing, kayaking, or just soak up the splendid scenery. There are private or shared cabins, mostly with shared bathroom facilities. All meals (probably some crayfish for dinner), fishing gear, and transfers from Manapouri are included in the price. ⊠ *Deep Cove, Doubtful Sound* ☎ *03/249–9005* ⊕ *www.fiordlandexpeditions.co.nz* ✉ *From NZ$695.*

★ **Real Journeys**

SPECIAL-INTEREST | Doubtful Sound is three times as long as Milford Sound and because there's no road access it receives far fewer visitors. The sides of the fjords aren't quite as in-your-face but they are just as beautiful, and there's a better chance of seeing dolphins and fur seals. Real Journeys runs a range of combined bus and boat trips. Most people take an eight-hour day trip from Lake Manapouri; there are bus connections from Te Anau and Queenstown. Between October and May the ultimate experience is an overnight on the sound, aboard the *Fiordland Navigator*. Rates include meals and kayaking, and if you're brave enough, you can take a swim in the frigid waters. ⊠ *Lakefront Dr., Te Anau* ☎ *03/249–6000, 0800/656–501* ⊕ *www.realjourneys.co.nz* ✉ *From NZ$267.*

Chapter 12

OTAGO, INVERCARGILL, AND STEWART ISLAND

Updated by
Gerard Hindmarsh

⦿ Sights	🍴 Restaurants	🛏 Hotels	🛍 Shopping	🍸 Nightlife
★★★★☆	★★★☆☆	★★☆☆☆	★☆☆☆☆	★★★☆☆

WELCOME TO OTAGO, INVERCARGILL, AND STEWART ISLAND

TOP REASONS TO GO

★ **Local Fare:** Partake in a fresh fillet of blue cod, salty muttonbird prepared the Māori way, succulent Bluff oysters, or a warm cheese roll.

★ **Bird-Watching:** See yellow-eyed penguins or an albatross on the peninsula or a kiwi on Stewart Island. Predator-free Ulva Island is the showcase jewel in the crown of Rakiura National Park.

★ **Kiwi Sports:** Rugby puts New Zealand on the world stage, and for many Kiwis it's a passion. Provincial and international teams ruck and maul at Dunedin's Forsyth Barr Stadium.

★ **Pubs and Clubs:** Thanks to the presence of 25,000 university students, Dunedin is full of cafés, funky bars, late-night pubs, and rocking music venues.

★ **The Southern Coastline:** The lower coast of the South Island is breathtakingly wild. Head south along the Catlins section of the Southern Scenic Route for ocean views, diving seabirds, and sandy beaches.

1 Dunedin. A university town, Dunedin is filled with history, a bustling harbor, and creative young academics.

2 Oamaru. This town is well-known for its Victorian buildings and nearby penguin colony.

3 Otago Peninsula. This claw-shape jut of land has an albatross colony, a hilltop castle, and some gorgeous scenery.

4 Invercargill. Thanks to its original Scottish immigrants, this seaside small city comes with plenty of European charm and architecture.

5 Stewart Island. Sparsely inhabited, Stewart Island contains New Zealand's newest national park and some of the world's best bird-watching.

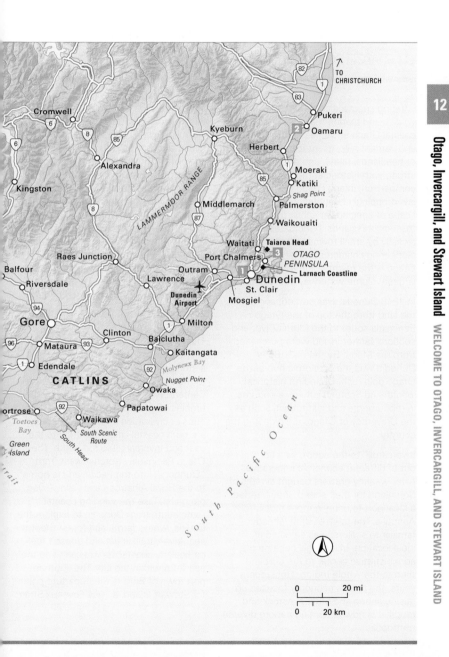

Otago Province takes up much of the southeast quadrant of the South Island and has two distinct regions, each a drawcard in its own right.

Offering spectacular opportunities for wildlife and marine mammal watching, coastal Otago stretches across moist and verdant hills, its intricate coastline of headlands, inlets, and misty beaches strung with historic settlements. By comparison, inland Otago is stark yet jaw-droppingly beautiful, a drier landscape of spectacular schist outcrops and tussock grasslands, punctuated occasionally by small towns that still exude pioneering character. Draining much of Otago is the mighty Clutha River, the largest-volume waterway in the country.

In 1848 Dunedin was settled, and all the land from the top of the Otago Peninsula south to the Clutha River and sections farther inland were purchased from the Māori. By the mid-1860s Dunedin was the economic hub of the Otago gold rush. Dunedin's historical wealth and Scottish influence endures in monuments and institutions such as the University of Otago, the oldest in the country.

Invercargill, to the south, was born out of different economic imperatives. After wealthy graziers bought swaths of Southland for their sheep, they needed a local port to bring in more stock from Australia. The town of Bluff, already familiar to sealers, was selected as an ideal location. Invercargill became the administrative center to the port and then to the whole region. Until recent years, the town's economy focused on raising sheep and other livestock and crops; it is now becoming a more diverse metropolis.

Hanging off the bottom of the South Island and separated by 30-km-wide (19-mile-wide) Foveaux Strait, Stewart Island is a world all of its own. Commercial fishing and tourism accounts for most of the commercial activity in the island's only settlement, which soon gives way to bushland that the kiwi bird still haunts. At night, the nocturnal birds can be seen wandering remote beaches. Another late night show is the aurora australis, the southern hemisphere equivalent of the northern lights, which can light up the sky (the best time to catch a viewing is from March through September).

GETTING ORIENTED

The region is bordered by the snow-capped Southern Alps to the west and a string of golden, albeit chilly, beaches to the east. The north is met by the wide Canterbury Plains and the south by the timeless Catlins region. The two major hubs of civilization in the "deep south" are both coastal cities: Dunedin to the east and Invercargill to the south. The Otago Peninsula stretches east from "Dunners" into the Pacific and is home to the Royal Albatross and yellow-eyed penguins. Take the winding coastal route south from Dunedin to explore the Catlins, where farms and forest meet the sea. Invercargill is flat and doesn't feel particularly coastal, as you can't see the sea from within the city. The southern port town of Bluff is the departure point for Stewart Island, across Foveaux Strait.

MAJOR REGIONS

Otago. The country's third largest province comprises the city of Dunedin, along with small towns along the coast like Oamaru. The region's peninsula is also popular with visitors thanks to its gorgeous scenery.

Southland. New Zealand's southernmost region centers around Stewart Island and the city of Invercargill. Due to its proximity to the sea, "Invers" has been called the "City of Water and Light." The wide flat roads of downtown and the enormous sweep of nearby Oreti Beach were perfect training grounds for homegrown hero Burt Munro (motorcycle land speed record holder).

Stewart Island. If your hand represents the island, your pinky fingernail would be the amount that is actually inhabited. Roads link the main township of Oban at Halfmoon Bay to the other "neighborhoods"—a few homes nestled around adjoining bays. Beaches are pristine; the sea is crystal green and bountiful. Flowers spill from grounded dories. Beyond town is wilderness teeming with wonderful birds.

Planning

Planning Your Time

Most people spend a few days in Dunedin and migrate south via State Highway 1. Once you reach Balclutha, you can continue south either by staying on the State Highway heading straight for Invercargill or by going via the Catlins on the Southern Scenic Route. The Catlins route is more demanding, but much more scenic. Whichever route you take, by the time you reach the Southland Plains, all roads are wide, flat, and point to Invercargill.

When to Go

Dunedin gets more visitors in summer, but during the university vacations it's quieter as students head home. Inland Otago remains dry year-round, and you can expect crisp, sunny days in winter, but the coast gets more rain, and Dunedin can have day after day of clouds and showers. Southland in winter isn't any colder, but it is wetter.

It's often said of New Zealand that you may experience all four seasons in one day; on Stewart Island you may experience them all in an hour. In winter, there's a better chance of seeing the aurora australis, but some of the island's walking trails may be closed or just too muddy to walk.

Getting Here and Around

AIR TRAVEL

Most Air New Zealand flights to Dunedin and Invercargill go via Christchurch or come direct from Wellington, while Jetstar connects Dunedin to Auckland. Fog occasionally causes delays, but Christchurch Airport has a slick and modern passenger-friendly terminal with shops and cafés as well as a family entertainment center where the little folks can wear themselves out. Stewart Island flights operate from Invercargill, or you can take a ferry to the island: one local described the choices as "either 60 minutes of fear or 20 minutes of terror," but that's true only on a bad day—both journeys afford breathtaking views.

BUS TRAVEL

InterCity's buses run once a day between Christchurch and Dunedin, departing at 7:45 am for a trip that takes six hours. A connecting daily InterCity bus continues on from Dunedin to Invercargill; this takes another 3 hours and 15 minutes. On both these routes the company makes an extra run on Friday and Sunday.

Other bus companies operating in the region include Atomic Shuttles, Bottom Bus, and Catch-A-Bus.

CAR TRAVEL

The best way to explore the lower South Island is by car, particularly if you want to take your time seeing the Catlins. You cannot ferry your rental car to Stewart Island; there is secure parking in Invercargill and Bluff. Buses serve most places of interest, including daily routes between South Island cities. They go the direct route between Dunedin and Invercargill on State Highway 1. If you are driving and want to see the Catlins, leave State Highway 1 at Balclutha and take the well-marked Southern Scenic Route.

Restaurants

Dunedin has the area's highest concentration of good restaurants. Seafood is a big player, in part because of Dunedin's coastal location but also because of its proximity to Bluff, the home of New Zealand's great delicacy, Bluff oysters. Many of the least-expensive options are café-like Asian restaurants; these tend to close early, around 9 pm. Locals don't usually dress up or make reservations for anything other than large groups or the more exclusive establishments.

Invercargill has a more limited selection of mostly moderately priced restaurants. Stewart Island has a reasonable selection considering its location, including some excellent takeaway spots, but in winter some places limit their hours or close entirely.

Hotels

Dunedin has a full range of accommodations, from modest hostels to luxury hotels, while Invercargill has more motels than anything else. Local motels generally provide clean rooms with kitchens and TVs. Stewart Island lodging options include camping, hostels, rental houses, hotels, motels, and boutique B&Bs. Throughout the region air-conditioning is a rarity, but given the temperate climate, this isn't a problem. Heating, on the other hand, is standard in most places.

It's a good idea to make reservations, especially in summer. In Dunedin, rooms can be scarce around special events, such as graduation ceremonies and high-profile rugby games.

Restaurant and hotel reviews have been shortened. For full information, visit Fodors.com. Restaurant prices are the average cost of a main course at dinner or, if dinner is not served, at lunch. Hotel prices are the lowest cost of a standard double room in high season.

What It Costs			
$	$$	$$$	$$$$
RESTAURANTS			
under NZ$15	NZ$15–NZ$20	NZ$21–NZ$30	over NZ$30
HOTELS			
under NZ$125	NZ$125–NZ$200	NZ$201–NZ$300	over NZ$300

Visitor Information

Both Dunedin and Invercargill have centrally located i-SITE visitor centers: you can find Dunedin's in The Octagon in the city center and a kiosk branch at the wharf that only opens to greet cruise ships; the Invercargill i-SITE is in the Southland Museum. On Stewart Island check out the Department of Conservation office or the Stewart Island Experience office (in the red building at the ferry wharf).

Dunedin

280 km (175 miles) east of Queenstown, 362 km (226 miles) south of Christchurch.

Clinging to the walls of the natural amphitheater at the west end of Otago Harbour, the South Island's second-largest city is enriched with inspiring nearby seascapes and wildlife. Because Dunedin is a university town, floods of students give the city a vitality far greater than its population of 128,500 might suggest. The city's manageable size makes it easy to explore on foot—with the possible exception of Baldwin Street, the world's steepest residential street and home to the annual "gutbuster" race, in which people run up it, and the "Jaffa" race, in which people roll the namesake spherical chocolate candy down it.

Dunedin, the Gaelic name for Edinburgh, was founded in 1848 by settlers of the Free Church of Scotland, a breakaway group from the Presbyterian Church. The city's Scottish roots are still visible; you'll find New Zealand's first legal whisky distillery (now there are seven), a statue of Scottish poet Robert Burns, and more kilts, sporrans, and gillies than you can shake a stick at. The Scottish settlers and local Māori came together in relative peace, but this wasn't true of the European whalers who were here three decades before, as places with names such as Murdering Beach illustrate.

Dunedin has always had a reputation for the eccentric. Wearing no shoes and a big beard here marks a man as bohemian rather than destitute, and the residents wouldn't have it any other way. The University of Otago was the country's first university and has been drawing writers ever since its founding in 1871, most notably Janet Frame and the poet James K. Baxter. Dunedin also has a musical heritage, which blossomed into the "Dunedin Sound" of the 1970s and '80s.

GETTING HERE AND AROUND

AIR TRAVEL
Dunedin Airport lies 20 km (13 miles) south of the city. Both Air New Zealand and Jetstar link Dunedin and Auckland daily; the flight takes just under two hours. Air New Zealand also flies daily from Dunedin to Christchurch and Wellington in around an hour, while Jetstar flies between Dunedin and Wellington three days a week. Virgin Australia flies between Dunedin, Brisbane, and Sydney four times a week.

AIRPORT CONTACTS Dunedin International Airport. ✉ *25 Miller Rd., Momona* ☎ *03/486–2879* ⊕ *www.dunedinairport. co.nz.*

BUS TRAVEL
Local buses to Portobello and other towns on the peninsula depart from Stand 5, out the back of City Centre New World on Cumberland Street.

BUS CONTACTS Dunedin Bus Station. ✉ *7 Halsey St.* ☎ *03/474–1699* ⊕ *www.orc. govt.nz.* **GoBus.** ✉ *1 Transport Pl., Princes St., Dunedin* ☎ *03/477–5577* ⊕ *www. gobus.co.nz.* **InterCity.** ✉ *7 Halsey St., Dunedin* ☎ *03/477–8860* ⊕ *www.inter-city.co.nz.*

CAR TRAVEL
You can rent a car to explore the region at Dunedin airport on arrival, but confusing one-way roads and twisting hills in the suburbs make driving in Dunedin itself a challenge. Street parking can be limited.

TOURS
City Walks Dunedin
GUIDED TOURS | Three separate walks showcasing Dunedin's rich history, architecture, and urban renewal are offered every day except Sunday and depart from the Dunedin i-SITE Visitor Information Centre. The one-hour Vogel Street Walk leaves from Vogel St Kitchen at 9 am daily. The walk season is mainly October through April, but a reduced winter

schedule applies; check the website for details. ✉ *Dunedin i-SITE Visitor Centre, 50 The Octagon* ☎ *027/356–9132, 0800/925–571 toll-free* ⊕ *www.citywalks. co.nz* ✆ *From NZ$30*.

Elm Wildlife Tours

GUIDED TOURS | Passionate and enthusiastic guides lead walks through private conservation areas to penguin, fur seal, and sea lion colonies. A moderate degree of fitness is required to negotiate hilly terrain. ✉ *19 Irvine Rd., The Cove* ☎ *03/454–4121, 0800/356–563* ⊕ *www. elmwildlifetours.co.nz* ✆ *From NZ$122*.

Mainland Air Scenic Flights

AIR EXCURSIONS | Scenic flights show off inland mountains and coastal sights as far south as Stewart Island. ✉ *Dunedin Airport, 3 Airport Dr.* ☎ *03/486–2200, 0800/284–284* ⊕ *www.mainlandair.com* ✆ *Flights from NZ$225 a person*.

VISITOR INFORMATION

CONTACTS Dunedin i-SITE Visitor Information Centre. ✉ *50 The Octagon* ☎ *03/474–3300* ⊕ *www.dunedin.govt.nz* **Dunedin NZ Official Tourist Information.** ⊕ *www. dunedinnz.com*.

◉ Sights

As you explore Dunedin's city center, do look down. Beneath your feet are bronze plaques embedded in the sidewalks that highlight the city's Victorian history and heritage buildings. Around The Octagon, the thoughts of popular New Zealand writers are captured in bronze pavestones.

Botanic Gardens

GARDEN | **FAMILY** | Relax and enjoy the birdsong of bellbirds, woodpigeon, and *tūi* amid 70 acres of international and native flora at New Zealand's first ever public garden. Some 6,800 plant species thrive on flatlands and hillsides ranging up from Central Dunedin, providing amazing seasonal displays of foliage. Attractions include an aviary, a winter garden

hothouse, a comprehensive native plant collection, and the spectacular Rhododendron Dell. Parking at the lower part of the gardens, off Cumberland Street, affords easier access than the Opoho end, which is steeper, but both parts are worth visiting. ✉ *50 The Octagon* ☎ *03/477–4000* ⊕ *www.dunedinbotanicgarden.co.nz* ✆ *Free*.

Dunedin Public Art Gallery

MUSEUM | The shell of an original municipal building has been paired with a sweeping, modern, glass facade to house a collection that includes European masters Monet, Turner, and Gainsborough, as well as New Zealand and Otago artists. A special gallery highlights Dunedin native Frances Hodgkins, whose work won acclaim in the 1930s and '40s. Hodgkins's style changed throughout her career, but some of her most distinctive works are postimpressionist watercolors. ✉ *30 The Octagon* ☎ *03/477–3240* ⊕ *www.dunedin.art.museum* ✆ *Free*.

Dunedin Railway Station

TRANSPORTATION SITE (AIRPORT/BUS/FERRY/TRAIN) | The 1906 Dunedin Railway Station, a cathedral to the power of steam, is a massive bluestone structure in Flemish Renaissance style, lavishly decorated with heraldic beasts, nymphs, scrolls, a mosaic floor, and even stained-glass windows of steaming locomotives. This extravagant building, considered one of the best examples of railway architecture in the southern hemisphere, earned its architect, George Troup, a knighthood from the king—and the nickname Gingerbread George from the people of Dunedin because of the detailing on the outside of the building. It was once the busiest station in the country, with up to 100 trains a day coming and going. The station is also home to the Sports Hall of Fame, the country's finest sports museum with displays celebrating rugby, cricket, and other athletic pursuits. ✉ *Anzac Ave. at Stuart St.* ☎ *03/477–4449 Station, 03/477–7775 Sports Hall of Fame*

Dunedin

KEY

1 Sights

1 Restaurants

1 Hotels

—+—+— Rail Lines

⊕ www.nzhalloffame.co.nz ✉ Sports Hall of Fame $6.

First Church of Otago

RELIGIOUS SITE | On the south side of Moray Place, the church is not vast, but it's still impressive, with a base of Oamaru stone topped by a delicate 200-foot spire. Check out the leaf patterns, dragon, and other carved details around the windows. ✉ 415 Moray Pl. ☏ 03/477–7118 ⊕ www.firstchurchotago.org ✉ Free.

Milford Galleries

MUSEUM | Milford Galleries, a major fine-art dealer, presents solo and group exhibitions of New Zealand paintings, drawings, sculpture, glasswork, ceramic art, and photography. Among the artists are Neil Frazer (who does large-scale abstract expressionist paintings) and Paul Dibble, one of New Zealand's most acclaimed sculptors. ✉ 18 Dowling St. ☏ 03/477–7727 ⊕ www.milfordgalleries.co.nz ⊘ Closed Sun.

The Octagon

PLAZA | The city's hub is the eight-sided town center, lined with several imposing buildings, and a smattering of market stalls, cafés, and bars with tables spilling onto the pavement. In summer it's a meeting place, and it's also the site for the occasional student demonstration. Dunedin City Council provides free Wi-Fi in this grand arena. A **statue of Robert Burns** sits in front of **St. Paul's Cathedral,** a part-Victorian Gothic, part-modern building with an imposing marble staircase leading up to a towering facade of Oamaru stone. On Stuart Street at the corner of Dunbar, check out the late-Victorian **Law Courts.** Their figure of Justice stands with scales in hand but without her customary blindfold (she wears a low helmet instead).

★ Otago Museum

MUSEUM | FAMILY | Galleries in an 1877 building are a throwback to Victorian times. The museum's first curator was a zoologist, and many of the original animals collected from 1868 are still on display in "Animal Attic," a restored, magnificent skylighted gallery. "Southern Land, Southern People" explores the cultural heritage of this region, and other galleries focus on Māori and Pacific Island artifacts, animal and insect specimens, and nautical items, including ship models and a whale skeleton. "The Tropical Forest" re-creates a jungle, complete with live butterflies and other tropical creatures. ✉ 419 Great King St. ☏ 03/474–7474 ⊕ www.otagomuseum.nz ✉ Free; Discovery World from NZ$10.

Speight's Brewery Heritage Centre

WINERY/DISTILLERY | For a tasty indulgence, head to the Speight's Brewery Heritage Centre for a 90-minute tour of the South's top brewery, which dates back to 1876 on this very same site. Here you can see the various stages of gravity-driven brewing, learn the trade's lingo such as wort and grist, and taste the results. Speight's makes several traditional beers, the most common being its Gold Medal Ale. The company claims that this is the drink of choice for every "Southern Man," which isn't far from the truth. Watch a video of various Speight's iconic television ads and learn to say the tough Southern way, Good on ya, mate. ✉ 200 Rattray St. ☏ 03/477–7697 ⊕ www.speights.co.nz ✉ NZ$29 ☞ Reservations essential.

Taieri Gorge Railway

TRANSPORTATION SITE (AIRPORT/BUS/FERRY/TRAIN) | FAMILY | A route along the now-closed Otago Central Railway runs from Dunedin to Pukerangi and Middlemarch, home of the annual Middlemarch Singles' Ball; each year this very train imports young city gals up to a dance with lonely Otago sheep shearers. The highlight of the trip is the run through the narrow and deep Taieri Gorge, with 10 tunnels and dozens of bridges and viaducts, all of which can be enjoyed from open-air viewing platforms. Also available is a

The extravagant Dunedin Railway Station is fronted by manicured grounds.

seasonal *Seasider* route from Dunedin up the coast to Palmerston. The train runs every day; check the timetable for its destination. Reservations are essential. Cyclists can connect at Middlemarch to the wonderful Otago Central Rail Trail. ✉ *Dunedin Railway Station* ☎ *03/477–4449* ⊕ *www.taieri.co.nz* ✉ *From NZ$91.*

Toitū Otago Settlers Museum

MUSEUM | Documents, works of art, technological items, and forms of transport tell the stories of all Otago settlers, from Māori and early European and Chinese to later Pacific Islanders and Asians. The museum hosts changing exhibits and events, with a charge for some. ✉ *31 Queens Gardens* ☎ *03/477–5052* ⊕ *www.toituosm.com* ✉ *Free.*

🔄 Beaches

St. Clair Beach

BEACH—SIGHT | FAMILY | The sea at Dunedin can be a little wild; in summer an area between flags is patrolled by lifeguards. St. Clair has some good surfing, and hosts some prestigious competitions. Don't be too spooked by the shark bell on the Esplanade: a fatal attack hasn't occurred for 50 years (although nonfatal attacks have occurred at least once a decade). Local residents show what they're made of at the annual "midwinter plunge" held on the beach at winter solstice. If the ocean is too cold for you, try the Hot Salt Water Pool at the southern end of the beach (NZ$5.70 admission). South of town is the Tunnel Beach Walkway, a sandstone tunnel cut in 1870 by Edward Cargill so that his family could get down to the pretty beach below (this walk is closed from August through October for lambing). **Amenities:** food and drink; lifeguards; parking (free); showers; toilets. **Best for:** surfing; walking. ✉ *Beach St., St. Clair* ✛ *Drive south on State Hwy. 1 or hop on Normanby–St. Clair bus from George St. or The Octagon.*

Restaurants

The Ale House Bar & Restaurant

$$$ | **NEW ZEALAND** | Authentic and quirky, the Ale House serves as a lively bar in a brewery-restaurant setting. The menu includes a "drunken" steak (steak marinated in dark, malty porter) and beer-battered fish, along with plenty of Speight's ales you can match with your meal. **Known for:** hearty meals featuring southern NZ fare; lively atmosphere; fine local ales including seasonal brews. ⑤ *Average main: NZ$28* ✉ *200 Rattray St.* ☎ *03/471–9050* ⊕ *www.thealehouse. co.nz.*

The Kitchen Table Cafe & Bake

$$ | **CAFÉ** | At this centrally located café and bakery, artisan bakers craft delicious wholesome food on-site. You can choose from, pancakes, French toast, or good old eggs Benedict for breakfast, or maybe a venison panini for lunch. **Known for:** cozy atmosphere; some of the best coffee in town; sweet treats and baked goods at reasonable prices. ⑤ *Average main: NZ$16* ✉ *111 Moray Pl.* ☎ *03/477–0232* ⊙ *No dinner.*

Little India Dunedin

$$$ | **INDIAN** | Influenced by the flavors of northern India (and the kitchen of founder Sukhi's grandmother), this family business began in Dunedin and has become a chain spanning the country. Spacious and modern eateries meet traditional cooking methods, and warm hospitality and generous portions of spicy vindaloos and Bengali fish preparations are among the hallmarks. **Known for:** authentic North Indian cuisine; great curries; Indian beers. ⑤ *Average main: NZ$24* ✉ *308 Moray Pl.* ☎ *03/477–6559* ⊕ *www.littleindia.co.nz* ⊙ *No lunch weekends.*

Plato Cafe

$$$$ | **NEW ZEALAND** | A favorite among locals, this waterfront eatery that was once a seafarers hostel provides great food and excellent service. Everything from the bread and house-made duck liver–cognac pâté to the perfectly cooked seafood and chicken dishes is delicious. **Known for:** impressive all-encompassing menu; great waterfront views; BYOB policy. ⑤ *Average main: NZ$35* ✉ *2 Birch St.* ☎ *03/477–4235* ⊕ *www.platocafe.co.nz.*

★ Salt Bar Restaurant

$$$ | **NEW ZEALAND** | In an iconic art deco building, this is the place to dine in St. Clair's, a leafy seaside neighborhood along a spectacular beach. Sate yourself with beef Burgundy pie or venison; the less carnivorous may wish to try the roast pumpkin risotto. **Known for:** sunny corner location close to beach; delicious food at reasonable prices; great brunch menu. ⑤ *Average main: NZ$29* ✉ *240 Forbury Rd., St. Clair's* ☎ *03/455–1077* ⊕ *www.saltbar.co.nz.*

Sampan Khmer Satay Noodle House

$ | **ASIAN** | **FAMILY** | This no-frills noodle bar is crowded with students and serves yummy, filling, and inexpensive soups. Try the spicy satay chicken burgers and fried rice. **Known for:** signature dishes of Thai, Khmer, and Chinese cuisine; quick service; popularity with university students. ⑤ *Average main: NZ$11* ✉ *362 George St.* ☎ *03/477–3782* ▭ *No credit cards.*

Thai Hanoi

$$$ | **THAI** | This Thai-Vietnamese fusion spot offers options like green or red Thai curries and a yellow or jungle (hot) Vietnamese curry. The Rialto Cinema is across the way, making this a convenient pre- or postmovie dinner spot—but reserving a table is a good idea. **Known for:** authentic curries; centrally located setting; BYOB policy. ⑤ *Average main: NZ$23* ✉ *24 Moray Pl.* ☎ *03/471–9500* ⊙ *No lunch weekends.*

🛏 Hotels

Bluestone on George

$$ | **RENTAL** | A short walk from restaurants and inner-city shopping, each of these contemporary-style studio

Otago Central Rail Trail

From Dunedin Railway Station, take the Taieri Gorge Train to Middlemarch (or Pukerangi, 19 km [12 miles] from Middlemarch), one end of the **Otago Central Rail Trail**. This 150-km (93-mile) pleasantly undulating bicycle path follows the old railway line and includes a dizzying wooden viaduct and a 500-foot-long tunnel, with places to eat, sleep, and drink along the way. The only traffic you'll encounter is the occasional herd of daggy (muddy-bottomed) sheep. The ride takes about five days to complete, passing through sheep farms and lovely wee towns such as Ranfurly, an "oasis of art deco," and Alexander, one of the busier hubs in Central Otago on the banks of the paint-green Clutha River. The trail eventually ends in Thyme-scented Clyde. The route can be traversed in either direction; Clyde is approximately 80 km (50 miles) from Queenstown. The trail provides a great way to experience the sheep stations, with their puzzling gates and similarly puzzling locks, as well as mud, wind, rivers, pubs, and old gold fields. ⊕ www.otagocentralrailtrail. co.nz.

apartments has a patio or balcony. **Pros:** centrally located; contemporary style; free Wi-Fi and parking. **Cons:** not much character; impersonal business-trip vibe; gym is on the small side. ⑤ *Rooms from: NZ$195* ✉ *571 George St.* ☎ *03/477–9201* ⊕ *www.bluestonedunedin.co.nz* ⤴ *15 rooms* ⦿ *No meals* ⌕ *No children allowed.*

Brothers Boutique Hotel

$$ | **HOTEL** | This centrally located historic hotel once housed members of the Christian Brothers, but now its family-run with plenty of charm, elegance, and character. **Pros:** quirky interior; free parking; great views over city. **Cons:** some street noise; no air-conditioning; some rooms could use an upgrade. ⑤ *Rooms from: NZ$190* ✉ *295 Rattray St.* ☎ *03/477–0043* ⊕ *www.brothershotel.co.nz* ⤴ *15 rooms* ⦿ *Free Breakfast.*

George Street Motel Apartments

$$ | **RENTAL** | One block from Dunedin's main shopping and dining area, these clean and spacious apartments come with full kitchens in one-bedroom units and refrigerators and microwaves in the studios. **Pros:** large open kitchen/lounge rooms; central location; free Wi-Fi. **Cons:** some bathrooms are small; can be dated but upgrades are ongoing; breakfast not included with price. ⑤ *Rooms from: NZ$160* ✉ *575 George St.* ☎ *03/477–9333, 0800/109–333* ⊕ *www.georgestreetmotel.co.nz* ⤴ *16 units* ⦿ *Breakfast.*

Hogwartz Hostel

$ | **RENTAL** | **FAMILY** | Just opposite St. Joseph's Cathedral, this late-1800s former bishop's residence (once called Rockmount) is now a comfortable hostel with a few touches of Harry Potter (fans may want to look for Hedwig in Room 9 3/4) and plenty of nice spaces. **Pros:** central location; affordable rates; lots of fun decor for Harry Potter fans. **Cons:** uphill access; some bathroom facilities are shared; Wi-Fi isn't free. ⑤ *Rooms from: NZ$93* ✉ *277 Rattray St.* ☎ *03/474–1487* ⊕ *www.hogwartz.co.nz* ⤴ *17 rooms* ⦿ *No meals.*

Hulmes Court Bed & Breakfast

$ | **B&B/INN** | An 1860s Victorian mansion just a three-minute walk to the center of town, Hulmes Court was originally built for one of the founders of the Otago Medical School (it maintains scholarly ties by employing University of Otago students) and is paired with a 1907 house. **Pros:** friendly staff; interesting decorations; quiet, residential neighborhood. **Cons:** not ideal for folks with cat allergies; located on a steep hill; not all rooms have en suite bathrooms. ⑤ *Rooms from: NZ$85* ✉ *52 Tennyson St.* ☎ *03/477–5319* ⊕ *www.hulmes.co.nz* ➟ *11 rooms* ⦿ *Breakfast.*

Lisburn House

$$ | **B&B/INN** | This Victorian-Gothic house is a romantic retreat set amid lovingly tended gardens and shows off such original details as decorative Irish brickwork, fishtail slate roof tiles, high, molded-plaster ceilings, and an impressive turn-of-the-20th-century stained-glass entrance. **Pros:** antique-style rooms; fabulous in-house restaurant; late breakfast and check-out. **Cons:** on the outskirts of city center; only one of the private baths is en suite; no televisions in rooms. ⑤ *Rooms from: NZ$175* ✉ *15 Lisburn Ave.* ☎ *0800/666–716* ➟ *3 rooms* ⦿ *Breakfast.*

▼ Nightlife

You could spend all night bar-hopping and never leave The Octagon, with its many drinking establishments. Many venues are on or near George and Princes streets, often down dark alleys with no signs, so follow the crowd. Information about what's going on can be found on Radio One 91 FM (⊕ *www.r1.co.nz*) and in the student paper (⊕ *www.critic.co.nz*) the *Critic*.

Bacchus Wine Bar and Restaurant

WINE BARS—NIGHTLIFE | Overlooking The Octagon, this high-ceilinged, upstairs wine bar and restaurant in 1880s surroundings is as elegant as the wines on offer. An accompanying fine dining menu showcases New Zealand beef and lamb. ✉ *12 The Octagon, 1st fl.* ☎ *03 /474–0824* ⊕ *www.bacchuswinebarrestaurant.co.nz.*

The Craic Irish Tavern

BARS/PUBS | The Irish term for fun and banter certainly applies to this cozy tavern that plays host to live music and serves good pub grub and an excellent choice of beer, whisky, wine, and cocktails. For its food, emphasis is on seafood and wild game, with a few Irish favorites. ✉ *24 The Octagon* ⊕ *www.thecraic.co.nz.*

Ironic Cafe and Bar

$$$ | **CAFES—NIGHTLIFE** | A decor of steel and concrete with lots of natural light gives this modern space a semi-industrial look and every table comes with a view of the iconic Dunedin Railway Station building just across the road. You can enjoy market-fresh light fare by day and a lively cocktail scene come sunset. Its brunch is also very popular. ✉ *9 Anzac Ave.* ☎ *03/477–9988* ⊕ *www.ironiccafe-bar.co.nz.*

Pequeno

BARS/PUBS | Possibly the snuggest bar in Dunedin came to notoriety as the hangout of choice for Gwyneth Paltrow and Chris Martin, of the band Coldplay, during the Dunedin shoot of the film *Sylvia*. Leather chairs, an open fire, and a good selection of whisky and cigars add to the lounge atmosphere. The wine list is good as well, if pricey, and there's live music some nights. ✉ *Savoy Bldg., 50 Princes St., lower ground fl.* ☎ *03/477–7830.*

Union Bar

BARS/PUBS | A prime spot at the heart of the university campus ensures a predominantly student clientele, though everyone is welcome. Nights are split between local or national (or even international) live rock acts and DJ-driven nights of 1980s hits, hip-hop, house, and drum 'n' bass music. ✉ *640 Cumberland St.* ☎ *03/479–5309* ⊕ *www.dunedinmusic.com.*

🎭 Performing Arts

Regent Theatre

THEATER | A historic building hosts large-scale musicals as well as dance and theater performances and those of the Royal New Zealand Ballet. It is also the scene of the New Zealand Film Festival and the World Cinema Showcase each year. Stylish, 1930s-era The Bund is a café and tapas bar. ✉ *17 The Octagon* ☎ *03/477–8597 ticket reservations* ⊕ *www.regenttheatre.co.nz.*

🛍 Shopping

Nearly all the good shops are clustered around George Street and Moray Place.

Design Withdrawals

BOOKS/STATIONERY | New Zealand artists and designers are well supported here. Unique jewelry, clothing, art, and housewares, including pieces by David Trubridge, Phizacklea, and Ian Blackwell, are on offer. ✉ *7 Moray Pl.* ☎ *03/477–9296* ⊕ *www.designwithdrawals.co.nz.*

Guilty by Confection

FOOD/CANDY | For sweets, drop by this shop for a hot chocolate or some terrific homemade fudge. ✉ *44–46 Stuart St.* ☎ *03/474–0835.*

Koru NZ Art

ART GALLERIES | An owner-operated gift shop and gallery that promotes New Zealand art. It houses the work of some 80 artists and craftspeople from all around the country and includes crafts made of *pounamu* (New Zealand greenstone), *paua* (abalone shell), and wood, as well as weaving and pottery. ✉ *2 Castle St.* ☎ *03/477–2138.*

Plume

CLOTHING | Plume carries great New Zealand labels among a selection of major international designer clothes. New Zealand labels include Nom D, Zambesi, Rick Owens, Ksubi, Jimmy D, Palladium, Serge Thoraval, and Workshop. ✉ *310*

George St. ☎ *03/477–9358* ⊕ *www. nomdstore.com/us/plume-store.html.*

Slick Willy's

CLOTHING | If you're looking for fun, funky sundresses, here's a great selection, along with women's denim, dresses, jackets, pants, skirts, shoes, shorts, skirts, and tops, not to mention snazzy shoes and jewelry. ✉ *323 George St., upstairs* ☎ *03/477–1406* ⊕ *www.slickwillys.co.nz.*

University Bookshop

BOOKS/STATIONERY | Bibliophiles will be in heaven amid this eclectic and diverse selection of books as well as a feast of quirky gifts, and bargain hunters will love the second floor, where there is a constant sale. ✉ *378 Great King St.* ☎ *03/477–6976* ⊕ *www.unibooks.co.nz.*

🏃 Activities

Mix up your city adventure with some sightseeing on the outskirts of town. And when that's finished, pop over to one of the parks to watch kids in rugby practice after school.

HIKING AND WALKING

"Walking with Wheels" is a collection of well-groomed walks put together by Dunedin City Council detailing those suitable for wheelchair users and families with strollers (the three-wheeled rugged terrain kind). You can download a leaflet from the Dunedin i-SITE website.

Signal Hill

HIKING/WALKING | This rise just northeast of the city center offers good views of the city below and the surrounding hills. It's a popular walking destination and an excellent mountain-biking venue. At the opposite end of town, Saddle Hill looks southward to Mosgiel and the Taieri Plain. The monument at the top was built in 1940 to mark 100 years of British sovereignty in New Zealand. Legend has it the flagpole here was made from the mast of the cutter once belonging to the notorious Bully Hayes, the South Pacific's only pirate. ⊠ *Signal Hill Rd.*

RUGBY

Forsyth Barr Stadium

LOCAL SPORTS | Is this real grass growing in a covered stadium? Originally developed for the space industry, a transparent polymer roof crowns this commanding 30,000 seater. Take a tour of the stadium; scream yourself hoarse at a rugby match; soak up the atmosphere of a soccer game; choose a concert; or shop at the Stadium Market on a Sunday. Home games for super-rugby's Highlanders are played here, as are provincial rugby team Otago, and soccer's Southern United. Tickets sell out quickly for international rugby fixtures; there's nothing like watching a pregame *haka* (Māori warrior dance) when national team, the All Blacks, are in town. Ticket prices start from NZ$25 but depend hugely on the type of match; internationals go well into hundreds of dollars. ⊠ *130 Anzac Ave.* ☎ *03/479–2823, 0800/246–464* ⊕ *www. forsythbarrstadium.co.nz* ⊠ *Tours NZ$20.*

Oamaru

112 km (69 miles) north of Dunedin, 85 km (53 miles) south of Timaru.

In Oamaru's port district New Zealand's best-preserved collection of historical landmarks still gleam with ornate, limestone Victorian facades. During the second week of November the town hosts the Victorian Heritage Celebrations. Festivities include the New Zealand Penny Farthing Championships, a Heritage Golf Classic, a Heritage Ball, and a Victorian Garden Party. The town's visitor center has information about the festival and the buildings themselves.

Oamaru's other claim to fame is penguins. Each evening, enthusiastic blue penguins—the world's smallest penguin breed—emerge from the sea and waddle up the beach to their nests. The penguin colony is a five-minute drive from the town center in Oamaru. An even more significant population of yellow-eyed penguins, or *hoiho,* come ashore south of Oamaru. The best places to view them are Bushy Beach and Katiki Point, where hides (camouflaged viewing huts) have been constructed. The hide at Bushy Beach is wheelchair-accessible. These penguins are one of the world's rarest breeds, and they are considered an endangered species. More recently the town has become known for a company called Steampunk, which creates quirky recycled industrial art throughout the town.

GETTING HERE AND AROUND

From Dunedin to Oamaru it's a 1½-hour drive north on State Highway 1. From Timaru to Oamaru it's a one-hour drive south on the same route. InterCity Coachlines connects Oamaru to Dunedin and Timaru three times daily. Exploring the mostly flat and ordered layout of Oamaru streets is easy and enjoyable on foot. South Hill Walkway follows the harbor to Lookout Reserve, which affords excellent views out over the town and port.

VISITOR INFORMATION

Oamaru i-SITE Info Centre

The town's visitor center has information about the locally popular Victorian Heritage Celebrations as well as the town's noteworthy buildings. ⊠ *1 Thames St.* ☎ *03/434–1656* ⊕ *waitakinz.com.*

⊙ Sights

Moeraki Boulders

NATURE SITE | These giant spherical rocks are concretions that were formed by a gradual buildup of minerals around a central core. Some boulders have sprung open, revealing—no, not alien life forms, but—interesting calcite crystals. The boulders stud the beach north of the town of Moeraki and south as well at Katiki Beach off Highway 1. Be warned that the boulders at Moeraki Beach have become a bit of a tourist attraction, and there are often whole busloads of people wandering the beach. Watch for little Hector's dolphins jumping in the surf just offshore; they're as interesting as the boulders. ⊠ *7 Moeraki Boulders Rd., Moeraki.*

Oamaru Blue Penguin Colony

LOCAL INTEREST | FAMILY | Penguins at Friendly Bay might be present any time of the year, and tours and viewing opportunities run day and evening. There's a small visitor center on-site with a shop and toilet facilities. The actual times penguins come ashore in the evening affects the nighttime open hours, but the center opens every morning at 10 am. Access to the public beach is free. ⊠ *Waterfront Rd.* ☎ *03/433–1195* ⊕ *www.penguins. co.nz* 🎫 *Tours from NZ$20.*

 ## Restaurants

Riverstone Kitchen

$$$ | NEW ZEALAND | FAMILY | The mouthwatering menu focuses on organic, locally grown, seasonal produce, offering regional New Zealand cuisine with a few Asian accents (a Thai duck salad, for instance). While the atmosphere is casual, the food is serious thanks to chef Bevan Smith, who trained in Christchurch and has published two cookbooks.
Known for: fresh seasonal fare; innovative and elegant menu; affordable prix-fixe option. ⑤ *Average main: NZ$30* ⊠ *1431 State Hwy. 1* ☎ *03/431–3505* ⊕ *www. riverstonekitchen.co.nz* ⊗ *Closed Tues. and Wed. No dinner Mon.*

Otago Peninsula

The main items of interest along the claw-shape peninsula that extends northeast from Dunedin are an albatross colony and Larnach Castle. The road on the west side of the peninsula consists of 15 km (9½ miles) of tight curves along the harbor, so be careful while driving, or you could find yourself having an impromptu marine adventure. Along the road are a handful of settlements; these get progressively more rustic as you near the peninsula's tip. On the east side of the peninsula there's a string of rugged beaches; some are accessible via walking paths. On the journey back to Dunedin, the Highcliff Road, which turns inland at the village of Portobello, is a scenic alternative to the coastal Portobello Road and gives easiest access to Larnach Castle. Allow an hour to drive from the city.

GETTING HERE AND AROUND

Driving to the peninsula gives you freedom to stop when and where you choose, and the route is quite scenic, as much of the road hugs the water. The Dunedin city bus leaves throughout the day from Cumberland Street to the peninsula; check the GoBus website for the schedule. You can also see the peninsula sights via a harbor boat cruise.

Visitor information is available at the Dunedin i-SITE Visitor Information Centre, but for facts specific to the peninsula, check out the Visit Otago Peninsula website.

CONTACTS GoBus. ☎ *03/474–5577* ⊕ *www.gobus.co.nz.* **Otago Regional Council.** ⊠ *Dunedin Passenger Transport, 1 Transport Pl., Dunedin* ☎ *03/474–1669* ⊕ *www.orc.govt.nz.*

TOURS
Monarch Wildlife Cruises

BOAT TOURS | Experience the area's prolific wildlife on a guided, hour-long cruise from Dunedin to Taiaroa Head, including visits to the breeding sites of the northern royal albatross, New Zealand fur seals, and up to 20 species of coastal and pelagic birds. Very likely, an albatross will fly over your boat—the huge wingspan of these birds makes this a spectacular sight. Other trips include landing stops at the yellow-eyed penguin reserve or the Taiaroa visitor center.

Otago Peninsula

Middlemarch

Sutton

Taieri Gorge Railway

Clarks Junction

Lake Mahinerangi

Lawrence

Outram

Mosgiel

Allanton

Westwood

Brighton

Kuri Bush

Milton

Balclutha

Invercargill

Kaitangata

Toko Mouth

TO CHRISTCHURCH

Palmerston

Waikouaiti

Cornish Head

Puketeraki

Evansdale   Warrington

Waitati

Orokonui Ecosanctuary

Aramoana

The Mole

Port Chalmers

Sawyers Bay

Portobello

Larnach Castle

Broad Bay

Waverley

St Clair

Dunedin see detail map

Royal Albatross Colony & Taiaroa Head

Yellow-Eyed Penguin Reserve

Otago Harbour

OTAGO PENINSULA

South Pacific Ocean

0   15 mi

0   15 km

✉ 20 Fryatt St., Dunedin ☎ 03/477–4276 ⊕ www.wildlife.co.nz 🖼 From NZ$54.

Natures Wonders Wildlife Tours

ADVENTURE TOURS | An all-terrain vehicle gets you to hard-to-reach parts of the Otago Peninsula. The one-hour Wildlife Tour includes visits to colonies of shags (cormorants), seals, and blue penguins, and you may even catch up with some yellow-eyed penguins coming ashore. The Sheep Shed Tour is exactly that and provides a look at life on a New Zealand sheep farm: watch talented shearers in action; feel the fleece; smell the lanolin (and the waft of a genuine sheep shed); walk alongside working dogs as they control the flow of sheep into holding pens. Make a day of it and combine both trips. ✉ Taiaroa Head, 1265 Harrington Point Rd., Dunedin ☎ 03/478–1150,

0800/246–446 ⊕ www.natureswonders. co.nz 🖼 From NZ$45.

VISITOR INFORMATION
CONTACTS Visit Otago Peninsula. ⊕ www. otago-peninsula.co.nz.

🔘 Sights

Larnach Castle

CASTLE/PALACE | High on a hilltop with commanding views from its battlements, the grand baronial fantasy of William Larnach, an Australian-born businessman and New Zealand politician, was a vast extravagance even in the free-spending days of the gold rush in the 1870s. Larnach imported an English craftsman to carve the ceilings, which took 12 years to complete. The solid marble bath, marble fireplaces, tiles, glass, and even much of the wood came from Europe.

Larnach rose to a prominent position in the New Zealand government of the late 1800s, but in 1898, beset by a series of financial disasters and possible marital problems, he committed suicide in Parliament House—when, according to one version of the story, his third wife, whom he married at an advanced age, ran off with his youngest son. The 35 acres of grounds around the castle include lodging, a rain-forest garden with kauri, *rimu*, and totara trees, statues of *Alice in Wonderland* characters (see if you can find the Cheshire Cat), a herbaceous walk, and a South Seas Walkway lined with palms and aloe plants. New Zealand's only castle is a 20-minute drive from Dunedin but can be tricky to find, so follow the directions on the website. ⊠ *145 Camp Rd., Otago, Dunedin* ☎ *03/476–1616* ⊕ *www.larnachcastle. co.nz* ✉ *From NZ$17.*

The Mole

TOUR—SIGHT | The Mole, which splits the picturesque white-sand beach at the end of the Aramoana Peninsula, is a 1-km-long (½-mile-long) artificial breakwater protecting the entrance to Otago Harbour. A walk atop the breakwater is especially exciting when there is a big running sea. The beach and sand dunes to the east are known as Shelly Beach, while to the west, Big Beach extends for more than 2 km (about a mile). At points along this stretch, steep rock faces come down to the waterline and are popular with rock climbers. Seals can be found sun bathing on the rocks.

Orokonui Ecosanctuary

FOREST | **FAMILY** | A 30-minute drive northeast of Dunedin is a 759-acre forest where native plants and wildlife thrive in relative safety surrounded by an 8.7-km (5-mile) predator-proof fence. This is necessary because much of New Zealand wildlife is threatened by pests and predators introduced into the country before settlers knew any better, and Orokonui is unique because it's the only mainland ecosanctuary on the South Island. The park offers good walking tracks, informative displays, a café, and souvenir shop. Parents, grab a "Kiwi Ranger" booklet from the front desk, which lists lots of activities to keep the kids amused during the day; if they complete the tasks, they earn a "Kiwi Ranger" badge. ⊠ *600 Blueskin Rd., Waitati* ☎ *03/482–1755* ⊕ *www.orokonui.org.nz* ✉ *Tours from NZ$20.*

★ **Royal Albatross Colony**

NATURE PRESERVE | The wild and exposed eastern tip of the Otago Peninsula is the site of a breeding colony of royal albatrosses. Among the largest birds in the world, with a wingspan of up to 10 feet, they can take off only from steep slopes with the help of a strong breeze. With the exception of this colony and those in the Chatham Islands to the east, the birds are only on windswept islands deep in southern latitudes, far from human habitation. Under the auspices of the **Royal Albatross Centre,** the colony is open for viewing all year, except during a two-month break between mid-September and mid-November when the birds lay their eggs; the visitor center is open year-round. The greatest number of birds is present shortly after the young albatrosses hatch near the end of January. Between March and September parents leave the fledglings in their nests while they gather food for them. In September, the young birds fly away, returning about eight years later to start their own breeding cycle. Access to the colony is strictly controlled, and you must book in advance. From the visitor center you go in groups up a steep trail to the Albatross Observatory, from which you can see the birds through viewing windows. ⊠ *1260 Harington Point Rd., Taiaroa Head* ☎ *03/478–0499, 0800/528–767* ⊕ *www. albatross.org.nz* ✉ *NZ$52.*

Taiaroa Head

Overlooking the albatross colony is the Armstrong "Disappearing" Gun at Fort

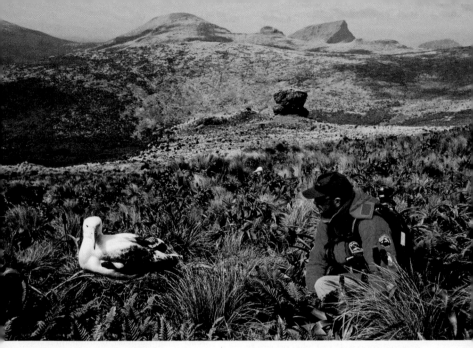

A tramper gets close to a Royal Albatross.

Taiaroa, a 6-inch artillery piece installed during the Russian Scare of 1886, when Russia was making hostile maneuvers through the Pacific. The gun was shot in anger only once, during World War II, when it was fired across the bow of a fishing boat that failed to observe correct procedures. Tours range from 30 to 90 minutes and can include albatross viewing, Fort Taiaroa, and an Albatross Insight presentation. ✉ *Taiaroa Head* 🚲 *Combined tour with Albatross Colony NZ$62.*

Yellow-Eyed Penguin Reserve

NATURE PRESERVE | FAMILY | This conservation project is entirely funded by guided tours of the private reserve. If you'd like to observe the world's most endangered penguin in its natural habitat, visit Penguin Place, where an ingenious network of tunnels has been disguised so that you can get close. The penguins, also known as *hoiho* (meaning "noise shouter" in Māori), are characterized by their yellow irises and headbands. Tours run throughout the afternoon but must be booked in advance. If you can't bring yourself to leave, Penguin Place Lodge offers basic and inexpensive farm-stay accommodation. ✉ *45 Pakihau Rd., Harrington Point* ☎ *03/478–0286* ⊕ *www.penguinplace.co.nz* 🚲 *NZ$55* 🚲 *Reservations essential.*

🍴 Restaurants

Bay Café

$$$ | CAFÉ | Located in the first settlement you reach on the peninsula, this well-known café has fine views across the harbor. Scallops, prawns, blue cod, and mussels are popular, as are the tasty pizzas with smoked salmon and prawns. **Known for:** charming surroundings; great seafood; popular brunch menu. Ⓢ *Average main: NZ$24* ✉ *494 Portobello Rd., Portobello* ☎ *03/476–0075.*

1908 Café & Bar

$$$ | ECLECTIC | There are good views of the harbor from this converted post office "where the high road meets the low road." The interior still feels Edwardian, and classic seafood dishes and steaks lead the menu. On a nice day sit outside in the courtyard or in winter beside the open fire. **Known for:** beautiful harbor views; gorgeous Edwardian decor; delicious seafood and steaks menu. $ *Average main: NZ$29* ⊠ *7 Harington Point Rd., Portobello* ☎ *03/478–0801* ⊕ *www.1908cafe.co.nz* ۩ *No lunch Mon. and Tues. in Apr.–Sept.*

 Hotels

Larnach Lodge

$$ | B&B/INN | It's hard to beat panoramic sea views, 35 acres of world-class gardens, having Larnach Castle as a neighbor, and the choice of a luxury room or a more modest yet still character-filled accommodation. **Pros:** impressive grounds; Scottish themed with period furniture; coastal walks nearby. **Cons:** cheaper rooms do not have private baths; a bit on the expensive side for what you get; more a manor house than a true castle. $ *Rooms from: NZ$180* ⊠ *145 Camp Rd., Otago, 14 km (8.6 miles) northeast of Dunedin, Dunedin* ☎ *03/476–1616* ⊕ *www.larnachcastle.co.nz* ⌐ *23 rooms* ۩⊙۩ *Breakfast.*

 Activities

DIVING

Dive Otago

DIVING/SNORKELING | A dozen or so small ships were sunk between 1920 and 1950 to protect the breakwater from the relentless Southern Ocean. You can check these ships out, and the tall kelp forest that protects them, with Dive Otago, which run trips to the Mole and other dive sites when the weather allows. Introductory dive courses and snorkeling trips also offered. ⊠ *2 Wharf St., Dunedin* ☎ *03/466–4370* ⊕ *www.diveotago.co.nz.*

Invercargill

182 km (113 miles) south of Queenstown, 217 km (135 miles) southwest of Dunedin.

Originally settled by Scottish immigrants, Invercargill has retained much of its turn-of-the-20th-century character, with broad main avenues (Tay Street and Dee Street) and streetscapes with richly embellished buildings. You'll find facades with Italian and English Renaissance styles, Gothic stone tracery, and Romanesque designs on a number of its well-preserved buildings.

Invercargill was featured in the movie *The World's Fastest Indian* (2005) starring Sir Anthony Hopkins as Invercargill-bred Burt Munro, a local "petrolhead" who raced his Indian motorcycle on Oreti Beach in preparation for breaking a world land speed record. Mayor Tim Shadbolt had a cameo in the film, which is worth seeing. Invercargill has a reputation to this day for "boy racers," and you'll notice them roaring up and down the city streets in tricked-out cars. Indignant Invercargillites blame the epidemic on "Gorons," boy racers from neighboring city Gore. You might have a '50s flashback if you're waiting at a light and a lowrider next to you starts to rumble and rev its engine.

GETTING HERE AND AROUND

Invercargill's airport (IVC) is 3 km (2 miles) from the city center. From Invercargill, Air New Zealand runs direct flights to Christchurch and Wellington, and Stewart Island flights hops over to Stewart Island. Several rental car companies operate in the terminal. Taxis from Invercargill Airport into town cost NZ$12–NZ$15. A shuttle run by Executive Car Services (⊕ *www.executivecarservice.co.nz*) costs NZ$10–NZ$14 per person, and there's usually a shuttle waiting for each flight. Executive Car Service also rents secure car storage (NZ$10 per night). Invercargill is extremely walkable, and also

Taking the Southern Scenic Route

The Southern Scenic Route, 440 km (273 miles) long, follows the coast south of Dunedin and the Otago Peninsula, picks up the highway to Balclutha, and swings around the Catlins coast before pushing through Invercargill to Milford Sound. The Catlins stretch (200 km, or 125 miles) is a treat, although some side roads can be rough. Split your journey over at least two days. The *Southern Scenic Route* brochure, available at the Dunedin visitor center, describes the sights; attractions are signposted. Visit ⊕ *www.southernscenicroute. co.nz.*

When you leave the highway at Balclutha, you'll notice that the native bush is dense and relatively untouched. This, coupled with rich birdsong, gives the countryside a subtropical quality.

The first stop is **Nugget Point**. Its Māori name, Tokatā, means "rocks standing up out of water." Wildlife abounds, including yellow-eyed penguins, fur and elephant seals, and sea lions. The town at Nugget Point is **Kaka Point**. There are several places to stay the night, and you should spend time at the "hide" observing the yellow-eyed penguins coming in from the sea. If you want a coffee served with an excellent sea view, stop in the **Point Café & Bar** at Kaka Point. Inland is **Owaka**, the Catlins' only town. With a population of roughly 400, Owaka has a cluster of shops, a Department of Conservation Field Centre, a small museum, and basic services.

At the settlement of **Papatowai**, there's a convenient picnic spot behind a tidal inlet. Here you can enjoy rock pools with bush on one side and coastline on the other. Just

south of here, stop at the **Florence Hill Lookout**. The view of Tautuku Bay is one of the best coastal views in New Zealand. There's a 30-minute loop walk onto the estuary at Tautuku Bay.

Farther on is **Curio Bay**, home to a petrified forest accessible at low tide. From Curio Bay a back road runs out to **Slope Point**, mainland New Zealand's southernmost point. Heavy rains or unusually high tides can make the road impassable. Slope Point is a bit of a disappointment— just some farmland sloping to the sea. However, it gets plenty of visitors, mainly because nearby Waipapa Point was the location of the country's worst ever civilian shipwreck when the *SS Tararua* sunk offshore on April 29, 1881. A memorial stands to the 131 people who died in the wreck and are buried in a paddock here. There is no access during the lambing season in September and October. If you skip Slope Point and continue on the main road, stop at the general store in Waikawa, where the art of the meat pie has been perfected. Worth checking out, too, is the Waikawa Museum and Information Centre, made from two old school buildings.

By now the rugged Catlins landscape smooths out into gentle green hills. From the township of Fortrose the roads are straight once more across the wide flats of Southland; before you know it, you've reached Invercargill. The road continues westward to Tuatapere, the self-proclaimed "sausage capital of New Zealand." Along the way check out the surfers at Colac Bay and make a detour to Cosy Nook, where a handful of fishing "cribs," or huts, have been likened to an old Cornwall fishing village.

particularly driver-friendly. Outside Reading Cinemas in Dee Street, BusSmart Central links the center of town with local districts; longer distance buses connect Invercargill to Christchurch, Dunedin, Te Anau, and Queenstown every day and leave from Queens Park adjacent to Southland Museum. Stewart Island Experience (⊕ *www.stewartisland-experience.co.nz*) operates the Bluff Bus, which stops at the museum and various accommodations (reservations essential).

AIRPORT CONTACTS Invercargill Airport.
✉ *106 Airport Ave.* ☎ *03/218–6366* ⊕ *www.invercargillairport.co.nz.*

BUS CONTACTS Atomic Shuttles.
☎ *03/349–0697, 0508/108–359* ⊕ *www.atomictravel.co.nz.* **Bottom Bus.** ☎ *0800/304–333, 03/477–9083* ⊕ *www.travelheadfirst.com.* **BusSmart.** ✉ *Dee St.* ☎ *03/211–1777* ⊕ *www.icc.govt.nz* **Inter-City.** ☎ *03/471–7143* ⊕ *www.intercity.co.nz.*

TOURS

Catlins Scenic and Wildlife Tours
ECOTOURISM | This company offers guided eco-tours that will take you to view sea lions, fur seals, yellow-eyed penguins, and seabird nesting sites, along with other top sights in the area. Tours all are three-four hours and include options for a sunrise tour and a waterfall tour; there's one full day, in-depth nature tour. ✉ *744 Catlins Valley Rd., Papatowai* ✛ *Tawanui* ☎ *03/415–8613* ⊕ *www.catlinsmohua-park.co.nz* 🍽 *From NZ$150.*

Lynette Jack Scenic Sights
PERSONAL GUIDES | Lynette Jack draws on an extensive knowledge of Invercargill and the surrounding area to illuminate local history during an exploration of gardens, beaches, historic houses, local hero Burt Munro, and even the local aluminium smeltery. ✉ *22 Willis St.* ☎ *03/215–7741, 027/433–8370* 🖋 *scenic.sights@xtra.co.nz* 🍽 *From NZ$105.*

CONTACTS Invercargill Visitor Information Centre. ✉ *Southland Museum, Wachner Pl.* ☎ *03/211–0895* ⊕ *www.invercargillnz.com.*

👁 Sights

Bluff
TOWN | In the tiny township of Bluff (*The Bluff* to locals) you can taste the coveted namesake oysters. An annual festival, held in May, wallows in seafood delicacies; oyster-opening and oyster-eating competitions and cook-offs are part of the fun. (If you miss the festival, the most spectacular place for oysters, in season, is Lands End Restaurant overlooking the sea.) Don't miss the Maritime Museum on the Foreshore Road (the Oyster boat *Monica* sits beside it). Bluff is also home to the frequently photographed Stirling Point signpost, at the southern end of State Highway 1, which gives directions to places all over the world, including the South Pole. If it's a nice day follow the signs up to Bluff Lookout: the views encompass the Catlins and Stewart Island, and give you an excellent lay of the land. Good walking tracks are around Bluff; many begin at Stirling Point. The town is also the main jumping-off point for Stewart Island. It's about 30 km (19 miles) from Invercargill to Bluff, an easy half-hour drive south on State Highway 1. ⊕ *www.bluff.co.nz.*

E. Hayes and Sons
STORE/MALL | Invercargill's most famous sight is a 100-year-old hardware store that stocks every little thing you can think of. It's totally yin-yang (grandma-grandpa) with one half devoted to little glass lemon juicers and whisks and the other half filled with tools and wheelbarrows. The store also has a popular Motorworks Collection where you can view memorabilia of Invercargill's famous son Burt Munro, the "World's Fastest Indian." ✉ *168 Dee St.* ☎ *03/218–2059.*

Queens Park

CITY PARK | FAMILY | These 200 acres in the center of town create a fine layout of public gardens. Included are two rose gardens with both modern and "antique" rose varieties; a Japanese garden complete with meditation area; and an impressive hothouse, which acts as a sanctuary on a wet day. The park has miles of gentle walking paths and waterways, an 18-hole golf course, a fitness trail, and a decent café. There's also a small zoo area and an aviary with a walk-through section that children love. The main entrance is through the stately Feldwick Gates next to the Southland Museum. ⊠ *Queens Dr. at Gala St.* ☎ *03/217–7368.*

Transport World

MUSEUM | More than 300 trucks and VW Kombis (that's a VW bus, to Americans) are on display, alongside motoring memorabilia and petrol bowsers—or, again for Americans, gas pumps. Kids who get bored looking at old cars will enjoy a special Lego learning space geared to them. There's something for everyone here, including a display of classic motorcycles and an interactive display of heavy machinery. ⊠ *491 Tay St.* ☎ *03/217–0199* ⊕ *www.transportworld.co.nz* ⊡ *NZ$30.*

Water Tower

BUILDING | An exceptional example of Victorian architecture can be seen peaking above the city's gentle landscape. Built in 1889 to pressurize the water supply, the structure was recognized by New Zealand's Historic Places Trust as one of the country's most outstanding industrial monuments. This ornate landmark is still completely functional. On Sunday afternoon you can sometimes scale the internal staircase of the 139-foot-tall structure. ⊠ *Doon St.* ⊕ *www.icc.govt.nz.*

Beaches

Oreti Beach

BEACH—SIGHT | The surf at this spot 11 km (7 miles) southeast of town is often too rough for swimming, but locals do swim in summer, and surfers and windsurfers take advantage of the wind and swells that whip the coast almost constantly. The annual Burt Munro Challenge in February sees motorcycles hurtle across the sand as riders pit their wits and machines against one another in honor of the local hero and motorcycle land speed record holder from whom the race gets its name. **Amenities:** none. **Best for:** solitude; surfing; walking; windsurfing. ⊠ *Dunns Rd.* ⊕ *www.burtmunrochallenge.com.*

Restaurants

Cabbage Tree

$$$$ | NEW ZEALAND | FAMILY | A spacious room done in wood and brick offers a supersize menu with more than 100 dishes. Popular choices are Stewart Island blue cod, lamb shanks, prawns, pan-seared venison, and Bluff oyster dishes. **Known for:** comprehensive menu including many New Zealand wines; deliciously fresh seafood; wonderful outdoor garden bar. ⑤ *Average main: NZ$32* ⊠ *379 Dunns Rd.* ☎ *03/213–1443* ⊕ *www.thecabbagetree.com.*

Little India Invercargill

$$$ | INDIAN | Influenced by the flavors of northern India (and the kitchen of founder Sukhi's grandmother) this family business began in Dunedin and now has restaurants spanning the country. Spacious and modern eateries offer traditional cooking methods; warm hospitality and generous portions keep diners coming back. **Known for:** exotic and authentic Indian cuisine; cozy and charming atmosphere; plenty of vegetarian options. ⑤ *Average main: NZ$21* ⊠ *11 The Crescent* ☎ *03/214–1555* ⊕ *www.littleindia.co.nz* ☉ *No lunch weekends.*

The Rocks Restaurant Bar

$$$$ | CONTEMPORARY | You could easily walk past this stylish place, tucked inside a shopping courtyard. The kitchen employs bounty from the nearby bush and sea paired with inventive sauces and sides. **Known for:** exquisite dining experience; specializing in steaks, fish, chicken, pork, venison, and lamb; Tuscany-inspired decor. $ *Average main: NZ$32* ✉ *11 Courville Pl.* ☎ *03/218–7597* ⊕ *www.shop5rocks.com* ☉ *Closed Sun. and Mon.*

Ziff's Café and Bar

$$ | NEW ZEALAND | This enormously popular restaurant on the way to Oreti Beach (past the airport) is a local favorite. Ziff's does steak, blue cod, chicken, and pasta, and customers love the home-smoked salmon and the venison hot pot. **Known for:** generous servings of simple but tasty cuisine; late breakfasts; local atmosphere. $ *Average main: NZ$18* ✉ *143 Dunns Rd.* ☎ *03/213–0501* ⊕ *www.ziffs. co.nz.*

Hotels

Many of Invercargill's motels are on Tay Street, handy if you're coming from Dunedin and North Road, convenient if you're arriving from Queenstown.

Ascot Park Hotel

$$ | HOTEL | The largest hotel in town, a five-minute drive from the town center, is a rambling complex with spacious, modern rooms, all with small balconies and those in a motel-style building with kitchenettes. **Pros:** big spacious rooms; some kitchenette units for cooking; free Wi-Fi and parking. **Cons:** restaurant is pricey; tiny pool; some rooms could use updating. $ *Rooms from: NZ$165* ✉ *Corner of Tay St. and Racecourse Rd.* ☎ *03/219–9076, 0800/272–687* ⊕ *www. ascotparkhotel.co.nz* ⬑ *106 rooms* ⦿| *No meals.*

Kelvin Hotel

$$ | HOTEL | The big advantage of this modern but somewhat bland full-service hotel is that it's really central, in just about the ideal location if you're not driving. **Pros:** couldn't be more centrally located; excellent restaurant; welcoming staff. **Cons:** no gym on-site but pass to nearby facility included; currently undergoing renovations on exterior; some rooms on the small size. $ *Rooms from: NZ$150* ✉ *20 Kelvin St.* ☎ *03/218–2829, 0800/802–829* ⊕ *www.kelvinhotel.co.nz* ⬑ *61 rooms* ⦿| *No meals.*

Mohua Park

$$$ | RENTAL | If you're traveling to Invercargill via the Southern Scenic Route, these four lovely self-catering cottages make a perfect rest stop before you get to the city. **Pros:** beautiful outlooks on 35 acres of native forest; eco-friendly; lots of privacy. **Cons:** no restaurants on-site; no TV or phone; no Wi-Fi. $ *Rooms from: NZ$225* ✉ *744 Catlins Valley Rd.* ☎ *03/415–8613* ⊕ *www.catlinsmohua-park.co.nz* ⬑ *4 cottages* ⦿| *No meals.*

Tuatara Backpackers Lodge

$ | HOTEL | The world's southernmost YHA hostel is in the center of Invercargill, next door to the Speight's Ale House and the main city library. **Pros:** inexpensive; centrally located; all necessary amenities on-site. **Cons:** can be noisy at night; very basic; only three private rooms. $ *Rooms from: NZ$28* ✉ *30–32 Dee St.* ☎ *03/214–0954, 0800/488–282* ⊕ *www.tuatara-odge.co.nz* ⬑ *26 rooms* ⦿| *No meals.*

⚡ Activities

Take a picture of yourself on some of the world's southernmost beaches and send it home. But Invercargill doesn't exactly have perfect tanning weather. Even in summer, the south can still get a few chilly days. Some Stewart Island trips depart from here and include the ferry costs in their rate.

HIKING

Estuary Walkway

HIKING/WALKING | Just 2½ km (1½ miles) south of Invercargill, this walking/cycling loop track where the Waihopai River meets the New River estuary traverses what was once a landfill site. The area has benefited from a community regeneration project and now provides a rich habitat for wildlife and people to enjoy. The walkway is accessible from the Stead Street Wharf parking lot. ✉ *Stead St.*

Sandy Point

HIKING/WALKING | This good walking spot can be reached by taking a left after crossing the Oreti River on the way out to Oreti Beach. A 13-km (8-mile) network of easygoing trails covers the riverbanks, estuary, and the bush. A leaflet detailing the paths is available from the Invercargill Visitor Information Centre. ✉ *Sandy Point Rd.*

Tuatapere Hump Ridge Track

HIKING/WALKING | On the western side of the Southern Scenic Route, this challenging, circular three-day, two-night walk combines beach, bush, and subalpine environments in its 53 km (33 miles). The track starts near Tuatapere, about two hours' drive west of Invercargill and right on the edge of the Fiordland National Park. It's no amble; you'll spend about nine hours walking each day, but two good huts along the route each sleep about 40 people. You'll need to buy hut tickets in advance. ✉ *31 Orawia Rd., Tuatapere* ☎ *03/226–6739* ⊕ *www. humpridgetrack.co.nz.*

Stewart Island

Stewart Island, home to New Zealand's newest national park, Rakiura, is the third largest and most southerly of New Zealand's main islands, separated from the South Island by the 30-km (19-mile) Foveaux Strait. Its original Māori name,

Te Punga O Te Waka a Maui, means "the anchor stone of Maui's canoe." Māori mythology says the island's landmass held the god Maui's canoe secure while he and his crew raised the great fish— the North Island. Today the island is more commonly referred to by its modern Māori name, Rakiura, which means "the land of the glowing skies." This refers to the spectacular sunrises and sunsets and to the southern lights, or aurora australis. The European name of Stewart Island dates back to 1809. It memorializes an officer William W. Stewart on an early sealing vessel, the *Pegasus,* who was the first to chart the island.

The island covers some 1,700 square km (650 square miles). It measures about 75 km (46 miles) from north to south and about the same distance across at its widest point. On the coastline, sharp cliffs rise from a succession of sheltered bays and beaches. In the interior, forested hills rise gradually toward the west side of the island. Seals and penguins frequent the coast, and the island's prolific birdlife includes a number of species rarely seen in any other part of the country. In fact, this is the surest place to see a kiwi. The Stewart Island brown kiwi, or *tokoeka,* is the largest species of this kind of bird. Unlike their mainland cousins, these kiwis can be seen during the day as well as at night. It's a rare and amusing experience to watch these pear-shape birds scampering on a remote beach as they feed on sand hoppers and grubs.

Māori have visited and lived on Stewart Island for centuries. Archaeologists' studies of 13th-century Māori *middens* (food refuse heaps) indicate that the island was once a rich, seasonal resource for hunting, fishing, and gathering seafood. A commonly eaten delicacy at that time, the *titi,* also known as the muttonbird, is still traditionally harvested and occasionally appears on menus.

In the early 19th century, explorers, sealers, missionaries, and miners settled the island. They were followed by fishermen and sawmillers who established settlements around the edges of Paterson Inlet and Halfmoon and Horseshoe bays. In the 1920s Norwegians set up a whaling enterprise, and many descendants of these seafaring people remain. Fishing, aquaculture, and tourism are now the mainstays of the island's economy.

Even by New Zealand standards, Stewart Island is remote, raw, and untouched. The appeal is its seclusion, its relaxed way of life, and its untouched quality. Stewart Island is not for everyone: if you must have shopping malls, casinos, or umbrella drinks on the beach, don't come here. Visitors should be prepared for the fact that Stewart Island can be chilly, windy, and rainy, even in the middle of summer.

GETTING HERE AND AROUND
AIR TRAVEL
Stewart Island Flights has three scheduled flights daily between Invercargill and Halfmoon Bay. The 20-minute flight costs NZ$220 round-trip; for the best views ask to sit up front with the pilot. The island's bare-bones-but-paved Ryan's Creek Airstrip is about 2 km (1 mile) from Oban (population 420). The shuttle that meets each flight is included in the airfare.

CONTACTS Stewart Island Flights.
☎ *03/218–9129* ⊕ *www.stewartisland-flights.com.*

BOAT TRAVEL
Stewart Island Experience runs the ferry between the island and Bluff. There are three departures daily November to April, and one during the low season. The cost is NZ$85 each way, NZ$148 return. The company also offers an extensive list of organized tours, including trips aboard submersible craft with viewing windows that afford a close-up look at dozens of fish species and the mesmerizing kelp forests.

CONTACTS Stewart Island Experience.
⊠ *Stewart Island Visitor Terminal, Main Wharf, Oban* ☎ *03/212–7660, 0800/000–511* ⊕ *www.stewartislandexperience. co.nz.*

CAR, MOPED, AND BICYCLE TRAVEL
There are cars, mopeds, and bicycles for rent on the island, but there are only 20 km (13 miles) of paved road. Most of the traffic road signs you'll see are big yellow caution ones depicting silhouettes of kiwi and penguins.

FOOT TRAVEL
The best mode of transportation on the island is the "10-toe express." There are some sidewalks, but when there isn't one, keep to the edge of the road and you'll endear yourself to locals by not strolling in the middle of traffic.

TAXI TRAVEL
Water taxis are an excellent option if you want to "mix it up" a bit when seeing the park. One-way fares start from NZ$45 depending on destination, and the Ulva Island return is NZ$25. Four taxis operate from Golden Bay Wharf, a scenic 15-minute walk from town. The visitor center can make a booking for you.

TOURS
Besides regular daily ferry services between Bluff and Halfmoon Bay (Stewart Island), Stewart Island Experience offers a range of island-based excursions. Get your bearings on the Village & Bays bus tour. There aren't many roads on Stewart Island but during the 90-minute tour you'll drive along most of them. Informative commentary, suitable for all ages, scheduled services at 11 am and 1 pm daily (more in summer). On the water: explore the coast near Halfmoon Bay and the underwater world on the Marine Nature Cruise. Sit beneath the waterline on a semisubmersible vessel and cruise past the kelp forests. From November through March, there are daily departures at noon (unsuitable for preschoolers). Or take a short cruise and

Stewart Island

guided walk on Ulva Island on the Paterson Inlet Cruise. From November through April there are daily departures at 12:45. Both cruises are 2 hours 30 minutes and are weather-dependent. Discounts are available for multibookings.

Island Explorer

BUS TOURS | If you're short of time, then hop on a scenic, 90-minute bus tour operated by Stewart Island Flights. There are no scheduled departure times (it's done on demand), so make sure to book ahead whenever possible. ⊠ *Stewart Island Flights, Elgin Terr., Halfmoon Bay* ☎ *03/218–9129* ⊕ *www.stewartisland-flights.com* 🎟 *From NZ$35.*

VISITOR INFORMATION

The Department of Conservation Rakiura National Park Visitor Centre is open daily. The Environment Centre, located next to the Glowing Sky Merino Shop, has information about the habitat recovery projects on the island. The village library in the Community Centre has a complete collection of books about Stewart Island, as well as field guides of native flora and fauna. (The library is open only five hours per week, however.) For biased, vulgar, and amusing information about island goings-on ("the goss"), belly up to the bar at the pub and do some earwigging.

CONTACTS Department of Conservation Rakiura National Park Visitor Centre. ⊠ *15 Main Rd., Oban* ☎ *03/219–0009* ⊕ *www. doc.govt.nz.* **Stewart Island Promotion Association.** ⊕ *www.stewartisland.co.nz.*

◉ Sights

Apart from the tiny township of Oban at Halfmoon Bay, Stewart Island is practically uninhabited. Directly behind Oban's waterfront is a short main street with a small collection of establishments. A handful of roads head up the surrounding hills. The hills are mostly thick bush, with houses poking their heads out for a view of the bay.

Bunkhouse Theatre

ARTS VENUE | *A Local's Tail* is a quirky 40-minute movie about life on Stewart Island as told by Lola the dog. At three daily screenings (11 am, 2 pm, and 4 pm from October to April) in this neat 53-seater cinema, you'll be introduced to local characters and learn about island living. Write a review on the blackboard, pose for a photo with Lola herself, and perhaps add your name to the rogues gallery of moviegoers past. Additional screening times can be arranged for groups. On some weekend evenings classic old movies are shown. Be sure to grab a bucket of popcorn from the foyer. ⊠ *10 Main Rd., Oban* ☎ *027/867–9381* 🎟 *NZ$10* ⊗ *Closed May–Sept.*

Rakiura Museum

MUSEUM | A charmingly eclectic collection includes Māori artifacts, ambergris, old schoolhouse memorabilia, tools from gold and tinning prospectors, and a china "moustache cup" (there's a story behind every item). The museum also forgivingly showcases an old-world globe that doesn't include Stewart Island. ⊠ *Ayr St., across from Community Centre, Oban* 🎟 *NZ$2.*

Rakiura National Park

NATIONAL/STATE PARK | More than 200 km (124 miles) of trail unfurl at your feet into pure wilderness when you enter Rakiura National Park: the rest of the world is indeed far removed. Even the most adventurous travelers are liable to experience a growing feeling of utter isolation as they go about exploring the lush, bush-clad hills, sand dunes, unspoiled inlets, and beaches strewn with driftwood. Since spring 2002, about 85% of Stewart Island has been designated as the national park. Memorable hikes include the three-day Rakiura Track and the challenging 11-day Northern Circuit. A popular adventure is taking a water taxi to the trailhead at Freshwater Creek on the east side of the island, and walking across to

Golden Pingao grows on sand dunes along the popular North West Circuit.

the West Coast's amazing Mason Bay Beach, where you can arrange to have a plane pick you up. It takes close to three hours to walk to the end of the beach; along the way you'll find one of the best places to spot a few of the island's 20,000 kiwi birds. ⊕ www.doc.govt. nz/parks-and-recreation/places-to-go/ southland/places/stewart-island-rakiura/ rakiura-national-park.

🍴 Restaurants

There are only a few places to eat on Stewart Island, and the only place open year-round for lunch and dinner is the South Sea Hotel Restaurant. The year-round center of island social life is the hotel's pub, where at happy hour you'll encounter the "five o'clockers," retired fishermen who gather for a "few pints" and trade improbable yarns. After a lifetime on the deck of storm-tossed boats, the sea stance remains—legs apart and knees slightly bent. There's almost an anti-dress code here: short-sleeved sweaters that are long in the back and often have burn holes from leaning against galley coal ranges and gum boots prevail. During oyster season, it's not uncommon to see customers in full wet suits squish-squashing around the bar. On Friday night a crowd gathers when the kitchen sends out platters of free greasy "nibbles"—heaps of fried mussels, cod, chips, and pies. The pool table is free. Be aware that folks play by "Island rules," which are posted on the wall. Locals take the "down-trow" seriously, and if you lose without sinking a ball and you are not willing to circle the table with your pants down, you ought to buy your opponent a drink. If you leave the jukebox idle, a certain resident will invariably play Three Dog Night and grab you for a whirl (whether you're a bloke or a lady) roaring "Jeremiah Was a Bullfrog." Overall, it's a great place to enjoy a couple of "coldies," hear some local lore, and have a laugh. If you need a ride home, or help up the stairs, ask the bar staff for assistance.

Planning Your Visit to Rakiura

Best Time to Go
The summer (November through March) is the best time to visit. Weather is unpredictable this far south, and Christmas barbecues have been known to see a sudden hailstorm. But generally this is the best bet for lovely long days (and the local businesses are all open as opposed to the off-season).

Best Ways to Explore
Mud Walk. Eighty-five percent of the island is national park, and it's thrilling to think that much of that is impenetrable wilderness, never seen or trodden upon by people. Over 200 km (124 miles) of walking trails create some of New Zealand's greatest hikes, including the three-day Rakiura Track and the challenging 11-day Northern Circuit. A popular adventure is taking a water taxi to the trailhead at Freshwater on the east side of the island, and walking across to the West Coast's amazing Mason Bay beach, where you can arrange to have a plane pick you up. It takes close to three hours to walk to the end of the beach, along which is one of the best places to spot a few of the island's 20,000 kiwi birds. Unless you happen upon the island after a rare dry spell, you are sure to encounter copious quantities of mud on these trails so come prepared.

Sea-Sighting. Local companies offer a variety of boat tours: go fishing for Stewart Island blue cod, do a bird-viewing cruise, or view the gorgeous kelp gardens beneath the surface. Water taxi companies can drop you at bird sanctuary Ulva Island or at destinations along the Rakiura coast, or show you the aquaculture (mussel, salmon, and oyster farms) of Big Glory Bay. If the weather is right, nothing beats a kayak trip in Paterson Inlet, where you can visit Ulva, circumnavigate half a dozen tiny islands, and observe penguins (little blue and yellow-eyed).

Flightseeing. Seeing the island by helicopter is an unforgettable experience. If you don't have a week or more to properly tackle the trails, then heli-hiking makes a lot of sense—get dropped at Mason Bay and walk back, or spend a day visiting various far-flung bays and beaches and be back in Halfmoon Bay in time for dinner. Tours can show you the magnificent southern coast, and you will be privy to views of Stewart Island that many lifelong locals have never seen.

Church Hill Boutique Lodge and Restaurant
$$$$ | SEAFOOD | At the heart of the menu is food of the sea, or *kai moana*. Stewart Island blue cod, salmon, mussels, oysters, and *paua* (abalone) are all cooked to perfection and accompanied by fresh vegetables from the garden just yards away. **Known for:** delicious muttonbird; hilltop views out over Foveaux Strait; popularity with locals. $ *Average main: NZ$40* ⊠ *36 Kamahi Rd., Oban*

☎ *03/219–1123* ⊕ *www.churchhill.co.nz* ⊙ *Closed Apr.–Aug. No lunch weekdays.*

Kai Kart
$ | NEW ZEALAND | Come here for good old-fashioned fish-and-chips wrapped in a newspaper. There isn't an ounce of pretense in this cheerful little place between the museum and the "skateboard park" (a wooden ramp). **Known for:** local mussels and cod; casual atmosphere popular with tourists and locals alike;

small space. ⑤ *Average main: NZ$12* ✉ *7 Ayr St., Oban* ☎ *03/219–1225* ⊙ *Closed May–Sept.*

Kiwi-French Cafe and Crepery

$$$ | **FRENCH** | Britt Moore runs this little establishment offering a nice selection of sweet and savory crepes, salads, and a panfried fish of the day, making this a great place to stop and watch the world go by. Grab a take-out packed lunch or stay for coffee and cake. **Known for:** best crepes in the region; cozy atmosphere; excellent coffee. ⑤ *Average main: NZ$25* ✉ *6 Main Rd., Oban* ☎ *027/314–6192* ⊙ *Closed June–Sept.*

South Sea Hotel Restaurant

$$$ | **NEW ZEALAND** | You can have a relaxed meal in the seaside restaurant or an even more relaxed meal in the bar at this popular local spot. Food such as local seafood (including oysters), pizza, pasta, and steaks offer good value: seafood chowder is a popular choice, and if you give a 24-hour notice, you can try the crayfish. **Known for:** excellent pub grub; ultimate local hang-out on the island; gets crowded year-round so reservations are a good idea. ⑤ *Average main: NZ$22* ✉ *South Sea Hotel, 26 Elgin Terr., Oban* ☎ *03/219–1059* ⊕ *www.stewart-island. co.nz.*

🛏 Hotels

In contrast with the lack of dining options there are scores of accommodations catering to every budget and fancy. All lodging is guaranteed to have a gorgeous view of bush, sea, or both. Look for accommodations on the Stewart Island website (⊕ *www.stewartisland. co.nz*). Around Christmastime and New Year's every available bed is often taken, including all the bunks in the DOC huts, so prebooking is a must.

Bay Motel

$$ | **RENTAL** | Clean, spacious, and comfortable apartment-like units and full apartments have decks with views that take in Halfmoon Bay, and from these "busybody" perches you can observe the comings and goings of the wharf and pub, as well as the antics of the *kakas* (bush parrots). **Pros:** central location; all rooms have cooking facilities; thoughtful amenities. **Cons:** a slight walk uphill from town; breakfast not included; some restrictions on what can be cooked in kitchens. ⑤ *Rooms from: NZ$180* ✉ *9 Dundee St., Oban* ☎ *03/219–1119* ⊕ *www.baymotel.co.nz* ⇄ *12 rooms* ⑩ *No meals.*

Glendaruel

$$$ | **B&B/INN** | At this beautiful B&B a short walk from town, you can have private views over Paterson Inlet from two double rooms and a cozy wee single. **Pros:** lovely garden with birds; nice views; transfer from ferries included. **Cons:** a bit of a walk uphill from town; minimum two night stay; gets booked up quickly. ⑤ *Rooms from: NZ$275* ✉ *38 Golden Bay Rd., Oban* ☎ *03/219–1092* ⊕ *www.glendaruel.co.nz* ⇄ *3 rooms* ⑩ *Breakfast.*

South Sea Hotel

$ | **HOTEL** | This handsome, historic building dominates the main road in Oban and offers comfortable rooms, some of which (in the front) have sea views. **Pros:** great value for a real island experience; in-house pub and restaurant; open year-round. **Cons:** can be noisy some nights; shared bathrooms in some rooms; breakfast not included. ⑤ *Rooms from: NZ$90* ✉ *26 Elgin Terr., Oban* ☎ *03/219–1059* ⊕ *www.stewart-island.co.nz* ⇄ *17 rooms* ⑩ *No meals.*

🏃 Activities

BIRD-WATCHING

In New Zealand, you will encounter birds you've never seen before, and most of the country's native bird species reside on Stewart Island. If you brush up on your whistling, you might find yourself a feathered friend following you along a Rakiura trail. Kiwi sightings can be one

Continued on page 520

BIRDING ON ULVA ISLAND

Ulva Island is not only a birdwatcher's paradise, but also a living time capsule. Visiting it gives you the chance to experience New Zealand in a time before human contact. Then, as now, birds seen nowhere else in the world find sanctuary and thrive here.

By Kathy Ombler

Isolated as it was for millions of years, New Zealand was the ideal environment for the evolution of unique birds and flora. Indeed, it was one of the last of the Earth's landmasses to be discovered, with only a 1,000-year history of settlement. Without native mammals, only those that could swim (sea lions, seals, and whales) made it to the islands, so flightless birds flourished absent of predators. It took just the last few hundred years of human contact to endanger many indigenous birds—some have become extinct.

In recent years, New Zealand conservationsts have developed ground-breaking techniques for creating predator-free sanctuaries on many islands, where native birds now flourish. Ulva Island's 250 hectares (618 acres) of forested land in a sheltered inlet of Stewart Island form one such sanctuary. Following the eradication of rats here in 1996 several previously endangered species are now flourishing.

The bird sightings begin on the 10-minute water-taxi ride from Golden Bay (Stewart Island), with glimpses of penguins, petrels, and, possibly, albatrosses. Beneath ancient rimu, totara, and miro trees, walk well-marked trails across rocky coasts and sandy beaches, while the forest resounds with bird chatter, song, and wing-flapping.

Above: Tui bird feeding on nectar of native Kakabeak flowers

ULVA ISLAND BIRDS

Early Maori settlers named New Zealand's distinctive birds, many according to the sounds of their calls. For example they gave the name "ruru" to the morepork, for its mournful nighttime cry and "whio" to the blue duck, echoing its high-pitched whistle. Many of these names (noted in parentheses below), some with tribal variations, remain in use along with more recently established English names.

Tui

(A) Possibly New Zealand's best-known native bird, the tui is abundant in both remote forests and private gardens, even in towns and cities. It's distinctive for the white tuft of feathers at its throat (some call it the parson bird) and loved for its melodious songs and mimicry.

Kiwi (Stewart Island tokoeka)

(B) One of New Zealand's five kiwi species, tokoeka live throughout Stewart Island where, unlike their strictly nocturnal mainland cousins, they feed during the day and night. The few that live on Ulva Island are rarely seen. However, Stewart Island guided tours—

such as the Ocean Beach evening tour with Bravo Adventure Cruises—provide excellent chances to see kiwi. You might also get lucky while taking a solo evening stroll around Oban—kiwis are sometimes spotted in the town's parks and on trails.

Fantail (piwakawaka)

(C) Its eponymous fanlike tail makes this tiny bird easy to spot. The tail isn't just for show, though; the bird catches flies and other insects with it and uses it to navigate. Like robins, fantails are attracted to track walkers.

Northern Royal Albatross (torea)

(D) One of the world's largest albatrosses and the only one to breed on New Zealand's mainland (on Otago Peninsula, just one hour's drive from Dunedin city), the torea is also seen on the boat trip to Ulva. They're more likely seen, however, on a fishing or pelagic bird watching cruise; ask at the visitor center for operator details. Alternatively, visit the Royal Albatross Centre on the Otago Peninsula, or take an Albatross Encounter cruise from Kaikoura.

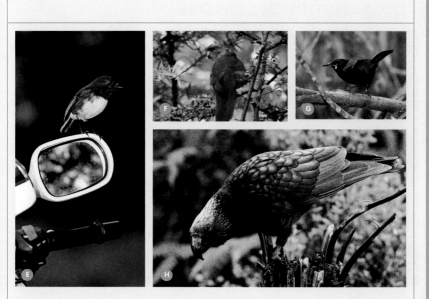

Stewart Island Robin (toutouwai)

(E) The island's "friendliest" birds have a habit of following you on treks. They're not just trying to get into photographs (and they do); they nab the insects disturbed by your feet. Ulva's robin population has grown to more than 200 since 2000, when just 20 birds were transferred here following the rat eradication.

Parakeet (kakariki)

(F) Both red- and yellow-crowned parakeets live on Ulva. The bright green, red, and yellow colorings of these small parrots stand out against the darker forest greens. Their high-pitched "ka-ka-ka" chatter is also distinctive.

Saddleback (tieke)

(G) Ulva is the only place to see the South Island saddleback, named for the distinctive saddle-like reddish stripe across its back. The species has recovered from near extinction in the 1960s. The more prolific North Island saddleback lives on several island and mainland reserves.

Kaka

(H) These colorful, boisterous bush parrots screech their greetings, congregate in loud social groups, and commute over long distances between islands and forests. Look for bark torn by the kaka foraging for grubs and for the spectacle of their bright red underwings.

Yellowhead (mohua)

Island sanctuaries such as Ulva have become bastions for yellowhead as mainland populations dwindle. Their presence is signalled by persistent chatter, and they're found mostly in flocks high in the trees, especially in winter.

TIPS AND TOUR OPERATORS

Stewart Island robin on Ulva Island

KEEP ULVA PREDATOR FREE. Check your clothes and boots for seeds. Check and re-pack your belongings before getting off the boat. Rats have been known to stow away!

TAKE YOUR TIME. You will see more birds. Most guided tours take an unhurried three to four hours. If walking on your own, purchase the Ulva Island Charitable Trust self-guided brochure (NZ$2) from the i-SITE Visitor Centre or Department of Conservation Visitor Centre.

ENJOY THE ISLAND'S FLORA. With no browsing from introduced animals the plants' abilities to fruit have increased and the forest has flourished. While giant totara, rimu, and miro dominate, there's also old, gnarled red-flowering rata; a tangled understorey of ferns; mosses; orchids; and rare, ancient plants now found in few other places.

COST. Guided Ulva Island trips cost around NZ$140, water taxi included. For independent trips, water taxis cost NZ$20 to NZ$35 return (depending on passenger numbers). Several companies operate both scheduled and private charter trips daily.

BEST TIME TO GO. You can go to Ulva any time of the year. Winter will be colder but the weather is more predictable.

TOUR OPERATORS

The DOC has approved the following guided tours: **Ulva's Guided Walks** (⊕ www.ulva.co.nz); **Ruggedy Range™ Wilderness Experience** (⊕ www.ruggedyrange.com) and **Sail Ashore** (⊕ www.sailsashore.co.nz)

USEFUL WEB SITES

Stewart Island i-SITE Visitors Centre (⊕ www.stewartisland.co.nz)

Department of Conservation and Ulva Island Charitable Trust (⊕ www.doc.govt.nz)

TOP BIRDING SPOTS IN NEW ZEALAND

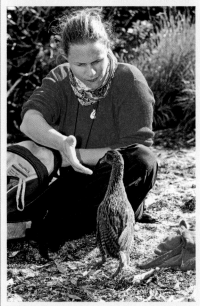

Native weka seeking food from a visitor on Ulva Island

There are plenty of exceptional birding areas, and all are simply great places to visit even if birds aren't your main thing.

NORTH ISLAND

Cape Kidnappers Nature Reserve, Hawke's Bay. The world's largest mainland concentration of Australasian gannets congregates on dramatic sea cliffs. Visit November–April.

Kapiti Island Nature Reserve, Kapiti Island. Located 5 km off North Island's west coast, near Wellington, the bird population includes endangered little spotted kiwi and takahe. The Department of Conservation can book day trips; overnight stays are available at Kapiti Island Lodge. Visit anytime.

Kiwi Encounter/Rainbow Springs Nature Park, Rotorua. Visit this kiwi hatchery and nursery to learn about the ground-breaking work raising chicks for release into the wild.

Daily tours are conducted all year; chicks hatch September to April.

Tiritiri Matangi Island Scientific Reserve, Hauraki Gulf (Auckland). This is one of the easiest places to see New Zealand's rarest birds, including takahe, kokako, saddleback, and stitchbird. Day trips depart from downtown Auckland. Walking treks range from one to five hours. Visit year-round.

Miranda Ramsar Site, Firth of Thames. From roadside viewings and hides, see some of the tens of thousands of Arctic migratory waders that live in the vast, tidal flats and shellbanks in the Firth of Thames. It's a one-hour drive south of Auckland. Visit September–March.

SOUTH ISLAND

Farewell Spit Nature Reserve, Golden Bay and Takaka. A massive sandspit and tidal flats at South Island's northeastern tip provide a summer home to thousands of Arctic waders and winter breeding grounds for other wetland birds. Guided 4WD tours are available. Visit year round; September–March for Arctic waders.

Kaikoura, between Christchurch and Picton. Feeding grounds, just a 10 minute boat trip from shore, attract some 16 albatross species, as well as prions, petrels, and more. Specialist pelagic tours and whale- and dolphin-watching cruises are available. Visit year round.

Otago Peninsula. A mainland colony of Northern Royal Albatross, several yellow-eyed penguin colonies, and a host of seabirds and shorebirds live on the peninsula's headlands, beaches, and tidal inlets, within one hour's drive of Dunedin city. Several guided tours operate from Dunedin. Visit year-round; summer is best for the Northern Royal Albatross.

of the most memorable experiences of your trip.

Birds are plentiful in Halfmoon Bay. If you walk up Argyle Street, which dead-ends into a drive, and continue up (where it turns into a path), you'll be certain to see the noisy kaka (bush parrots) clowning in the trees around you. Ducks loiter at Mill Creek (locals have named many of them) and a little kingfisher often sits on the phone wire above them. Rare albino wood pigeons (*kereru*) reside in the *rimu* tree by the "*rimu* tree phone" on the road leading down into Horseshoe Bay. Little blue penguins are seen in Paterson Inlet, ditto yellow-eyed penguins and Stewart Island shags. Mollymawks soar past Acker's Point. *Tūi*, bellbirds, fantails, and robins can be seen throughout Halfmoon Bay gardens and on day walks. *Weka* have been reintroduced to the area and favor the gardens of Deep Bay Road (they cut through homes and steal shiny objects if residents leave the doors open). Oystercatchers live on every one of the town's beaches, and pied oystercatchers like grazing the schoolyard. Kiwis are rarely seen around town but they are there; telltale tracks have been seen at Traill Park and their shrill unmistakable cry is heard some nights.

One of the best places for bird-watching is Ulva Island, 620 acres of thick native bush. The rare birds that live here have no predators, so they have an excellent survival rate. Among the resident species are the weka, saddleback, kaka (a parrot), and kiwi. The forest, which has walking paths accessible to the public, is made up primarily of *rimu, rata*, and *kamahi* trees. To get here, take a boat or water taxi from Halfmoon or Golden Bay, or paddle a kayak from Thule Bay. You can also join a tour; the best guide is the aptly named Ulva Goodwillie.

Aurora Charters

BIRD WATCHING | Full- or half-day pelagic bird-watching tours are offered aboard the *Aurora, a* comfortable 58-foot catamaran on which to get your fix of seabirds. It's not uncommon to see five species of albatross during these trips, as well as penguins, petrels, terns, shearwaters, and more. The large open deck out back provides an excellent platform for spotting the birds (bring your binoculars but most of the birds get pretty close), and if the wind picks up the cabin can comfortably seat 20 to swig a hot drink. Advance booking is strongly recommended. A full-day trip usually goes to Port Pegasus, a rarely seen part of southern Stewart Island. Fishing charters for large groups are available, too. ☎ *03/219–1394* ⊕ *www.auroracharters. co.nz* ✉ *From NZ$105.*

Ulva's Guided Walks

BIRD WATCHING | Let Ulva Goodwillie and her team of guides share their knowledge of flora, fauna, avian, and wildlife expertise with you on a three- to four-hour amble through this ancient podocarp forest. An open sanctuary since 1997, this predator-free refuge allows rare and endangered birds and plants to thrive. Ulva's guiding team all live and work on Stewart Island, and this becomes immediately apparent as they share their passion and enthusiasm for Ulva Island with you. Advanced booking is essential. Keen birders opt for the Birding Bonanza, a full-day wildlife trifecta of land birds, seabirds, and kiwi. ✉ *The Stewart Island Gift Shop, 20 Main Rd.* ☎ *03/219–1216* ⊕ *www.ulva.co.nz* ✉ *From NZ$130.*

FISHING

If you go fishing, your catch will likely be the succulent Stewart Island blue cod. Go with a guide and he or she will fillet and bag it for you. Some will cook it for your lunch. The best way to experience fishing in this region is to go out with one of the real salt dogs who have fished these waters all their lives. Aurora Charters can also arrange group fishing excursions.

Lo Loma Fishing Charters

FISHING | Richard Squires (aka Squizzy) runs an old-school operation with a historic wooden boat and traditional hand-line fishing. You'll hear him belting out of *Lo Loma* as you near the wharf, and be regaled with some great stories once you're on board for a relaxed half-day fishing trip. Advance booking is recommended (half- or full-day charters are also possible). These trips are not suitable for preschoolers. ✉ *Oban* ☎ *03/219–1141* ⊕ *www.loloma.co.nz* ⊠ *From NZ$100.*

Rakiura Charters & Water Taxi

BIRD WATCHING | FAMILY | Hop on board the *Rakiura Suzy,* a custom-built modern boat with heated cabin to experience full and half-day bird-watching tours, scenic cruises, and custom charters. Advance booking is recommended, and children are welcomed (under five are free). A water-taxi service is also available; the price depends on the destination. ✉ *10 Main Rd., Oban* ☎ *0800/725–487, 03/219–1487* ⊕ *www.rakiuracharters. co.nz* ⊠ *From NZ$125.*

Tequila Charters

FISHING | Want to crew for the day on the commercial fishing vessel *Tequila?* Learn how to prepare cod pots, process the catch, fillet fish, and use hand lines to catch your own blue cod to take home. "Chook," aka Anthony, has more than 28 years of experience in commercial fishing and will show you how things are done in the "roaring forties" (so called due to the unpredictable weather at 47 degrees south). Wet weather gear and equipment is provided; trips depart Halfmoon Bay wharf twice daily, weather permitting. Reservations are essential. ☎ *03/219–1334, 027/251–7122* ⊕ *www. stewartislandfishing.com* ⊠ *NZ$100.*

HIKING

Numerous day hikes on well-maintained trails are in and around the township. Free street maps are available at the Flight Centre–Post Office and Ferry Terminal; detailed maps and information are available at the Department of Conservation Office. Some walks, such as the Observation Rock and Fuchsia walks, are measured in minutes; others, such as the walks to Fern Gully, Ryan's Creek, and Horseshoe Point, are measured in hours.

For information on Rakiura National Park's walks, contact the Department of Conservation Rakiura National Park Visitor Centre in Oban.

If you only have a few hours, the walk from town out to the Acker's Point lighthouse is marvelous and encompasses town, boat sheds, a historic homestead, lush forest, and ocean views. This is nesting ground for *titi* (sooty shearwaters or muttonbirds), and little blue (fairy) penguins, which can often be seen from the lookout, along with albatross and fishing boats.

Kiwi Wilderness Walks

HIKING/WALKING | Get back to nature with a four- or five-day guided walk out in the Stewart Island bush. Highlights include Mason Bay with its staggering sand dune system; the possibility of seeing wild kiwi; historic Māori Beach, once the site of sawmills and a school in the early 1900s; and Port William's early sealing location. These tours depart from Invercargill and include return flights. ☎ *021/359–592* ⊕ *www.nzwalk.com* ⊠ *From NZ$1695.*

North West Circuit

HIKING/WALKING | This 9- to 11-day walk from Halfmoon Bay circles the north coast and then cuts through the interior. If that's not enough for you, five days can be tacked on by including the Southern Circuit. Stewart Island's climate is notoriously changeable, so be prepared for sun, wind, rain, and *lots* of mud. Take the usual safety precautions for these hikes: bring suitable boots, clothing, food, and a portable stove. Complete an Outdoors Intentions form at ⊕ *www.adventures-mart.org.nz* (or at the DOC office) before setting out; and, ideally, bring along with you a locator beacon (available for hire from the Department of Conservation) or a guide who knows the trails. This hike may well reward you with a wild kiwi encounter.

Rakiura Track

HIKING/WALKING | One of New Zealand's great walks covers 32 km (19 miles) and takes three days. Day 1 goes from Half-moon Bay to Port William Hut via Horse-shoe and Lee bays. Day 2 heads inland through native bush and wood across the ridge, allowing for good views of Paterson Inlet and the Tin Range. Day 3 connects back to Halfmoon Bay via *rimu* and *kamahi* forest. Two huts on the route each accommodate up to 30 people on a first-come, first-served basis. They come with mattresses, a wood-burning stove, running water, and toilets. (If you're relatively fit and you leave early, you can do this track in one day, but you will be sore.)

Sails Tours

BIRD WATCHING | With 80 years combined island experience, let Peter and Iris Tait escort you around Ulva Island for a four-hour tour. Group sizes are small; courtesy transfers to and from your accommodation are included. Or you can take a leisurely road tour and learn what island life is like (at a discounted rate if you book and pay for both tours). Accommodation on Stewart Island can also be arranged. ✉ *11 View St.* ☎ *03/219–1151* ⊕ *www. sailsashore.co.nz* ✉ *From NZ$175.*

KAYAKING

Share the water with penguins, seals, and occasionally dolphins in the mostly uninhabited Paterson Inlet; 100 square km (38 square miles) of bush-clad, sheltered waterways, it has 20 islands, four DOC huts, and two navigable rivers.

Phil's Sea Kayak

KAYAKING | Suitable for beginners and experienced paddlers, this half-day guided trip in peaceful Paterson Inlet close to the shoreline is hard to beat. A full-day trip will get you into exposed coastal and intertidal waters, while a sunset/twilight tour rounds off the day as little blue penguins come home. Phil is very modest about his 30 years' experience on the water (which includes a circumnavigation of Stewart Island and crossing Foveaux Strait) and makes an amiable and patient guide. Small groups; tailored to experience; prices start from NZ$90 per person. ✉ *7 Leonard St., Oban* ☎ *027/444–2323* ✉ *phil_dove500@ hotmail.com.*

Index

Photo Credits

Front Cover: SIME / eStock Photo [Description: Southland, Fiordland National Park, Milford Sound, New Zealand.] Back cover, from left to right: Shutterstock / Pichugin Dmitry; Shutterstock / irakite; Pichugin Dmitry/Shutterstock. Spine: Pichugin Dmitry/Shutterstock. Interior, from left to right: Cloudia Spinner/Shutterstock (1). Winston Tan/Shutterstock (2-3). Rob Suisted/www.naturespic.com (5). **Chapter 1: Experience New Zealand:** MikeDrago.cz/Shutterstock (8-9). Guaxinim/shutterstock.com (10). Courtesy of Hobbiton Movie Set Tours (11). Jeff McEwan/Courtesy of Destination Wairarapanz (11). Courtesy CoCA (12). Andy Belcher/Courtesy of Destination Coromandel (12). Courtesy CoCA (12). Martin Dworschak/Shutterstock.com (12). Photosport Ltd/www.photosport.nz (13). Courtesy of Ngāi Tahu Tourism (13). Vašek Vinklát [Flickr_CC BY 2.0] (14). Chris McLennan/Courtesy of Polynesian Spa (14). Courtesy of Tourism New Zealand (14). Courtesy of Discover Waitomo (14). Andy Woods/Courtesy of Glacier Helicopters (15). Jet Productions NZ Ltd. / Courtesy of Tourism New Zealand (16). Michael Williams/Dreamstime.com (16). Courtesy of Tourism New Zealand (16). Moha Nadly Aizat Mohd Nudri /Dreamstime.com (16). premysl luljak/Shutterstock(17). Courtesy of Wellington City Council (17). Shotover Canyon Swing & Canyon Fox, Queenstown New Zealand (18). Michael Williams/Dreamstime. com (18). Courtesy of Destination Queenstown (18). Tourism New Zealand (18). Courtesy of AJ Hackett Bungy NZ (19). Courtesy of Tourism New Zealand (24-26). ChameleonsEye/Shutterstock (26). Courtesy of Tourism New Zealand (26-27). Patrick Hamilton / www.photosport.co.nz / Courtesy Tourism New Zealand (27). CSNafzger/Shutterstock 28). Krzysztof Golik/Wikimedia.org (CC BY-SA 4.0) (28). DestinationsInNewZealand/Shutterstock (28). Aidil/Shutterstock (28). aaronj9/ Shutterstock (28). Dmitry Pichugin/Shutterstock (29). Phattana Stock/Shutterstock (29). Courtesy of Tourism New Zealand (29). Gabor Kovacs Photography/Shutterstock (29). Courtesy of Department of Conservation (29). Courtesy of Mt. Difficulty Wines (30). Courtesy of Allan Scott Wines (31). Rudmer Zwerver/Shutterstock (32). Patricia Hofmeester | Dreamstime. com (32). Vincent Bovey/Shutterstock (32). Rob Tucker (33). Winston Tan/Shutterstock (33). Rob Suisted/www.naturespic. com (43). Jason Friend / www.jasonfriend.net (45). Rob Suisted/www.naturespic.com (45). Rob Suisted/www.naturespic. com (46). Cate Starmer (46). Rob Suisted/www.naturespic.com (48). **Chapter 3: Auckland:** Rudy Balasko/Shutterstock (73). Filip Fuxa/Shutterstock (86). Joe Gough/Shutterstock (89). Chris Gin/Shutterstock (101) **Chapter 4: Northland and the Bay of Islands:** Christina Fink/Shutterstock (109). Rob Suisted/www.naturespic.com (118-119). Kim Westerkov/ www.hedgehoghouse.com / Tourism New Zealand (120). Marc von Hacht/Shutterstock (125). GARDEL Bertrand / age fotostock (128). Holger Leue/Tourism New Zealand (130). Destination Northland/Tourism New Zealand (131). jamie thorpe/Shutterstock (132). Gareth Eyres/Tourism New Zealand (132). Ruth Black/Shutterstock (132). Scott Venning/Tourism New Zealand (133). Destination Rotorua (133). Small World Productions/Tourism New Zealand (133). Rob Suisted/ www.naturespic.com (134). Scott Venning/Tourism New Zealand (134). Becky Nunes/Tourism New Zealand (134). Scott. Venning/Tourism New Zealand (135). Adventure Films/Tourism New Zealand (135). Fay Looney/Tourism New Zealand (135). **Chapter 5: Coromandel and the Bay of Plenty:** Colin Monteath / age fotostock (141). Michaela Mazurkova/ Shutterstock (150-151). Rob Suisted/www.naturespic.com (157). Rob Suisted/www.naturespic.com (163). ian woolcock/ Shutterstock (174). Greg Balfour Evans / Alamy (177). **Chapter 6: East Coast and the Volcanic Zone:** Pichugin Dmitry/Shutterstock (196). Rob Suisted/www.naturespic.com/ Tourism New Zealand (201). Rob Suisted/www.naturespic.com (213). David Wall / Alamy Stock Photo (217). **Chapter 7: North Island's West Coast:** Andy Belcher / age fotostock (221). Colin Monteath / age fotostock (229). Shaun Jeffers/Shutterstock (233). Daniel Sockwell/Shutterstock (237). christian_b/Shutterstock (244-245). Don Fuchs / age fotostock (248). Don Smith / age fotostock (251). PK289/Shutterstock (255). **Chapter 8: Wellington and the Wairarapa:** byvalet/Shutterstock (261). Naruedom Yaempongsa/Dreamstime (273). stefano brozzi/age fotostock (274). Nick. Servian/www.nickservian.com/Tourism New Zealand (276). Rob Suisted/ www.naturespic.com (280-281). New Line Cinema/Courtesy Everett Collection (291). Rob. Suisted/www.naturespic.com (292). David Wall (www.davidWallPhoto.com) / Tourism New Zealand (292). Rob Suisted/www.naturespic.com (293). Miles Holden/Tourism New Zealand (294). Gilbert van Reenen/Tourism New Zealand (294). travellight/Shutterstock (297). **Chapter 9: Upper South Island and the West Coast:** Mi-chi/Shutterstock (299). Whale Watch Kaikoura (311). Rob Suisted/www.naturespic.com (318). David Wall/www.davidWallPhoto.com / Tourism New Zealand (319). Rob Suisted/ www.naturespic.com (320). Cherryfarm22/wikipedia.org (320). David Wall/Tourism New Zealand (320). Rob Suisted/ www.naturespic.com (321). Filipe Raimundo/Shutterstock (321). Ian Trafford/www.iantraffordphotos.com/Tourism

Notes

Notes

Notes

Notes

Notes

Notes

Notes

Notes

Notes

Notes

Notes

Fodor's ESSENTIAL NEW ZEALAND

Editorial: Douglas Stallings, *Editorial Director*; Margaret Kelly, Jacinta O'Halloran, Amanda Sadlowski, *Senior Editors*; Kayla Becker, Alexis Kelly, Teddy Minford, Rachael Roth, *Editors*; Jeremy Tarr, *Fodors.com Editorial Director;* Rachael Levitt, *Fodors.com Managing Editor*

Design: Tina Malaney, *Design and Production Director*; Jessica Gonzalez, *Production Designer*

Photography: Jill Krueger, *Senior Photo Editor*, Ashok Kumar, *Photo Researcher*

Maps: Rebecca Baer, *Senior Map Editor*; Ed Jacobus, David Lindroth, Mark Stroud (Moon Street Cartography), *Cartographers*

Production: Jennifer DePrima, *Editorial Production Manager*; Carrie Parker, *Senior Production Editor*; Elyse Rozelle, *Production Editor*

Business & Operations: Chuck Hoover, *Chief Marketing Officer*; Robert Ames, *General Manager*; Stephen Horowitz, *Director of Business Development and Revenue Operations*; Tara McCrillis, *Director of Publishing Operations*

Public Relations and Marketing: Joe Ewaskiw, *Manager*; Esther Su, *Marketing Manager*

Writers: Anabel Darby, Gerard Hindmarsh, Claire Kenny, Kathy Ombler, Richard Pamatatau, Mike Stearne

Editor: Amanda Sadlowski

Production Editor: Carrie Parker

Production Design: Liliana Guia

2nd Edition

ISBN 978-1-64097-154-7

ISSN 2470–9441

Library of Congress Control Number 2018914619

All details in this book are based on information supplied to us at press time. Always confirm information when it matters, especially if you're making a detour to visit a specific place. Fodor's expressly disclaims any liability, loss, or risk, personal or otherwise, that is incurred as a consequence of the use of any of the contents of this book.

SPECIAL SALES

This book is available at special discounts for bulk purchases for sales promotions or premiums. For more information, e-mail SpecialMarkets@fodors.com.

PRINTED IN THE UNITED STATES OF AMERICA

10 9 8 7 6 5 4 3 2 1